KANSAS ARCHAEOLOGY

KANSAS ARCHAEOLOGY

EDITED BY
Robert J. Hoard and William E. Banks

Foreword by Alfred E. Johnson

Published in Association with
the Kansas State Historical Society
by the University Press of Kansas

© 2006 by the University Press of Kansas

All rights reserved

Published by the University Press of Kansas (Lawrence, Kansas 66045), which was organized by the Kansas Board of Regents and is operated and funded by Emporia State University, Fort Hays State University, Kansas State University, Pittsburg State University, the University of Kansas, and Wichita State University

Library of Congress Cataloging-in-Publication Data
Kansas archaeology / edited by Robert J. Hoard and William E. Banks ; foreword by Alfred E. Johnson.
p. cm.
Includes bibliographical references and index.
ISBN 978-0-7006-2445-4 (pbk. : alk. paper)
ISBN 978-0-7006-2459-1 (ebook)
1. Indians of North America—Kansas—Antiquities. 2. Prehistoric peoples—Kansas. 3. Kansas—Antiquities. 4. Kansas—History. I. Hoard, Robert J. II. Banks, William E.
F683.K36   2006
978.1'01—dc22   2005022569

British Library Cataloguing in Publication Data is available.

Printed in the United States of America

10 9 8 7 6 5 4 3 2 1

The paper used in this publication is recycled and contains 30 percent postconsumer waste. It is acid free and meets the minimum requirements of the American National Standard for Permanence of Paper for Printed Library Materials z39.48-1992.

CONTENTS

Foreword, *Alfred E. Johnson*   vii

Acknowledgments   xiii

1. Introduction   1
   Robert J. Hoard and William E. Banks

2. Late Quaternary and Modern Environments in Kansas   10
   Rolfe D. Mandel

3. The Effects of Late Quaternary Landscape Evolution   28
   on the Archaeological Record of Kansas,
   Rolfe D. Mandel

4. The Paleoarchaic of Kansas   46
   Jeannette M. Blackmar and Jack L. Hofman

5. Woodland Adaptations in Eastern Kansas   76
   Brad Logan

6. Plains Woodland Complexes of Western Kansas and
   Adjacent Portions of Nebraska and Colorado   93
   John R. Bozell

7. The Central Plains Tradition   105
   Donna C. Roper

8. The Late Prehistoric on the High Plains of Western Kansas:
   High Plains Upper Republican and Dismal River   133
   Laura L. Scheiber

9. Late Prehistoric Oneota in the Central Plains   151
   Lauren W. Ritterbush

10. The Great Bend Aspect   165
    Donald J. Blakeslee and Marlin F. Hawley

11. Looking South: The Middle Ceramic Period
    in Southern Kansas and Beyond   180
    Scott D. Brosowske and C. Tod Bevitt

12. Wichita Ethnohistory   206
    Susan C. Vehik

13. The Kansa   219
    James O. Marshall

14. The Pawnee in Kansas: Ethnohistory and Archaeology   233
    Donna C. Roper

15. Paleoethnobotanical Research in Kansas   248
    Mary J. Adair

16. Kansas Lithic Resources   264
    C. Martin Stein

    Appendix   283

    References Cited   329

    The Contributors   401

    Index   405

FOREWORD

As I reviewed my library in preparing to write these prefatory comments, I was struck by the exceptionally worn condition of a single volume, Waldo Wedel's 1959 *Introduction to Kansas Archaeology*. Reporting fieldwork accomplished in 1937, 1939, and 1940, the book, in the words of the author, was intended to serve as "a comprehensive review of the available ethnohistorical, archaeological, and geographical data bearing on the aboriginal occupancy of Kansas" (Wedel 1959: xiii). The success of this review, as an orientation and stimulus for archaeological research in Kansas over the past 42 years, can only be described as exceptional. The present publication is an attempt to build on Wedel's feat, this time with 19 authors summarizing the results of a vastly intensified research effort financed with a great deal more than the $4,000 expended during Wedel's (1959: xiv) early fieldwork.

Archaeology is a cumulative discipline requiring patient and dedicated efforts by numerous individuals, over lengths of time, to amass the data necessary to chronicle the events of the past and to interpret those events in an approximation of their original cultural context. In Kansas, both professional and avocational archaeologists have contributed to this effort.

PROFESSIONAL ARCHAEOLOGY

Beginning with the University of Kansas in 1948, and more recently with Kansas State (1965) and Wichita State (1970), the Board of Regents has supported professional archaeologists, who in turn have provided educational opportunities for undergraduate and graduate students through direct involvement in field and laboratory research into the prehistory and early history of Kansas. The master's theses, Ph.D. dissertations, and publications resulting from this work form a major portion of the corpus of data on Kansas archaeology. For example, at the University of Kansas, 40 master's theses and 10 Ph.D. dissertations have been written on Kansas archaeology to date. In addition, there are now 104 numbers in the Project Report Series from the Museum of Anthropology at the university.

In 1961, with the hiring of Roscoe Wilmeth as the first state archaeologist, another Kansas institution, the Kansas State Historical Society, recognized the important part that archaeology could play in the understanding and the preservation of Kansas' cultural heritage. Since that time, archaeologists from the Kansas State Historical Society have worked across the state to record the location of historic and prehistoric sites, to mitigate the effects of natural and manmade destructive forces on these sites, and to see to their long-term preservation through purchase of the land on which the sites are located. Examples of the latter include the extremely important Tobias site in Rice County, one of the sixteenth-century Great Bend sites perhaps visited by the Coronado expedition, and an early nineteenth-century Pawnee village in Republic County. Other contributions of significance are state laws to protect important historic and prehistoric sites on state, county, and municipal lands (KSA 75-5401 to 75-5408) and the Kansas Unmarked Burial Sites Preservation Act (KSA 75-2741 to 75-2754). Archaeological research projects from the Kansas State Historical Society are reported to the profession and the public by means of the Anthropological Series (17 volumes) and the Contract Archeology Publications (25 volumes).

During the 1970s, a number of federal laws were passed with the cumulative effect of mandating full consideration of the impact of development projects involving federal funds or permits on significant historic and prehistoric sites. One important consequence has been the creation of new positions for archaeologists to administer federally funded cultural resource management programs and to review federal undertakings. Usually filled at the M.A. or Ph.D. level, these positions have added an important new force to the archaeological enterprise in Kansas. Prior to development, surveys are conducted to determine location and significance, followed by plans and implementation of appropriate mitigation efforts. A small percentage of development costs is available for archaeological work. In addition, federal agencies, such as the Bureau of Reclamation, the U.S. Army Corps of Engineers, and the U.S. Forest Service, are required to survey and determine the significance of historic and prehistoric sites on their landholdings. This work is often contracted out to private contractors or to state agencies. Federal dollars for archaeology for these two purposes have provided most of the financial support enjoyed by Kansas archaeology over the past 20 years.

AVOCATIONAL ARCHAEOLOGY

My earliest awareness of the varied and little-known prehistory of Kansas came from association, during my teenage years, with two avocational archaeologists in my hometown of Ellsworth, Kansas. Both were avid collectors, usually from the surfaces of sites in plowed fields. Later, while doing survey work, as a professional-in-training, I became aware of the widespread popularity of archaeology across Kansas and the tremendous resource for information on site locations on the part of interested and motivated members of the public. Most were willing to share this information, especially in return for the answers to questions on the temporal, spatial, and cultural meaning of artifacts recovered. Fortunately, archaeologists at the Kansas State Historical Society who encouraged the development of the Kansas Anthropological Association following its formation in 1955 also appreciated this trade-off. Training sessions in professional field and laboratory procedures were instituted, and as a consequence, major contributions have been made, especially in the statewide record of site locations and in the excavation of important sites across the state. Professional archaeologists from the State Historical Society, assisted by archaeologists from the universities in Kansas and from federal agencies, have coordinated and supervised this work. A backlog of unpublished data remains, but recent efforts to involve graduate students at the universities are bringing these data to the attention of the profession and the public (e.g., Huhnke 2000; Bevitt 1999a).

Further direction and encouragement for the state's avocational archaeologists came with Patricia O'Brien's *Archaeology in Kansas* (1984). Written for "the Kansan interested in Kansas archaeology," this summary of the prehistory and early history of the state also identifies a series of ways for avocational archaeologists to contribute to recovery, recording, and preservation of the cultural heritage of Kansas.

Although not strictly from Kansas, perhaps the best example I can give of the potential of avocational involvement in furthering the archaeological endeavor is the R. B. Aker collection at the Museum of Anthropology at the University of Kansas. Aker was a masonry contractor in Parkville, Missouri, on the Missouri River at the north edge of Kansas City. As a young man, he began collecting prehistoric artifacts from sites in the vicinity of Parkville, eventually expanding his collecting territory northward to St. Joseph, Missouri. This linear strip was narrowly defined to include the terraces and bluff tops of the hills along the Missouri. Over approximately 50 years, Aker returned many times to collect from the same sites, while expanding his sample to include new discoveries. During evenings and periods of inclement weather, Aker cataloged his collection, identifying where each artifact was found. As a consequence, the approximately 40,000 artifacts donated to the university in 1989 provide the best sample we will ever have of the first 10,000 years of human occupation along the lower Missouri River valley (Estep 1993: 12–17; Feagins 1993: 12–18).

COORDINATION

Fortunately, when one considers the immensity of the task (12,000 years of occupation spread over 82,158 square miles of territory), archaeologists working in Kansas follow a number of procedures that facilitate cooperation and coordination. Perhaps primary among these are the reports and discussions held each year during the Plains Anthropological Conference and the more localized Flint Hills Conference. Publication of the results of research is an exceptionally strong ethical stance that ensures that new work can build on previous accomplishments. Most of the archaeology done in the state is funded by federal agencies. Reviews, often of work in the field and laboratory as well as of final reports, are usual. Funding can be and has been withheld if the product is not acceptable. Another important mechanism of coordination is the statewide archaeological survey record maintained by the Kansas State Historical Society, with a duplicate copy at the Museum of Anthropology at the

University of Kansas. The transfer of the paper record into a Geographical Information System (GIS) format has significantly increased the potential of this resource.

Finally, the recent formation of the Professional Archaeologists of Kansas (PAK) (bylaws ratified 1996) bodes well for the enhancement of all of the cooperative measures noted above and the development of others as needed. Major goals of PAK include the encouragement of research designed to increase our understanding of the prehistory and history of Kansas, dissemination of the results of the research to as wide an audience as possible, and long-term preservation of the database on which the research depends.

RESULTS

The chapters in this volume summarize the accumulated knowledge of the many Kansas archaeologists, both professional and avocational, along with the institutions that have supported them, and serve to build upon the story of the earliest human occupancy. Themes include placing the events of prehistory in their proper chronological order (often called culture history). Studying changes in material culture is the essential first step, followed by attempts to explain the nature of the events.

To date, culture-historical studies have been most successful in eastern Kansas, the portion that has received most of the federal financial support and, consequently, the most archaeological attention. Here we have a basic understanding of the time block from ca. 2500 B.C. to the present (Late Archaic, 2500–500 B.C.; Early Woodland, 500 B.C.–A.D. 1; Middle Woodland, A.D. 1–750; Late Woodland, A.D. 750–1000; Early Plains Village, A.D. 1000–1500; Late Plains Village, A.D. 1500–1700; Historic, A.D. 1700–present). Numerous local variants of these generalized periods have been named over the eastern third of the state.

As we have begun to understand the archaeology of eastern Kansas, we also have been able to recognize detailed similarities with prehistoric developments in the eastern United States. Eastern Kansas (to and including the Flint Hills) fits much more comfortably with the diversified pattern of the East than with the focal orientation characteristic of the Plains. This is especially noticeable for the post–2500 B.C. periods noted above, but preliminary indications suggest that this relationship was probably true throughout prehistory (R. B. Aker collection, Museum of Anthropology, University of Kansas).

To the west of the Flint Hills, our record is much less detailed. This is, in part, a result of limited fieldwork, but also a reflection of lower population density and mobile lifeways. Early periods remain little known, with increasing knowledge available for more recent time spans, especially after A.D. 1000.

An important focus of culture-historical studies in Kansas has been the application of the Direct Historical Approach (Wedel 1938a). The logic of this approach is to work from the known to the unknown, by tying the ethnohistorical record of Kansas area Indian tribes to the prehistoric record. Perhaps the best example, to date, is the research by Mildred Wedel (1982) and Waldo Wedel (1970a), which convincingly relates the Late Plains Village Great Bend culture (ca. A.D. 1400–1700) to the Wichita Indians. A strong case has also been built that ties the Dismal River culture of western Kansas to the Plains Apache (Champe 1949: 285–291; D. A. Gunnerson 1974; J. H. Gunnerson 1960). The Oneota tradition that extends into northeastern Kansas has been suggested as the origin of both the Chiwere (Iowa, Missouria, Oto) and the Dhegiha (Quapaw, Osage, Kansa, Omaha, Ponca) Siouan groups (Buffalohead 2004; Henning and Thiessen 2004), although the latter association has been challenged on the basis of similarities between the architecture and settlement patterns of the Kansa and the prehistoric eastern Kansas Pomona culture (A. E. Johnson 1991: 57–66).

Beyond identification, Kansas archaeologists have been equally interested in providing meaning to the temporal and spatial changes recognized in the archaeological record of material culture. The first step in this process involves inferences believed to approximate the context of an activity or event in the culture of the past. Recontextualization has primarily involved (1) inferences derived from relationships among items of material culture, and (2) the ethnohistoric record of Plains Indians. Point one is exemplified by Waldo Wedel's (1970b: 36–45) report of antler tine handles for plano-convex endscrapers from central Kansas Great Bend sites. A more recent example is the recognition of spatial patterning in the small-scale debris recovered from Steed-Kisker sites (Logan and Hill 2000: 241–56). This example is based on the analysis of data from the increasingly precise excavation procedures that characterize most archaeological endeavors in Kansas. Point 2 is illustrated by Wedel's (1979: 85–98) formula for estimating population based on house floor size, which draws heavily on the ethnohistoric records for the Pawnee and Wichita.

An important approach to understanding the reasons behind reconstructed cultural settings, and probably first applied in Kansas by Wedel (1959), emphasizes man-natural environmental interactions. The locations of most Kansas City Hopewell sites, for instance, are apparently a function of the availability of potable water, protection from floods, and ready access to a variety of environmental niches from which first-line resources could be extracted (e.g., deer, turkey, fish, nuts, wild plant seeds) (A. E. Johnson 1976a: 7–15). Beyond such deterministic first attempts, more sophisticated understandings require an appreciation of the crucial role of social interaction in explaining human behavior. A recent study by Pugh (2001: 269–282), attempting to account for the aberrant location of the Kansas City Hopewell Aker site by reference to trade and periodic aggregation to maintain social cohesion, is an interesting example. Appreciation of the overarching significance of worldviews, based both on celestial and terrestrial principles, is another recently explored explanatory framework of great potential (P. J. O'Brien 1986: 939–946; Blakeslee and Hawley, chapter 10, this volume).

A trend important to mention is that with the vast growth in knowledge of the prehistoric and early historic record of Kansas, predictably, has come the need for specialization. As a consequence, studies centering on geomorphology (Artz 1983; Mandel, chapter 3, this volume), paleoethnobotany (Adair 1988; Adair, chapter 15, this volume), zooarchaeology (M. E. Brown 1981; M. E. Hill 1996), lithic sources (Haury 1984; Stein, chapter 16, this volume), ceramic technology (Beck 2001: 5–20), and historic sites archaeology (M. King 1996a, 1996b, 1996c, 1997, 1999a, 1999b, 2004; Larson, Madson, and Mather 2004; Lees 1986; Schoen 1994) are all important aspects of our current interpretive framework.

As demonstrated by this book, advances in our understanding of the prehistory and early history of Kansas, since the last comprehensive overview in 1959 (Wedel), have been significant. We can only hope for similar progress in the future. Certainly an increasing threat to such progress is how rapidly important archaeological sites are destroyed as a result of economic development projects. Preservation laws, both state and federal, at best, only ensure consideration of cultural resources in development situations on land owned, leased, or permitted by government agencies. Most of the land in Kansas is in private hands, with protection of cultural resources entirely at the discretion of the landowner. Governmental ownership of the sites themselves seems the solution, and we can only hope that the Kansas State Historical Society continues and expands its efforts to purchase important sites, perhaps with the assistance of the Archaeological Conservancy.

As the resource base of archaeological sites diminishes, Kansas archaeological repositories that hold the collections and records of previous work become even more important. Many of the collections already at hand have only been superficially examined, and all deserve periodic attention as new interpretive devices appear. It is crucial, therefore, that these collections and associated documentation are conserved according to the most up-to-date procedures. In this regard, it is heartening to see the federal agencies that own many of the collections now devoting attention to long-term care.

Over the past 50 years, I have had the good fortune to be a part of the Kansas archaeological community in its effort to build and provide an understanding of the pre- and early history of the state. Looking back, it is possible to see significant change both in the procedures available for interpreting the past and in the concomitant interpretations themselves. Although our numbers always have been few and the task immense, I believe we can all be proud of the contributions we have made to understanding and preserving the cultural heritage of our state. With a solid base of knowledge to build on, the future can only be productive.

Alfred E. Johnson

ACKNOWLEDGMENTS

The initiative to produce this volume began at a meeting of the Professional Archaeologists of Kansas in 2000. At that meeting, nearly everyone in the room agreed that there was a need for a single reference to summarize the current understanding of the archaeology of Kansas. Soon after, those best equipped to address this need volunteered to produce chapters, and we thank those authors for their dedication and patience. W. Raymond Wood and an anonymous individual reviewed a draft of the volume and offered useful and constructive comments that the authors have worked to address. We appreciate the encouragement, latitude, and financial support provided by Jennie Chinn, Dick Pankratz, Christy Davis, and Terry Marmet of the Kansas State Historical Society. The authors provided the figures, but significant assistance was also provided by Christine Ewing of the Kansas State Historical Society, Kelli Bacon and René Botts of the Nebraska State Historical Society, Mary Adair and Jeannette Blackmar of the Kansas University Museum of Anthropology, and Tod Bevitt.

Much of the information in this volume is the result of state and federal agencies meeting their obligations under Section 106 of the National Historic Preservation Act (PL 89-665; USC 470 *et seq.*). Without naming each agency, we wish to thank them for the financial and logistical support they have provided for archaeological investigations and publications in Kansas. Researchers from the University of Kansas, Kansas State University, and Wichita State University have undertaken important field investigations and reported their findings at conferences and in a variety of publications. Another significant contributor to the archaeological record of Kansas is the Kansas Anthropological Association, whose members have recorded a large percentage of the state's documented sites and have contributed countless hours of survey, excavation, and artifact processing. The Kansas City Archaeological Society and the Archaeological Association of South Central Kansas also have made substantial contributions to the understanding of the state's prehistory.

Finally, we thank Fred Woodward and Susan McRory, as well as the entire staff of the University Press of Kansas, for making this publication possible.

1. Introduction

Robert J. Hoard and William E. Banks

Much is known about the archaeology of Kansas, and much has come to light in recent years. The existing summaries of Kansas archaeology (P. J. O'Brien 1984a; W. R. Wedel 1959) predate the more recent research. Recent overviews (Hofman 1996; Wood 1998) describe the archaeological record in Kansas but do so against a large regional backdrop.

Much of the work carried out in Kansas since the 1970s has been the result of compliance with federal law. Since the passage of the National Historic Preservation Act in 1966 (PL 89-665; 16 USC 470 *et seq.*), any project that receives federal permits or funding—roads, housing projects, water treatment plants, gas pipelines, cellular telephone towers—must have its impact on archaeological sites taken into account. As a result, there has been an enormous volume of data generated. These data often remain in technical reports accessible only to professional archaeologists, and little of this work has been synthesized for presentation to other professionals, much less the interested public. With this volume we intend to change that situation.

In addition to the archaeological work done because of federal laws, a significant amount of academically oriented research has been carried out since the 1970s in Kansas. In addition, avocational groups, working in conjunction with professional archaeologists, have made significant contributions. This research has been published in a variety of professional journals and books, but more recent work has not been synthesized in one publication. That is another major goal of this volume—to provide discussions of current archaeological research for all major time periods in one readily accessible resource. Therefore, each chapter draws together data on a topic, summarizing what we know and in many cases focusing on those questions that remain unanswered and on topics or issues that warrant further investigation.

This volume provides a summary of the material remains that have been found in Kansas and also sheds light on issues such as how people adapted to environmental shifts, as well as the impact of technological change or innovation on social behavior. Of course, every question we answer raises additional questions. By bringing this information together, we hope this book will help guide future research.

Another goal of this volume is to provide information that may help facilitate the preservation of the state's archaeological record. There are nearly 12,000 known sites in Kansas, but these sites are being lost at an alarming rate due to both natural processes and human action. Unless we find out where sites are, understand the nature of these sites, and know what it takes to obtain information about the past from them, we will not be able to save them. It is our hope that this book will help to foster a deeper appreciation of the record of human occupation in Kansas.

TIME DEPTH

Currently, the earliest evidence of human occupation in Kansas comes from the end of the Pleistocene period approximately 12,000 years ago. At this time, people lived alongside and hunted now-extinct Ice Age mammals such as mammoth and species of giant bison. Since the end of the Pleistocene, the climate and, accordingly, the vegetation and landscape of Kansas have changed, as did human groups living off available resources. We find a gradual diversification of technology through time until approximately A.D. 1, when evidence of pottery technology and horticulture came on the scene. This is a significant shift in lifestyle, with a gradually reduced dependence on wild food sources and a growing dependence on cultivated crops, requiring more sedentism, investment of labor, planning, and cooperation. After A.D. 1000, we find the remains of hamlets and villages with substantial houses and deep food storage pits, evidence that growing crops had made a fundamental change in people's lives. The next major change began when the influence of people from Europe began to be felt in Kansas. It is likely that European trade goods and diseases preceded Coronado's journey into the area in A.D. 1541. These influences had a significant impact on the native people living in the state, changes that influenced the creation of the Plains Indian culture that many are familiar with through the popular media.

Native tribal people were dealt a devastating blow, first by Europeans looking to trade and acquire raw materials and later by settlement of Americans of European and African descent. But native people have not vanished from the scene. Although most citizens of the Indian Nations present in Kansas at European contact were moved—forcibly—to Oklahoma, they live on in the twenty-first century. Their story has not ended but coexists with that of immigrants to the land we now call Kansas. Figure 1.1 gives a generalized sequence of events in Kansas.

ARCHAEOLOGICAL DATING

Knowing the age of an archaeological site is critical to understanding the broader archaeological record and thus understanding the developments of human actions over time. Many techniques have been used to estimate or quantitatively determine the age of archaeological sites and artifacts. The stratigraphic position of objects in the soil, assuming that deeper artifacts are older than those closer to the surface, gives archaeologists a relative measure of time. Changes in manufacturing techniques from different stratigraphic layers allow a researcher to extrapolate the relative ages of specific types of artifacts at sites that do not have stratigraphic control.

Methods, including dendrochronology, which uses tree ring sequences to determine the age of wood samples (Dean 1997), and archaeomagnetic dating, which uses the magnetic properties of soils that track dated shifts in the location of magnetic north (Sternberg 1997), are available but not widely used in Kansas. However, radiocarbon dating has seen wide use in Kansas since its earliest development and a brief discussion is warranted.

Willard F. Libby and others developed the radiocarbon dating method in 1949 at the University of Chicago (R. E. Taylor 1987: 147–170). Radiocarbon dating is based on a property of a carbon isotope, Carbon 14 or ^{14}C. This radioactive isotope is taken in from the atmosphere by living organisms, which have amounts of ^{14}C within them that is the same as that of the surrounding environment while they are alive. But when an organism dies, the intake of ^{14}C ceases. The ^{14}C decays at a known rate, known as a half-life, into stable isotopes. A half-life is the amount of time it takes for a given amount of a radioactive isotope to decay to half its mass. For ^{14}C, the half-life is 5,568 years.

The radiocarbon age of an archaeological sample is determined by measuring how much ^{14}C has decayed from the sample and, using the half-life, determining how many years it took for that amount of decay to take place. The radiocarbon age of a sample is a statistically derived number with an associated single standard deviation of statistical error. An example of a typical radiocarbon age would be expressed as 2,545±50 B.P. This means that the sample material died somewhere between 2,495 and 2,595 years before present (or B.P., with present arbitrarily set at A.D. 1950). Because a radiocarbon age is a statistical estimate, the most accurate assessment of a radiocarbon age is to consider the date range that includes the two-standard-deviation date range.

There have been fluctuations in the level of atmospheric ^{14}C through time. By radiocarbon dating samples of known age such as individual tree rings, researchers have been able to document the fluctuation of ^{14}C values in the atmosphere and have produced a method by which radiocarbon ages can be calibrated and assigned calendrical (B.C. or A.D.) dates. Radiocarbon ages that have been calibrated are expressed as calendrical dates, for example, cal A.D. 422 to 216 cal B.C., with cal referring to calibrated years (R. E. Taylor 1997: 73–76).

Early radiocarbon dates were determined by counting the beta particles emitted as a result of the radioactive decay of ^{14}C from a sample measured over a known period of time. More recently, physicists have developed a technique to directly count ^{14}C atoms. This technique is accelerator mass spectrometry, or AMS, described in R. E. Taylor (1997: 78–83). AMS dating allows the use of much smaller samples, weighing milligrams instead of samples weighing several grams that are needed for conventional radiocarbon dating. The AMS dating method has allowed small samples such as seeds to be accurately dated. The appendix of this volume lists all known, well-documented radiocarbon dates from archaeological sites in Kansas as well as some relevant dates from surrounding states. These dates have proven invaluable in

Cultural Period			Date	Physiographic Provinces					Subsistence Pattern
				Dissected Till Plains	Osage Cuestas	Flint Hills	Arkansas River Lowlands	High Plains	
Historic	Modern		A.D. 1950	Americans, including Indian Nations, and immigrants of many cultures					Service economy, light industry, mineral & petroleum exploitation, farming, ranching
			A.D. 1900	Industrialization, Mechanized Agriculture					
	Historic		A.D. 1870	Iowa, Sac & Fox, Kickapoo, Potawatomi, Delaware, Wyandotte, Shawnee	Shawnee, Sac & Fox of Mississippi, Ottawa, Peoria & Kaskaskia, Wea & Piankeshaw, Chippewa, Potawatomi, Miami	Osage, Kansa	Cherokee	Comanche, Cheyenne, Arapahoe, Kiowa, Kiowa-Apache, Sioux, Pawnee	Reservations, Equestrian Bison Hunting; Maize-based Horticulture East; Equestrian Nomads West
Proto-historic	Late Ceramic			Immigrant Tribes					
			A.D. 1800	Kansa	Osage, Kansa, Wichita	Osage, Kansa, Wichita	Wichita, Comanche, Cheyenne, Kiowa, Kiowa-Apache	Comanche, Cheyenne, Arapahoe, Kiowa, Kiowa-Apache, Sioux, Cuartelejo Apache, Pawnee	Equestrian Bison Hunting, Equestrian Nomadism; Maize-based Horticulture & Trapping East
			A.D. 1700	Oneota Tradition	Neosho Focus		Dismal River Aspect	Dismal River Aspect	
Prehistoric	Middle Ceramic		A.D. 1500	Great Bend Aspect White Rock, Nebraska, & Steed Kisker Phases, Pomona Variant	Great Bend Aspect	Great Bend Aspect, White Rock Phase, Smoky Hill Phase, Pomona Variant	Great Bend Aspect Pratt Complex, Bluff Creek Complex	Great Bend Aspect; White Rock, Upper Republican, Smoky Hill, & Odessa Phases; Pratt Complex	Hunting, Gathering; Maize Horticulture East; Some Supplemental Horticulture West
			A.D. 1000		Pomona Variant				
	Early Ceramic			Grasshopper Falls Phase, Valley Variant, Kansas City Hopewell	Greenwood, Grasshopper Falls, & Cuesta Phases	Grasshopper Falls, Greenwood, Schultz & Cuesta Phases	No Known Early Ceramic Cultural Manifestation	Keith Phase	Hunting, Gathering; Cultivation & Domestication of Native Plants East
			A.D. 1	Nebo Hill Phase	Nebo Hill & El Dorado Phases	Walnut & El Dorado Phases	Unclassified Archaic Cultural Manifestations		
			500 B.C.						Hunting, Gathering; Incipient Cultivation of Native Plants East
		Paleo-Archaic		Munkers Creek Phase	Munkers Creek Phase	Vermillion, Chelsea, & Munkers Creek Phases	McKean Complex		
			3000 B.C.						
			5000 B.C.	Logan Creek Phase	Stigenwalt Complex	Logan Creek Phase			
			7500 B.C.		Dalton, Cody Complex, Allen, Fredrick				Hunting, Gathering
			10,000 B.C.		Clovis, Folsom, Plainview				

Figure 1.1 The chronological sequence of Kansas cultures by physiographic provinces

tracking changes in the archaeological record through time. For detailed information of the history, methods, assumptions, and sample requirements for radiocarbon dating, the reader should consult R. E. Taylor (1987, 1997).

While radiocarbon dating has become routine, there have been problems in the past. Adjustments in sample preparation and atmospheric ^{14}C calculation were made to correct problems related to samples from bone and shell and from marine samples, respectively. Also, in the 1990s it became clear that the Gakushuin laboratory in Tokyo was producing inaccurate dates (Blakeslee 1994), and archaeologists now know to be skeptical of these age assessments. Advances continue to increase the precision of ^{14}C dating.

ARCHAEOLOGICAL EVIDENCE

Indian Nations have oral traditions that explain their past. It is the domain of history and ethnography to document and interpret those histories. Archaeology, on the other hand, focuses on the material remains of the past and employs scientific methods to understand the everyday activities not recorded in any history. While oral history often is used to guide understanding of how artifacts were used, archaeologists rely primarily on the material objects themselves to draw their conclusions.

Some basic principles of archaeology need to be explained for those not familiar with the discipline. Material remains are classified as artifacts or features, and their locations and associations with one another are used to define sites—the locations of prehistoric human activity. Generally, an artifact is any movable object that was created by people or subjected to direct or indirect human manipulation. This definition includes a broad range of items. Some of the more obvious examples are chipped-stone projectile points (arrowheads and spear points), stone tool-manufacturing debris, pottery vessels or fragments of them, and animal bone fragments resulting from the butchery and processing of hunted animals. A feature is defined as any unmovable manifestation of human activity. Examples would include fire pits (often referred to as hearths), house floors, trash dumps or middens, and burials.

Another important concept to keep in mind is that the archaeological record exists in the present. It is true that sites were created by events that occurred in the past, but natural processes (e.g., deposition, erosion) may have altered them, and later human activities may have altered materials deposited during an earlier occupation. Therefore, when investigating a site, one cannot assume that the site exists in the same state as it did when the human activity that created it ceased. If we are to reconstruct past events and understand what they tell us about human culture, we must determine which patterns or associations among artifacts are the result of natural processes and which associations are likely the results of human action (see Schiffer 1987 for a review). In other words, we must understand the relationships between the present archaeological record and the past dynamics that created it.

Binford (1981, 1983) describes the need to develop a body of theory that describes these relationships and terms it middle-range theory. Middle-range research (Binford 1983) is the expression of middle-range theory that allows archaeologists to give meaning to the archaeological record that we investigate. This can be done in a variety of ways. For example, an archaeologist might observe a modern hunter-gatherer group and describe the patterns of features and artifacts it left behind at a location or in a region and then compare those patterns to remains found at an archaeological site (e.g., Binford 1978a; Yellen 1977).

Moreover, archaeologists have used the work of researchers (e.g., Hunt 1978; Voorhies 1969) who have studied natural animal death sites (no human involvement) to understand the natural processes that affect carcasses prior to their burial and preservation. These types of studies are done so that archaeologists can compare their results with what is observed at a kill site, thereby allowing them to infer what natural processes and human behaviors created the patterns we see in the bonebed.

To find behavioral patterns in assemblages of artifacts, archaeologists create classification systems. These provide a means of conveying a substantial amount of information in a single word or phrase. For example, if someone mentions the Forty-niners, this term calls to mind a set of ideas about a group of people that traveled to California in the mid-1800s in search of gold. Likewise, when archaeologists talk about Paleoindians, the term describes the earliest known people in North America, their nomadic lifestyle, their well-made projectile point technology, and their hunting of large Ice Age mammals.

Several terms are used to describe sets of artifacts at archaeological sites. Terms such as phase, focus, aspect, tradition, variant, period, and complex are all found in the following chapters. These terms arise primarily from two different taxonomic systems, which demand a brief explanation. For in-depth analysis of the topic see Dunnell (1971, 1986), Lyman, O'Brien, and Dunnell (1997), and Willey and Phillips (1958). For information on the history and application of classification schemes in the Great Plains, see Krause (1998).

The first explicit attempt at archaeological classification was the Midwestern Taxonomic Method. Published in 1939 by W. C. McKern and widely used for about 20 years, it established six hierarchical units—component, focus, aspect, phase, pattern, and base—to describe morphological similarities between groups of artifacts. As a result of the establishment of this system, specific names for archaeological manifestations were established, published, and brought into common use: the Nebo Hill phase, the Great Bend aspect, the Glen Elder focus. The following is a brief summary of McKern's units (1939: 307–310).

> Focus: A complex of traits exhibiting "characteristic peculiarities" (distinctive traits, such as a particular pattern of designs on pottery), occurring in more than one site.
>
> Component: The manifestation of a focus at a site. A site may contain one or more components.
>
> Aspect: A grouping of foci, sharing more general traits. An aspect might include several foci.
>
> Phase: A phase is more general than an aspect, and may include foci and aspects all of which have several similarities in traits such as pottery construction and decoration, patterns of house construction, and disposal of the dead.
>
> Pattern: An aggregation of phases sharing even more general traits. For example, one pattern may include pottery-bearing phases, one of which includes crushed

stone inclusions in the pottery and projectile points with stemmed bases, with another phase represented by pottery with crushed shell inclusions and projectile points with side notches.

Base: A term that encompasses broad sets of fundamental traits, such as the presence of pottery and evidence of horticulture in the sites of a particular region, as opposed to sites with basketry containers and no evidence of horticulture, but instead remains that indicate a strong reliance on fish as a food source.

The terms *pattern* and *base* quickly fell from use.

Those who felt that the Midwestern Taxonomic Method was not entirely satisfactory chose to use labels that included *complex* and *culture* (Krause 1998: 61), referring to assemblages of artifacts and to sites that shared similarities, respectively, but had not yet been placed in a taxonomic scheme. As time went on, archaeologists became dissatisfied with McKern's system, primarily because it focused on the similarity or dissimilarity between artifacts but did not address two factors critical to archaeological studies: time and space.

Gordon R. Willey and Philip Phillips's publication *Method and Theory in American Archaeology* added the dimensions of time and space to that of artifact form (1958: 17). They established three major taxonomic units:

Tradition: "a (primarily) temporal continuity represented by consistent configurations in single technologies or other systems of related form" (Willey and Phillips 1958: 37).

Phase: "An archaeological unit possessing traits sufficiently characteristic to distinguish it from all other units similarly conceived, whether of the same or other cultures or civilizations, spatially limited to the order of magnitude of a locality or region and chronologically limited to a relatively brief interval of time" (22).

Horizon: "A primarily spatial continuity represented by cultural traits and assemblages whose nature and mode of occurrence permit the assumption of a broad and rapid spread" (33).

Then, in 1971, Lehmer proposed the term *variant* to describe "a unique and reasonably uniform expression of a cultural tradition which has a greater order of magnitude than a phase, and which is distinguished from other variants of the same tradition by its geographic distribution, age, and/or cultural content"(1971: 32).

To further complicate matters, Central Plains archaeologists occasionally assign sites to one of three periods referred to as the Early, Middle, and Late Ceramic. These periods were first described by Nebraska archaeologist John Champe (1946: 85, 89–90) as a means of distinguishing ceramic-bearing sites of the Great Plains from their midwestern counterparts. These period designations apparently followed Champe-trained Thomas Witty, Jr., to Kansas when he took the position of Kansas State Archeologist in 1960. Use of Early, Middle, and Late Ceramic to describe sites begins to appear in Kansas site reports at about that time, and O'Brien uses it in her handbook on Kansas archaeology (P. J. O'Brien 1984a).

Date	Geographic Region		
	Midwest	Eastern Kansas	Central and Western Kansas
A.D. 1800	Historic	Historic	Historic
A.D. 1500		Late Ceramic (Kansa, Osage)	Late Ceramic (Wichita, Comanche, Cheyenne, Arapahoe, Kiowa, Kiowa-Apache, Sioux, Cuartelejo Apache, Pawnee, Kansa, Osage)
A.D. 1000	Mississippian	Middle Ceramic (White Rock, Nebraska, Steed Kisker Phases, Pomona Variant)	Middle Ceramic (Great Bend Aspect, White Rock Oneota, Smoky Hill, Upper Republican, Odessa Phases; Pratt & Bluff Creek Complexes, Steed-Kisker, Pomona)
A.D. 750	Late Woodland	Early Ceramic (Grasshopper Falls, Kansas City Hopewell, Greenwood, Schultz, & Cuesta phases; Valley Variant)	Plains Woodland (Keith Phase)
A.D. 500	Middle Woodland		
A.D. 1			No Pottery-Bearing Sites
500 B.C.	Early Woodland	No Pottery-Bearing Sites	
2500 B.C.	Late Archaic	Late Archaic	Late Archaic

Figure 1.2. Comparison of taxonomic conventions by geographic region

In the eastern United States, pottery-bearing sites are divided into general periods of Woodland and Mississippian. The Woodland period is further divided into the Early Woodland (ca. 1000–500 B.C.), Middle Woodland (ca. 500 B.C.–A.D. 500), and Late Woodland (ca. A.D. 500–1000), followed by the Mississippian period and its subperiods. In eastern Kansas, we find pottery closely similar to that found in Middle and Late Woodland sites of the eastern United States, though none that is similar to Early Woodland.

In Champe's ceramic periods, Great Plains sites that are called Middle Woodland in the Midwest are referred to as Early Ceramic sites, and further west, Late Woodland sites are referred to as Plains Woodland (Figure 1.2). These sites have traits similar to their eastern woodland counterparts—thick pottery vessels, corner-notched projectile points, and burial mounds—with differences that reflect the adaptation to a semiarid grassland environment (A. M. Johnson and A. E. Johnson 1998: 201). Sites on the Plains with similarities to eastern Late Woodland sites are referred to as Middle Ceramic or Plains Village sites. Later pottery-bearing sites, referred to as Late Ceramic, are less similar to coeval sites in the Midwest and instead are identified with historically known Kansas tribes such as the Kansa, the Pawnee, and the Wichita.

Clearly archaeologists have adopted and adapted various systems in an attempt to create a classification system that is unique to the discipline. Although these systems make some intuitive sense through the use of examples and repeated use, they ultimately remain poorly defined. Lyman, O'Brien, and Dunnell (1997: 180–181) express this succinctly: "Unfortunately, Americanist archaeology still lacks a theory for specifying what aggregates of artifacts should consist of and how to specify temporal-spatial boundaries of the aggregates such that they are relevant to the analytical problems at hand."

The following chapters discuss the major time periods and associated changes in human behavior that are reflected in the artifacts and features that people made. Also included are discussions of the changing environment through time and the use of critical resources such as plants for food (chapter 15) and stone for tools (chapter 16). Mandel's chapter (chapter 3) on geomorphology and archeological site location demonstrates how sites are lost to natural processes.

Many other important topics are not addressed directly in this volume. For example, burial sites and mortuary practices receive only limited treatment. Petroglyphs and pictographs—designs engraved and painted, respectively, on stone exposures—are mentioned only in passing. Readers interested in this topic should refer to *Kansas Rock Art* by Brian O'Neill (1981). Finally there is a rich and diverse archaeological record that tells the story of European, Euro-American, African, and American Indian people who lived in Kansas during the Historic period. Although written history speaks to major social, political, and economic movements, it rarely addresses the everyday lives of the common person, much less those of minority populations (c.f. Beaudry, Cook, and Mrozowski 1996; Mullins 1997; Rotman and Nassaney 1994). However, the archaeological record of the Historic period is not discussed in this book. It is our hope that this volume serves to synthesize much of what we know about Kansas prehistory and to make that diverse knowledge base accessible to a large number of people with a variety of interests.

2. Late Quaternary and Modern Environments in Kansas

Rolfe D. Mandel

Environmental features of Kansas, such as climate, vegetation, landforms, and surface geology, have undoubtedly influenced prehistoric people who occupied the region. For example, it is likely that the availability of high-quality lithic resources, which is related to bedrock geology, attracted prehistoric people to specific areas of Kansas. Because subsistence strategies of people depend on plant and animal resources, the composition and distribution of vegetation affected the spatial pattern of human groups. Furthermore, certain landforms, such as the playas in western Kansas, were microenvironments that attracted game and people. Hence, researchers must have some understanding of the environments that formed the setting for prehistoric human occupation in Kansas.

The environments of Kansas have not been static over the past 12,000 years. There have been significant climatic changes that not only affected vegetation, game, and people but also influenced landscape evolution that in turn affected the material record of human occupation. The nature of late Quaternary environmental change is described in this chapter, but its effects on the archaeological record of Kansas are considered elsewhere (see chapter 3). This chapter presents a general overview of the physiography, geology, climate, and vegetation of Kansas, thereby providing an environmental backdrop for many of the other chapters in the volume.

PHYSIOGRAPHY AND GEOLOGY

Compared to mountainous terrain, such as the Rocky Mountains or Appalachians, Kansas is almost featureless. However, if this comparison is set aside, one realizes that Kansas has a diverse landscape with many interesting features. Although most of the broad stream divides in western Kansas are monotonously flat, there is dramatic relief in areas such as the Flint Hills of east-central Kansas and the dissected High Plains of western Kansas. There also are prominent landforms in some areas of the state, such as the pyramids, castle rocks, monument rocks, and other badland features where the Smoky Hill River and its tributaries have dissected the soft Cretaceous-age (136 to 65 million years ago) chalks of western Kansas.

The modern land surface in Kansas slopes gently eastward from the highest point of 1,260 m above mean sea level in Wallace County (northwestern Kansas) to the

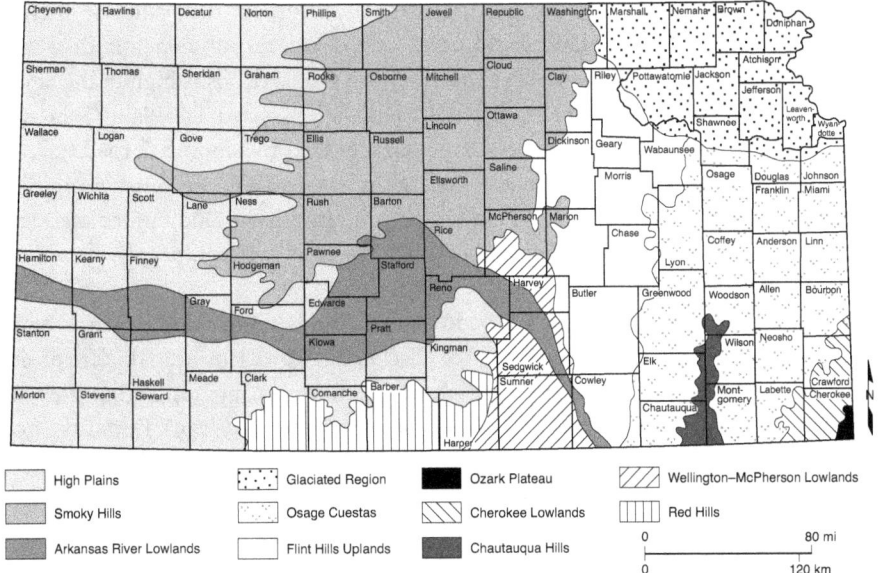

Figure 2.1. Generalized physiographic map of Kansas

lowest point of 213 m above mean sea level in Montgomery County (southeastern Kansas). Eastward inclination of this surface is discordant with the regional structure of all outcropping rocks predating the Tertiary period (65 to 2.5 million years before the present) (Merriam 1963: 161). Thus, the present slope of the land probably was established during Tertiary time.

Two of Fenneman's (1931) physiographic provinces compose most of Kansas: the Central Lowland and the Great Plains. The Central Lowland forms nearly all of eastern Kansas, and the Great Plains province spans the western two-thirds of the state. A third province, the Ozark Plateau, extends across a small portion of the southeast corner of the state. The Central Lowland portion of Kansas is divided into five subprovinces: the Glaciated Region, the Osage Questas, the Cherokee Lowlands, the Chautauqua Hills, and the Flint Hills. The Great Plains province in Kansas is divided into five subprovinces: the Arkansas River Lowlands, the Wellington-McPherson Lowlands, the Red Hills, the Smoky Hills, and the High Plains (Figure 2.1). The physiographic subprovinces are briefly described below.

Glaciated Region

The Glaciated Region is in the northeast corner of the state. It is bordered on the south by the Kansas River and on the west by the Flint Hills. During the Pre-Illinoian glacial episodes of the Pleistocene, a continental ice sheet that extended slightly beyond the Kansas River in places and overlapped portions of the Flint Hills covered this area. The ice sheet buried pre-glacial stream valleys, cut new valley segments, and leveled the uplands (Mandel and Bettis 2001). Streams subsequently dissected the drift plain that was left by the ice sheet, leaving glacial deposits high in the landscape. Hence, this region is often referred to as the Dissected Till Plain (Schoewe 1949). Interstream areas, or divides, are characterized by smooth, broad, gently rolling hills. Approaching the valleys of large rivers, the land becomes more dissected. The most rugged portion of the Glaciated Region is the land immediately adjacent to the Missouri River. There, the upland surface has been deeply incised by streams, and the hills have steep convex slopes.

Pennsylvanian and Permian-age bedrock formations similar to the bedrock formations of the Osage Cuestas underlie the Glaciated Region. However, thick deposits of till, glacial outwash, and loess conceal the cuesta-type topography that prevails south of the Kansas River (Frye and Walters 1950; Schoewe 1949: 289). Deposits associated with at least two and as many as five Pre-Illinoian glacial episodes have been described from localities in northeastern Kansas (Aber 1988, 1991; Bayne et al. 1971; Dort 1966, 1985; Frye and Leonard 1952; Mandel and Bettis 2001). Two glacial tills are commonly recognized in Kansas (Mandel and Bettis 2001). The lower till has been called the Nebraskan, Nickerson, Iowa Point, or lower Kansan till, and the upper till has been called the Kansan, Cedar Bluffs, or upper Kansan. Recently, Aber (1991) proposed the Independence Formation to include all these glacial tills and the stratified sediments associated with them. The Independence Formation is mantled by late-Quaternary loess and/or colluvium (for a detailed description of the loess stratigraphy, see Mandel and Bettis 2001).

The landscape and surface geology along the western fringe of the Glaciated Region has not been greatly affected by glaciation, and much of this area lacks a thick loess mantle. The most common evidence for glaciation in this area consists of large boulders, or glacial erratics, scattered over the land surface (Dort 1987). Many of the erratics are distinctive reddish Sioux quartzite, a Precambrian metamorphic rock that does not have a source in Kansas. Outcrops of Sioux quartzite are restricted to a small area in southwestern Minnesota and nearby parts of Iowa and South Dakota (Dort 1987). The Laurentide ice sheet dislodged pieces of Sioux quartzite, as well as other "foreign" rock types, and transported them into Kansas during Pre-Illinoian glacial episodes, where they were deposited on the Pleistocene landscape.

Osage Cuestas

The Osage Cuestas region, which is immediately south of the Glaciated Region, is the largest subprovince of the Central Lowland. In Kansas, the Osage Cuestas is bounded by the Kansas River to the north, the Flint Hills to the west, and the Cherokee Lowland to the east (Figure 2.1). Long, low, rolling hills and wide, shallow valleys characterize the topography of the Osage Cuestas. The regional bedrock, which consists of alternating layers of Pennsylvanian-age limestone and shale, has strongly influenced the physiography of the Osage Cuestas (F. W. Wilson 1984: 16). Specifically, the cuestas formed as a result of differential erosion of these alternating hard and soft rock layers. The more resistant limestone strata compose the upland scarp and dip-slope of each cuesta, and the thicker and softer shales, which erode more easily, form the intervening lowlands. All of the strata slope gently toward the west-northwest. The dipping strata form a series of ridges with gently sloping west faces and steeply sloping east faces. Although the escarpments generally exhibit an irregular northeast-southwest trend, the major streams flow to the east and southeast, transverse to the direction of the escarpments and against the westward dip of the rock formations.

Cherokee Lowlands

The Cherokee Lowlands region includes portions of Bourbon, Cherokee, Crawford, and Labette counties in the southeastern corner of Kansas. This region is an erosional plain that slopes to the west at an average rate of about 1.5 m/km (Self 1978: 42). The bedrock of the Cherokee Lowlands consists of weak shales and sandstones of the Pennsylvanian-age Cherokee Group. The landscape is nearly flat and featureless, except for some low rolling hills and a few broad, flat-topped erosional remnants or "mounds" capped by resistant sandstone. The major streams and rivers of the region flow to the south or southeast, passing through wide, shallow, flat-bottomed valleys.

Chautauqua Hills

The Chautauqua Hills region, which includes portions of Montgomery, Chautauqua, Elk, Wilson, Woodson, and Greenwood counties, is a narrow belt of rolling uplands that extends northward into the Osage Cuestas from the Oklahoma-Kansas state line. Erosion of the thick Pennsylvanian-age sandstone in this region has formed a series of low, rounded hills that sharply contrast with the cuesta-form ridges of the surrounding Osage Cuestas.

Flint Hills

The Flint Hills trend north-south along the western edge of the Osage Cuestas and the Glaciated Region of Kansas. The Flint Hills region derives it name from the abundance of chert, or flint, scattered across its surface. Like the Osage Cuestas to the east, the Flint Hills were formed by erosion of westward-dipping strata. The rock units are Permian in age, and limestone members in the region contain many bands of chert. Because chert is much less soluble than the limestone that encloses it, weathering of the softer rock forms a clay-rich soil that contains a large volume of chert fragments (F. W. Wilson 1984: 19). This gravel-rich soil armors the rocky uplands and causes slower erosion than in adjacent areas where the limestone does not contain chert.

Surface features and the geologic structure of the Flint Hills are similar to those in the adjacent Osage Cuestas, but a prominent rocky escarpment nearly 100 m high separates the two regions. This escarpment, which forms the eastern border of the Flint Hills region, is the most rugged surface feature in Kansas (Self 1978: 44). The east-facing slope of the escarpment is composed of resistant cherty limestone interbedded with softer shale layers. Weathering of the shales has created a landscape that resembles steplike benches. The highest of these benches form the uplands of the Flint Hills. The uplands are gently rolling, especially toward the western boundary of the Flint Hills. Major rivers and streams have dissected portions of the uplands, forming prominent strath terraces. These terraces are erosional surfaces cut across bedrock as stream channels laterally migrated and downcut, leaving little to no alluvium on the rock-cut straths. The smaller streams in the region usually have steep gradients and deeply entrenched channels bordered by rocky ledges.

From an archaeological perspective, the abundance of chert bands in the limestones is perhaps the most important characteristic of the Flint Hills environment. Because of its superior flaking qualities, Flint Hills chert provided excellent raw material for chipped-stone tools and was heavily exploited by prehistoric inhabitants of the region.

Arkansas River Lowlands

The Arkansas River Lowlands region follows the Arkansas River from the Kansas-Colorado border in Hamilton County eastward to the Kansas-Oklahoma border in Cowley County. The Arkansas River meandered across this region throughout the Quaternary, leaving a complex record of alluvial deposits that mostly consist of sand and gravel. In many areas of the Arkansas River Lowlands, winds swept the sands into low, rolling dunes.

Fenneman (1931) and Schoewe (1949) subdivided the Arkansas River Lowlands into the Finney Lowland and the Great Bend Lowland. The Finney Lowland is 10 to 40 km wide and includes the entire Arkansas River valley in Kansas west of Dodge City. The floodplain, alluvial terraces, and side slopes of the Arkansas River valley collectively form the Finney Lowland. The north side of the Finney Lowland is bordered by high bluffs that stand nearly 30 m above the valley floor.

The Great Bend Lowland is an undulating plain with little relief that parallels the great northward bend of the Arkansas River in south-central Kansas. This area extends from about Dodge City in Ford County northward to Great Bend in Barton County, then southward to Arkansas City in Cowley County. The Great Bend Lowland is 50 to 80 km wide, and elevations range from approximately 320 to 670 m above mean sea level. The Arkansas River traverses the middle of this region. Fent (1950) suggested that the great bend of the Arkansas River migrated laterally from the south to its present position via successive captures by its own northern tributaries.

Unconsolidated Quaternary deposits of alluvial and eolian origin dominate the surface geology of the Great Bend Lowland. The valley fill of the Arkansas River has a maximum thickness of about 120 m and consists of sediment derived from local and distant sources. Rosner (1988) identified five lithostratigraphic units in the Arkansas River valley (from bottom to top): (1) basal sand and gravel; (2) alternating sequences of sandy silt-clay, sand, and gravel; (3) near surface silt-clay beds; (4) loess; and (5) sand. The uppermost sand unit is 1–15 m thick and has been reworked by the wind in many areas. Dunes and dune fields have formed where this sand is thickest (Arbogast 1995; Bayne 1956; Fent 1950; W. C. Johnson 1991; Latta 1950; Layton and Berry 1973; Logan, Arbogast, and Johnson 1993; Rosner 1988; Schoewe 1949: 293). An extensive sand-dune belt that is about 8 km wide occurs on the north side of the Arkansas River northeast of Hutchinson and trends southeast between the Arkansas and Little Arkansas rivers. Smaller dune fields are scattered throughout the Great Bend Lowland.

A large natural depression, known as the Cheyenne Bottoms, lies north of the city of Great Bend. The total area of this depression is approximately 30,000 acres. There are also some spring-fed lakes in the region, such as James Lake in southeast Pawnee County, and small ponds often form between sand dunes during the rainy season (C. C. Williams 1946).

Wellington-McPherson Lowlands

The Wellington-McPherson Lowlands form a triangular-shaped region in south-central Kansas. This region is divided by the Arkansas River Lowlands. The Wellington Lowland lies southwest of the Arkansas River and includes most of Sumner County and portions of Harper, Kingman, and Reno counties. The landscape of this area is more rolling than the McPherson and Arkansas lowlands to the northeast. Elevations in the Wellington Lowland region range between approximately 350 and 400 m above sea level. The eastern border of the Wellington Lowland gradually merges into the Arkansas River Lowlands. To the west, however, a prominent escarpment, known as the Gypsum Hills, marks the boundary between the Wellington Lowland and the Red Hills.

Permian salt deposits, shales, siltstones, sandstones, and gypsum underlie the Wellington Lowland. The beds of salt and gypsum have been dissolved by groundwater near the land surface. Consequently, these deposits are seldom seen in outcrops. Instead, the Permian "redbeds" are exposed at the surface over wide areas of the region. The redbeds are composed of dark-red shales, siltstones, and sandstones (Swineford 1955: 164), and the soils derived from these rocks have distinct red hues.

Frye and Leonard (1952: 206) noted that the Wellington Lowland is geologically related to the Red Hills to the west. The landscapes of both regions are products of the erosion of Permian bedrock. However, the topography of the Wellington Lowland is predominantly a complex of different-aged pediments lacking the prominent scarps and buttes that characterize the Red Hills. The absence of scarps and buttes in the Wellington Lowland region is largely due to the lack of bedrock layers that could serve as resistant caprocks.

The McPherson Lowland lies northeast of the Arkansas River and includes most of McPherson County and portions of Harvey, Rice, and Marion counties. This area is a flat plain underlain by gravels, sands, silts, and clays. Deposits of sands and gravels are as much as 35 m thick and are overlain by 15–20 m of loess (Frye and Leonard 1952: 190). The coarse-grained deposits are referred to as the "Equus beds" (Haworth and Beede 1897: 295–296) or the McPherson Formation (Lohman and Frye 1940). The Equus beds overlie impervious Permian-age shale. Lohman and Frye (1940: 846) suggested that the Equus beds represent the alluvial fill of a channel that connected the Smoky Hill River with the Arkansas River during the early Pleistocene.

Sand dunes are prominent features in portions of the McPherson Lowland, especially within a 10-km-wide east-west belt that extends from points south of Medora and Buhler eastward to the Little Arkansas River and Kisiwa Creek. In addition, there are many small depressions scattered across the McPherson Lowland. The largest depression is about 3 km long and 1 km wide, and many hold water.

Red Hills

The Red Hills physiographic subprovince, also called the Cimarron Breaks, forms part of the highly dissected southern border of the High Plains. In Kansas, the Red Hills extend across most of Harper, Barber, Comanche, and Clark counties. The Red Hills are named after the red soils and bedrock exposed throughout this region. The surface bedrock is predominantly red shales, siltstones, and sandstones of the Permian redbeds (Swineford 1955: 164). The name Cimarron Breaks refers to the sharp break in topography marking the edge of the High Plains along the Cimarron River valley (Schoewe 1949: 302). Beds of gypsum and dolomite cap the highly erodible shale hills; hence, the region is characterized by butte-and-mesa topography. The landscape of Barber County is especially rugged, with many steep-sided buttes and pinnacles.

Smoky Hills

The Smoky Hills physiographic subprovince extends across north-central Kansas from the western edge of the Flint Hills to the eastern edge of the High Plains. The Arkansas River Lowlands and the Wellington-McPherson Lowlands bound the Smoky Hills on the south. The Smoky Hills region consists of a broad belt of hills formed by differential erosion of Cretaceous rock units. Thick sandstones of the Dakota Formation cap the easternmost range of hills. This area is commonly referred to as the Dakota Hills (F. W. Wilson 1984: 24), and it is characterized by hills and buttes that abruptly rise above the surrounding plains.

The Greenhorn Formation caps uplands in the central portion of the Smoky Hills. This stratigraphic unit is composed of thick beds of gray shale interbedded with thin limestone. Erosion of the softer shale layers has formed a rolling landscape interspersed with flat-topped buttes and mesas capped by resistant limestone.

The western segment of the Smoky Hills is developed on thick chalks of the Niobrara Formation. Erosion of the relatively soft chalk has produced a rugged "badlands" landscape with many high, flat-topped buttes and mesas. A common lithic resource associated with the chalk is Smoky Hill Jasper (Hattin 1982; Stein 2005; see also Stein, chapter 16, this volume).

High Plains

The High Plains physiographic subprovince forms most of the western one-third of Kansas, and a peninsula of the High Plains surface extends as far east as eastern Reno and Kingman counties in south-central Kansas. The eastern limit of the High Plains is defined by the prominent scarp of the Cretaceous-age Fort Hays limestones along the Smoky Hills Border (Frye and Swineford 1949: 74) and by the scarps of the Tertiary-age Ogallala Formation that extend from northern Clark County southward to the Kansas-Oklahoma state line (Frye and Leonard 1952: 202). Although the edge of the High Plains is heavily dissected, this region is essentially a plateau characterized by broad reaches of flat uplands with poorly developed surface drainage. Hundreds of shallow depressions, or playas, of various shapes and sizes are scattered across the uplands.

The geologic history of the High Plains can be traced back to the evolution of the Rocky Mountains. As this great mountain system was slowly uplifted during the Tertiary period, large volumes of rock were eroded from its slopes and transported eastward by streams. These streams eventually carried the sediments into eastern Colorado and western Kansas. Frank W. Wilson (1984: 33) commented: "So great was the mass of eroded material that it literally overflowed the stream valleys and spread out over the uplands. By the end of the Tertiary period, the upper surface of this immense sheet of sand and gravel formed a gently eastward-sloping plain extending from the eastern front of the Rockies to the west slopes of the Flint Hills in central Kansas." The High Plains of western Kansas represent the uneroded remnants of this extensive plain, and the deposits of pre-Quaternary sand and gravel that lie below the surface are part of the Ogallala Formation (Frye, Leonard, and Swineford 1956).

In Kansas, the Ogallala Formation mostly consists of Miocene and Pliocene deposits of fluvial sand and gravel (Merriam 1963: 22). There are many pedogenic caliche layers in the Ogallala Formation; the most distinct of these horizons is the resistant "caprock" caliche that forms the upper surface of the Ogallala (C. C. Reeves 1976). The "caprock" typically is several meters thick and preserves the plateau topography of the High Plains. Because of the thick package of Quaternary deposits (loess and alluvium) on the High Plains, surface exposures of the Ogallala Formation are confined to deeply dissected or eroded areas, especially along the High Plains escarpment. The Ogallala is also exposed in the valley walls of major streams. The Ogallala is a major aquifer; hence, springs are common along the High Plains escarpment and where the Ogallala is exposed in the walls of stream valleys. Given that these springs were probably reliable sources of water for game and people during the past 12,000 years, it is not surprising that archaeological sites are often located at or near them.

The High Plains surface is mantled by a sheet of late Quaternary loess that is generally 2–3 m thick but is more than 10 m thick in some areas near major river valleys. The loess directly overlies Pleistocene alluvium or the Ogallala Formation.

Shallow playas with diameters ranging from a few meters to several kilometers are common on the High Plains (Frye 1950; Mandel 2000). Most of these playas are less than 3 m deep, but some of the larger ones are as much as 15–20 m deep. Radiocarbon ages determined on soils developed in playa fills suggest that many of these depressions formed during the Holocene (Mandel 2000). Their development has been attributed to several causes, including wind deflation, solution subsidence, and wallowing of bison. Frye (1950) suggested that most, if not all, of these processes played a role in the development of depressions on the High Plains. There is also evidence indicating that some playas formed when ephemeral drainage systems were blocked by sand dunes (Mandel 2000). Like springs, the playas attracted game and people during prehistoric times. The Winger site (14ST401), a Late Paleoindian bison bonebed contained in playa fill on the High Plains of southwestern Kansas, is a case in point (Mandel and Hofman 2003).

Sand dunes are common features on the High Plains. Most of the dunes are concentrated on the south side of the Arkansas and Cimarron rivers. In fact, one of the largest dune fields in North America is located on the south side of the Cimarron River in Morton, Stevens, and Seward counties. The Cimarron National Grassland is located within this dune field.

Many geologists during the late 1800s and early 1900s held the view that the present surface of the High Plains is the original surface developed by stream deposition during late-Tertiary (Pliocene) time, kept essentially unchanged throughout the Quaternary because of a protective cover of grass (e.g., G. I. Adams 1903; Fenneman 1931: 107; Haworth 1897; W. D. Johnson 1901). However, as Frye (1946: 73) correctly noted, "there are many indications that the area has been extensively modified by several cycles of erosion and deposition since Pliocene time, and it seems clear that most of the present High Plains surface was shaped in Pleistocene and recent (Holocene) times." In other words, late Quaternary landscape evolution has greatly modified the High Plains surface. This is an important point because the processes of late Quaternary landscape evolution (erosion and deposition) have "filtered" the region's archaeological record (see chapter 3, this volume).

CLIMATE

The modern climate of Kansas is continental; summers are very hot, and winters are very cold. There also are extremes in precipitation, with years of drought sometimes followed by periods of excessive annual rainfall.

There is a distinct longitudinal (east-west) precipitation gradient across Kansas. Mean annual precipitation ranges from a high of about 106 cm (42 in.) along the eastern edge of the state to a low of about 40 cm (16 in.) along the Kansas-Colorado border (Institute for Public Policy and Business Research 2000). June and January are normally the wettest and driest months, respectively, for all regions of the state. Approximately 75 percent of the precipitation falls during the six months of the growing season, April through September (Self 1978: 56). This period of high precipitation is largely a result of frontal activity. Maritime polar (mP) and continental polar (cP) air masses that flow into Kansas during spring and early summer usually converge with warm, moist, maritime tropical (mT) air that is flowing north from the Gulf of Mexico. The overrunning of mP and cP air by warmer mT air often produces intensive rainfall of short duration along the zone of convergence. During late summer, convectional thunderstorms can also produce heavy rainfalls.

The mean annual temperature for Kansas is approximately 12.8° C (55° F), with mean monthly temperatures ranging from a high of 26.2° C (79.2° F) in July to a low of 0.9° C (33.6° F) in January. A wedge of warm, humid air often extends into central Kansas during the summer, whereas temperatures tend to steadily decrease northward across Kansas during the winter.

Kansas lies in the zone of the prevailing westerly winds. Consequently, cyclonic frontal cells associated with invading Pacific air masses are largely responsible for short-term (daily and weekly) changes that affect the weather across the state. However, climate, which is the average of weather conditions over a period of many years, is not uniform across Kansas. Thornthwaite (1948) recognized four distinct climatic zones in Kansas: humid (B4), moist subhumid (C2), dry subhumid (C1), and semiarid (D). The moist subhumid (C2) zone covers most of the eastern half of Kansas, but the humid (B4) climatic zone edges into the southeastern corner of the state. Similarly, the dry subhumid (C1) zone covers nearly all of the western half of Kansas, but there is a strip of the semiarid (D) climatic zone along the western edge of the state.

The east to west climatic variability that characterizes Kansas is related to dominance of certain air masses over different portions of the state. Specifically, warm, humid, mT air from the Gulf of Mexico usually blankets eastern Kansas during the summer, providing a source of moisture for convectional thunderstorms and occasional mid-latitude cyclones. The presence of mT air steadily decreases westward from central Kansas.

The western third of Kansas is in a "rain shadow" on the eastern side of one of the highest segments of the Rocky Mountains. Although Pacific air is initially cool and moist as it crosses the mountains, it loses much of its moisture on the windward side of the Rockies. The air becomes warm and dry as it descends the eastern slopes of the mountains. This warm, dry air spreads out across the High Plains and has a drying effect on the environment of eastern Colorado and western Kansas. The dominance of Pacific air in western Kansas during the winter and summer results in low annual precipitation for the region.

The weather patterns of western Kansas have a tendency to produce frequent droughts. Climatic records indicate that severe droughts tend to afflict the High Plains about every 21 years (Frison 1978: 25), producing near-arid conditions in the short-grass prairie of extreme western Kansas and semiarid conditions in the tall-grass prairie of eastern Kansas. Borchert (1950) suggested that drought occurs when the strong westerlies of winter persist into spring and summer. Intensification of westerly (zonal) air flow in the upper atmosphere has the effect of blocking the northward penetration of moist Gulf air into the mid-continent (Bryson and Hare 1974: 4), thus promoting drought.

Prolonged severe drought can have significant effects on ecosystems of the Plains. For example, short-grass prairie in western Kansas may respond to drought by expanding eastward into the area of mixed- and tall-grass prairie. Also, increased aridity tends to increase fire frequency on the Plains. The dynamics of drought-related vegetational perturbations and their implications for late Quaternary landscape evolution and prehistoric human adaptations are discussed elsewhere in this volume (see chapters 3 and 4).

VEGETATION

Kansas lies in the extensive North American grassland region commonly referred to as the Great Plains, Prairie and Plains, or Interior Grasslands. This region extends from the Central Plains of Canada to the Gulf Coastal Plain of southern Texas. Explorers and settlers usually described the Great Plains as a vast, homogeneous prairie. However, it is actually a complex biogeographical region. Kuchler's (1974) map of the natural vegetation of Kansas illustrates how the composition of plant communities varies across the state (Figure 2.2). Although most of the variability is related to climate, other factors, such as topography, drainage, and soils, affect the distribution of plant communities.

Three broadly defined plant communities dominate Kansas: the short-grass, mixed-grass, and tall-grass prairies. The short-grass prairie covers most of the High Plains of western Kansas and is dominated by blue grama (*Bouteloua gracilis*) and buffalo grass (*Buchloe dactyloides*). At the eastern edge of the High Plains, the short-grass prairie is gradually replaced by mixed-grass prairie. The bluestem-grama prairie forms the largest portion of the mixed-grass prairie and extends eastward to the poorly defined western edge of the Flint Hills. There, the tall-grass prairie begins and extends eastward to its boundary with the eastern deciduous forest in northeastern Kansas and portions of western Missouri. The tall-grass prairie is dominated by big bluestem (*Andropogon gerardi*) and little bluestem (*Andropogon scoparius*).

Although the flora of the tall-grass prairie and eastern deciduous forest are clearly different, the boundary between these plant communities is far less obvious. Most of the eastern quarter of Kansas is actually a mosaic of forest and prairie. In a

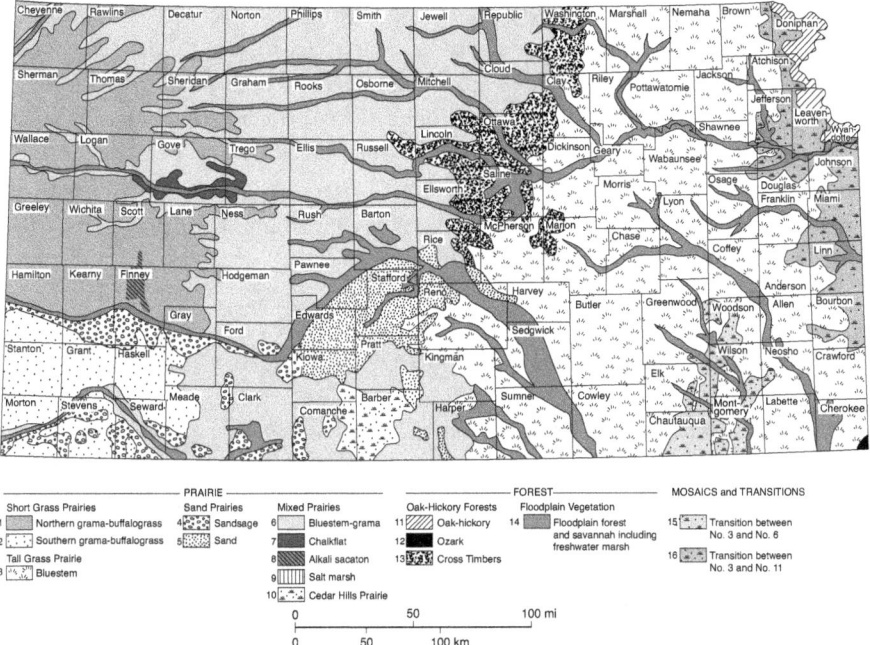

Figure 2.2. Generalized vegetation map of Kansas

mosaic, the species of one vegetation community are not mixed with those of the other. Instead, each community retains its unique character (Kuchler 1974: 586). For example, in northeastern Kansas, the oak-hickory forest keeps its identity and does not gradually open up into a savanna; the tall-grass prairie does likewise. Going westward from the Kansas-Missouri border, forests with "islands" of prairie gradually change into a forest-prairie mosaic, and finally into tall-grass prairie with isolated patches of forest.

There are four forest communities in Kansas: the oak-hickory forest in the extreme northeastern corner of the state, the Ozark oak-hickory forest in the southeast corner of Cherokee County, the cross timbers in the Chautauqua Hills of southeastern Kansas, and riparian forests restricted to the valley floors of streams and rivers. The oak-hickory forest of northeastern Kansas is dominated by white oak (*Quercus alba*), red oak (*Quercus borealis*), black oak (*Quercus velutina*), bitternut hickory (*Carya cordiformis*), and shagbark hickory (*Carya ovata*). These species, plus Shumard's oak (*Quercus shumardii*), also dominate the plant assemblage of the Ozark oak-hickory forest in the southeast corner of the state.

The cross timbers of southeastern Kansas are characterized by low, broadleaf, deciduous trees scattered singly or in groves among medium-tall, rather dense stands of various grass species (Kuchler 1974: 599). The dominant trees are post oak (*Quercus stellata*) and blackjack oak (*Quercus marilandica*).

Riparian forests form narrow bands along streams and rivers across Kansas and are dominated by cottonwood (*Populus deltoides*), hackberry (*Celtis occidentalis*), willow (*Salix* sp.), and elm (*Ulmus* sp.). The riparian forests tend to become narrower and less dense and diverse going from east to west across the state. These ribbons of trees allow woodland fauna, such as white-tailed deer, to penetrate into the prairies of western Kansas. Hence, in addition to providing botanical food resources, such as hackberry seeds, riparian forests played a role in providing game for prehistoric people who occupied the grasslands of Kansas.

LATE QUATERNARY ENVIRONMENTS OF KANSAS

This section is intended to briefly summarize the late-Quaternary paleoenvironmental history of the Central Plains, including the area of Kansas. Mandel (1987) and W. C. Johnson and Park (1996) have presented more thorough accounts of this history. Such a summary provides important context for understanding the cultural history of the region. It also helps explain temporal and spatial patterns of landscape evolution that affected the archaeological record of Kansas (see chapter 3, this volume).

Pleistocene-Holocene Transition (12,000–9000 B.P.)

The Pleistocene-Holocene transition was a period of major environmental change in North America. By 12,000 B.P., the influence of the Laurentide ice sheet diminished, insolation increased during summers, and there was increased seasonality (Kutzbach and Webb 1993). The shift from a glacial to a nonglacial climate was accompanied by a dramatic change in vegetation. The pollen record from Muscotah Marsh in northeastern Kansas suggests that at about 12,000 B.P., spruce began to disappear from the region (Grüger 1973). The demise of spruce was accompanied by an increase in deciduous trees, especially oak and elm, and nonarboreal taxa (grasses and forbs). A similar trend is recorded in pollen records for eastern Nebraska (Kilinska 1995); Moon Lake, North Dakota (Laird et al. 1996, 1998); Lake Okoboji, northwest Iowa (Van Zant 1979); and Pickerel Lake, eastern South Dakota (Watts and Bright 1968). At Muscotah, spruce continued to decline and disappeared from the region by ca. 10,500 B.P., whereas deciduous species continued to increase until ca. 9000 B.P. By 9000 B.P., the pollen record at Muscotah was dominated by grass (Grüger 1973).

Unfortunately, relatively little paleoenvironmental data are available for the Pleistocene-Holocene transition in the Central Plains. At Cheyenne Bottoms, a large depression in central Kansas, the pollen record suggests that grasslands had fully developed by 10,500 B.P. (Fredlund 1992, 1995). The pollen record for the Rosebud site in northern Nebraska suggests that the Holocene opened with an abrupt transformation from mixed spruce–deciduous forest to prairie, with no substantial intermediate phase of deciduous forest such as occurred farther east (Watts and Wright 1966).

Major changes in the composition of vegetation in the Great Plains at the onset of the Pleistocene-Holocene transition were accompanied by dramatic changes in animal assemblages. The paleontological record indicates that the complex Pleistocene faunal communities began to disappear from the Plains by approximately 12,000 B.P., and that by 10,000 B.P. approximately two-thirds of the region's large mammal genera (megafauna) became extinct (for detailed accounts of late-Pleistocene megafauna extinction, see P. S. Martin and Wright 1967; P. S. Martin and Klein 1984). The collapse of Pleistocene faunal communities has been attributed to various causes, including increased seasonality (Axelrod 1967; Graham 1979; Lundelius 1967, 1976; Slaughter 1967); increased aridity and associated changes in vegetation (Grayson and Meltzer 2002, 2003; Guilday 1967; Guthrie 1990; J. E. King and Saunders 1984; Lundelius 1967, 1976; S. D. Webb 1969, 1977); inability of some taxa to adjust reproductive habits to changing climates (Slaughter 1967); ecological disequilibrium initiated by rapid glacial retreat (Dreimanis 1968; Graham 1979); competitive exclusion (Guilday 1967; Krantz 1970); and over-hunting by humans (Alroy 2001; Edwards 1967; Fiedel and Haynes 2004; Haynes 2002; Jelinek 1967; P. S. Martin 1967, 1973, 1984; V. L. Smith 1975). Whatever the cause(s) of extinction (for ongoing debate, see Fiedel and Haynes 2004; Flannery 1999; Grayson and Meltzer 2003), the demise of megafauna undoubtedly affected the subsistence strategies of people who occupied the Plains at that time (see chapter 4, this volume).

Early through Middle Holocene (9000–4000 B.P.)

Generally, air-mass circulation models indicate that beginning at approximately 9000 B.P., the Great Plains was dominated in summer by the warm, dry Pacific air that flowed down the eastern side of the Rocky Mountains (Bryson 1966; Bryson and Hare 1974; COHMAP 1988; Kutzbach 1987; Kutzbach and Guetter 1986; Kutzbach, Guetter, et al. 1993; Whitlock et al. 2001). Strong zonal airflow at the surface restricted the northward penetration of moist tropical air masses into the Central Plains, thereby triggering a warm, dry, climatic period that continued to approximately 5000 B.P. (Antevs 1955; Bryson, Baerreis, and Wendland 1970; Deevey and Flint 1957; T. Webb and Bryson 1972). This period is often referred to as the Altithermal (after Antevs 1955), but it is also know as the Hypsithermal (Deevey and Flint 1957) or Atlantic climatic episode (Baerreis and Bryson 1965).

In the South Fork Big Nemaha River valley of southeastern Nebraska, a combination of pollen, plant macrofossil, and stable carbon isotope ($\delta^{13}C$) data suggest that drier conditions between ca. 9000 and 8500 B.P. eliminated upland and riparian forests and accentuated the dominance of prairie (R. G. Baker et al. 2000). As the Pacific air masses increased in strength and frequency during the early Holocene, prairies were pushed eastward from the Central Plains in a broad bisecting wedge often referred to as the "Prairie Peninsula" (H. E. Wright 1976). Paleobotanical evidence suggests that prairies expanded far eastward into Missouri, Iowa, and Illinois as the

Altithermal intensified during the middle Holocene (Brush 1967; Durkee 1971; J. E. King and Allen 1977; Van Zant 1979; H. E. Wright 1968, 1970, 1971). The warming and drying trend responsible for the eastward expansion of the prairies reached a maximum by ca. 7000 B.P. and continued until ca. 4000 B.P.

Two localities in the east-central Plains show evidence of warming and drying from the early through the middle Holocene, i.e., Muscotah Marsh and the South Fork Big Nemaha River valley. At Muscotah Marsh, arboreal pollen reaches a minimum between ca. 8000 and 5000 B.P., and there are peaks in ragweed, other Asteraceae, Chenopodiineae, and Amorpha pollen percentages (Grüger 1973). These trends suggest that the Holocene climate was driest at this time. In the South Fork Big Nemaha River valley, pollen, plant macrofossil, and $\delta^{13}C$ data suggest that all the upland deciduous trees except oak disappeared between ca. 8500 and 5800 B.P., and except for willow, riparian trees are largely missing (R. G. Baker et al. 2000). Shrubs, wetland, and aquatic taxa remain at low levels, but pollen and plant macrofossil indicate an increase in grasses and forbs, and several prairie taxa reach peak values during this period (R. G. Baker et al. 2000). Although the regional signal is weak at Cheyenne Bottoms, the Holocene pollen record in this basin shows a depression in Chenopodium and Amaranth percentages from ca. 8500 to 3700 B.P. (Fredlund 1995). These pollen signals suggest that vegetative successional processes may have been reclaiming former mudflats within the basin as a result of increased aridity.

Some researchers (e.g., Benedict 1978; Malouf 1958; Syms 1969) have suggested that the paucity of recorded Early and Middle Archaic sites in the core of the Central Plains indicates that this region was largely abandoned by people as aridity intensified during the early to middle Holocene. However, recent geoarchaeological studies have demonstrated that the archaeological record has been filtered by geomorphic processes; Early and Middle Archaic sites are either deeply buried or they have been removed by erosion (see chapter 3, this volume). Nevertheless, it is likely that subsistence strategies of people were affected during the Altithermal (see chapter 4, this volume), and game and people were probably tethered to reliable water sources, such as springs, during the period of maximum aridity.

Late Holocene (4000 B.P.–Recent)

Climatic models show a change of atmospheric circulation from frequent zonal dominance during the early and middle Holocene to mixed zonal and meridional (south to north) dominance during the late Holocene (Bryson 1966; COHMAP 1988; Kutzbach, Guetter, et al. 1993). The increased frequency of meridional atmospheric circulation after ca. 4000 B.P. is significant because it allowed warm, moist tropical air masses from the Gulf of Mexico to penetrate deep into the Central Plains (Mandel 1994a). Mean annual precipitation probably increased significantly because of frequent frontal activity in the collision zone between polar and tropical air masses (Knox 1983: 39). Vegetation density increased in upland areas of the Central Plains as mixed and tall-grass prairies replaced short-grass prairies and forests expanded across floodplains and hillslopes in the Midwest (H. E. Wright 1971). At Muscotah Marsh, the end of the "prairie interval" came soon after ca. 5100 B.P. and is marked by an increase in the frequency of oak and hickory pollen (Grüger 1973). According to Grüger, a mosaic of upland prairies and forested valley walls and floors was in place by 4000 B.P.

In the South Fork Big Nemaha River valley, plant macrofossils indicate that from ca. 5800 to 3100 B.P., riparian forests were well established, upland trees were mainly absent except for oak, wetland species increased in frequency, and prairie plants and weeds were well established (R. G. Baker et al. 2000). Pollen, phytoliths, and $\delta^{13}C$ values fluctuate widely for this period, suggesting periodic droughts within a somewhat moister climatic interval (R. G. Baker et al. 2000). However, these data indicate a rapid change in vegetation and stream behavior from 3100 to 2700 B.P. With the exception of elm, all trees, upland and riparian, disappear, aquatic and wetland plants become more common, and there is a dramatic increase in prairie plants and weeds. The decrease in trees and increase in prairie plants and weeds suggests a return to consistently drier conditions (R. G. Baker et al. 2000). The abundance and diversity of aquatic and wetland plants seems to contradict this interpretation, but these plants tend to grow around quiet water, such as oxbow lakes, not in flowing streams. The geomorphic evidence suggests that a shallowly incised meandering channel belt characterized the South Fork Big Nemaha River during the early part of the late Holocene (Mandel 1996; Mandel and Bettis 2001). Increased wetland and aquatic plants may result from this more meandering stream pattern, where numerous oxbow lakes provided quiet-water environments.

The presence of Juniper stumps in place on paleofloodplains in central Oklahoma, dating to ca. 3200 to 2600 B.P. (Hall and Lintz 1984), supports evidence from the South Fork Big Nemaha River valley indicating a late Holocene interval of aridity. All Juniper species grow in dry areas where the water table is far below the ground surface. Their presence on floodplains is strong evidence that from 3200 to 2600 B.P. the water table was at least 4 to 5 m lower than it is today (R. G. Baker et al. 2000).

Further evidence for a late Holocene dry interval comes from the Sand Hills of Nebraska. Ponte, Loope, and Swinehart (1994) cored the central Sand Hills and detected a period of dune activation from ca. 3800 to 2800 B.P. Earlier work by Ahlbrandt and Fryberger (1980) and Ahlbrandt, Swinehart, and Maroney (1983) in the Sand Hills produced radiocarbon-controlled stratigraphic records indicating dune activity between ca. 3000 and 1500 B.P.

The pollen record for the Cheyenne Bottoms shows an increase in Chenopodium and Amaranth percentages from 3700 B.P. to the present (Fredlund 1992). This pattern points to frequent water-level fluctuations and exposed mudflats. Hence, at Cheyenne Bottoms, the late Holocene appears to have been punctuated with episodes of basin-wide drying (Fredlund 1995).

In the South Fork Big Nemaha River basin, the record of environmental change since 2700 B.P. is not complete (R. G. Baker et al. 2000). However, the available pollen, phytolith, plant macrofossil, and $\delta^{13}C$ data suggest that an intermediate bioclimate was in place, with oak returning to the uplands and/or high Pleistocene terraces and diverse riparian forests becoming reestablished. After 2700 B.P., the vegetation apparently was not much different from that present shortly before Euro-American settlement in the region. The plant macrofossil record for the postsettlement period is marked by a dramatic decline in prairie taxa and an increase in weedy taxa, including several introduced species (R. G. Baker et al. 2000). The disturbances that these weedy taxa require are present both on the uplands, where cultivation is widespread, and on the floodplains, where increased flooding and siltation produce fresh erosional and depositional surfaces.

In northeastern Oklahoma, pollen spectra suggest that hickory increased in the Cross Timber oak forest from ca. 2000 to 1000 B.P. (Hall 1977, 1982). During this same period, moist-habitat land snails became more abundant in rock-shelter deposits (Hall 1982). According to Hall (1982, 1990), this evidence, as well as paleontological data and records of fluvial activity, suggests that there was a moist climate from 2000 to 1000 B.P. across the Southern Plains. At 1000 B.P., however, there appears to have been a shift to much drier conditions, as indicated by channel incision of valley floors in the Southern Plains (Hall 1990). Similar channel entrenchment at ca. 1000 B.P. has been documented in the Central Plains and may be related to a dry climatic interval (Mandel 1994a, 1996).

There is strong paleobotanical evidence for a distinct climate change around 400 years ago in the Eastern Plains. This change marks the beginning of the cool, moist, Neo-Boreal climatic episode, or Little Ice Age, that persisted for about 250 years (Bernabo 1981; Fritts, Lofgren, and Gordon 1979; Swain 1978).

In sum, the late Holocene, including modern times, has been a period of climatic fluctuation and extremes. Although effective moisture increased in the Central Plains after ca. 4000 B.P., frequent droughts lasting a few years to decades characterize this period. There is also evidence for protracted aridity, such as the apparent dry period from ca. 3100 to 2700 B.P., as well as episodes of greater effective precipitation, such as the Little Ice Age. The boundaries of plant communities (ecotones) probably shifted in response to some late Holocene climatic perturbations, which in turn affected the distribution of plant and animal resources exploited by people on the Plains. For example, bison probably accompanied eastward shifts of the short-grass prairie during dry periods, whereas deer followed westward expansion of forests during moist intervals (Shay 1978). Also, late Holocene climatic variability and extremes likely were factors in the development of alternative subsistence strategies and related technologies, such as agriculture and food storage. Finally, certain aspects of the late Holocene climate shaped the archaeological record. For example, increased frequency of intense rainfalls and associated high-magnitude floods during the late Holocene (Knox 1983) contributed to rapid aggradation of floodplains and, therefore, deep burial of cultural deposits. The effects of climate-driven landscape evolution on the archaeological record of Kansas are described in chapter 3.

SUMMARY

The region of the Central Plains that we now call Kansas has experienced dramatic climatic changes over the past 12,000 years. These shifts in climatic conditions influenced the structure and distribution of plant and animal communities. As will become apparent in the following chapters, this floral and faunal diversity influenced human adaptation in Kansas throughout prehistory. One must be careful to avoid environmentally deterministic explanations of human behavior, but it is also impossible to ignore the influence of floral and faunal variability on cultural behavior. Climate change over the last 12,000 years has also influenced the archaeological record that we observe and study today. Issues of natural site destruction and site preservation must be addressed if we are to understand prehistoric settlement patterns and human use of the Kansas landscape.

3. The Effects of Late Quaternary Landscape Evolution on the Archaeological Record of Kansas

Rolfe D. Mandel

The record of human occupation of the Central Great Plains, including the area of Kansas, spans the past 11,500 years and may go even further back in time. Although the number of recorded sites in Kansas predating Euro-American settlement is substantial (7,580 sites as of December 1, 2003), 79 percent of the 3,389 sites that can be assigned to a cultural period are Woodland or younger ceramic sites and, therefore, are less than approximately 2,000 years old. The paucity of recorded preceramic sites may be more related to lower population densities in the Central Plains prior to 2000 B.P. than population densities during later periods. However, the effects of geologic processes on the archaeological record also must be considered.

Many studies (e.g., Artz 1985; Bettis 1990; Bettis and Hajic 1995; Bettis and Mandel 2002; Mandel 1992, 1995, 1996; Mandel et al. 1991; Stafford and Creasman 2002; Thompson and Bettis 1980) have demonstrated that patterns of erosion and deposition strongly influence the preservation and visibility of archaeological deposits. For example, Thompson and Bettis (1980) suggested that during the early and middle Holocene, erosion and net transport of sediment out of second- and third-order streams in western Iowa removed most of the Archaic record from these small drainage elements. However, they pointed out that during the same period, Archaic sites were buried in floodplain settings and alluvial fans within large valleys that were zones of net sedimentation. The results of their investigation and other basin-wide studies (e.g., Mandel 1992, 1994a, 2005a, 2005b, 2005c; Mandel et al. 1991) indicate that different geologic processes operating concurrently within a single drainage basin may differentially preserve the archaeological record and lead to erroneous conclusions about prehistoric settlement patterns. In other words, the remains of human occupation pass through a geologic filter to become the archaeological record. Understanding the nature of the temporal and spatial patterns that this filter has imposed on the archaeological record is the first step in identifying archaeological patterns that reflect human choices (Bettis and Mandel 2002).

This chapter describes how temporal and spatial patterns of late Quaternary landscape evolution have influenced the archaeological record of Kansas. In order to address relationships between patterns in the archaeological record and temporal/spatial patterns of late Quaternary landscape evolution, the discussion is separated into four periods: Pleistocene-Holocene transition (12,000–9000 B.P.), early Holocene (9000–7000 B.P.), middle Holocene (7000–4000 B.P.), and late Holocene (< 4000 B.P.). For each period, different geomorphic systems are considered, including fluvial, colluvial, eolian, and lacustrine systems. However, the discussion focuses on alluvial systems because (1) most of the recorded archaeological sites in Kansas are in stream valleys, (2) alluvial stratigraphies are well defined for the region, and (3) a recent statewide study of late Quaternary landscape evolution yielded sufficient radiocarbon ages to permit an evaluation of temporal patterns in the alluvial and archaeological records at several spatial and temporal levels.

I take a basin-wide approach in assessing landscape evolution in alluvial systems. Streams are separated into small (< fifth-order), intermediate (fifth-order), and large (> fifth-order) drainage elements based on Strahler's (1964) stream classification system. Only those drainage elements shown as dashed or solid blue lines on USGS 7.5-minute topographic maps were rank-ordered. The objective is to detect patterns of late Quaternary erosion and sedimentation within drainage systems and thereby determine whether alluvial deposits of certain ages are differentially but systematically preserved in the basins. It is reasonable to assume that archaeological sites dating to a specific cultural period, such as the Archaic, will be found only where there are deposits old enough to contain them. A corollary is that where sufficiently thick deposits postdating the Archaic are present, evidence of these sites will not be found on the modern land surface. Hence, interpreting the chrono-stratigraphy of late Quaternary alluvial deposits is an important aspect of this study.

Another important aspect of landscape evolution considered in this chapter is soil stratigraphy. Buried soils in late Quaternary deposits represent previous land surfaces that were exposed for sufficient periods to develop recognizable soil profile characteristics. Hence, they represent former stable land surfaces. If one assumes that the probability of cultural utilization of a particular landscape position is equal for each year, it follows that the surfaces that remain exposed for the longest time would represent those with the highest probability of containing cultural materials (Hoyer 1980: 61). Because buried soils represent former stable surfaces, evidence for human occupation would more likely be associated with them. This reasoning also implies that a soil that had the most time to develop before it was buried would have the highest potential for containing cultural materials at any given location. Thus, buried soils are useful indicators for locating archaeological deposits and for assessing an important aspect of the geologic potential for buried cultural deposits. Knowledge of the temporal and spatial pattern of buried soils in a landscape provides archaeologists with a powerful tool for identifying areas with high potential for buried cultural deposits and for assessing prehistoric cultural patterns.

TEMPORAL AND SPATIAL PATTERNS OF LATE QUATERNARY LANDSCAPE EVOLUTION

Pleistocene-Holocene Transition (12,000–9000 B.P.)

The transition from the Pleistocene to the Holocene occurred from about 12,000–9000 B.P. This was a time of major climatic and vegetative change in the Central Plains of North America (see chapter 2, this volume). The effects of this change on landscape evolution are recorded in the alluvial-stratigraphic records of streams throughout the region. At ca. 12,000 B.P., sedimentation slowed in the valleys of large rivers, and from ca. 11,000 to 10,000 B.P., thick, organic-rich, cumulic soils developed on floodplains (now terraces) in these valleys (Mandel 2005a, 2005b, 2005c). With cumulic soils, pedogenesis and sedimentation occur simultaneously because the rate of sedimentation is very slow (Birkeland 1999). In other words, soil development keeps up with sedimentation. A deeply buried cumulic soil dating to the Pleistocene-Holocene transition has been recorded in the valley fill of large streams, including the Neosho and Kansas rivers in eastern Kansas (Mandel 2005a), the Chikaskia, Ninnescah, and Walnut rivers in south-central Kansas (Mandel 2005a), the Smoky Hill, Saline, and Solomon rivers in north-central and west-central Kansas, and the Pawnee and Cimarron rivers in southwestern Kansas (Figures 3.1 and 3.2). This soil has been traced into the lower reaches of major tributaries of the trunk streams. For example,

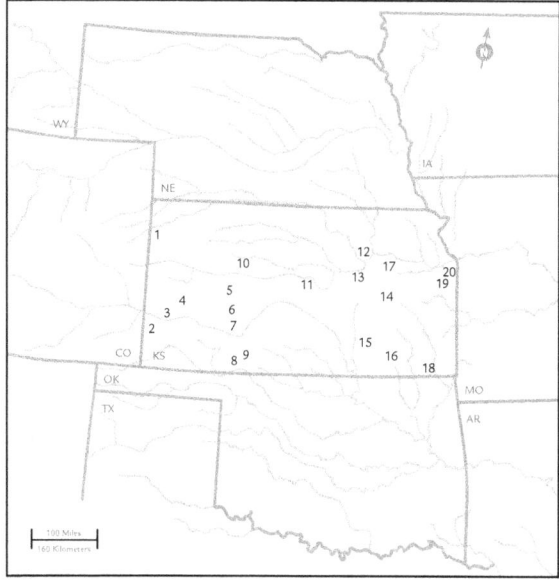

Figure 3.1. Map of Kansas showing localities and archaeological sites mentioned in the text. 1. Kanorado Locality (Sites 14SN101, 14SN105, 14SN106); 2. Winger Site (14ST401); 3. Bahntge Ranch Alluvial Fan; 4. Simshauser Alluvial Fan and Site 14KY102; 5. Site 14HO316; 6. Buckner Creek Site (14HO306); 7. Ft. Dodge Alluvial Fan; 8. Adams Ranch Alluvial Fan; 9. Pike Ranch Site (14CK321); 10. Delaney Site (14TO341); 11. Eagle's Roost Site (14EW174); 12. Ft. Riley Alluvial Fans; 13. Clements Section; 14. Diamond Creek Site (14CS1338); 15. Augusta Site (14BU306); 16. Site 14CT399; 17. Claussen Site (14WB322); 18. Stigenwalt Site (14LT351); 19. Site 14DO417; 20. Lower Mill Creek.

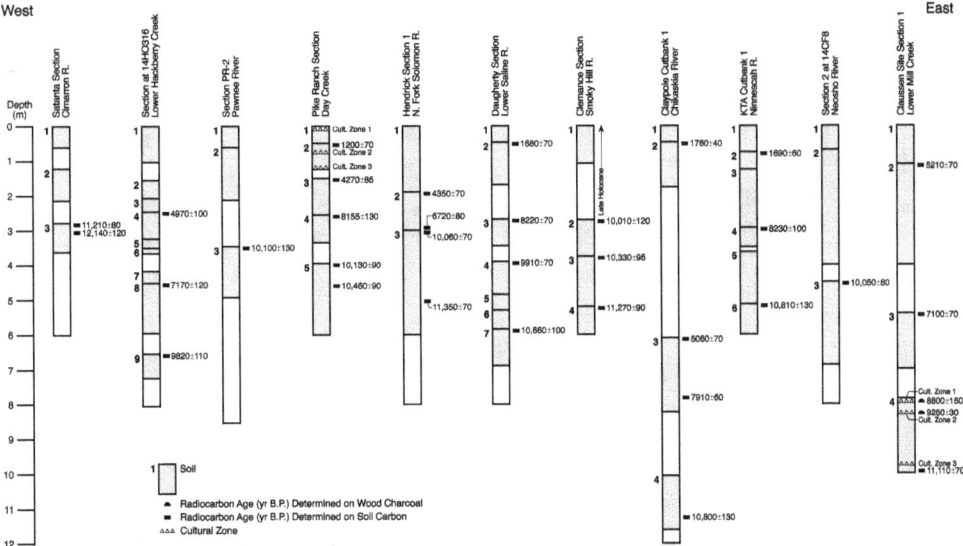

Figure 3.2. Soil stratigraphy and geochronology of localities in the valleys of large streams (> sixth order) in Kansas

at site 14HO316 at the lower end of Hackberry Creek in the Pawnee River basin of southwestern Kansas, organic carbon from a deeply buried alluvial soil yielded a radiocarbon age of ca. 9800 B.P. (Mandel 1994a). At the Pike Ranch site (14CK321) on lower Day Creek in the Cimarron River basin, organic carbon from the upper and lower 10 cm thick, deeply buried, cumulic A horizon yielded radiocarbon ages of 10,130±90 and 10,460±90 B.P., respectively. At the Claussen site (14WB322) in the valley of lower Mill Creek, a tributary of the Kansas River in northeastern Kansas, radiocarbon ages for a deeply buried cumulic soil range from 11,110±70 B.P., determined on total organic carbon near the bottom of the soil, to 8800±150 B.P., determined on charcoal from a cultural feature in the upper 10 cm of the soil.

In striking contrast to the large trunk streams, there is no trace of a soil or, for that matter, alluvium dating to the Pleistocene-Holocene transition in the valleys of most intermediate and small streams (Figure 3.3). The absence of this alluvium is attributed to net sediment removal in the middle and upper segments of drainage networks between ca. 12,000 and 9000 B.P. (Mandel 1995; Bettis and Mandel 2002). There is, however, an exception to this pattern of sediment removal in low-order streams. Recent investigations determined that thick deposits of alluvium with multiple buried soils dating to the Pleistocene-Holocene transition are stored in the valleys of first- and second-order intermittent streams, or draws, in areas of the High Plains with a thick loess mantle (Mandel 2005b) (Figures 3.4 and 3.5). The loess is a major source of silty alluvium, which accounts for the large volume of sediment in the draws. The draws lie high in the drainage networks and are inset into late Pleistocene loess and older Quaternary and/or late Tertiary deposits. Waves of entrenchment

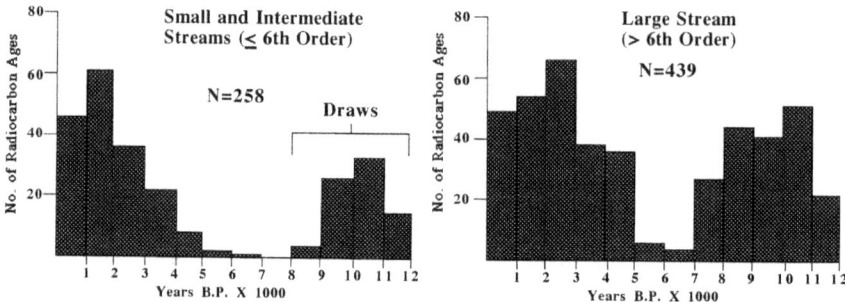

Figure 3.3. Histograms showing the number and temporal range of radiocarbon ages determined on samples from alluvial fills in the valleys of large, intermediate, and small streams in Kansas

postdating the Pleistocene-Holocene transition did not extend into these draws until the late Holocene (generally after 2000 B.P.). Consequently, there has been insufficient time for complete removal of the vast quantity of terminal Pleistocene and early Holocene alluvium stored in the draws. The soil-stratigraphic record preserved in the draws indicates very slow aggradation punctuated by episodes of landscape stability and soil development beginning as early as ca. 11,600 B.P. and continuing as late as ca. 8200 B.P. However, most of the radiocarbon ages assigned to buried soils in the draws range between ca. 11,000 and 9000 B.P. (Figure 3.5). For example, at the Kanorado locality in the upper Middle Beaver Creek valley (Figure 3.1), XAD-purified collagen from bones associated with a Clovis-age cultural component in the lower 10 cm of a buried A horizon yielded AMS ^{14}C ages of 10,150±500, 10,950±60, and 11,005±50 B.P. (Mandel, Holen, and Hofman 2005). Radiocarbon ages determined on decalcified soil carbon from the upper 10 cm of the buried A horizon range between ca. 9400 and 8900 B.P.

In the High Plains of western Kansas, there is evidence showing alluvial fan development throughout the Pleistocene-Holocene transition. Like the accumulation of alluvium in the draws, aggradation of fan deposits was slow and punctuated by soil development during this period. For example, at the Adams Ranch Fan in the Cimarron River valley near Ashland, Kansas (Fig-

Figure 3.4. Photograph of Mattox Draw in Kearny County, southwestern Kansas. All of the sediment exposed in the cutbank is alluvium deposited between ca. 13,500 and 8,000 years ago.

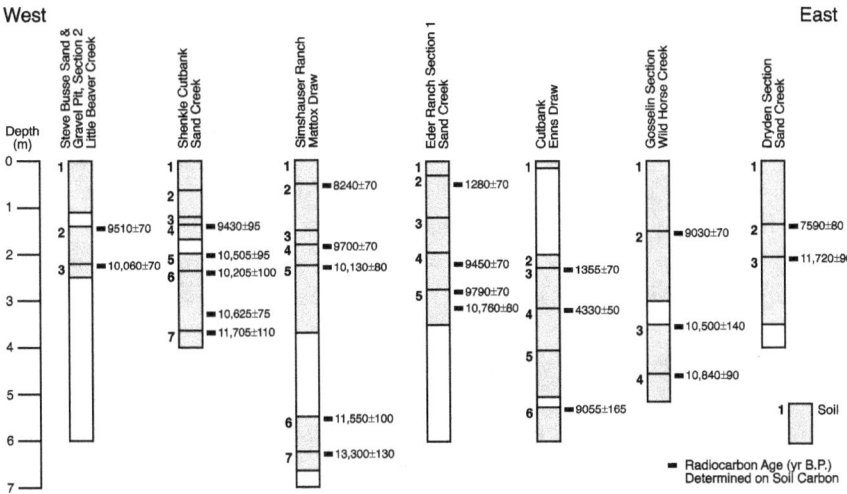

Figure 3.5. Soil stratigraphy and geochronology of localities in draws in western Kansas

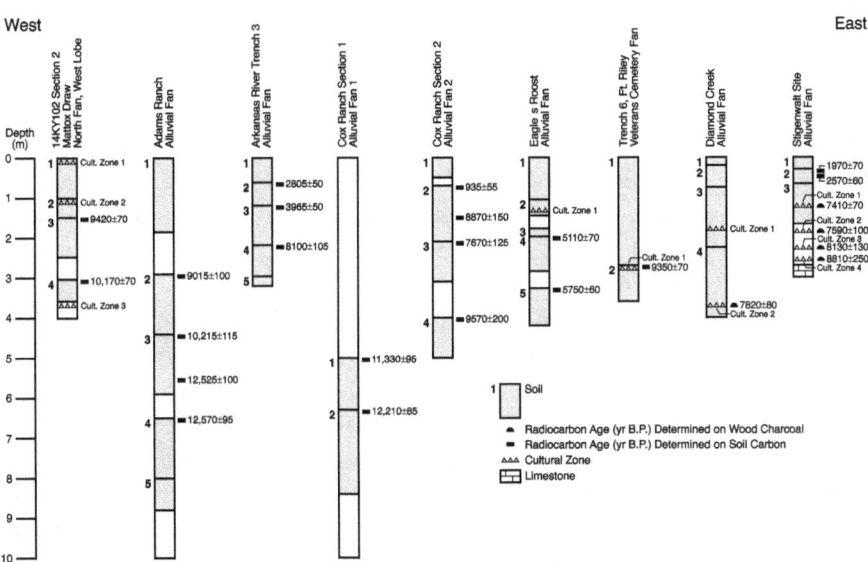

Figure 3.6. Soil stratigraphy and geochronology of alluvial fan localities in Kansas

ure 3.1), slow aggradation was accompanied by three episodes of soil development (cumulic profiles) between ca. 13,000 and 9000 B.P. (Figure 3.6). At the Bahntge Ranch Fan in Sand Creek valley near Lakin, Kansas (Figure 3.1), aggradation was interrupted by a major episode of soil development that continued until at least 10,700 B.P. (Figure 3.6). The Simshauser Fan (14KY102) in Mattox Draw north of Lakin (Figure 3.1) has at least two buried soils dating to the Pleistocene-Holocene transition.

Organic carbon from lowest and middle buried soils at Simshauser yielded radiocarbon ages of ca. 10,170 and 9420 B.P., respectively, and a chipped-stone flake and bison bones were recorded 70 cm below the top of the lowest soil (Mandel 2005b) (Figure 3.6).

Radiocarbon data suggest that fan development began during the latter part of the Pleistocene-Holocene transition in the Flint Hills of northeastern Kansas. Organic carbon from deeply buried soils in alluvial fans in the Kansas River valley at Ft. Riley, Kansas (Figure 3.1), yielded radiocarbon ages of ca. 9700 and 9350 B.P. (Figure 3.6).

There is also evidence for landscape stability and associated soil development on the loess-mantled uplands of Kansas during the Pleistocene-Holocene transition. Accumulation of Peoria loess, the dominant surficial deposit on uplands in Kansas (Frye and Leonard 1952), ceased by ca. 13,000–12,000 B.P. (W. C. Johnson, May, and Diekmeyer 1993; Mandel and Bettis 1995a; C. W. Martin 1993; May and Holen 1993). As accumulation of the Peoria loess slowed, pedogenesis occurred and produced a thick, strongly expressed soil in the upper 1–2 m of this unit of silty, wind-blown sediment. In some areas of Kansas, especially along the bluffs of the Arkansas, Kansas, and Missouri rivers, the soil at the top of the Peoria loess is mantled by Bignell loess. Where this occurs, the buried soil developed in Peoria loess is referred to as the Brady soil (Feng et al. 1994; C. B. Schultz and Stout 1945). W. C. Johnson and Willey (2000) noted that the widespread development of the Brady soil between ca. 10,500 and 9000 B.P. implies that the loess-mantled uplands were stable during much of the Pleistocene-Holocene transition. Where it is not buried by Bignell loess, the soil at the top of the Peoria loess has either been overprinted by modern pedogenesis (Dreeszen 1970; Thorp, Johnson, and Reed 1950) or removed by erosion, along with the overlying Bignell loess (W. C. Johnson and Willey 2000). From an archaeological perspective, understanding the distribution of the Brady soil is important because it has potential for containing buried Paleoindian cultural deposits and may, therefore, yield important information about human occupation of uplands.

Landscape stability during the Pleistocene-Holocene transition is also indicated by the occurrence of a strongly developed soil in sand dunes and sheets in Kansas. In the Great Bend Sand Prairie, a large sand sheet in south-central Kansas, organic carbon from buried soils yielded radiocarbon ages ranging between ca. 12,000 and 10,000 B.P. (Arbogast 1995). According to Olson and Porter (2002), a stable period began approximately 11,000–10,000 B.P. in the dune field of the Cimarron Bend of southwestern Kansas, resulting in soil formation (Brady soil).

Soil- and chrono-stratigraphic information gleaned from a recent study of playas on the High Plains of western Kansas (see chapter 2, this volume, for a description of playas) suggests that at least some of these upland basins were stable during the Pleistocene-Holocene transition (Mandel 2000, 2005b). The radiocarbon chronology supporting this interpretation is based on relatively few samples (Figures 3.7 and 3.8). Nevertheless, radiocarbon ages determined on organic carbon from buried paleosols at the Sullivan and Knudsen playas, as well as the playa at the Winger site

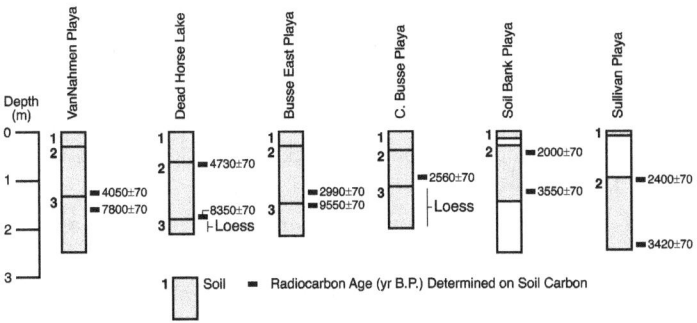

Figure 3.7. Soil stratigraphy and geochronology of playa basins in Kansas

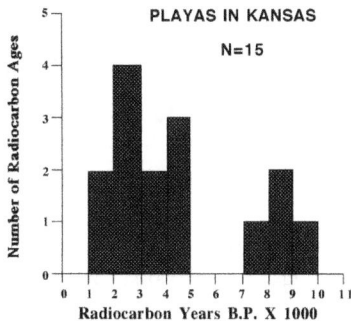

Figure 3.8. Histograms showing the number and temporal range of radiocarbon ages determined on samples from playa basins in Kansas

(14ST401) (Figure 3.1), indicate soil development in playa basins between ca. 12,500 and 9000 B.P. (Mandel 2005b).

Early Holocene (9000–7000 B.P.)

The general trend of warming and drying that characterized the climate of the Central Plains at the end of the Pleistocene-Holocene transition continued and intensified during the early Holocene (ca. 9000–7000 B.P.) (see chapter 2, this volume). The response of fluvial systems to this change was similar across the region, and spatial patterns of stream erosion and aggradation varied systematically within drainage networks during this period (Bettis and Mandel 2002; Mandel 1994a, 1995). Specifically, small streams (< fifth-order) were actively downcutting and lengthening between ca. 9000 and 7000 B.P. Although there may have been temporary storage of early Holocene alluvium in low-order drainage elements, there is no record of it in terrace fills of small streams (Figure 3.3). Even in the draws of western Kansas, there is little to no evidence of early Holocene alluvium (Figure 3.5).

Large volumes of sediment transported out of small drainage elements during the early Holocene accumulated as alluvial fill in the valleys of intermediate and large streams (> fourth-order). The soil-stratigraphic record indicates that accumulation of early Holocene alluvium on floodplains (now terraces) of large streams in Kansas, including the Saline, Solomon, Ninnescah, Chikaskia, and Pawnee rivers, was punctuated by landscape stability and soil development (Figure 3.2). Buried soils dating to ca. 8000 to 7000 B.P. are especially common in valley fills of large streams. However, there are some exceptions to this pattern of early Holocene aggradation punctuated by soil development. For example, in the valley of lower Mill Creek (sixth-order stream) near the community of Holliday in northeastern Kansas (Figure 3.1), alluvium rapidly accumulated between ca. 9000 and 5000 B.P.; there is no evidence for soil development during this period (Mandel 1994b). Also, in segments of some large rivers, early Holocene alluvium has been partially or completely stripped off. For example, at the Delaney site (14TO341) in the Saline River valley near Wa-Keeney, Kansas (Figure 3.1), a truncated cumulic soil dating from ca. 12,300 to 10,300 B.P. is overlain by middle Holocene alluvium (Figure 3.2). At the Clements Section in the lower Smoky Hill River valley near Salina, Kansas (Figure 3.1), a thick unit of stratified late Holocene alluvium mantles a truncated cumulic soil that dates to the Pleistocene-Holocene transition (Figure 3.2).

In the High Plains region of western Kansas, aggradation of alluvial fans that began during the Pleistocene-Holocene transition (e.g., Adams Ranch Fan and Simshauser Fan [Figure 3.1]) generally slowed or ceased during the early Holocene as fan-head trenches downcut and sediment bypassed the fans (Mandel 2005b). One exception is the Fort Dodge Fan in the Arkansas River valley near Dodge City (Figure 3.1). Radiocarbon ages determined on organic carbon from buried soils in this fan indicate stability at ca. 8100 B.P., followed by a brief episode of sedimentation not long before ca. 4000 B.P. (Figure 3.6). However, in the Central Lowland of eastern Kansas, alluvial fans began to develop around 9000 B.P. where third-order and smaller streams enter the valleys of large streams. For example, at the Stigenwalt site (14LT351) in Big Hill Creek valley in southeastern Kansas (Figures 3.1 and 3.6), a small alluvial/colluvial fan developed at the mouth of an intermittent first-order stream during the early Holocene (Mandel 1990). Radiocarbon ages determined on charcoal from stratified cultural deposits indicate that most of the alluvium and colluvium composing the fan accumulated between ca. 8800 and 7400 B.P. (Mandel 1990) (Figure 3.5). At the Diamond Creek site (14CS1338) near the community of Elmdale in northeastern Kansas (Figure 3.1), charcoal from a hearth near the bottom of an alluvial fan yielded a radiocarbon age of 7820±80 B.P. (Mandel 2005c) (Figure 3.6).

Playas in western Kansas appear to have been zones of very slow sediment accumulation and soil development during the early Holocene (Mandel 2000). This interpretation is based on the suite of radiocarbon ages determined on organic carbon from buried cumulic soils in six playas (Figure 3.7). Four of these ages lie between ca. 8600 and 7800 B.P. Hence, the pattern of upland stability that began during the Pleistocene-Holocene transition continued into the early Holocene.

There is little evidence for eolian activity in the dune fields and sand sheets of Kansas during the early Holocene. Arbogast (1995) reported a radiocarbon age of ca. 7850 B.P. on organic carbon from a buried soil developed in alluvium beneath a sand dune in the Great Bend Sand Prairie. In the dune fields of the Cimarron Bend area of southwestern Kansas, early to middle Holocene alluvium is mantled by middle to late Holocene eolian sediments (Olson and Porter 2002). Paleosols developed in the early Holocene alluvium are usually truncated (Porter 1997; Olson and Porter 2002). Olson and Porter (2002) attribute this truncation to fluvial erosion associated with relatively mesic conditions in the Cimarron Bend during the early Holocene. Dune activity appears to have been quite localized, slowed possibly by increased vegetation at this time (Olson and Porter 2002).

Middle Holocene (7000–4000 B.P.)

The middle Holocene was perhaps the warmest and driest postglacial period in the Central Plains. The first two millennia of this period (7000–5000 B.P) correlate with the warm, dry interval commonly referred to as the Altithermal (see chapter 2, this volume). Geomorphic evidence indicates that the Altithermal was generally a time of landscape instability (i.e., erosion and sedimentation) throughout the interior of North America (Bettis and Hajic 1995; Bettis and Mandel 2002; Mandel 1995). In Kansas, most small streams (< fifth-order) were characterized by erosion and net transport of alluvium, with little or no long-term sediment storage (Bettis and Mandel 2002; Mandel 1992, 1994a, 1995). Small streams were actively downcutting, migrating laterally, and lengthening during this period. Consequently, there is a mid-Holocene erosional hiatus, or gap, in the late-Quaternary stratigraphic record of many small streams in the region (Bettis and Mandel 2002; Mandel 1995).

Some of the sediment transported out of small drainage elements accumulated in the valleys of large streams (Mandel 1992, 1994a, 1995). For example, in southwestern Kansas, there is evidence of middle Holocene alluvium beneath a remnant of a high terrace (T-2) of Hackberry Creek near its confluence with the Pawnee River (Figures 3.1 and 3.2) (Mandel 1994a). At site 14CT395 in the Caney River valley in southeastern Kansas (Figure 3.1), a large volume of early through middle Holocene alluvium is stored beneath a broad terrace (Mandel 2005a). In west-central Kansas, middle Holocene alluvium has been documented beneath the T-1 terrace of the Saline River at the Delaney site (Figures 3.1 and 3.2). At the Claussen site (14WB322) in northeastern Kansas (Figure 3.1), early through middle Holocene alluvium underlies the T-2 terrace of lower Mill Creek. It is important to note that organic carbon from a buried soil developed in terrace fill at Claussen and Delaney yielded radiocarbon ages of 5210±70 and 6200±70 B.P., respectively. If these ages are accurate, the valleys of lower Mill Creek and the middle Saline River are two of the few localities in the Central Plains where there is evidence for mid-Holocene landscape stability.

Although the valleys of large streams were zones of sedimentation during the middle Holocene, long-term storage of mid-Holocene floodplain deposits is the exception, not the rule. Stratigraphic sequences for many large streams in Kansas have gaps between ca. 7000 and 5000 B.P. (Figure 3.2). Furthermore, there are few radiocarbon ages determined on all materials (wood, charcoal, soil carbon, etc.) between ca. 7000 and 5000 B.P. for terrace fills of large streams (Figure 3.3). Given that early Holocene soils are often truncated and overlain by late Holocene alluvium, and soils dating to this period appear to be rare in terrace fills, the common mid-Holocene gap in the valleys of large streams is due to floodplain erosion instead of nondeposition. Hence, channel migration was a very active process in the valleys of most large streams from 7000 to 5000 B.P., resulting in removal of large volumes of mid-Holocene valley fill.

Although most floodplains were zones of erosion during the middle Holocene, there is evidence for accumulation of sediment along the margins of valley floors in some areas of Kansas during this period (Mandel 2005a, 2005b, 2005c). For example, thick deposits of mid-Holocene sediment compose large, low-angle alluvial fans along the southern margin of the valley floor of the Smoky Hill River in central Kansas (Mandel 1992). At the Eagle's Roost site (14EW174) in the Smoky Hill valley near Kanopolis, Kansas (Figure 3.1), packages of silty and loamy sediment derived from the uplands form a large, low-angle alluvial fan (Mandel 1992). There are multiple fining-upward sequences beneath the midsection of the fan, with soils developed at the top of most sequences. Organic carbon from two of the buried soils at Eagle's Roost yielded radiocarbon ages of 5750±60 and 5110±70 B.P. (Figure 3.6).

In many areas of the Central Plains, including Kansas, evolution of alluvial fans during the middle Holocene was accompanied by development of colluvial aprons along footslopes and toeslopes (Mandel 1995; Mandel and Bettis 1995b). There is good evidence for this at site 14DO417 in northeastern Kansas (Figure 3.1) where a Middle Archaic human burial was recorded in a colluvial apron at the foot of the valley wall of Coal Creek (Hoard et al. 2004). A deer bone in direct association with the burial yielded an AMS radiocarbon age of 6160±35 B.P. (Hoard et al. 2004).

Stratigraphic and chronometric data for dune fields and sand sheets in Kansas generally support the alluvial and colluvial evidence for mid-Holocene landscape instability. In the Cimarron Bend of southwestern Kansas (Figure 3.1), thick deposits of eolian sand mantle truncated alluvial soils radiocarbon dated at 5870±60 and 6480±120 B.P. (Olson and Porter 2002; Porter 1997). Farther north near the Arkansas River, eolian sands mantle alluvial soils radiocarbon dated between ca. 6100 and 6700 B.P. (Olson et al. 1997). According to Olson and Porter (2002), the burial of alluvial soils by eolian sands during the middle Holocene indicates a shift toward drier conditions in southwestern Kansas. Increased aridity apparently triggered landscape instability and dune reactivation. A similar dune reactivation period occurred in central Kansas ca. 5670 B.P. on the Great Bend Sand Prairie (Arbogast 1993) and ca. 5370 B.P. in Reno County, Kansas (Arbogast 1996).

The mid-Holocene gap that appears in the stratigraphic record of most small streams and many large rivers is also common in playas on the High Plains of western Kansas. In fact, of the 15 radiocarbon ages determined on organic carbon from soils developed in playa fill, none date to 7000–5000 B.P., and only three of the ages range between 5000 and 4000 B.P. (Figure 3.8). In most of the playas that have been studied, late Holocene pond deposits mantle truncated soils developed in early Holocene playa fill or late Wisconsinan loess (Mandel 2000). Hence, the playas underwent deflation (i.e., they were zones of landscape instability) during most of the middle Holocene.

Late Holocene (4000 B.P.–Present)

A major shift in the locus of sediment storage occurred in stream valleys during the late Holocene. Following the mid-Holocene episode of entrenchment and lateral erosion, small streams, formerly zones of net erosion and sediment transport, became zones of sediment storage. Although valley bottoms of small streams experienced cut-and-fill episodes during the late Holocene, net storage of alluvium is shown by preservation of large volumes of late-Holocene valley fill beneath low terraces and floodplains. The late Holocene alluvium in small valleys is often inset against bedrock or Pleistocene alluvial deposits.

From ca. 4000 to 1000 B.P., aggradation in small valleys was often interrupted by episodes of floodplain stability and soil formation. Consequently, buried soils are common in the late-Holocene valley fills of these streams (Figure 3.9). This has important implications for archaeological research in these valleys, which will be discussed later.

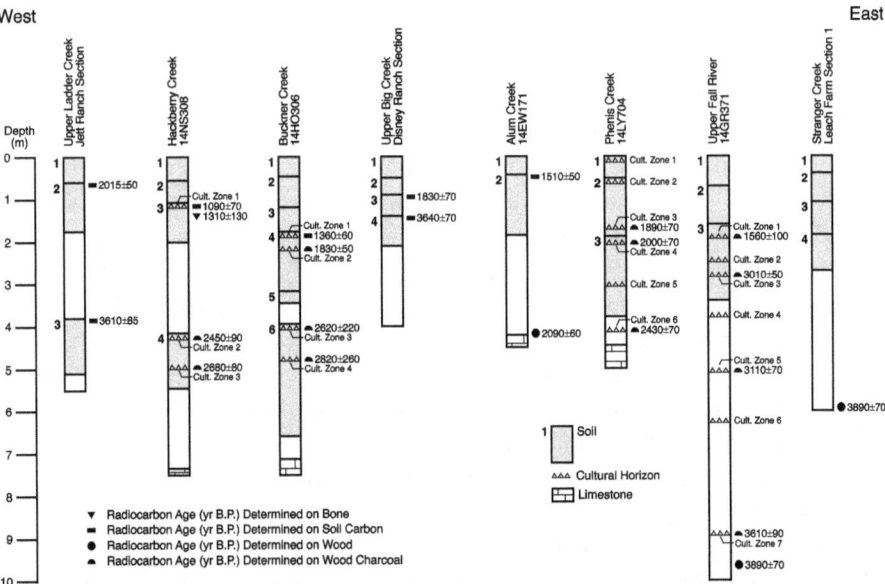

Figure 3.9. Soil stratigraphy and geochronology of localities in the valleys of small and intermediate streams (< sixth order) in Kansas

The number of buried soils developed in late-Holocene valley fills of small streams tends to increase from east to west across Kansas. For example, in southeastern Kansas, there is usually only one buried soil developed in late-Holocene valley fill beneath low terraces (Mandel 2005a). In most places, this buried soil has a thick, organic-rich cumulic profile and dates to between ca. 1900–900 B.P. Hall (1977) recognized this ubiquitous buried soil in northeastern Oklahoma and named it the Copan Paleosol.

In western Kansas, multiple buried soils are common in late-Holocene valley fills of small streams. For example, at site 14HO306 in Buckner Creek valley (Figure 3.1), five buried soils are developed in late Holocene alluvium beneath the T–1 terrace (Mandel 1992, 1994a) (Figure 3.9). Three of these soils have thin, weakly expressed Ak-ACk profiles and are not always traceable throughout the valley. However, two of the buried soils, the Hackberry Creek Paleosol and the Buckner Creek Paleosol, have thick, well-expressed Ak-Bk profiles and occur in the valleys of all second- through fourth-order streams in the Pawnee River basin (Mandel 1994a). Radiocarbon ages indicate that these paleosols developed around 2800–2400 B.P. and 1600–1000 B.P., respectively.

Unlike eastern Kansas soils, most buried soils in late-Holocene valleys fills of small streams in western Kansas are probably related to the longitudinal climatic gradient. Eastern Kansas has a humid to moist subhumid climate with mean annual precipitation ranging from about 100 to 80 cm (39.4 to 31.5 in.), whereas western Kansas has a dry subhumid to semiarid climate with mean annual precipitation ranging from about 60 to 40 cm (23.6 to 15.7 in.) (see chapter 2, this volume). Throughout the Holocene, there has been more effective precipitation and, therefore, a higher flood frequency in eastern Kansas than in western Kansas. Hence, rapid alluviation associated with frequent flooding prevented soil development on late Holocene floodplains of small streams in eastern Kansas until aggradation slowed ca. 2000 B.P. In western Kansas, however, there has been relatively low effective precipitation during the Holocene, and the modern precipitation pattern characterized by infrequent but intensive rainfall was in place by ca. 8000 B.P. (Bryson, Baerreis, and Wendland 1970). In the loess-mantled High Plains of western Kansas, this precipitation pattern generates infrequent, high-magnitude floods with large volumes of suspended sediment. Therefore, floods and concomitant sedimentation would have frequently interrupted episodes of landscape stability and soil development on late-Holocene floodplains. In western Kansas, the sequence of buried soils in late-Holocene valley fills of small streams, such as Buckner Creek, is a product of these cycles of landscape stability and instability.

The valleys of intermediate and large streams in Kansas also were zones of sediment storage during the late Holocene. In eastern Kansas, increased effective precipitation produced frequent high-magnitude floods during the late Holocene. Those floods delivered large volumes of sediment to floodplains. Initially, sedimentation was rapid, forming thick packages of late-Holocene valley fill (Mandel 2005a). However, by ca. 3000 B.P., sedimentation slowed and cumulic soils developed on late Holocene floodplains (now terraces). For example, in the middle and lower reaches of the Neosho River, soil development was under way on the late-Holocene floodplain ca. 3000 B.P. and continued until ca. 1300 B.P., producing a thick, dark soil. This soil was buried soon after ca. 1300 B.P. and is a prominent soil-stratigraphic marker in the upper part of the T–1 fill (Figure 3.2). At site 14BU1311 near Augusta, Kansas (Figure 3.1), a prominent buried soil in the T–1 fill of the lower Whitewater River is firmly dated between ca. 2200 and 1900 B.P. The radiocarbon data for streams in southeastern Kansas suggest that late-Holocene floodplain stability was time-transgressive through drainage networks. Specifically, soil development dating to ca. 3000–1300 B.P. in the T–1 fill of high-order streams dates to ca. 1900–900 B.P. (Copan Paleosol) in the T–1 fill of low-order streams.

In the valleys of large streams in western Kansas, there are two discrete episodes of late-Holocene soil development represented by buried soils: one at ca. 2750–2600 B.P. and the other at ca. 2000–1600 B.P. (Mandel 1994a). The older of these two episodes of stability and soil development partially coincides with the soil-forming period radiocarbon-dated to ca. 2800–2400 B.P. in the valleys of small streams (Mandel 1992). However, the period of soil development dated to 2000–1600 B.P. precedes the beginning of the major soil-forming episode dated to 1600–1000 B.P. in the valleys of small streams. Hence, at least one episode of late Holocene landscape stability appears to be time-transgressive in drainage networks.

In the Central Plains, most large and small streams went through a major episode of entrenchment around 1000 B.P., leaving their late-Holocene floodplains as terraces. During this time of stream erosion, large volumes of early, middle, and late Holocene alluvium were removed from channel belts. However, aggradation and development of new floodplains were under way soon after ca. 1000 B.P.

The drainage networks of most streams in the Central Plains received large volumes of sediment soon after the region was settled by Euro-Americans. Reduced vegetative cover associated with clearing and cultivating land increased surface runoff, which in turn increased both flood frequency and sediment delivery to all drainage elements. Large volumes of modern alluvium accumulated on floodplains (T–0) in large and small valleys, and in places formed thick deposits on low terraces. Consequently, prehistoric geomorphic surfaces at low positions in valley landscapes are often mantled by recent (< 300 B.P.) alluvium. This has had a profound effect on the visibility of prehistoric cultural deposits in stream valleys.

The late-Holocene stratigraphic records for dune fields and sand sheets in Kansas resemble late-Holocene alluvial stratigraphic records for small streams in western Kansas. Over the past 3,000 years, episodes of eolian sedimentation and dune development were interrupted by periods of landscape stability and soil formation. For example, stratigraphic evidence for the Great Bend Sand Prairie indicates that environmental conditions fluctuated between relatively moist and dry during the late Holocene (Arbogast 1995). In general, landscapes were unstable during arid intervals, resulting in mobilization of dune sand. As effective moisture increased, dunes stabilized and soils formed. Based on the radiocarbon ages of weakly developed buried soils in the Great Bend Sand Prairie, Arbogast (1995) suggested that there were five brief episodes of landscape stability and soil formation during the late Holocene: 2300, 1500, 1000, 700, and 200 B.P. In the Cimarron Bend of southwestern Kansas, dune development was interrupted by at least two episodes of stability and soil formation: one ca. 1500 B.P., and the other ca. 1100 B.P. (Olson and Porter 2002).

Playas in western Kansas, which were zones of net sediment removal via wind erosion during the middle Holocene, became zones of net sediment storage and soil formation during the late Holocene. Buried cumulic soils dating to the late Holocene are common in playa basins on the High Plains (Mandel 2000). Of the 15 radiocarbon ages determined on organic carbon from buried soils developed in playa fills, 11 date to 1000–500 B.P. (Figure 3.8).

SUMMARY AND CONCLUSIONS

This description of temporal and spatial patterns of late Quaternary landscape evolution in Kansas provides the basis for answering the following question: How have geomorphic processes (i.e., erosion and deposition) shaped the archaeological record of the state? In addressing this question, the following discussion summarizes the temporal and spatial patterns of landscape evolution during specific periods of the late Quaternary and considers the effects of these patterns on cultural deposits in valleys of different size streams (low-, intermediate-, and high-order streams). Other geomorphic settings, including playas and sand dunes and sheets, also are considered.

During the Pleistocene-Holocene transition (ca. 12,000–9000 B.P.), many landscapes in Kansas were quasi-stable to stable, as indicated by the existence of one or more buried soils in terrace fills, alluvial fans, loess deposits, sand dunes and sheets, and playa basins. It is important to note that these buried soils represent buried Paleoindian landscapes often more than 1 m below the modern land surface (Mandel, Hofman, et al. 2004). However, buried Paleoindian landscapes are not preserved throughout drainage networks. In fact, with the exception of the draws on the High Plains, soils dating to 12,000–9000 B.P. rarely occur in the valleys of small or intermediate streams. Hence, the fact that there are few recorded Paleoindian sites in Kansas (91 as of February 2004, most of which are isolated projectile points) may be more related to their lack of visibility (i.e., they are deeply buried) as well as their removal by channel erosion than to low human population densities in the region during the Pleistocene-Holocene transition.

As noted earlier, the Central Plains, including the area of Kansas, became generally warmer and drier toward the end of the Pleistocene-Holocene transition. This trend continued and intensified during the early and middle Holocene (ca.

9000–4000 B.P.). Small streams (< fifth-order) responded by downcutting and lengthening. Early and middle Holocene alluvium may have been stored temporarily in low-order drainage elements, providing habitable surfaces for human occupation on valley floors. However, small streams were zones of net sediment removal during this period. Hence, as early and middle Holocene alluvial deposits were removed by stream erosion, Middle Archaic and older sites associated with these deposits also would have been removed. In this case, the geologic filter has resulted in an archaeological record that is not a complete record of human activity.

Sediment transported out of the valleys of small streams during the early and middle Holocene was delivered to and stored in alluvial fans. It was also stored in floodplains of some large and intermediate streams (> fifth-order). During the warm, dry Altithermal (ca. 7000–5000 B.P.), it is likely that floodplains (now terraces) and alluvial fans were frequently occupied by Archaic hunters and gatherers attracted to more dependable water supplies and abundant food resources in the valleys of large streams. Hence, their cultural remains would likely have been rapidly buried and preserved in situ on fan and floodplain surfaces. From an archaeological perspective, this is a double-edged sword (Mandel 1995). Although terrace fills and alluvial fans have great potential for containing stratified Paleoindian and Archaic materials, there may be limited or no exposure of the artifact-bearing deposits. Detecting these buried cultural deposits without deep trenching or systematic surveys of cutbank exposures is, therefore, unlikely. The recent discovery of the Claussen site (14WB322) and other deeply buried cultural deposits in lower Mill Creek valley underscores this point. In 1999, a preliminary survey of cutbanks along Mill Creek resulted in the detection of stratified cultural deposits (mussel shells, bone fragments, chert flakes, and charcoal) in a paleosol about 10 m below the surface of the broad T–2 terrace (Mandel 2005c). Charcoal from features in the deeply buried cultural components yielded radiocarbon ages ranging from ca. 9250 to 8800 B.P. In 2003, a systematic survey of cutbanks along approximately 15 km of lower Mill Creek resulted in the discovery of six buried sites, including three that consist of Early Archaic cultural deposits at depths of 9–10 m below the surface of the T–2 terrace. Given the tremendous volume of early Holocene alluvium stored below the T–2 terrace, lower Mill Creek valley and similar large streams in the Flint Hills probably harbor many Early Archaic cultural deposits. Although some of these deposits may be visible in cutbanks, it is likely that most of them are not exposed.

In sum, the paucity of recorded Early Archaic sites in the valleys of large streams (> fifth-order) throughout Kansas is probably related to lack of visibility. The same can be said for the few recorded Middle Archaic sites in the valleys of some large streams. However, mid-Holocene erosion probably removed Middle Archaic cultural deposits in the valleys of many large streams, just as it did in the valleys of small (< fifth-order) and intermediate streams (fifth-order).

Playas in western Kansas were zones of slow sedimentation and soil development during the early Holocene (9000–7000 B.P.). It is likely that they contained water during moist periods, but were occasionally dry, thereby allowing soil development. The playas would have attracted game and people, and episodes of sedimentation (i.e., accumulation of slope wash and/or pond deposits) would have resulted in burial of Late Paleoindian and Early Archaic cultural deposits. The Winger site (14ST401) in southwestern Kansas (Figure 3.1) demonstrates the significance of playas as geomorphic settings for buried cultural deposits dating to the early Holocene. At Winger, an extensive bison bonebed with Late Paleoindian Allen projectile points was recorded in a deeply buried cumulic soil developed in playa deposits (Mandel and Hofman 2003). A radiocarbon age of 9080±90 B.P., determined on rib fragments from the bonebed, indicates that the playa basin was relatively stable as late as ca. 9000 B.P., and soil development was under way immediately before that time (Mandel and Hofman 2003). Subsequent accumulation of pond deposits and alluvium sealed the cultural deposits about 2.5 m below the modern land surface.

Mid-Holocene soil-stratigraphic evidence suggests that from ca. 7000 to 5000 B.P., a period corresponding to the peak of the Altithermal (H. E. Wright 1968), playas and sand dunes/sheets in western Kansas became zones of landscape instability. While playas were being deflated during most of the middle Holocene, sand dunes were mobilized. Deflation of the playa basins would have compromised the integrity of Middle and late Early Archaic cultural deposits in these geomorphic settings. However, in dune fields, depositional processes associated with mobilization of the sands probably resulted in deep burial of Middle and late Early Archaic cultural deposits. Although deep burial generally favors preservation of cultural deposits, they are difficult to detect except in modern blow-outs in the dunes.

During the late Holocene (4000 B.P.–present), small, intermediate, and large streams in Kansas were characterized by episodes of sedimentation punctuated by landscape stability and soil development. Consequently, buried soils (i.e., buried landscapes) are common in late Holocene valley fills. Modern surfaces of terraces, floodplains, and alluvial fans that compose valley floors throughout drainage networks are geologically quite young, often postdating 1500 B.P., whereas buried soils with high potential for containing Late Archaic and Early Woodland materials are usually several meters or more below the land surface. Also, thick deposits of alluvium postdating Euro-American settlement in Kansas are common on floodplains and low terraces, especially in the valleys of large streams. Therefore, even late Prehistoric and early Historic cultural deposits may be buried. Hence, in valley landscapes of Kansas, it is not surprising that most of the recorded surface sites assigned to cultural affiliations are Middle Woodland or younger.

The late Holocene soil-stratigraphic record of playas and sand dunes/sheets in Kansas is similar to the late-Holocene record preserved in stream valleys. Sedimentation in playa basins, dune fields, and eolian sand sheets was punctuated by episodes of landscape stability and soil development. This is especially apparent in dune fields and eolian sand sheets. As with floors of stream valleys, modern geomorphic surfaces of playas and sand dunes/sheets are typically less than 1,500 years old, and many are much younger than that. Buried soils that may harbor Late Archaic and younger cultural deposits tend to be 1–3 m below the modern land surface. Hence, what we know about human occupation in playa basins, dune fields, and eolian sand sheets is biased because most of the recorded archaeological sites are on young, exposed geomorphic surfaces. The paucity of recorded Late Archaic and older sites in these geomorphic settings is probably a result of deep burial of cultural deposits rather than limited human occupation in these settings.

Several conclusions important to the interpretation of Kansas' archaeological record arise from the information presented in this chapter. First, late Quaternary landscapes, especially those in stream valleys, are mosaics of landforms and underlying sediments. The temporal and spatial patterns of these landform sediment assemblages have influenced many spatial and temporal patterns observed in the archaeological record. Second, the success of strategies for archaeological sampling of stream valleys and other landscapes, such as playa basins and dune fields, depends in large part on the level of understanding of soil-stratigraphy and geologic patterns. Finally, the geologic filter *strongly* controls the archaeological record. Temporal and spatial patterns of erosion and sedimentation, which may have produced differential preservation and visibility of past human activity, must be assessed in order to distinguish the effects of geomorphic processes from those of human choices in the archaeological record. Without this assessment, an accurate understanding of prehistoric peoples' use of the landscape is impossible.

4. The Paleoarchaic of Kansas

Jeannette M. Blackmar and Jack L. Hofman

> *Paleoindian and Archaic constructs obscure rather than illuminate early human behavior in the Great Plains . . . and [these terms] need to be subdued to better recognize behavioral plasticity and adaptive variability.* (Simms 1988: 41)

Hunting and gathering economies were dominant in the Central Great Plains of North America for a period spanning approximately 8,000 years. Beginning with the entry of people into North America, the Paleoarchaic (cf. G. T. Jones et al. 2003) concluded roughly with the introduction of ceramic technology and the increased importance of horticulture and utilization of domesticated plants. These new developments had their greatest impact in the eastern two-thirds of Kansas. The use of wild plant and animal resources, through implementation of strategies dating back thousands of years, continued into the Historic period, sometimes as a supplemental and in other cases as the dominant strategy. Some bison hunters and traders on the western plains never adopted horticulture as a primary mode of subsistence, but the archaeological record of these peoples is thin.

Hunting and gathering lifeways were dynamic and do not represent one homogeneous, unchanging adaptation. In fact, these cultural groups varied socially, economically, and technologically. Human societies during this period occupied a wide range of natural settings from the High Plains to the Missouri River valley, using a broad array of economic strategies, and we must assume that their social organizations and conditions were equally diverse. Much of the archaeological literature about these earliest archaeological complexes has been previously summarized, but fortunately we have substantially more and different information than has been available for previous syntheses (Greiser 1985; Hofman 1996: 41–100; Hofman and Graham 1998: 87–139; Kay 1998: 173–200). In particular, this chapter aims to integrate the early archaeological record of the Kansas area with newly available data from deeply buried archaeological sites and to document, explore, and evaluate past behavioral variability as shown in the limited but diverse hunter-gatherer archaeological record. We use information on recorded hunter-gatherer sites, material remains (features and artifacts), as well as nonsite evidence of isolated finds, to address problems of site patterning and resource use and to monitor changes in these material records through time. Economic, technological, and social changes are the result of many selective forces, including a dynamic environment, population growth, social competition, technological constraints, and the effectiveness of social and information systems.

Traditionally, archaeologists have divided the Paleoarchaic record, the time period from at least 11,500 to 3000 B.P. (based on uncorrected radiocarbon dates [see Appendix]), into the Paleoindian and Archaic. Paleoindian complexes in the Great Plains region generally encompass the late Pleistocene and earliest Holocene archaeological evidence, which at many sites has included evidence for hunting and processing large animals such as mammoth and bison. Paleoindian archaeological complexes included diverse groups with diversified economies, some of which focused more on the use of large herbivores, while others had much more generalized economic pursuits for part or all of their seasonal economic cycles. Paleoindian archaeological complexes certainly do not represent a single homogeneous adaptation.

For the central North American Great Plains, the Archaic period is usually characterized as one of generalized hunter-gatherer economies focused on locally available resources. This Archaic concept has been extended from its initial use in the eastern United States, where the early Archaic period begins about 2,000 years earlier than on the High Plains, and temporally overlaps the late Paleoindian Plains complexes. Because of the east-to-west environmental diversity of Kansas, the early Archaic of eastern Kansas is more similar to that of the eastern deciduous forests than to that of the western Kansas High Plains. The Dalton complex, which is well represented in eastern Kansas (Wetherill 1995), arguably represents an early broad spectrum, locally focused, economic orientation (Morse 1997). Economically this could be considered to mark the beginning of the Archaic. Beginning before 10,000 B.P., the Dalton complex is contemporary with late Paleoindian complexes in the Plains region and shares many technological traits with Paleoindian assemblages (Goodyear 1982; Morse 1997; M. J. O'Brien and Wood 1998: 75–84). Several authors (e.g., Knudson 2002) have discussed the presence of Dalton and Dalton-like projectile points and technology in the Plains region. However, some of the Plains Archaic complexes had economic strategies that, at least during some seasons and years, were comparable to those of the earlier Paleoindian bison hunters (e.g., Bement and Buehler 1997; Frison, Wilson, and Wilson 1976). Table 4.1 highlights selected Paleoarchaic sites located in Kansas.

These examples are among the many reasons we have elected to combine the diverse hunter-gatherer cultural groups of the Kansas region for an integrated presentation that makes no prior assumptions as to whether they represent specialized big game hunters, localized foragers, or some combination of both.

As shown in Table 4.2, many complexes have been recognized within the Paleoarchaic period in the Central Plains. These archaeological complexes are classified based on specific artifact types, including distinctive projectile point forms, their associated technologies, economic evidence, and primary prey species. Figure 4.1 shows a selection of the distinctive projectile point types recognized in the region. Paleoindian and Archaic points are recognizable based on attributes of shape and technological features such as flaking patterns and the presence or absence of grinding. Typically, the final forms of chipped-stone artifacts vary greatly due in part to

Table 4.1. Selected Kansas Paleoarchaic Sites

Site Name	Site Number	County	Selected References	Cultural Affiliation*
12 Mile Creek	14LO2	Logan	M. E. Hill 1994, 1996; Rogers and Martin 1984; W. R. Wedel 1959; Williston 1902	Clovis, Folsom
Claussen	14WB322	Wabaunsee	Mandel 2003; Widga and Hofman 2003; Mandel, Widga, et al. 2004	Paleoarchaic
Coffey	14PO1	Pottawatomie	Schmits 1976, 1978, 1981	Munkers Creek, Black Vermillion, El Dorado, Walnut
Cow Killer	14OS347	Osage	Reynolds 1984	Munkers Creek
Eckles	14JW4	Jewell	Hoard et al. 1993; Holen 1998, 2001	Clovis
Kanorado Locality	14SN101 14SN105 14SN106	Sherman	Mandel, Hofman, et al. 2004a; Mandel et al. 2005	Pre-Clovis? Clovis?
Laird	14SN2	Sherman	Hofman and Blackmar 1997, 2004; Mandel, Hofman, et al. 2004	Dalton
Norton	14SC6	Scott	Hofman 1996	Cody, Allen-Frederick
Snyder	14BU9	Butler	Grosser 1970, 1973, 1977; Klepinger 1972	Chelsea, El Dorado, Walnut
Stigenwalt	14LT351	Labette	Thies 1990	Archaic
Sutter	14JN309	Jackson	Katz 1971, 1973	Allen-Frederick, Logan Creek, McKean
William Young	14MO304	Morris	Witty 1962, 1982	El Dorado, Munkers Creek
Williamson	14CF330	Coffey	Schmits 1980a, 1987a	El Dorado
Winger	14ST401	Stanton	Buckner 1970, 1973; Hofman 2002; Mandel and Hofman 2002, 2003	Allen-Frederick

*Some sites also have post-Archaic components.

Table 4.2. Recognized Paleoarchaic Complexes in Kansas

Complex/ Phase[a]	Age Estimate (B.P.)	Defined by	Type Site	Area Distribution
Walnut	3150–1950	Grosser 1970	Snyder, KS	Flint Hills
Colvin	3450–2000	Rohn et al. 1977	14CF519, 14CF524	Osage Cuestas
El Dorado	3950–3250	Grosser 1970	Snyder, KS	Flint Hills, Osage Cuestas
Nebo Hill	4550–2900	Shippee 1948	Nebo Hill, MO	Eastern Prairie Plains; Kansas City area, western Missouri
Chelsea	4800–3950	Grosser 1970	Snyder, KS	Flint Hills
Black Vermillion	5650–4850	Schmits 1981	Coffey, KS	Flint Hills, Osage Cuestas
Munkers Creek	5800–4950	Witty 1982	William Young, KS	Flint Hills, Osage Cuestas
Logan Creek	6150–5200	Kivett 1962	Logan Creek, NE	Eastern Prairie Plains
Stigenwalt	8750–7350	Thies 1990	Stigenwalt, KS	Big Hill Creek, eastern Kansas
Allen-Frederick[b]	9400–7800	Mulloy 1959	James Allen, WY	North American Great Plains[c]
Cody	9400–8800	Jepsen 1951	Horner, WY	North American Great Plains
Alberta	10,200–9400	Wormington and Forbis 1965	Fletcher, Alberta	North American Great Plains
Hell Gap	10,500–9500	Agogino 1961; H. T. Irwin 1968	Hell Gap, WY	North American Great Plains
Agate Basin	10,500–10,000	R. P. Wheeler 1954	Agate Basin, WY	North American Great Plains
Plainview	10,200–9800	Krieger 1946	Plainview, TX	North American Great Plains
Dalton	10,600–9300	C. H. Chapman 1948	Dalton site, MO	Southeast, Prairie Plains
Folsom	10,900–10,200	E. B. Howard 1935	Folsom, NM	North American Great Plains
Clovis	11,500–10,900	Sellards 1952	Clovis, NM	North America

[a]Data collected from Holliday 2000: 227, Brown and Simmons 1987, Hofman and Graham 1998: 87–139.

[b]Frederick was defined at Hell Gap by Irwin 1968.

[c]As defined by Fenneman 1931.

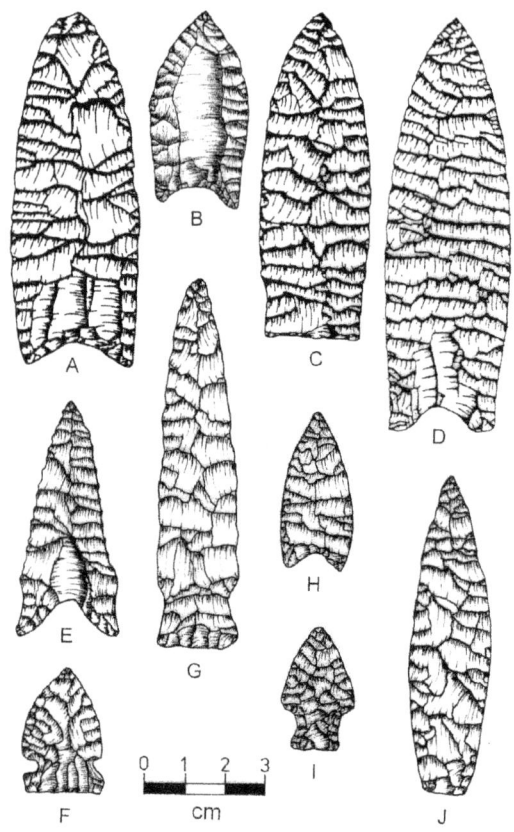

Figure 4.1. Selected Paleoarchaic projectile point types. A. Clovis; B. Folsom; C. Cody (Firstview); D. Allen; E. Dalton; F. Logan Creek; G. Munkers Creek; H. McKean; I. Late Holocene Stemmed; J. Nebo Hill.

tool recycling, the abilities of stone toolmakers, and the variation in stone quality. However, projectile point types alone provide insufficient evidence to adequately define archaeological complexes. Archaeological complexes should be defined using the broader evidence of technological assemblages, land-use patterns, economies, and, as much as possible, the entire lifeway represented. Our current knowledge is indeed limited, and many prehistoric artifacts found in Kansas do not fit neatly into the defined typologies or with specific archaeological complexes. Our goal in this chapter is to emphasize diversity and variation as key components in understanding hunter-gatherer lifeways of the earliest peoples of Kansas. Following Simms (1988: 41), we subscribe to the view that "the archaeological record reflects gradual or punctuated frequency shifts in the use of alternative strategies that incorporate technologies and behaviors in various mixes." In other words, we expect that a group might operate like big game hunting specialists during some periods while, during other periods, the same group would embrace a broad spectrum economic strategy. Such variation probably occurred on seasonal, yearly, and generational time scales.

SITE AND NONSITE DISTRIBUTION

The 1987 Kansas Archaeological Preservation Plan indicates 504 Archaic sites and 27 Paleoindian sites (K. L. Brown and Brown 1987). The past 16 years have seen a substantial increase in this documented evidence in Kansas. As of 2005, 970 sites designated as Paleoindian or Archaic have been recorded in Kansas, of which 23 sites include at least one Paleoindian and one Archaic component (Figure 4.2). Ninety-four sites are assigned as Paleoindian and 876 as Archaic sites. Additional Paleoindian evidence includes isolated point finds that have not received site number designations. Key sites in the wider area that are mentioned here or that have yielded critical information are shown in Figure 4.3.

Dunnell and Dancey (1983: 272) suggest that "the archaeological record is most usefully conceived as a more or less continuous distribution of artifacts over the land surface with highly variable density characteristics." For regional studies, recognizing the distribution of artifacts across the landscape is equally important and complementary to documentation of sites (Ebert 1992; Foley 1981a, 1981b; D. H. Thomas 1975). Furthermore, "many patterns of landscape and resource use will simply not be visible if we only study a selected handful of 'productive' sites" (Hofman 1996: 77). This is especially true for hunter-gatherer archaeology on the Plains.

Avocational archaeologists provided much of the nonsite information as reported in part by studies listed in Table 4.3. Based on the incorporation of nonsite and site data for Clovis and Folsom fluted points, Figure 4.4 shows 61 Clovis loca-

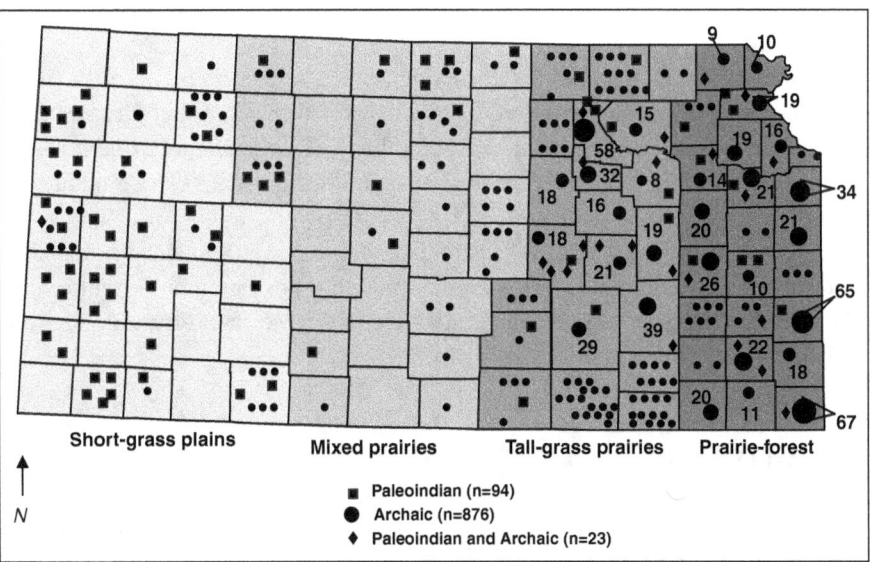

Figure 4.2. Distribution of recorded Paleoarchaic sites in Kansas

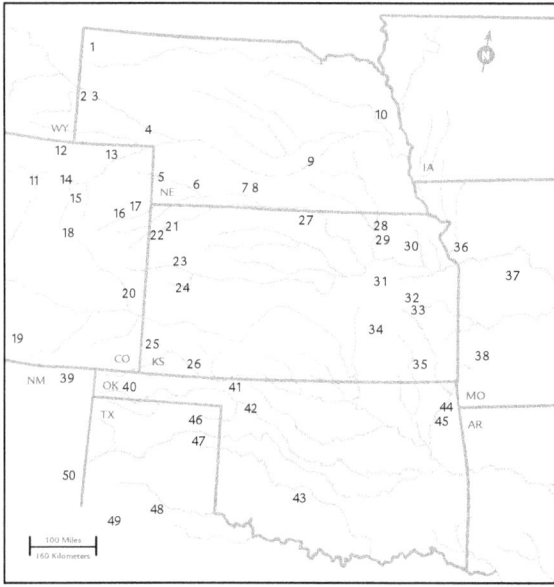

Figure 4.3. Locations of key sites in Kansas and bordering states.
Nebraska: *1. Hudson-Meng; 2. Scottsbluff; 3. Signal Butte; 4. Clary Ranch; 5. Nolan; 6. Spring Creek; 7. Lime Creek; 8. Red Smoke, Allen; 9. Meserve; 10. Logan Creek.* Colorado: *11. Dent; 12. Lindenmeier; 13. Dipper Gap; 14. Jurgens; 15. Lamb Spring; 16. Claypool; 17. Jones Miller, Selby/Dutton; 18. Westfall; 19. Cattle Guard; 20. Olsen-Chubbuck.* Kansas: *21. Busse, Laird; 22. Kanorado; 23. 12 Mile Creek; 24. Norton; 25. Winger; 26. Sailor-Helton; 27. Eckles; 28. Diskau; 29. Coffey; 30. Sutter; 31. William Young; 32. Cow Killer; 33. Williamson; 34. Snyder; 35. Stigenwalt.* Missouri: *36. Nebo Hill; 37. Rodgers Shelter; 38. Big Eddy.* New Mexico: *39. Folsom; 50. Blackwater Draw.* Oklahoma: *40. Nall; 41. Waugh; 42. Cooper, Jake's Bluff; 43. Domebo; 44. Afton; 45. Packard.* Texas: *46. Lipscomb; 47. Miami; 48. Lake Theo; 49. Lubbock Lake.*

tions and 63 Folsom locations. Potentially significant differences between the Clovis and Folsom records may partly reflect different economic and mobility strategies used by the makers of these distinctive technologies (Blackmar 2001). Clovis people may have been more generalized in their adaptation and resource exploitation patterns than were Folsom folks (cf. Meltzer 1993; Hofman and Todd 2001). Figure 4.5 illustrates the distribution of late Paleoindian sites and nonsite evidence. Included within the Late Paleoindian, based on chronological position and technology, are Allen-Frederick, Agate Basin, Cody, Dalton, Hell Gap, Meserve, Plainview, and undesignated "late Paleoindian."

SITE PATTERNING

Modern vegetation communities across Kansas are known to have changed substantially during the Holocene and are distinct from those that existed during the terminal Pleistocene (see chapter 2, this volume). During this change to warmer, more seasonal continental climate, the paleontological and archaeological records indicate

Table 4.3. Publications Using Paleoarchaic Data Collected by Avocational Archaeologists

Reference	Complex [a]
Beaver 1998	Hell Gap
Blackmar 2001	Clovis, Folsom, Cody
K. L. Brown and Logan 1987	Clovis, Folsom, Plainview, Agate Basin, Hell Gap, Cody, Frederick, Dalton, Meserve
Glover 1978	Cody
Hofman 1994	Folsom
Hofman and Blackmar 1997	Folsom
Hofman and Hesse 2002	Clovis
Holen 2001	Clovis
Rogers 1984	Paleoindian and Archaic in the Arkansas River drainage and Wichita sandpit localities
Schmits 1987b	Clovis
Stein 1984	Paleoindian
Wetherill 1995	Clovis, Plainview, Agate Basin, Hell Gap, Scottsbluff, Milnesand, Frederick, Dalton, Meserve in the Bonner Springs locality
Yaple 1968	Paleoindian

[a] Statewide unless noted.

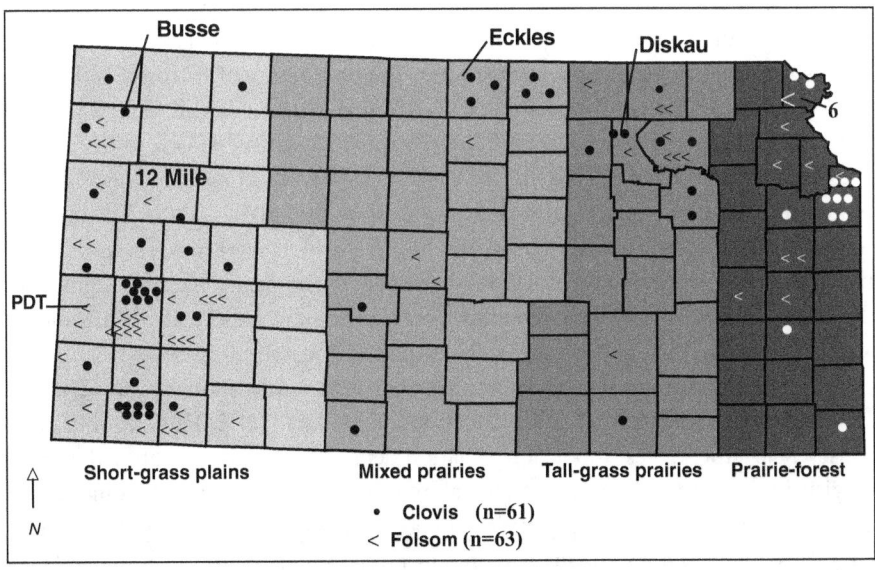

Figure 4.4. Distribution of fluted point sites and isolates by county

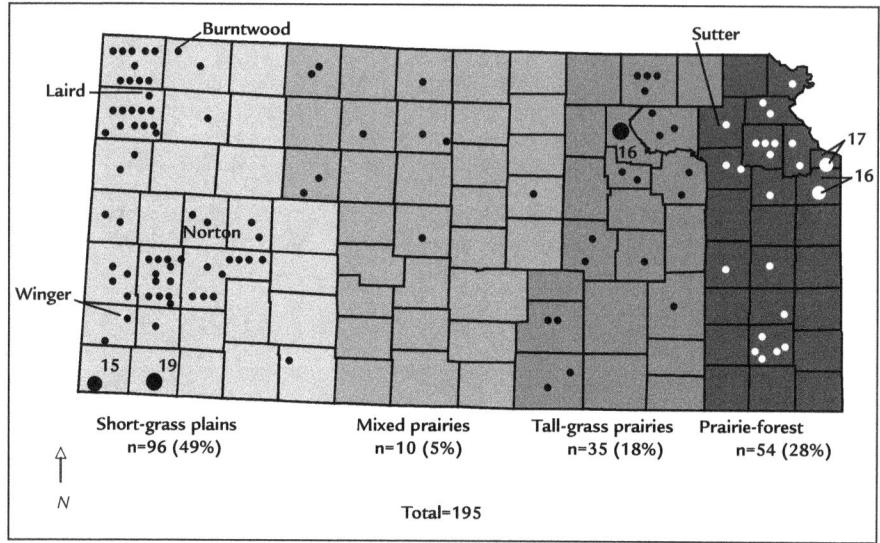

Figure 4.5. Distribution of late Paleoindian sites and isolates by county

the reorganization of plant and animal communities (Graham 1987; Graham and Lundelius 1984; Graham and Mead 1987). We use these broad vegetation regions here as a coarse proxy measurement for the variety of physiographic regions that exist and have existed in Kansas during the period of human occupation.

Modern vegetation types in Figure 4.6 compare Paleoindian site and nonsite distributions. While broadly similar, the differences in frequency of localities by area, shown in Figure 4.6, signal the importance of including all available information, not just site-specific records, in such studies. The dominance of Paleoindian finds in the western short-grass region of the Kansas Plains is probably the result of several combined factors. Obviously, early hunter-gatherers used the area, and during the late Pleistocene and early Holocene, the western Kansas environment was apparently more hospitable and better watered than during the middle and later Holocene. It was a prime environment for herbivores, hunters, and general foragers. Erosion of the High Plains, including the upland divides, playas, and draws, has been significant during the Holocene, exposing many surfaces that contain sediments of Paleoindian age, 12,000 to 8000 B.P. (see chapter 3, this volume). Focused research on Paleoindian evidence in this region during the past decade has also contributed to this pattern. However, most archaeological investigations in Kansas (M. E. Hill, Hofman, and Kinsey 1996), the highest modern population density, and most avocational archaeologists in Kansas are all in the eastern half of the state. Even though Paleoindian age sediments are commonly deeply buried along the draws in western Kansas (see chapter 3, this volume), these deposits represent a relatively small portion of the landscape, which is dominated by broad uplands. These uplands contain dune fields and

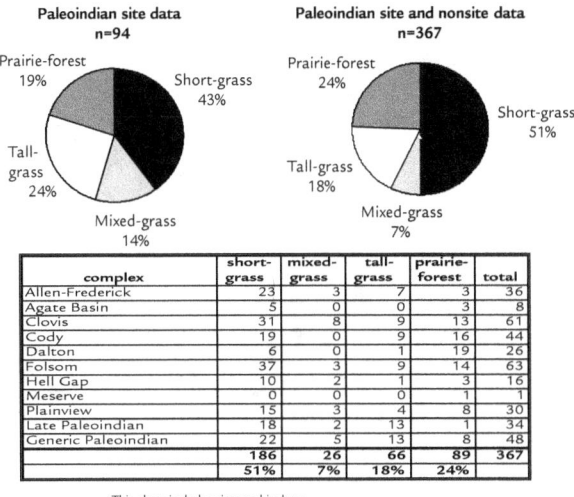

Figure 4.6. *Site and nonsite Paleoindian distribution by vegetation type*

playa lakes that are very susceptible to wind erosion, especially in areas that are under cultivation or have previously been broken open. In these areas, Paleoindian artifacts commonly occur as surface and near-surface deposits.

Paleoindian artifacts and sites are least well documented in the mixed-grass portion of Kansas. Landscapes in this area are generally better vegetated and less vulnerable to erosion, there are proportionately more streams, and Paleoindian-age deposits are again deeply buried (see chapter 3, this volume). In the tall-grass prairie area of Kansas, including the Flint Hills, the Paleoindian record is very poorly represented. This is almost certainly a reflection of modern land-use patterns and geomorphology. The uplands in the Flint Hills are typically grass-dominated pastureland, uncultivated because soils are relatively rocky. As a result, we see net deposition of wind-borne sediments rather than erosion. The combination of grass cover and loess deposition results in land surfaces on which Paleoindian artifacts are buried (probably shallowly) and covered by grass. The drainages in the tall-grass region have cultivated terraces, but the terrace surfaces are typically later Holocene in age, and Paleoindian-age sediments are again deeply buried (see chapter 3, this volume). Deep excavations in the tall-grass and Flint Hills region of Kansas show stratified Archaic sites where Paleoindian levels were never reached if they were even present (Schmits 1978; Witty 1982).

The prairie-forest mosaic of eastern Kansas includes the Till Plain region north of the Kansas River, which is essentially an eastern extension of the Plains habitat dissected by deep drainages with abundant water. In this area are both eroded and cultivated uplands that have yielded important Paleoindian evidence (e.g., W. R. Wedel

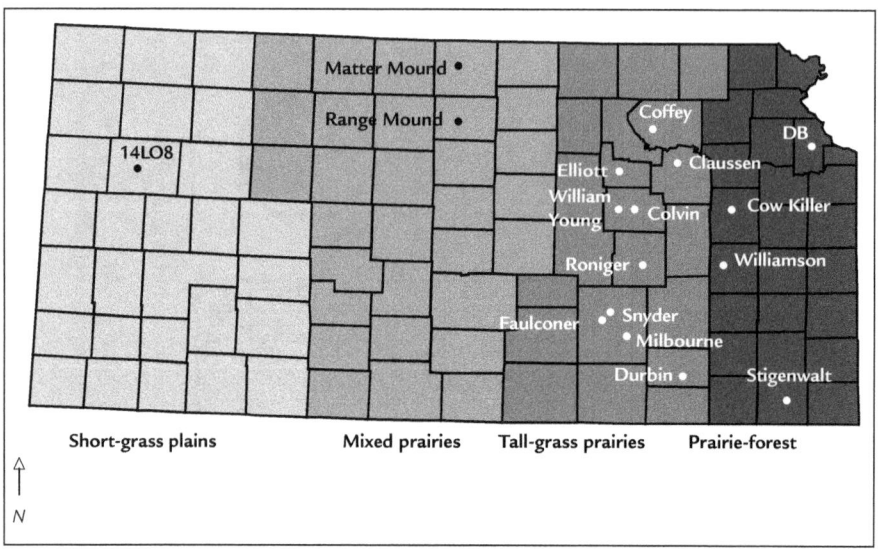

Figure 4.7. Distribution of selected Archaic sites

1959), but again the early prehistoric record in alluvial stream deposits is deeply buried. Buried Paleoindian sites in this portion of Kansas undoubtedly exist, although as yet none have been investigated in detail. Early Holocene stream terrace sites that were deeply buried are now regularly being recognized and documented in this region (see chapter 3, this volume). In the last few years, a number of fluted points have been documented in eastern Kansas south of the Kansas River, indicating that the earliest Kansas hunter-gatherers were certainly not limited to the western prairie and plains regions. In particular, Paleoindian point finds in the Kansas River near Bonner Springs are evidence of cultural material in deeply buried Pleistocene-Holocene boundary deposits, eroded out by river channel movement (Wetherill 1995).

When we look at the specific Paleoindian complexes, even with our limited data, strong patterns clearly exist. Cody artifacts are common in the west and the east, while Folsom, Allen-Frederick, Plainview, and Hell Gap finds come mostly from the High Plains area. Clovis is somewhat more evenly distributed but is still most common in the west.

The limited number of tested or excavated Archaic sites is shown in Figure 4.7, and key sites in neighboring areas are plotted in Figure 4.3. The Kansas sites lie mostly in the eastern third of the state where most federally contracted archaeological excavations have occurred. If we compare Paleoarchaic sites (not isolates) across the vegetation regions of Kansas, we witness a dramatic difference (Figure 4.8). The Archaic site distribution pattern is dominated by recorded sites in the prairie forest region of easternmost Kansas with very few sites recorded for the mixed-grass and short-grass prairie of western Kansas. The intensive archaeological investigations related to reservoir construction and other major federal projects in eastern Kansas, in-

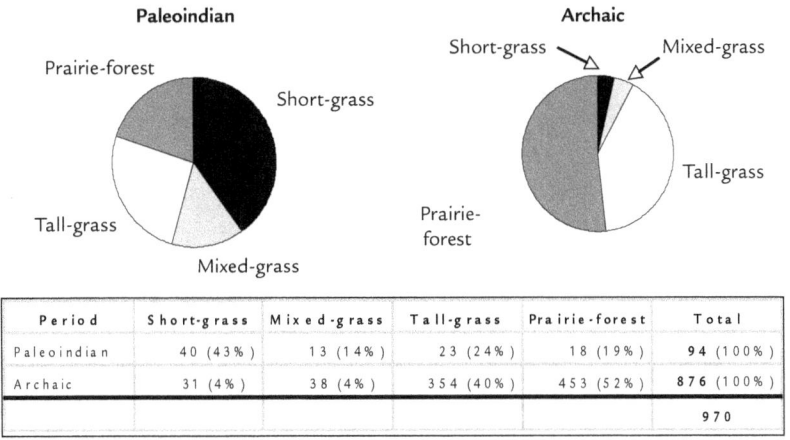

Period	Short-grass	Mixed-grass	Tall-grass	Prairie-forest	Total
Paleoindian	40 (43%)	13 (14%)	23 (24%)	18 (19%)	94 (100%)
Archaic	31 (4%)	38 (4%)	354 (40%)	453 (52%)	876 (100%)
					970

Figure 4.8. Comparison between Paleoindian and Archaic site distribution by vegetation type

cluding the Flint Hills, accounts for some of this pattern. The density of recorded sites as seen in Figure 4.2 is obviously weighted by the history of archaeological research in eastern Kansas.

The overall trend during the Holocene was toward a progressively drier, warmer, and more variable climate, with a more seasonal distribution of rainfall and greater seasonal variation in temperature (see chapter 2, this volume). It has also been argued (Hurt 1966; W. R. Wedel 1963) that there were periods when the High Plains environment was relatively inhospitable, notably during the middle Holocene Altithermal interval when there was an increase in aridity and temperature climaxing between 7,500–4,500 B.P. (Antevs 1955; Holliday 2000; W. C. Johnson and Park 1996; Wendland 1978; H. E. Wright 1976). However, the environment may not have kept human groups from using the region, although the severe erosion and deposition cycles of the middle Holocene have destroyed and buried the archaeological record so that the true intensity of middle Holocene human activity has not been recognized (Artz 1981; Bettis 1995; Mandel 1995; Mandel, chapter 3, this volume; B. Reeves 1973).

The diverse landforms on which Holocene archaeological sites occur are noteworthy. In particular, we have inadequate documentation of the use of playa lakes in the High Plains region, where Paleoindian and especially Archaic sites occur but have yet to be systematically documented. Likewise, the use of rockshelters and cave sites, which should be locally common in parts of eastern Kansas, remain remarkably underreported. Two rockshelters, Ernie's rockshelter (14CT303) and Dry Creek Rockshelter (14WO224), yielded evidence for multicomponent occupation, including Archaic components (J. H. Howard 1964: 347–353). These examples simply indicate that our current knowledge of hunter-gatherer sites in Kansas cannot capture the full diversity of the evidence. Recognizable patterns are, at least in part, a direct result of the uneven nature and limited extent of our investigations of the archaeological record.

HUNTER-GATHERER TECHNOLOGY IN THE CENTRAL PLAINS REGION

Paleoarchaic people are most well known through their durable stone artifacts and less so from their more rarely recovered bone technology. We have only sporadic evidence of perishable technologies from the region, notably netting, sandals, and other textiles in caves and rockshelters, such as Graham and Arnold Research caves in central Missouri, where preservation is generally much better than on the common open sites of the Plains (Chapman 1975: 158–163; M. J. O'Brien and Wood 1998: 12, 78). From the earliest occupants through the late Holocene hunter-gatherers, hunters used spears and atlatl-propelled darts but apparently did not have bow and arrow technology.

The atlatl or spearthrower was a central element of the hunting equipment used by early Americans and was still in use at the time of European contact by the Aztecs and some other groups. Upper Paleolithic hunters in Europe and Eurasia used spearthrowers by at least 20,000 B.P. (Cattelain 1989; Garrod 1955; Klein 1999), and we assume this technology was carried early into the New World. Some varieties of atlatl forms are known from dry caves in the Ozarks, western Texas and Oklahoma, the Southwest, the Rocky Mountain region, and the Great Basin (e.g., Harrington 1971; W. Baker and Kidder 1937). These include simple to elaborate forms that sometimes have distinctive atlatl weights or "boatstones" attached (Fenenga and Wheat 1940). Boatstones or atlatl weights have been found throughout Kansas but have only recently received systematic study (Ryan 2004). They were commonly used into the Woodland period. Elements of the wood technology associated with atlatls, darts, and foreshafts are also represented in dry cave deposits on the margins of the Plains (e.g., Frison 1965, 1991), reflecting aspects of hunter-gatherer technology we generally do not recover from the open-air sites that dominate the Kansas archaeological record.

Other wooden artifacts would have included fire-making equipment such as drills, which also are common in some dry cave sites. Digging sticks, hunting clubs or throwing sticks, pegs, stakes, and elements of traps and snares probably were part of the everyday technology of hunter-gatherers in the Kansas area.

Bone technology is somewhat better preserved but still minimally represented at most Kansas hunter-gatherer sites. Bone awls, flintworking tools, weaving needles, tubes (flutes, pipes, or sucking tubes), fishhooks, needles, scraping and cutting tools, and other implements either have been recovered or probably were used, although we have little evidence for it. Two bone awls were recovered from the Stigenwalt site (14LT351) and one each from the Coffey (14PO1) and Williamson (14CF330) sites.

Needles are present in several early Paleoindian contexts from the Plains region (Frison 1991), and it is probably only a matter of preservation and sampling that they have not yet been recovered from Kansas sites. Ornaments, especially beads, are known but have at present been found at only a few Kansas sites. One small bird bone bead was recovered at Stigenwalt, but its cultural assignment is unclear. A bone bead was also recovered from the Snyder site (Grosser 1973).

Netting, matting, fiber ropes, twine, sandals, and basketry were elements of hunter-gatherer personal, domestic, gathering, processing, and hunting technologies and are generally not preserved at open-air sites. These materials constitute a significant proportion of the artifacts in archaeological sites where preservation enables their recovery and documentation. Clues from dry cave sites in the Ozarks, the arid Southwest, the Rocky Mountain region, and the Great Basin indicate that Native American hunter-gatherers had sophisticated perishable technologies, dating back to the earliest occupations (e.g., C. H. Chapman 1975: 158–163; Frison et al. 1986; Harrington 1971; M. J. O'Brien and Wood 1998: 12, 78). Collecting, processing, and storing many resources would have required a variety of such technologies for prehistoric foragers in the Plains region.

Transportation technology probably included the dog and use of packs and travois. The importance of dogs in Plains Indian cultures is unquestioned, and their uses in hunting, as camp guards, as beasts of burden, and as a food source apparently have a long tradition in the region (Bozell 1988; Ewers 1955; Snyder 1991; Walker 1982; G. L. Wilson 1924; Witty and Frantz 1964). A dog burial was recovered from the Williamson site (Schmits 1987a) and another from the Coffey site (P. J. O'Brien, Hixon, et al. 1973: 8; Schmits 1978: 136). Water transportation along major rivers was probably also important and began early in the New World. In Florida, over 100 canoes dating from 5000 to 2300 B.P. have been found, as well as others from earlier time periods (R. Wheeler et al. 2003). Imagery and direct evidence of canoes from late prehistoric times also have been found (Phillips and Brown 1983; C. H. Chapman 1948).

The degree of mobility in the Great Plains is reflected in part by the movement of lithic materials. This is well exemplified by studies of the north-central Kansas Eckles site (14JW4) collection (Holen 2001), which provides an example of long-distance movement of high-quality lithic materials. White River Group chalcedony, probably from the Flattop source in northeast Colorado, dominates this assemblage (Hoard et al. 1992; Hoard et al. 1993) and was widely used during Paleoindian and later times on the Plains (Holen 2001; Hofman 2003). Most Archaic sites, in contrast, have chipped-stone assemblages dominated by local lithic materials, perhaps reflecting less extensive and more focused use of resources.

Chipped-stone artifact technology is well represented at Kansas hunter-gatherer sites, and the assemblages from selected sites are summarized in Table 4.4. There are few excavated Paleoarchaic sites, and many of these show multiple occupations. Their materials have become mixed, making it difficult to determine the potential chronological and cultural relationships among the multiple types of artifacts found. Projectile points are among the more diagnostic of chipped-stone artifacts, but samples from unmixed contexts are few. The Stigenwalt, Snyder (14BU9), and DB (14LV1071) sites are examples of this problem. Nevertheless, assessing technological and morphological variation in projectile points/knives remains the primary method for determining archaeological complexes and for comparing assemblages.

Table 4.4. Chipped-Stone Artifacts from Selected Hunter-Gatherer Sites*

Site Number	Site Name	Complex	Material	Total	Points	Bifaces
14SN101	Kanorado•	Clovis?	Alibates, jasper, Hartville, silicified wood	7+	-	1
14SN105	Kanorado•	Clovis?	Alibates, flattop	6	-	-
14SN106	Kanorado•	Clovis?	Hartville	4	-	-
14WB416		Clovis	?	2	2	-
14JW4	Eckles	Clovis	Flattop	87	2	3
14RY303	Diskau	Clovis	Flattop, KRF, Hartville	124	8	4
14SW302	Sailor-Helton	Clovis	Alibates	166	-	-
14LO1	12 Mile Creek	Folsom	Alibates?	1	1	-
14NT604	Tim Adrian	Hell Gap	Jasper, KRF	112	1	40
14SN2	Laird	Dalton	Flattop, jasper, Hartville, silicified wood	48	2	-
14SC6	Norton	Cody/Allen-Frederick	nonlocal[d]	209+	5	-
14RW2	Burntwood Creek	Allen-Frederick	-	-	-	-
14JN309	Sutter	Allen-Frederick	local	523	4	5
14ST401	Winger	Allen-Frederick	local, Alibates	10+	3	-
14LT351	Stigenwalt	Stigenwalt	local	113	18	30
14PO1	Coffey	Munkers Creek	local	10,931	18	66
14OS347	Cow Killer	Munkers Creek	local	520	6	12
14MO304	William Young	Munkers Creek	local	4315	31	389
14MO304	William Young	El Dorado	local	298	6	6
14CF330	Williamson	El Dorado	local	160	26	46
14BU25	Milbourn	El Dorado	local	834	69	274
14BU50	Faulconer	El Dorado	local	779	8	32
14BU9	Snyder	Walnut	local	50[e]	9	43
14BU9	Snyder	El Dorado	local	94[e]	13	77
14BU9	Snyder	Chelsea	local	4	4	-
14SN1	Busse Cache	Paleoindian	Jasper	88	-	38

*Does not include groundstone and unmodified cobbles.
•Kanorado data through 2003.
[a]Scrapers include endscrapers and sidescrapers.
[b]Flake tools include retouched flakes, modified flakes, gravers, spokeshaves, flake knives, burins.
[c]Perforators include drills.
[d]Norton lithic material includes Edwards, Alibates, Niobrara Jasper, and Flattop.
[e]Total does not include flakes since flakes were not broken down by complex.

Scrapers[a]	Flake tools[b]	Unmodified Flakes	Perforators[c]	Knives	Cores	Reference
1	1	3+	-	1	-	Mandel, Hofman et al. 2004
-	2	4	-	-	-	Mandel, Hofman et al. 2004
1	-	3	-	-	-	Mandel, Hofman et al. 2004
-	-	-	-	-	-	KSHS site form
9	21	51	-	-	1	Holen 1998
62	17	1	3	26	-	Holen 2001
-	5	151	-	-	10	Mallouf 1994
-	-	-	-	-	-	M. E. Hill 1994
45	11	3	-	-	13	P. J. O'Brien 1984b
4	-	41	-	1	-	Hofman and Blackmar 2004
2	2	200+	-	-	-	Hofman, unpublished manuscript
-	-	-	-	-	-	
6	226	282	-	-	-	Katz 1971
-	1	5+	-	1	-	Mandel and Hofman 2002
-	15	-	-	-	25	Thies 1990
31	36	10,726	3	51	-	Schmits 1978
1	4	440	-	2	55	Reynolds 1984
7	73	3652	1	14	148	Witty 1982
-	6	257	-	-	23	Witty 1982
9	73	-	3	3	-	Schmits 1987a
-	52	414	-	-	25	Root 1981
1	2	730	2	-	4	Bradley 1973
4	-	-	-	-	-	Grosser 1973
1	-	-	3	-	-	Grosser 1973
-	-	-	-	-	-	Grosser 1973
-	2	48	-	-	-	Hofman 1995

Most of the projectile points represented were probably hafted on short foreshafts and could be used either as handheld hafted knives or inserted in dart shafts to tip atlatl darts. These artifacts typically show evidence of being reworked after having been broken or dulled through use.

Many other chipped-stone artifacts are also integral to hunter-gatherer technologies, including unmodified flake tools used for a great variety of tasks; steep-edged scrapers for hide and woodworking; gouges for woodwork and hide or fiber processing; bifacial knives used for butchering or cutting plants; double- and single-bitted chipped-stone axes for felling trees and woodworking; adzes for woodworking; perforators for drilling holes in wood, bone, and stone objects; cores as sources of flakes; and preforms representing stages in the reduction process of stone tool manufacture but that can also serve as tools themselves. Some chipped-stone artifacts, such as Munkers Creek gouges and knives and Dalton adzes, are diagnostic for specific hunter-gatherer complexes, and spurred scrapers are indicative of Paleoindian sites (Morse and Goodyear 1973; Hester 1972; Witty 1982).

Groundstone artifacts have been found in a variety of forms at Paleoarchaic sites in the region. Abraders and small grinding stones of Paleoindian age have been recovered. The grinding stones typically show evidence of being used to grind hematite or other pigments. Boatstones or atlatl weights of various forms occur widely in the state. Plant food processing equipment becomes very important during the Holocene and is well represented on some hunter-gatherer sites. Often the hand stones (manos) and grinding basins (metates) are rough or of irregular form, but nicely pecked and shaped groundstone artifacts predominate by the late Holocene. There is every reason to assume that plant foods were essential to the diets of all native Kansans, but our archaeological evidence for plant use during the Paleoarchaic is limited (see chapter 15, this volume).

A summary of groundstone tool occurrences at selected Kansas hunter-gatherer sites is provided in Table 4.5. The earliest age site with manos, metates, and perhaps a celt is the Sutter site (14JN309). Manos and metates are also present in seven other Archaic age sites. Beyond the groundstone processing tools, many stone features and rock-filled or rock-lined pits probably reflect processing of roots and tubers for food. Processing of nuts, such as hickory, acorns, and walnuts, for their meats and butter is probably also reflected by some pit features used for stone boiling. Stone boiling was a common cooking procedure before ceramics were introduced or when groups were highly mobile. A suspended skin bag or a pit lined with a hide or leaves could be used for cooking by adding heated rocks from a nearby hearth.

Other economic pursuits required very little in the way of technology. Honey was probably collected whenever beehives were found. Beeswax was also useful for waterproofing. Insects, including moths and grasshoppers, could also be collected en masse in some situations or eaten incidentally as encountered. Snares and deadfall traps were probably used habitually near camps or along common foraging routes, providing a passive and more or less continuous acquisition of resources.

Table 4.5. Groundstone Tools

Site Number	Site Name	Complex	Mano	Grinding Slab	Hammer Stone	Abrader	Axe	Celt	Ochre[a]	Other	Total	Reference
14JN309	Sutter	Allen-Frederick	2	2	-	-	-	1[b]	-	-	5	Katz 1971
14LT351	Stigenwalt	Stigenwalt	2	18	2	-	1	-	1	-	24	Thies 1990
14PO1	Coffey	Munkers Creek	15	7	18	-	1	-	several	9[c]	50+	Schmits 1978
14OS347	Cow Killer	Munkers Creek	1	-	1	-	-	-	5	-	7	Reynolds 1984
14MO304	William Young	Munkers Creek	-	5	8	-	-	-	-	-	13	Witty 1982
14MO304	William Young	El Dorado	1	-	-	-	-	-	-	-	1	Witty 1982
14BU9	Snyder	El Dorado	5	-	-	-	-	-	-	-	5	Grosser 1973
14CF330	Williamson	El Dorado	2	2	-	4	-	-	4	-	12	Schmits 1987a
14BU25	Milbourn	El Dorado	-	-	-	-	-	-	-	-	21[d]	Root 1981

[a]Ochre includes hematite and limonite.

[b]Material is limestone; author questions functional efficiency of the implement.

[c]Includes a spheroid, a whetstone, and fragments of manos and grinding slabs.

[d]Tool types not specified.

Limited evidence of ceramic technology appears during the Middle Holocene. Current evidence includes a ceramic bead from the Coffey site and small effigy heads from William Young (14MO304). These are the earliest ceramic figures known in the United States.

RESOURCE DIVERSIFICATION: BROAD SPECTRUM ECONOMY

Fauna Diversity

People who lived in the Kansas area from before 11,500 B.P. until 3000 B.P. depended in part on wild animal resources (Table 4.6). The diversity of environments across this region and through time meant using many economic orientations and mixes of plant and animal procurement strategies. The dramatic ecological changes through this period, at scales ranging from seasons to millennia, also required that human groups respond to different economic opportunities. Some had access to mammoth, mastodon, ground sloth, bison, and other species, which became extinct or for which the availability varied dramatically. In Kansas, there is evidence of exploitation, either by scavenging or hunting, of mammoth at 14CK421. The Diskau site (14RY303) yielded mammoth and camel remains, along with 123 chipped-stone tools (Holen 2001: 98; Schmits 1987b). Recent investigations at the Kanorado locality (sites 14SN101, 105, and 106) revealed evidence of mammoth and camel in Clovis-age and earlier deposits (Mandel, Hofman, et al. 2004; Mandel, Holen, and Hofman 2005).

Reorganization of plant and animal communities at the close of the Pleistocene offered opportunities as well as problems. A broad range of food sources, as well as backup resource options for times when productivity or availability of key or preferred resources was low, was necessary. The mix of resources also needed to include a range of complementary food types to yield sufficient protein, lipids, carbohydrates, and nutrients to sustain women, men, and children of all ages and conditions. The subsistence patterns reflect both diffuse and focal economies (Cleland 1976: 42). Site data in Kansas indicate bison hunting in the uplands and the hunting of smaller fauna in riverine woodland habitats as well as plant use. Settlement patterns are directly related to environmental parameters, including spatial ranges and seasonal variations of availability, resulting in a "seasonally shifting subsistence-settlement system" (Thies and Witty 1992: 144). This is well exemplified at the Cow Killer (14OS337) and Coffey sites.

Moving and carrying necessities and supplies for future use required continual compromise. Binford's (1980) discussion of hunter-gatherer organizational variability, with foragers and collectors representing alternative strategies at opposite ends of the mobility and storage spectrums, has provided archaeologists with a valuable framework for investigating and comparing hunting and gathering societies. The combination of certain resources, technology, and environments enabled food storage in some cases, but necessitated high mobility and limited fixed storage in others.

Table 4.6. Flora and Fauna Exploitation

Site Number	Site Name	Complex	Seeds	Mussels	Bison[a]	Deer/Antelope[a]	Small Mammals[a]	Reptile[a]	Amphibian[a]	Fish[a]	Bird[a]	Reference
14SC6	Norton	Cody/Allen-Frederick	-	-	+	+	-	-	-	-	-	Hofman et al. 1995
14JN309	Sutter	Allen-Frederick	-	-	2	?	1	?	?	?	1	Katz 1971
14PO1	Coffey	Munkers Creek	+	-	5	4	4	6	6	172	16	Schmits 1978
14OS347	Cow Killer	Munkers Creek	+	-	2	2	+	+	-	+	-	Reynolds 1984
14CF330	Williamson	El Dorado	-	-	+	+	+	+	-	-	+	Schmits 1987a
14BU9	Snyder	El Dorado	+	+	+	+	?	?	?	+	?	Grosser 1973
14MO304	William Young	Munkers Creek	-	-	-	4	7	1	-	-	-	Witty 1982
14LT351	Stigenwalt	Stigenwalt	+	+	-	1	13[b]	3	2	-	3	Thies 1990
14BU50	Faulconer	El Dorado	-	+	-	4	15	-	-	-	1	Bradley 1973
14BU25	Milbourn	El Dorado	+	-	1	5	11	1	-	2	1	Root 1981
14WB322	Claussen	Paleoindian, Archaic	?	+	?	?	?	?	?	?	?	Widga and Hofman 2003
14CT35	Fulsom	Archaic	?	+	?	?	?	?	?	?	?	Mandel, personal communication
14CO1306	Winfield	Archaic	?	+	?	?	?	?	?	?	?	Mandel, personal communication
14GR371	Eureka	Archaic	?	+	?	?	?	?	?	?	?	Mandel, personal communication
14EK343	Wiseman	Archaic	?	+	?	?	?	+	?	?	?	Mandel, personal communication
14BU1308		Archaic	-	-	+	-	+	+	-	-	+	Bevitt et al. 2003

[a]Quantities reflect MNI values.
[b]Stigenwalt also contained charred rodent remains that may be indicative of human consumption (Finnegan and West 1990: 160–164).

The combination of mobility, resource transportation options, and decisions as to where and how long to camp and whether to move people to resources or move resources to people all served to create variability in the behaviors of Paleoarchaic groups and in the behavior of specific groups during different seasons or years. Entire groups could move from one residential location to another, or individuals or small logistical groups could travel for specific tasks or purposes. Kelly (1992) has discussed the anthropological problem of the mobility-sedentary continuum. The same group could be mobile in different ways and at different rates or sedentary on a seasonal or situational basis, such as when a windfall of key resources became available. The length of site occupation would affect the nature of construction and features, and the frequency and distance of group movement would have influenced the type of shelter, of clothing, and of transport technology.

Locations that were used repeatedly probably were used as cache sites for storable or durable supplies, food, or technological materials. Areas likely to be reoccupied include rockshelters, chert sources, gravel shoals where shellfish were common, and springs or other locations that provided reliable water, wood for fuel and technological needs, plants for food and fabrication materials, shelter from inclement weather, or good hunting areas. In these places, the archaeological record accumulated, leaving more visible evidence of hunter-gatherer activities. Such locations include William Young, Coffey, and Williamson. Other locations were useful for a limited time or on an unpredictable basis. These sites, unless they happen to be the location of animal kills that left abundant skeletal remains such as bison, tend to be less visible to archaeologists and represent the many ephemeral occupations of thousands of hunter-gatherer groups who used the Kansas region for thousands of years in a wide variety of ways.

Shellfish

Holocene hunter-gatherers in many coastal and riverine areas of North America utilized seasonally abundant shellfish as a recurrent element of their diets. Although the archaeological visibility of shellfish middens can tend to exaggerate their economic contribution (Klippel and Parmalee 1974; Klippel and Morey 1986), there is no question about the importance of shellfish as a predictable source of food and nutrients. Recurrent use of mussel-rich shoals in rivers and mussel beds in coastal bays often created highly visible archaeological sites that are typically well preserved because of the microenvironmental conditions of shell concentrations.

Shellfish use in prehistoric times is not uncommon in Kansas, but shell middens are essentially nonexistent. A few sites do have shell-filled features and small or shallow midden accumulations. These deeply buried sites include Claussen, Fulsom (14CT395), Winfield (14CO1306), Eureka (14GR371), and Wiseman (14EK343) (Mandel 2005a; Mandel, Widga, et al. 2004). Associated with the mussel shell are fire cracked rock and charcoal. Along with other faunal remains, mussel shell was also recovered from Snyder, Stigenwalt, and Faulconer (14BU25).

Economically, shellfish can be grouped with a variety of other foods that are easily collected but not highly ranked in terms of food value or return for the investment of energy required to collect and process them. The nutritive potential of many shellfish makes them little more than starvation fare, but the intensive use of shellfish does not become common in North America until human populations are relatively high. Evidence for the collecting of shellfish indicates seasonally recurrent land-use patterns. Shellfish use is thus often taken as an indication of a broad-spectrum economic strategy generally associated with Archaic hunter-gatherers in the Americas who used a broad range of local resources (aquatic, terrestrial, plant, and animal) and had economies that could vary dramatically from season to season and year to year, depending upon local and regional productivity of key species and upon competition from other human and animal foragers.

Flora

Plant use by hunter-gatherers in Kansas can be inferred directly from actual seed remains, indirectly by groundstone tools at several sites, and by ethnographic records. Charred seeds were recovered from five Paleoarchaic sites in Kansas: Cow Killer, Coffey, Stigenwalt, Milbourn, and Snyder. Floral remains were also recovered at the DB site in northeastern Kansas, but it is unclear whether these remains were associated with the Archaic occupation or the later prehistoric Steed-Kisker occupation. Charred seeds and charcoal were recovered from Cow Killer, but the seeds are not identified, and their association remains unclear (Reynolds 1984: 76). Identified plants at Coffey included goosefoot, knotweed, hackberry, bulrush, grape, and Solomon's seal (Schmits 1978: 146–147). Charred bulbs identified as wild onion, *Alium* sp., were found at Stigenwalt (Thies 1990: 104). Chenopodium seeds and walnuts were recovered from features at the Snyder site (Grosser 1977). Chenopodium seeds were also recovered at Milbourn (Root 1981: 194).

Bison

Archaeologists now recognize that the Paleoindian period was one of considerable economic diversity (Bamforth 1988; Frison 1991; Kornfeld 1996; Meltzer 1993). Even so, several Kansas Paleoindian sites represent bison kills, which were discovered because of the high visibility of exposed bone. These sites include 12 Mile Creek (14LO1), Norton (14SC6), Winger (14ST401), and Laird (14SN2), as well as Burntwood Creek (14RW2) and Gardiner (14CK320). The variability of bison evidence from Paleoarchaic sites is summarized in Table 4.7.

By approximately 11,000 years ago, many species that had been common in the region we now recognize as the Central Great Plains had become extinct or soon would be, due to rapid changes in climate and ecosystems (Graham 1987; Grayson 1988; Guthrie 1990; L. D. Martin 1996). We commonly think of bison as the quintessential Plains herbivore adapted to the vast grassland region. Prior to 12,000 B.P.,

Table 4.7. Bison Utilization

Site Number	Site Name	Complex	Date (B.P.)	Site Type	Vegetation	Season	MNI	Other Fauna	Reference
14WB416[a]		Clovis	none	camp	tall grass	?	?	no	KSHS site form
14LO1	12 Mile Creek	Folsom	10,400 (avg.)	kill	short grass	winter-spring	12+	no	M. E. Hill et al. 1996
14KY102	Simshauser	?	10,170±70[b]	?	short grass	?	?	no	Mandel, personal communication
14SR319	Pat Allen	?	9440±90	?	tall grass	?	?	no	Mandel, personal communication
14SN2	Laird	Dalton	8495±40	kill/processing	short grass	?	3+	no	Hofman and Blackmar 1997, 2004
14SC6	Norton	Cody/Allen-Frederick	9080±60	kill/ processing	short grass	?	8+	yes	Hofman et al. 1995
14ST401	Winger	Allen-Frederick	9080±90	kill/processing	short grass	?	?	no	Mandel and Hofman 2002, 2003
14JN309	Sutter	Allen-Frederick	7825 (avg.)	camp	prairie forest	?	2	yes	Katz 1971
14RW2	Burntwood Creek	Allen-Frederick	none	kill	short grass	spring-summer	31	no	M. E. Hill, Hofman, et al. 1992
14CK320	Gardiner	Allen-Frederick	none	kill	short grass	?	?	no	KSHS site form
14OS347	Cow Killer	Munkers Creek	4980±100	village	prairie forest	?	~2	yes	Reynolds 1984
14PO1	Coffey	Munkers Creek	4818 (avg.)	camp	prairie forest	summer-fall	5	yes	Schmits 1978
14MO304	William Young	El Dorado	4785 (avg.)	camp	tall grass	?	?	no[c]	Witty 1982
14BU25	Milbourn	El Dorado	4568±100	base camp	tall grass	spring-summer?	1	yes	Root 1981
14BU9	Snyder	El Dorado	3598 (avg.)	village	tall grass	?	?	yes	Grosser 1973
14CF330	Williamson	El Dorado	3550 (avg.)	camp	prairie forest	fall	3	yes	Schmits 1987a
14LO8[d]		Archaic	none	camp	short grass	?	1-3	no	Schock 1965

[a] 14WB416 yielded two Clovis points and bison bone. Site visited by Thies in 1995; not investigated further.
[b] Soil above bonebed.
[c] The Munkers Creek, Zone III, component at William Young contains no bison remains but does contain other fauna.
[d] Bone assumed to be bison.

however, several other herbivores were actually much more common than bison, including horses, camels, mammoths, and antelope. After 11,000 B.P., bison populations expanded rapidly to fill this herbivore niche and changed in their size, behavior, and grazing patterns.

Large bison herds, as indicated by bonebeds containing skeletons of dozens of animals apparently killed at one time, first appear in the archaeological and paleontological records after 11,000 B.P., before which time bonebeds with more than about 30 bison are unknown. Bison become smaller and more gregarious during the early Holocene, and by about 4000 B.P. had reached their modern size. Seasonal variation in bison behavior and condition is pronounced, as is their sexual dimorphism (Speth 1983). Bison behavior and condition significantly influenced how they were used during prehistory, which provides valuable clues about bison ecology and behavior of bison hunters in the past.

Bison meat, fat, bone grease, and bone marrow provided essential nutrition (Speth and Spielmann 1983), and these were often supplemented with rumen content and organs (Wheat 1972). Organs had other uses as well. The stomach was commonly used as a water bladder for transporting drinking water as people moved in the Plains environment. Hides, which varied significantly in thickness, pliability, size, quality, and hair condition by season and the age and sex of the animals, were used for shelter and clothing as well as footwear and containers. Other technological essentials were derived from the sinew, hair, bones, horns, hooves, and organs of bison (Ewers 1955; Roe 1951). Differential use of bison carcasses at kills resulted from this great seasonal range of bison condition and the persistent and changing needs of their hunters. For many groups, bison resources were key to everyday survival and for life even weeks or months after bison kills had occurred. We suspect that in many archaeological situations, bison products are underrepresented in proportion to their importance and use (Hofman and Todd 2001).

SITE ARCHITECTURE

Hearths and Burned Rock Features

Hearths, burned limestone concentrations, roasting pits, and earth ovens are commonly found dating to the Paleoarchaic in the Great Plains, although no systematic study of the features has been undertaken. Hearths tend to be more ephemeral during the Paleoindian period, which may be due to a bias in site types and preservation, lack of recognition, or simply not excavating large enough areas. At the Waugh Folsom site (34HP42) in northwestern Oklahoma, two shallow or near-surface hearths had considerable ash and charcoal but few associated hearthstones. Hearths served many technological purposes, among them cooking, heating, light, and preparing lithic material (Shippee 1948). They also served as an important center for family and social functions for ceremonial dancing, festivities, celebration, and ritual.

Table 4.8. Site Architecture: Hearths, Burned Rock Features, and Postmolds

Site Number	Site Name	Complex	Hearths	Burned Limestone	Post-molds	Reference
14JN309	Sutter	Allen-Frederick	-	6	-	Katz 1971
14ST401	Winger	Allen-Frederick	1[a]	-	-	Mandel and Hofman 2002, 2003
14LT351	Stigenwalt	Stigenwalt	-	+	-	Thies 1990
14OS347	Cow Killer	Munkers Creek	7	4	2	Reynolds 1984
14PO1	Coffey	Munkers Creek	19	19	1	Schmits 1978
14MO304	William Young	Munkers Creek	16	-	-	Witty 1982
14MO304	William Young	El Dorado	3	-	4	Witty 1982
14CF330	Williamson	El Dorado	+	21	-	Schmits 1987a
14BU9	Snyder	El Dorado	-	2	+[b]	Grosser 1973
14BU25	Milbourn	El Dorado	-	6	-	Root 1981
14BU50	Faulconer	El Dorado	4	-	2	Bradley 1973
14EK331	Durbin	Archaic	2	+	-	KSHS site files
14LO8		Archaic	1	-	-	Schock 1965
14BU1308		Archaic	-	+[c]	-	Bevitt et al. 2003

[a]Evidence of a small hearth suggested by burned bison bone in a concentrated area.
[b]Postmolds defined as concentrations of burned earth and daub.
[c]Feature 1 represents an earth oven measuring 240 cm × 152 cm × 55 cm deep with associated faunal remains.

The construction of earth ovens, however, seems to be an innovation associated with the Archaic (Thies and Witty 1992: 154). Earth ovens are "evidenced by large amorphous masses or 'beds' of burned rock with or without clear indications (charcoal, burned earth) of firing in place" (Thies and Witty 1992: 154). Rocks were heated and packets of food were placed on top of them and subsequently covered by grass or hides and then earth, providing slow, thorough cooking. Earth ovens efficiently regulate heat and conserve energy and were often used to process plant foods, specifically bulbs and tubers (Thoms 1989). Site 14BU1308 in Butler County, with an estimated date of 6000 to 5000 B.P., is an excellent example of an earth oven (Bevitt, Mandel, and Bauer 2003).

Table 4.8 lists the sites that yielded burned rock or hearth features. Some of the burned limestone concentrations may have functioned as earth ovens, especially at Stigenwalt where there is direct evidence of onion bulbs. Although no actual hearth remains were recovered at the Eckles site, a hearth likely was present: pieces of burned lithic material were recovered from the site (Holen 2001: 107). Likewise, a hearth was likely present at the Winger site, explaining a small concentration of burned bison bone (Mandel and Hofman 2003).

Structures

A variety of native habitations were widely used in the Plains region during historic times, including tipis, earth lodges, brush arbors, and bark-covered structures. Tipis were in use at least by middle Holocene time (Davis and Wilson 1980) but were apparently more common to the north and west of Kansas. Season, terrain, precipitation, mobility, group size, permanence of settlement, and similar factors determined the habitation structures prehistoric Kansas hunter-gatherers used.

More ephemeral skin tents or brush-covered "wickiups" are apparently represented at several Paleoindian sites, such as Agate Basin and Hell Gap in Wyoming and possibly Waugh, in Oklahoma. Kansas-area hunter-gatherers presumably used them for thousands of years. Small skin-covered structures supported by poles that also served as poles for dog travois continued to be used in the Plains well into historic times (G. L. Wilson 1924).

Pit houses, or semisubterranean structures covered with logs, branches, and sod, also were common from the northern to the southern plains by middle Holocene time (Cassells 1997; Lintz, Treece, and Oglesby 1995; M. L. Larson 1990; M. L. Larson and Francis 1997; M. Metcalf and Black 1991). Though such structures have not been documented in Kansas, this lack is almost certainly a result of sampling, excavation strategies, knowledge of the size and form of these features, preservation, and visibility. Only five Kansas Paleoarchaic sites show postmolds (Table 4.8), which may or may not indicate domestic structures. Posts were also used in a variety of nonhabitation structures such as drying racks or tethers for dogs.

BURIALS

Current evidence of mortuary practices in Kansas during the Paleoarchaic is extremely limited. Only a few sites have yielded evidence of human remains, and these sites typically contain few individuals (Owsley and Bruwelheide 1996; Owsley and Jantz 1989). A fundamental problem in hunter-gatherer mortuary studies is that most models that have been developed and applied by archaeologists for interpreting patterning in mortuary behavior use cemeteries of sedentary groups. Differences in graves and their offerings are commonly explained based on gender, age, and status of the individuals. These factors are compounded with others, including seasonal variation (frozen ground, for example), high mobility, lack of formal cemetery areas, and situational factors impacting the treatment and movement of the dead (Hofman 1985, 1986). The mortuary practices of later, seasonally mobile groups were also not immune to these situational problems when trying to implement preferred burial rituals.

Among hunter-gatherers in the Kansas region, a variety of mortuary practices are likely, based on evidence from surrounding areas. In most known burials from this period, bodies were not extended but were flexed or folded. There is not enough information to see patterns in the orientation of the bodies, the side, or the position within the grave. Secondary burials may occur as bundled collections of bones or cremations. Associations occur, but the current sample is too limited to extract meaningful patterns about potential differences based on age or gender. Information on the limited mortuary evidence is provided in Table 4.9.

SUMMARY

The diverse environments across the Kansas region from east to west and the long time frame during which hunting and gathering societies lived here guarantee a richness in the history and record of these peoples and the social, technological, economic, and ideological aspects of their cultures. Many important questions and areas of research remain, and the potential to learn more about the past of Kansas hunter-gatherers is great. Some basic questions that remain unanswered and in need of research include (1) the origins of the first Kansans; (2) the domestic life and organization of hunter-gatherer families and groups; (3) the impact of major climatic changes on the technology, economy, and organization of social groups; (4) the general health and changing health patterns of these foraging peoples; (5) documentation of the variation in hunter-gatherer lifeways across the region through time; and (6) how oral traditions, later cultural evidence, and modern cultural patterns can be used to enhance our inquiries and our understanding of the archaeological record of these peoples.

The origins of the first Kansans remain unknown. Origin stories of Native American tribes should be considered as a source of information relevant to this issue (Echo-Hawk 2000). From an archaeological perspective, we do not know when people first came to Kansas, the specific nature of their technology, from which direction they came, or the cultural tradition that they represented (Hofman 1996: 46–49). Concerted research focused on late Pleistocene land surfaces (25,000 to 11,000 B.P.), many of which are now deeply buried, will help in identifying sites and in studying an archaeological record critical to addressing the problems of peopling of the Central Plains and Kansas area (see chapter 3, this volume). Ongoing investigations at the Kanorado locality sites are yielding important new information on the archaeology and paleontology of this critical time period (Mandel, Hofman, et al. 2004; Mandel, Holen, and Hofman 2005). Stratified deposits with Clovis-age and earlier camel, mammoth, and stone tool associations are being studied.

The study of domestic life, families, and organization of prehistoric hunter-gatherers in Kansas will require different strategies for archaeological research than have generally been employed in the past. The scale of hunter-gatherer campsites is

Table 4.9. Paleoarchaic Burials

Site Number	Site Name	Complex	MNI	Sex	Burial Type	Beads	Points	Other Artifacts	Reference
14LT351	Stigenwalt	Stigenwalt	2–3	?	?	0	0		Thies 1990: 107
14BU9	Snyder	El Dorado	1	female	flexed	0	2	137 flakes, 2 knives, 2 Scallorn points, charcoal, fired clay	Klepinger 1972
14ML307*	Range Mound	El Dorado?	several	?	?	25	4	scrapers, bifaces, flakes, core, faunal remains, sherds	Reynolds 1977
14CF330	Williamson	El Dorado	2	female	flexed	0	1	biface, charcoal, burned rock	Schmits 1987a
14JW303*	Matter Mound	El Dorado?	23+	?	primary, secondary	+	+		Finnegan 1981
14DO417		Archaic	1	male	flexed	0	1	limestone slab, flakes, drill	Hoard et al. 2004
14GL401*	Herl	Archaic?	4	?	secondary	0	1	bone awl, flakes	Bowman 1961
14LC501*		Archaic?	1	?	?	0	0		KSHS site form
14LV315*	Lansing Man	Archaic	2	?	?	0	0		Hrdlička 1903, W. M. Bass 1973
14RY302*		Archaic?	1	male	?	0	0		W. M. Bass and Wiley 1966

*Chronological and cultural assignments remain unclear

typically expansive (O'Connell 1987), but the scope of archaeological excavations and site studies, especially for deeply buried sites, has been limited. Extensive block excavations, like those witnessed at the relatively shallow Nebo Hill site (23CL11) (Reid 1980), approach the order of magnitude needed if we are interested in identifying structures and activities associated with hearth areas and learning about the behaviors of families and larger groups in the domestic arena. Generally a space of at least three meters around a hearth or similar feature will "capture" the activities of people using it (Binford 1978b; Gamble 1986). However, determining relationships among features at an occupation site requires more extensive coverage, and to identify structures and the activities conducted in and around them requires even larger areas.

Typically, our excavations have been too small to address questions of family and group organization as reflected at hunter-gatherer sites in the region. The lack of well-documented and thoroughly studied structures from hunter-gatherer sites in Kansas is an indication of how much we have yet to learn. This is further exacerbated by the lack of studies of rockshelter or cave sites with hunter-gatherer occupations. The limited nature of our current knowledge about hunter-gatherers in Kansas is also shown by the number of counties for which we currently have no records of Paleoarchaic sites (Figure 4.2). These counties represent almost one-fifth of the state of Kansas for which we lack documentation of hunter-gatherer activity for a 9,000-year period! This illustrates how much research documentary work remains to be done, but this is not a problem unique to Kansas (e.g., Hofman and Brooks 1989).

Moreover, with few exceptions, such as Munkers Creek and Nebo Hill, archaeological complexes used to recognize Paleoarchaic groups in Kansas remain minimally defined and generally lack documentation of the seasonal and technological variability that we expect among mid-latitude hunter-gatherer groups (e.g., Binford 2001). In many cases, our archaeologically defined units are primarily based on projectile point types from limited time periods, a few other stone tools, and relatively little else.

The range of technology, economic orientations, land-use patterns, and organizational studies requires not only detailed and extensive site investigations, but integrated use of region-wide archaeological evidence as well. Cooperation among avocational archaeologists, students, professional archaeologists, and Native Americans is necessary in order to gain more complete and mutually beneficial perspectives on the lives of the earliest Kansans. The health and diets of these people can be better understood with investigation of plant and animal remains found at the archaeological sites. Documentation and study of human remains, when treated in a diligent and respectful manner, can also be of great service to such studies. Remains of very few Paleoarchaic individuals have been documented in Kansas, although this probably reflects in part their relatively mobile life styles, the rarity of cemeteries, factors of preservation, and the limited nature of many site investigations.

Prehistoric hunter-gatherers in Kansas hunted mammoth, bison, deer, antelope, rabbits, turkeys, and many other animals. The changes in hunting and diet reflect extinctions, seasonal changes, yearly variation, and local availability of resources. Dogs were used to protect camps, to hunt, to carry packs, and sometimes for food. People fished with hook and line, nets, and fish traps and poisoned small pools by using the broken husks of black walnuts. A wide range of aquatic plants and animals were used, and some riverine locations were habitually used because they provided a reliable source of mussels, fish, turtles, deer, and smaller animals; nuts and green plants; and usable cobbles of chert. Plants of many varieties were used both for food and for technological needs. Although we do not have direct evidence from Kansas sites, yucca fiber was probably used for sandals, matting and cattails leaves likely were made into mats, and cattail roots were probably used as food. Many seedy plants, such as lamb's-quarter, knotweed, sunflower, gourds, grasses, and others, were probably used for thousands of years; some eventually were domesticated. We know or can surmise many basic aspects of hunter-gatherer life in the Central Plains region, but we know only the broadest outlines of variation and developments. We know details concerning the organization and lives of these people in very few times and places, and it is this rich history and variety that archaeological researchers must study and document in the coming years.

5. Woodland Adaptations in Eastern Kansas
Brad Logan

From approximately 500 B.C. to A.D. 1000, the eastern Central Plains was home to ceramic-making populations of hunter-gatherers who increasingly relied on agriculture. Assigned to the Woodland tradition (A. E. Johnson 2001; A. M. Johnson and Johnson 1998), these populations appear to have derived much of their subsistence practices, and the ceramic and stone tool technologies they adopted to employ them, from Eastern Woodland contemporaries. Since the 1930s, archaeologists have noted striking parallels between these aspects of the Woodland cultures of the lower Illinois River valley and some of those in eastern Kansas. More recently, archaeologists have found further parallels in lithic technologies dating back to the Late Archaic (e.g., Logan 1998; Reid 1980, 1983, 1984). Undoubtedly, the Eastern Woodland populations played an important role in the development of Woodland populations in the eastern Central Plains. A more persistent question, however, is whether this influence occurred indirectly through the diffusion of ideas, or directly via the periodic migration of splinter groups from Illinois along the lower Missouri River valley. Both perspectives are simplistic and artificially dualistic; they mask what was likely a more complex process that involved both the communication and sharing of concepts and technologies along the Missouri River valley and the movement of persons or population segments from the east. The latter process was probably facilitated by a fluid kinship system throughout the Woodland tradition areas that included real or fictive kin ties and adoption, practices common among historic groups of the eastern United States but difficult to document archaeologically.

Braun (1977, 1985, 1987, 1991) and Braun and Plog (1982) have suggested that the appearance of Hopewellian cultures throughout much of what is now the eastern United States resulted from communication among groups who had more social interaction as they became more sedentary, sharing widely recognized ceramic decorative motifs as communicative symbols. These researchers interpret this communication as likely an attempt to mitigate risks, such as periodic food shortages, inherent in hunter-gatherer-gardener adaptations. This process developed during a long period of horticultural experimentation through Archaic and Early Woodland times that, in the Midwest, reached a critical threshold of various demographic or environmental factors by ca. 200 B.C.

M. J. O'Brien and Wood (1998) suggest that Kansas City Hopewell, a Middle Woodland variant of the lower Missouri River valley on the eastern edge of the Central Plains, was part of this adaptive process. Logan (2005a) has argued that discounting migration as a factor in the establishment of a Hopewell culture in the Kansas City locality is premature; given the as yet poorly documented Early Woodland adaptation there, Kansas City Hopewell still exhibits a site unit intrusive character. Indeed, we lack any evidence of occupation in the Kansas City locality for about 100–200 years prior to the earliest acceptable dates of Kansas City Hopewell. Moreover, scant evidence supports the use of native cultigens in the floral assemblages from the few Early Woodland sites in the Kansas City locality, in contrast to the clear trend of increasing reliance on native cultigens in the Hopewell core areas in Illinois and Ohio (Adair 1996; cf. B. D. Smith 1987, 1992a).

Still, the process that Braun describes for the development from Middle to Late Woodland periods in the Midwest mirrors changes in the eastern Central Plains. Such changes include a trend from the use of plain-surfaced pottery with Havana-like decorative motifs within zones to pottery with motifs on the upper rim and lip to, ultimately, the near lack of classic Hopewell elements such as cross-hatching and rocker-marking. Late Woodland wares in the Midwest are characterized by cord-marked exteriors and limited decoration. With the increasing reliance on maize agriculture in Late Woodland to Late Prehistoric adaptations (Adair 1988, 1996), vessel form changed from large, elongate jars to globular pots. Braun (1983, 1987), who links changes in ceramic morphology to changes in food preparation and diet, found a "lockstep" correlation between a shift toward construction of thinner-walled vessels and the increased use of cultivated seeds. This coevolution of cooking technology and cultivation culminates in the globular pot, which is more likely to survive the expansion and contraction of repeated heating and cooling (Braun 1983, 1987). The Late Prehistoric Pomona variant (K. L. Brown 1985; Witty 1967, 1978) derives from a regional Late Woodland adaptation, shown by the retention of some ceramic attributes, including high, straight to slightly everted rims, exterior cord-marking, and the relative lack of decorative treatment. This indigenous development is not clear with regard to the various phases of the Central Plains tradition.

What follows is a review of the Early, Middle, and Late Woodland periods, including a critique of the various taxa recognized in eastern Kansas, and further discussion of the developmental process that culminated in the tenth century A.D. transition to the Late Prehistoric.

EARLY WOODLAND IN KANSAS

An Early Woodland adaptation in Kansas has been described from limited data at a few sites in Brown and Johnson counties in the northeastern part of the state (A. E. Johnson 1992; Logan and Hedden 1990). The Walnut phase of the southern Flint Hills has also been interpreted as a transitional Late Archaic–Early Woodland manifestation (A. E. Johnson 1992). More substantive data come from a similarly small number of Early Woodland sites in the Little Blue River drainage of northwestern Missouri (A. E. Johnson 1992; Schmits and Bailey 1989; C. A. Wright 1980). Where radiocarbon dates are available from these sites, they fall within the general range of 500–100 B.C. Recovered pottery, always sparse when present, compares favorably with ceramics of the Early Woodland Black Sand culture of the lower Illinois River valley, the source of subsequent influence on Hopewell developments in the lower Missouri River valley. Contracting-stemmed dart points may be diagnostic of the period (A. E. Johnson 1992; T. L. Martin 1997).

T. L. Martin (1997: 88–93) suggests that few Early Woodland sites in Missouri have been identified because of (1) the short duration of the period (ca. 600 B.C.–A.D. 1 in Missouri) relative to the preceding Late Archaic period; (2) a settlement pattern that, in response to the drier conditions of the Sub-Atlantic climatic episode, focused on the occupation of small camps on terraces in stream valleys where subsequent alluviation led to their burial beyond the range of traditional methods of archaeological site discovery; and (3) the misidentification as Late Woodland of some ceramic sites that yield small sherds.

Site 14BN26, in Brown County, yielded the first concrete evidence of an Early Woodland presence in Kansas. Its location 20 miles west of the Missouri River encourages "the search for additional evidence of Early Woodland occupations in portions of the Plains long believed not to have been exposed to Woodland influences until Middle Woodland times (ca. A.D. 1–500)" (A. E. Johnson 1992: 129, 131). Both a Liverpool-like sherd and a bifacial knife from the site are similar to types diagnostic of the Black Sand culture (A. E. Johnson 1992: 130). Other materials with Black Sand counterparts have been recovered from the Shields (23CL1) and Traff (23JA139) sites, both in the Kansas City area in northwestern Missouri. Schmits and Bailey (1989: 231–232) assign these sites to the Bowlin phase (cf. A. E. Johnson 1992: 131–132).

The ceramic-impoverished nature of Early Woodland sites in eastern Kansas and western Missouri, the few shallow pit features, the lack of definable house structures, and the short-term occupation reflected by the nature of their lithic assemblages point to seasonal habitations. This suggests that the regional Early Woodland adaptation differed little from that of the Late Archaic in eastern Kansas. In western Missouri, a shift to lowland settings for settlement is a change from the late summer-autumn occupation of bluff tops by band aggregates during the preceding Nebo Hill phase (T. L. Martin 1997: 88–90; Reid 1983, 1984). At least one cultigen, marsh elder, appears, but the few sites where systematic flotation was used do not provide sufficient reasons to infer that gardening was important in Early Woodland subsistence in the region (Adair 1996). Indeed, the Early Woodland period remains so poorly known in Kansas that we cannot yet track continuity between it and the subsequent Middle Woodland period. Consequently, the processes that resulted in the Kansas City Hopewell culture, that is, whether they entailed the immigration of populations from the east, the acceptance by indigenous groups of diffused technologies from that area, or some combination of these, are still unclear (Logan 2005a).

MIDDLE WOODLAND IN KANSAS

Various Middle Woodland cultures in Kansas and adjacent states have been defined, including Kansas City Hopewell, the Valley variant of the Missouri River valley, the Cooper variant of northeastern Oklahoma, the Cuesta phase of southeastern Kansas, and the Schultz phase of north-central Kansas (A. E. Johnson 2001; A. M. Johnson and Johnson 1998). All share attributes of the ceramic and lithic technologies of the Hopewell cultures of the Eastern Woodlands, particularly Havana of the Illinois River valley. With regard to pottery, this includes the predominant vessel form—elongate straight-walled jars with rounded or conoidal bases—and various forms of rim and body decoration (Figure 5.1).

The best-known Middle Woodland culture in the Central Plains is Kansas City Hopewell, for which most data come from sites in northwestern Missouri. Recent investigations in northeastern Kansas have shed more light on this variant there (Logan 1993; Logan 2005a). In particular, the Quarry Creek site (14LV401), on a high terrace along an intermittent stream on the Ft. Leavenworth reservation, is comparable to Trowbridge (14WY1), a Wyandotte County base camp in a similar upland context. Before investigation of the Quarry Creek site, Trowbridge had been considered anomalous. A. E. Johnson (1976a, 1979, 1981) presented a dissimilar settlement pattern model derived from sites in northwestern Missouri. In that area, base camps were situated at the mouths of Missouri River tributaries, and through time, in response to population increase, satellite camps were established upstream to support the growing population. Eventually, base camps could no longer be sustained, and by Late Woodland time, settlements were smaller habitations distributed rather evenly along the tributaries.

In Kansas (and possibly in Missouri, where future surveys may find upland base camps),

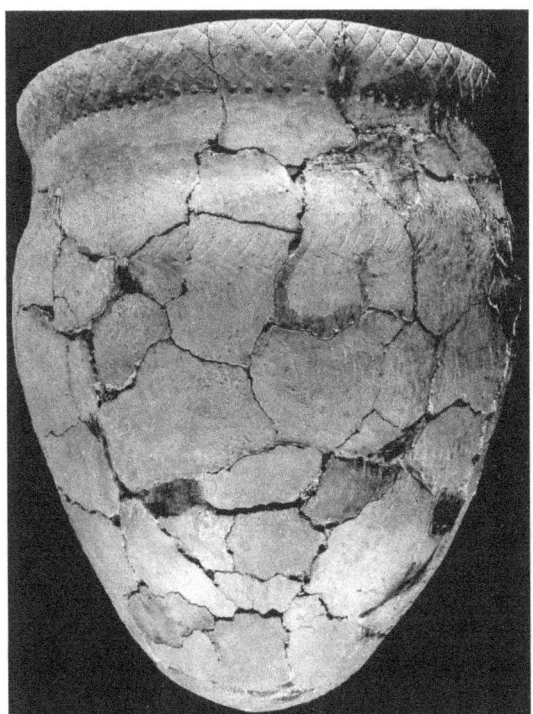

Figure 5.1. Kansas City Hopewell (Kansas City phase) vessel from the Trowbridge site (14WY1). Museum of Anthropology, University of Kansas. Vessel height is 43 cm. (Courtesy of the Kansas State Historical Society)

the Kansas City Hopewell settlement pattern was characterized by greater variability (Logan 2005a). Major settlements in more varied settings focused more directly on the Missouri and Kansas rivers and offered proximity to stable backwater niches. Perhaps not as rich or reliable as the backwater lakes and sloughs of the lower Illinois River valley, these habitats in the Kansas City locality still provided an important supplement to other woodland and prairie resources. Hopewell sites in Kansas are found along the Missouri River, within the Stranger Creek watershed, and in the lower Kansas River valley westward to the Delaware River. The correlation between these site locations and the oak-hickory habitat and the woodland-prairie ecotone is evident, reflecting Hopewell preference for woodland-riverine resources (Logan 2005a).

A. E. Johnson (1976b, 1979, 1984) and A. M. Johnson and Johnson (1998) date the Kansas City Hopewell variant at ca. A.D. 1–750. This range is derived from 30 radiocarbon dates. However, the one sigma values of several of these assays are rather large (100+), and the initial range did not benefit from samples that had been corrected for isotopic fractionation and subjected to more recent calibration curves. As more radiocarbon ages from better samples, such as AMS assays from annual plant remains, are obtained, corrected, and calibrated, this range may be refined. Based on a series of four radiocarbon dates (Appendix) from the Quarry Creek site, the terminus of the Kansas City Hopewell occupation there was ca. A.D. 600, the more probable end of this archaeological culture (Logan 1993).

Changes in ceramic decorative treatments of Kansas City Hopewell pottery parallel those in Illinois, beginning with dentate and embossed elements in zoned panels during the Trowbridge phase (ca. A.D. 1–250), changing to incised elements that include cross-hatched lines and rocker marks separated by punctates and plain zones during the Kansas City phase (ca. A.D. 250–400), and ending with limited decorative elements such as punctates and crenulated lips or a lack of decorative treatment during the Edwardsville phase (ca. A.D. 400–600). Again, these changes mirror those documented among Middle to Late Woodland populations of the Illinois River valley and point to at least some form of communication with them (A. E. Johnson 2001; A. E. Johnson and Johnson 1975; A. M. Johnson and Johnson 1998: 203; Logan 2005a).

Changes in projectile point styles in Kansas City Hopewell also parallel those of the lower Illinois River valley. Broad-bladed, corner-notched dart points of the Snyder type characterize the Trowbridge phase, whereas more narrow-bladed, corner-notched forms, such as Steuben, are typical of the Kansas City phase. A significant technological change during the late Kansas City or early Edwardsville phase is the adoption of the bow and arrow, indicated by the appearance of Scallorn points (P. Bell 1976; A. E. Johnson 1976a; Montet-White 1968).

Treatment of the dead entailed periodic primary and secondary interment of remains, the latter often cremated, in stone-lined, earth-covered mounds on bluff tops (W. R. Wedel 1943). A. M. Johnson and Johnson (1998: 208) note a striking contrast between the size of burial mounds of the Kansas City Hopewell and the Schultz phase, with the mean size of the former nearly twice that of the latter. This reflects a larger population in the Middle Woodland groups of the lower Missouri River valley and the lower Republican River valley that is in turn a reflection of the available natural resources of the two areas. When present in mound burials, grave goods rarely include exotic items (e.g., copper celts and earspools, sheet mica artwork, conch shells) often found in burial mounds in the Hopewell core areas in Illinois and Ohio. Indeed, relatively few exotic artifacts indicative of what has been called the Hopewell Interaction Sphere (Struever 1964; Struever and Houart 1972) have been found in the Kansas City locality, and most of those were recovered in habitation site contexts (A. E. Johnson 1979; Logan 1993; W. R. Wedel 1943). These include ceramic anthropomorphic figurines, platform pipes, miniature celts of hematite and copper, hematite and quartz cones, a few small pieces of helmet shell and sheet mica, and a single flake of obsidian from the Yellowstone Park area (R. E. Hughes 1995; A. E. Johnson 1979).

The community-based context of Kansas City Hopewell exotics does not differ dramatically from that of the Havana Hopewell of Illinois, where such artifacts are also found at habitation sites. However, the absence of Interaction Sphere items from mounds and their paucity at base camps in the Kansas City locality suggest that the relations between the Hopewell of the two localities were not cemented through trade and may have been more tenuous than is suggested by the parallels in ceramic and projectile technologies.

The Valley variant, contemporary with Kansas City Hopewell, is known from a number of occupation and burial sites in the Missouri River valley of western Iowa through the Platte River basin as far west as the High Plains of western Nebraska (A. E. Johnson 2001). Only in the northeastern corner of Kansas does the Valley variant appear. It shares some aspects of Kansas City Hopewell, including the use of such ceramic decorative elements as embossing, dentate stamping, cord-marking, incised lines, and punctates (Bozell and Winfrey 1994), as well as mound burial of the dead in stone-lined, earth-covered cists (P. J. O'Brien 1971). Taylor Mound, located on a high bluff on the west banks of the Missouri River near White Cloud, is the best-known example of such mound burials. It has been known for more than a century and was the unfortunate victim of extensive, uncontrolled excavations by the early "archaeologists" of the lower Missouri River Valley, Mark Zimmerman and Ed Parks. In the early part of the twentieth century, they removed the remains of several individuals from the mound, leaving no adequate documentation of their contexts (Logan 1985). The mound retained some significant information, however, as demonstrated by excavations directed by P. J. O'Brien (1971) under the auspices of the Great Plains Archaeological Field School in 1968. She described two separate cremations that yielded remains of at least three individuals, an adult male in one and, in the other, an adult of indeterminate sex and a child. These were recovered from fill overlying a stone cist that contained a single male, interpreted by P. J. O'Brien (1971) as a high status individual. Her interpretation of the supra-cist remains as evidence of human sacrifice following interment of the latter person is speculative. Archaeologists have differed in their interpretations of status differentiation reflected in mortuary mounds among

Woodland groups in the Midwest, some inferring the evidence as indicative of ranked social organization (Buikstra 1976) and others seeing no evidence of hereditary rank (Braun 1979). However, ritual sacrifice does not appear to have been part of Woodland burial practices.

The distinction between Cooper and Cuesta (Brogan 1981; Marshall 1972; Witty 1999) may be spurious. Given their proximity, poorly known chronologies, and general formal similarity, it is possible that both should be assigned to a single regional variant of the Middle Woodland period. There is evidence that Middle Woodland groups of southeastern Kansas and northeastern Oklahoma were in contact with Kansas City Hopewell. Similarities in the development of ceramic wares represented at the Cooper sites and those of Kansas City Hopewell have been described recently by Cook (2001). She also notes six sherds in one Cooper site assemblage (DlCoI) with pastes and tempering agents that are strikingly similar to those from Kansas City Hopewell sites, pointing to contact between these Middle Woodland communities (Cook 2001: 111). Witty (1999: 171–172) suggests that the distinction between Cooper and Cuesta be maintained, although he admits they share several traits. This distinction is to be "maintained because of what has been identified as to the settlement pattern and subsistence within the middle and upper Verdigris as well as Elk River and a portion of the Cottonwood River drainage" (Witty 1999: 172). Yet there is so little basis for comparison, given the paltry amount of published data from the few Cooper sites excavated prior to World War II, that taxonomic differences or similarities cannot be properly weighed. Until more Cooper sites have been dug or collections analyzed, it seems more prudent to consider the Cooper-Cuesta problem unresolved.

Middle Woodland sites in the Verdigris and Cottonwood drainages do, however, provide a good picture of adaptation in southeastern Kansas (Marshall 1972; Rowlison 1977, 1978; Witty 1999). Several houses have been excavated, revealing large (e.g., 42 by 28 ft. [Witty 1999: 36]) dwellings of oval to circular outline. Pit features have been found both within the structures and outside them. Houses occur singly or in closely spaced pairs and are distributed in an apparently random pattern across the site (Witty 1999: 169). Burials of humans and dogs have been found in middens. Two ceramic wares have been identified. Naples occurs in two varieties or types and Cuesta in six. Hopewellian motifs include dentate stamping, punctates, and cordmarking. Crenulated lips, which appear late in the Kansas City Hopewell sequence, also occur. Projectile points include a variety of dart points, predominately contracting-stem types (Gary, Langtry) but also include a number of corner-notched types (Snyder, Ensor) and the Scallorn arrowpoint (Witty 1999: 169). The population subsisted on hunting and gathering of wild resources. AMS radiocarbon dating of maize samples putatively associated with Cuesta components shows that they date to a much later time (Adair 2000).

The Schultz phase (W. E. Banks et al. 2001; Eyman 1966; S. G. Parks 1978; Phenice 1969; Roper 2000a) is known primarily from mound cemeteries comparable in many respects to those of the Kansas City Hopewell variant (F. Schultz and Spaulding 1948)

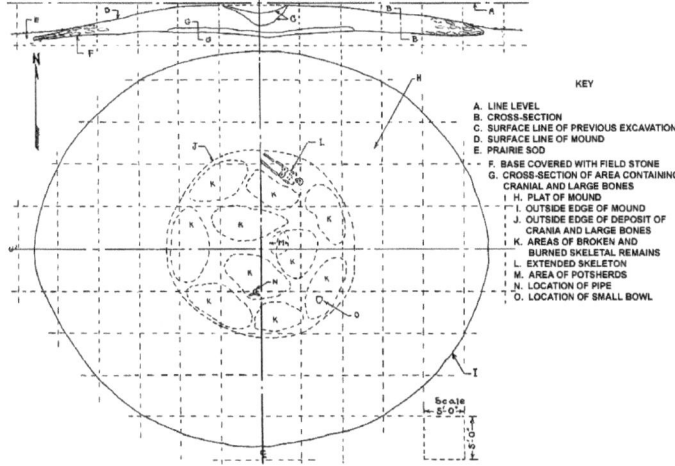

Figure 5.2. Cross section of Younkin Mound (14GE6) (Schultz phase). Modified from the original drawing in the Floyd and Adah Jane Broceus Schultz Collection, Museum of Anthropology, University of Kansas.

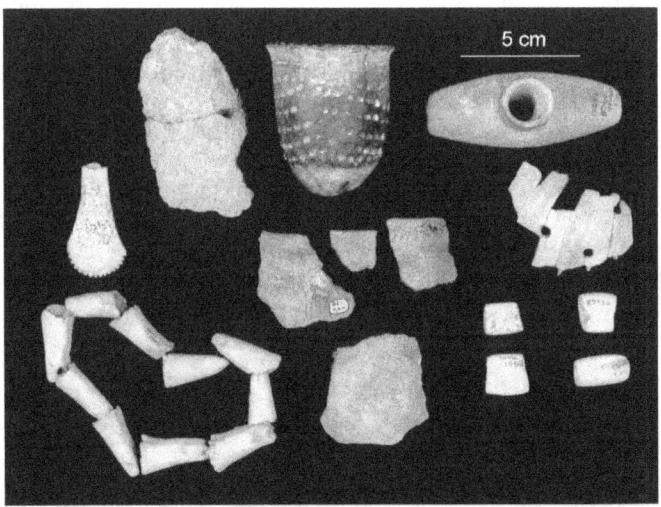

Figure 5.3. Selected artifacts from Younkin Mound. Floyd and Adah Jane Broceus Schultz Collection, Museum of Anthropology, University of Kansas. (Courtesy of the Kansas State Historical Society)

(Figures 5.2 and 5.3). Its relationship with the Kansas City Hopewell may reflect a migration from the lower Missouri River valley or the diffusion of traits to Late Archaic groups in the upper Kansas River and Blue River valleys, but these relationships are poorly understood. A few habitations of this north-central Kansas complex have been described (P. J. O'Brien 1972; P. J. O'Brien, Larsen, et al. 1973; P. J. O'Brien, Caldwell, et al. 1979; S. G. Parks 1978). The stratified deposits at the Macy site (14RY38) in Manhattan provide baseline chronological data (W. E. Banks et al. 2001; Benison, Banks, and Mandel 2000). Macy contained five components, at least four of which are identified as Woodland. It is intriguing that the lower two components with radiocarbon dates in the two sigma range of A.D. 2–456 lacked ceramics, whereas the two components above them, which dated A.D. 531–654 (two sigma range), contained pottery with cross-hatched rim decoration, oblique cord-marking, and dentate-stamping, although these differences may be due to sampling. Hypothetically, Macy may document a temporal lag in the introduction of Hopewellian ceramic technology from the Kansas City locality and the persistence of a Late Archaic or Early Woodland adaptation until the sixth century A.D.

LATE WOODLAND IN KANSAS

Late Woodland cultures are distinguished from those of the Middle Woodland chronologically by their general temporal placement ca. A.D. 500–1000 and by the pottery, in which the Woodland form is retained but decorative treatment is lacking or restricted to the lip. Seven phases have been assigned to this period in eastern Kansas: Grasshopper Falls, Wakarusa, Deer Creek, Greenwood, Hertha, Butler, and Bemis Creek. Except for Bemis Creek, they have much more in common than they do in difference. Bemis Creek, dated ca. A.D. 1000 at the single site assigned to the phase (14BU55; Adair and Brown 1981: 253–254), appears to represent an adaptation transitional in some respects to the Late Prehistoric, in particular to the Pomona variant. The others share the following: pole-supported, wattle-and-daub structures that were circular to oval in outline and of sufficient size for an extended family; subsistence that was broadly based on wild prairie-woodland-riverine species and that demonstrated a marked increase in dependence on domesticated plants

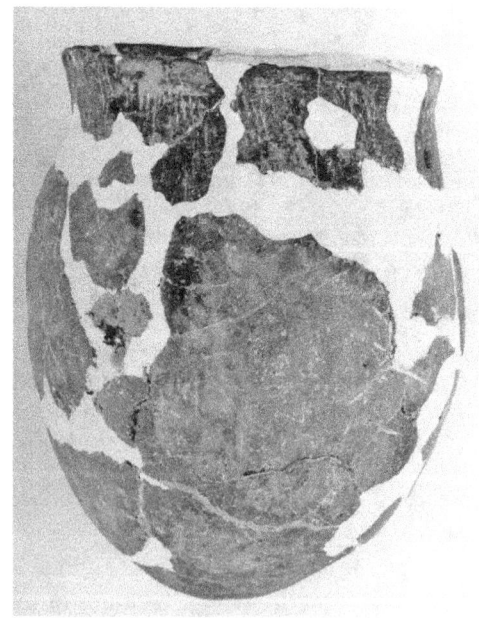

Figure 5.4. Verdigris-type vessel from Greenwood phase site 14GR301. Vessel height is 21.5 cm. (Courtesy of the Kansas State Historical Society)

(Adair 1988); pottery of Woodland form using regionally varying tempering agents and showing exteriors that are generally cord-marked (Figures 5.4 and 5.5); chipped-stone and groundstone assemblages with drills, scrapers, axes, celts, manos and metates, abraders, and a projectile technology that apparently entailed use of both the atlatl and dart and bow and arrow (Adair 1996; A. E. Johnson 1983, 1984, 1987, 2001; A. M. Johnson and Johnson 1998). Mortuary practices, while not well known, include continued practice of cremation and mound burial, as well as primary pit interment of extended or semiflexed individuals (Calabrese 1967; Logan 1990a; F. Schultz and Spaulding 1948).

One of the more intriguing problems of regional Woodland archaeology is the continued use of two forms of projectile propulsion, atlatl and dart and bow and arrow, from ca. A.D. 500, when the Scallorn arrowpoint type appears in the regional archaeological record, until the Late Prehistoric period (ca. A.D. 900), when the bow and arrow was used exclusively. The timing of the appearance of the bow and arrow near the end of the Middle Woodland period suggests that the impetus for this technological change was increasing population pressure on, or competition for, game resources. This evolutionary (in the Darwinian sense) perspective precludes an alternative view that its appearance on the Central Plains was just one more instance of indigenous groups accepting the latest innovation from the Eastern Woodlands, where the selective advantage of the bow and arrow may have been more critical (Logan and Beck 1996: 93–94). Both abandonment of the atlatl and dart and the coincidental increase in reliance on maize agriculture during the Late Prehistoric may reflect the same process: resource competition among growing populations.

The plethora of regional Woodland cultures defined by archaeologists in the twentieth century is probably unjustified (Logan and Beck 1996: 60–64), reflecting instead an absence of critical review that facilitated recognition of many phases or variants. Archaeological taxonomy should be a conservative enterprise, particularly when too little spatial, temporal, and formal data are available for identifying complexes or when formal variability is not sufficiently understood. Once

Figure 5.5. Grasshopper Falls phase vessel from site 14JN349. Vessel height is 44 cm. (Courtesy of the Kansas State Historical Society)

defined, unjustified taxa are difficult to drop. Some examples of this problem are illustrated below.

The Grasshopper Falls phase (Reynolds 1979, 1981) was defined without reference to the previously recognized Wakarusa and Deer Creek phases (A. E. Johnson 1968) of the same general geographic area. They are so similar that we may legitimately question their distinction. Kampschroeder (14DO27), in the Clinton Lake area on the Wakarusa River, remains the only excavated site assigned to the Wakarusa phase, and in nearly all respects it is comparable to the many sites since assigned to the Grasshopper Falls phase. Only one excavated site, Anderson (14DO32), was initially assigned to the Deer Creek phase, and it lacks information regarding house form, storage facilities, hearth placement, and other activity areas. The only apparent difference between the Wakarusa and Deer Creek phases was the absence from Wakarusa and presence in Deer Creek of corner-notched (Scallorn) arrowpoints. At the time of their definition, no radiocarbon dates confirmed the relative temporal placement of Wakarusa as ca. A.D. 1–500 and of Deer Creek to ca. A.D. 500–1000. More recent excavations at Richland (14SH101), a Deer Creek phase candidate in the Clinton Lake area, yielded radiocarbon dates supporting its relative placement ca. A.D. 500–1000 based on recovery of a few Scallorn points (Logan 1990a, 1987). While no dart points were found there, the recovered lithic assemblage is too small to make the absence of any particular artifact a basis for chronological interpretation. Likewise, we should not assume that the small lithic assemblages from the two type sites of these phases reflect the range of potential variability in this regard. Of the three type sites of the Grasshopper Falls phase, all had dart points, but one (Teaford, 14JF333) also contained Scallorn points (Reynolds 1979); similar mixtures of dart points and arrowpoints have been found at other Grasshopper Falls phase sites, such as Avoca (14JN332; Baugh 1991) (Figure 5.6). Until further research indicates otherwise, none of these phases deserves distinction. Rather, Grasshopper Falls, Deer Creek, and Wakarusa all manifest the same general adaptation to the Dissected Till Plains and Attenuated Drift Border drained by the lower Kansas and Missouri rivers.

The Grasshopper Falls phase has since become much more extensively identified throughout northeastern Kansas, with the result that the name is much better known than Wakarusa, which has prior taxonomic status. The temporal range, based on a small number of radiocarbon dates (Logan and Fosha 1991), falls within the general span of the Plains Woodland period (ca. A.D. 500–1000). Several houses, all found on terraces in valley settings, have been documented. These are of oval outline, of sufficient size for a nuclear or extended family, and are sometimes paired, perhaps reflecting another aspect of the social organization of these people (Reynolds 1979; Logan and Fosha 1991). Hunting and gathering remained paramount, although there is botanical evidence of marsh elder, sunflower, and maize in the diet (Adair 1988, 1991, 1996: 118). Burial practices are poorly understood. Reynolds (1979: 74) notes that human remains from Grasshopper Falls phase sites were limited

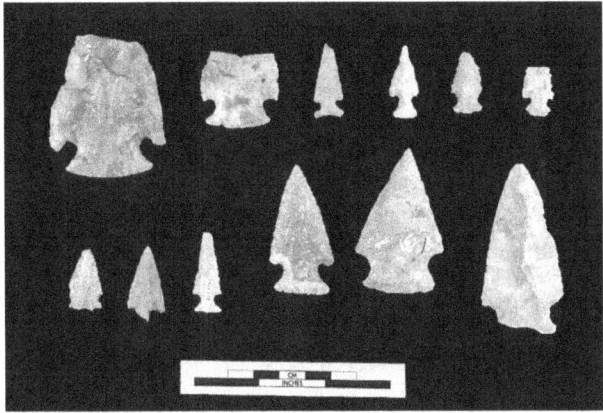

Figure 5.6. Dart points and arrowpoints from the Avoca (14JN332) (top row and second from left bottom row) and Teaford (14JF333) sites (Grasshopper Falls phase). These are representative of Late Woodland sites in eastern Kansas that yield both forms of projectiles. (Courtesy of the Kansas State Historical Society)

to "sections of an adult mandible and associated skull fragments and a primary infant burial, both recovered from site 14JF350 (Barr 1971)." Reynolds (1979) suggests that the several mound sites recorded on bluff tops along the Delaware River may reflect a continuation by Late Woodland groups of the mound burial practice of preceding Hopewell groups centered to the east. That burial of the dead may have varied more is suggested by 14BN1332, a cemetery exposed on the west bank of the Delaware River. Excavation in 1991 revealed primary burials of nine individuals (two adult females, three adult males, and four subadults of indeterminate sex) with a few grave goods (a complete dart point, a bone awl, a piece of limonite, and a dozen shell beads), a few pieces of debitage, and eight sherds (Kansas State Historical Society site files). On the basis of the ceramics, the site was assigned to the Grasshopper Falls phase, although data from the excavation have not been published.

Just as the Grasshopper Falls and Wakarusa phases are essentially indistinguishable, the Butler phase of the southern Flint Hills (Grosser 1973) differs little from the Greenwood phase (Witty 1982), also located in the southern Flint Hills as well as in the Osage Cuestas. The ceramics of both are limestone-tempered and cord-marked, and both have projectile point assemblages that include a variety of corner-notched and contracting-stemmed dart points as well as Scallorn arrowpoints. In his description of the Curry site (14GR301), one of the first excavated sites of what was later defined as the Greenwood phase by Witty (1982), Calabrese (1967: 80–99) finds its assemblage comparable to that of sites assigned to the Keith variant, which is now recognized only in the western portion of Kansas and Nebraska (chapter 6, this volume; Bozell and Winfrey 1994). In Keith and Greenwood pottery, only the use of calcite temper and the vertical orientation of cord-marking appear to distinguish the diagnostic ware of the former, called Harlan Cord Roughened (Kivett 1953), from Verdigris ware. Again, it is apparent that the differences among most, if not all, of the Late Woodland complexes in the Central Plains are slight.

DISCUSSION

Previous emphasis on minor differences among some Middle and Late Woodland cultures in the eastern Central Plains, often restricted to behavior that may have been influenced by environmental factors within the geographically broad range of these cultures, such as the use of different materials as ceramic temper, has kept us from appreciating the significance of what they shared. In this case, the prevailing taxonomy has led us to emphasize the minor regional variability that inherently characterizes any widely distributed population, causing us to lose sight of the importance of those common factors that reflect their greater cultural proximity. Two of these factors are critical to understanding Woodland adaptations in Kansas: (1) population increase through time and space and (2) ceramic surface treatments as a means of interregional communication.

A. E. Johnson (1976a, 1979, 2001) noted a trend of population increase throughout Middle Woodland time on the eastern edge of the Central Plains. The continuation of this trend during Late Woodland time is evident in the notably greater number and density of sites of that period throughout eastern Kansas. For example, there is scant evidence of Kansas City Hopewell in the Delaware River drainage or of any known contemporaries, but 115 Late Woodland sites have been identified there (Logan 1990b; Schmits and Parisi 1987: 207). Similarly, only 7 Middle Woodland sites have been recorded in Stranger Creek basin, on the western edge of the Kansas City Hopewell area, yet 43 sites there have been assigned to the Late Woodland period (Logan 1985). Given that the Late Woodland period spanned no more than 5 centuries, comparable to the duration of the Hopewell occupation in northeastern Kansas, the number of sites must reflect a greater population and/or the broader dispersal of groups throughout the region.

Obviously, the more numerous Late Woodland settlements must have maintained communication, and it is unlikely that this interaction was restricted to specific drainages or geographic areas, as our taxonomic units imply. Some archaeologists (Deuel 1952; Dragoo 1976; Ford 1974; Griffin 1952; Struever 1960; Tainter 1977) have suggested that the diminishing amount of pottery decoration and general homogeneity of Woodland ceramics throughout the terminal Middle Woodland and Late Woodland in the Midwest signal a breakdown in communication. The general homogeneity of Late Woodland ceramics in Kansas is sometimes maligned as uninspired and lacking in the variation valued by archaeologists to define the "cultures" that they consider meaningful or the short temporal periods they hope to recognize.

Other archaeologists (Braun 1977, 1985, 1987, 1991; Braun and Plog 1982) interpret the diminishing decoration and increasing ceramic homogeneity as evidence of increasing social interaction. When lines of communication are tenuous and communities need to hedge against the risk of resource failures by fostering ties with other, often distant, communities, ceramic decorative treatments become more elaborate and varied. Seen in the light of these two factors, we can better understand the process of post-Archaic adaptation to the region as one of fluid movement of ideas and people across the prairie-plains landscape. This entailed acceptance of these ideas and, likely, some of the people who brought them, expansion of the subsistence base to include more domesticated plants, more prolonged settlement of camps that storage of some surplus goods permitted, and the cementing of social ties through various means of communication, including the adoption over broad areas of comparable decorative treatments on pottery. This trend continued to Late Prehistoric time, and probably beyond, and likely explains the replacement of Late Woodland cultures throughout eastern Kansas and some areas of northwestern Missouri by a similarly widespread and homogeneous adaptation, the Pomona variant.

Despite the general similarity of Late Woodland ceramics, the variability of some site assemblages in this regard is valuable for tracking significant changes from Woodland to Late Prehistoric lifeways. This applies to Greenwood, which is represented at some sites by two types of pottery called Verdigris and Greenwood (Calabrese 1967: 80–83). The former exhibits attributes typical of Plains Woodland wares—elongate body form with straight walls and conical bases and cord-marked or smoothed exteriors. The Greenwood type is globular in form with sloping shoulders and more constricted mouths, a form comparable to Pomona pottery. Indeed, the appearance of this type at Greenwood sites supports the interpretation that the Pomona variant descended directly from Plains Woodland cultures, such as Greenwood, in eastern Kansas (K. L. Brown 1985; Reynolds 1982: 207; Witty 1978, 1982). Some sites in southeastern Kansas have yielded ceramic assemblages with Greenwood phase pottery, either Verdigris or Greenwood or both, and Pomona pottery, supporting such a connection. It is not always apparent, however, that the wares were associated contemporaneously. For example, the ceramics at the Wiley site (14OS312) in Osage County (P. S. Moore and Birkby 1964) were from horizontally discrete areas, suggesting different occupations (Logan 1981). The wares of the two complexes were vertically stratified at the Cow Killer site (14OS347), indicating subsequent occupation by a Pomona group (Reynolds 1982).

Descent relations among other Late Prehistoric cultures and Late Woodland groups are not as evident as between the Late Woodland and Pomona, although Roper (1995: 217; cf. Roper 2000a: 54) has suggested that the Central Plains tradition may have developed from Woodland. Part of the problem is that wares diagnostic of some of these cultures, such as the Steed-Kisker phase (Calabrese 1969; C. H. Chapman 1980; Shippee 1972; Wedel 1943), lack the attributes of Pomona ware that are more clearly transitional from Woodland pottery (i.e., cord-marking, general lack of decorative treatment, and higher, straight rims). Lacking such evidence of transition,

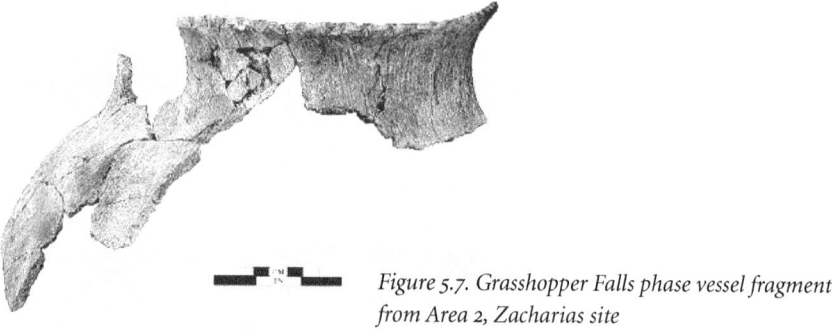

Figure 5.7. Grasshopper Falls phase vessel fragment from Area 2, Zacharias site

Figure 5.8. Steed-Kisker phase loop handles from Area 2, Zacharias site. The handle to the left was associated with the Woodland vessel fragment shown in Figure 5.7 at a depth of 30 cm.

Figure 5.9. Steed-Kisker phase rimsherd (left) found below the Grasshopper Falls phase rimsherd (right) at a depth of 45 cm in Area 3, Zacharias site

we must rely on contextual evidence, and this remains ambiguous at sites in northeastern Kansas and northwestern Missouri that have yielded ceramic assemblages of both Late Woodland and Late Prehistoric wares. In such cases, their contextual association is not always clearly attributable to contemporaneity and, thus, interpretable as evidence of development from one form of adaptation to the other.

For example, excavations at the Keen site (14JF303) in Jefferson County and the Zacharias site (14LV380) in Leavenworth County recovered ceramic assemblages dominated by Late Prehistoric pottery, including both Pomona and Steed-Kisker wares, as well as Late Woodland pottery assigned to the Grasshopper Falls phase (Logan 1990c; Logan and Ritterbush 1994; Witty 1983a). At the Keen site, the Woodland ware was found in houses and a pit feature identified as Pomona, suggesting contemporaneity and a developmental relationship, although an earlier occupation may also explain its presence (Witty 1983a: 109). Similarly, sherds of Woodland ware were consistently found in each of three areas excavated at the Zacharias site, including two areas that revealed house remains interpreted as Late Prehistoric. In several cases, Woodland sherds were found in direct association with Late Prehistoric pottery (Figures 5.7–5.9). Evidence of postdepositional mixing was absent, but that absence was not sufficient to discount sherd association through various disturbance processes, either cultural (i.e., Late Prehistoric intrusion into Late Woodland middens or activity areas) or natural (i.e., rodent burrowing or tree growth) that left no discernible traces. Given the contrast in their respective ceramic wares, which is insufficient grounds per se for ruling out direct descent, we must rely on incontrovertible evidence that is archaeological (contextual) or biological (e.g., genetic evidence from human remains), neither of which is at hand. For that reason, we cannot yet demonstrate a lineal descent of some, or any, Central Plains tradition culture from a Late Woodland predecessor. However, the ceramic evidence from sites like Keen and Zacharias justifies inquiry into this important research problem.

CONCLUSIONS

The Woodland period in eastern Kansas represents a time of critical change from the Archaic adaptations that had persisted throughout much of the Holocene. Some aspects that came to characterize Woodland cultures made their first appearance during the Late Archaic, including production of ceramic vessels and interment of the dead in earthen mounds. However, there is little evidence of regional continuity in these traits. Indeed, there is no evidence of mound burial in the Early Woodland period in Kansas, and the small amount of pottery found shows clear influence from Black Sand cultures in Illinois. The evidence of midwestern influence on subsequent Middle Woodland adaptations in eastern Kansas is even more apparent in the use of stone-lined cists in burial mounds and parallel changes in the styles of dart points and various ceramic decorative motifs. It is not yet clear whether these relations reflect the migration of Havana groups via the Missouri River valley from their homeland along the lower Illinois River, the adoption of these traits as a form of communication among groups that shared common concerns with periodic food shortages in woodland-prairie habitats, or some combination of both historical and adaptive processes.

The Late Woodland period in eastern Kansas is characterized by a dramatic increase in the number of sites along stream valleys. This has been seen as a response to demographic pressures that began during the Middle Woodland period, when larger groups then able to occupy base camps on a long-term basis eventually depleted resources in their vicinity. Archaeologists in Kansas have overemphasized minor differences among these Late Woodland groups, generally limited to such ceramic attributes as temper, at the expense of the greater homogeneity among their various material inventories. These commonalities reflect the close lines of communication among these groups and the fluid movement of people and ideas throughout the region that continued into Late Prehistoric time. While the descent from Late Woodland cultures is more apparent for some Late Prehistoric groups, such as Pomona, it is less evident for others, such as those of the Central Plains tradition. There is, however, enough tantalizing evidence of such developmental continuity to spur more research into this aspect of Kansas archaeology.

6. Plains Woodland Complexes of Western Kansas and Adjacent Portions of Nebraska and Colorado

John R. Bozell

From the broad perspective of North American prehistory, Woodland refers to a widespread series of cultural complexes found in the eastern and midwestern United States from 2500 to 1000 B.P. Woodland complexes also influenced Great Plains and Rocky Mountain cultures. Some Kansas complexes, particularly Kansas City Hopewell (see chapter 5, this volume), bear significant social similarity to Woodland societies in the east, but the Woodland peoples of western Kansas and Nebraska and eastern Colorado and Wyoming possessed a lifestyle much more similar to that of the preceding nomadic or semi-sedentary Archaic hunter-gatherers.

Woodland period sites are scattered throughout both the Central Plains and the High Plains of Kansas, but the most extensively investigated include Woodruff Ossuary (14PH4, Kivett 1953), Coal Oil Canyon (14LO1, 14LO401; Bowman 1960), West Island (14PH10, Witty 1966), Pfaff (14NS319, Craine 1956), Young (14SC2, W. R. Wedel 1959: 468–475), Pottorff (14LA1, W. R. Wedel 1959: 381–413), and Vohs (14OB401, Witty 1969a). Several complete and partial overviews of Woodland in the Central and High Plains have been developed in recent years and provide greater detail on select topics than does this summary. Readers interested in the subject are strongly encouraged to consult Adair (1996), Bozell and Winfrey (1994), W. B. Butler (1988), Gilmore (1999), A. E. Johnson (2001), A. M. Johnson and Johnson (1998), Kivett and Metcalf (1997), and W. R. Wedel (1959, 1986) as well as primary sources.

ENVIRONMENT

According to researchers in the 1960s and 1970s, the Plains Woodland tradition existed during the course of three poorly understood climatic episodes (Bryson, Baerreis, and Wendland 1970). The Sub-Atlantic (2500–1700 B.P.) dominated at the emergence of the tradition and appears to have been cooler and moister than today's climate. The Scandic episode began about 1700 B.P. and persisted until 1300 B.P. The Scandic was warmer and perhaps dryer than today and was followed by a period of increased moisture termed the Neo-Atlantic (1300–800 B.P.). However, the timing and nature of these shifts have been called into question during recent decades. More recent climatic models for the Southern and Central Plains suggest that much of the Woodland period was characterized by increased precipitation (Kay 1998: 28). The moist conditions may have encouraged horticultural experimentation by Woodland people.

In general, the eastern portion of the Central Plains is rolling and covered with tall-grass prairie and hardwood forest along streams. Summers are warm and humid, and winters are cold and snowy. The central and western portions of the region are typically drier and less humid than the east but with comparable temperatures. Vegetation there is dominated by mixed- and short-grass prairie with fewer trees. Faunal resources available in the east included deer and a wide variety of smaller mammals, birds, reptiles, and fish typical of Midwestern and Eastern Woodland communities. A broad assortment of fauna (although slightly less diverse than in the east) was also available in the west with the important addition of bison and pronghorn. High-quality lithic material was available at several locations throughout the region with concentrations in the Republican and Smoky Hill river valleys as well as various locations in the High Plains and Rocky Mountain foothills (Holen 1991; Miller 1991; Stein, chapter 16, this volume).

TAXONOMY

This brief review does not address taxonomic issues in detail but does touch on several broad divisions of the western Kansas Woodland (Figure 6.1). The Keith phase (Central Plains) is centered in the Republican River valley of Nebraska and Kansas with sites also present in the Solomon, Saline, Smoky Hill, and Arkansas river drainages. The South Platte phase (High Plains), in this context, also includes previously defined taxa such as Ash Hollow and Parker and is much more widespread, extending from the Nebraska Sand Hills through western Nebraska and at least northwestern Kansas and into a large area of northeastern Colorado and portions of eastern Wyoming and southwestern South Dakota. Much of what we know of South Platte is derived from research in Colorado (W. B. Butler 1988; Gilmore 1999). The Arkansas phase is a separate Colorado taxon (W. B. Butler 1988) and is centered along the Arkansas River of southeastern Colorado and the Front Range. W. B. Butler (1988: 461–462) and Kalasz, Mitchell, and Zier (1999) caution that the Arkansas phase is poorly defined and in need of substantial additional research. Scattered Woodland sites in southwestern Kansas may relate to this complex. The Valley phase (see chapter 5, this volume) occurs in central Nebraska and northeastern Kansas and is not formally treated in this chapter, but it likely influenced Woodland developments to the west.

Traditionally, Woodland archaeological complexes are divided into Early, Middle, and Late stages—each with distinct temporal, formal, and sociopolitical characteristics. These distinctions are meaningful in the Midwest but become less so on the Central Plains and High Plains. In fact, they simply may not be applicable for the region.

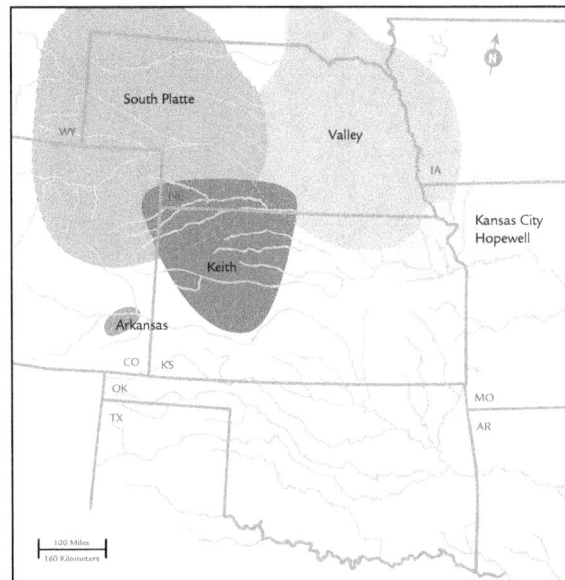

Figure 6.1. Distribution of select Woodland complexes in the Central and High Plains

Radiocarbon dates for the Keith and South Platte components are few and most suggest a temporal duration from roughly A.D. 500 to A.D. 1100. However, both phases, as well as some of the southeastern Colorado components, have produced a few dates stretching back as far as 100 B.C. (see Appendix). If those early dates are reliable, Woodland in the High Plains emerged early in the common era (during the Middle Woodland stage) and possibly was associated very loosely with developments in the Valley and Kansas City Hopewell phases. However, by approximately A.D. 500, when a clear shift from Middle Woodland to Late Woodland was taking place in the east, Woodland populations in the west remained relatively stable. These peoples' economy, material culture, mortuary customs, and settlement patterns persisted until as late as A.D. 1100 in much the same form as when they emerged between 500 and 1,000 years earlier. Using radiocarbon dates and a refreshingly innovative analysis of ceramic technological evolution, Krause (1995a) suggested that Keith may ultimately be divided into two phases: one early and one late. Until chronological refinement is achieved, considering these phases as Middle or Late Woodland is premature. Clearly, however, most Woodland occupancy of western Kansas took place after A.D. 500.

SETTLEMENT AND ARCHITECTURE

Keith phase architecture and settlement is well documented (Bozell and Winfrey 1994: 135; Grange 1980: 108–112; Kivett and Metcalf 1997: 11–22; Winfrey 1991: 85). This complex is characterized by small villages, normally consisting of one to several oval to circular enclosed structures placed in shallow basins up to seven meters in diameter

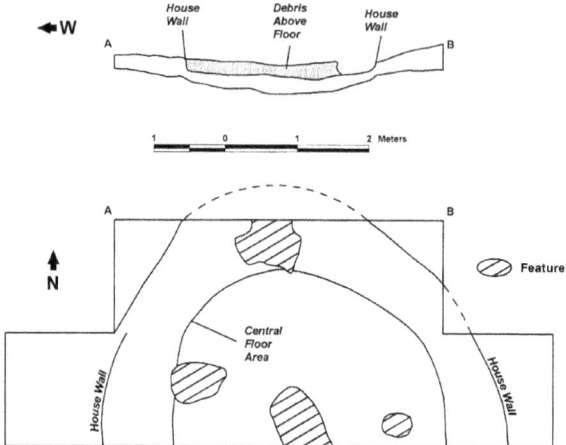

Figure 6.2. Woodland house floor at the Doyle site, 25RW28 (from Grange 1980)

(Figure 6.2). Superstructures were fairly light, were constructed of small poles, and were likely covered with skins, mats, or possibly wattle and daub. Most had central fire basins, posthole patterns, and occasional pit features. Many Woodland habitation sites are situated on low alluvial terraces of creek and rivers. Occasionally, Woodland sites are found on ridges and bluffs above stream valleys.

Woodland sites in the High Plains do not typically produce much evidence of domestic structures. Most contain little more evidence than sparse midden deposits, hearths, and shallow pit features. Woodland sites in these areas can also be found in rockshelters. Several exceptions have been identified in eastern Colorado where circular, oval, and square dry-laid masonry structures are associated with both the South Platte and Arkansas phases (W. B. Butler 1988: 460). Several oval pit house features similar to those in Nebraska have also been identified in Colorado.

Woodland settlement appears to include groups of hunter-gatherers, perhaps family units, living in small, semi-permanent, streamside households or hamlets (Bozell and Winfrey 1994: 135), seasonally occupied based on resource availability. Kivett (1970: 100) suggests that these small and dispersed Woodland hamlets may have been loosely organized and linked to communal burial sites.

Woodland complexes of the High Plains are defined by what appears to be a significantly more mobile hunting and gathering lifeway, which apparently involved seasonal occupation of the Rocky Mountains and the foothills (W. B. Butler 1988: 459). During the Late Archaic and Woodland periods, large-scale communal bison hunting was fairly common on the High Plains at sites such as Ruby (48CA302), Muddy Creek (48CR324), and Wardell (48SU301) (Frison 1991: 194–217). What relationship these big game hunters had with the Woodland people on the Central Plains remains uncertain.

PHYSICAL ANTHROPOLOGY

The remains of dozens of Woodland individuals have been recovered from Nebraska, northern Kansas, and northeastern Colorado, although only about one-half of those have been even partly studied (Owsley and Bruweldheide 1996, 1997). The Plains Woodland life expectancy was generally longer than for the subsequent Plains Village period. Approximately 40 percent of recovered Woodland individuals were below the age of 15, whereas between 60 percent and 65 percent of Plains Village interments represent people under 15 years of age (Owsley and Bruweldheide 1997: 19). Infant mortality was about 15 percent less frequent among Woodland people than among Plains Villagers (Owsley 1992).

The largest single analyzed skeletal series from a Woodland component on the Central Plains is that from the Keith phase Woodruff Ossuary on the Nebraska/Kansas border (Kivett 1953: 137–140). In that series of 54 individuals, the following age classes are represented: infant–2.5 years (21 percent), 2.5–7 years (23 percent), 7–12 years (1 percent), 12–25 years (0 percent), 25–55 years (39 percent), 55–75 years (16 percent). The gender division in this population is about equal. The average female height at Woodruff was 5 feet 2 inches, and the average male height was 5 feet 5 inches. The few Woodland period skeletons discovered on the High Plains are those of adults (W. B. Butler, Chomko, and Hofman 1986; Gill 1991; Gill and Lewis 1977). Woodland people on the High Plains had a tendency to be rather robust with individuals occasionally reaching over 6 feet in height. This robustness appears to increase to the north and west. Plains Woodland crania are somewhat distinctive in their dolichocranic (long-headed) nature.

Overall health of Plains Woodland peoples is not particularly well known, largely because skeletal remains have not been completely analyzed. In general, skeletal signatures of disease, infection, and trauma occur at lower frequencies than those observed for late prehistoric and post-contact Native American populations (Owsley and Bruweldheide 1997: 26–56; Owsley 1997: 298–301). Periostitis and osteomyelitis, probably the result of trauma and various infections, occur on several skeletons, as do fractures and dislocations. Dental caries are not common, but significant dental wear suggests a diet low in corn but high in abrasive vegetal and protein materials. Some skeletal series do provide evidence of considerable nutritional stress in the form of hypoplasia, bone porosity, and growth arrest lines.

ECONOMY

Plains Woodland populations were, in general, semi-sedentary hunter-gatherers. The overall configuration of Woodland adaptation in the Central Plains is probably related to environmental gradients. Developing a clear picture of Plains Woodland subsistence is hampered because relatively few fine-screen-recovered botanical and faunal samples exist (Adair 1996, 2003a). Examples of well-recovered useful samples include those reported by Winfrey (1991) and Adair (1988, 1991, 1996). The eastern complexes show more evidence of horticulture and sedentism than do western expressions. In the west, subsistence evidence suggests primary protein reliance on deer, bison, and pronghorn, with lesser (yet remarkably diverse) dependence on mussels, small mammals, birds, and fish. Increased use of mussels, fish, and birds occurs during the later Woodland period. Bison use decreases somewhat through time but remained important to subsistence throughout the tradition. In the High Plains, bison was the principal meat item throughout the Plains Woodland period.

Adair (1988, 1996, 2003a) synthesized all available archaeobotanical information for Woodland complexes on the Central Plains. Wild plant foods commonly used throughout the Plains Woodland period include goosefoot, pigweed, sunflower, grape, and various nuts and grasses. Although small quantities of maize and other domesticates occur, in all cases, serious provenience problems exist, and use of domestic plants by western Plains Woodland people remains uncertain. Stable isotope analysis of human skeletal remains is generally consistent with analysis of faunal and floral remains (Tieszen, Reinhard, and Foreshoe 1997). During the Plains Woodland period, $\delta^{13}C$ values range from –23 parts per thousand to –17 parts per thousand, which is typical of a broad-spectrum diet not based on maize. Most Plains Village carbon isotope ratios vary from –18 parts per thousand to –10 parts per thousand, which is much more consistent with a maize-based diet.

MATERIAL CULTURE

One of the most important technological innovations of the Plains Woodland period was the manufacture and use of ceramic cooking vessels. Braun (1983) reasoned that pottery was initially developed to simmer and boil hard and starchy plant resources to maximize nutritional value. Most Woodland pottery from the Central and High Plains is thick and elongated, with only occasional decoration, usually in the form of bosses, punctates, and incised lines. Pottery is typically cord-marked across the entire surface of the vessel (Figure 6.3). Thick conical pottery continued to be made in the central and western portions of the Plains throughout the Plains Woodland period, but distinctive ceramic technological changes are evident in the east beginning about A.D. 500 and characterized by increasing use of cord-marked rim decoration and a tendency toward rounding at the base of the vessel. Keith phase pottery, known as Harlan Cord-Roughened Ware, often contains crushed calcite temper. South Platte ceramics are classified as Ash Hollow Cord-Roughened. Both normally exhibit little or no decoration. These two wares are very similar, the primary distinction being the lack of calcite tempering in Ash Hollow pots.

Stone tools and debris are not particularly abundant at Woodland sites (Figure

Figure 6.3. Ceramics from Keith phase site 14PA303

Figure 6.4. Stone knives, scrapers, and projectile points from Keith phase sites 14PA303 and 14PA307

6.4). Most projectile points are corner-notched and decrease in size through time. Smaller points likely relate to increased use of the bow and arrow. Bow and arrow technology increased hunting range and accuracy, the equipment was lighter, and points were simpler to manufacture. Other chipped-stone tools include scrapers,

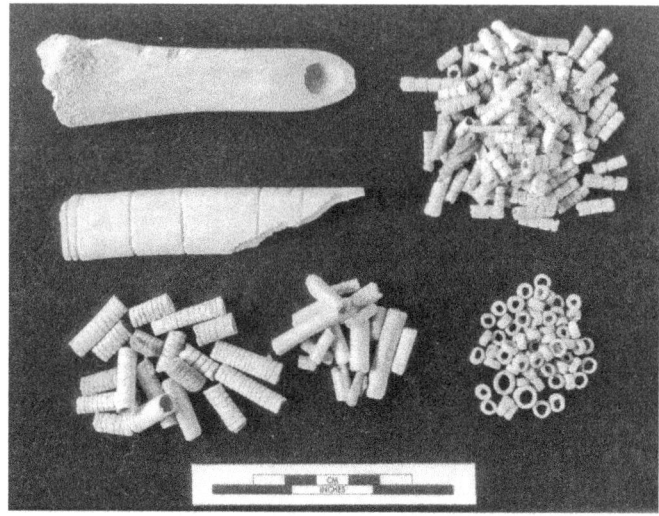

Figure 6.5. Bone artifacts from Keith phase sites. Upper left: digging stick tip from 14PA303. Right and center: beads from the Pfaff site, 14NS319. Lower left: beads from 14PA303. Left center: scored bone, 14PA303.

wedges, ovate or rectangular knives, drills, and retouched and utilized flakes. Ground- and pecked-stone implements include hammerstones, grinding stones, and the diagnostic three-quarter grooved celt or ax.

Bone and antler artifacts include flaking tools, awls, expedient butchering tools, perforated phalanges, pendants, beads, and shaft wrenches (Figure 6.5). Shell artifacts are not particularly common in earlier assemblages but do increase rather dramatically in frequency after about A.D. 500. Shell objects are either scraping or butchering tools or ornamental beads and pendants (Figure 6.6). Decorative shell items are particularly common in the Republican River area (Kivett 1953) where they are associated with communal ossuaries. Most shell is local, but marine species such as *Olivella* and *Busycon* occur.

SOCIOPOLITICAL ORGANIZATION AND RELIGION

Woodland social and political structure on the Central and High Plains is poorly understood. What has been offered on the topic (Benn 1990), while quite productive, remains speculative. Lifestyles ranged from nomadic bison hunters to semi-sedentary hunter-gatherers. Typically, Woodland people lived as isolated nuclear or extended families or in small hamlets. Given that sites are small, exogamy was probably practiced, and the emphasis on hunting and gathering suggests patrilocal residence. Descent reckoning is uncertain. Scattered habitation sites may reflect loosely affiliated bands or lineage groups. In Woodland society, the family or extended family

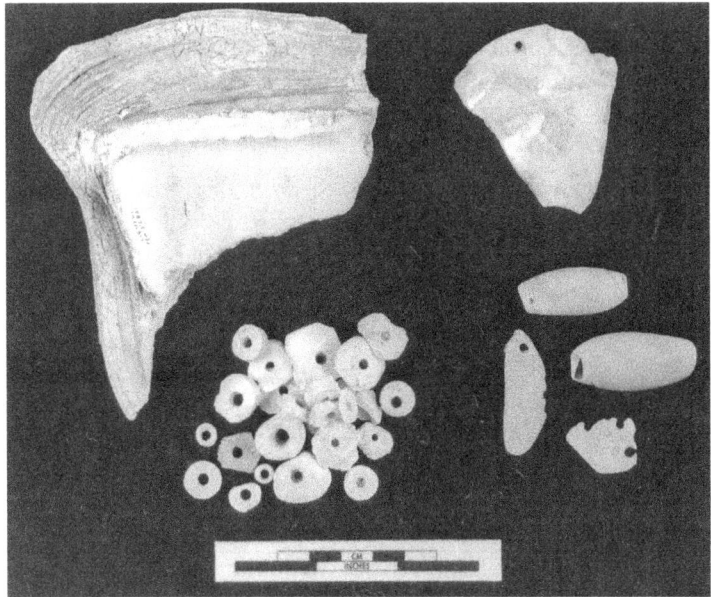

Figure 6.6. Shell artifacts from Keith phase sites. Upper left: large Busycon fragment, 14PA317. Upper right: drilled shell pendant, 14PA307. Lower right: drilled Olivella shells, pendant, and gorget, Pfaff site, 14NS319. Lower left: shell beads in various stages of manufacture, Woodruff site, 14PH4.

band was the primary unit of production. Although there is no reason to suspect that sharing of food and resources did not take place, there is no evidence for large-scale systematic redistribution of goods. It is not unreasonable to assume that cooperation took place among multiple Woodland bands in resource procurement activities. What level of social stratification Woodland people defined for themselves is vague. Mortuary offerings and grave preparations at some Plains Woodland sites suggest a ranked society (Kivett 1953; P. J. O'Brien 1971). An adolescent at the Woodruff Ossuary was lavishly wrapped in a "blanket" of shell beads, suggesting that social status may occasionally have been ascribed and not solely achieved. Certainly, artifact styles present at these and other Woodland sites are influenced or adapted from the Hopewell culture of the mid-continent, but exotic items suggesting active sustained involvement in developments in the Illinois or Ohio river valleys are not abundant. Neither widespread cultural interaction nor widespread conflict appears to have taken place. Skeletal evidence bears only limited evidence of warfare.

Religion played a part in Woodland life in at least portions of the region. What little is known of religious custom is derived from observation of mortuary patterns (Adair 1996; Bozell and Winfrey 1994; W. B. Butler, Chomko, and Hoffman 1986; Kivett 1953; P. J. O'Brien 1971; Oothoudt 1976). Woodland burials in the east are normally found within or below mounds containing multiple secondary interments, sometimes in stone-lined cysts. P. J. O'Brien (1971: 180–181) even suggests that nobility were buried with sacrificed low-status individuals (but see chapter 5, this volume). Woodland burials in the Central Plains normally did not involve mounds (see Craine 1956 for a possible exception). Large basin ossuaries containing multiple burial pits such as the Woodruff Ossuary (Kivett 1953) are more typical. Grave goods at ossuaries were sometimes rather lavish for certain individuals, suggesting that they held high status. High Plains Woodland burials are more likely to be single, articulated interments with personal offerings, although ossuaries are also known from the High Plains (Oothoudt 1976). The seemingly more elaborate mortuary customs in the Eastern and Central Plains may be a reflection of the more sedentary population required for cooperative construction of mounds and ossuaries.

ORIGIN, DEVELOPMENT, AND TERMINATION

The initial incursion of Woodland peoples or ideas onto the Central High Plains was probably a product of influence or migration of Woodland cultures from the east, particularly Kansas City Hopewell and Valley, as well as influence from the north and west, primarily Pelican Lake, Besant, and Avonlea. Woodland presence in the west may be linked to the Hopewell Interaction Sphere and the resultant acquisition of goods and food from the region, although this cannot be substantiated with available information.

Available evidence indicates that, for the most part, Woodland people in the Central and High Plains did not have regular contact with peoples in the Eastern Plains or the Midwest. They persisted as a relatively autonomous, static, and homogenous tradition of scattered groups for perhaps a thousand years. Craniometric data suggest that Keith and Valley populations may be related to one another but are distinct from Kansas City Hopewell (Key 1994). The fate of these Woodland peoples is unclear, although the development of the Central Plains tradition swiftly replaced Woodland culture. Woodland people may have been incorporated into the Central Plains tradition, although the skeletal record suggests that Woodland involvement in that tradition was limited. Keith and Valley crania do, however, bear some similarity to Late Woodland Great Oasis and Initial Middle Missouri populations (Key 1994), suggesting a possible northeastern movement out of the Central and High Plains. Krause (1995a), however, proposes a technological continuity from Keith Phase pottery to Upper Republican pottery, perhaps reflecting biological/cultural continuity.

CONCLUSIONS AND FUTURE RESEARCH

Plains Woodland is an important, and often overlooked, "formative" period in that it reflects the initial development of prehistoric semi-sedentary horticultural societies on the Great Plains (Adair 1996: 104). Woodland marked the beginning of the end of 10,000 years of a largely nomadic, hunting-gathering, nonhorticultural existence on the Plains. Those Woodland cultures wedged between the Rocky Mountains and the central and eastern Plains are of particular research value because they reflect the most obvious blending of High Plains nomadism and emerging eastern sedentism. Members of the Keith, South Platte, and possibly other unrecognized taxa clearly have strong roots in High Plains hunting and gathering. However, they also participated, in a limited fashion, in rapidly developing cultural changes in the east. These groups reflect a persistent link to a High Plains lifeway. Hunting and gathering always remained the primary economic framework. Similarly, although ceramics were in use, pots rarely display the elaborate decoration evident in the east in Middle Woodland wares (Kansas City Hopewell and to a lesser extent Valley) and Late Woodland wares (Loseke Creek, Great Oasis, Sterns Creek). Other aspects of Woodland life on the Central and High Plains clearly echo developments in the east, such as construction of substantial dwellings, elaborate mortuary customs, and possibly social stratification.

To solve nagging problems involving culture history, environment, social issues, technology, and economy, Woodland archaeological research on the Central and High Plains needs to accelerate in several critical areas (Hofman, Logan, and Adair 1996: 214–217).

Systematic Survey and Excavation, Including Geomorphology

Variation in the location and density of Plains Woodland sites is poorly understood. Woodland components, unlike more highly visible Plains Village sites, are more likely to be buried in lower alluvial settings. A geoarchaeological research program to identify Plains Woodland–age deposits will enhance our ability to develop settlement pattern models and amass a larger pool of sites to investigate and will allow better management of the Woodland portion of the continually degrading archaeological record.

Taxonomic Refinement and Radiocarbon Dating

Remarkably, when Plains Woodland in the Central and High Plains emerged remains vague. While a few radiocarbon dates suggest development as early as 100 B.C., most dates fall after A.D. 500. Resolution of the issue is critical. Similarly, with the limited evidence available, it would appear that the Keith and South Platte phases continued for a thousand years. Clearly that is an oversimplification. If these two cultural complexes lasted that long, further taxonomic division may ultimately be warranted. An aggressive program of radiocarbon-dating materials in solid association with diagnostic material culture will eventually provide a more accurate culture history.

Additional Fine-Screen Recovery of Faunal and Floral Samples

From the broad perspective of the evolution of Great Plains Native American culture from the Archaic to the Plains Village periods, a firmer handle on Woodland subsistence and paleoenvironmental information is sorely needed. Only a handful of fine-screen samples are available, and, although certainly useful, they indicate that the type and diversity of faunal and floral materials present in Central and High Plains Woodland deposits vary sharply through time and across space. More archaeological evidence will ultimately result in a clearer understanding of the role Woodland peoples played in the rather dramatic cultural changes that took place in Native American history from 3,000 years ago to the nineteenth century.

Reexamination of Select Extant Collections

Some of the major Central and High Plains Woodland collections housed in Kansas, Nebraska, Colorado, Wyoming, and South Dakota institutions may be candidates for reexamination. Krause's (1995a) reconsideration of Keith and Upper Republican ceramic evolution is an excellent case in point of what can be accomplished with curated collections and innovative thought. Looking at older collections can prove productive from an almost limitless number of perspectives. Some obvious research avenues include clay and temper sourcing, lithic raw material analysis, extraction of stable isotope values on animal bone to record environmental conditions, and fine-grained technological analysis of weaponry, ornaments, and tools.

7. The Central Plains Tradition

Donna C. Roper

In a work published in 1954, Donald J. Lehmer (1954a: 143–147) formulated the Central Plains tradition as one of three traditions, joining the Plains Village pattern as a Central Plains counterpart to the Middle Missouri tradition of the Dakotas. Lehmer did not define finer-scale units within the Central Plains tradition, as he did for the Middle Missouri tradition, but he did recognize that the sites assigned to it "certainly show enough cultural variation to warrant the recognition of several foci and are generally grouped into two aspects" (Lehmer 1954a: 146). These were the Upper Republican and Nebraska aspects, each defined in Nebraska two decades earlier by William Duncan Strong (1933, 1935), drawing on earlier work by Robert F. Gilder (1926) in the case of the Nebraska aspect. In 1959, Waldo Wedel defined the Smoky Hill aspect as a separate cultural complex (W. R. Wedel 1959: 566) and, by implication, subsumed it within the Central Plains tradition. Aspects are units of the Midwest Taxonomic Method (MTM) (McKern 1934), which began to fall from use in the 1960s after the publication of Willey and Phillips's (1958) method of culture-historical integration. In 1966, therefore, Lionel Brown (1966) converted the Upper Republican, Nebraska, and Smoky Hill aspects to phases, the first two of which had several subphases. Since then, Krause (1969) reconfigured these units as regional variants, each with several phases, and Blakeslee (1999) has attempted to recast the Central Plains tradition as the Central Plains mosaic with several phases subsumed under it. Neither of these schemes has won particular favor. Lehmer's concept of a Central Plains tradition, therefore, remains fundamental to the taxonomy of Middle Ceramic period cultures in the Central Plains.

Central Plains tradition sites date to the period of about A.D. 900–1400 and occur over an area that includes the valley and immediate drainage of the Missouri River in northeastern Kansas, northwestern Missouri, southwestern Iowa, and all of eastern Nebraska and beyond to the southern part of the Missouri River valley of South Dakota and the Kansas River basin of Kansas and southern Nebraska to about 100° W longitude (Figure 7.1). Units within it include the Upper Republican, Nebraska, and Smoky Hill phases. The Itskari (formerly called the Loup River phase and, before that, the Sweetwater focus of the Upper Republican aspect) and St. Helena phases of central and northeast Nebraska also are Central Plains tradition units. The Steed-Kisker phase and the Initial Coalescent variant previously were assigned to other traditions (Mississippian and Coalescent, respectively) but are better accommodated by assignment to the Central Plains tradition and are so considered here.

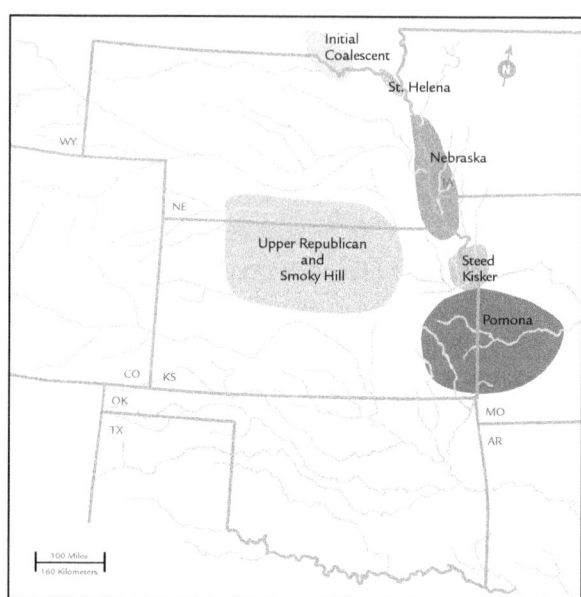

Figure 7.1. General locations of the Central Plains tradition phases

The area throughout which the sites assignable to the Central Plains tradition are found is much larger than the spatial scope of this volume. This chapter covers, therefore, the Missouri River valley and the Kansas River basin. In cultural terms, this includes remains assignable to the Steed-Kisker, Nebraska, Smoky Hill, and Upper Republican phases or variants (Figure 7.1). These taxa, however, are really just arbitrary divisions of a continuum. Thus, the phase terms are used here as spatial referents, but overall the discussion will treat the remains as a somewhat diverse group of sites, in which material culture variation often characterized as having phase-level significance may be attributable as much to available raw materials as to cultural differences.

INVESTIGATIONS OF CENTRAL PLAINS TRADITION SITES IN KANSAS

Early investigations of Central Plains tradition sites in Kansas include work conducted by Brower (1898), Zimmerman (1918), Fowke (1922: 152–156), and Schultz (reported in Hawley 1993). This, along with work in Nebraska by Straley (1909), Gilder (1907, 1908, 1909, 1911, 1913, 1926), and Sterns (1914, 1915a, 1915b), served to bring to light data that led to the later definition of the Central Plains tradition and the subunits subsumed under that broad taxon.

The 1930s was a very productive decade for archaeological research throughout the Central Plains, and the beginning of the modern study of the Central Plains tradition was an important part of the investigations. William Duncan Strong defined the Upper Republican culture on the basis of materials from his 1930 excavation of a lodge at the Lost Creek or Dooley site (25FR1) and another one nearby that local collectors had excavated the year before (Strong 1933, 1935). Understanding of the Upper Republican phase was reinforced by the work of A.T. Hill, E. E. Blackman (1930), and Waldo Wedel (1933, 1934a; see also Roper 2002a). Excavation of the Minneapolis site (14OT5), brought to Hill's attention by avocational archaeologists Guy and Mabel Whiteford, led Wedel, who reported the excavation, to designate a separate focus of the Upper Republican aspect that eventually became the Smoky Hill aspect (later phase) (W. R. Wedel 1934b: 252; 1959: 562–566). Other important Smoky Hill sites investigated in the 1930s include 14SA1, the Whiteford site or Salina Burial Pit, excavated by the Whitefords and run as a tourist attraction for decades (Roper 2001a, 2003, 2005a), and the Griffing site (14RY21) (W. R. Wedel 1938b: 106; 1959: 178–187).

Around this same time, in 1938, Wedel excavated two houses and part of a cemetery at the Steed-Kisker site (23PL13) in the Missouri River valley in extreme western Missouri, considering the site to represent "a local variant of the late Middle Mississippi culture" (W. R. Wedel 1943: 213). Subsequent work has revised that assessment. By the end of the 1930s, therefore, what now would be called Central Plains tradition sites were identified throughout Kansas and the adjacent parts of Nebraska and Missouri, and key elements of the taxonomic framework had been recognized.

Work with Central Plains tradition sites changed direction after about 1939. After a work hiatus during World War II, attention immediately turned to investigating sites to be inundated by reservoirs proposed by the Corps of Engineers and the Bureau of Reclamation. This work was conducted under the auspices of the River Basin Surveys (RBS) from the mid-1940s through the late-1960s, by which time all the reservoirs actually built had filled, and the RBS was phased out.

Particularly important to an understanding of the Upper Republican and Smoky Hill phases was work at Tuttle Creek Lake on the Blue River (Cumming 1958; A. E. Johnson 1973; Schmits, Mandel, et al. 1987), Milford Lake on the lower Republican River (Sperry 1965; Witty 1963), Kanopolis Lake on the Smoky Hill River (C. S. Smith 1949a), Wilson Lake on the Saline River (Blakeslee, Blasing, and Garcia 1986; Witty 1962), and Waconda Lake on the Solomon River (Blakeslee 1999; Krause 1970, 1995a; Lippincott 1976), all in Kansas; and at Harlan Lake on the Republican River (Champe 1950; Kivett 1947a), Harry Strunk Lake on Medicine Creek (Kivett 1947b, 1949; Kivett and Metcalf 1997; Roper 1991, 1993, 1996a; W. R. Wood, ed. 1969), and Hugh Butler Lake on Red Willow Creek (Grange 1980), all in southern Nebraska. Reporting of all this work, particularly that from the RBS era, is uneven, and some collections that were reported decades ago would reward reanalysis with significant new information.

Reservoir work does not account for all investigations into Upper Republican and Smoky Hill phase sites in the last six or so decades. The activities of avocational archaeologists, often through the efforts of the Kansas Anthropological Association (KAA) and its annual training program, the Kansas Archeology Training Program (KATP), have added significant information from localities that lie between lakes and might not otherwise attract attention (Fosha 1994; Roper 2002b; Roper and Reed

2003; Witty 1968a, 1970, 1971, 1974). Likewise, universities have sometimes investigated sites away from the major dams and reservoirs, and cultural resources compliance efforts on federal lands other than those for lakes, particularly on Fort Riley (Richardson 1997; Root 2000), have yielded information on the Smoky Hill phase. Additionally, a number of master's theses from the University of Kansas (Beck 1995; M. E. Brown 1981; Fosha 1994; Greatorex 1998; Hedden 1992; Macy 2002; Nickels 1971) and the University of Nebraska (Carlson 1971; Roll 1968; Sperry 1965; Steinacher 1976) have covered various topics of Central Plains tradition culture in the Kansas River basin, as have one master's thesis (Gilliland 2003) and one doctoral dissertation (Lippincott 1976) from the University of Missouri–Columbia.

The situation is somewhat different for the Central Plains remains in eastern Kansas. Here, surveys for reservoir projects such as Perry Lake on the Delaware River (Witty 1983a) or Clinton Lake on the Wakarusa River (Chambers and Tompkins 1977; A. E. Johnson 1968) have shown that Central Plains tradition sites seem to be largely absent from these Kansas River drainage valleys. Very little additional work has been done with the known Nebraska phase sites in northeast Kansas. The major exception is the 1967 University of Missouri–Columbia excavation of a rather poorly defined house with a low density of artifacts at the Nuzum site (14DP10) in Doniphan County (W. R. Wood, ed. 1969: 63–81). Investigations of Steed-Kisker sites in Kansas also have been limited, in part because most Steed-Kisker phase sites are in northwest Missouri and because the number of known components in Kansas is rather small. Nevertheless, a Steed-Kisker cemetery in Wyandotte County, the Calovich Mound (14WY7), was excavated in the early 1960s (Barnes 1977), and Steed-Kisker habitation components have been investigated recently at the DB (14LV1071) and Scott (14LV1082) sites, both in Leavenworth County (Logan 2001, 2002; Logan, ed. 1998; Logan and Hill 2000).

SITE DISTRIBUTION

Nearly a century of work on Central Plains tradition sites has led to a general understanding of their distribution (Figure 7.2). Steed-Kisker and Nebraska phase sites are more or less continuously distributed throughout the immediate drainage of the extreme lower Kansas River north of the river and the valley and immediate drainage on both sides of the Missouri River from the mouth of the Kansas River north into Nebraska and southwestern Iowa. Steed-Kisker sites in Kansas appear in the Missouri River valley or on the bluffs above and near the mouth of the Kansas River. They also are known from some of the tributary valleys of both the Kansas and Missouri rivers, including the lower Stranger Creek valley in Leavenworth County. Nebraska phase sites lie north of the Steed-Kisker phase sites and, in Kansas, are essentially confined to the valley of the Missouri River in the Doniphan County area.

Most Central Plains tradition sites in Kansas are assigned to the Smoky Hill and Upper Republican phases. Smoky Hill phase sites appear on both sides of the Blue

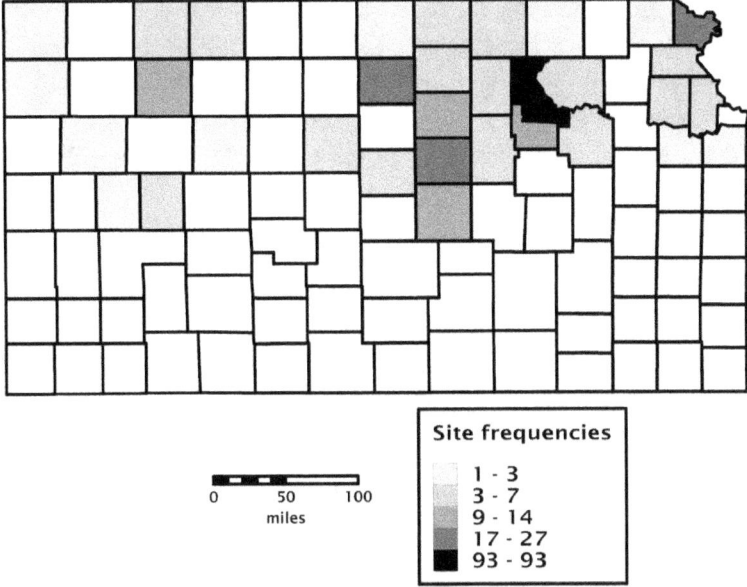

Figure 7.2. Distribution of Central Plains tradition sites in Kansas, by county, as recorded in the Kansas archaeological site files

River valley and are continuously distributed to the west through the valleys of tributaries of the upper Kansas River proper and in the lower valleys and larger tributary valleys of the Smoky Hill, Saline, Solomon, and Republican rivers. Sites farther west in the valleys of these rivers or their larger tributaries are assigned to the Upper Republican phase or to a phase that historically has been connected to the Upper Republican culture. Thus, Central Plains tradition sites in Kansas extend throughout, but not to the south of, the Kansas River basin. Their western limit is at about the 100th meridian.

Several generalizations can be made about the distribution of Central Plains tradition sites in Kansas. First, as W. R. Wedel (1953: 503) long ago pointed out, the western limit of Central Plains tradition sites, excluding those sites with some diagnostic artifacts but not the agricultural remains, features, and settlement patterns of Central Plains tradition sites, is near the 100th meridian, which approximates the 20-inch average precipitation line. This is significant because farther west summer precipitation is not sufficient to support dryland agriculture on a year-to-year basis. A class of sites west of this line, in far northwestern Kansas and adjacent Nebraska and in northeastern Colorado and southeastern Wyoming, yields artifacts diagnostic of the Central Plains tradition, particularly the Upper Republican phase, but the assemblages from many of these sites are inconsistent with those from the sites east of 100° W longitude (Roper 1990), and some archaeologists have been reluctant to include them within the Central Plains tradition (see chapter 8, this volume). Second, Central Plains tradition sites are found along the edges of, but are sparse within, the Dissected Till Plains of northeast Kansas (Figure 7.2). Third, Central Plains tradition sites extend from the mixed oak-hickory forest and tall-grass prairies of the Missouri River valley and eastern Kansas, across the mixed prairies, to the edge of the short-grass plains, and thus are not strongly correlated with any biotic zone within the Central Plains.

CHRONOLOGY

Efforts to develop a chronology for the Central Plains tradition have used several common approaches with varying degrees of success. Early on, stratigraphy was useful for placing the Central Plains tradition in its proper place relative to other Ceramic period complexes (Champe 1946; Sterns 1915b; Strong 1935: 274). Some form of seriation has been applied in a number of studies (Carlson 1971; Hedden 1992; Lippincott 1976; Roll 1968; Steinacher 1976), but the results are inconsistent and not one of the orderings has been validated by external means. In an attempt to assign calendar ages to the Central Plains tradition component at Ash Hollow Cave site in the North Platte River valley of Nebraska, John Champe incorporated Harry Weakly's dendrochronological analysis of charcoal into his stratigraphic analysis of excavations. From this, he estimated an age of A.D. 1300–1500 for the Upper Republican occupation (Champe 1946: 90). Dendrochronology has not seen further use in the region. In the end, therefore, the Central Plains tradition chronology relies primarily on radiocarbon age determinations to place sites and phases in both relative and calendar time.

Excluding age determinations from the Gakushuin laboratory, which have been shown to be unreliable (Blakeslee 1994), the corpus of radiocarbon age determinations for Central Plains tradition sites now numbers well over two hundred, with about a hundred of them from Central Plains tradition sites in Kansas or immediately adjacent parts of Missouri and Nebraska (see Appendix, including several of the dates on cultigens from Central Plains tradition sites). Collectively, they date the Central Plains tradition as a whole to around cal A.D. 900–1400. This date range, however, does not apply evenly throughout the Central Plains. Most of the earliest dates are from the tenth century and are from sites in the eastern Central Plains, including some of the Steed-Kisker phase sites and some of the Nebraska phase sites in the Glenwood locality of southwest Iowa (Roper 1995: 208). Central Plains tradition material culture subsequently becomes identifiable in central and western Kansas and the adjacent portion of Nebraska during the latter part of the eleventh, through the twelfth, and into the thirteenth centuries, during which time Central Plains tradition sites were thriving throughout the region. Numerous central Kansas and some eastern Kansas dates continue into the late thirteenth through the fourteenth or even very early fifteenth centuries, but fewer Central Plains tradition sites are represented in western Kansas and southwest Nebraska by the end of the thirteenth century. The dynamics behind this apparent chronological distribution are reviewed later in this chapter.

MATERIAL CULTURE

In Lehmer's formulation of the Plains Village pattern, its diagnostic traits included a mixed hunting and agricultural subsistence base, semi-permanent villages located adjacent to floodplains, earthlodges with cache pits both inside and between houses, grit-tempered pottery, small projectile points, endscrapers, scapula hoes, and bone hide-working tools (Lehmer 1954a: 139–140). In his formulation of the Central Plains tradition, he suggested that villages typically were small and unfortified, and that the houses were square, with four interior support posts around a central hearth and with the entryway to the east or west. Artifact traits of this tradition's definition included grit-tempered plain or cord-marked pottery vessels with flared or collared rims and tool-impressed decoration, notched arrowpoints, diamond-beveled knives, chipped celts in Upper Republican sites, elbow pipes, deer metapodial bone awls, bone or antler shaft wrenches, and figurines. The dead were disposed of in ossuaries with multiple, disarticulated burials with pottery and other artifacts as funerary objects (Lehmer 1954a: 146). Subsequent phase distinctions, by others, have been based on even more specific partitioning of the variability among assemblages and within artifact classes, and continued work in the last half century has considerably refined what we know about the Central Plains tradition.

Pottery

The basic ceramic vessel form throughout the Central Plains tradition is a grit-tempered globular to subglobular jar, with a circular orifice, restricted neck, and rounded to subangular shoulders that are the widest part of the vessel (Figure 7.3). Vessel walls converge to a rounded or slightly elongated base. Vessel rims may be direct and usually flaring, or they may be collared. "Collared" rims, though, may be true collared rims or S-shaped rims, and collars may vary considerably in height. Variations on these forms, such as a thickened lip or a wedge lip, occasionally are observed (Figure 7.4). The predominant exterior surface treatment is overall vertically oriented cord-marking. Exteriors may also be smooth, particularly in some of the eastern and central Kansas sites, but other surface treatments such as simple stamping are entirely absent. Vessel interiors are invariably smooth, and a very few exhibit a fugitive red wash. When present, and except in rare instances, decoration is confined to the rim and/or the lip. The most common decorative techniques include incising, tool-impressing, and pinching or some other means of producing small nodes. Tool-impressing usually is a lip decoration technique; incising and noding are applied to rim panels. Incised decoration motifs, far more common on collared or S-rims than

Figure 7.3. (at left) Typical Central Plains tradition vessel from the Minneapolis site, 14OT5. Vessel height is 28.5 cm. (Courtesy of the Kansas State Historical Society)

Figure 7.4. (opposite) Variation in Central Plains tradition pottery vessel rims. All sherds from the Minneapolis site, 14OT5, except the sherd on the bottom right, which is from the Kohr House site, 14SA414. (Courtesy of the Kansas State Historical Society)

on direct rims, may consist of parallel incised lines, chevrons, filled chevrons, or occasional other motifs, and they may appear in combination with pinched or gouged nodes. Pinching or noding on direct rims usually appears alone. Handles or lugs may be applied but often are not.

Shell-tempered pottery that Scott (1995) named Majors Opposed Diagonal is a minority ware in some Central Plains tradition assemblages. Shell-tempered vessels are predominantly globular jars with low rolled rims, loop handles, and, if decoration is present, incised or trailed shoulder decoration. They are most common in the east, in Steed-Kisker and Nebraska phase context. Their incidence declines toward the west, to the point that they are absent in the Waconda Lake and Medicine Creek localities, and nearly absent even in the Saline County area. Some shell-tempered vessels in Steed-Kisker context are identified as, or are at least similar to, Ramey Incised vessels from the Cahokia site in the Mississippi River valley. Beck (1995) used petrographic analysis to consider the question of whether the shell-tempered material is trade ware or was locally manufactured, with inconclusive results. It is an important question, though, and it deserves further attention.

A minority grit-tempered pottery vessel form in the Kansas River basin is a small, neckless, globular, almost spherical jar, in the older literature sometimes called a "coconut pot" after the vessel's resemblance to a coconut. The term "seed bowl" is also applied. Cord-marked and undecorated, these vessels are distinct and are explicitly noted when present. The type, however, is not formally defined within any of the pottery typologies.

Bowls appear in Nebraska phase and Steed-Kisker phase sites and in some of the

eastern Smoky Hill phase sites. These vessels are grit-tempered and generally not decorated. They may have attachments comprising lugs or occasionally zoomorphic effigies attached to their rims.

Formal typologies of Central Plains tradition pottery have proliferated over the years. Waldo Wedel (1943: 73–79) first described Steed-Kisker pottery; Calabrese (1969: 69–74) and Chapman (1980: 159) later designated wares and types for this material. J. H. Gunnerson (1952) developed a Nebraska phase typology for the Harvard collections from Sterns's work, and both Ives (1955) and Anderson and Anderson (1960; see also Anderson 1961) adapted it to the Glenwood locality pottery. Waldo Wedel (1959: 183–184) defined Riley cord-roughened as the diagnostic ware of the Smoky Hill phase, without defining types within the ware. Later, Hedden (1992, 1994) defined types of Riley cord-roughened pottery using material from ten central Kansas sites. Waldo Wedel (1934a: 185–188) also produced the initial formulation of Upper Republican phase types, and Sigstad (1969) later formalized the typology. Blakeslee (1999: 103–108) recently presented a separate typology for the Waconda locality pottery. All these typologies deal exclusively with the grit-tempered material, accommodating both the predominant jar form and the bowls, when applicable, but not the neckless "coconut pots" or the shell-tempered vessels.

Typological criteria are consistent. A first distinction is based on rim form, particularly direct versus collared. The distinction between true collars and S-rims may or may not be made, but the other rim form variations are overlooked. The second distinction, which crosscuts rim form, is made on the basis of decorative technique. Incising, tool-impressing, and noding are accommodated, and the lack of decoration is equally definitive. Individual decorative motifs or combinations of decorative techniques are not considered. Overall, typologies are built extensionally (Dunnell 1971: 15–16) from a limited set of material from a limited area. As a result, they are neither exhaustive nor mutually exclusive when used more widely.

Chipped-stone

Chipped-stone assemblages on Central Plains tradition sites usually are reasonably voluminous but are not particularly diverse (Figure 7.5). Their basic composition has been understood for almost a century. Triangular arrowpoints, notched and unnotched, are prominent. Unnotched forms are the more common form in the Nebraska phase sites (Blakeslee and Caldwell 1979; Bozell and Ludwickson 1994); notched forms are more common, often considerably more common, in Smoky Hill and Upper Republican phase assemblages, but unnotched specimens do appear regularly (e.g., Blakeslee 1999; Kivett and Metcalf 1997; Roper 2001a). Notched points occur in several varieties, including side-notched, double side-notched, side- and basal-notched, and, more rarely, other notching combinations. Strong's (1935: 88) "classification chart for chipped points" remains a useful way to unambiguously describe the various combinations of side- and basal-notching and base form that occur, especially since Central Plains tradition archaeologists do not use projectile point type names. Strong's chart, however, does not account for the notable variation in point size, particularly blade size, that is evident throughout the region, nor does resharpening necessarily account for the variability in arrowpoint blade size. The technology involved in arrowpoint manufacture may also vary. Very well-made, exquisitely chipped specimens can be observed in many assemblages, but so also can more casually chipped points, and even forms with fairly minimal chipping to form the specimen.

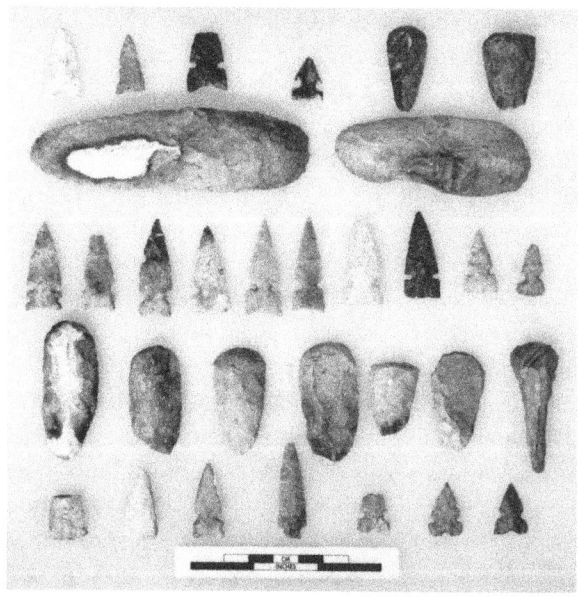

Figure 7.5. Chipped-stone projectile points and scrapers from Central Plains tradition sites. Top row: Albert Bell site, 14SD305. Second and third rows: Minneapolis site, 14OT5. Bottom two rows: Kohr House, 14SA414. (Courtesy of the Kansas State Historical Society)

Bifacial knives in Central Plains tradition assemblages occur in a variety of forms. Triangular specimens, similar in form and proportion but otherwise notably larger than triangular unnotched points, occur regularly. Another common form is the alternately beveled diamond-shaped "Harahey" knife. Variations on this form are elongated and exhibit the characteristic flat-faced cross-section and steep-edge beveling on some part or parts of the outline. Ovoid bifaces may be pointed on one end or rounded on both ends. Large, long, and proportionally very thin ovoid bifaces are occasionally found. They are best described from mortuary context at the Smoky Hill phase Whiteford site (Indian Burial Pit) (Reynolds 1990), but similar specimens, often fragmentary, have been recovered from habitation sites. With the exception of these latter, which are excellent examples of outrepassé flaking, the technology of Central Plains tradition bifaces, like that of projectile points, can vary considerably.

Drills are a usual part of assemblages, though neither ubiquitous nor abundant. Morphologically, they vary considerably in size and haft morphology. Some of the smaller drills may have been used in shell bead manufacture, but the function or functions of larger specimens have not been addressed through microwear studies.

Endscrapers are ubiquitous and common on Central Plains tradition sites. Endscrapers varied more in length than in width. They probably were manufactured on blades or bladelike flakes (Wilke, Carlson, and Reynolds 2002), which would explain the high degree of uniformity in their width. Working ends are convex, steeply retouched, and oriented perpendicular to the longitudinal axis of the blade. Variability in scraper length probably results from a combination of resharpening and unequal blade sizes. Endscrapers may or may not have retouched lateral margins and may or may not have been formed by extensive chipping on the dorsal surface of the blade. Ridges, or keels, on the dorsal surface of endscrapers reflect their origin on blades and also would reinforce the tool against transverse fractures from torsion around the end of the haft.

Chipped celts appear unevenly. They are found in Nebraska phase assemblages and are very common on Upper Republican sites, but absent or rare in Smoky Hill phase sites. These latter, however, have groundstone celts, which the Upper Republican sites do not. Suitable materials for groundstone celt manufacture are largely absent from the Upper Cretaceous and Tertiary landscapes of the Upper Republican phase, however. Chipped versus groundstone celts is a supposed phase difference, but obviously this is less a cultural factor than a geographic factor reflecting locally available raw materials. Chipped celts are thick and have heavy bifaces, rarely exhibiting more than early stage reduction. They often exhibit heavy battering and presumably were used for woodworking, but this is not yet conclusively demonstrated.

Other chipped-stone artifacts include specimens called side scrapers. These are essentially heavily retouched large flakes or blades. Retouched flakes are very common and grade from the "side scrapers" to very lightly retouched or flakes modified only through use. Debitage, of course, is found, and often in considerable quantity. Cores are usually freehand percussion cores and, for all the apparent presence of blades, polyhedral blade cores are largely absent. Blade core platform rejuvenation flakes, however, have occasionally been recovered (e.g., Roper 1999).

When lithic raw materials are reported, assemblages are dominated by cherts that are available locally or, when raw material is not locally available, are from the closest source area. Thus, Upper Republican assemblages are dominated by Smoky Hill jasper (sometimes called Republican River or Niobrara jasper, or Niobrarite), while Smoky Hill phase assemblages are dominated by Permian chert from the northern Flint Hills, and Pennsylvanian cherts predominate in Nebraska and Steed-Kisker assemblages. Rarely, however, are assemblages composed entirely of these local or nearby raw materials—usually a small percentage of the raw material is from sources farther away, and characteristically these are high-quality tool stones. Thus, assemblages from the western sites may have varying quantities of White River Group chalcedonies (particularly Flattop chalcedony) and other materials from the High Plains and Colorado Piedmont, while assemblages from sites in central Kansas may have a small proportion of Alibates agatized dolomite from the Texas panhandle and Florence-A chert from the Kansas/Oklahoma border area of the southern Flint Hills (see chapter 16, this volume, for descriptions of Kansas lithic resources). Obsidian is exceedingly rare in Central Plains tradition sites.

Raw materials were differentially used within assemblages. Projectile points may be the most diverse class in terms of raw materials used. Scrapers were, when possible, preferentially made of high-quality cherts and chalcedonies, and it is in this part of the assemblage that some of the imported raw materials may stand out. Chipped celts, on the other hand, were made of poorly silicified low-quality raw material that probably was somewhat tougher and better suited to the heavy use these implements received than were the higher-quality lithic materials. Expedient tools often are made from local cherts, but may be of imported cherts when they appear in more than incidental proportion (M. G. Hill 1997; Roper 1993: 120–122; 1996a: 142–145).

Technological systems in the Central Plains tradition are not well studied. It is clear that at least some Central Plains tradition flintknappers were producing blades (Roper 1999; Wilke, Carlson, and Reynolds 2002). Percussion techniques varied, with hammerstones attesting to the use of hard-hammer percussion in some places, and antler flakers elsewhere attesting to soft-hammer percussion as the basic reduction technique. Pressure-flaking is ubiquitous for at least certain tool classes, and specialized techniques are occasionally observed.

Groundstone Artifacts

Groundstone assemblages (Figure 7.6) vary considerably in size and diversity, depending on the raw materials locally available for groundstone tool manufacture. Shaft abraders are common, and the most suitable raw material for their manufacture was Dakota sandstone, which outcrops in central Kansas. Not surprisingly, therefore, abraders of this material not only appear but also may be abundant on

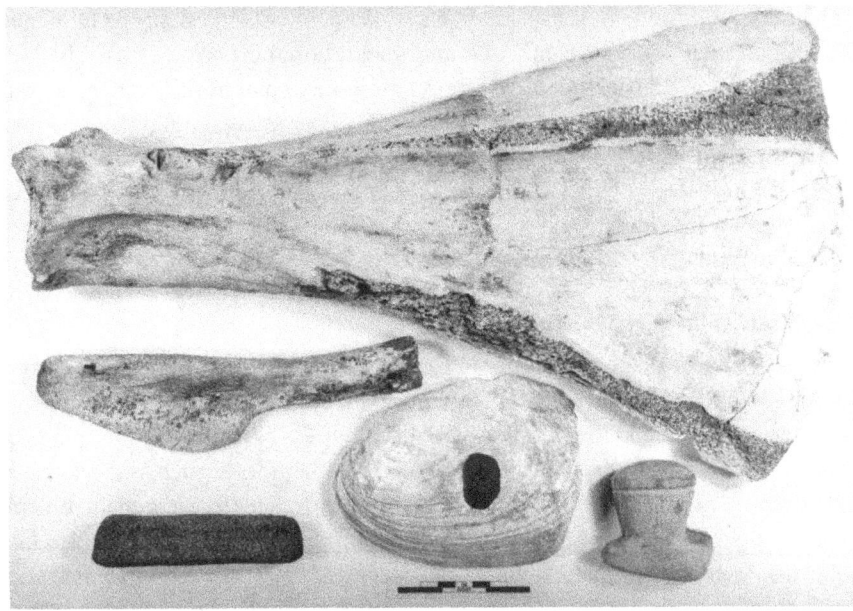

Figure 7.6. Bone, shell, and groundstone tools from Central Plains tradition sites. Bison scapula hoe, squash knife, and sandstone abrader from 14OT5; shell hoe from 14SA402; and pipe blank from 14SA414. (Courtesy of the Kansas State Historical Society)

sites in this area. Farther west, the Dakota formation has no surface expression, and abraders are more likely made of the local Ogallala formation conglomerate, a material that was reasonably well suited for this purpose.

Proximity to sources of Dakota sandstone seems also to be correlated with the appearance, or lack of appearance, of metates and manos. These objects, particularly the large metates, often are prominent on the Central Plains tradition sites in the heart of Dakota sandstone country, but lacking on sites away from sources of suitable material. Metates, when found, are generally large, rectangular objects, with depressions on one face. Manos are fist-size or larger.

As noted above, groundstone celts appear in sites in areas where suitable raw material is available, and conversely, in areas where the tougher cherts used for chipped celts are not available. Groundstone celts are smaller than their chipped counterparts. They feature a distinct bit and poll end, and the bit may be well formed and sharp. Occasional hematite specimens are smaller but no less well formed than groundstone celts of other rock types.

Hammerstones are another object class whose presence or absence seems to be correlated with availability of suitable materials. Hammerstones may be very abundant in the glaciated areas of northeast Kansas and even in central Kansas, which was not glaciated but probably has a considerable quantity of cobbles in river gravels. They are, however, absent in the western part of the area of Central Plains tradition sites.

Other groundstone objects include pipes and pigment. Pipes may be little more than pebbles with two perpendicular and joined bore holes or they may be well-formed elbow or effigy forms carved from limestone or pipestone. Pigments usually are hematite or its earthy form, ochre, available in some stream gravels or as small nodules in the Dakota sandstone. In the Upper Republican sites, where hematite is not locally available, chalk of various hues is found in a condition suggesting it was substituted for true hematite as a pigment.

Bone, Antler, and Shell Objects

Bone, antler, and shell objects appear in Central Plains tradition assemblages in some diversity, although not always in large quantity (Figure 7.6). A basic and common artifact type is the hoe made on a bison or deer scapula by removing the spine and articular end. Scapulae also may be modified into other forms, such as the so-called squash knife. Awls, another common bone artifact, frequently were made on split mammal metapodials and may or may not retain an articular end. Large bird long bones also were used to manufacture awls. Other bone or antler tools include beamers, fleshers, and shaft wrenches. Flakers may appear, particularly where hammerstones are not present, and soft-hammer percussion is evident in the chipped-stone assemblages. Bone beads and tubes, made by ringing and snapping bird bones or, sometimes, smaller mammal long bones, are common. Rare bone ornaments, such as bracelets or bow guards and pendants are known. Bone fishhooks are found from the Missouri River valley all the way west to the Medicine Creek valley and the Albert Bell site (14SD305), each just west of the 100th meridian.

Shell objects were made on freshwater mussel shells. In areas where large heavy shells, particularly of species with ridges on the dorsal surface of the shell, were available, hoes may be made of shell instead of or in addition to scapulae. Shell beads are common and appear in both domestic and mortuary context. Cut shell pendants have also been recovered at a number of both domestic and mortuary sites.

SETTLEMENT

The basic Central Plains tradition dwelling unit was the rectangular lodge. Posts set into the ground framed the walls, and ideally four interior support posts formed a rough square around a central fire hearth (Figure 7.7). Beams laid in crotches of these uprights supported the ends of wall leaners and roof rafters. An entryway extended from one side, usually to the east, southeast, or south, and thus away from the prevailing winds of the colder seasons. The arrangement of large pieces of charred wood on the floors of excavated lodges suggests that rafters probably were not, or at least not always, laid in a radial arrangement, as they consistently were in Historic period lodges, and it is possible that the roofs were flat (e.g., W. R. Wedel 1934b: 223;

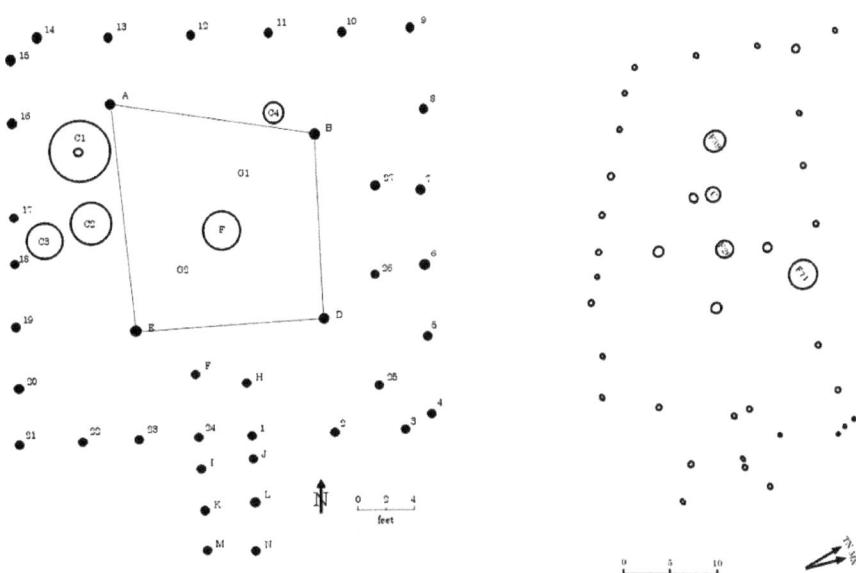

Figure 7.7. Two examples of Central Plains tradition house floor plans

Blakeslee 2002: 176). Also debatable is whether the outer layers of these late Prehistoric dwellings were constructed in the same manner as the outer layers of the Historic lodges. (G. L. Wilson 1934 is an excellent source on Historic period lodge construction; Roper and Pauls [2005] review the variability in lodge construction throughout the Plains Village period of the Central Plains and Middle Missouri subareas.) The presence of grass-impressed daub in many excavated lodge sites, however, suggests that even if they were not fully comparable to their Historic counterparts in construction detail, they were at least wattle-and-daub structures.

Lodges varied in their appearance. Their sizes varied from ca. 4 m to 15 m in maximum dimension, with many toward the middle of this range. Length-to-width proportions varied between about 0.85:1 and 1.15:1, with some outliers and with many near 1:1. The floor plan of some lodges tended more toward circular than rectangular (A. E. Johnson 1973: 224; Roper 2001a: 117, 139; W. R. Wedel 1959: 384). The number of posts observed when a lodge floor is excavated varies considerably from perhaps a dozen or so to well over a hundred. Some of the variability may be a product of lodge design and construction, some undoubtedly represents repair episodes, and some may be a product of excavation techniques and soil conditions at the time of excavation. Available woods also affect lodge size and shape since stronger and more moisture-resistant woods, such as oak, are available only sporadically, if at all, in the western parts of the Central Plains tradition area (Roper 2002c).

The central point of a Central Plains tradition lodge is the hearth, typically basin-shaped and often not stone-lined. Cache pits are another common lodge feature.

Cache pits in a single house number from none to over a dozen, with five or so the modal value. Cache pits are cylindrical to bell-shaped and only occasionally more than a meter deep. Pits may also appear outside the house. Other feature types on a lodge floor might include small basins or "pocket caches" and seemingly extraneous post molds that represent house repair, internal constructions such as beds or dividers, or other internal amenities.

Central Plains tradition sites may contain isolated lodges, but they usually are present in groups ranging from two to two dozen or so. Some of the Nebraska phase sites in the larger river valleys of Nebraska may contain as many as several dozen lodges, but that is rare. Throughout Kansas, Central Plains tradition lodge numbers vary from one, at sites such as the Albert Bell site in Sheridan County, to the two dozen or so at the Minneapolis site in Ottawa County (W. R. Wedel 1934b). The concept of a site is strained in many instances, however, for sites are never fortified, and houses may be only loosely grouped in particular places on the landscape. It is highly debatable as to whether these represent contemporaneous dwellings or whether they are simply accumulations of lodge locations representing dwelling abandonment and rebuilding or reoccupation of favorable locations. Evidence of noncontemporaneity seems clear in some instances, and the argument for rebuilding or reoccupation seems secure in these cases. Some combination of simultaneous occupation of several houses coupled with rebuilding or reoccupation might best account for some of the other cases, particularly the larger sites.

Frequently associated with the lodges are middens that can be a valuable source of subsistence remains and artifacts. Specialized activity areas associated with the lodges and middens have been recognized and investigated in the Upper Republican phase sites in Nebraska's Medicine Creek valley (Roper 2002b: 186–191) and in the contemporaneous sites in the Waconda Lake area of the Solomon River valley of north-central Kansas (Blakeslee 1999). A retrospective look at previously investigated sites such as the Root site (14LC301) in the Wilson Lake area (Witty 1962) and the current analysis of the Albert Bell site suggest that this is more common than has been recognized to date. It presents the Central Plains tradition sites as organized farmsteads, perhaps on the model of those described for some contemporary peasant cultivators in Mesoamerica (e.g., Graham 1994; Killion 1987). This would have far different implications for social and economic organization than would a settlement arrangement featuring small villages or hamlets. Nor should it be assumed that, even if some sites do contain contemporaneously occupied lodges, a village social organization transcended the household.

Sites are found within the valleys of both main rivers and their larger tributaries. Some of the Nebraska phase sites of extreme eastern Kansas and the adjacent area are on river bluffs overlooking large bottomlands, but the more usual location is the front edge of an alluvial terrace or morphologically similar low upland ridge or toe. This type of location placed sites near water and the timber that followed the streams, but above flood levels. It also provided access to the floodplain soils that were best suited for cultivation with bone- or shell-hoe technology and to the rich and varied stream and streamside fauna. Evaluation of site distributions relative to floodplain soils in the Medicine Creek valley shows that known lodge sites are always positioned so that at least a few acres of floodplain soils were available within 400 m of the lodge, and conversely, that otherwise characteristic locations with no lodges often also had no floodplain soils available within 400 m (Roper, unpublished data). If this were found to be the case elsewhere, it might indicate that one factor in the distribution of lodges and their apparent discontinuous distribution (or, conversely, their apparent aggregation) is simply that favorable spots on the landscape were repeatedly used, while less favorable spots were avoided.

SUBSISTENCE

In the 1930s, William Duncan Strong (1933, 1935) startled the anthropological world by suggesting a Late Prehistoric sedentary and agricultural horizon on the Central Plains. His inference was based on the results of excavations at the Lost Creek and other sites and was somewhat remarkable, for although the evidence for sedentism seemed good, the inference of agriculture was not based on the recovery of cultigen remains. Nevertheless, in the same decade, Waldo Wedel (1934a: 185) reported the remains of corn, beans, and squash in Central Plains tradition sites in the Republican River valley, and Guy Whiteford (1937: 7) reported corn from a Smoky Hill phase lodge (Kohr House No. 1, 14SA414) in the Smoky Hill River valley. Strong's conclusion should not have been so remarkable, for Gilder (1907: 715; 1926: 19) and Sterns (1915a: 263) had both previously reported corn and beans from Nebraska phase sites, Sterns even noting that corn "was found in nearly all the sites and in some of them it was very abundant." In the years since, evidence of plant remains has accumulated, albeit slowly, and is yielding a more comprehensive picture of plant utilization (see chapter 15, this volume). As Sterns had found, corn is essentially ubiquitous and usually is the most abundant plant represented in a site. Corn, however, is only one of several important cultigens in these assemblages. Squash (*Cucurbita*), beans (*Phaseolus*), sunflower (*Helianthus*), chenopod (*Chenopodium*), marsh elder (*Iva*), maygrass (*Phalaris*), little barley (*Hordeum pusillum*), smartweed (*Polygonum*), and tobacco (*Nicotiana*) may be present in variable quantities and sometimes as prominent species in an assemblage (Adair 1999, 2003a; Adair, chapter 15, this volume). Tobacco, of course, is not a subsistence plant, but it is a cultigen. Adair (2003a: 311–312), however, suggests that crop diversity was more limited in the western (especially Upper Republican) than in the eastern (Nebraska, Steed-Kisker) Central Plains tradition sites.

Central Plains tradition macrofloral assemblages contain more than cultigens. In sites in the oak-hickory woodlands of the large river valleys of the eastern Central Plains, nuts such as hickory (*Carya*), walnut (*Juglans*), and hazelnut (*Corylus*) may be represented. More widely, chokecherry (*Prunus*), wild plum (*Prunus*), hackberry (*Celtis*), and grape (*Vitis*) have been recovered (e.g., Adair 1999, 2003a; Puseman 1996). Wild or weedy varieties of plants such as goosefoot (*Chenopodium*), knotweed (*Polygonum*), and pigweed (*Amaranthus*) also are found. Although not directly represented by macrofloral remains, the prairie turnip (*Psoralea*) likely was used, as presumably were a variety of other greens and tubers that leave no macrofloral remains.

Just as agriculture included, but did not focus on, corn, so also did faunal procurement include, but not necessarily focus on, bison. Even from the earliest reports (Strong 1935: 100–101), faunal assemblages have routinely showed a high species diversity. Bison (*Bison*) usually is present. Its proportion within an assemblage, however, may vary from almost negligible, as at Medicine Creek valley site 25FT22, House 4, where bison constituted a small fraction of a percent of an assemblage recovered by screening all house fill and floating all feature sediment (Turnmire 1996), to dominant, as at the Albert Bell site, also excavated using comprehensive recovery techniques and currently undergoing detailed analysis. The latter, though, is an unusual case. Also represented in most collections are other ungulates, including white-tailed and/or mule deer (*Odocoileus*), wapiti (*Cervus*), and pronghorn (*Antilocapra*). Medium to small mammals include canids and other carnivores (*Canidae*), lagomorphs (*Leporidae*), and a variety of rodents (*Rodentia*). Birds include waterfowl, raptors, and game birds. Reptiles include both land and water turtles, but little else. Fish, particularly large game fish such as catfish, can be very prominent in collections recovered using fine-mesh screen, and freshwater mussels can also be abundant (Bozell 1991; M. E. Brown 1981; Falk 1969; Turnmire 1996).

Nepstad-Thornberry, Cummings, and Puseman (2002) proposed a model of Upper Republican subsistence that consisted of about 30 percent fauna, 30 percent maize, 20 percent other cultigens, and 20 percent wild plant resources, showing it to be nutritionally complete and adequate, and, with its diversity, able to counteract the risks of a diet that, compared to earlier periods, relied increasingly on cultigens and bison. The picture of Central Plains tradition subsistence that now is emerging, therefore, is one of a generalized or broad-spectrum economy. Agriculture was important. Although corn was an important cultigen, this was not the dual-focus corn-bison economy of later centuries, and both wild plants and smaller fauna were prominent and critical elements of the diet. Put differently, it seems realistic to view Central Plains tradition subsistence as an example of what B. D. Smith (2001) has termed low-level food production.

MORTUARY PRACTICES

Early excavations of Central Plains tradition burial sites found that they tend to be communal, secondary burials often within a natural or constructed mound in eastern sites (Gilder 1909: 76–84; Strong 1935: 266). More recent work at both Nebraska and Steed-Kisker sites in Missouri (Feagins 1988; Finnegan 1977; Nickels 1971; P. J. O'Brien 1977) and Kansas (Calovich Mound, 14WY7; Barnes 1977) confirms that burial in this area also was communal. Funerary objects included pottery and some shell objects. Associations with individuals are unclear, and no analyses of mortuary programs have been attempted.

Farther west, surely the most prominent of all Central Plains tradition mortuary sites is the Indian Burial Pit, or Whiteford site (14SA1), a cemetery in the Smoky Hill River valley near Salina. Here are both primary (62.5 percent) and secondary (32.5 percent) burials of about 151 individuals of both sexes and ages ranging from fetal/neonatal to old adult (45+). Primary burials are flexed and laid with the head generally to the south but randomly placed on one or the other side. Secondary burials consist of crania alone and also were laid with the vault to the south. Funerary objects are relatively sparse and consist mainly of ceramic vessels, ceremonial knives (Reynolds 1990), and shell bead necklaces, with an occasional other object (Roper 2005a).

The Whiteford site cemetery is in a moundlike but natural rise (a small sand dune) in the river bottoms. A careful analysis of other mortuary sites shows that the Central Plains tradition people routinely interred their dead in rises not of their own construction, which is to say either natural rises or mounds built by their Woodland predecessors in the region. Particularly notable are the Central Plains tradition burials in the mounds that Floyd Schultz excavated in Clay and Geary counties (Eyman 1966; see also Krause 1995b: 137). Secondary burial seems to have been the predominant but not exclusive mode of burial. Well-reported primary burials are scarce enough that it is not possible to readily determine how they were oriented in the ground and how that and other aspects of the mortuary program compare with that of the Whiteford site.

Still farther west, Central Plains tradition ossuaries are documented in southern Nebraska and northern Kansas (Strong 1935; Thies 1982). The individual primary, extended burials on a bluff top overlooking 25FT13 in the Medicine Creek valley are unique for the Central Plains tradition (Kivett and Metcalf 1997: 56). One of the most common contexts from which human remains were recovered in the valley, however, is house floors, cache pits, and middens (Kivett and Metcalf 1997: 170). These are not complete skeletons, and most certainly they are not formal burials, and what they represent is one of the unsolved problems of archaeology in this region.

Compliance with the Native American Graves Protection and Repatriation Act (PL 101-601; 25USC 3001 *et seq.*), the Kansas Unmarked Burial Sites Preservation Act (KSA 75-2741 to 2754), and other repatriation or reburial requirements has served to bring together much information on burials of the Central Plains tradition and other cultures in Kansas. Much of this work, however, has been the requisite documentation of the individual cases held (or formerly held) at the various institutions practicing archaeology in the region. To date, a synthesis of Middle Ceramic period mortuary practices is lacking. A recent study of the Whiteford site (Roper 2005a), with its attempt to put that cemetery into a broader regional context, takes a step toward addressing this.

POMONA: A NON–CENTRAL PLAINS TRADITION MIDDLE CERAMIC PERIOD COMPLEX

A prominent Middle Ceramic cultural complex of eastern Kansas that has never been considered part of the Central Plains tradition is Pomona, variously called a focus (Witty 1967, 1981: 78–79) and a variant (K. L. Brown 1985). Pomona sites are recorded throughout the eastern quarter of Kansas, from Doniphan to Cherokee to Morris counties (Figure 7.8) and also are identified in western Missouri. Their distribution crosscuts drainages, with sites in the Missouri, Kansas, Marais de Cygnes, and Arkansas (Neosho and Verdigris) river drainages. In physiographic terms, Pomona sites in Kansas are found almost throughout the Dissected Till Plains and Osage Cuestas and into the eastern Flint Hills. Their distribution, at least in the northeast part of the state, is largely complementary to that of Central Plains tradition sites.

Pomona chronology has always been difficult to assess since the suite of available dates is small, contains many unreliable age determinations, and seems to encompass a large amount of time (see Appendix). Excluding the Gakushuin age determinations and one other early and seemingly anomalous date (I–11165), 28 calibrated dates place Pomona around cal A.D. 700 to 1500. This, of course, makes the earliest Pomona earlier than the earliest Central Plains tradition and the latest Pomona later than the latest Central Plains tradition (in northeast Kansas, at least). This seemingly long time range need not be a problem, although surely more age determinations on well-selected samples are needed.

Pomona material culture has been analyzed in considerable detail by K. L. Brown (1985: 129–386). Pomona differs from Central Plains tradition material culture more in detail than in overall composition. The pottery resembles eastern Central Plains tradition in many ways except for its distinctive paste and temper (Witty 1981: 80). The original definition of Pomona pottery was that it was tempered with crushed sherds or indurated clay and that grit temper was lacking (Wilmeth 1970: 26; Witty 1967: 2–3). Since then, grit-tempered pottery otherwise identified as Pomona has been reported (B. G. Williams 1986: 29). The basic vessel form is a jar, apparently globular or nearly so, with a circular orifice, restricted neck, and cord-marked exterior. Rims may be direct and flaring or a channeled rim that externally resembles a collared rim. Decoration is very rare.

Chipped-stone inventories include triangular side-notched and unnotched arrowpoints similar to Central Plains tradition specimens. They also include small corner-notched arrowpoints and larger corner-notched or stemmed dart points similar to those of Woodland tradition complexes. Other forms of bifaces appear, but do not include the distinct diamond-shaped knives so characteristic of the Central Plains

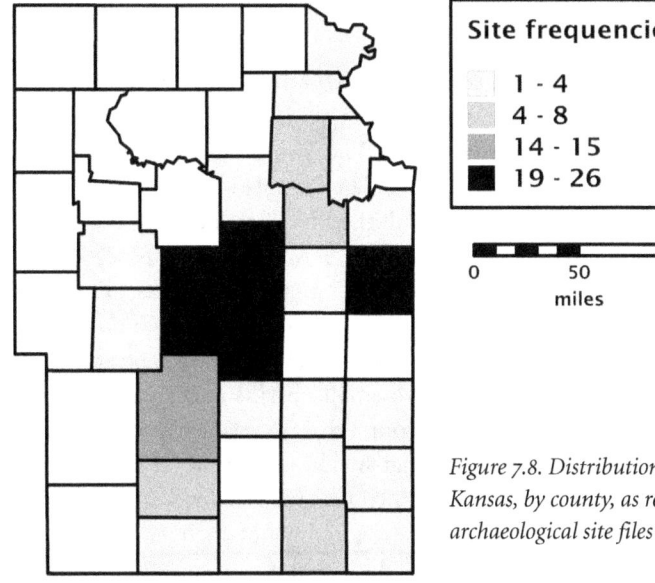

Figure 7.8. Distribution of Pomona sites in Kansas, by county, as recorded in the Kansas archaeological site files

tradition. Endscrapers are common, as are the usual assortment of retouched flakes, expedient tools, and debitage. Groundstone tools include shaft abraders and some celts. Bone tools are not common, possibly because they are not preserved in the more acidic soils of the eastern part of the state.

Small houses have been excavated at several Pomona sites (Brogan 1982: 29–34; A. E. Johnson 1968: 29–34, 56–62; Schmits 1980b: 137–149; Williams 1986: 16–18; Wilmeth 1970: 20–25; Witty 1981: 22–269, 1982: 29–38). These are small, ovoid, pole-and-thatch constructions. Sites may contain multiple houses, but, as with Central Plains tradition sites, they may simply represent reuse of particular locations and accumulations of noncontemporaneous houses. Features within and outside houses include hearths, small storage pits or basins, and rock concentrations.

Subsistence is not well documented, because of both poor preservation of faunal remains in particular and lack of comprehensive recovery techniques in most excavations on Pomona sites. The two best-documented floral assemblages are those from 14AT2 and 14BO319 (the Roth site). Storage pits at 14AT2 yielded goosefoot, pigweed, bulrush (*Scirpus* sp.), grass (*Sporobolus* sp.), walnut, and one partial corn kernel (Williams 1986: 46–47). Similarly, a few Roth site soil samples subjected to flotation yielded goosefoot, smartweed, bedstraw (*Galium* sp.), wild grape, and pecan (*Carya illinoiensis*) (Brogan 1982: 65–66). The few faunal remains that have been recovered are the expected large mammals. Mussel shell also was prominent at the Hart site (14OS305) in Osage County (Wilmeth 1970: 40–41).

Mortuary practices are poorly documented. Witty (1967: 2; 1981: 80) indicated that, at the single excavated mortuary site (14OS312), inhumations were made in individual graves covered with limestone slabs. Bodies were flexed and placed with the head to the south or southeast in this particular case. Funerary objects included ceramic vessels.

An important site that does not fit comfortably within Pomona or any other recognized cultural complex is the Two Deer site (14BU55) in the El Dorado Reservoir area of Butler County (Adair and Brown 1981). The Two Deer site pottery shares some similarities with Pomona and some of the late Woodland complexes (Greenwood, Cuesta) of southeastern Kansas and with the Bluff Creek complex of south-central Kansas. The predominance of bone temper, however, distinguishes it from these other complexes. Chipped-stone tools, including the arrowpoints, are similar to many Early and Middle Ceramic period assemblages from throughout eastern Kansas. Two excavated structures seem to be ovoid and probably were wattle-and-daub constructions. Features were limited to small hearths and shallow pits or basins. Flotation yielded carbonized seeds from a diverse set of plants, including squash, maize, domesticated sunflower and marsh elder. Radiocarbon age determinations (see Appendix, Pomona section) obtained when the site was excavated suggest an early eleventh century (calibrated) date; recently obtained AMS dates obtained on corn and marsh elder are fully consistent with this (see Appendix, cultigens section).

DISCUSSION

Two observations made earlier in this chapter are keys to understanding what the Central Plains tradition represents, other than a set of material culture traits of the Middle Ceramic period on the Central Plains. One of these is the identification of the Central Plains tradition as a low-level food production society; the other is the overall later dates of first appearance of Central Plains tradition culture in a progressively westward direction. Woodland tradition people were less sedentary than were the Central Plains tradition people, and agriculture, while in evidence at least at the end of the Woodland period, was as yet limited and was considerably more limited than it was among contemporaneous Woodland societies to the east in the Prairie Peninsula (Adair 1996, 2003a; Johannessen 1993). The trend during the time of the Central Plains tradition, therefore, was toward greater sedentism and an intensification of agriculture, including an increase in crop diversity. Maize, in particular, became considerably more important. The other cultigens, some of which had appeared during the late part of the Woodland period, were still used, as were wild and weedy plants and a diverse terrestrial, aquatic, and avian fauna. In a real sense, then, the Central Plains tradition occupied an intermediate position between the reduced mobility and incipient, but limited, agriculture of the Woodland tradition and the village-based intensive maize-beans-squash agriculture and communal bison hunting of the period from about the fifteenth century on. Empirical models of the transition to farming in Neolithic Europe reflect this same three-step sequence of the increasing importance of cultigens. On the first step, foraging remained dominant, but cultigens accounted for a small portion of subsistence. On the following step, the use of cultigens substantially increased and farming strategies were developed even as foraging was still conducted. On the final step, cultigens became dominant and foraging was insignificant (see also Zvelebil 1986; 1996: 324–325). In this view, then, the Central Plains tradition is a major step in, although not quite the beginning of, the neolithization of the Central Plains. Beyond being merely a transitional stage, though, it represents a distinctive adaptive system that must be studied in its own right.

Turning to the chronological data, plotting the radiocarbon dates by their geographical position (Roper 1995) indicates that the Central Plains tradition, as identified by its material culture traits, first becomes identifiable in the Steed-Kisker phase area of western Missouri and in the Glenwood locality of southwestern Iowa (Billeck 1993). The earliest dates for the Central Plains tradition in the more westerly localities are overall later and appear to reflect a time-transgressive appearance of Central Plains tradition assemblages and styles in an overall westerly direction. This is an important observation, but per se implies nothing about the mechanism of the expansion of this material culture complex. That is, it does not preclude nor require an influx of people and their expansion (much less a movement) throughout the Kansas River basin (see Roper 2005b for a considerably expanded discussion).

To begin to put these two points together, it is pertinent to observe that although maize has been dated to as early as ca. A.D. 100 in the Mississippi River valley it was a minor element of the diet there for about a millennium. Its use, however, was greatly intensified after about A.D. 800 in that area of the valley associated with the Mississippian societies at Cahokia and surrounding polities (Fritz 1990: 397–398). Maize-centered agriculture subsequently spread throughout the western Mississippi River drainage basin in the following four or so centuries, reaching the portion of the Missouri River valley in what is now northwestern Missouri and southwestern Iowa (as well as places to the north such as the Mill Creek phase area of northwest Iowa and the Cambria area of southwest Minnesota) probably in the tenth or early eleventh century. In the Central Plains, and specifically in the area considered in this chapter, it spread along the valleys of the rivers composing the Kansas River basin during the later eleventh and especially the twelfth century, reaching the limits allowed by rainfall adequate for agriculture sometime in the twelfth century. In this view, the material culture traits that epitomize the Central Plains tradition, while representing a seemingly notable change in styles from the earlier Woodland tradition assemblages, can also be viewed as the introduction and development of the technology of a sedentary population partially dependent on maize and other starchy seeds and a diverse fauna. This technology would include sturdier housing, storage facilities (cache pits), hoes, and cooking pots designed with thinner walls and a more globular body, each of which would better conduct heat to more thoroughly cook the starchy foods (Braun 1987). It also would include a settlement pattern in which the permanent habitations were placed on elevated ground but near the diversity of resources necessary for fulfilling the daily needs of a sedentary population. These would include water for drinking and cooking; the floodplain soils suitable to a bone- or shell-hoe agricultural technology; timber for lodge construction, firewood, and what may have been a notable assemblage of wooden objects, none of which preserves; and the diverse fauna of the streams, stream banks, and bottomlands. Dispersing small farmsteads along the stream valleys would allow each farmstead to satisfy its needs with minimal travel, except perhaps to procure larger and more mobile game.

Zvelebil and Lillie (2000: 60–67) proposed several possible mechanisms for the similar transition in the European Neolithic. One of these, which they called Individual Frontier Mobility, may approximate the situation in the Central Plains. Individual Frontier Mobility operates "through contact and partner exchange [that] involves mostly single individuals or small groups linked by kinship, who move between hunter-gatherer and farming communities within the framework of established ties, marriage alliances, trading/exchange partnerships, or other social ties of reciprocity and obligation" (62–63). Individuals moving across this frontier, not necessarily people who differ in a social, political, or linguistic sense, are adults who carry with them new foods and techniques for raising them, as well as their technologies and styles as encoded in ceramics and probably other aspects of material culture.

Under such a scenario, the Central Plains tradition, including the Steed-Kisker phase, represents a continuity of population whose subsistence regime and material culture was modified by the assimilation of a small proportion of adult individuals bearing the new technology and probably also by contacts through exchange across long-established trade routes essentially paralleling the Missouri River. As Alfred E. Johnson (1992: 134) pointed out, developments in the Kansas City area mirrored those in the Mississippi River valley for millennia, a statement that resonates well with J. A. Brown, Kerber, and Winters's (1990: 258; italics added) comment about "development of new, *and the revival of old,* trade networks" at the time of the Emergent Mississippian period in the Mississippi River valley. This might suggest not a succession of immigrants, but cyclical renewal and lapsing of contact and exchange between the two areas.

The eastern phases of the Central Plains tradition, then, began as the agricultural frontier reached the eastern edge of the Central Plains; the rest followed as the frontier passed up the Kansas River and the streams that converge to form the Kansas River. The exception, though, may have been the Dissected Till Plains, where the Pomona culture appears to reflect the persistence of a less sedentary and largely foraging lifeway. This need not mean that two separate and distinct cultures coexisted in the region—only that some members of the population did and some did not adopt the new agricultural and technological system. The few cultigens recovered from Pomona sites and the Two Deer site do not contradict this, for very limited agriculture did precede the beginnings of the Central Plains tradition. Continued casual cultivation by overall foraging people is possible; nor should the possibility be overlooked that corn was obtained by exchange with neighbors and relatives more committed to agriculture.

A corollary, or perhaps a result, of this passage of the frontier along the waterways is the form in which styles, particularly ceramic styles, are distributed across the Central Plains. As we have seen, some of the purported phase differences, such as chipped versus ground celts or presence/absence of Dakota sandstone metates, are as much products of the types of locally available resources as culturally conditioned raw material selection. Ceramic typologies have tended to follow the designation of phases and have reified the arbitrary division of the Central Plains tradition into phases. But both phases and ceramic typologies were defined for specific collections from widely scattered localities. As areas between these localities are investigated, it becomes more and more clear that ceramics show more of a style continuum than a series of discrete style clusters. Further, stylistic gradients may follow rivers from east to west, and styles vary more noticeably from river valley to river valley than along a single river valley. To be sure, what we might term microstyle zones are recognizable and probably reflect loosely conceived communities, but the borders are fuzzy. The goal should be to create a single ceramic typology for the entire Central Plains tradition or, better yet, to dispense with typologies and instead develop a system based on paradigmatic or attribute analyses of pottery assemblages. Some (e.g., Beck 1998; Bozell and Ludwickson 1999: 29; Gilliland 2003; Roper 1996a: 85–96) have done this on a site-specific basis. An expansion of these analyses to develop a single analytical system applicable across the entire Central Plains tradition would better serve the study of ceramic variability.

The Middle Ceramic period mode of life was not monolithic across the Central Plains. Evidence from the Medicine Creek valley and probably also the Albert Bell site convincingly indicates that agriculture was practiced as far west as 100° W longitude. Yet the evidence suggests that the agricultural system, while sufficiently productive, was not stable—that is, yields of both cultigens and weedy or wild foods varied over runs of years (this is readily observed in the present). Independent evidence suggests that the valley was cyclically abandoned and reoccupied, probably in response to variability in resource yield. The system, however, while somewhat unstable, was nevertheless sustainable, or at least persisted for a century and a half or so (see Marten 1988 on the concepts of productivity, stability, and sustainability in agricultural systems). To the east, where annual precipitation was higher, and where crop diversity also was higher, system instability probably was less marked and periodic abandonment less a factor.

The Central Plains tradition lifeway, somewhat varied as it was across the region, flourished in the Kansas River basin to the 100th meridian throughout the twelfth and into the thirteenth century. The chronological evidence, though, suggests that by the latter part of the thirteenth century, the western part of the region was substantially abandoned, never really to be reoccupied by permanent agriculturalists until the influx of Euro-American farmers in the late nineteenth century. This may have been triggered by a decline in agricultural system sustainability. But, contrary to some proposed scenarios (cf. Blakeslee 1993), there was no overall dramatic event of the people of the Central Plains tradition picking up and moving north, but rather the less dramatic and more gradual process of a contraction in the area permanently settled by people bearing a Central Plains tradition culture. Radiometric evidence suggests a continued presence of at least some Central Plains tradition people in eastern Kansas and adjacent parts of Nebraska, Iowa, and Missouri at least through the fourteenth century, with their disappearance perhaps sometime near the end of that century. It is hard to see a decline in agricultural system sustainability as a factor here, but the apparently increasing presence of, and pressure from, Oneota culture peoples in and near the Missouri River valley (Henning 1998b) may have rendered untenable the continued occupation of the area by people of the Central Plains tradition. As good a guess as any is that they contracted to the north, becoming part of the St. Helena phase and Initial Coalescent variant. Pomona, which appears to persist somewhat longer in eastern Kansas, is found away from the larger valleys and also south of the area where Oneota intrusions are most in evidence.

The situation was different in central Kansas. Here, abundant radiometric evidence attests to a continued occupation by people with a Central Plains tradition material culture through the fourteenth century, and possibly even into the early fifteenth century. The area of this continued occupation was west of the Dissected Till Plains of northeast Kansas and east of the Blue Hills, and thus in the Flint Hills and immediately adjacent Smoky Hills (Schoewe 1949: 276) in the lower parts of the valleys and drainages of the rivers that contributed to the upper Kansas River proper. Or, in culture-history terms, the Smoky Hill phase lasted longer than the Upper Republican phase and is identifiable throughout much of the fourteenth and possibly even the early fifteenth century. Again, sustainability of the agricultural system probably was not a particular problem. This late Central Plains tradition occupation was in an area essentially adjacent to that of the White Rock phase and was contemporaneous with it, thus contradicting the notion of an Oneota "hegemony that quickly led to the displacement of the [Central Plains tradition]" (Logan 1998a: 263).

The Central Plains tradition disappeared from the upper Kansas River watershed sometime in the fourteenth or possibly the early fifteenth century, and it is obvious that this involved depopulation rather than a transformation to a new material culture complex. This depopulation likely occurred as Smoky Hill phase people or their descendants joined people of the Pratt and other complexes of southern Kansas and adjacent areas to "become" the Great Bend aspect, probably more specifically the Little River focus of the Great Bend aspect. Some assemblage characteristics of late Smoky Hill phase sites, such as is seen in the collection from the late thirteenth-century/fourteenth-century Markley site house (14OT308) (Roper 2001a: 122–137), seem to anticipate Great Bend aspect assemblages. Further, the Little River cord-marked pottery of early Great Bend sites, such as 14RC306, is largely identical to the

Riley cord-roughened pottery of the Smoky Hill phase sites (except for paste and temper details—but this likely reflects the characteristics of the locally available clays), and lithic raw material use patterns also are similar. The presence of occasional Florence-A chert and Alibates agatized dolomite in Smoky Hill phase sites and the occurrence in the Whiteford site of a Crockett Curvilinear Incised vessel and large ceremonial knives resembling those at Spiro are among the indicators of existing Smoky Hill phase connections to the south, as perhaps, going the other way, is the presence of Flint Hills cherts in the contemporaneous Pratt complex levels of the Lewis site (Ranney 1994; S. C. Vehik 2002a). In essence, folding the last of at least parts of the Smoky Hill phase into the early Great Bend works temporally does not really require a spatial displacement of any note and can be seen in material culture contributions to the emerging Great Bend culture.

This leaves, then, the problem of the identity of the descendants of the Central Plains tradition, which is to say, Is the Central Plains tradition ancestral Pawnee, as has been suggested or outright claimed in some form since the publication of Strong's (1935) seminal Nebraska monograph? The answer is a nicely definitive "yes and no." No, in the sense that the Historic-period people called the Pawnee did not have a single origin. Yes, in the sense that the cultural traditions from which the Pawnee emerged were at least partly formed as Central Plains tradition peoples joined with others. And further no, in the sense that the Central Plains tradition is not wholly and exclusively ancestral Pawnee. Obviously, then, this is not a productive way to ask the question.

A better approach to the problem is to inquire into the nature of the relations among the Central Plains tradition, the Great Bend aspect, the Lower Loup phase, the Wichita, and the Pawnee. As discussed in chapter 14 of this volume, prior to the late eighteenth century two divisions of the Pawnee were recognized (Skiri and South Bands, or *Panimaha* and *Pani*), and no single term denoted all the people who came to be called Pawnee. This and other evidence suggests separate origins for the two divisions, and the situation in the Central Plains in the fifteenth through seventeenth centuries provides a mechanism. By the late fourteenth century/early fifteenth century, what had been the Central Plains tradition was merging into either the Initial Coalescent variant of the Middle Missouri subarea to the north or the Great Bend aspect of central Kansas to the south of the area of the Central Plains tradition. Between them, at least for a time, and perhaps driving something of a wedge between them, were the Oneota communities in the Missouri River valley and, west of the Missouri River, the White Rock aspect, which may represent a Siouan (Oneota) intrusion into the Central Plains (Logan 1998a).

The time-honored scenario, which would derive the Protohistoric Pawnee Lower Loup phase of east-central Nebraska from the Extended Coalescent variant of South Dakota (itself derived from the Initial Coalescent variant) might, with some wrinkles, approximate the historical trajectory leading to the Arikara and the Skiri; but only the Skiri band of the people came to be called Pawnee. Tradition holds that the

South Bands were once one, the Kawarahki, and that they arrived in the Historic Pawnee heartland in the Loup and Platte river drainage from the south, differentiating into the three Historic bands after, or at least as, they arrived. Several lines of evidence suggest that the Kawarahki may, prior to their northward movement to the Platte River valley, have been people whose material culture archaeologists call the Great Bend aspect. Of course, the Great Bend aspect is generally regarded as Wichita. Both Pawnee and Wichita, though, are names for closely related peoples of the eighteenth century to the present, while both the Central Plains tradition and the Great Bend aspect are archaeological cultures of earlier times. As Barth (1969: 38) has pointed out, culture need not be constrained by ethnic boundaries, indicating, of course, that cultures and ethnic groups are not necessarily synonymous. The problem here is that when we talk of the Central Plains tradition we are talking about a culture, but when we talk about the Pawnee we are talking about an ethnic group or society, and it is difficult to make the equation. The problem is further complicated by the extensive culture change and flux in ethnic group configuration on the Plains in the Protohistoric period. Inasmuch as the Great Bend aspect is at best only partially derived from the Central Plains tradition, and the Initial Coalescent variant is at best derived from only a part of the Central Plains tradition, an ancestor-descendant relation between the Central Plains tradition and the Pawnee cannot be monolithic; nor can an ancestor-descendant relation between the Central Plains tradition and the Great Bend aspect be monolithic; nor can the Great Bend–Wichita equation be monolithic. Certainly, therefore, a Central Plains tradition–Pawnee equation cannot be monolithic either. Identifying all of these cultures and ethnic groups as Northern Caddoan, however, seems warranted.

8. The Late Prehistoric on the High Plains of Western Kansas: High Plains Upper Republican and Dismal River

Laura L. Scheiber

Late Prehistory in western Kansas (approximately A.D. 1000–1750) is represented by at least two distinct archaeological signatures: the High Plains Upper Republican and the Dismal River cultural complexes. The gradual intensification of horticulture and more settled lifeways characterized this period on much of the Plains. Native peoples differentially acted and reacted to these changes, spending some of their time as foragers and some as farmers. One of the challenges for the archaeologist is to recognize the differences and fluidity between foraging and farming ways of life and to realize that the same people may have been involved in both practices. On the Plains, the term Late Prehistory refers to the approximately 800 years before active European settlement, or from the pre-contact era about 1,000 years ago through the Late Prehistoric/Protohistoric transition about 250 years ago. In the archaeological literature, the two periods that fall within these 750 years are sometimes referred to as Middle Ceramic and Late Ceramic. I will provide a brief overview of major archaeological topics for each of these periods, including typology and history of investigations, site distributions, recent investigations, chronology, subsistence, trade and contact, and settlement patterns. In the final section, I will summarize the similarities and differences between these periods and suggest some avenues for future research.

Western Kansas is part of the High Plains, which are on the western edge of the Central Plains and extend from the Pine Ridge escarpment at the South Dakota/Nebraska border to the Llano Estacado in the Texas Panhandle (Fenneman 1931; Mandel, chapter 2, this volume). Wide expanses of short-grass plains, occasionally bisected by stream and river riparian zones, characterize the area (J. H. Gunnerson 1987). Although professional archaeological research on the High Plains of Kansas has been limited (McLean 1996), the Upper Republican and Dismal River cultures have also been studied in adjoining states.

HIGH PLAINS UPPER REPUBLICAN

Typology and History of Investigations

The Upper Republican phase of the Central Plains tradition (A.D. 1000–1350/1400) is documented at localities such as the Medicine Creek area of south-central Nebraska (Grange 1980; Kivett 1949; Roper 1996a; Roper, chapter 7, this volume; W. R. Wedel 1935a) and the Solomon River area of north-central Kansas (Blakeslee 1999; Krause 1970; Lippincott 1978) (Figure 8.1). Most Upper Republican archaeological sites are small farming hamlets with many earthlodge traces, although it is unclear how many of these semisubterranean houses were simultaneously occupied (Geisel 1999). Houses of the Central Plains tradition are typically square to rectangular with extended entry passages and four central roof-support posts around a central fire hearth, with subfloor storage pits and several associated extramural features or middens (Steinacher and Carlson 1998). Typical material culture includes globular cord-marked pottery vessels, triangular side-notched and unnotched projectile points and preforms, bifacial knives and choppers, scrapers, flake tools, celts, sandstone abraders, hammerstones, bison scapula hoes and knives, bone tools and ornaments,

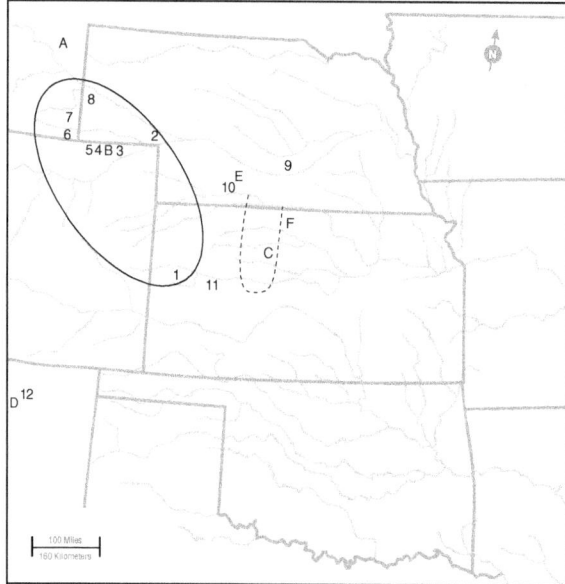

Figure 8.1. High Plains Upper Republican site distribution. 1. Coal-Oil Canyon (14LO201); 2. Ash Hollow Cave (25GD2); 3. Donovan (5LO204); 4. Peavy (5LO1); 5. Biggs (5WL27); 6. Seven Mile Point (48LA304); 7. Gurney Peak Butte (48LA302) and Gurney Peak Bench (48LA305); 8. Signal Butte (25SF1); 9. Hulme (25HL28); 10. Mowry Bluff (25FT35); 11. Pottorff (14LA1); 12. Northern Rio Grande Pueblos. A. Hartville Uplift; B. Flattop Butte; C. Smoky Hill jasper (several locations within dotted line); D. Jemez Mountains obsidian sources; E. Medicine Creek locality; F. Solomon River locality. Solid line indicates the approximate distribution of High Plains Upper Republican sites.

shell beads and ornaments, and spindle whorls for use in spinning thread (Bozell and Ludwickson 1998a; Logan 1996a) (see also Figures 7.3 to 7.6).

Related sites to the west of this "core" area have been known since the 1930s (E. H. Bell and Cape 1936; Champe 1946; Strong 1935). These sites contain material culture similar to that of the Upper Republican sites to the east, including distinctive cord-marked pottery, triangular side-notched projectile points, beveled-edge knives, tubular bone beads, and bone and shell ornaments. Yet these western sites lack evidence of houses and horticulture, which are criteria used to define the Upper Republican phase (and Central Plains tradition in general) in the traditionally defined core areas.

These western sites are known more for what they lack (houses, hoes, and corn) than for what they possess. Many archaeologists include High Plains sites in their discussions of the Upper Republican phase, calling these people either local populations, an unnamed subphase within Upper Republican, or simply "High Plains Upper Republican" (Logan 1996a; Roper 1990, 2002b). However, ceramic sherds and vessels in both areas share identical forms, construction techniques, and styles (W. R. Wood 1971). Comparisons of ceramics from several sites on the High Plains and Central Plains reveal that variations in mean number of design elements per rim and rim type (collared or flared) do not vary according to geography (Midgett and Reher 1996; Reher 1973).

Two issues are relevant for this discussion: (1) How do we classify the sites located in western Kansas and in the adjoining areas to the west? (2) What is their relationship to the Central Plains tradition sites of eastern and central Kansas? Our understanding of the relationships among the village groups composing the Central Plains tradition (e.g., Upper Republican, Smoky Hill, Nebraska, Itskari) who lived at approximately the same time was originally based on location and differences in the ceramic assemblages found in the various areas, where "each is a regional adaptation to available resources of the Central Plains–tradition pattern" (Bozell and Ludwickson 1998a: 131). Besides some variation in architecture and ceramic styles, the main differences seem to be based on the river valley or valleys in which the material culture is found. Certainly people from these villages interacted with one another, although whether they conceived of themselves as loosely related or ethnically distinct is unknown. The sites on the High Plains, however, are neither well contained in space, nor is the material culture clearly distinct from that found at contemporaneous Kansas and Nebraska villages. Although these western cousins present problems for a neatly ordered typological framework, they are nonetheless essential for gaining a more complete picture of Upper Republican (and Central Plains tradition) lifeways.

Site Distribution

High Plains Upper Republican sites are distributed over a wide area in northeastern Colorado (Reher et al. 1994; Scheiber 2001; J. J. Wood 1967; W. R. Wood 1971), southeastern Wyoming (Reher 1973; Reher and Scheiber 1999), western Kansas (Bowman

1960; McLean 1996), and southwestern Nebraska (Bell and Cape 1936; Champe 1946; Strong 1935). To date, more than 50 sites have been documented (Scheiber 1997). Some of the better-known or more recently investigated sites include Signal Butte (25SF1) (Strong 1935), Ash Hollow Cave (25GD2) (Champe 1946), Gurney Peak Butte and Bench (48LA302/305) (Reher 1973; Reher and Scheiber 1999), Donovan (5LO204) (Reher et al. 1994; Scheiber 2001), and Coal-Oil Canyon (14LO1/401) (Bowman 1960; McLean 1996). Most of these sites are located along bluffs and rock outcrops with views of the surrounding areas (Eighmy 1994). Some of these butte-top sites, especially those in southeastern Wyoming, have limited access and may have been preferred for their defensive advantages (Reher 1973). The sites in southeastern Wyoming are located more than 400 km (250 miles) from the hamlets at Medicine Creek, whereas the sites in western Kansas are much closer to the farming communities, approximately 160 km (100 miles) from the Solomon River area.

Sites in Kansas

Located in the middle of the High Plains, Upper Republican sites in western Kansas lie between the better-known village sites and the clusters of identified High Plains campsites to the west. The best documented is the site of Coal-Oil Canyon. This site is strategically located at the eastern and southern edge of the High Plains Upper Republican landscape and, as such, plays an important role in understanding interactions between east and west as well as north and south. Coal-Oil Canyon lies along a tributary of the Smoky Hill River in Logan County, Kansas, 80 km (50 miles) farther west than the site of Pottorff (14LA1), which has the westernmost earthlodge feature in Kansas known to date (W. R. Wedel 1959; Witty 1978). The Kansas Anthropological Association (KAA) excavated the Coal-Oil campsite between 1955 and 1960 (Bowman 1960). Under the direction of Peter Bowman (Bowman 1960), KAA placed test excavations in almost 20 different areas around the canyon. A recently published history of investigations and artifact analysis summarizes and clarifies the earlier work (Bowman 1996; McLean 1996).

Although the site spans several time periods, occupations dating to the Middle Ceramic or Upper Republican are the best represented. No radiocarbon dates have been obtained. More than 2,000 ceramic sherds, representing more than 40 vessels, were recovered (Roper 1996b), along with more than 600 arrowpoint fragments and other diagnostic lithic materials (Bowman 1960). Large quantities of bison bone were also present, but following the standard field methods of the day, much of it was immediately discarded. No evidence of house foundations was uncovered. Although the material culture inventory is fairly similar to that found at other High Plains Upper Republican sites, especially in terms of lithics and faunal remains, the number of ceramic vessels is much higher, resembling counts of pots recovered from village sites (Blakeslee 1999; Kivett and Metcalf 1997; Reher 1973; Reher and Scheiber 1996). Perhaps these vessels were cached at the site for future visits by Upper Republican travelers. A majority of the analyzed pottery sherds from Coal-Oil campsite are chemically similar to ceramics found at sites to the north in Nebraska and to the west in Colorado, although it is likely that most pots at the site were made of local clays (Roper et al. 2004).

Recent Investigations

Currently, archaeologists from the High Plains Archaeology project are actively researching several High Plains Upper Republican sites, focusing their attention on southeastern Wyoming and northeastern Colorado (Reher 1989; Scheiber 1997). The most extensive work has been conducted at the Donovan site, a multiple occupation processing/hunting camp located in the South Platte River drainage of northeastern Colorado. Containing at least 11 stratified Upper Republican cultural levels or occupations, this site was occupied and reoccupied for at least 200 years by several generations of Upper Republican peoples (Reher et al. 1994; Reher and Scheiber 1996). Numerous stone tools, small side-notched projectile points, ceramic sherds, bone beads and ornaments, and heavy densities of stone debitage and bone fragments have been recovered, using modern archaeological recovery techniques. Absolute dates from the Donovan site suggest that the earliest occupation probably occurred in the decades shortly after A.D. 1000, and the last occupation probably occurred 200 to 300 years later (between A.D. 1240 and 1380) (Scheiber and Reher 2000).

Of the more than 16,000 artifacts that have been point-plotted, more than half are butchered bison bone fragments (Scheiber 2001). The faunal assemblages from the first and last levels provide evidence for intensive bone disarticulation and processing of at least ten bison at this site, which is located away from the kill locale. Although separated by time and generations, the methods of butchery and discard and the spatial organization of activities changed little between the two occupations. Despite these redundancies in the practice of animal processing, the kinds of activities undertaken narrowed by the last Upper Republican occupation. The families who first occupied the Donovan site practiced a range of domestic activities in addition to marrow and bone grease extraction, including cooking, tool maintenance, and hide preparation. The last occupants instead focused more specifically on pemmican production (Scheiber 2001, 2005). The presence of fewer than expected scapulae and metapodials (bone elements made into agricultural and hide-scraping tools in eastern sites) may indicate exchange or transport to eastern village sites.

Temporal Framework and Absolute Dates

As currently understood, the florescence of the Upper Republican phase in the Central Plains occurred between A.D. 1000 and 1250, followed by a less intense occupation lasting until the mid- to late-1300s (Blakeslee 1999; Ludwickson and Bozell 1998). One of the difficulties in defining and discussing this time period on the High

Plains is a paucity of good chronometric dates, although this is slowly changing (Scheiber 2001; Scheiber and Reher 2000; W. R. Wood 1967).

Dates obtained from several High Plains sites, such as Donovan, Peavy (5LO1), and Biggs (5WL27) in northeastern Colorado and Seven Mile Point (48LA304) in southeastern Wyoming, suggest that the High Plains Upper Republican phase of the western area lasted from the first decades of the A.D. 1000s until well into the 1300s, which means that the High Plains were first occupied as early as the hamlets at Solomon River in Kansas and at Medicine Creek in Nebraska. After utilizing resources on the High Plains and potentially living there for years, these Upper Republican groups left the region at the same time as the villages in the east were abandoned.

Subsistence and Diet

Hunting in the High Plains primarily focused on bison, although deer, rabbit, and pronghorn were also commonly procured (W. B. Butler 1997). This pattern differs from the more diverse animal taxa recovered on the Central Plains, at least in terms of specimen frequencies (number of identified specimens) if not diet diversity (Bozell 1991, 1995; M. E. Brown 1981; Falk 1969; Koch 2004; Scheiber and McCabe 2003; Turnmire 1996; Watson 1996). Faunal remains from the hamlet sites include large and small mammals, amphibians, fish, and reptiles. Upper Republican groups have been characterized as broad-spectrum hunter-gatherers who also practiced horticulture, or as subsistence generalists who farmed and hunted in different areas depending on resource zones (Blakeslee 1999; Bozell 1991, 1995; Roper 1990), not unlike Fremont peoples who occupied the Great Basin in Utah during roughly the same time (Kelly 1997; Madsen and Simms 1998).

The importance of bison hunting, especially long-distance hunting, once emphasized by archaeologists (W. R. Wedel 1986: 123–126; W. R. Wood 1971: 80–81), has been minimized recently in favor of a consideration of more localized hunting strategies (Bozell and Ludwickson 1998a: 132). At many of these eastern sites, bison account for only a small part of the faunal assemblage (Blakeslee 1999). However, all of these faunal remains were recovered from village sites. Larger bison bones may have been left behind at primary butchering areas (Koch, Nelson, and Bozell 1999). The many bison scapula farming implements in Central Plains sites may have originated from local hunting (in which case we lack evidence for these locations), from trade with western High Plains groups, or from hunting expeditions on the High Plains by Central Plains residents (Bozell and Ludwickson 1998b: 557). The actual number of bison locally available to farming hamlets and the consequent travel distance to obtain these bison resources, however, is unknown.

Given the environmental limitations, horticulture on the western High Plains is unlikely. The characterization of High Plains residents as nonhorticultural is based on a lack of recovered cultivated macrobotanical remains as well as the absence of plant processing and gardening tools such as the bison scapula hoes commonly found in the eastern sites. If scapulae (either unfinished or as formal hoes) were being traded or brought back to the east, their numbers should be lower than expected in the assemblages of the western sites, which they are.

Evidence for Contact and Trade

Trading networks have been documented throughout all of the Central Plains tradition phases, both between the Central Plains villages and to more remote areas such as the southern Plains and the American Bottom (Bozell and Ludwickson 1998b; Logan 1996a; Logan and Ritterbush 1994). The presence of exotic goods and artifact styles at these sites usually indicates exchange. For instance, nonlocal resources in assemblages of Upper Republican sites at Medicine Creek may reflect interaction with the Texas panhandle (lithics), the Midwest (freshwater snails), the Southwest (malachite and turquoise), and the Southeast (conch shells) (Logan 1996a; Roper 1988: 531; W. R. Wedel 1986: 111). Turquoise and malachite at Medicine Creek house sites are evidence of trade between Upper Republican people and the Southwest pueblos, perhaps via Antelope Creek phase peoples (a possible Caddoan group) on the Southern Plains (Brosowske and Bevitt, chapter 11, this volume; Roper 1988).

Archaeologists also acknowledge that some villagers of the Central Plains tradition may have moved to new areas to take advantage of trading contacts. Nebraska phase groups moved along the Missouri River after A.D. 1250, possibly to "interdict the export of bison products to, and the import of status symbols from, the Mississippian-period Cahokia site in Illinois by Initial Middle Missouri tradition and Mill Creek people via the Missouri River" (Bozell and Ludwickson 1998b: 557). It seems reasonable to suggest that if the people of the Central Plains were moving to different areas to take advantage of various trading opportunities, they may have also expanded into the western area for the same reason.

Evidence for trade and contact between the western High Plains and other areas is primarily based on material sourcing of lithics and ceramic clays. For instance, the Donovan site lithic assemblage contains small quantities of Smoky Hill jasper (also known as Republican River jasper), a brown-yellow-red jasper that outcrops in numerous locations within north-central Kansas and south-central Nebraska (Holen 1991; Reher et al. 1994; W. R. Wedel 1986). Additionally, some of the ceramics recovered from the Donovan site are made of clays from the Medicine Creek area (Cobry and Roper 2002; Roper et al. 2004). More widespread trading networks are suggested by obsidian found at the Gurney Peak site in southeastern Wyoming. Several flakes came from one of the Valles Caldera obsidian sources located in the Jemez Mountain of north-central New Mexico, a distance of approximately 640 km (400 miles) (Glascock, Kunselman, and Wolfman 1999; Scheiber and Reher 2000).

Similarly, site assemblages in the east commonly contain nonlocal lithics from the High Plains, most notably purple-gray Flattop Chalcedony from the Flattop quarry in northeastern Colorado (Greiser 1983; Hoard et al. 1992; Hoard et al. 1993;

Miller 1991). Average assemblages usually contain no more than 2 percent Flattop, although a few sites in both the Medicine Creek and Solomon River areas have produced much higher percentages of this nonlocal resource (closer to 20 percent) (Blakeslee 1999; Roper 1996a).

Bison scapula hoes and other bone tools may also have been imported from the west (Blakeslee 1999; Bozell 1995). The high frequency of bison scapula hoes in Central Plains sites could be evidence for nonlocal procurement strategies since the number of animals represented by scapula tools is much higher than other unmodified bison bone at various village sites (M. E. Brown 1982; Drass and Flynn 1990; Fishel 1999a; Gilbert 1969; P. C. Johnson 1972; Ludwickson 1978; White 1953; 1954: 258; J. J. Wood 1967: 184). For example, at the Hulme site (25HL28), an Upper Republican village in Central Nebraska, the number of individual bison counted when considering only unmodified bison bone is 1, whereas the number of individuals based on bison scapulae is 20 (Bozell 1991). Similarly, 86 percent of the bison bones from the Mowry Bluff site (25FT35) are tools and scapula fragments (Falk 1969). The bison must have been hunted and processed somewhere away from the villages, but these other sites have generally not been found (Bozell 1995).

Overall, ties between the Donovan area in northeastern Colorado and the Medicine Creek area seem to be stronger than those between Donovan and the Solomon River area. Perhaps future investigations will demonstrate a stronger connection between the western Kansas and south-central Colorado and Solomon River sites.

Settlement Patterns

One of the central issues of High Plains Upper Republican sites is understanding why these people were on the High Plains. Beginning in the 1930s, archaeologists recognized Central Plains tradition pottery in the western area and presumed that these sites represented hunting parties from the east, similar to the activities of several historic tribes such as the Pawnee and the Arikara (Bell and Cape 1936; W. R. Wood, ed., 1969). Several early publications list these sites as evidence of long-distance hunting trips (Lehmer 1954b). Others countered that local resources were sufficient on the Central Plains for year-round residency and that the High Plains site assemblages were more extensive and incorporated too many local High Plains resources to be the result of hunting parties alone (Reher 1973; W. R. Wedel 1970c; W. R. Wood 1971, 1990).

If hunting parties created the sites on the High Plains, the recovered material should conform to the definition of a "hunting camp." However, Central Plains tradition hunting camps have not been found archaeologically. Instead, we have evidence of hunting camps from Protohistoric Pawnee (Lower Loup phase) archaeological sites in Kansas and Nebraska, as well as written descriptions of Pawnee hunting from the 1830s (Roper 1991b, 1992, 1994). Roper (1990, 2002b) and others (Bozell 1995; Steinacher and Carlson 1998) have demonstrated, though, that these models are probably not best applied to Late Prehistoric settlement strategies. This does not mean that the High Plains Upper Republican sites are not hunting camps or that people at the High Plains sites were unrelated to those in the Central Plains, or even that the High Plains ceramics were necessarily locally produced. The important point to keep in mind is that Upper Republican subsistence and settlement strategies do not appear to conform to models based on a dual economy focused on corn and bison.

High Plains Upper Republican Summary and Conclusions

In recent literature, the High Plains Upper Republican continues to await "proper classification" (Bozell 1995; Bozell and Ludwickson 1998a: 131). While the inhabitants were not likely to be simple hunting parties, neither were they just "local" populations. Not knowing how to classify these sites, archaeologists routinely cite the same debate. The mechanism by which the "Upper Republican culture" arrived in the western parts of Kansas and adjacent areas remains unexplored. Trade for acquiring buffalo meat and other products from peoples of the western fringe is occasionally mentioned, but an understanding of how the people in this vast area related to one another and to the people in the more constricted "core" area remains largely unknown.

Several ways of conceptualizing these groups have been proposed (Steinacher and Carlson 1998). I advocate that Upper Republican hunting parties from the east moved west as part of their seasonal movement, soon after intensification of horticultural practices and construction of the first earthlodges. After several years or generations, these hunting parties essentially moved onto the High Plains and re-created their identity there, possibly considering themselves a new people, what we recognize archaeologically as High Plains Upper Republican. Whether or not this scenario is correct, if it can ever really be teased apart, the High Plains Upper Republican people are more than mere satellites of a larger phenomenon. At the same time, neither were they totally independent of the activities occurring in the east. High Plains Upper Republican should be considered the western manifestation of the Central Plains tradition in an east-west continuum. The sites in western Kansas have strong potential for further elucidating these relationships.

DISMAL RIVER

Typology and History of Investigations

The Dismal River aspect refers to a Late Ceramic or Protohistoric archaeological manifestation (A.D. 1675–1725) that incorporates a large area of northwestern Kansas, western Nebraska, eastern Colorado, and southeastern Wyoming. Sites that are characteristic of this period were first identified along the Dismal River in the Sand Hills of west-central Nebraska during the early 1930s (Strong 1932; 1935: 212–217). By 1935, Waldo Wedel (1935b: 181) began calling this the "Dismal River culture." Investigators from the University of Kansas, the University of Nebraska and Nebraska State Historical Society, and the Bureau of American Ethnology of the Smithsonian Institution excavated several Dismal River sites between 1898 and 1949. The most well-studied Dismal River sites are in Nebraska, and many of them were excavated under the auspices of the Works Project Administration (WPA) and the River Basin Survey (RBS) Projects.

Based on his excavations at White Cat Village (25HN37) in Harlan County, Nebraska, John Champe (1949) linked the Dismal River material culture with Protohistoric Athabascan-speaking Plains Apacheans, using both cartographic and ethnohistoric data. Although this correlation has been generally accepted for 50 years (J. H. Gunnerson 1960; Schlesier 1972), some continue to disagree (Opler 1971, 1982). The Gunnersons, especially James Gunnerson, have been the most influential synthesizers of this material and have published numerous articles and books on the subject (D.A. Gunnerson 1956; J. H Gunnerson 1960, 1968, 1987; Gunnerson and Gunnerson 1971). Most of the published summaries of the Dismal River aspect are based on excavations at three sites: White Cat, Lovitt (25CH1), and the Scott County Pueblo or El Cuartelejo (14SC1). However, the degree to which these sites represent the norm in Dismal River lifeways or are unique situations is not currently known. Researchers should, therefore, be aware that many lists of traits draw heavily on only a few examples.

Dismal River sites are characterized by the presence of triangular, side-notched and un-notched projectile points (Figure 8.2) and distinctive gray-black pottery with smooth or stamped surfaces (Figure 8.3) (Champe 1949; J. H. Gunnerson 1960, 1968). The northern sites located in Nebraska are sometimes further assigned to the Stinking Water phase of the Dismal River aspect (A. T. Hill and Metcalf 1941), while the

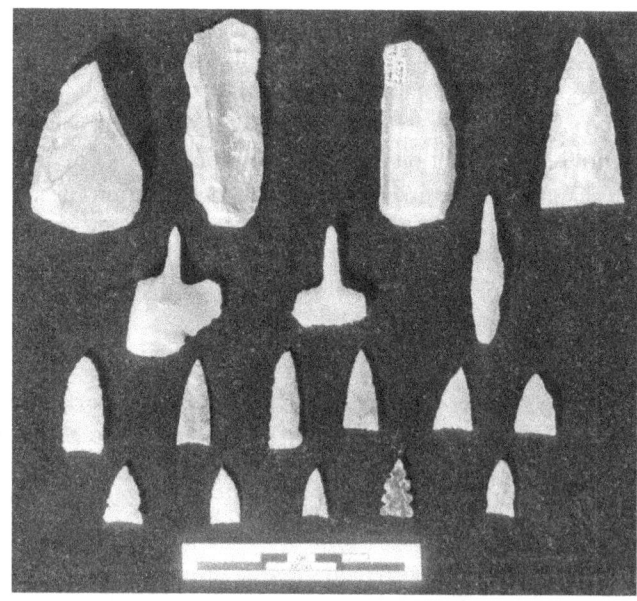

Figure 8.2. Stone tools from 14SC1 (El Cuartelejo, Scott County Pueblo). Top row: scrapers, alternately beveled knife at far right. Second row from top: drills. Third and fourth rows from top: projectile points. The dark projectile point in the bottom row is made of obsidian. (Courtesy of the Kansas State Historical Society)

Figure 8.3. Reconstructed Dismal River pottery vessel from 14SC1. Vessel height is 16 cm. (Courtesy of the Kansas State Historical Society)

Kansas sites are at times referred to as the Scott phase (W. R. Wedel 1959), based on differences in pottery styles. Likewise, the eastern portions of the culture area in Nebraska and Kansas are occasionally paired together as Eastern Dismal River and considered separate from the Western Dismal River sites in Wyoming and Colorado (Brunswig 1995), again based on differences in pottery. These differences probably relate to regional variation in production techniques and design styles but may not necessarily indicate separate groups.

Semi-permanent circular residences measuring 4.5 to 7.6 m (15 to 25 feet) in diameter with five main posts around a central hearth have been documented at several Dismal River sites (Champe 1949; J. H. Gunnerson 1968; A. T. Hill and Metcalf 1941). These structures may have been covered with poles, grass, and packed earth. Bell-shaped roasting or baking pits are also common, ranging from 1.5 to 2.4 m (5 to 8 feet) in diameter and 60 to 90 cm (2 to 3 feet) in depth (Champe 1949; A. T. Hill and Metcalf 1941; W. R. Wedel 1959).

Site Distribution

Dismal River sites extend from the Sand Hills of west-central Nebraska to just south of the Smoky Hill River of west-central Kansas, and from the Goshen Hole in southeastern Wyoming to the Republican River in south-central Nebraska (Figure 8.4). Sites have been identified along the Dismal River in Hooker County, Nebraska (Strong 1935), Stinking Water Creek (a tributary of Frenchman's Creek) in Chase County, Nebraska (J. H. Gunnerson 1960; A. T. Hill and Metcalf 1941), Medicine Creek in Frontier County, Nebraska (W. R. Wedel 1935b: 180–182), Prairie Dog Creek (near Harlan County Reservoir) in Harlan County, Nebraska (Champe 1949), and Ladder Creek (a tributary of the Smoky Hill River) in Scott County, Kansas (W. R.

Figure 8.4. Dismal River site distribution. 1. El Cuartelejo (Scott County Pueblo, 14SC1); 2. White Cat Village (25HN37); 3. Lovitt (25CH1); 4. Nichols (25DN1); 5. Humphreys/ Matthews (25HO21); 6. Ash Hollow Cave (25GD2); 7. Petsch Springs (48LA303); 8. Northern Rio Grande Pueblos. A. Hartville Uplift; B. Flattop Butte; C. Smoky Hill jasper (several locations within dotted line); D. Alibates Quarry. Solid line indicates the approximate distribution of Dismal River sites.

Wedel 1959; Witty 1983b). Farther west are sites in Ash Hollow of Garden County, Nebraska (Champe 1946), and along Horse Creek and Lodgepole Creek in Laramie County, Wyoming (Reher 1973). Other sites are not well documented but are found scattered between these concentrations and also farther south and east into Colorado (Brunswig 1995; J. H. Gunnerson 1960).

Sites in Kansas

The most well-known Dismal River site in Kansas is the Scott County Pueblo (14SC1) located in the Ladder Creek valley, south of the Smoky Hill River. The site is one of the identified locations of El Cuartelejo, a set of villages described in early Spanish accounts associated with the Cuartelejo Apache (see D. A. Gunnerson 1956; A. B. Thomas 1935). Known to local European and Euro-American settlers as early as the 1880s (Williston 1899), this large site consists of a seven-room pueblo structure and associated Dismal River middens. Many additional concentrations of Dismal River archaeological deposits have also been identified throughout the valley (Witty 1983b).

Investigators have conducted a number of archaeological excavations both around and within the Scott County Pueblo structure, often referred to as El Cuartelejo. S. W. Williston and Handel T. Martin, geologists from the University of Kansas, exposed the walls of the pueblo and excavated within the structure in 1898 and 1899 (H. T. Martin 1909; Williston 1899; Williston and Martin 1900). In addition to thousands of artifacts, they uncovered several slab-lined fireplaces, a small oven, and an adobe grinding trough (measuring more than 60 by 90 cm [2 by 3 feet]). Small postholes in most rooms suggest ladders for ceiling entrances into the rooms (Witty 1983b). Under the auspices of the Smithsonian Institution, Waldo Wedel returned to the site in 1939 but focused on the refuse pits and middens located around the stone building (W. R. Wedel 1940, 1959). In his excavations, Wedel recovered almost 4,000 ceramic sherds (W. R. Wedel 1959: 441). He writes that the site "middens yielded potsherds and artifacts of stone, bone, and horn, as well as rare objects of copper, iron, and glass. Charred maize, and squash or gourd rinds indicate horticulture, but quantities of animal bones suggest that subsistence was mainly through hunting" (W. R. Wedel 1940: 83).

James Gunnerson, then of Northern Illinois University, uncovered two Dismal River house floors less than a mile from the main part of the site in 1965 (J. H. Gunnerson 1968). In 1971, Thomas Witty, Jr., and the Kansas State Historical Society reexcavated the pueblo structure and adjacent area. At that time, the architecture was reconstructed as part of an interpretive display in the Scott County State Park (Witty 1971, 1983b). In addition to these formal projects, Scott County Pueblo has also been visited by local collectors throughout the years (Witty 1983b). All of the work at the site makes Scott County Pueblo the "most frequently excavated site in Kansas" (Reynolds 1996). More recently, reanalysis of the excavated materials from the Witty project was conducted at the University of Kansas, and the results were presented in a Plains Anthropological Conference symposium. Analysis of two large features (one with Dismal River pottery, no corn, and high quantities of bison bone, and the other with southwestern pottery, burnt corn, scapula hoes, and low quantities of bison bone) suggests different hunting strategies possibly corresponding with two distinct residents of the site (J. A. Jacobson 2004).

Several archaeologists have focused their attention on the interpretation of the pueblo architecture itself, believing it to be the remains of a structure built by refugees from the northern Rio Grande Pueblos of Picuris and/or Taos during the late seventeenth and early eighteenth centuries. These puebloan people would have traveled approximately 480 km (300 miles) north and east in order to reach modern-day Scott County. Documentary and artifactual evidence does not refute this assessment, although proving it has been difficult (W. R. Wedel 1986). Some material culture is diagnostic of the Southwest, but features and artifacts that are common and distinctive to Dismal River sites (e.g., stone, pottery, bones) compose most of the recorded materials (W. R. Wedel 1959; Witty 1983b). Figure 8.3 shows a variety of stone tools from the site, and Figure 8.4 shows a reconstructed Dismal River pottery vessel.

The site was probably occupied by both Dismal River peoples (who were more than likely Plains Apache) and one or more pueblo groups from the Rio Grande. As one of the only Protohistoric archaeological sites on the High Plains with possible corroborating written documentation and as a site demonstrating evidence of daily contact between two or more identified groups on the Plains, this site provides a unique opportunity for unraveling some of the questions about Plains-Pueblo relationships.

Chronology and Dating

Current evidence suggests that Dismal River people occupied the High Plains minimally between A.D. 1675 and 1725 (J. H. Gunnerson 1968; Logan 1996b; W. R. Wedel 1986), although Patricia J. O'Brien (1984a) widens this date range to A.D. 1525–1725. The more commonly cited A.D. 1675–1725 assessment is based on several criteria: tree ring dates obtained from charcoal from four sites in the late 1940s (Champe 1946; J. H. Gunnerson 1960; A. T. Hill and Metcalf 1941: 205; Weakly 1946), the presence of a limited number of European-manufactured trade goods (Champe 1949; Strong 1935), cross-dating with Rio Grande ceramic sherds and pipe fragments (Witty 1983b), and the lack of horse bones, which presumably would be more common in later assemblages (J. H. Gunnerson 1960). Two recently reported AMS radiocarbon dates of macrobotanical remains from the Scott County Pueblo are starting to fill the gaps in knowledge (A.D. 1463–1638 and A.D. 1640–1949) (see Appendix).

The "end" date range of A.D. 1725–1750 seems to be relatively secure, primarily because of the sparsity of more European-introduced materials in site collections. The beginning date, however, could potentially be pushed back several decades or more if Dismal River is securely associated with Apachean people, who may have migrated through the High Plains as early as A.D. 1300–1400 (Palmer 1992). Additionally, it is still unclear if the entire geographic area was occupied at the same time, sequentially over time, or in different areas on a seasonal basis.

Diet and Subsistence

People associated with the Dismal River aspect used a range of subsistence practices, from a mixed economy of hunting and farming in the east to more broad-based hunting and gathering strategies in the west. Several archaeologists have suggested that hunting and the gathering of wild plants actually dominated Dismal River subsistence strategies, while farming was an occasional enterprise (J. H. Gunnerson 1960; W. R. Wedel 1986). However, very few formal analyses of faunal remains or botanical remains have been conducted.

Dismal River groups primarily hunted bison, although other species have been identified, including pronghorn and deer, beaver, fox and dog, small mammals, fish, turtles, and birds (J. H. Gunnerson 1960; Jacobson 2004; A. T. Hill and Metcalf 1941). The presence of numerous scrapers, knives, and fleshers suggests that people spent a significant amount of time preparing bison hides (Champe 1949; J. H. Gunnerson

1960; W. R. Wedel 1986), in addition to drying and eating the meat. Edible wild plants recovered from Dismal River sites include wild plums, chokecherries, and black walnuts (J. H. Gunnerson 1960; A. T. Hill and Metcalf 1941; W. R. Wedel 1959: 440).

These communities also practiced at least some horticulture, as shown by corncob fragments, charred corn (*Zea mays*) and squash (*Cucurbita pepo*), and scapula digging tools and hoes (Adair 1996; J. H. Gunnerson 1960; A. T. Hill and Metcalf 1941: 196; H. T. Martin 1909; Williston 1899). Other cultigens such as watermelon (*Citrullus* spp.) appear for the first time in the archaeological record during this time, possibly coming from the southwest (see chapter 15, this volume). Food was also probably prepared by baking or roasting in large, often bell-shaped pits, although the kind of food processing that they represent remains unclear.

Culture Contact, Mobility, and Trade

Evidence for contact or trade between Dismal River people living on the High Plains and other groups, particularly those in the Southwest, is indicated by the presence of Euro-American–manufactured metal (such as an ax found in a hearth at White Cat Village), gunflints, catlinite, turquoise, micaceous ceramics, and puebloan painted pottery (Champe 1949; J. H. Gunnerson 1960; A. T. Hill and Metcalf 1941; Roper 1996b; W. R. Wedel 1959). However, these materials do not occur in high quantities. Perhaps Dismal River Apachean people occasionally traded prepared buffalo hides for agricultural products at New Mexico pueblos as part of a Plains-Pueblo regional interaction sphere (Habicht-Mauche 1995; Spielman 1991; S. C. Vehik 2002a). The lack of these materials is another indication of an earlier time frame. Euro-American–introduced materials become more common later in the eighteenth and nineteenth centuries.

Other methods for determining interaction and settlement patterns rely on sourcing traditional items, such as lithics used to make stone tools and clays used to make ceramic vessels. These types of analyses have for the most part been descriptive, rather than quantitative, and await more formalized studies (but see T. Butler 1997; Roper 1984–1985). Most of the raw material at the eastern sites in Nebraska and Kansas consists of Smoky Hill jasper (T. Butler 1997; J. H. Gunnerson 1960; W. R. Wedel 1986). This yellow-brown silicified chalk is found along tributaries of the Smoky Hill and Republican rivers in north-central Kansas and south-central Nebraska, indicating that Dismal River groups in the eastern areas obtained most of their raw material from local or nearly local sources. Alibates agatized dolomite from the Texas panhandle, more than 300 kilometers (200 miles) south, is also present at Scott County Pueblo (T. Butler 1997; Witty 1983b).

On the other hand, Dismal River sites in southeastern Wyoming instead contain materials from the closer Hartville Uplift in eastern Wyoming, i.e., Hartville Cherts and Spanish Diggings Quartzite (Reher 1973, 1991). Interaction or travel from west to east is not well expressed in terms of raw material procurement, although at least one site in the Medicine Creek valley may have contained materials from Hartville (Roper 1984–1985).

As long ago as 1932, Strong noted the "rather common occurrence" of obsidian at Dismal River sites (Strong 1932: 152). Since that time, small quantities of obsidian continue to be recovered and observed in Dismal River assemblages (Champe 1949; J. H. Gunnerson 1960; A. T. Hill and Metcalf 1941: 192; Strong 1935: 217; W. R. Wedel 1959: 455). Roper (1984–1985) suggests that obsidian found at Dismal River sites macroscopically resembles northern sources near Yellowstone in northwestern Wyoming and eastern Idaho. However, more recently Hughes and Roper (1999: 80) imply that pieces of obsidian from Dismal River sites are likely from southwest sources because of the presence of other southwestern materials at these same sites. Clearly, until actual source analyses are conducted, various assumptions cannot be substantiated. Obsidian has also been recovered from several sites in southeastern Wyoming. X-ray fluorescence data from these sites suggest that some of the obsidian came from southern sources in New Mexico, while other pieces originated at northern sources in the Yellowstone area (Reher and Kunselman 1990).

Dismal River Summary and Conclusions

Dismal River is a Late Prehistoric/Protohistoric cultural complex that extends across much of the High Plains. People associated with this material culture practiced mixed subsistence strategies, including some maize horticulture in the eastern sites. Resource use focused on locally available items, although some material was obtained from outside the vicinity, especially in areas to the south.

If the Dismal River archaeological complex is the material manifestation of Plains Apachean peoples (and overwhelming evidence points in that direction), then the wide distribution of Dismal River sites may be the result of multiple bands or divisions of Apaches, such as the Cuartelejo Apache in western Kansas and the Paloma Apache in the Sand Hills of Nebraska (Roper 1984–1985; Schlesier 1972). Based on ethnographic evidence, Dolores and James Gunnerson believe that some of the northern groups may have later become the Kiowa Apache, while others joined the Jicarilla and Lipan Apaches during the early eighteenth century (Gunnerson and Gunnerson 1971; D. A. Gunnerson 1974). Farther west in Wyoming and Colorado lived either different unnamed bands or these same eastern groups during different parts of the year.

Although connecting Dismal River archaeological sites with historically known groups is appealing, several questions remain unanswered. For instance, how typical over the broader area are the few sites that serve to define Dismal River? To what degree did these people rely on horticulture, and for how long during the year did they stay in the more settled communities? Do the sites in this large area represent sequential occupation or seasonal occupation by the same or related peoples or more permanent territories of unrelated groups? And finally, what is their relationship (if any) to the Central Plains tradition/Upper Republican?

CONCLUSIONS AND GOALS FOR FUTURE RESEARCH

In summary, the last 750 years of prehistory in western Kansas reflect dynamic changes occurring throughout the Plains and provide crucial links in the long-term histories of several Native American groups. The diagnostic criteria used to define these sites are clear. Ceramic and projectile point styles have been studied and identified for more than 60 years. Archaeologists also have some ideas about the subsistence practices of the groups of people in this broad region, although the relationship between farming and foraging practices, and farmers and foragers in general, remains uncertain. The diagnostic artifacts for both periods are found across wide areas but are recognized mainly based on "types" defined at the eastern villages, not the western sites.

Archaeologists studying Upper Republican and Dismal River peoples have been preoccupied with linking these complexes with cultural identities, especially how and why the High Plains Upper Republican differ from the other Central Plains tradition phases and how Dismal River materials relate to the ethnohistoric accounts of the Plains Apache. The current prevailing opinion is that Upper Republican and Dismal River peoples probably moved across large areas and practiced diverse lifeways within specific regions. Cultural identity was reflected and expressed in unique ways within these various river valleys, although connections among groups were maintained.

The transitions between the peoples and cultures of the Upper Republican phase and the Dismal River aspect are not clear. Many of the stratified sites on the western Plains represent multiple occupations, in which Dismal River levels overlie Upper Republican levels. The relationship between the Upper Republican and Dismal River occupations is rarely considered (instead separating time into tidy packages of Middle Ceramic and Late Ceramic), even though the migration of Central Plains tradition peoples during the late 1300s might be related to early Athabascan arrivals.

Although both groups occupied a similar area, practiced a range of subsistence strategies, and are primarily defined by their distinctive ceramic vessels and small triangular arrowpoints, numerous differences exist as well. For instance, the large Dismal River baking pits are absent in Upper Republican sites, whereas Central Plains tradition storage pits are absent in Dismal River sites. Domestic architecture also varies between groups, especially in the eastern sites where house features have been recovered. The use of nonlocal resources, especially lithic raw materials, suggests an east-west movement and exchange during the Upper Republican phase (with Flattop Chalcedony found in the east and Smoky Hill jasper found in the west) but more of a north-south trend during the Dismal River time period (with Alibates and obsidian found in High Plains sites). Archaeologists are just beginning to unravel some of these questions, extending traditional debates of typology to include other ecological and social issues.

Early archaeologists studying these sites on the High Plains focused primarily on typology and classification of material remains. Further work from recent excavations and the reanalysis of old collections using more sophisticated theoretical and methodological approaches have led to new interpretations of the variability within High Plains Upper Republican and Dismal River lifeways. These results will contribute greatly to our understanding of the dynamics of Kansas prehistory. Additional questions can be better explored with further problem-oriented research:

1. Researchers can conduct multi-scalar analyses that explicitly incorporate both macroscale models of hunter-gatherer and farmer interaction and microscale daily activities at single sites.
2. Researchers can reanalyze museum collections, specifically targeting the materials that can be sourced, such as lithics and ceramics, as well as faunal and paleoethnobotanical remains. Although biased recovery techniques hamper some kinds of analyses, preliminary assessments written 50 years ago often represent the only data that were collected.
3. Researchers can conduct fine-scale excavations at selected sites, focusing on intensive recovery techniques.
4. Researchers can participate in interregional collaboration. Because these cultural groups are found within the modern boundaries of four states, special efforts would help combine and synthesize data, resources, and conceptual frameworks.

9. Late Prehistoric Oneota in the Central Plains

Lauren W. Ritterbush

The Oneota tradition is an Upper Mississippian complex best known from archaeological investigations in the Midwest. Oneota sites in that region have been dated between about A.D. 1000 and the earliest portion of the Historic period. Several well-known, but until recently little-studied, sites in Kansas and Nebraska are clearly affiliated with this archaeological tradition. Those sites in the Central Plains that contain Oneota components dating to the Late Prehistoric period are the Leary (25RH1), Ashland (25CC1, 25SD147), and various White Rock phase sites (Figure 9.1). Additional Oneota artifacts have also been found among late prehistoric assemblages from southern Kansas.

Modern studies of Oneota sites in Kansas and Nebraska indicate westward migration of certain midwestern populations in the late thirteenth or early fourteenth centuries. Little is known about their fate after about A.D. 1450, although this cultural tradition continued in the Midwest, including along the eastern edge of the Central Plains, into the Protohistoric period. The expansion of Oneota peoples into the

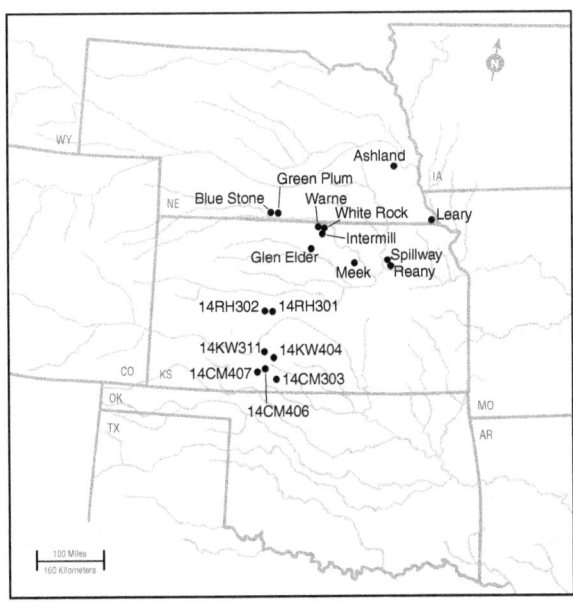

Figure 9.1. Map of the Central Plains showing locations of the Leary and Ashland sites and White Rock phase sites, as well as those Plains Border variant sites in southwestern Kansas that include Oneota materials in their assemblages

Plains during the Late Prehistoric period coincided with movements of various Oneota populations and those of the Central Plains tradition (see chapter 7, this volume). Likewise, trans-Plains exchange involving Oneota, Central and Southern Plains, and more western populations can be documented during this period. As a result, study of Oneota sites in Kansas and Nebraska promises to help us understand Oneota processes of expansion and adaptation to the Plains environment, as well as the cultural dynamics of the Central Plains and neighboring regions during the Late Prehistoric period.

This chapter describes Oneota finds in Kansas and Nebraska that date to the Late Prehistoric period. Discussion starts with the Leary site in extreme southeastern Nebraska. Remains from this site are most comparable to those from midwestern Oneota sites, which have been used to define this broad cultural tradition. The Leary site likely represents a major point of entry for Oneota peoples into the Central Plains after about A.D. 1250. Westward expansion and adaptation to the Plains environment is evident in the Ashland and especially the White Rock sites of southern Nebraska and north-central Kansas. Here, Oneota populations focused on bison hunting and the procuring of quality lithic materials from regional sources. Direct interaction between Oneota and native Plains populations is not evident in the heart of the Central Plains but is indicated by limited evidence from sites along the eastern, southern, and northern margins of the region (Ritterbush 2005). The apparent absence of interaction in the Central Plains may be due to Oneota aggression or perception thereof. Evidence of interaction in peripheral areas may signal more friendly ties with neighboring groups who facilitated the exchange of materials and ideas across the Plains.

LEARY SITE

The largest western Oneota site in the Central Plains is the Leary site, located in Richardson County, Nebraska (Figure 9.1). Archaeologists interested in the Central Plains have known of this site since the early twentieth century (Ritterbush 2002a; Sterns ca. 1915). Hill and Wedel (1936) published the first major description of Leary based on excavations conducted there in 1935 by the Nebraska State Historical Society. Their analysis of the recovered assemblage resulted in its identification with the Oneota archaeological tradition. Since that time, additional excavations have been conducted at the site, including those by the Nebraska State Historical Society in 1965 and the University of Kansas in 1968. Ongoing analyses of these assemblages seek to gain more detailed information about the culture history of the site and its role in late prehistoric cultural processes in the Central Plains (Ritterbush 2002a).

The Leary site is situated along the right or east bank of the Big Nemaha River not far above its confluence with the Missouri River. This location allowed easy access to diverse plant, animal, and geological resources available in both large and small streams, bottomlands, Missouri River bluffs, and other uplands. Arable land and a favorable climate made gardening feasible, while hunting, fishing, and gathering in the various habitats surrounding the site furnished additional foods and materials for tools. Water routes and possible overland trails provided means of travel and communication in all directions.

The site's size, location, deposits, and abundance and variety of artifacts suggest that Leary was a village that was occupied over an extended period. Unfortunately, few structural remains have been found. Only two houses (discussed below) have been identified despite extensive field investigations. Temporary structures of poles, bark, or mats and surface fires instead of prepared fire pits provided shelter and warmth. The most substantial and numerous features identified are bell-shaped pits. The Nebraska State Historical Society excavated more than 175 pits during 1935 and 1965 excavations. These were likely used to store dried foodstuffs, tools, or raw materials. Fishel (1999b) has emphasized the importance of storage pits to Oneota peoples, especially when villagers left their home base to travel into the Plains for hypothesized communal bison hunts.

The Leary site was also used as a burial ground. At least 22 burials have been documented during excavation of different portions of the site. Oneota burials are also present in burial mounds located on the nearby bluffs (W. M. Bass 1961; Hill and Wedel 1936). Extended burials with few associated material remains are common, although other finds of human bone may represent secondary or disturbed inhumations. This pattern of extended and secondary burial within the limits of an occupation site is not uncommon for Oneota sites in the Midwest (Kreisa 1993).

Many of the varied activities of the prehistoric occupants of the Leary site are reflected in the artifacts recovered from the site. The stone artifacts include small triangular unnotched arrowpoints, endscrapers and sidescrapers, alternately beveled and flake knives, sandstone and clinker abraders, celts, manos and metates, "nutting" stones, mauls, hammerstones, possible discoidals, worked hematite, and disk and elbow pipes. Many of the chipped-stone tools were formed through minimal edge modification of flakes and blades. This informal or expedient form of stone tool manufacture is commonly associated with Oneota assemblages.

The abundance of artifacts made of locally available materials indicates adaptation to this portion of the Central Plains. Many of the chipped-stone tools were made of chert obtained from the Permian- and Pennsylvanian-age deposits exposed in the general region surrounding the site. Local glacial tills provided materials for groundstone tools. The exact source of the red stone used to make pipes and other objects has not been identified, although it would have been derived from local glacial deposits or from catlinite quarries in southwestern Minnesota. The latter would likely indicate contact with other Oneota populations to the northeast. Other exotic materials, such as Smoky Hill jasper from northwestern Kansas and Alibates agatized dolomite from the Texas panhandle were obtained through travel to source areas or down-the-line trade with peoples from western and southwestern regions. The

Figure 9.2. Oneota pot recovered from the Leary site (catalog no. R1-1115). Vessel is 19.3 cm high. Note interior lip decoration, flaring rim, strap handles molded directly to the lip of the rim, vertical tool trails decorating the handles, and shoulder decoration, including trailed lines forming nested chevrons bordered by a row of punctates and sets of oblique tool trails. (Courtesy of the Nebraska State Historical Society)

White Rock Oneota sites and Oneota finds in southern Kansas provide evidence of the western Oneota role in these procurement strategies.

Bone and antler tools are also present in the Leary assemblage. Bison scapula hoes are abundant and provide evidence (in addition to the plant remains) of gardening. Other bone and antler tools include awls, needles, a shaft wrench, an antler billet, antler projectile tips, and other worked, but as yet unidentified pieces. Mussel shells have been recovered from the site but do not appear to have been commonly used as a raw material for tools, other than as temper for ceramics.

These tools compare favorably with those recovered from other Oneota sites. However, the most diagnostic evidence of Oneota occupation of the Leary site is seen in the ceramic artifacts. Numerous potsherds recovered from the site are from small to large shell-tempered jars with smooth exterior surfaces (Figure 9.2). Rims flare or curve outwards from the neck. Decoration of the rims and shoulders of these pots compares well with those found on ceramics from more eastern Oneota sites. Roughly 90 percent of the rims were decorated with tool or finger impressions made on the top of the lip or the interior portion of the lip-rim juncture. Occasionally, trailed lines are found on the interior surface of the rim. The outflaring or outcurving rim form makes the interior rim decoration clearly visible from above. Loop and strap handles were appended to some vessels (Figure 9.2). Many of these were decorated with trailed lines, tool or finger impressions, or punctates.

The shoulders of Leary pots provide the most extensive area for adornment, where rectilinear designs, formed by trailing a tool or finger through the damp clay, are commonly found (Figures 9.2 and 9.3). These trailed lines are often arranged in parallel sets that combine to form motifs of chevrons, opposed horizontal, vertical, or diagonal lines, or other repeated elements. In some instances, a row or set of punctates was arranged as a border to a set of lines (Figure 9.2) or used to fill trian-

Figure 9.3. Reconstructed Oneota pot recovered from the Leary site in 1935 (catalog no. R1-815). Vessel is 19.5 cm high. Note the oblique tool impression on the lip, paired strap handles attached below the lip, elliptical orifice, and wide vertical (finger) trails on the shoulder similar to those on Koshkonong Bold ceramics found at many Midwestern Oneota sites. (Courtesy of the Nebraska State Historical Society)

gular spaces between designs. Individual elements, such as a large punctate, bull's-eye, or spiral, are also occasionally found within these motifs.

Potsherds at the Leary site indicate the use of ceramic vessels for storage and cooking. Additionally, certain ceramic attributes provide clues to the age of the Oneota occupation of the site. Interior lip notching, handles attached directly to the lip of the vessel, and rectilinear motifs with punctate borders are often found on the Leary ceramics (Ritterbush 2003). These attributes have been found to co-occur at other Oneota sites of the Developmental Horizon or Middle (Developmental) Horizon I (Boszhardt 1998). Based on radiocarbon ages from other Oneota sites, this horizon is dated to A.D. 1250–1450. Calibrated radiocarbon dates obtained from charcoal and residue associated with Oneota ceramics from the Leary site (WIS-151, WIS-155, UCR-3945) fall within this range (see Appendix). Other ceramic attributes represented at the Leary site may indicate a somewhat later occupation (Garst 2002; Henning 1961: 39; 1970: 145; 1998a: 393–394; Ritterbush 2003). These include fine lip-top decoration, handles commonly attached well below the lip, narrow or fine tool trails, and punctate-filled design elements. The co-occurrence of these attributes has been found at other Oneota sites associated with the Classic Horizon or Late (Classic) Horizon I, which has been dated to about A.D. 1450–1650 (Boszhardt 1994, 1998; Henning 1961). One of the above-mentioned chronometric dates (UCR-3945) overlaps with the earliest portion of this range. The residue sample from which this date was obtained derives from a body sherd decorated with sets of narrow opposed lines associated with a punctate-filled zone.

Other data also hint that Oneota peoples occupied Leary at multiple times, over a long period of time, and into the Classic horizon. The observation that some pit features intrude into others suggests that the site was occupied repeatedly and over a long enough period of time to allow them to fill. Similarly, some time elapsed before surface evidence of burials was obscured before reoccupation. In addition, worked catlinite or pipestone, including at least three fragments of disk pipes (and two sandstone disk pipe fragments), is present at the site. Catlinite is believed to have been used by Oneota peoples, especially for disk pipes, more frequently during the Classic Horizon than earlier times (Boszhardt 1998: 215).

In addition to extensive or multiple Oneota occupations of the Leary site is the likelihood that a Central Plains tradition population or populations once occupied at least one portion of the site. This, as well as the temporal overlap of the Oneota and Central Plains traditions, raises the question of whether Oneota and Central Plains tradition peoples interacted directly or indirectly with one another and, if so, in what manner. Data relevant to these issues are present at the Leary site in the form of house features and Central Plains tradition ceramics.

Crews of the Nebraska State Historical Society excavated remnants of two houses in different portions of the Leary site in 1935 and 1965. The earliest of these two structures was found 2.5–3.5 feet below the surface in an area near the Big Nemaha River (Ritterbush 2002a). Grit-tempered and cord-marked ceramics typical of the Central Plains tradition (Nebraska phase) were found with this feature (Bozell et al. 1999; Frantz 1966; Middleton 2003; Ritterbush 2002a). However, Oneota ceramics were also recovered during excavation of this house and its overlying deposits. Provenience information for the artifacts and features in this portion of the site is limited, making it impossible to develop a clear interpretation of the cultural affiliation of the house and other features uncovered there. One possible interpretation is that Central Plains tradition peoples built and occupied a lodge at the Leary site before Oneota people occupied it. After it was abandoned and partly buried by flood deposits from the nearby river, the site was occupied by Oneota peoples who excavated storage pits into the underlying stratum containing debris produced by the site's earlier occupants. As a result of these later activities, Oneota and Central Plains tradition artifacts became mixed. Although this interpretation seems plausible, an alternative hypothesis is that Central Plains tradition and Oneota peoples lived side by side, possibly within the same lodge, indicating close and direct interaction.

The age of this early occupation is estimated at between A.D. 1275 and A.D. 1425. Four radiocarbon dates (BGS 2301, BGS 2302, SI-617, SI-618) have been obtained from charcoal posts from the floor of this lodge (see Appendix) (Ritterbush 2002a). One date (SI-618) is much too early for either the Central Plains or Oneota traditions. The other three samples produced overlapping ranges most closely associated with the fourteenth century. These dates are compatible with both the Oneota and Central Plains traditions and do not distinguish this lodge from other dated Oneota occupations at the site (Ritterbush 2002a).

A second house feature was excavated in the eastern portion of the site in 1935 (Hill and Wedel 1936; Ritterbush 2002a). Unlike the house uncovered in 1965, this structure was found near the surface and overlying Oneota artifacts and features. The house floor, clearly outlined by posts and associated with a central fire pit, four central support posts, two interior cache pits, and an extended entry, is very comparable in form to well-documented Central Plains tradition lodges. The only similar type of lodge found at an Oneota site is House 3 at the Ashland site (discussed below). Hill and Wedel (1936) argued, based on the style of the associated ceramics, that Oneota peoples occupied this lodge. Seventeen decorated sherds from this lodge exhibit typical Oneota attributes. However, close reinspection of the assemblage indicates that one restored pot and two body and three rim sherds excavated from the house are unlike typical Oneota wares. The restored pot has a smooth exterior surface pockmarked with small voids left by platy shell temper. The out-curving rim, rounded shoulder, and globular body are undecorated and reminiscent of Central Plains tradition ceramic forms. The individual body sherds are grit-tempered and have partially smoothed-over cord-marked exterior surfaces (comparable to Central Plains tradition ceramics). One rim sherd is also grit-tempered but with a smooth surface. Two of the unusual rims have low, almost-rolled rim forms with plain, rounded lips. The third is from a small constricted-mouth bowl decorated with a single trailed line encircling the mouth. Although grit-tempering and cord-marking are associated with a few Oneota sites (Henning 1992; Moffat 1998: 171, 178–180), the lack of these attributes on clearly identifiable Oneota ceramics from Leary and the presence of some definite Central Plains tradition ceramics and features suggests a non-Oneota, possibly eastern Central Plains tradition, origin for these sherds. These three rims compare favorably with several sherds recovered from Steed-Kisker sites in northeastern Kansas and northwestern Missouri (Ritterbush 2002a: 257).

The form and ceramic association of this house raise important issues regarding potential interaction between Oneota and indigenous populations during the Late Prehistoric period. The Central Plains tradition form but Oneota association may suggest that Oneota peoples learned this type of construction through interaction with Central Plains tradition peoples or knowledge of their means of successful adaptation to the region (Ritterbush 2005). Another scenario is that Oneota and Central Plains tradition peoples may have jointly occupied this shelter. This may explain the presence of mixed ceramics. Yet another hypothesis is that an as-yet-unidentified non-Oneota (Central Plains tradition or Steed-Kisker) population built this lodge after the Oneota occupants abandoned the site (or that portion of the site). This hypothesis assumes that few ceramics were left with this structure and that Oneota remains were present because underlying deposits were disturbed, or Oneota debris exposed on the surface of the site was reused.

Understanding the order and timing of different occupations of this and other Oneota and Central Plains tradition sites in the region is essential for addressing the question of cultural interaction. The general stratigraphy suggests that the initial occupation of the Leary site included a Central Plains tradition population. This was followed by what appears to have been more than one or a continuous occupation of the site by Oneota peoples. Eventually, an unidentified group of people, possibly Oneota cohabiting with Central Plains tradition or Steed-Kisker peoples, Oneota peoples influenced by native populations, or a Central Plains tradition or Steed-Kisker household, occupied at least a portion of the site. Available radiocarbon dates and ceramic styles indicate that each of these occupations occurred during the Late Prehistoric period.

ASHLAND SITE

The multicomponent Ashland site, located near the confluence of Salt Creek and the Platte River in eastern Nebraska (Figure 9.1), is similar to Leary in that it has a late prehistoric Oneota component associated with a Central Plains tradition house form. Other major components at the site are represented by Central Plains tradition and protohistoric (Oto?, Lower Loup-influenced) remains (Hill and Cooper 1937: 248–278; Pepperl 2000a, 2000b). These components are, for the most part, spatially discrete. The late prehistoric Oneota occupation is confined to an upland ridge. A few Oneota sherds are also mixed with non-Oneota materials on the terrace below (Occupation C of 25CC1) (Hill and Cooper 1937; Pepperl 2000a, 2000b). These materials likely represent the interaction of protohistoric Oneota (Oto?) with Pawnee peoples. Both Developmental and Classic Horizon attributes appear to be associated with the ceramics from the upland Oneota component (Occupation B of 25CC1 and 25SD147) (Bozell and Carlson 1999; Pepperl 2000a, 2000b). An AMS date of charred material from a recently excavated Oneota pit provides a calibrated range of A.D. 1283–1418 (Beta-133384) (Pepperl 2000a: sec. 7, p. 12; Pepperl 2000b: 63). This is comparable to dates from Leary (see Appendix).

In addition to Oneota pit features, Hill and Cooper (1937: 267) reported the disturbed remains of a house in the upland portion of the Ashland site (Occupation B). These included the lower portion of a basin-shaped hearth, four central support posts, scattered wall posts, and a bell-shaped cache pit (Pepperl 2000a: Fig. 5). The overall form of this structure is comparable to houses assigned to the Central Plains tradition, as well as to the house feature excavated in the upper portion of the Leary site in 1935. The ceramics associated with this house are reportedly Oneota (field notes of George Lamb, quoted in Pepperl 2000b: 2: B-6). Like the house excavated at Leary in 1935, this feature and its associated artifacts hold potential for understanding possible Oneota interaction with or influence from Central Plains tradition people (Ritterbush 2005). An unrelated pit containing a burial was also found in the area of the Ashland Oneota house but appears to have underlain that floor. This burial is tentatively identified as Woodland, based on a single associated sherd (Pepperl 2000a: sec. 8, p. 12).

Further analysis of the late prehistoric Oneota and other components at the Ashland site is needed. Like Leary, Ashland promises to provide information for understanding the cultural dynamics of the Late Prehistoric period of the Central Plains, as well as of the westward expansion of Oneota peoples.

WHITE ROCK PHASE

The most direct evidence of expansion of Oneota peoples into the heart of the Plains is provided by sites in north-central Kansas and southern Nebraska that exhibit Oneota characteristics and that define the White Rock phase (Logan 1998a). Radiocarbon dates from two of these sites overlap those of the late prehistoric Oneota components at Leary and Ashland (see Appendix). White Rock sites differ from the more prevalent Central Plains tradition sites of this region in their settlement form, ceramic styles, various tool forms, and a lack of evidence for substantial houses.

The White Rock (14JW1), Warne (14JW2, 14JW8, 14JW24), Intermill (14JW202), Glen Elder (14ML1), Blue Stone (25HN45), Green Plum (25HN39), Meek (14CY5), and possibly the Spillway (14PO12) and Reany (14PO13) sites are assigned to the White Rock phase of the Oneota tradition (Figure 9.1). White Rock and Warne are extensive sites located on low upland ridges above White Rock Creek, a tributary of the Republican River in north-central Kansas. George Lamb and Paul Cooper of the Nebraska State Historical Society excavated two possible house floors at the White Rock site in 1937 (Cooper 1937; Lamb 1937; Rusco 1960). These houses were not well-defined but appeared to the excavators as an amorphous scatter of postmolds around a hearth. No other house features have been identified at any White Rock phase site, but bell- or basin-shaped pits are common (Logan 1995; Logan and Banks 1994; Neuman 1963). These features, the extensive nature of these sites, and the abundance and variety of artifacts have led researchers to interpret the White Rock and Warne sites as villages or long-term occupations (Ritterbush and Logan 2000; Rusco 1960).

Rusco (1960), who completed the first analysis of materials from the White Rock, Glen Elder, Blue Stone, and Green Plum sites, also identified the Glen Elder site as a village. Like the White Rock site, Glen Elder is extensive, situated in an upland setting overlooking, in this case, the Solomon River. Pits, postholes, a hearth, and a variety of artifacts were uncovered (Marshall 1969; Rusco 1960). Blakeslee, Peck, and Dorsey (2001: 100–101), in a recent reanalysis of Glen Elder, reinterpreted this site as a large, short-term bison-hunting camp rather than a village. This new interpretation is based on the abundance of hunting and processing tools and a reported "relative lack of in-ground storage facilities."

The Blue Stone and Green Plum sites differ in several respects from the White Rock, Warne, and Glen Elder sites. They are situated on low terraces of Prairie Dog Creek in southern Nebraska and are not as extensive as those described above. In addition, the tool inventory is not as diverse. These observations led Rusco (1960) to interpret them as temporary camps used during bison-hunting and lithic-procurement expeditions. The Meek site and possibly the Intermill site, located in similar settings, also may have served as temporary camps for Oneota peoples (Neuman 1963; Ritterbush and Logan 1991). The function of the Spillway site and the Reany site, which lie on a ridge overlooking the Big Blue River, is indeterminate. A small sample of artifacts was collected during their destruction (Cumming 1958: 56–57). The few tiny sherds generally have a fine, hard paste tempered with fine shell (visible in many cases as platy voids) and smooth (sometimes almost burnished) exterior surface. Fine trailed lines and punctates are visible on several of the body sherds. These are generally similar to White Rock phase ceramics.

The occupants of the White Rock phase sites certainly had strong ties to Oneota populations. This is most evident in the ceramic artifacts. My ongoing reanalysis of the potsherds recovered in 1935 and 1937 from the White Rock site reveals that they are very similar to Oneota ceramics in terms of rim form and decoration. Jars with out-flaring or out-curving rim forms predominate. The lip is commonly decorated (Rusco 1960). More than half of the rims have perpendicular or oblique tool (or finger) impressions on top of the lip. One-third are decorated with oblique, vertical, or horizontal tool impressions on the lip interior. The exterior portion of the rims is undecorated, and in only four instances has the interior surface of the rim been decorated with oblique trailed lines (probably part of a nested chevron).

In addition to lip and interior rim decoration, White Rock shoulder sherds exhibit trailed (or smoothed-over trailed) line and punctate motifs. Because of the small size of the White Rock sherds, it is often impossible to determine how these decorative elements were arranged relative to one another and other decorative elements. However, lines were oriented vertically, diagonally, and horizontally and in various arrangements with one another. Sets of opposed lines are common, sometimes in combination with punctates. Most of the punctates are aligned singly along a trailed line to form a border. Those associated with horizontal lines appear immediately below the neck of the vessel and above the lines. Punctates fill the area between two sets of opposed diagonals on only one decorated body sherd in this assemblage. Other White Rock assemblages include sherds with punctate-filled zones, although these have not yet been quantified. At least some of the White Rock site pots had strap handles, most of which were attached at the lip and were plain or decorated with vertical lines.

White Rock rim form and decoration are very comparable to those in Oneota ceramic assemblages (cf. Boszhardt 1989, 1994; Fishel 1999b; Harvey 1979; Henning 1961, 1970; O'Gorman 1993, 1995). As a set, they are not comparable to ceramics found in other assemblages from the Central Plains (e.g., Central Plains tradition). Similar sets of trailed lines occur on shell-tempered pots recovered from Smoky Hill and Steed-Kisker phase ceramics, but rim form and lip decoration differ. It is on the basis of these comparisons that the White Rock phase is assigned to the Oneota tradition rather than an indigenous Central Plains tradition (Logan 1998a; Ritterbush and Logan 2000).

Despite the strong similarity between White Rock and other Oneota ceramics, some notable differences occur. The primary contrasts are in surface treatment and temper. Most Oneota ceramics, by far, have smooth exterior surfaces. Cord-marking only occurs occasionally in certain assemblages (e.g., Moingona phase [Moffat

1998]). Smooth exterior surfaces predominate in White Rock assemblages, although simple stamping also occurs. Nearly 5 percent of the White Rock site assemblage recovered during the 1930s and 14.8 percent of the Glen Elder site ceramics show evidence of simple stamping (Blakeslee, Peck, and Dorsey 2001). Possible cord-marking is present on less than 1 percent of the White Rock site ceramics.

The most common temper used in Oneota ceramics is crushed shell. This temper is generally clearly visible as white to gray, platy particles visible on the surface and on broken edges of sherds. Similar indicators of shell temper are rarely seen in the White Rock sherds. Instead, sand is common. In defining the Walnut Decorated Lip type and describing most of the sherds at the Blue Stone and Green Plum sites, Rusco (1960: 30) identified "moderate amounts of medium- to coarse-grained sand" in these ceramics. Ceramics from the White Rock and Glen Elder sites were also classified as Walnut Decorated Lip with sand temper. Shell temper was noted in very few of the potsherds from the White Rock sites (Marshall 1969; Neuman 1963; Rusco 1960). A more recent analysis reveals that shell temper has traditionally been overlooked in White Rock ceramics because the shell particles in these ceramics are so small and are also degraded (Ritterbush 2001). Nonetheless, sand temper predominates in White Rock ceramic subassemblages. The reason for this variation from more typical Oneota ceramic attributes is unclear at this time. Adaptation to the Plains environment in terms of available resources and refocused subsistence activities, as well as possible contact with other groups, may have influenced change in ceramic technology among Oneota migrants to the Plains.

Nonceramic artifacts recovered from the White Rock sites are similar to those from other Oneota sites. The inventory of stone implements includes small triangular arrowpoints (predominately unnotched), beveled knives, endscrapers, various flake and blade tools, mauls, disk pipes, abraders, and nutting and grinding stones. Informal chipped-stone tools were produced through minimal retouch of flakes and blades (Padilla and Ritterbush 2005). Lithic raw materials from the Central Plains, namely Smoky Hill jasper from northwestern Kansas and cherts from the Permianage bedrock of the Flint Hills, were heavily used (Logan 1998a; Ritterbush and Logan 2000). More exotic materials, such as Alibates agatized dolomite from the Texas panhandle and obsidian from the Jemez Mountains of New Mexico and the Malad region of Idaho, constitute a minor portion of the lithic materials used by White Rock peoples (Logan, Hughes, and Henning 2001). Despite the limited availability of exotic materials, their presence indicates long-distance travel or exchange.

One of the most distinctive differences between the White Rock migrants and the Oneota to the east is the focus of the subsistence base. Preserved corn and agricultural implements (e.g., scapula hoes) at Oneota sites in both the Plains and Prairie Peninsula indicate farming as one subsistence activity. Hunting was also important. In the Plains, bison were the primary game as indicated by their proportions in assemblages from White Rock sites. Little species diversity as well as instances of extensive processing are represented (Logan 1998a, 1998b). As noted by Logan (1998a,

1998b), the White Rock phase is characterized by a focal (rather than diffuse) economy (Cleland 1976) adapted to the bison-rich environment of the Plains. Mobile bison hunting may explain the quantity and distribution of White Rock sites in the Central Plains. This mobility may also account for the abundance of nonlocal, yet Plains-derived, lithic materials at White Rock sites.

The White Rock people may have been drawn to the Plains, in part, by its abundant bison resources (Ritterbush 2002b). It appears from the archaeological record of this region that they were the first peoples of the latter portion of the Prehistoric period to emphasize bison hunting as a mode of subsistence. This pattern of combined farming and bison hunting continued into the Protohistoric and early Historic periods by other populations. Although gardening implements and dependence on lithic materials derived from the Central Plains suggest that the White Rock people occupied the Plains year-round (Ritterbush and Logan 2000), they did not become permanent occupants of the Plains. At this time, no evidence suggests continuity between the White Rock phase and later archaeological complexes of the Central Plains. It appears from limited radiocarbon dates that Oneota peoples abandoned the heart of the Central Plains by about the middle of the fifteenth century. The relationship of the late prehistoric Oneota of the Plains to protohistoric and historic Oneota has yet to be studied.

OTHER ONEOTA REMAINS IN KANSAS

In addition to the Oneota remains discussed above, occasional finds of Oneota ceramics are reported in association with indigenous Plains assemblages from southern Kansas. At present, clear Oneota ceramics with smooth surfaces and trailed line decorations on the lip and shoulder, sometimes in association with punctates or bull's-eye, have been identified in assemblages from Comanche, Kiowa, and Rush counties, Kansas (Figure 9.1) (Bevitt 1999a; Christine Garst, personal communication, 2002; Ritterbush 2002c). These Oneota sherds are associated with Plains ceramics, which are more typically cord-marked. These assemblages are assigned to the Plains Border variant of the Late Prehistoric period (Bevitt 1999a).

The co-occurrence of Oneota artifacts with the more numerous remains of indigenous Plains populations in southern Kansas suggests direct interaction between Oneota and Plains peoples. This interaction may have been based on an exchange network that linked populations from widespread regions, namely from the Southwest, Southern Plains, Central Plains, and Midwest. Given the distribution of Alibates agatized dolomite, obsidian from New Mexico sources, and turquoise at these Plains sites, as well as at certain White Rock and other Oneota sites, Oneota contacts with populations in southern Kansas provide a logical connection for the exchange of these and less tangible materials and ideas (Ritterbush 2002c).

LATE PREHISTORIC ONEOTA IN THE CENTRAL PLAINS

The careful study of Oneota sites in Kansas and Nebraska has identified the presence of a nonindigenous population in the Central Plains during the Late Prehistoric period. The Leary, Ashland, and White Rock phase sites document the movement of Oneota peoples westward from their traditional homelands around A.D. 1250–1450. From the remains at these sites, we can learn about the adaptations these migrants made as they established their home in a new land. At the Leary and Ashland sites, Oneota peoples established settlements along tributary streams near their confluences with major rivers. These locations are comparable to those of many of the major Oneota sites to the east. Travel would have been facilitated by their situation along or near major streams. Arable land and rich, diverse flora and fauna were also easily accessible in these locales, allowing continuation of a village farming, hunting, and gathering way of life. Adapting to the regional environment included using local resources, including quality lithic materials. Proximity to bison herds gave direct access to these animals, although deer, fish, and other fauna continued to be important to the diverse subsistence base of the Oneota occupants of Leary and Ashland.

The more western White Rock people emphasized bison hunting, and as a result the diversity of utilized resources decreased. Oneota migration deep into the grasslands and their focus on bison hunting necessitated specific adaptations. Temporary camps near bison herds and preferred lithic material source areas were established, in addition to expansive villages or base camps, such as the Warne and White Rock sites. Mobility likely increased with this focus on bison hunting, yet farming continued to be practiced, as evident from gardening tools and floral remains at the larger White Rock sites (Blakeslee, Peck, and Dorsey 2001; Ritterbush and Logan 2000).

The lifeways of these western Oneota migrants, especially the settlement form and focus on bison hunting, contrast with that of the indigenous Central Plains tradition populations that also occupied this region during the Late Prehistoric period. Evidence for the direct interaction of Oneota and Central Plains tradition peoples is limited, especially in the heart of the Central Plains (Ritterbush 2005). The presence of less than one dozen Oneota sherds at the Kullbom sites (13ML12, 13ML13) in the Glenwood locality of eastern Iowa suggests possible short-term interaction on the eastern edge of the Plains. Oneota ceramics in southern Kansas assemblages suggest more direct interaction along the southern margin of the Central Plains. Furthermore, the mingling of Oneota attributes with Plains attributes in Initial Coalescent ceramics hints of Oneota influence along the northern margin of the Central Plains (Ritterbush 2005).

The general coincidence in timing of Oneota migration into portions of the Central Plains with the movement of indigenous (Central Plains tradition) populations within the Plains suggests a possible link between these phenomena. The application of recent interpretations of general Oneota development and expansion suggests that Central Plains tradition populations were displaced by more competitive Oneota societies. Although both Oneota and Central Plains tradition societies were likely kin-based, Benn (1989) proposes that the Oneota developed social structures above the level of the household that allowed efficient manipulation of social labor. Stable economic production was possible because people were organized for the varied and often simultaneous tasks necessary for survival and growth. The resultant tribal form of organization may have incorporated views of hegemony within the society, as well as over others. This hierarchical ideal is reflected in symbolic motifs present on ceramic vessels that may also represent the importance of warfare in this social system (Benn 1989). Hollinger (2001), through a broad review of archaeological evidence from the Midwest and Plains, suggests that Oneota were establishing dominance over foreign lands through aggressive acts of warfare. Although direct evidence of violence between Oneota and Central Plains tradition peoples is uncertain, a combination of social dominance and threat of aggression could have influenced the cultural dynamics of the Plains during the Late Prehistoric period. Relatively isolated Central Plains tradition populations, with little or no cohesive organization above the household, would likely have been unable to compete with the more cohesive and aggressive Oneota. This cultural dynamic, it is speculated, may have led to Central Plains tradition populations shifting away from some of their traditional homelands within the Central Plains (Logan 1998a: 263; Ritterbush 2002b). These movements likely made way for Oneota immigrants, such as the White Rock people of northern Kansas and southern Nebraska.

Although evidence for direct Oneota–Central Plains tradition interaction is limited, it is now clear that Oneota peoples established ties with other Plains populations in southern Kansas. These ties no doubt helped the Oneota peoples adapt to the Plains. This adaptation extended the social network of the late prehistoric immigrants and provided them with access to nonlocal materials such as Alibates agatized dolomite, New Mexican sources of obsidian, and possibly turquoise. Similar ties may have been made with other populations, as indicated by obsidian from the Malad region of Idaho at the Warne site. Western Oneota ties with their kinsmen to the east extended this trans-Plains exchange to the Midwest (Boszhardt 2000; Ritterbush 2002c).

In summary, Oneota archaeological remains in the Central Plains reveal that prehistoric migration into this region from the east played a complex role in the cultural dynamics of the Central Plains and surrounding regions during prehistoric times. Advanced study of these and other remains from Kansas and surrounding states promises to lead to a more complete understanding of Kansas' prehistoric past.

10. The Great Bend Aspect

Donald J. Blakeslee and Marlin F. Hawley

This chapter is a review of the archaeology of the late prehistoric to early historic Wichita bands in Kansas. Waldo Wedel (1935a, 1959), who conducted excavations in two of three known settlement clusters, classified the remains in the McKern taxonomic system as the Great Bend aspect. He classified the sites in Rice and McPherson counties as the Little River focus and those along the Kansas-Oklahoma border as the Lower Walnut focus (Figure 10.1). Since then, there has been work on a third cluster of villages near Marion (Lees 1988; Lees et al. 1989; Rohn and Emerson 1984). In addition, recent studies have dealt with sites other than village clusters. Wedel also explored sites that are called council circles, and in recent decades, work has been done on ground figures or intaglios, on quarries, and on hunting camps (Blakeslee and Rohn 1986; Mallam 1982; Stein and Reynolds 1994).

Also since Wedel's classic work, we have learned something about Great Bend houses, and, as archaeological methods have improved, we have gained important knowledge about the economy of these people, including hints regarding the extent of individual band territories. Great Bend sites contain some of the finest stone and bone artifacts to be found on the Great Plains, and the chapter summarizes and illustrates the artifacts as well.

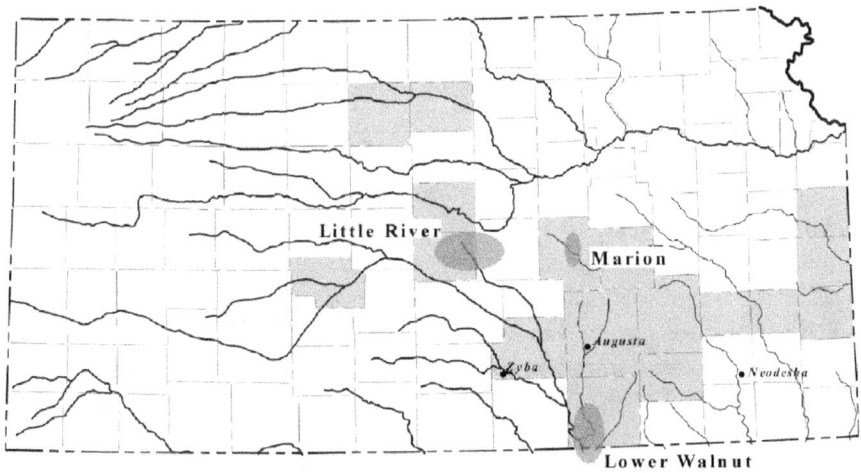

Figure 10.1. Location of village clusters and isolated sites mentioned in the text. Counties known to contain Great Bend hunting camps are shaded.

HISTORY OF WORK

The Great Bend aspect is easily the most studied archaeological complex in Kansas, and very early reports include both surface investigations (Billings 1882; Mead 1890: 64; Mudge 1873; Richey 1904; West 1880) and excavations (Gould 1898a, 1898b, 1899; C. P. Johnson 1897; O. T. Mason 1881; Putnam 1880). The most significant investigations of the era were conducted in the early 1880s by Johan Udden of Bethany College. Over a five-year period of time, he excavated at the Paint Creek site (14MP1) in McPherson County and concluded that the inhabitants were probably horticulturalists and were ancestral to the Wichita or the Pawnee. He attributed a rusted mass of chain mail armor to a visit by the Spanish, perhaps Coronado (Udden 1900: 73–78). Udden's important contribution has been reprinted recently, along with a number of important accompanying contributions in volume 23 of *Kansas Anthropologist* (2002). Also of considerable importance was the work of the Jones brothers in Rice County that generated the hypothesis that the Great Bend sites there were the ones visited by Coronado (H. Jones 1928; P. A. Jones 1929, 1937; Ross 1928).

Starting in 1934, systematic scientific study of sites in Kansas was initiated by Waldo R. Wedel, first with the Nebraska State Historical Society and later with the Smithsonian Institution (Wedel 1935a, 1935b). Wedel not only named the complex, for the location of a major concentration of its sites north of the great bend of the Arkansas River, but also determined its approximate age and its affiliation with the Wichita bands, and he provided the description of its material traits that established the baseline for all future research (Wedel 1942, 1959). Based on his fieldwork, he defined two foci (Little River and Lower Walnut) for two of the three major site clusters of the Great Bend aspect (Figure 10.1). Later investigations revealed that the third cluster, near Marion, was roughly equivalent in age and composition to the other two (Barr 1973; Emerson 1977; Lees et al. 1989; Rohn and Emerson 1984; Roper 2000b, 2000c). Keller (1961) investigated a series of sites in the vicinity of the city of Augusta in Butler County, which he related to those in the vicinity of Arkansas City. Other work has been carried out by seven Kansas Archeology Training Program excavations between 1977 and 1993 (Lees and Mandel 1993; Loosle 1991; Rowlison 1981, 1983a, 1983b; Stein 1992; Witty 1977, 1986, 1992; Wulfkuhle 1993). The majority of the resulting collections await intensive analysis. Much recent work has been done in the vicinity of Arkansas City (Rohn 1994; Rohn, Larson, and Davis 1982), especially a massive project done by the Kansas State Historical Society in advance of levee construction and highway relocation (Hawley 1994, 1995, 2000; Hawley and Haury 1994; Hawley et al. 1994; Holland 1998; Perttula, Hawley, and Scott 2001; Thies 1991a, 1991b; Wulfkuhle 1993). The final report on this work is in preparation (Stein, personal communication, 2005) and will be a major contribution to our understanding of Great Bend archaeology. An annotated bibliography for Great Bend archaeology is now available (Hawley and Blakeslee 2003).

CHRONOLOGY

Chronological understanding of the Great Bend aspect is based primarily on radiocarbon dates, with seriation ages of southwestern trade ceramics providing additional insights (Hawley 2000; Rucker 1971; Terry and Terry 1961; Thies 1987; W. R. Wedel 1950, 1982). A large series of radiocarbon dates is now available for the Lower Walnut focus sites (see Appendix), with a smaller but still reliable set from the Little River focus sites and only a few dates from the cluster of villages at Marion. In general, the dates suggest that the Great Bend aspect began at about A.D. 1425 and lasted up to the last quarter of the seventeenth century. There is, however, a cluster of early dates from the excavations in the Lower Walnut sites that suggest an occupation in the late thirteenth to early fourteenth centuries. Whether or not these dates derive from a pre–Great Bend occupation of the Lower Walnut valley has not been determined.

SITE TYPES AND SETTLEMENT PATTERN

Most Great Bend aspect habitation sites lie in three clusters: around Marion, near the junction of the Walnut and Arkansas rivers (Lower Walnut focus), and in Rice and McPherson counties (Little River focus). Each cluster consists of a scattering of large and small sites, and early Spanish visitors noted the extensive nature of the Wichita settlements they visited (cf. M. M. Wedel 1979, 1982). Roper (2002d) relates the settlement pattern to the style of floodplain agriculture known from the Mississippian tradition. There are also a few isolated habitation sites, such as those at the Zyba site in Sumner County and the Augusta site (14BU501) (Figure 10.1). Finally, near Neodesha on the Verdigris River, there was once an earthwork and related sites that appear to be of late Great Bend aspect affiliation (Wedel 1959: 526–534; Weston and Lees 1994).

Prior to agricultural disturbance, low midden mounds marked the village sites. For instance, the Tobias site, as mapped by Wedel, contained 19 such mounds. It also featured numerous small depressions that marked the locations of cache pits. The village sites yield a wide range of artifacts, including pottery. This distinguishes them from a second kind of site present in the Lower Walnut focus. These sites are located adjacent to the village cluster and lack pottery. In such sites near Winfield, D. Hill and Blakeslee (1983: 29–33) found assemblages that differed significantly from those Wedel had excavated from Lower Walnut villages. In addition to the absence of pottery, these sites had a much higher proportion of heavy chopping tools and far fewer endscrapers than the village sites. Apparently these sites were created by people engaged in extracting a limited variety of resources.

Great Bend aspect hunting camps are widespread in Kansas (Figure 10.1). First reported by O'Bryant (1947) in Sedgwick County and by C. S. Smith (1949a) on the Smoky Hill River, they were later found as far east as Hillsdale Lake in Miami County

(Blakeslee and Rohn 1986), at Toronto Lake in Woodson County (J. H. Howard 1964), and in Bourbon County and in Vernon County, Missouri (Feagins 1996). The most intensively occupied hunting camp found so far is the multicomponent Lewis site (14PA307) at Larned (Monger 1970; Ranney 1994). The hunting camps suggest that Great Bend aspect territory extended much farther east and north than previously suspected, and the easterly distribution of some of them suggests that the Osage, who later claimed the area and presumably excluded Great Bend aspect people, arrived in western Missouri sometime during the early Historic period.

Several Great Bend aspect village sites contain features known informally as council circles. These are low mounds surrounded by a series of shallow depressions. When Wedel (1959: 215–229) tested one such feature at the Tobias site (14RC8), he found the central mound to be composed of earth mixed with midden material underlain by some cache pits. While the depressions that were tested proved to be devoid of cultural material, Wedel did uncover two structures that were not marked by surface features. The structures were elongated, rather sausage-shaped, and apparently had earth- and sod-covered superstructures. They contained a complex set of features including cache pits, hearths, postmolds, sandstone slabs, and human skeletal remains (Figure 10.2).

The contents of the central mound and associated structures did not provide a clear indication of the purpose of the council circles, but Wedel (1967) found solstice alignments between three of the council circles in the Little River locality. More recently, Susan Vehik (2002a, 2002b) has interpreted the structures in the council circles as the residences of priestly leaders.

On a ridge above the council circles in Rice County is a ground figure in the form of a giant serpent. An intaglio (the reverse of a bas-relief), it was formed by removal of the sod and topsoil. Today it is marked by a low depression that supports only short grasses in contrast to taller grasses all around it. The serpent is 48 meters long and appears to hold an oval object in its open jaws (Figure 10.3). Mallam (1982) determined that the jaws align with two of the council circles in the vicinity. This alignment and the recovery of two

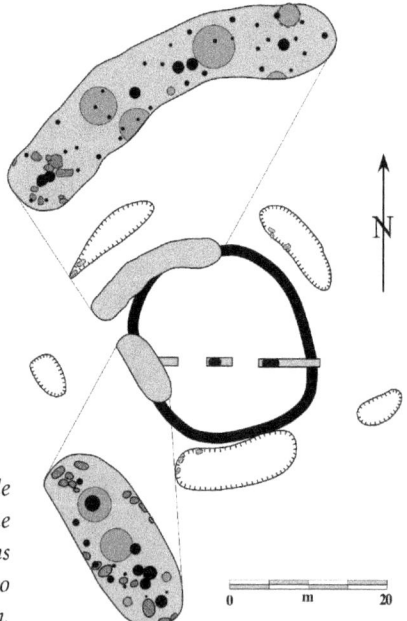

Figure 10.2. Wedel's excavations in the council circle at the Tobias site. Dark gray open ring marks the limits of the central mound. Wedel's excavations are shaded light gray. Enlarged views of the two excavated structures are shown at top and bottom.

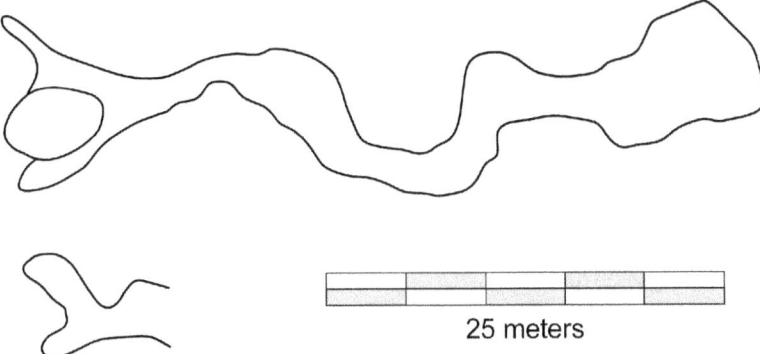

Figure 10.3. Comparisons of the depressions at two Kansas intaglios. The left-hand side of the Sage site intaglio (bottom) has been obscured by modern activities.

small flakes of Alibates agatized dolomite from a test trench are the only evidence that associates the serpent with the Great Bend aspect. The significance of the Alibates is explained below.

The serpent is one of three intaglio sites known to exist in Kansas. The other two also lie within Great Bend aspect territory as it is defined by the distribution of hunting sites. The Sage site, on the south side of Waconda Lake, is two miles south of Waconda Spring, a major sacred site. This site has been disturbed by historic activities, but the portion that remains bears a close resemblance to the open mouth of the serpent in Rice County (Figure 10.3). The third site, the Walter Hutchinson site (14SG557), is located west of Wichita. It contains low earthen walls and shallow ditches as well as four apparent intaglios, but no artifacts have been recovered from it, and there are no reported sites in the immediate vicinity (Figure 10.4).

Other sites likely to be associated with the Great Bend aspect include cairns, petroglyphs, and quarries. There are petroglyphs at the Peverly site (14RC10), which lies between the Serpent intaglio and the Tobias site, and there are other petroglyphs in the vicinity of the Lower Walnut sites (Wedel 1959: 492). It is interesting that there is rock art near Thompson Creek, a hunting camp, and in the Woodson County rockshelters. J. H. Howard (1964), using content as his criterion, believed that people from Great Bend aspect sites created the rock art in the shelters. Wedel (1970d) made the same point. Recently, local residents have reported a piece of rock art near Fall River that is described as a depiction of a serpent with an object in its mouth, i.e., very similar to the intaglio near Lyons but on a much smaller scale and in a different medium.

On the bluff above the Peverly site are three stone cairns. Only the spatial association ties them to the Great Bend aspect. Major quarries of Florence A chert exist near Maple City, Kansas, and Hardy, Oklahoma (Gould 1898b, 1899; Stein, chapter 16, this volume; Wedel 1959: 476–480). Both appear to have seen heavy use by Great Bend aspect populations. Other lithic sources used by them are discussed below.

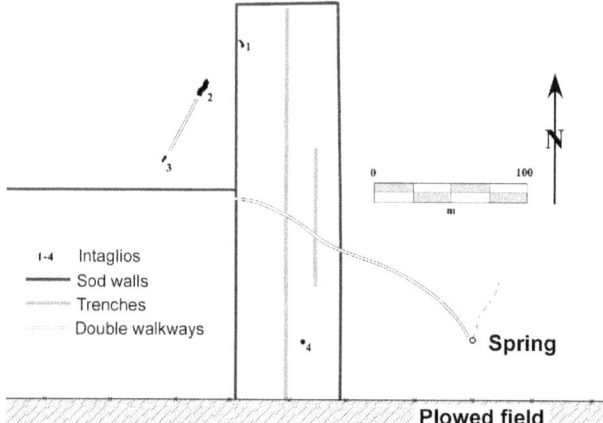

Figure 10.4. Map of the Walter Hutchinson site, Sedgwick County, Kansas. The four intaglios at this site include a possible duck (1), two worm or caterpillar-like figures (2 and 3), and a turtle (4). The walls were formed from piled sod. The two trenches run diagonally with respect to the slope of the ground and are interrupted by causeways where they are crossed by the double walkway.

A type of site that is missing from the Great Bend complex is any form of mortuary site. In fact, purposeful human interments of any sort appear to be absent. There are no cemeteries, no burial mounds, no ossuaries, and no cremations for the many thousands of people who lived in Kansas for centuries, producing the remains that we classify as Great Bend. More than a century of investigation has yielded little more than scraps of human bone, usually from cache pits.

During the massive recent and as-yet-unreported excavations near Arkansas City, the only human remains that were found were some smashed cranial bones in shallow basin features at 14CO1509, modified and unmodified long bones in a pit at 14CO331, and a skull in a pit at 14CO3. In his earlier excavations in the same village cluster, Wedel (1959: 85–86) found fragments of an adult human skull in one pit and scraps of an infant skeleton in another. Neither was complete enough to suggest purposeful burial. In a 1917 dig, Harry Martin (Wedel 1959) and John Sterling found a fully articulated burial in a pit at 14CO3, but gun parts found in the pit fill indicate that the burial is later than the Great Bend occupation of the site.

Farther north, human remains are even scarcer. Rohn and Emerson (1984) report none from their extensive work at Marion, but there are two isolated human mandibles at Wichita State University in a donated collection from the Zyba site. Extensive collections that the senior author has examined from three sites on tributaries of the Smoky Hill River contained no human remains at all. However, Horace Jones reported some human teeth from the council circle at the Hays site, and Wedel found human remains on the floor of a structure in the council circle at the Tobias site (Wedel 1959: 66, 218–222). Susan Vehik (2002b: 39) suggests that the remains are not those of the inhabitants of the site but of enemies sacrificed there.

By the time that the Wichitas were visited by anthropologists, they were burying their dead in individual pits on hilltops (Dorsey 1904: 12). If their ancestors had been doing so during the time that they created the Great Bend sites, many thousands of graves would have been created. There are some hints that there was an earlier pattern of disposal that involved exposing the body on the prairie so that wild animals would consume the body. For instance, Dorsey (1904: 13) reports that "a man injured in fighting would be told not to go into the timber to die, but to go out on the prairie, where the wolves would eat him," and that if two men were wounded in battle, they were told to stay close enough together that a crow could hop from one body to the other. One of the stories in Dorsey's compilation of myths mentions a dead woman who was not buried but instead placed on top of the ground (Dorsey 1904: 92). The rationale for this practice may be reflected in another myth in which Thunderbird was restored to life from one shred of flesh still clinging to one of the bones of his hand, "for there was still life in the hand" (Dorsey 1904: 105). Thus, early Wichita mortuary behavior may have been predicated on the belief that any flesh (life) remaining on the bones would prevent the dead person from reaching the afterlife. If the ancestors of the Wichitas placed their dead out on the prairie, not only would we have an explanation for the lack of Great Bend burials, but it would also have interesting implications for the Native American Graves Protection and Repatriation Act.

ARCHITECTURE

Historic sources document a variety of structures for the historic Wichita, including not only houses (Dorsey 1904: 4; Hammond and Rey 1953: 754; Winship 1896: 591) but raised platform granaries, summer arbors (for resting and sleeping during the summer months), corn drying arbors (W. R. Wedel 1982: 19), sleeping arbors (distinguished from summer arbors, as these were used apparently exclusively for young, unmarried women), and sweatlodges (Dorsey 1904: 6). Good evidence of dwellings turned out to be difficult to find because many of the houses were lightly built and had been erected on the ground surface, where the evidence was subsequently plowed away or obscured by later activities at the site. Recent work, however, has documented pit houses, surface houses, and arbors, along with smaller and less easily interpreted structures. Table 10.1 summarizes the structures that have been reported to date.

The measurable house pits average 30 cm in depth, and access to the floor was by ramp or simply via the sloping pit wall. Some pit houses have well-defined wall post patterns, while others do not (e.g., Wedel 1959: 351). Some structures, such as Structure 1 at 14MN328 and House 2 at 14PA307, feature some paired posts in the wall lines (Lees et al. 1989; Monger 1970: 4). Wall posts were not large—the average diameter is less than 10 cm. This contrasts with the granary or work platform supports found at 14CO501, where a square 1.8 m on a side was defined by four posts that averaged 20 cm in diameter.

Table 10.1. Great Bend Architecture

Site	Shape	Type	Size (Meters)	References
Little River Village Cluster				
14RC306	circular	pit house	2.7	Loosle 1991
	circular	pit house	4.0	Loosle 1991
14RC8	circular (?)	surface house	8.0	Lees et al. 1989
	oval	surface house	7.9 x 5.5	Lees et al. 1989
14RC9	oval	surface house	5.5	Lees et al. 1989
Lower Walnut Village Cluster				
14CO2	circular	pit house	3.1	W. R. Wedel 1959
14CO501	square	granary or work platform	1.8	Hawley 1995, 2000
	pair of posts	drying rack (?)	1.8	Hawley 1995, 2000
14CO385	oval	arbor or 2 houses	10.5 x 7.2	Hawley 2000
	oval	arbor	10.7 x 6.9	Stein 2005
	oval	arbor	13.5 x 5.4	Stein 2005
Marion Village Cluster				
14MN328	oval	pit house	2.3 x 3.0	Lees et al. 1989
	oval	arbor	4.6 x 4.0	Lees et al. 1989
	line	rack or screen	2.2	Lees et al. 1989
	line	rack or screen	3.5	Lees et al. 1989
Hunting Camps				
14PA307	oval	arbor	4.5 x 5.5	Monger 1970
	circular	surface house	3.0	Monger 1970
	oval	surface house	3.0 x 4.0	Monger 1970
	circular	surface house	4.9	Monger 1970

Most of the excavated structures contain one or more hearths. For instance, the three structures at 14CO385 that are interpreted as arbors each contained two hearths. When a house contains a single hearth, it usually lies slightly off-center within the structure. This tendency of hearths in Great Bend aspect houses to be off-center may be related to how the structures were built. Because the poles to form the house were pulled together and lashed at the top, there was no possibility of a central hole in the roof to allow smoke to vent. Vent holes were then necessarily placed down the roof/walls, away from the center of the structure (John Reynolds, personal communication, 1994). Sometimes hearths were placed directly on the house floor; others were placed in shallow basins.

Interior features were usually restricted to hearths. At 14PA307, however, Monger (1970) found that three structures contained large posts located near the central hearth, each about 20 cm in diameter. He interpreted them as "crane posts" for internal support of the roof. For instance, House 1, which measured 4.5 m by 5.5 m, contained a central post 18 cm in diameter.

At 14MN328, there were four sets of widely spaced posts, which "may indicate the presence of a bench along the southwest wall" (Lees et al. 1989: 48). The bench would have had a length of around 2.8 m to as much as 4.1 m.

The cache pits in Great Bend aspect sites are often quite large—up to 2.5 m deep. For instance, the sample of pits excavated by Wedel (1959: 229) at the Tobias site had depths below plow zone of from 0.76 to 2.03 m and had storage capacities of 1400 to 7040 liters. This implies a reliance on stored foods that was much greater than is found in earlier sites in the region.

Plowing has erased the evidence of many surface structures in shallowly buried Great Bend aspect components, and this makes analysis of site structure difficult. The lower portions of cache pits usually survive plowing and erosion, however, and clustering of pits is common on Great Bend aspect sites. At 14MN328, however, six storage pits were found in apparent association with Structure 2 (Lees et al. 1989: 52), and it may be that the clustering in other sites is related to the placement of storage pits in proximity to no-longer-visible dwellings. On the other hand, the three oval structures at 14CO385 that are interpreted as arbors are separated by 30 or more meters from intense concentrations of pits (Stein, ed., 2005).

ECONOMY

The Great Bend aspect subsistence economy included a mix of agriculture, hunting, gathering, and fishing. The primary crops were maize, beans, squash, and sunflowers (Adair 1989; Bozarth 1989, 1990; Rohn and Emerson 1984: 189; Wedel 1959: 231). Tobacco was also grown (Adair, personal communication). Gathered foods that have been recovered from sites include walnut, hickory, plum, hackberry, and grape. It is likely that the prairie turnip was important in the diet, but this tuber is seldom preserved in archaeological sites. Greens also would not preserve.

A wide variety of animals was eaten. These appear to have included dogs. In the three sites that Wedel (1959: 233, 304, 329) tested in the Little River focus, dog ranked just behind bison as the most numerous in terms of elements identified. All of the large game animals in the region—bison, elk, deer, and pronghorn—were hunted (Haury 2005; Rohn and Emerson 1984: 189; Wedel 1959). Medium-sized mammal bones in the collections include all of the species in the region that were normally eaten: muskrat, beaver, otter, raccoon, badger, coyote, wolf, jackrabbit, and cottontail. Smaller mammals, including the larger rodents such as prairie dog, thirteen-lined ground squirrel, and pocket gopher, are also likely to be food remains, but the smaller rodents such as kangaroo rats, moles, and various species of mice do not appear to be as common as in earlier sites (Blakeslee 1999: 77–85) and thus may not reflect diet. The large water-flotation collections from the Lower Walnut sites that are now being analyzed should clarify which species were regularly used for food.

Bones of various species of reptiles and amphibians along with freshwater mussels may reflect the gathering of these animals for their meat. Both eastern and ornate box turtles, pond terrapins, snapping turtles, soft-shelled turtles, frogs, toads, snakes, and ten species of freshwater mussels are present in the collections. Bones of wild turkey, bobwhite, and possibly sandpiper are found, as well as a wide variety of water birds, including black duck, wood duck, ducks/teals, snow goose, great blue heron, terns, hooded merganser, and the pied-billed grebe. Other birds that may have been taken more for their feathers or other parts than for their meat include the great horned owl, flicker, bald eagle, crow, and raven. Finally, fish remains are also found and include catfish, buffalo, gar, and drum. It is not yet clear how important they were in the diet, but the large Lower Walnut collections now being analyzed should make this clear.

The lithic economy is also interesting. The primary sources of the chipped stone in Great Bend aspect sites appear to be bedrock quarries, as opposed to scattered sources such as upland and riverine gravels. Use of the quarries at Maple City, Kansas, and Hardy, Oklahoma, has already been mentioned. Other lithic types commonly found in at least some Great Bend aspect sites include Smoky Hill jasper from northwestern Kansas, Alibates agatized dolomite from the panhandle of Texas, the gray Permian-age cherts from the Flint Hills, and Mississippian cherts from the Ozark uplift. Acquisition of these types of stone may have been embedded in long-distance hunts, as demonstrated by Holen (1991) for Lower Loup sites in Nebraska (cf. Blakeslee, Peck, and Dorsey 2001). Nearby sources not present in large amounts include Florence D chert from the northern Flint Hills, Nehawka chert from southeastern Nebraska, and Winterset chert from the Kansas City locality. Zehnder (1998) analyzed the chipped-stone debitage from two Little River focus sites to show that these people drew their stone from two very different regions. The lithics from one of them, the Sharps Creek site (14MP408), match nicely with the pattern present in sites at Marion (Rohn and Emerson 1984; Roper 2000b). Zehnder's work suggests strongly that Wedel's Little River focus will have to be revised and that the sites on tributaries of the Smoky Hill should be separate from at least some of those along the tributaries of the Arkansas River. The lithic sources that dominate the various village assemblages suggest the pattern of band territories illustrated in Figure 10.5.

Raw material from the various quarries was carried to Great Bend aspect sites in several forms. Rohn and Emerson (1984: 150–151) report the presence of large biface blanks in Marion sites, at least one of which appears to have shattered during heat-treatment in the village. Bifacial blanks have also been found in a pit at the Lower Walnut Radio Lane (14CO385) site, while similarly heat-shattered and unheated blanks have been recovered from the surface of the Maple City quarry (14CO5) (Gould 1898b, 1899; Hawley and Haury 1994; Reynolds, Reed, and Jackson 2001).

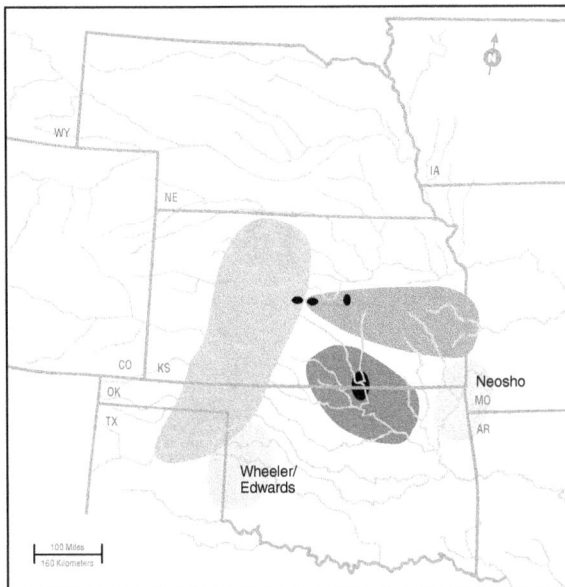

Figure 10.5. Approximate band territories suggested by analysis of the sources of the lithic materials found in Great Bend village sites. Darker shading indicates village clusters.

Rohn and Emerson report some large percussion flakes that apparently were also blanks. These very large flakes appear to have been detached from the core with a hard hammer, subsequent to which the thick bulbs of percussion were reduced with a soft hammer, apparently to allow them to pack better for transport. Another form of quarry blank is represented by true blades struck from polyhedral cores.

Glacial drift in the northeastern corner of Kansas was another important source of stone for pecked- or groundstone implements. Cobbles of Sioux quartzite were fashioned into mauls, and Kansas pipestone (not true catlinite) was obtained for pipe making. Some of the quartzite cobbles used for hammerstones may also come from this source, as well as from riverine gravels. The Dakota sandstone from the Smoky Hills region was used for arrow shaft smoothers and for other abraders. Limestone for milling stones and manos probably derives from a variety of sources.

Exchange was the source of a variety of exotic goods, and exchange with the puebloan peoples of the Southwest was especially important. Southwestern pottery, New Mexico obsidian, occasional pieces of turquoise, southwestern-style shaft straighteners and tubular pipes, and Olivella shell beads all derive from this source (Hawley 2000). Occasional sherds of Lower Loup and Caddoan pottery also occur in Great Bend aspect sites (Perttula, Hawley, and Scott 2001; Roper 2000d).

MATERIAL CULTURE

Great Bend aspect ceramics consist almost entirely of utilitarian wares, most of which were formed by the paddle and anvil technique. Also present are a few miniatures

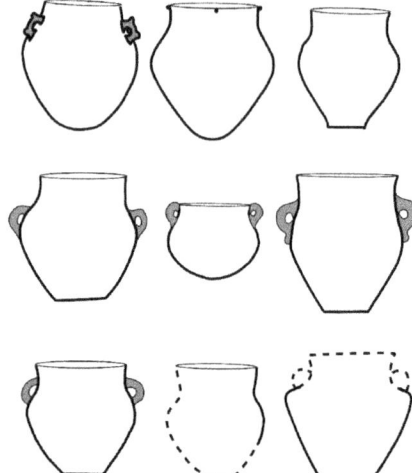

Figure 10.6. Typical Great Bend vessel shapes. Top row: Little River. Middle row: Lower Walnut. Bottom row: Marion (after W. R. Wedel 1959; Rohn and Emerson 1984).

formed by pinching. The most common vessel form is an amphora-shaped jar, the maximum diameter of which is usually above mid-height. The rims are fairly tall and vertical to slightly flaring (Figure 10.6). Both flat and convex bases occur. Also present are deep bowls that have lower rims and convex bases.

A few bottle forms are present in the Paint Creek site. Those that the senior author has examined are unique in several ways. They have a red slip that appears to have been applied after an initial firing of the vessel. The vessel was then fired a second time. They also feature loop handles that were oriented horizontally rather than vertically as on the jars. Analyses of the vessels' clay pastes are needed to determine whether they are trade items or of local origin. Vessel form, surface treatment, and temper type vary among the three main village clusters. Shell temper dominates Lower Walnut assemblages, surfaces are usually smoothed, and flat bases are common. In Little River sites, sand is the most common temper type, flat bases are rare, and simple-stamped surfaces occur. The sites near Marion have both shell and sand temper, some simple-stamping, and more flat bases than the Little River sites. A few cord-marked vessels occur in both the Little River and Marion sites. Jars frequently sport a pair of loop handles, as do a few deep bowls. On the jars, the handles are usually placed at the base of the rim. The handles are attached by riveting. Decoration is rare, especially below the rim. Incised and punctate decoration is usually restricted to the lip and handles, but appliqué nodes and fillets (some of which are incised) occur on upper rim exteriors.

Great Bend aspect arrowpoints are small and triangular, both with and without side notches. They usually have slightly convex blade edges and straight to concave bases. Many exhibit portions of the original flake scar on one or both faces. Three basic forms of knives are present. Some are plain ovate specimens. Others are stemmed or hafted, and on these the long blade edges usually exhibit alternate bevel-

Figure 10.7. Typical Great Bend chipped-stone artifacts. Points, a–e; pipe drill bit, f; stone awls, g, h; hafted beveled knives, i, n; endscrapers, j–l; blade fragments m, o.

ing (Figure 10.7). The third form, what Rohn and Emerson called Marion blade knives, consists of blades that most often are unifacially worked on one edge only.

Endscrapers are common. They are usually small and triangular to teardrop-shaped. The lateral edges are usually carefully straightened and smoothed, and the proximal ends are usually fairly thin. When more than one is present in a site, they are readily distinguished from assemblages from all earlier archaeological units in the region.

Drills are also common, and they come in several forms. The large, straight, double-ended drills are the most distinctive. The ends of used-up or broken beveled knives were also used as drills. Pipestone dust still adhering to some specimens demonstrates that both forms were used to drill stone pipes. Other smaller perforators that probably functioned as stone awls are also common, and these often have an expanding stem. Most of the smaller specimens do not have a thick cross section and hence probably did not function as drills. Instead they may have been used as stone awls to perforate the edges of hides so that they could be stretched for drying and scraping. Choppers and other heavy bifaces are frequently present. They include a tool type distinctive to Great Bend aspect sites. These have the form of choppers and have heavily battered edges. In fact, the edges on some are so blunted that they appear to have been used as hard hammers. These tools may have been used to re-roughen the surfaces of milling stones that had become slick from wear.

Groundstone artifacts include elbow pipes with very tall bowls (Figure 10.8). This form of pipe was usually fashioned from Kansas pipestone to form an angle of

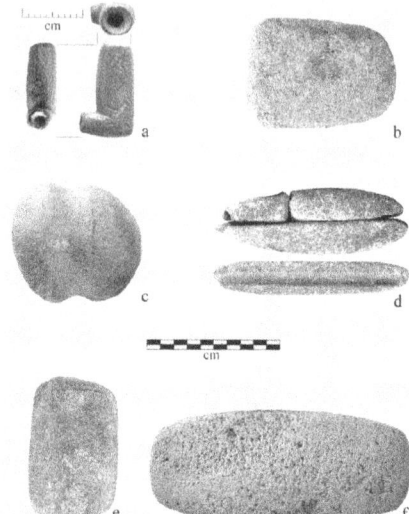

Figure 10.8. Typical Great Bend groundstone artifacts. Miniature pipe, a; nutting stone, b; round-headed maul, c; arrow shaft smoothers, d; manos, e, f.

slightly less than 90 degrees. Also present in large numbers are stone mauls (e.g., Wedel 1959: 276–280). These occur in two forms, those with flat ends and those on which the ends are quite convex. Apparently, the two forms of maul were used for very different purposes. Manos long enough to have been held in both hands and heavy grinding slabs are common. The pipes and milling stones are rare in earlier sites in Kansas. Other groundstone tools, such as arrow shaft smoothers and hammerstones, are not as distinctive.

Artifacts of bone, antler, and shell are also common in Great Bend aspect sites (Figure 10.9). Ubiquitous in the village sites are bison scapula hoes, hafted by a variety of techniques (Wedel 1959: 251, 365). Also made from bison scapulae, and often from broken hoes, are more or less triangular tools that functioned either as squash knives or digging tools (Rohn and Emerson 1984: 172–173). Another agricultural tool, digging stick tips made from the tibias of bison, are common in the Cowley County sites. Flaking tools, arrowpoints, shaft wrenches, and bone and antler endscraper handles are all found. Animal bone was also used to make hide grainers, beamers, awls, beads, and pendants. Some scored pieces of bison rib may have functioned as musical rasps; others may have been used to create simple stamping on pottery. Mussel shell was used primarily for making beads and pendants, but at least one hafted shell knife has been recovered from a Great Bend aspect site.

European goods show up in small numbers in some Great Bend aspect sites. Spanish chain mail (Terry and Terry 1961; Udden 1900; Wedel 1975) has drawn the most attention, but an axe head, glass beads, and beads of copper or brass are also present. Most of these materials appear to derive from the Spanish, as befits the early historic age of the sites.

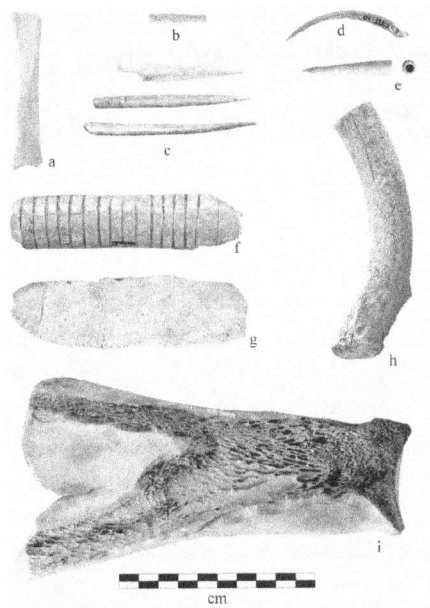

Figure 10.9. Typical Great Bend bone artifacts. Polished bison hyoid, a; pendant, b; awls, c; beaver incisor chisel, d; antler arrowpoint, e; bison rib rasp, f; knife, g; antler billet, h; scapula hoe, i.

CURRENT WORK AND FUTURE PROSPECTS

Work on Great Bend aspect archaeology continues. Susan Vehik (2002a, 2002b) has reanalyzed some of Wedel's data, examining them for evidence of status differences. Michelle Peck (2003) compiled a summary of Great Bend aspect hunting camps. Other work needs to be done. Zehnder's (1998) thesis points to the need for a revision of Wedel's Little River focus that recognizes the use of different territories by individual villages. No one has yet addressed in any detail the relationship of Great Bend aspect to the contemporary Neosho phase of northeastern Oklahoma and southwestern Missouri or to the Wheeler/Edwards complex of western Oklahoma. More work also needs to be done on the origins of the Great Bend aspect (Roper, chapter 7, this volume; S. C. Vehik 1976; Wedel 1968). A basic problem here is that so little is known of the Bluff Creek, Pratt, and Uncas complexes that preceded the Great Bend aspect in the southern half of Kansas (see chapter 11, this volume). Much more work is also needed on the demise of the Great Bend aspect and the transformations generated by increasing European contact (cf. Bell, Jelks, and Newcomb 1967; Odell 2002; S. C. Vehik, chapter 12, this volume; Wedel 1981). Finally, there are unanalyzed collections awaiting study. Zehnder looked only at the lithic debitage from two of the Kansas Archeology Training Program excavations; there are seven such collections that contain the full range of ceramic, lithic, and other artifacts, along with houses and other features.

11. Looking South: The Middle Ceramic Period in Southern Kansas and Beyond

Scott D. Brosowske and C. Tod Bevitt

Archaeological complexes lying south of the Arkansas River and dating to the Middle Ceramic period (A.D. 1100–1500) represent the Plains Village tradition on the Southern Plains. Until recently, the period has remained poorly documented in the Plains Border region of southwestern Kansas, northwestern Oklahoma, and the eastern half of the Texas panhandle compared to adjacent areas. Archaeological investigations in this area have been sporadic and have resulted in the identification of a number of cultural complexes that have long remained inadequately defined. While sharing many similarities with Central Plains Village societies, the frequent use of Alibates agatized dolomite also indicates that these groups developed trade relationships with Antelope Creek phase populations to the south. Overall, the material remains left by these groups suggest that this portion of the region represents an important transitional area, both spatially and temporally. As such, it occupies a key position for understanding many significant topics of long-standing interest.

This discussion focuses on results provided by recent investigations as a means of updating our understanding of the Middle Ceramic period in southern Kansas and beyond. Particular attention is on the recently defined Odessa phase of southwest Kansas and the panhandle region of Oklahoma and Texas (Brosowske 2002a). Delineation of this phase has been the result of fieldwork carried out over the last several years. While this research has shed much-needed light on the period, it has also served to illuminate the complex and variable nature of groups straddling the Central and Southern Plains border region. Included here are summaries on the Pratt and Bluff Creek complexes and other unaffiliated Middle Ceramic sites in southern Kansas and adjacent areas of Oklahoma (Figure 11.1). Because little fieldwork has been conducted on these neighboring cultural complexes during the last few decades, many crucial details about these groups still remain unknown. Despite these shortcomings, given the spatial and temporal focus of this chapter it is worthwhile to also consider these societies here.

It should be noted that even though the Odessa phase, Pratt and Bluff Creek complexes, and other unaffiliated sites are examined here within a single chapter, this does not necessarily imply that they shared similar origins or historical trajectories. Ideally, all of these entities could be combined within a single taxonomic framework; however, the information currently available precludes such an endeavor. But it is clear that these archaeological entities do share a number of similarities. This is likely

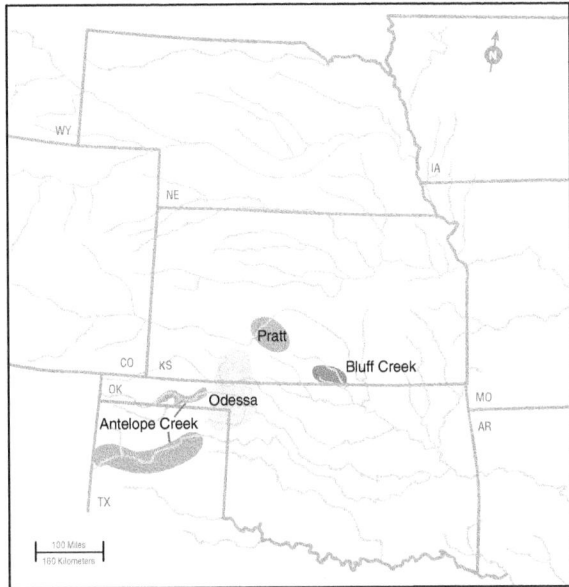

Figure 11.1.
Archaeological manifestations of the Plains Border

a consequence of regional patterns of interaction and exchange, the natural landscape they inhabited, and a shared dependence on horticulture.

THE ODESSA PHASE (A.D. 1250–1475)

Previously, the Middle Ceramic period on the Southern High Plains has been synonymous with the stone architectural sites of the Antelope Creek phase and the Buried City complex (see D. T. Hughes and Hughes-Jones 1987; Krieger 1946; Lintz 1986, for review of past investigations). Indeed, that sites with stone architecture have long dominated previous discussions is not surprising since these Middle Ceramic populations have been proposed to have occupied an enormous area covering portions of four different states (see Lintz 1986: fig. 1). Recent investigations, however, have demonstrated that the area inhabited by these societies is substantially smaller than previously estimated (e.g., Boyd 2004; Brosowske 2002a).

Despite an absence of stone foundation architecture, many Middle Ceramic sites along the northeastern margins of the Southern High Plains have been attributed to either the Antelope Creek phase or Buried City complex (e.g., R. Brooks 1986, 1994a; Drass and Turner 1989; J. N. Howard and Brown 1973; D. T. Hughes and Hughes-Jones 1987: 105; Kay County Chapter of the Oklahoma Anthropological Society 1963; Lintz 1986: fig. 1, pp. 29–30). Until recently, however, the sporadic nature of research conducted in this area has precluded the assignment of cultural affiliation to sites found here. In this chapter the results of recent and past archaeological work are summarized to present a new Middle Ceramic taxonomic unit for the northeastern margins of the Southern High Plains: the Odessa phase (Brosowske 2000, 2002a; Brosowske, Drass, and Maki 2000).

Delineation of the Odessa phase is largely a result of intensive investigations conducted in the study area since 1998. This work has included three yearlong survey projects, four archaeological field schools, documentation of many private collections, and extensive geophysical survey at several sites (Bement and Brosowske 2001; Bevitt 1997, 1998, 1999a, 1999b; Brosowske 1999, 2002a; Brosowske and Bement 1998a; Brosowske, Drass, and Maki 2000; Brosowske and Maki 2002; Maki 2000; Maki and Jones 1998, 2001; Maki, Jones, and Brosowske 1999). To date, systematic excavations have been conducted at nine different sites. Thirty-four radiocarbon dates indicate occupation from A.D. 1250 to A.D. 1475. It is worth noting that these studies have been greatly augmented by the efforts of local avocational archaeologists and landowners who have actively participated in all stages of fieldwork (Bevitt 1999a; Brosowske and Bement 1998; Brosowske, Drass, and Maki 2000).

Although a great deal more research is required, a fairly detailed picture of the Odessa phase can be assembled at this time. Key traits examined here include spatial and temporal distribution, settlement patterns, domestic architecture, subsistence, composition of material assemblages, involvement in intersocietal exchange, and mortuary practices. Most of these traits are very distinct and serve to differentiate the phase from other surrounding Middle Ceramic entities of the Southern Plains.

Spatial and Temporal Distribution

Odessa phase sites occur from southwest Kansas, across northwest Oklahoma, and into adjacent areas of the Texas panhandle (Figure 11.1). The northern and eastern borders of the distribution are still poorly defined, but the southern and western margins present a fairly abrupt cutoff or boundary with Antelope Creek phase sites. Pedestrian survey and analysis of site collections suggest that Odessa phase sites do not extend south of the Wolf Creek valley or west of the Palo Duro valley (see Bement and Brosowske 2001: 76–77; D. T. Hughes 1991: 142).

From north to south, important sites include Lundeen (14MD306), Lonker (34BV4), Odessa Yates (34BV100), Sprague (34BV99), Schwab (34BV130), and Miller (34EL25). In addition, sites attributed to the Buried City complex, which have previously been included in the Antelope Creek phase (Lintz 1986), are also included in the Odessa phase. These include 41OC1, 41OC26, 41OC27, 41OC29, 41OC43, and 41OC48.

Settlement

Two main types of settlements are known for the Odessa phase: homesteads and large extended villages. The presence of domestic structures, cache pits, substantial middens, and burials support the idea that each of these site types was a permanent settlement.

Homesteads. These sites are designated largely by site size (i.e., <5000 m^2) and are known primarily from northern portions of the study area. Excavations have been conducted at several homesteads, including Lundeen, Lonker, Miller, and Wynn (34BV63) (Bevitt 1999a; R. Brooks 1994a; Drass and Turner 1989; Oklahoma Archeological Survey Site Files 2002). Homesteads are situated atop low terraces overlooking small-to-large drainages and are invariably located adjacent to perennial springs and small patches of fertile soil. These sites are generally dispersed, although some drainages contain two or three closely spaced homesteads, which, if contemporaneous, probably represent hamlets.

Extended Villages. In southern portions of the distribution, sites of all sizes are densely concentrated along Clear, Duck Pond, Kiowa, Sand, and Wolf creeks to form large extended villages reminiscent of those described by Coronado in 1541 at Quivira (see Bolton 1949: 292). Although site boundaries are constrained by topographic features, such as terraces and ravines, and are recorded as individual sites, it is clear that they form continuous settlements 6 to 12 km in length (Bement and Brosowske 2001; Brosowske 2002a; Brosowske, Drass, and Maki 2000; D. T. Hughes 1991: 142). To date, systematic excavations have been conducted at large villages along Clear and Wolf creeks (i.e., the Buried City locality). Barring complete excavation and an extensive radiocarbon program, estimating the population of these villages is difficult. Nevertheless, if these villages were occupied at a minimal rate of five families per linear km, at least 30 to 60 families could have inhabited these settlements.

The resource base needed to support aggregated populations is much different than that required for homesteads occupied by nuclear or extended families. In general, an abundance of fertile soils and potable water are two of the more important resources that aggregations of horticulturalists require. As such, it is not surprising that large villages in the study area are found in settings where fertile floodplain soils are abundant, the risk of catastrophic flooding is minimal, and where water is not saturated with chemical impurities that render the water undrinkable (see Marine and Schoff 1962: 56). Settings meeting each of these requirements are limited in the study area but are most often found in the upper ends of tributaries.

That Odessa phase habitation sites are situated near agriculturally productive soils supports the interpretation that these populations were heavily dependent on horticulture. Although this is typical of most horticultural societies, fertile floodplain soils, which retain water well and are easily tillable, are particularly important in the study area where only 20–23 inches of precipitation falls annually. Floodplain soils with these characteristics are often classified as Spur, Bippus, Canadian, St. Paul, or Roxbury series or another equivalent. Odessa phase settlements are almost always associated with these loam or clay loam soils. Soil capability classification systems rate these as the most productive bottomland soils in the region (see Allgood 1962: 28). Interestingly, these soils compose less than 2 percent of all soils, which suggests that they were a limited resource.

Initially, it was thought that the density and size of Odessa sites across the distribution was directly correlated with the abundance of arable land; however, it is likely that other factors also influenced these patterns. For example, aggregated populations were probably necessary to defend or maintain claims to productive soils, horticultural fields, bison pounds, storage facilities, trade routes, and other valued resources. This interpretation gains further support when one considers the fact that most of the aggregated settlements are clustered along the margins of their distribution. That Odessa populations may have not maintained particularly amiable relations with their neighbors, particularly those of the Antelope Creek phase, seems to be a distinct possibility (see R. Brooks 1994b; Green 1986; S. C. Vehik 2002a).

Radiocarbon dates suggest that numerous homesteads and extended villages were contemporaneously occupied throughout the area between A.D. 1250 and A.D. 1350. This indicates the presence of a sizable population of Odessa phase groups rather than smaller numbers of people who made frequent residential moves. In contrast, the number of settlements dating from A.D. 1350–1475 is much lower. Even though these dates are primarily from large settlements, it is not clear whether the phase underwent increasing aggregation through time or if the area was undergoing depopulation.

Architecture and Other Features

The primary domestic house forms observed at Odessa phase sites are oval-to-circular subterranean pit structures (Bement and Brosowske 2001: 32; Bevitt 1999a; R. Brooks 1994a; Brosowske, Drass, and Maki 2000; D. T. Hughes 1991; Oklahoma Archeological Survey Site Files 2002). The dozen or so pit houses examined thus far are about 20–30 square m in size and were excavated between 0.9 and 1.5 m in depth below the aboriginal ground surface. One completely excavated structure at the Odessa Yates site (34BV100) is probably typical of the phase and provides a great deal of information regarding construction details (Brosowske 1999: 2). This house contained two large central posts with smaller posts closely spaced around the perimeter and a small basin-shaped hearth along a pit wall (Figure 11.2). Structures are usually oriented from northwest to southeast with a sloped or stepped entry along the latter side.

A second distinct house form has been identified at several Odessa phase sites. These structures are circular, 40–60 cm deep, and about 2.0 to 2.5 m in diameter. Many of these shallow pit houses have basin-shaped hearths located off center, a central post, and in some cases, posts along the perimeter (Figure 11.2). Identical house forms are documented for the Little River focus at 14RC306 (Figure 11.2). Roof configurations for this and other Odessa phase houses remain unknown, as all of the structures excavated appear to have been dismantled and usable posts and beams salvaged (Brosowske 1999). Following abandonment, houses were typically backfilled with trash.

Odessa phase sites at the Buried City locality include both types of pit houses described above and large, square surface structures outlined in stone (Figure 11.2) (Brosowske and Maki 2002; Brosowske et al. 2003; D. T. Hughes 1991; D. T. Hughes

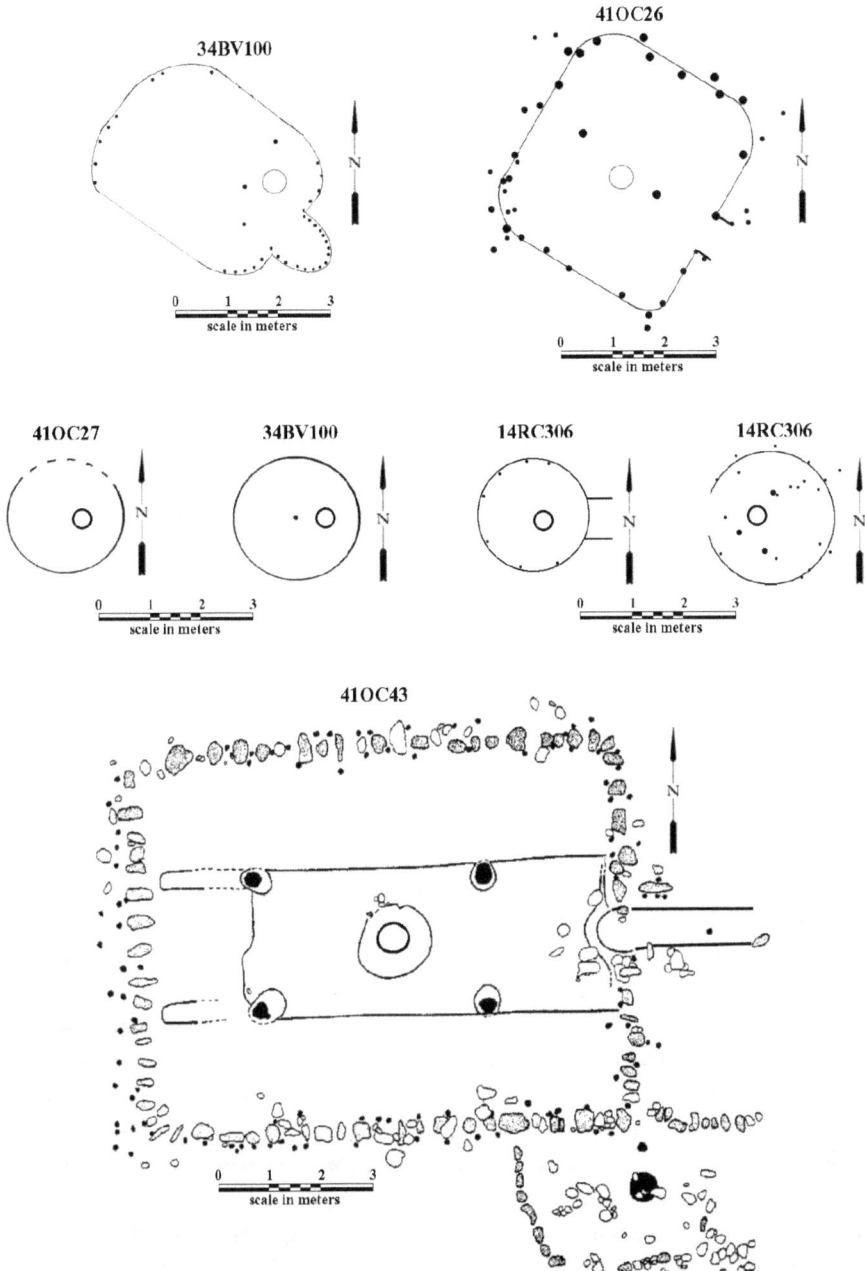

Figure 11.2. Odessa phase houses

and Hughes-Jones 1987). Stone houses have not been documented downstream from this locality or at any other Odessa phase sites. Recent work suggests that pit houses are widespread at Buried City and probably represent the dominant house form (Brosowske and Maki 2002; Brosowske et al. 2003). The relationship between semi-subterranean and surface stone structures at Buried City remains unclear, although given the close proximity of this locality to the Antelope Creek phase, some form of competitive emulation or simply the diffusion of ideas may be indicated.

Subterranean storage facilities are very common at Odessa phase habitation sites and include both bell-shaped and cylindrical storage pits. These pits are usually unlined, though examples lined with caliche plaster have also been identified. Typical dimensions are 1.0–1.5 m diameter and depth. Multiple cache pits are often found outside individual house structures and following abandonment were backfilled with trash. The abundance of storage facilities at Odessa phase sites is aptly demonstrated at the Odessa Yates site, where more than 150 cache pits have been documented in one area. Most were found by shallow surface geophysical survey, testing, and positive cropmarks (areas within the field crop exhibiting more luxuriant growth) (Maki, Brosowske, and Drass 2003).

Subsistence

The character of Odessa phase subsistence economies is fairly well known, since a number of systematic investigations have been conducted at several homesteads and extended villages. Information regarding floral and faunal assemblages are known from well-dated contexts at Lundeen, Lonker, Odessa Yates, and Miller and at several along Wolf Creek (see Bevitt 1999a; R. Brooks 1994a; Brosowske 2002a; Brosowske, Drass, and Maki 2000; Brosowske et al. 2003; Drass and Turner 1989; D. T. Hughes 1991; D. T. Hughes and Hughes-Jones 1987). These data indicate that while all settlements were reliant on a mixture of cultivated and wild plants, a great deal of variability seems to exist among resident hunting economies.

As noted above, settlement patterns and the abundance of subterranean storage facilities suggest that all Odessa phase populations were heavily dependent on horticulture. This conclusion is further supported by the abundance and ubiquity of domesticated plants in macrobotanical samples and high frequencies of horticultural tools at all sites (Bevitt 1999a; R. Brooks 1994a; Brosowske 2000; 2002a; Brosowske, Drass, and Maki 2000; Drass and Turner 1989). Domesticated species present include corn, beans, squash, marsh elder, and sunflower. Groups also utilized a variety of wild plants, such as sunflower, purslane, goosefoot, sand plums, knotweed, marsh elder, bulrush, and carpetweed (Bevitt 1999a: 60, 107, 163; R. Brooks 1994a: table 8; Brosowske 2002a; Brosowske et al. 2003; Drass and Turner 1989).

The available data suggest that substantial differences in hunting strategies existed among homesteads and large extended villages. At small sites, hunting appears to have focused on a broad range of species, and nearly every animal found in the region is recovered in the faunal inventory (e.g., Bevitt 1999a; R. Brooks 1994a; Drass and Turner 1989). In contrast, faunal assemblages from extended villages display little species diversity and are dominated (i.e., >90 percent) by bison (Brosowske 2002a; D. T. Hughes, personal communication, 2001). These assemblages also suggest that all portions of bison were transported back to villages and were intensively processed for marrow and bone grease. Bison remains from these sites suggest that kills were conducted close to villages by bison-hunting specialists.

The economic variability observed among Odessa phase sites does not appear related to differences in climate or environment but rather to whether subsistence activities were organized at the household level or some level beyond the household (e.g., clan, lineage). Faunal assemblages recovered at homesteads appear to document opportunistic hunting of dispersed prey sources by one or two individuals, while people living in or near extended villages hunted bison in large cooperative groups. Albeit tentative, the above model is supported by numerous examples in the ethnographic record, which demonstrate that diet breadth is highly correlated with the size of foraging groups (see chapters in Winterhalder and Smith 1981).

Material Assemblage

Odessa phase artifact inventories are comparable to other Plains Village tradition sites and include the usual suite of diamond beveled knives, triangular projectile points, distal endscrapers, drills, bison tibia digging sticks and scapula hoes, bone awls, cord-marked ceramics, and abrading stones (Figures 11.3 and 11.4). However, if one looks in greater detail at specific features of material assemblages, it is clear that

Figure 11.3. Odessa phase ceramics. (Courtesy of the Kansas State Historical Society)

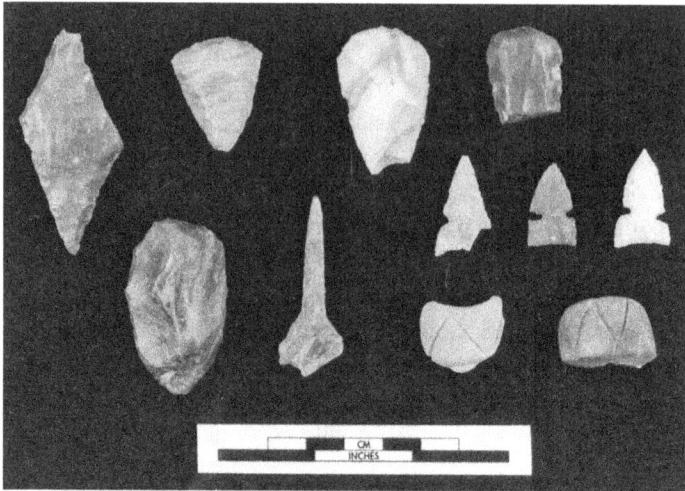

Figure 11.4. Odessa Phase stone tools and pipe fragments. (Courtesy of the Kansas State Historical Society)

Odessa phase sites are distinctive. In fact, combined with information on settlement locations, it is often possible to differentiate Odessa phase sites from those associated with other Middle Ceramic groups to the west, south, and southeast purely on the presence or absence of specific material traits. Particularly important are lithic raw materials utilized, the high percentages of decorated ceramics, and the near ubiquitous presence of southwestern trade items.

Located near the boundary of the Central and Southern Plains, lithic raw material use and decorated ceramics suggest cultural ties to both regions. While lithic assemblages from Upper Canark and Redbed variant sites are usually dominated (i.e., >90 percent) by Alibates agatized dolomite or local materials (Drass 1997; Lintz 1986), Odessa phase site assemblages contain a combination of Alibates agatized dolomite and Smoky Hill jasper (Brosowske 2000, 2002a; Brosowske, Drass, and Maki 2000). Individual site samples vary, but Alibates usually makes up 50–60 percent and Smoky Hill about 25–35 percent of all chipped stone. The high percentages of Smoky Hill are extremely unusual compared to other Southern Plains Village assemblages. Cherts derived from the Flint Hills do occur at most sites (i.e., usually <5 percent), but are more common at the easternmost Odessa phase sites (i.e., 20 percent). Various local and nonlocal materials round out the remaining portion of lithic assemblages.

Globular cord-marked vessels with vertical to flaring rims characterize the ceramic assemblage. Rims are frequently decorated, usually greater than 50 percent, with a variety of techniques (Bevitt 1997, 2005a; Brosowske 2000, 2002a; D. T. Hughes 1991, 2002; D. T. Hughes and Hughes-Jones 1987). Although a wide variety of decorations are represented, the most common are finger-pinching or -impressing and parallel impressed lines along the neck and rim (Figure 11.3). While lip tabs and handles are present in many assemblages, they generally occur on less than 5 percent of ceramics. Surface treatment varies from unmodified to completely smoothed cordmarking, although some examples with corncob impressions are also present (Bevitt 1997, 2005a; D. T. Hughes 2002). Tempers most often consist of sand (>80 percent) but also include bone, crushed stone, grog, and grit.

In general, most other aspects of Odessa phase material assemblages are comparable to other Plains Village tradition sites. Nonetheless, several points are worthy of mention. First, projectile points usually include various corner-notched forms (8 percent), Washita (55 percent), and Fresno (37 percent) varieties. Second, although bison tibia digging sticks were produced in essentially the same manner as in other areas, scapula hoes were manufactured by the removal of the glenoid process. Lastly, groundstone metates are rare at some sites and suggest the use of wooden mortars and pestles.

Intersocietal Exchange

The Middle Ceramic period marks the beginning of widespread intersocietal exchange in the region. This is most readily seen in an increased reliance on specialized stone tools produced from high-quality lithic materials. As such, it is no surprise that the period also coincides with the establishment of large permanent settlements near important quarries of the region as groups laid claim to these valuable resources (see Bandy 1976; Brosowske 2002a; Lintz 1986; S. C. Vehik 1990). The wide variety of nonlocal materials recovered indicates that Odessa phase sites were actively involved in a widespread exchange network. Although exchange with other Plains populations is most readily apparent, nonlocal items of southwestern origin are also common and suggest direct trade with the eastern Pueblos (Brosowske 2004; Brosowske and Bement 1998). The goals of exchange were undoubtedly multifaceted and provided access to both utilitarian and nonutilitarian or status items.

Previous research indicates that Antelope Creek groups controlled access, production, and distribution rights to Alibates agatized dolomite, the highest-quality tool stone on the Southern High Plains (Bandy 1976; Brosowske 2002a; Lintz 1991). While Alibates is certainly a common lithic material at Odessa phase sites, the fact that bedrock sources for this material are located over 100 km away clearly indicates that this material should not be regarded as a local resource. A comparison of chipped-stone assemblages from Odessa and Antelope Creek phase sites indicates that substantial differences in the availability of Alibates existed among sites and provides some important insights into the nature of regional interaction at this time. These differences are especially clear when Odessa and Antelope Creek sites (e.g., Stamper [34TX1], Roy Smith [34BV4], and Two Sisters [34TX32]), located at similar distances from the quarry, are compared. The size and frequency of tools and debitage from Antelope Creek sites suggests that these groups enjoyed relatively unrestricted access to Alibates. In contrast, debitage is scarce and largely limited to late stage production or resharpening activities at Odessa phase sites. In addition, Odessa phase tools are often heavily exhausted or recycled into other tools.

The heavily curated appearance of chipped-stone assemblages at Odessa phase sites, particularly extended villages, suggests that groups were regularly faced with shortages of chipped stone. Although other lesser-quality cherts and quartzites were available in the area, these groups seem intent on using high-quality tool stone. As noted above, while Alibates agatized dolomite typically composes the majority of chipped-stone materials recovered at Odessa phase sites, other high-quality lithic sources are also represented. In particular, the abundance of Smoky Hill jasper at Odessa phase sites, whose nearest sources are at least 250 km away, is intriguing. It is possible that groups established and maintained trade relations with unknown groups in north-central Kansas as a means of offsetting their dependence on trade with Antelope Creek populations.

Overall, the composition and appearance of Odessa phase chipped-stone assemblages suggest that, while trade did occur between Odessa and Antelope Creek societies, it seems likely that interaction was irregular and may have been strained. Although difficult to assess at this time, given the examples provided by Keeley (1996), LeBlanc (1999), and others (e.g., R. Brooks 1994b; Green 1986; A. W. Johnson and Earle 2000; Wilkens 2001) it is likely that warfare was prevalent among these societies.

Materials obtained from the eastern Pueblos most often represent evidence for interregional exchange at Odessa phase sites. Southwestern trade goods regularly occur at most sites, although frequencies are quite variable from site to site. Puebloan trade items include obsidian, marine shell beads and ornaments, turquoise or amazonite, ceramics, Mimbres Valley greenstone, mica, and others. Trade items from regions other than the Southwest include conch shell ornaments, a wide variety of nonlocal lithics, and Kansas and South Dakota pipestone (Bevitt 1999a; Brosowske 2002a; Brosowske and Bement 1998; D. T. Hughes and Hughes-Jones 1987). The latter usually shows up as finished items, but pipe manufacturing debris does occur at some sites.

Mortuary Practices

Mortuary practices of the Odessa phase are not well understood, but burials can include both single and multiple interments on or overlooking habitation sites (Bement and Brosowske 2001: 67; Brosowske and Maki 2002; D. T. Hughes 1991; D. T. Hughes and Hughes-Jones 1987: 104–105; Oklahoma Archeological Survey Site Files 2002). In some instances, burials are capped by rock-covered cairns. In contrast to surrounding groups, burial of the dead within house structures does not appear to have been a common practice among Odessa populations. Burials in houses have been documented along Wolf Creek, but these appear to represent reuse of Middle Ceramic sites by later occupants (D. T. Hughes, personal communication, 2003; D. T.

Hughes and Hughes-Jones 1987: table 7). Overall, considering the size and population of the phase, burials are noticeably rare. Although the reasons for this are unclear, it is possible that groups may have practiced some form of excarnation, such as scaffold burial. Several burials contain evidence for intersocietal warfare, but these examples are poorly documented. Associated grave goods are common and often include mussel shells, elbow pipes of Kansas pipestone, caches of Alibates flakes, large bifaces, Olivella shell beads, celts produced from nonlocal materials, cord-marked vessels, bone awls, tibia digging sticks, conch and abalone shell ornaments, and turquoise beads and pendants. Marked concentrations of status items are not known from burial contexts.

THE PRATT COMPLEX (A.D. 1300–1500)

The name "Pratt complex" came into common usage as a result of Wedel's (1959) commentary on a surface collection from a site along the upper reaches of the South Fork of the Ninnescah River near Pratt, Kansas, but our understanding of this complex of sites is nearly as poor today as it was more than 50 years ago. Subsurface investigations near Pratt are limited to amateur excavations of cache pits at several sites, as well as some little-known investigations conducted by Dr. Paul Baker of the University of Southern Maine, who had local ties to the Pratt area. Experienced amateur archaeologists in the area have made significant contributions through reporting of sites and through allowing access to their collections.

Spatial and Temporal Distribution

The Pratt locality includes sites along an eight-kilometer stretch of the Ninnescah River and centered on the city of Pratt (Figure 11.1). This area includes a wide range of site sizes. The smallest sites are less than five acres (2 hectares) and include sites 14PT402, 14PT405, 14PT407, and 14PT425. Somewhat larger sites, approximately 10–15 acres (4–6 hectares), include 14PT301, 14PT302, 14PT409, 14PT410, and 14PT414. Moderately large sites range up to 25 acres (10 hectares) and include 14PT1 and a complex group of sites situated along the south edge of Pratt consisting of sites 14PT304, 14PT405, 14PT406, and 14PT420. Large sites in the Pratt locality include 14PT408, occupying approximately 43 acres (17 hectares), and perhaps 14PT415 covering roughly 60 acres (24 hectares) and including areas both north and south of the river (suggesting that the site could be divided into at least two discrete areas).

Currently, the best-documented Pratt complex component comes from the Lewis site (14PA307). Lewis is a multicomponent, stratified site yielding several Great Bend levels, a Pratt component, and an apparent Smoky Hill–like component (Monger 1970; Ranney 1994). The site has been interpreted as a hunting camp of some permanence since several houses are represented but evidence of horticulture is limited.

Specifically, there are no bone-digging implements, scant evidence of corn or other cultigens, and no deep storage facilities (Monger 1970: 14). As such, the site is not necessarily representative of Pratt settlement and subsistence patterns or even a good measure of the material culture overall.

Related Pratt complex sites are found on Elm Creek, a major tributary of the Medicine Lodge River approximately 15 miles south of the city of Pratt. Significant among these is the Lemon Ranch site (14BA401), briefly tested by the Kansas State Historical Society in 1972. There is also a sizable collection of material from several pits uncovered during ranch activities and subsequently salvaged by amateur archaeologists. One final component has previously been linked to the Pratt complex: the Seuser site (14RH301), which has been the subject of a recent analysis (Bevitt 1996, 2005b). That analysis suggested the traits exhibited at the site bore stronger similarities to other sites in southwest Kansas (see Unaffiliated Middle Ceramic Sites of the Plains Border Region, below).

The original temporal span for the complex of A.D. 1400–1500 was suggested by Wedel (1959: 505–506) on the basis of puebloan ceramic cross-dates from 14PT1. Additional puebloan ceramics from that site, as well as one from 14PT408, confirm this range. Limited salvage excavations in Pratt have produced two radiocarbon dates from separate features (one from 14PT420 and one from the adjacent 14PT304) that serve to strengthen the ranges initially provided through cross-dating. The ^{14}C dates suggest an occupation beginning sometime in the 1300s and continuing into the latter portion of the 1400s (see Appendix).

Architecture and Other Features

Currently, information on architectural and other features of the Pratt complex is limited. One complete and several partial surface structures at the Lewis site represent the bulk of the sample. The complete house exhibited slightly flattened sides and rounded, braced corners with an entrance facing east (Figure 11.5). Basin-shaped hearths were centrally located within structures. Other hearths (circular basin form and simple surface hearths) were noted outside the identified structures (Monger 1970: 9). A single ovoid shallow basin containing a single post near the center was excavated at 14BA401, suggesting that subsurface structures are also present. From both the Pratt and Elm Creek localities, trash-filled storage pits have been excavated, but little concrete information on size and form is available. Various accounts suggest both cylindrical and bell-shaped pit forms and pit dimensions of approximately one meter in diameter and up to one meter deep.

Subsistence

Of all the poorly defined characteristics of the complex, subsistence is by far the most poorly quantified. Ranney (1994: 61) notes that bison were common in all levels

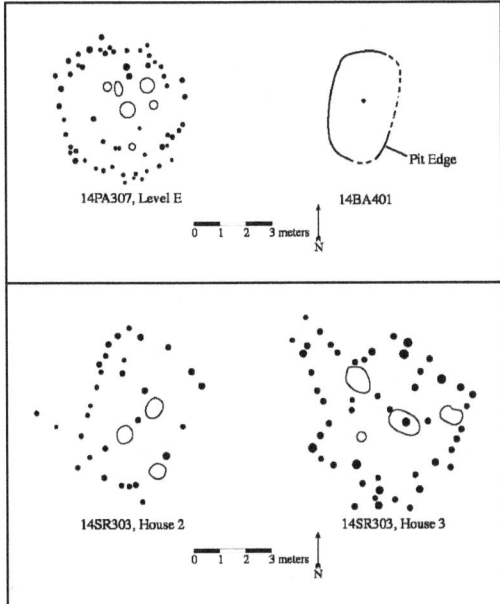

Figure 11.5. Pratt (top row) and Bluff Creek complex (bottom row) houses

at the Lewis site, while deer-sized elements, various avifauna, turtle, fish, and small mammal remains were noted occasionally. Bison bone overall exhibits breakage patterns characteristic of marrow extraction and at least some bone grease reduction. Charred pits of *Prunus* sp. were collected from Lewis, and corn has been collected from Pratt locality sites (particularly 14PT1). Digging implements typically associated with horticultural activities are common at most sites except Lewis and are secondary evidence of widely practiced horticulture. Bone tools are dominated by three items in particular: bison tibia digging stick tips, bison scapula hoes (glenoid articulation removed), and awls formed on long bone shaft fragments, rib edges, and from deer/pronghorn metapodials. Tubular bone beads and finely pointed needles are also present.

Material Assemblage

The Pratt complex tool kit is varied, but overall similar in many respects to most Plains Village assemblages. Chipped-stone tools include small triangular arrowpoints (Washita variety is most common), beveled knives, plano-convex endscrapers, and flake drills. The groundstone inventory includes tool manufacture and maintenance equipment such as arrow shaft abraders and hammerstones (Figure 11.6). Domestic processing equipment includes manos and metates and grooved mauls.

Lithic raw material patterning suggests an interesting, if unquantified, dichotomy between the Lewis site and some other Pratt complex sites in the Pratt locality and elsewhere. At Lewis, the only site for which quantification is available, Alibates agatized dolomite composed 56 percent of the Pratt level. Smoky Hill jasper totaled nearly 32 percent, Flint Hills cherts (primarily Wreford) were noted to be 6 percent of the assemblage, miscellaneous materials made up 5.2 percent, and obsidian was found in isolated instances (Ranney 1994: 58). Examination of collections from 14PT408 suggests a higher frequency of Alibates and a much lower occurrence of Smoky Hill jasper. Likewise, artifacts recovered primarily from feature contexts at

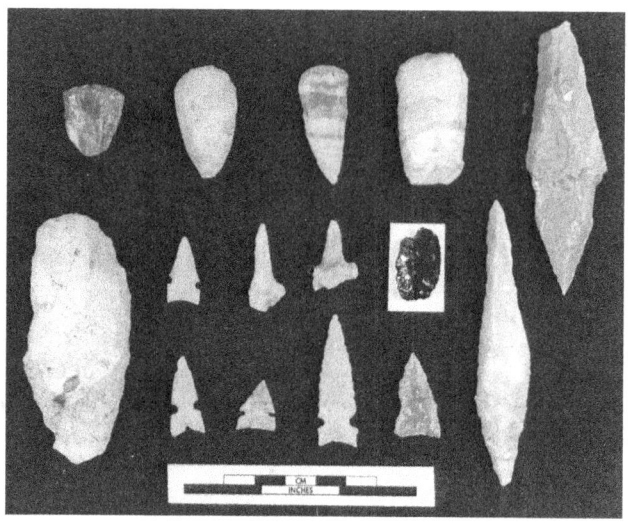

Figure 11.6. Pratt complex stone tools. (Courtesy of the Kansas State Historical Society)

14BA401 indicate a high proportion of Alibates in the sample, perhaps as high as 80 percent. In that same collection, several Florence A and Smoky Hill tools were noted, but debitage related to these types was limited.

Ceramics are predominantly cord-marked (80–85 percent), often exhibiting at least partial smoothing of the impressions. Occasional unmodified cord-markings are present, particularly on the rim. Plain wares are present at all sites (15–20 percent). In general, sites in the Pratt locality and elsewhere are dominated by sand-tempered ceramics. Other temper agents occur in low frequencies at most sites and include bone and calcium-carbonate material ($CaCO_3$), such as limestone or caliche. In addition, isolated examples of untempered ceramics are found at some sites. In contrast, bone tempering is very common at Lewis where nearly 79 percent of the collection had bone as either the only temper or bone mixed with sand (Ranney 1994: 46).

The typical vessel form consists of globular jars of moderate size, with slightly out-flaring rims (Figure 11.7). Handles and lugs are noted only in very rare instances. Based on reconstructed vessel pieces at Lewis, vessels were usually less than 20 cm tall (Ranney 1994: 51). Vessels of similar and slightly larger sizes have been found at other Pratt complex sites, including Pratt, 14PT408, and 14BA401. A miniature plain ware vessel exhibiting a subconical base, slight shoulders, and flaring rim was also recovered from 14BA401.

Decoration is generally confined to the vessel lip and includes punctates and obliquely incised or impressed lines. Six of nine vessels represented by rimsherds at Lewis exhibited obliquely impressed lip decoration (Ranney 1994: 52). In a collection of ceramics from Pratt, 21 percent of the rimsherds exhibit lip decoration, all but one of which were notched, a term synonymous with the previously mentioned oblique line decorative form (Wilcox 1981: 112). Vertical appliqué tabs are rarely found. When

Figure 11.7. Pratt and Bluff Creek complex ceramics. The Bluff Creek complex ceramics are in the top two rows; the Pratt complex ceramics are in the bottom row. (Courtesy of the Kansas State Historical Society)

present, this decoration is found on the vessel neck.

Evidence of exotic materials of southwestern origin is nearly universal in the Pratt complex, though the quantity of these items is small. Isolated puebloan potsherds occur at many sites. Obsidian is found in limited quantities at nearly every site, typically as flakes, but the occasional projectile point or flake tool is also found. Turquoise beads and fragments, Olivella shell beads, and other marine shell ornaments are found at some sites, particularly those from which features have been excavated. While this information cannot quantify the degree of interaction Pratt complex populations had with other groups, these exotic goods, found at nearly every site regardless of size, suggest that these materials arrived in the area occasionally, although the low numbers also suggest that Pratt complex populations were not too involved in the regional exchange of exotic materials.

Mortuary Practices

Our understanding of Pratt complex mortuary practices is limited to a single instance from 14BA401 where a child was discovered in a flexed position on the floor of a bell-shaped pit exposed in a trench silo wall. Material collected from the fill in the vicinity of this interment included ceramics, a Kansas pipestone pipe fragment, and faunal material (bison, turtle, shellfish). A skull and femur portion of an adult was also recovered from this site, although little is known of its specific provenience; it was recovered from an apparently disturbed context.

THE BLUFF CREEK COMPLEX (A.D. 1100–1300)

Much of the material assemblage that today is included in the Bluff Creek complex was originally recognized and discussed by Keller (1961) as a component of the Mid-Arkansan focus. The complex was defined sometime after excavation at the Buresh and Nulik sites in 1969 (Witty 1969b). Before this complex was named, the University of Kansas conducted excavations at Anthony (14HP1) in 1959 and 1960, and the Kansas State Historical Society excavated Armstrong (14HP5) in 1966 (Witty 1969b; R. Gould 1974). More recently, the Kansas Archeology Training Program excavated at Hallman (14HP524) (Huhnke 2000; Thies 1989). A better understanding of the complex requires not more excavated materials but rather more quantification of the results of the excavations, as well as limited dating of features from the various sites to better establish a chronological framework.

Spatial and Temporal Distribution

The complex is situated along Bluff Creek and its tributaries in south-central Kansas (Figure 11.1). Bluff Creek is a major tributary of the lower Chickaskia River. Intensive site survey along portions of Bluff Creek has yielded abundant evidence of extensive settlement along the drainage during the Middle Ceramic period (R. Gould 1975). Soils may have played an important role in the settlement pattern along Bluff Creek. Gould (1975: 97) noted that Bluff Creek complex sites were not found in the upper portion of the drainage system where soils tended to be rocky and where alluvial terrace settings were less common. This pattern may be further supported when comparing those soils with the alluvial settings in the Caldwell and Bluff City localities where numerous Bluff Creek complex sites have been identified.

The dating of the complex is difficult because several radiocarbon dates from Gakushuin radiocarbon laboratory are among the few samples that have been submitted. Gakushuin dates have been determined to be unreliable (Blakeslee 1994). In general, however, the complex is thought to date to A.D. 1100–1300.

Architecture and Other Features

Typical features associated with the complex include surface structures of ovoid to subrectangular form (Figure 11.5). When found in native prairie settings, house sites have been identified as low mounds (Witty 1969b). Excavation feature clusters suggest a pole framework with interior supports and possible partitions. In at least one instance, an extended entryway was identified. House sizes cluster around 25 square m. Interior hearths typically are not found. Other pole structures near house structures may include domestic work areas such as drying racks and scaffolds. Other features include shallow oval-shaped basins and cylindrical storage pits typically less than one m deep.

Subsistence

Subsistence data are available in part for several sites including Armstrong, Anthony, and Hallman. At these sites, evidence of horticulture is ubiquitous: primarily, charred maize (i.e., kernels, cobs, etc.) and, secondarily, the common occurrence of bison scapula hoes and tibia digging stick tips. Quantified faunal resources suggest a heavy reliance on bison, though other mammalian taxa are present and include deer, pronghorn, canid (i.e., coyote and wolf-sized dogs), raccoon, skunk, squirrel, cottontail, jackrabbit, prairie dog, and box and pond turtle. Further, several species of avifauna include raptors, waterfowl, and songbirds. Fish include bass, catfish, and sunfish. The remains suggest a generalized subsistence economy exploiting various local microenvironments, although bison and other large mammal species were the primary source of food.

Material Assemblage

Bluff Creek lithic assemblages exhibit many of the traits typically associated with the Plains Village period overall: various types of small triangular arrowpoints (dominated by the Washita variety), small plano-convex endscrapers, diamond-shaped beveled knives, and flake drills (Figure 11.8). A distinguishing characteristic of these lithics is the nearly exclusive occurrence of Flint Hills cherts, dominated by the Florence A variety that often occurs in frequencies of 90 percent or higher. The complex is located approximately 30 miles west of the primary sources of Florence A chert in southern Cowley County, Kansas, and Kay County, Oklahoma. Notable exotic lithic

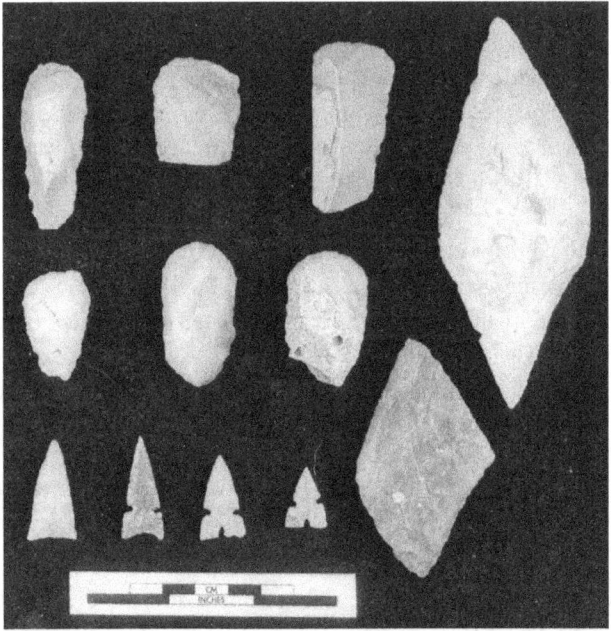

Figure 11.8. Bluff Creek complex stone tools. (Courtesy of the Kansas State Historical Society)

types are rare and include Alibates agatized dolomite and miscellaneous Mississippian cherts.

Bluff Creek ceramic assemblages include a wide range of attributes and types, some of which likely represent evidence of trade rather than local variation or innovation. The typical ceramic type is a cord-marked, globular vessel that is coarsely tempered with one or more of a variety of materials, including sand, bone, various mineral forms of calcium carbonate, and occasionally shell (Figure 11.7). Vessel base forms vary considerably; rounded, flat, and conical forms have been identified (Bevitt 1995).

Decoration is rare, found on less than 10 percent of the collection. Decoration associated with the common cord-marked ceramics includes incised zigzag lines on rim necks (both interior and exterior), punctates, finger-pinching, and oblique-incised lines on lips. On vessels without cord-marking, shell-tempered wares with appliqué nodes and strips are common and appear to represent something beyond the local ceramic tradition. Occasional strap handles present in this group appear to have similar decoration applied, although handles are typically undecorated (Bevitt 1995).

Mortuary Practices

Information on mortuary practices associated with the Bluff Creek complex comes from several of the investigated sites. At 14HP1, on a bluff north of a creek running through the site, a largely complete burial was excavated, as was a portion of a cranium found in association with more than 300 beads (283 hackberry seed, 24 bone) during fieldwork conducted by the University of Kansas (Munsell 1961: 112). On another occasion, during road construction, the largely complete remains of a third individual were recovered by a local person from what was likely a trash-filled storage pit (Kansas State Historical Society Site Files 2003). During salvage excavations at 14HP5, partial sets of remains were identified in flexed or semiflexed positions in the floors of trash-filled pit features truncated by road construction. In one instance, approximately 25 marine shell disk beads were found in direct association with a child burial. The other individual (an adult) was associated with a piece of red ochre and several ceramic sherds (R. Gould 1974: 11–12). Finally, at 14HP524, cranial fragments of at least two individual adults were recovered from a trash-filled, irregularly shaped basin and from surface contexts.

UNAFFILIATED SITES OF THE PLAINS BORDER REGION

In addition to sites attributed to the Odessa phase and the Pratt and Bluff Creek complexes, there are at least another 100 Middle Ceramic sites in south-central Kansas and north-central Oklahoma that are known but not currently assigned to any existing cultural complex (Oklahoma Archeological Survey Site Files 2003; Kansas State Historical Society Site Files 2003). Combined, these sites represent a siz-

Figure 11.9. Map of unaffiliated Middle Ceramic sites of the region

able population of dispersed family groups that practiced a mixed economy. Although these homesteads seem isolated in the landscape, the frequent presence of Alibates agatized dolomite and/or Flint Hills cherts at these sites, as well as occasional obsidian, puebloan ceramics, and marine shell ornaments, indicates regular interaction with neighboring groups to the west and east. Among the more notable of these sites are Fred Loomis (34WD12) (Kay County Chapter of the Oklahoma Anthropological Society 1963); 34MJ11 (J. N. Howard and Brown 1973); Trader's Creek (34WD5) (Buehler 1991, 1992); Shadid (34WO45) (Wyckoff and Jackman 1988); Wilson (34WO10) (Drass 1999); Nelson (34WO57) (Drass 1999); Nichols Ranch (14KW311); Rogers (34HP5); Hedding (34WD2) (Brosowske 2002b; Drass and Turner 1989; Shaeffer 1965); Bell (14CM407) (Bevitt 1999a); Booth (14CM406) (Bevitt 1999a); and Seuser (14RH301) (Bevitt 1996, 2005b). Figure 11.9 shows the location of some of these sites, and Figure 11.10 depicts known house forms. These sites have been investigated to varying degrees in the past and collectively provide additional insight into

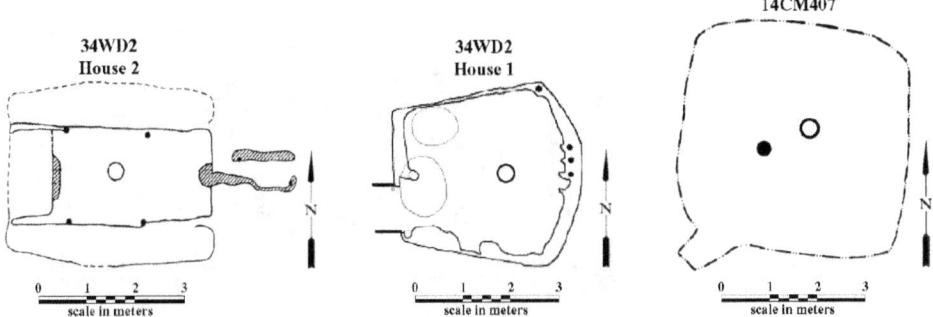

Figure 11.10. Excavated houses at the Hedding and Bell sites

Figure 11.11. Unaffiliated Middle Ceramic site ceramics. (Courtesy of the Kansas State Historical Society)

Figure 11.12. Unaffiliated Middle Ceramic site stone tools. (Courtesy of the Kansas State Historical Society)

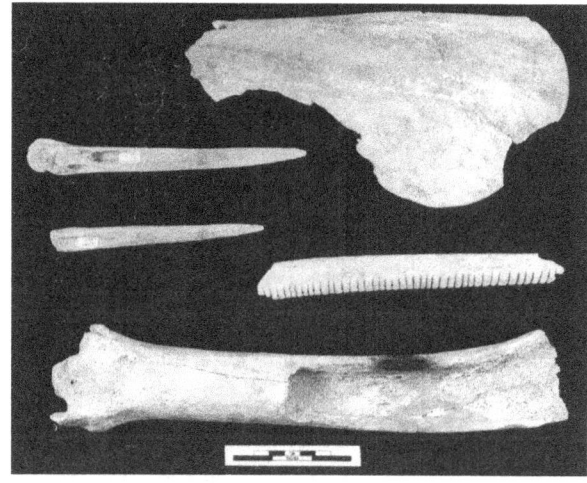

Figure 11.13. Unaffiliated Middle Ceramic site bone tools. (Courtesy of the Kansas State Historical Society)

Middle Ceramic occupants of the region. Although an abundance of cultural materials and features is documented from some of these sites, these assemblages appear sufficiently distinctive that they are not assigned to any cultural complex (see Bevitt 1999a; Brosowske 2002a). Selected artifacts from these sites are shown in Figures 11.11–11.13. The reader is urged to consult the various original sources for more detailed discussions of these sites.

DISCUSSION: THE PLAINS BORDER REGION

Geographically, the societies examined in this chapter inhabited an area nearly 200 km north to south and 260 km east to west. Groups in this area occupied a landscape between A.D. 1100 and A.D. 1500 that was both physically and culturally intermediate to the Central Plains tradition (see chapter 7, this volume) and other complexes of the Southern Plains, such as Antelope Creek, Paoli, Custer, Washita River, and Turkey Creek phases and the Zimms complex (R. L. Brooks et al. 1992; Brosowske 2002b; Drass 1997; Lintz 1986) to the south. Until recently, archaeological work in this area has been sporadic at best and has resulted in the accumulation of information from a number of widely scattered sites whose relationship to each other and to better known taxonomic entities was far from clear. In many ways this situation remains little changed; however, the adoption of a regional perspective involving systematic comparisons between sites has begun to shed light into what has long been viewed as an in-between or peripheral cultural area (e.g., Bevitt 1999a).

While compiling this chapter, we have been fortunate to view most of the sites and collections discussed here, as well as many other sites of adjacent complexes. These field trips, coupled with discussions with other researchers, have been invaluable for assessing the cultural units examined here. In particular, the recognition of variability has been equally important, for, as Thurmond (1991: 138) notes, "the patterns in any given data set are usually more readily discernable in comparison to a contrasting sample." This has certainly been the case for both comparing sites within each of the complexes presented here and comparing them with those of neighboring areas.

As noted at the beginning of the chapter, taxonomic relationships among the entities of the Plains Border area are far from well understood. Unfortunately, since the area seems to have been characterized by considerable interaction and exchange, the identification of discrete cultural units beyond what is currently identified will undoubtedly be difficult without considerably more excavation and radiocarbon dates. Even then, unless some clear temporal patterning exists among sites, the development of a more refined taxonomic framework will be challenging, as the traits used to create taxonomic groups grade from one site to another across the region. These problems, coupled with a lack of systematically collected data, or in some cases the lack of quantification of data, make it difficult to discern the differences and similarities that exist between groups occupying the study area.

Nevertheless, there are a number of trends that link the cultural units and sites discussed here. First, it is clear that societies occupying the Plains Border area shared many traits held by groups of the Central Plains tradition. Currently, whether these similarities resulted from frequent interaction and/or if societies of the area represent an expansion of peoples from the Central Plains is not known. This trend is most aptly demonstrated by the types of decorations applied to ceramic vessels. In general, rim and neck design elements present at Odessa phase and Pratt and Bluff Creek complex sites, such as finger-pinching, oblique impressions, incising, and lip tabs, all appear to be derived from the Central Plains rather than the Southern Plains. In addition, although there is certainly some gradation from east to west, semisubterranean house forms, the presence of large, extended villages, and subsistence economies heavily dependent upon horticulture seem more characteristic of the Central Plains.

From our perspective, the apparent similarity noted by early researchers between societies of the Plains Border area and the Southern Plains, most notably the Antelope Creek phase, is based primarily on an abundance of Alibates agatized dolomite at sites. Indeed, the majority, if not all, of the sites discussed here do contain an abundance of this material. We suggest, however, that the preponderance of Alibates agatized dolomite at Plains Border sites may have little to do with cultural relatedness or a close affiliation with these groups. Instead, because the Plains Border is devoid of local sources of high-quality stone, the acquisition of Alibates from Antelope Creek societies may simply reflect the need to offset shortages of an important resource. Similar economic systems involving Smoky Hill jasper or Flint Hills cherts either never developed or began sometime after A.D. 1400 (see S. C. Vehik 1990).

Beyond the Antelope Creek phase, there is little evidence to indicate that societies of the Plains Border area frequently interacted with or were closely related to other Southern Plains villagers, such as the Paoli, Custer, Washita River, and Turkey Creek phases (see Drass 1997). The lack of similarity with these societies may indicate that the Cross Timbers prohibited sustained interaction between the two areas. Although there does not appear to have been any geographical barrier that impeded contact, a similar situation also seems to apply to the nearby Zimms complex. The rectangular house forms, Quartermaster Plain ceramics, and types of tool stone documented for this complex all show little resemblance to the Odessa phase or other Plains Border groups (see R. L. Brooks et al. 1992; Brosowske 2002b).

Although seldom discussed in detail, Middle Ceramic groups of the Central and Southern Plains have traditionally been viewed as materially and culturally distinct from one another. If societies of the Plains Border are not included, this scenario certainly seems to hold true. Assuming that nonlocal items are a reliable measure of contact and interaction, then the primary reason for these differences is that societies of the two regions rarely interacted directly with one another. This is not entirely surprising considering that they were separated by 200–300 km. In contrast, sites throughout the Plains Border area contain abundant evidence for contact with both areas. Although this is certainly evident in ceramics, tool forms, subsistence economies, and architecture, it is most readily seen in the types of tool stone used by these societies. Sites of the Plains Border area contain a combination of Alibates agatized dolomite and Smoky Hill jasper, Alibates and Flint Hills cherts, or all three.

The large-scale abandonment by Southern Plains villagers during the fifteenth century has been a topic of long-standing interest to researchers of the region. Two of the more popular hypotheses proposed to explain this event are climate change and the incursion of Athabaskan groups into the region. We have little to add to current models at this time. However, a large bell-shaped pit excavated at the Odessa Yates site contained abundant charred corn remains and numerous scapula hoes and tibia digging sticks. Maize from this feature yielded an AMS date of A.D. 1475 (Beta–169791). This suggests that not only was corn horticulture possible, but that groups expected to harvest significant yields. Whatever the specific reasons surrounding an abandonment of the region may be, radiocarbon dates do suggest that populations of the Plains Border region were on the decline following A.D. 1400 or 1450. While the details surrounding the origin of Plains Border groups remain uncertain at this time, knowledge of what happened during the fifteenth century is on a much firmer foundation.

For years, archaeologists have discussed Waldo Wedel's notion that the Pratt complex may be a direct antecedent to the Little River focus of the Great Bend Aspect due to its relative age and proximity to central Kansas (Wedel 1959: 510). A major argument against this idea is that Pratt populations appear to have been too small to account for the later Little River populations. Extensive surveys by local avocational archaeologists, many of which are associated with the Kansas Anthropological Association, suggest that most of the Pratt complex sites have been documented. The recent findings discussed here clearly suggest that groups of the Plains Border area, specifically the Odessa phase and the Pratt complex, are likely ancestral to Little River. This is most unquestionably evident in architecture, ceramics, raw material use, subsistence economies, tool forms, and settlement patterns of these groups. Importantly, an abandonment of the area between A.D. 1400 and 1475 also fits well with the establishment of Little River settlements.

Assessing the potential role that Bluff Creek groups may have played in the formation of Little River is severely limited by the paucity of available radiocarbon dates for this complex. However, it is noteworthy that Odessa phase and Pratt and Bluff Creek complex groups all removed the glenoid process during the manufacture of bison scapula hoes. This is the same method used by Little River focus societies (S. C. Vehik, personal communication, 2002).

Currently, many of the specific details regarding the Little River focus remain unclear at this time, although the general consensus seems to be that there is a great deal of variability among localities of the focus. The simplest explanation for this variability is that the Little River focus represents a coalescence of a number of materially distinct cultural groups. While it is not possible to present a detailed argument outlining the nature of relationships at this time, groups of the Plains Border region seem to be most similar to Little River focus groups along the Little Arkansas River.

CONCLUSIONS AND SUGGESTIONS FOR FURTHER RESEARCH

In general, the Plains Village or Middle Ceramic period in Kansas has attracted more research attention than many other periods. As is often the case, however, as questions are answered, many more complex issues seem to be raised. This is certainly true of the Plains Border area. Nevertheless, this discussion has incorporated old and current data to summarize three archaeological groups that represent the Plains Village tradition along the northeastern margins of the Southern Plains.

Although a variety of information has been presented, perhaps the single most important contribution of this chapter has been to draw attention to the sizable populations that inhabited the Plains Border area from A.D. 1200 to 1500. Given the physiography of the region, the area contains many perennial streams with abundant patches of fertile soil on adjacent terraces. Middle Ceramic period settlement in the area varies from relatively isolated homesteads and hamlets to large extended villages. The fact that the study area likely contained population densities equal to or greater than those of adjacent areas will undoubtedly come as a surprise to many who may have viewed the region, both in a cultural and ecological sense, as a peripheral or marginal portion of the Plains. We hope that this chapter has demonstrated that the richness of the archaeological record found here requires us to reassess this perspective. As is evident by this discussion, we suggest that the term "Plains Border" is useful for understanding Middle Ceramic period groups of the region and their relationship to other known cultural entities.

The preceding discussions highlight several key questions, issues, and problems regarding Middle Ceramic populations of the region. These are briefly addressed here.

Data Recovery and Analysis of Existing Collections

Further data recovery and analysis of extant collections is particularly pertinent to a better understanding of Bluff Creek and Pratt, but additional work on previously unstudied sites of all three units discussed, as well as the large number of unaffiliated Middle Ceramic period sites, would create a set of quantified data needed to answer current questions and direct future research.

Taxonomic Definitions

Bluff Creek. There is an abundant source of material already awaiting formal analysis that, when coupled with existing site analyses and known survey data, would allow a formal characterization of the material assemblage and spatial distribution of the complex. The other, and more important, shortcoming in the data available currently lies in the paucity of radiocarbon dates for the complex as a whole. Additional dates would help refine the already recognized temporal range. Resolving these two glaring deficiencies will allow a more confident refinement of the taxonomy.

Pratt. The paucity of excavated collections is a significant problem. Additional fieldwork is necessary from more than one site and/or locality to formally define the complex.

Unaffiliated Plains Border Region Sites. It is apparent that this is a diverse group of sites, many of which have been studied very little. In spite of this, it appears that there are additional complexes/phases that could be delineated within the region using existing data and additional fieldwork together.

Temporal Refinement

This is less of a problem with the Odessa phase where numerous dates from a wide range of sites across the entire area have already been acquired. Although Bluff Creek has several dates, most are problematic (i.e., Gakushuin dates), though all suggest a similar time span. Existing collections can yield useful material for dating, although this would likely require some consideration of other materials besides wood charcoal: corn (ideally), faunal material, carbonized matter adhering to sherds, and so on. Pratt has few radiocarbon assays; however, existing dates roughly complement ceramic cross-dates. Further excavation would be necessary in order to collect datable samples.

Regional Perspective

Perhaps most importantly, discussion in the future should move beyond simple site analyses and intersite comparisons and seek to study these complexes and sites from a regional perspective to answer broader cultural questions such as, To what degree does the archaeological record allow us to determine the interrelationship among these and other complexes? What are the antecedents of the widespread Plains Village tradition in the Plains Border area? In other words, are Plains Woodland populations solely responsible or is there evidence for migration in some instances?

12. Wichita Ethnohistory

Susan C. Vehik

To many people, Wichita refers to a culture whose members today live near Anadarko, Oklahoma. Anthropologists and historians sometimes consider this to be the "generic" meaning because the modern-day Wichita are made up of people who centuries ago were members of several different cultural groups. Over the years, through population loss, conflict, and pressure from Euro-American governments, these different cultural groups have increasingly lived together. Although these groups are no longer distinct, they also have not totally disappeared (as can be seen from the listing of some of their names on present-day tribal license plates).

These cultural groups are often described as subdivisions, which are sometimes called bands, of the modern Wichita tribe. The principal subdivisions of the Wichita included the Wichita, Taovaya, Tawakoni, Iscani, and Waco. This chapter looks at how these subdivisions came to be and at their activities in Kansas. Thus, two meanings exist for the term "Wichita" as it is used in this chapter: when the Wichita subdivision is of concern it will be so designated; otherwise the meaning is simply generic and refers to any and all subdivisions.

This chapter will not cover all of the subdivisions equally. Some subdivisions either developed late in time or were not recorded until late. For example, Waco was once believed to be just another name for the Iscani (Bolton 1910: 1002; Lesser and Weltfish 1932: 11; Newcomb 1961: 250; S. C. Vehik 1992: 327–328). This perspective is wrong (Newcomb 1993: 41). Instead, the Waco probably were a subgroup of the Tawakoni (S. C. Vehik 2002a). Although use of the name Waco first appeared in 1783 after all Tawakoni had left Kansas (Kinnaird 1946: 84), the people making up the Waco and other Tawakoni likely differed when both lived in Kansas. However, it is presently difficult to discern this difference in the archaeological and early historic records (S. C. Vehik 2002a). Other subdivisions never lived in Kansas. The Iscani and their ancestors lived mostly in Oklahoma and Texas (S. C. Vehik 1992). Because of this, most of the discussion below is concerned with the Tawakoni, Taovaya, and Wichita subdivisions.

GENERAL WICHITA PREHISTORY

A.D. 900–1200

Archaeological evidence shows that the early ancestors of the Wichita were among the horticulturist societies of the Plains Village tradition scattered across the South-

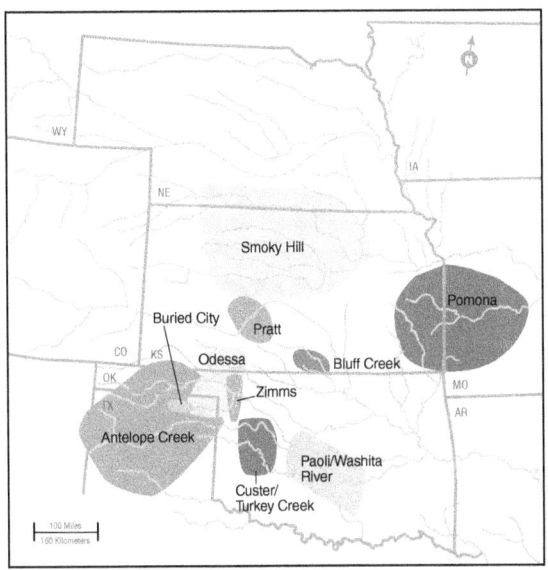

Figure 12.1. Some Southern Plains Village tradition complexes of A.D. 900–1450

ern Plains in Kansas, Oklahoma, and northern Texas (Figure 12.1). Between A.D. 900 and 1200 these people lived in scattered villages with only a few households. They made their living from a mixture of hunting, gathering, and horticulture, although horticulture was not as important in the more westerly communities of the Plains Village tradition. However, dependence on horticulture increased through time. Hunting emphasized deer, but bison were of greater importance westward (Adair 1988; Brosowske and Bevitt, chapter 11, this volume; Drass 1997, 1998).

A.D. 1200–1450

Between A.D. 1200 and 1450, horticulturist communities covered a similar area as in the preceding period. Bison numbers increased during this time, as did their eastward distribution (Creel 1991; Creel, Scott, and Collins 1990; Dillehay 1974; Huebner 1991; Ricklis 1992). The use of horticulture increased until sometime between A.D. 1350 and 1450, but some groups in the west were beginning to rely more on bison hunting. Cultures in more eastern areas increasingly depended on farming during this period (Drass 1997, 1998; Lintz 1991). Even though community size and/or number likely increased as well, most settlements are best described as small villages (R. Brooks 1987; Drass 1997, 1998).

A.D. 1450–1541

Around A.D. 1400, settlement and subsistence patterns changed significantly. Farming communities in the western parts of the Southern Plains disappeared or were replaced by societies emphasizing bison hunting at the expense of horticulture (Drass

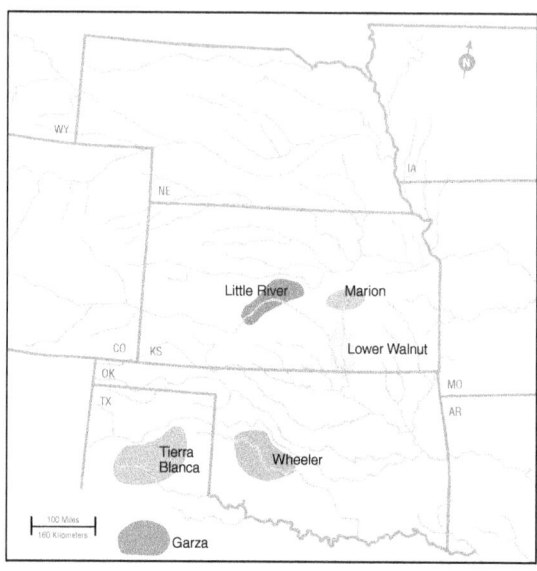

Figure 12.2. Southern Plains cultural complexes ca. A.D. 1450

1998: 421). The Wheeler phase and Garza complex are archaeological examples of bison-hunting societies that may have been part of the ancestry of the Wichita (Figure 12.2). These people lived in northwest Texas and western Oklahoma where they depended heavily on bison hunting but also did some farming. Wheeler phase people lived in villages but abandoned them seasonally for communal bison hunting. During the fall, some bison-hunting camps were fortified (Matchen 2002; Savage 1995). The Wheeler phase and, possibly, Garza complex can be associated with the Iscani (S. C. Vehik 1992).

To the northeast, across the Arkansas River, there were a series of large settlements in the Little Arkansas River/Cow Creek/Smoky Hill River area of central Kansas (Figure 12.2). Archaeologically, these settlements make up the Little River focus (Blakeslee and Hawley, chapter 10, this volume; W. R. Wedel 1959: 210–344). Additional settlements were in the Cottonwood River area around Marion, Kansas. These settlements are generally referred to as Marion Great Bend aspect (Blakeslee and Hawley, chapter 10, this volume; Rohn and Emerson 1984; Roper 2002d). A third large cluster of settlements existed near the confluence of the Walnut and Arkansas rivers. Archaeologists refer to this cluster as the Lower Walnut focus (Blakeslee and Hawley, chapter 10, this volume; W. R. Wedel 1959: 344–379). Other settlement concentrations are likely, including one around Augusta, Kansas, near the confluence of the Whitewater and Walnut rivers (Keller 1961: 106; R. Vehik 1967).

These large site concentrations resulted from the coalescence of the earlier dispersed horticulturists (S. C. Vehik 2002c; W. R. Wedel 1953: 507). This coalescence no doubt brought together several groups associated with the phases and complexes named earlier. For instance, it is likely that some members of the Smoky Hill variant, the Pratt complex, and the Buried City complex (Figure 12.1) were all involved in the ancestry of Little River focus. People in the new, larger settlements depended heavily on farming, but they also hunted bison and other animals (Hawley 1994; Loosle 1991; W. R. Wedel 1959: 210–344). In contrast to peoples of the Wheeler phase, the peoples of the Great Bend aspect utilized specialized task forces made up of a small number of individuals to hunt bison (Ranney 1994; Winship 1990: 197, 209).

Coalescence was a product of increased conflict (S. C. Vehik 2002c). The likely cause of conflict was competition over access to bison. People who decrease farming activities and increase dependence on animal resources need to procure more animals to replace the calories and nutrients that were once derived from farming. At the same time, the creation of large farming villages increased the distances over which people had to hunt compared to when they lived in small, dispersed villages. An increase in hunting distance places more reliance on large energy packages, such as bison. The intrusion of bison-hunting groups from elsewhere, such as the Tierra Blanca complex (Figure 12.2), which may reflect the movement of some Plains Apache groups into the Texas panhandle (Habicht-Mauche 1992), also increased competition. Coalescence resulted in more trade, and bison were an important aspect of this trade (S. C. Vehik 2002c). Because bison were a mobile and clumped resource, the costs entailed in locating herds and the consequences of not exploiting them after they were encountered were likely responsible for the conflict over bison.

THE EARLY HISTORIC WICHITA

Just as the various Wichita subdivisions were forming through coalescence during the fifteenth and early sixteenth centuries and adjusting to their new lifeways, the first Euro-Americans appeared on the Plains. The Wichita's earliest contacts were with Spanish explorers, missionaries, and traders (Bolton 1949; Hammond and Rey 1940, 1953; Winship 1990). The French followed a century or more later (Bolton 1914a, 1914b).

Figuring out the historic record on the Wichita can be quite confusing. Euro-Americans used a variety of names for the various subdivisions of the Wichita, and quite often, they were unclear as to exactly whom a particular name applied. The modern subdivision names could have been used in this chapter instead of the names employed in the early records, but that implies constancy to group identity that is not valid. Additionally, it makes it difficult to compare this chapter to that record. As a result, I am keeping the original names that were used, although I have standardized their spelling, and, in Table 12.1, I list their equivalences to the subdivisions as they are presently recognized. The archaeological representatives of the various subdivisions are also listed. However, the situation is much more complex than is represented in the table, and it should be stressed that the subdivisions were not closed groups and that their membership changed frequently.

Table 12.1. Wichita Subdivisions and Their Proposed Correlations

Archaeological Complex	A.D. 1541	A.D. 1601	A.D. 1630–1654	La Harpe	Dutisné	A.D. 1720–1734	A.D. 1750	Modern
Garza	Teya							
Wheeler		Escanjaque	Escanjaque	Aucanis				Iscani
Little River	Quivira	Tancoa	Quivira	Touacara		Panis Blanc		Tawakoni
Lower Walnut		Etzanoa	Jumano	Ouitsitas		Jumano and Pani Noir		Wichita
Marion		Uayam	Aijaos	Touajas and Ahouaho	Paniouassa	Panis Picques	Panis Picques	Taovaya

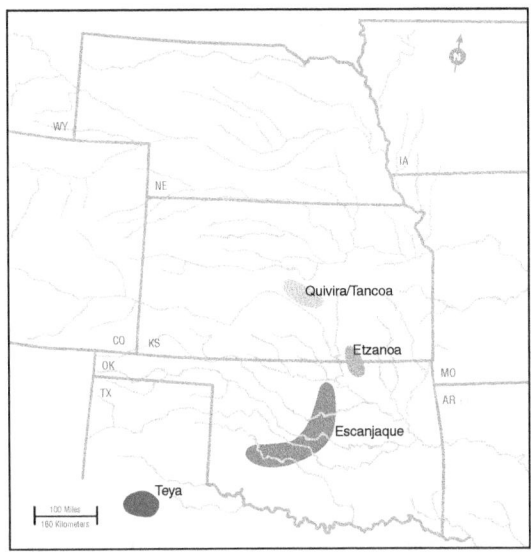

Figure 12.3. Wichita of A.D. 1541–1601

Coronado's Expedition: The Wichita in the Mid-Sixteenth Century

As far as is known, the first Euro-Americans to encounter the Wichita were members of Coronado's expedition in A.D. 1541. The Coronado expedition came into contact with possible ancestors of the Wichita when it met the Teya (Figure 12.3) in Blanco Canyon north of Lubbock, Texas (Word 1994). The archaeological manifestation of the Teya is known as the Garza complex (Habicht-Mauche 1987: 177). The Teya were bison hunters and perhaps became part of the Iscani (Habicht-Mauche 1992: 255–256; S. C. Vehik 1992: 328; 2002a).

Coronado's ultimate destination, however, was Quivira (Winship 1990: 297). Quivira (Figure 12.3) has long been associated archaeologically with the Little River focus of the Great Bend aspect in central Kansas (W. R. Wedel 1942). Quivira and the Little River focus represent the Tawakoni (M. M. Wedel 1981: 23) and thus also the Waco.

Oñate's Expedition: The Wichita at the Beginning of the Seventeenth Century

In A.D. 1601, the Juan de Oñate expedition visited a place they called the "Great Settlement." While there, the Spanish expedition captured a man whom they called Miguel. This man belonged to another culture that was an enemy of those who lived in the Great Settlement. Miguel knew the Great Settlement or its general area by the name of Etzanoa (Figure 12.3) (Hammond and Rey 1953; Newcomb and Campbell 1982; S. C. Vehik 1986). Etzanoa was in north-central Oklahoma and south-central Kansas in the area of the juncture of the Walnut and Arkansas rivers (S. C. Vehik 1986). Thus, Etzanoa is reflected archaeologically by the Lower Walnut focus. Etzanoa and the Lower Walnut focus represent the Wichita subdivision (S. C. Vehik

1986, 1992). Miguel also described a place called Tancoa (Figure 12.3). Tancoa was Miguel's original home, but he had been captured from there by another group of Indians. Tancoa was in central Kansas and is represented archaeologically by the Little River focus. Thus, Quivira and Tancoa are the same and reflect the Tawakoni (S. C. Vehik 1986: 23) and Waco subdivisions.

Miguel knew of another place called Uayam (Figure 12.3). Its location is not clear (S. C. Vehik 1986: 23). If the map is correct, the Marion Great Bend aspect sites may represent Uayam (S. C. Vehik 1992: 327). Uayam is possibly a component of the Taovaya. Miguel also described the Escanjaque. The Escanjaques had captured Miguel in a raid on Tancoa. The Wheeler phase of western Oklahoma is the archaeological representation of the Escanjaque (S. C. Vehik 1986: 24, 26). The Escanjaque were later recognized as the Iscani and are thus related to the Wichita (J. T. Hughes 1968: 319; Newcomb and Campbell 1982: 37; Schroeder 1962: 18; S. C. Vehik 1992: 18).

Thus, in 1601, three of the Wichita subdivisions, the Tawakoni, Wichita, and Iscani, are documented. The Waco were not formally recognized but would have been a component of the Tawakoni. The Taovaya are less certainly represented in the documentary record at this point. Most of the subdivisions may be tied to archaeological complexes dating back to the beginning of the fifteenth century at least.

The Wichita in the Mid-to-Late Seventeenth Century

Several accounts of Southern Plains Indian groups that may be relevant to understanding Wichita ethnohistory come from the mid-1600s. First, I will present summaries of these accounts. Then, I will discuss the problems and significance of the accounts as they relate to the Wichita of the mid-to-late seventeenth century. Table 12.1 will make the connections of the accounts to the Wichita clearer. Distances in these accounts are given in leagues. Most commonly, values of 2.6 miles or 4.2 km per league are used in conversion (see discussion in S. C. Vehik 1986: 14).

In A.D. 1630, one of the first accounts places the Jumano 112 leagues (291 miles or 466 km) east of Santa Fe at 37° north latitude (see Figure 12.4 for latitude/longitude locations). This distance (466 km) is just east of 101° west longitude in the eastern Oklahoma and Texas panhandles. Quivira and the Aijaos were 30–40 leagues (78–104 miles, 125–166 km) farther to the east (Ayer 1965: 63–64; A. B. Thomas 1982: 14).

Four years later Alonzo Baca went 300 leagues (780 miles, 1,248 km) east of Santa Fe and encountered the Great River in the process. Quivira was on the other side (A. B. Thomas 1982: 34). The 300-league distance from Santa Fe terminates at about 92° west longitude midway through the state of Arkansas.

Martín and Castillo in 1650 left Santa Fe and traveled 200 leagues (520 miles, 832 km), where they ultimately found the Jumano on the Rio de las Nueces. The Escanjaques and Aijaos were downriver to the east with a declination to the south. Another 50 leagues (130 miles, 208 km) brought the expedition to the boundary of the Texas (Caddo) nation. The Quivira were on the northern border of the Texas nation (A. B.

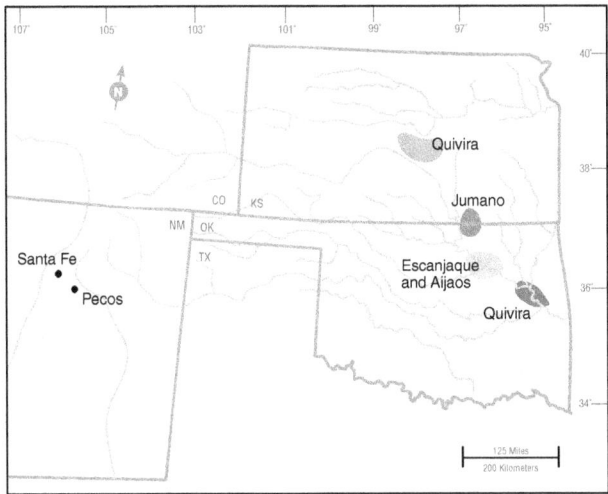

Figure 12.4. Wichita of A.D. 1650–1700

Thomas 1982: 27). The 200 leagues of distance east of Santa Fe ends at 97° west longitude in central Oklahoma. The extra 50 leagues extend to near the Oklahoma-Arkansas state line. In 1654, Guadalajara traveled 200 leagues (520 miles, 832 km) to the Rio de las Nueces where he found the Jumano. The Escanjaque and Aijaos were 30 leagues (78 miles, 125 km) to the east (A. B. Thomas 1982: 29).

Several problems are encountered in assessing these accounts, as well as Posada's 1686 synthesis (A. B. Thomas 1982). First, the name Jumano, or some version of it, was applied to a number of tattooed and painted people, including the Wichita. As a result, the Wichita get confused with others, especially tattooed and painted people living in southwest Texas. Second, and connected to the first problem, the Nueces River of the 1650 and 1654 accounts is often placed in Texas (A. B. Thomas 1982: 5n20). However, Hodge (cited in Bolton 1912: 69) suggested that the Nueces was the Arkansas River. Third, distances in the various accounts vary so widely that they must be viewed very cautiously. Fourth, Quivirans seem to be widely scattered across the landscape and not necessarily only in central Kansas where the Little River focus is defined. That leaves the impression that the location of Quivira was really unknown.

The fourth problem is partly clarified by noting that some Quivirans had moved south by the mid-1680s (S. C. Vehik 1992: 327; M. M. Wedel 1982: 110, 130). These Quivirans settled in the general area of the Three Forks, at the junction of the Arkansas, Verdigris, and Neosho or Grand rivers in east-central Oklahoma (see Figure 12.4). Thus, by the latter part of the seventeenth century Quivirans were in both central Kansas and east-central Oklahoma. That means that during the seventeenth century, some Quivirans were moving south through eastern Kansas and northeastern Oklahoma, and thus placing them in an easterly or even southeasterly direction from Santa Fe is not an error in the accounts. The comment that Quivira was on the northern border of the Texas nation is also not necessarily a mistake. Such a positioning suggests Quivirans were in southeast Oklahoma as the Caddo lived in northeast Texas and northwest Louisiana, but the Caddo traditionally claimed land as far north as the Arkansas River in eastern Oklahoma (Long 1818). In that sense, then, those Quivirans who moved south were on the northern Caddoan border. Nonetheless, the Spanish were not always clear about whom the name Quivira referred to, and it was sometimes applied to Wichita speakers generally. So, each usage needs careful consideration.

As for the varying distance estimates, the distance at which Quivira was located in the earliest two accounts is clearly wrong for both the central Kansas and east-central Oklahoma areas. The distance in the 1650 account is more accurate in placing Quivira in the vicinity of the Three Forks or to the north in northeastern Oklahoma or eastern Kansas. Some Quivirans may have left central Kansas to move to east-central Oklahoma by 1630–1650. Of the various distance estimates, the later ones are likely more accurate.

The following discussion considers where the Jumano were located and whom they represented. Hodge's identification of the Nueces River as the Arkansas River in these accounts is likely correct. Almost all expeditions came east from Santa Fe, and a latitudinal location of 37° in one account places the Jumano well north of Texas at the present-day Oklahoma/Kansas state line. If the distances given to Quivira are wrong in 1630, it is likely that the distance to the Jumano is in error. The more accurate distance to Quivira given in 1650 makes it probable that the distance to the Jumano also is more correct. The distance given to the Jumano in 1654 is the same as in 1650. Two hundred leagues travel from Santa Fe terminates near the Arkansas River. Further, early estimates of latitude generally are more accurate than distance estimates; so the early latitude measure is more acceptable for the Jumano. Combining the latitude of the early account with the later distance information places the Jumano of these accounts in north-central Oklahoma and south-central Kansas (Figure 12.4). This associates the Jumano with the Lower Walnut focus and the Wichita subdivision (S. C. Vehik 1986: 26–27; 1992: 327, 2002a).

A variety of cultural correlations have been suggested for the other groups mentioned in these accounts (Bolton 1910: 705; Newcomb and Campbell 1982: 39, 41; Schroeder 1962: 18). Of those with relevance to Kansas are the Aijaos. The Aijaos most likely were a group of Taovaya. The origins of the Taovaya may have been in the Marion, Kansas, group of Great Bend aspect settlements (S. C. Vehik 1992: 327). Because the Taovaya were the largest of the Wichita subdivisions in the early eighteenth century (R. A. Smith 1959a: 529), the Taovaya were probably more broadly distributed over eastern Kansas, not just restricted to the Marion locality.

Late in the seventeenth century, Spanish exploration met French expansion. The French used the word Pana and various versions thereof when describing Wichita groups. LaSalle in the 1680s had a Pana slave who said his people lived in two villages near each other on a tributary of the Missouri River. These Pana villages were near the Smoky Hill River in central Kansas where they are represented archaeologically by Little River focus sites (M. M. Wedel 1981: 19). Thus, at the end of the seventeenth century, there were still some representatives of the Tawakoni (and Waco) living in central Kansas.

In sum, during the seventeenth century, components of some of the Wichita subdivisions began to move to other locations further south, specifically to the Arkansas River area in Oklahoma. The first group to migrate came from those who lived in the northernmost portions of Wichita territory, namely the Tawakoni. As discussion in the next section will indicate, elements of the more easterly Taovaya probably moved south later in this century as well.

The Wichita in the Early Eighteenth Century

Two French expeditions contacted the Wichita in 1719. Jean Baptiste Bénard de La Harpe led one of the expeditions. He visited the Mento or Touacara somewhere in the Three Forks area of eastern Oklahoma (R. A. Smith 1959a; S. C. Vehik 1992: 321). The Mento were actually a multiethnic group that included the Touacara, along with some Taovaya, Iscani, and Wichita subdivision people and representatives of other cultures. The Touacara were descendants of the Quivirans who left central Kansas during the seventeenth century, and thus they represent part of the Tawakoni. The second expedition was that of Claude-Charles Dutisné, who headed west from Kaskaskia, Illinois. He ultimately ended up at a Paniouassa village on the Verdigris River near its confluence with Fall River in eastern Kansas (S. C. Vehik 1992: 319–320; M. M. Wedel 1973). Other Panis were to the northwest (remaining Little River focus people, possibly). The Paniouassa have been identified as a group of Taovaya (M. M. Wedel 1981: 31).

There are two maps relating to these expeditions. The first (Figure 12.5) likely predates La Harpe's knowledge of the Dutisné expedition (S. C. Vehik 1992: fig. 7; M. M. Wedel 1981: fig. 10). On the Touacara or Arkansas River are four cultural groups who represent several Wichita subdivisions. Most of them were in what would become Oklahoma (Conrad 1971: 140, 149; R. A. Smith 1959b: 374). Farthest downstream were the Touacara (Tawakoni). To their north were the Aucanis (Iscani) and then the Touajas (Taovaya). Further upstream were the Ouitsitas (Wichita subdivision), probably in the lower Walnut River area of extreme southern Kansas. To the northeast of the Ouitsitas were the Ahouaho. Linguistically, Ahouaho is very similar to Aijaos. The Ahouaho were another group of Taovaya who lived in east-central Kansas, possibly the same group Dutisné visited.

On the second map (S. C. Vehik 1992: fig. 8), made after La Harpe obtained information from the Dutisné expedition, most of the groups on the first map disappear. The Touacara become Mento, and the Ahouaho are replaced with Paniouassa (Ahouaho and "ouassa" being similar linguistically). The reason the others disappear

Figure 12.5. Wichita and Osage in A.D. 1719 (adapted from M. M. Wedel 1981: fig. 10)

is uncertain, but perhaps La Harpe assumed these people no longer lived where the earlier map indicated but had instead left to join the Touacara and form the Mento.

Although other Panis (i.e., Little River focus) were still living to the northwest of the Ahouaho or Paniouassa, neither La Harpe nor Dutisné said much about them. The last of the Little River focus people were definitely gone from central Kansas by the time Bourgmont visited the area in 1724 (Norall 1988; Reichart 1979). Ultimately, this second group of Tawakoni (along with the Waco) moved to the Neosho River where they lived with other Wichita (probably Taovaya) for a time in the eighteenth century (P. B. Hunt 1881: 77; A. C. Williams 1877a: 112, 1877b).

Exactly when and where these Neosho River settlements were established is not clear. No settlements are indicated on any of La Harpe's early-eighteenth-century maps for the area northeast of the Touacara/Mento, save for the Anahouo or Grand Osage (Figure 12.5) (S. C. Vehik 1992: figs. 7 and 8). Furthermore, Dutisné did not encounter, nor did he seem to expect to find, people living between the Osage and the Paniouassa. In 1726, however, the Wichita were only two days away from the Grand Osage village in west-central Missouri (Piazza 1995: 16–17). This Wichita settlement was probably not established until after the La Harpe and Dutisné expeditions. The Neosho River location was abandoned sometime between 1730 and 1740 as conflict with the Osage increased (S. C. Vehik 2002a).

There are other sources of information that also suggest the Wichita lived in eastern Kansas early in the eighteenth century. On some eighteenth-century maps as well as in written descriptions, the Panis Blanc and Panis Picques are found south of the Missouri River in eastern Kansas (Hutchins 1797: 293; Schoolcraft 1853: 557, 559). This information was probably derived from Le Page du Pratz (1972: 305) and reflected conditions from 1718 to 1734 when he was in North America. The name Panis Blanc

(White Panis) is most often associated with the Pawnee (M. M. Wedel 1979: 191, 193). At one time, though, the Osage River, which has its headwaters in eastern Kansas, was called White Waters or White River (Pike 1889: 176; M. M. Wedel 1973: 150). Thus, Panis Blanc in this case probably reflects a Wichita occupation. In fact, later the Panis Blanc were identified as Panis Picques (Jefferson 1852: 1075; Thwaites 1905: 95n55; 1908: 87n28). Panis Picques was a term usually used by the French and others to refer to the Taovaya or Wichita subdivisions but could be more broadly applied to Wichita speakers in general (Jackson 1978: 534–535; Jefferson 1852: 1075). It is unlikely that Panis Blanc and Panis Picques would be used in the same context if their meanings were the same. Thus, Panis Blanc in these cases could refer to the last of the Tawakoni (along with the Waco) to leave central Kansas.

Regardless, this second group of Tawakoni did not stay long in the Neosho River location. In the 1870s, the Tawakoni were described as having left the rest of the Wichita (probably meaning Taovaya) on the Neosho River about a century earlier. It is here that the Waco enter the picture. They are described as having left the Neosho River group of Wichita as well. One of the two (probably the Waco) ultimately moved to Texas, and the other established a village near modern-day Wichita, Kansas (P. B. Hunt 1881: 77; S. C. Vehik 2002a; A. C. Williams 1877a: 112, 1877b). The settlement established near Wichita, Kansas, has not been found. In 1883, Niastor, a Tawakoni political leader, indicated it was somewhere below the city (Teller 1883: 52). The settlement may even have been at the confluence of the Walnut and Arkansas rivers where other Wichita continued to live.

During the early eighteenth century, some Wichita appear to have moved fairly often. Most of this movement involved people who lived in the more northern and eastern portions of Wichita territory, specifically the Tawakoni and Taovaya. Niastor claimed that people moving downriver drove the Tawakoni out of their original home (Teller 1883: 47). This river is likely the Smoky Hill, and the hostile group was probably Apache. By 1730–1740, Osage expansion forced Wichita living in more easterly locations to move. The one setting with any stability in settlement was the Arkansas River in south-central Kansas and north-central Oklahoma where the Wichita subdivision had long resided. But even so, members of the Wichita subdivision were on the move as well because some of them were among the people called Mento.

The Wichita at the Middle of the Eighteenth Century

By the mid-eighteenth century, few Wichita, if any, were left in Kansas. Sometime around 1730, a group of Taovaya who had been with the Mento moved up the Neosho River to establish a village in northeast Oklahoma. After a very short stay, courtesy of the Osage, this group of Taovaya moved to north-central Oklahoma where they established a village near one occupied by members of the Wichita subdivision (S. C. Vehik 1992, 2002a). Around 1749, numerous references place villages of the Jumano and/or Pani Picque (Wichita and Taovaya subdivisions) on the Rio Napestle or Arkansas River (Bolton 1917: 394; Hackett 1941: 302, 322; M. M. Wedel 1981). The Deer Creek (34KA3) and Bryson-Paddock (34KA5) sites in north-central Oklahoma just south of the Kansas/Oklahoma state line are two of these villages. A third village likely existed. The French had a plan to erect a trading establishment on the Rio Napestle above the three villages of Pani Picques (Hackett 1941: 337). The Shrope site (14CO331) on the Walnut River in south-central Kansas may be that third village (Hawley and Holland 1996: 7).

In 1751–1752, one of the Pani Noir (likely Wichita subdivision) and Pani Picque (Taovaya) villages was destroyed. The village was first hit by a measles and smallpox epidemic and then attacked by the Grand Osage (Nasatir 1952: 357; Pease and Jenison 1940: 357; Thwaites 1908: 87). There is no indication as to where this village may have been, but the Shrope site is a possibility because people continued to live in the other two villages. Even though the two subdivisions stayed in north-central Oklahoma a few more years, they also began moving south. The last members of the Taovaya and Wichita subdivisions abandoned the Arkansas River in north-central Oklahoma around 1758 (Castañeda 1939: 111; Flores 1985: 48; Weddle 1964: 113). The southward removal took some of them to the Wichita Mountains and Red River areas of southern Oklahoma and others as far as central Texas where the first group of Tawakoni also ultimately moved.

CONCLUSIONS

By the time the various Wichita subdivisions entered the historic record, they had already undergone a period of profound social, political, and economic change that began in the fifteenth century (S. C. Vehik 2002c). Climatic change, alterations in subsistence strategies, and increasing conflict during the fifteenth and sixteenth centuries brought about the formation of large population aggregations from small, dispersed, mixed-subsistence villages. It is from these aggregations that the various Wichita subdivisions formed. About 150–200 years later, population loss from European diseases and escalating conflict, along with internal political events, brought fragmentation and realignment to these groups, ultimately forcing their removal from Kansas. Although the Wichita made a short return to Kansas during the Civil War, their stay was marked by very high loss of life, which only served to escalate the disintegration of the subdivisions as distinct cultural entities and ultimately culminated in the application of one subdivision's name (Wichita) to all who were left.

13. The Kansa
James O. Marshall

A REVIEW OF AN INCOMPLETE CULTURE HISTORY

The Kansa have been the subjects of the state and local history of Kansas since before the turn of the twentieth century. Founders of the Kansas State Historical Society began by locating and identifying Kansa villages and collecting reminiscences of eyewitnesses of the villages. This unique and detailed record represents much of the initial research on the history of Kansas. A history of the Kansa was published in 1908 (Morehouse 1908: 327–368). Other histories have been written as adjuncts to archaeological investigations (Marshall 2000: 57–89; W. R. Wedel 1946: 1–35; 1959: 19–54). One study is presented as a collection of historical anecdotes that recount the activities of the Kansa in the upper Kansas River valley from 1848 to 1867 (Staab 1995: 24–45). William E. Unrau (1971, 1989) has written major histories of the Kansa, but he notes that adequate archaeological information was lacking for the Kansa in prehistoric times or the time before European contact (Unrau 1971: xxii).

The archaeological record is obscure for the Kansa and for other linguistically related tribes, the Omaha, Ponca, Osage, and Quapaw, that have been historically identified (O'Shea and Ludwickson 1992: 16–17). They are collectively perceived as being Dhegiha speakers of the Siouan language family (Rankin 2001).

This review of the cultural history of the Kansa includes the inadequacies that cause the narrative to be incomplete. Archaeology can now only suggest that the five tribes that are related by language may also have been related before the time of European contact as manifestations of the Oneota tradition (Buffalohead 2004; Henning and Thiessen 2004; O'Shea and Ludwickson 1992: 16; Ritterbush, chapter 9, this volume). In this study, the anecdotal history of the Kansa is introduced as a source that can be used by archaeologists. This record demonstrates that the extent of the Kansa occupation of the Kansas River valley has not been fully appreciated.

James Owen Dorsey collected information on the Kansa from native informants in the 1880s. David T. Bushnell (1922: 89), who reviewed Dorsey's notes, comments that the Kansa list 20 villages that they occupied along the Kansas River before moving on to Council Grove. The names of these 20 villages are found in Dorsey's translated and typewritten list, but 27 villages can be counted in his handwritten notes (Bushnell 1922).

THE KANSA REMEMBRANCE OF THE PAST

The five related tribes, particularly the Omaha and the Quapaw, have a tradition in which they speak of the Ohio River valley in Kentucky and Southern Indiana as their ancient homeland. They moved west to the mouth of the Ohio River where the Quapaw descended the Mississippi River. The others ascended the Mississippi to the mouth of the Missouri River and divided further as they ascended that river. The Kansa finally settled at the mouth of the Kansas River, wandered a bit, and then ascended the Kansas River (Buffalohead 2004; W. R. Wedel 1959: 49).

The Kansa informed Dorsey that they came up the Missouri River when there were no white men. They resided at a village on the Missouri River called *Ma-da-qpa-ye* with the Osage, Omaha, and Ponca. They stopped at the Kansas River, as the story goes, for several years, perhaps 11 years. The white men were met for the first time, and the white men gave them calico, kettles, knives, and cups. Then the Kansa moved further north to *Nicudje ga'ga* (near the Iowa state line) where they stayed about a year. Here the Kansa were attacked by the Cheyenne, and many were killed on each side during a battle that lasted for two days. After the battle with the Cheyenne, the Kansa retreated south to the mouth of the Kansas River and, after staying for a year, ascended the Kansas River (to a vicinity southeast of Topeka) where they stayed for six years. The white men came again with more presents. The next move was to somewhere east of Junction City and finally to Mission Creek, where the Potawatomi came. White men came again with presents during these last moves, and six chiefs and six braves traveled to Washington, D.C. (Dorsey 1882).

A REVIEW OF THE CULTURAL HISTORY OF THE KANSA

The first historical records that identify the Kansa are the maps that were drawn after the Marquette and Jolliet exploration of the Mississippi River in 1673 (Delanglez 1985 [1946]). Research on the Spanish explorations of the Central Plains (see chapter 12, this volume) has led to a suggestion that three documented Indian contacts—the Guas in 1542, the Escansaques in 1601, and the Canceres in 1720—are, in fact, the Kansa. A Kansa identification has been deemed inconclusive, if not improbable, by W. R. Wedel (1959: 51). Brief descriptions of these Indians in the chronicles seem to more closely describe a Plains Apache tribe. However, it is not improbable that the Canceres (or Cances; see chapter 14, this volume), who were allied with the French in 1720, were the Kansa. The Kansa and other tribes were certainly affected by the Spanish before the eighteenth century, even if not by direct contact. The French were in contact with the tribes on the Missouri River by the beginning of the eighteenth century, and they saw for themselves that most of the tribes were in possession of mules that had been stolen from the Spanish (Rydjord 1956: 22).

The French explorers were familiar with Algonquian languages, and they used Algonquian references. Henry de Tonti, who was La Salle's lieutenant, explained in a letter to his brother that the Oyo River (Ohio) was called by the Indians "Akanceasipi" (Tonti 1700, as cited by Delanglez 1985 [1700]: 230). Akanceasipi is the Algonquian word for "River of the Kansa" (Rankin 2001). Tonti placed the Kansa living at an approximate distance of an 18-day canoe journey from the mouth of the Missouri River (232).

There is no Algonquian word that refers specifically to the Kansa as a tribe. Linguists believe that "the five related tribes were being called Kansa to identify one group of people and that when the Algonquian tribes passed the identification on to the French, the Algonquian prefix A was also passed on, forming a word such as Akanceasipi" (Rankin 2001). Robert L. Rankin, an expert on the Kansa language, goes on to explain that the Kansa believe their own name identifies them as the "people of the south wind" or has some connotation of wind. Rankin (2001) states, "Kansa is pronounced [kk'a-ze] in their own language but the word for wind is [ttaje] and south wind is [ak?a]. These wind-words are almost identical when spoken by the other related tribes so it must be inferred that the meaning of the word 'Kansa' is something else other than having to do with the wind." There is a Kansa clan in the social organization of the Kansa, as Rankin (2001) explains, "and within that clan are sub-clans named *ttaje onikkasjga* 'wind people', *ak?a onikkasjga* 'south wind people', and *ttaje zjga* 'little wind.'" The Osage and the Omaha tribes each had a Kansa clan, and the Quapaw, called the Arkansea by the French, remarked to Dorsey that "we are Kansa too" (Rankin 2001).

As noted earlier, the Kansa were on the Missouri River in 1700 at a location that can be reached by an 18-day canoe journey from the river's mouth. The Kansa remembrances note only one village following the occupation at *Ma-da-qpa-ye* and that is a village named *Tcexe styedje*. The next village, *Nicedje*, is on the Kansas River, about four miles from Kansas City (Dorsey 1882).

A VILLAGE ON THE MISSOURI RIVER

The Kansa come into focus on July 7, 1724. Etienne de Véniard Bourgmont arrived at a Kansa village on the west bank of the Missouri River to have these and other Indian allies escort him and his military detachment to the Padouca (Plains Apache) far out on the western plains. The locus of the village is probably site 14DP1 at present-day Doniphan, Kansas, where Independence Creek joins the Missouri River (W. R. Wedel 1959: 29). The Kansa village component at this site carries the distinction of being the earliest documented Kansa village and the earliest identifiable contact-period Indian village in eastern Kansas (W. R. Wedel 1959: 29, 51).

French mapmakers were just beginning to label the Kansas River as the "Grande Riviere des Cansez" by the 1720s. Bourgmont's firsthand accounts were included in the Delisle map of 1718 on which the Kansas River is labeled as such for the first time (W. R. Wedel 1959: 28). When encountered by Bourgmont in 1724, the Kansa were a fully developed horse and gun culture involved in raiding and trade. The village, 14DP1, had an estimated 150 lodges ruled over by two head chiefs and 14 war chiefs and an estimated 300 warriors, 300 women, and 500 children, as well as 300 dogs, which served as pack animals. The villagers who were with Bourgmont were escorting him to their familiar hunting grounds. Other Kansa were met who were hunting, and others were already returning to their village. When the Frenchmen and Kansa showed themselves to the Padouca, panic ensued because the Padouca and Kansa were traditional enemies. The diplomatic purposes of the expedition prevailed, however, and the two tribes voluntarily disarmed and engaged in ceremonial trade and feasting (Norall 1988: 141).

The occasion called for an exchange of visits to each other's villages. Fifty Kansa and five Podoucas returned to the village on the Missouri to escort Bourgmont to the council meeting. (An illness had forced Bourgmont to stay behind until he recovered.) The journal relates that the party was met when it was three days away from the Kansa villages (Norall 1988: 142). This implies that there were villages other than the one where Bourgmont was waiting.

The Kansa come into focus suddenly and briefly as aggressive hunters and raiders, as committed French allies, and as being supported by French trade. They are in place on the Missouri River at the time of the first official French expeditions of exploration and probably had already begun the process of becoming an equestrian culture before the end of the seventeenth century.

THE WESTERN VILLAGES

The Kansa disappear from the record until some 70 years later, when they are found in a village at the mouth of the Blue River, which is now known as the Blue Earth village (14PO24). The locus of this village is in the vicinity of present-day Manhattan, Kansas. The village was apparently occupied by 1796 (W. R. Wedel 1959: 52). The historical record indicates that after the Doniphan village occupation the Kansa moved south where a French outpost on the Missouri known as Fort Cavagnolle attracted them, but they may have not stayed there continuously (W. R. Wedel 1959: 51). The record of the Lewis and Clark expedition confirms that the Kansa had moved away from the Missouri River and resided on the Kansas River before the beginning of the nineteenth century. These explorers saw the remains of the Doniphan village and the French outpost.

The reason for the Kansa move from the Missouri to the Kansas River is not well understood. One cause might be a Kansa defeat. The precise time is not known, but apparently the Doniphan village was attacked by the Otoes, who captured the village, took it over, and forced the Kansa to move some 80 miles west (W. R. Wedel 1959: 38).

The Blue Earth village is noted on the Collot map of 1796. The defeat by the Otoes may very well have affected one village, and a shift to the west where there may have been other villages in familiar territory would have been a logical choice. Lewis and Clark mentioned two villages, on hearsay, on the Kansas River. One of these appears to be the Blue Earth village, which may be the village where the Kansa grand chief, *Shone-ge-ne-gare*, hosted George Sibley in 1811 (W. R. Wedel 1959: 38–39, 52).

Sibley (1927: 198) stated that he was on the Republican River. He estimated that he was about 100 miles above the mouth of the Kansas River. However, W. R. Wedel (1959: 52) pointed out that the mouth of the Republican River is 135 miles above the mouth of the Kansas River, and that Sibley's description of the area and the village fits just as well to the Blue Earth village. There was no known village site beyond the mouth of the Blue River (W. R. Wedel 1959: 52–53). Sibley's estimation of distances may be inaccurate but, as W. R. Wedel (1959: 42) points out, he was not a newcomer to the region, and Osage Indians guided him. There is no firm evidence that he was in the Blue Earth village or that he was confusing the Blue River and the Republican. And W. R. Wedel (1959: 52) again notes, "Strangely enough, the Lewis and Clark map . . . does indicate an 'Old Konza Vill' on a narrow neck of land between the Republican and Kansas Rivers immediately above their junction. This would appear to be on the spot now occupied by Junction City."

The village is described as follows:

> The town contains one hundred and twenty-eight houses or lodges; which are generally about 60 feet long and 25 feet wide, constructed of stout poles and saplings arranged in form of an arbor and covered with skins, bark and mats, they are, in general, neat, commodious and comfortable. The place for fire is simply a hole in the earth, under the ridgepole of the roof, where an opening is left for the smoke to pass off. All of the larger lodges have two, sometimes three fireplaces; one for each family dwelling in it. The town is built without much regard to order; there are no regular streets or avenues. The lodges are erected pretty compactly together in crooked rows, allowing barely space sufficient to admit a man to pass between them. The avenue between these crooked rows are kept in tolerably decent order and the village on the whole rather neat and cleanly than otherwise. Their little fields or patches of corn, beans and pumpkins, which they had just finished planting, and which constitutes their whole variety, are seen in various directions, at convenient distances around the village. The prairie was covered with their horses and mules (they have no other domestic animals except dogs). (Sibley 1927: 198)

Members of Major Stephen Long's scientific expedition visited Blue Earth village in 1819. The village was described as consisting of 120 lodges. The lodges were circular, domed earthlodges scattered about in no particular pattern. A circular area was excavated to a depth of one to three feet before poles were set to support the structure (Bushnell 1922: 92). The visitors described in detail the lodge they occupied:

> The lodge, in which we resided, is larger than any other in the town, and being that of the grand chief, it serves as a council house for the nation. The roof is supported by two series of pillars, or rough vertical posts, forked at top for the reception of the transverse connecting pieces of each series; twelve of these pillars form the outer series, placed in a circle; and eight longer ones, the inner series, also describing a circle; the outer wall, of rude frame work, placed at a proper distance from the exterior series of pillars, is five or six feet high. Poles, as thick as the leg at base, rest with their butts upon the wall, extending on the cross pieces, which are upheld by the pillars of the two series, and are of sufficient length to reach nearly to the summit. These poles are very numerous, and, agreeable to the position, which we have indicated, they are placed all around in a radiating manner, and support the roof like rafters. Across these are laid long and slender sticks or twigs, attached parallel to each other by means of bark cord; these are covered by mats made of long grass, or reeds, or with the bark of trees; the whole is then covered completely over with earth, which, near the ground, is banked up to the eaves. A hole is permitted to remain in the middle of the roof to give exit to the smoke. (James 1966, 1: 120–121)

Two contemporaneous but different types of Kansa villages have been described. One is a bark lodge village and the other is an earthlodge village. The bark lodges are recognized as something different than the earthlodges in which most of the other tribes on the Missouri River lived. The Kansa women could build a bark lodge in just a few days, but the construction of an earthlodge involved some planning and considerably more labor (Sibley 1927: 202). Sibley's (199, 202) descriptions of the Kansa confirm that they were aggressive hunters and traders. Horticulture was practiced, but only on a small scale. Little patches of corn, beans, and pumpkins were cultivated. The Kansa were no doubt dependent on trade, but the French no longer intimidated them; thus trade with the Kansa was profitable but hazardous. Fur traders risked having their goods stolen and being subjected to abuse (Sibley 1927: 199).

The goods that came into the village consisted of milled blankets, blue and red strouding (a woolen cloth that may have been of British manufacture), coarse scarlet cloth, brass and copper kettles, fusils (muskets), ball and powder, knives, axes, hoes, awls, traps, vermilion, silver ornaments, wampum, beads, tobacco, cotton prints, and black silk handkerchiefs. Traded for these goods were the fur and hides of beaver, otter, bear, raccoon, fox, deer, and bison. Bison, deer, and elk tallow was also traded, as well as a few prepared bison robes (Sibley 1927: 200). Later accounts describe the Kansa mode of dress and personal appearance in the 1800s:

> The men wore a blue or red breech cloth secured by a girdle, deerskin leggings, moccasins with no ornamentation, and sometimes a blanket over the upper part of the body. Shells, beads, or metal ornaments were attached to the rim of the ear. Sometimes in great profusion, and long, slender hair pipes were often worn. The head was shaven, leaving only the scalplock uncut. Sometimes the edge of

this lock was colored with vermilion, or an eagle feather was inserted. More striking was attachment to it, on top of the head, of a tail of a deer, dyed red and parted longitudinally by a silver plate. Facial hair was plucked. Women wore moccasins, knee-length leggings of blue or red cloth, a short skirt, and occasionally a cloth thrown over one shoulder. Their hair was worn long, parted on the midline, and the part covered with vermilion. Like the men, many of the women tattooed the body. (James 1966: 1, 126–128)

THE KANSA REMEMBRANCE OF THE WESTERN VILLAGES

Dorsey's map (Figure 13.1) shows a village located at the junction of the Republican River with the Kansas River where present-day Junction City is also noted. The place is named *Mi-xu-tci u-i-jan-ka,* and Dorsey translates the word to mean "the fork of the Republican (and the Kansas rivers)." Dorsey (1882) does not refer to the location as a village, but it is marked exactly like all the other villages on the maps. The Kansa name for the Blue River is *Ni-tu.* The word *Igama-sabe* also identifies the Blue River on the map (Dorsey 1882). Dorsey's map shows a village at the junction of the Blue River with the Kansas River. The village is identified on the map and in the field notes as *Ma-yin-katu-hu n-dje,* which is the lower village. An upper village is named *Igama-sabe.*

The Kansa moved to the Blue Earth village from a village named *Padje gadji.* Prior to this occupation, they were in a village called *Tce dungu-ma yi-wama-yu.* Blue Earth village was abandoned for a village named *Ba-he qu-be* from where, as Dorsey (1882) relates the move, they returned to Mission Creek and established *Ga-qu'-li u-li' be.* The interpretation has been that the Blue Earth village is the oldest known Kansa village that has been located on the Kansas River. The village was occupied for at least 30 years but probably was not the only village in the vicinity. It may be that Sibley stayed at another village on the Republican River, not yet identified archaeologically but suggested by the remembrances of the Kansa, with possible corroboration from a Lewis and Clark map (W. R. Wedel 1959: 52).

THE LAST VILLAGES IN THE KANSAS RIVER VALLEY

The Kansa began to drift to the east and by 1825 had settled in three villages near present-day Topeka. Two villages were established on Mission Creek, named for a Methodist mission that was built on the creek in 1835, and the third was on Soldier Creek (Marshall 2000: 66–67, W. R. Wedel 1959: 52–53). These villages are known as Hard Chief village, American Chief village, and Fool Chief village. One of the Mission Creek villages was called *Ga-qu'-li u-li' be;* its chief's name was *Waji-waqa.* Also at this time, Frederick Chouteau moved from Horseshoe Lake in 1830 and built his

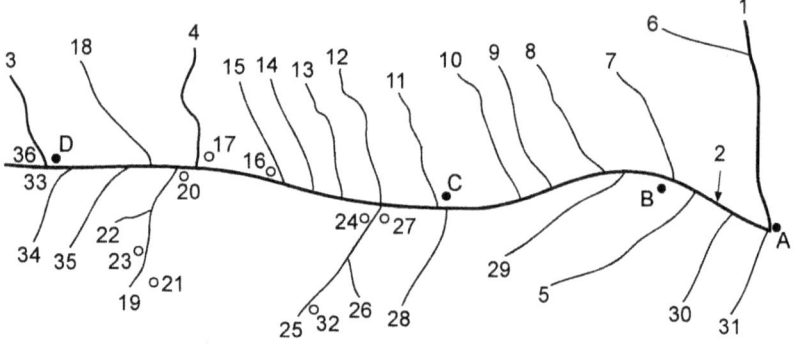

Figure 13.1. A schematic representation of two maps drawn by Kansa Indian informants for James Owen Dorsey. Geographical and cultural features are identified along an approximate 115-mile length of the Kansas River. A. Kansas City; B. Lawrence; C. Topeka; D. Junction City. 1. Missouri River; 2. Kansas River (Tu'-pi-ki'e Ga-qa'); 3. Republican River (Mi-xautci or Ni-tu'); 4. Blue River (I'-ga-ma Sa'-be); 5. Wakarusa River (Wa-gle' yu-ze'); 6. Yu-dje cku'-be, a tributary of the Missouri River; 7. U-ku'-tce sun-ga, a tributary of the Kansas River; 8. Ga-qa' ni-bu-ze, a stream of dry water; 9. Ni'-cku-be, a tributary of the Kansas River; 10. Wa-ja'-je-pa, a tributary of the Kansas River where there is a possible village (the name refers to Osage nose or head); 11. Sa-ba' sa'-be, a tributary of the Kansas River northwest of North Topeka; 12. Ga-dji' jin-ga, a name of a stream and of a camping place near Ja-i-tci *or Wooden House village (Wooden House village may be Fool Chief's village); 13. Ma-ja, a small stream or a small tributary of the Kansas River; 14. Ga-dji' jin-ga, a tributary of the Kansas River; 15. Tce-xu'-li, a stream on which there is a village of the same name; 16. Tce-xu'-lii, an ancient village that was also called Uzuli; 17. Ta-ma-gi'-le, an ancient village on the Blue River; 18. Mi'-da-yin-ga ts'e'-ya-be, a tributary that is identified as being Wildcat Creek; 19. Wa-nin'-dje hu', a tributary of the Kansas River; 20. Ma'-haz-u'-li, a village identified as the village at the yellow bank that superseded* Pasuli *village; 21. Ga-qu-li u-ki-stce, a village under the chief Ali kawahu; 22. Wa-ji-wa-qa t s' e, a tributary of* Wa-nin'-dje hu'; *23. Ga-qu-li-u-ki-stce, a village under the chief* Waji-waqa *on the stream named* Wa-ji-wa-qa t s'e; *24. Pasuli, a village on the hilltop or Hard Chief's village (this village location has been confirmed by archeological excavations and is designated as archaeological site 14SH301); 25. Zan-dje' jin'-ga, a tributary of the Kansas River that has been identified as Mission Creek (another name for the creek is* Co-to jinga ili-be, *which means "where young Chouteau dwelt"); 26. Ma-ze-ga'-xe-u-li-be, a tributary of Zan-dje' jin'-ga (Mission Creek) (the creek has been referred to as Blacksmith Creek, and the Kansa name means "where Blacksmith dwelt"); 27. Chouteau's store; 28. Cu-mi-ka-se-uli-be, a tributary of the Kansas River; 29. Dje-stye'-dje, a tributary identified as Long Lake Creek (a village having the same name is located near Lawrence); 30. Zan-dje-ga-dji, a tributary of the Kansas River; 31. Ga-hi-ge wa-da'-yin-ga i-ku'-ya ga-qa', a stream that empties into the Missouri River at Kansas City (the Kansa name means "the stream of the friend of Saucy Chief"—Saucy Chief may refer to Fool Chief); 32. Ga-qu'-li u-li'-be, a village to which the people from Ba-he' qu'-be moved after Chouteau established his trading post on Mission Creek; 33. Ba-he' qu'-be, a mountain near a village (this village was occupied after the Kansa left the mouth of the Blue River [Ma yinka tuhu udje], and then a move was made to Mission Creek and* Gaquli-uli-be, *which may be American Chief's village); 34. Pa-dje' ga-dji' kye, a tributary of the Kansas River (this name identifies a village that was probably on the north side of the Kansas River and was occupied after the Kansa left* Tcedunga-ma yi-wamu-yu); *35. Tci-ye'-da cun'-ge na-sa'-gi-be, which denotes a village that was occupied after* Yuje-maka-tce-ubuqpaye *and before the Kansa removed to* Wahehe-ijinge-t s'eyabe; *36. Mi'-xu-tci' u-i'-jan-ka', which denotes the junction of the Republican River with the Kansas River.*

trading post, "Chouteau's store," on the east side of the mouth of Mission Creek (Dorsey 1882). He associated his post with American Chief village, which forces the conclusion that *Ga-qu'-li u-li' be* was the Kansa name for American Chief village (Marshall 2000: 67).

American Chief village consisted of 20 lodges, which were large, permanent earthlodges (F. G. Adams 1904: 425). American Chief was thought to have been about 75 years old in 1841. As a young man, he traveled to Washington, D.C., where he met and received medals from President Thomas Jefferson, this visit being the probable source of his name. Hard Chief village, at the mouth of Mission Creek and on the west side of the stream, had a population of 500 to 600 people (F. G. Adams 1904: 425). This village, designated 14SH301, has been located and confirmed by archaeological excavations (Marshall 2000: 57–89; Reynolds 1987: 1–3; Thies 1988a: 86–108; 1988b: 67–75). The Kansa name for this village is *Pa-su-li* village, and the name identifies "the village on the hilltop" (Dorsey 1882). The site has been described as sitting 130 feet above the bottomland (Marshall 2000: 58). The German physician Dr. Frederick Adolph Wislizenus, then traveling with a party to the west, walked into the deserted Hard Chief village in 1839. He left a description of what he saw:

> The village was on an elevation from which one can enjoy a pleasant and wide view. The whole village consists of 50 to 60 huts, built all in one style, in four somewhat irregular rows. The structure is very simple. On a round, arched frame of poles and bark, earth is placed with grass or reeds: at the top, in the middle, an opening is left for light and smoke; in front, at the ground, a similar opening as an entrance; and the shanty is finished. At the open door there is usually a reed-covered passage, extending a few steps into the street. There are about twelve cut braces inside the house; the fireplace is under the opening in the roof; at the side are some bunks of plaited strips of wood. The whole is rather spacious. (Barry 1972: 368–369)

Ja-i-tci village identifies Fool Chief village, located on the north side of the Kansas River between the river and Soldier Creek. Fool Chief village was larger than the two Mission Creek villages, with the population estimated to have been between 700 and 800 people. The number of lodges was estimated to be as many as 80, assuming that a lodge housed between six and ten individuals (F. G. Adams 1904: 425). The name means "Wooden House" village. Principal chiefs apparently lived in log houses that were built for them by government agents instead of in lodges (Farnham 1966: 139). The well-known Kansa chief White Plume lived in a government-built stone house near the agency at Williamstown before he became dissatisfied with this mode of living and moved to Fool Chief village (Marshall 2000: 69). White Plume has been described as a Kansa Indian who had the heart, mind, and tongue of a Frenchman, which illustrates just how completely the French were assimilated into the Indian culture. Approximately 50 percent of the French-speaking tribal members were descended, in part, from the French, who had been present from the early eighteenth century (Hoffhaus 1984: 137, 142).

KANSA HUNTING

The Kansa refused to abandon their traditional life of hunting and raiding to become farmers. But game was becoming scarce in the 1830s, forcing longer journeys to the buffalo country. One band left the Mission Creek villages and moved some 40 miles west to be nearer the herds. By this time, the Kansa were traveling 200 miles or more to reach a hunting ground (Marshall 2000: 69). The villages were empty when a hunt was on or when an epidemic occurred. Normally, a village would be deserted one-third of the year, but during an epidemic, the villages would stand empty two-thirds of the year (W. Johnson et al. 1925: 232).

A traveler, Thomas Jefferson Farnham, came upon a Kansa hunting camp at Council Grove in 1839 and later in the same trip witnessed the summer hunt in the vicinity of Pawnee Forks. The camp consisted of a number of small domed structures covered with blankets and buffalo hides. Boughs that were about two inches in diameter had been inserted into the ground and tied together at the top to form an arch. Grass covered the floors, and a fire hearth was located outside of each structure. The lodges covered a semicircular piece of ground enclosed by outer lodges. The lodges were arranged in straight lines running from the diameter to the circumference. Large stakes had been set around the periphery of the huts to secure horses (Farnham 1966: 58–59).

A similar hut was described at the scene of the hunt. Branches had been inserted into the ground, tied at the top, and covered with hides. The hides gathered on the summer hunt had short hair and were used to make conical tents. Hides gathered on the winter hunt had long hair, and these were used for robes.

When on the hunt, warriors riding in a file pounced upon the herd. At the head of the file was the head chief carrying a lance, which was about six feet long. A three-foot blade was attached to the lance. Sometimes a broken saber blade was used (Din and Nasatir 1983: 22). Lesser chiefs used a shorter lance. The chiefs brought down five or six animals with their lances, and then the warriors, armed with muskets, pistols, and bows, commenced with the harvest. George Sibley had been an eyewitness of a Kansa hunt 28 years earlier, and he noted that more than 100 bison had been killed and were about to be processed (Sibley 1927: 210). Finally, 700 to 800 horses and mules were loaded with the spoils of the hunt. The women's tasks included finishing meat and hide preparation in the villages as well as cultivating corn, beans, and melons (Farnham 1966: 86–87, 139).

THE KANSA REMEMBER THE LAST VILLAGES ON THE KANSAS RIVER: RESERVATION LIFE

The Kansa were positioned right on the major trails, over which was moving a dominant culture that insisted on change and now was determined to move the Kansa out of the way. The Kansa initially refused to give up their traditional way of life but eventually were moved to a reservation. Even upon arrival at the reservation villages, the Kansa were described as being "as retched as human beings can be" (Barry 1972: 183). A severe winter in that year destroyed their horses, preventing them from going out on the hunt. The Kansa were reduced to begging and stealing food and horses from settlers who were already on their reservation lands. Their desperation caused them to intensify their raids upon the Pawnee in order to capture horses. The Kansa endured until a disastrous flood in 1844 broke their resolve (Barry 1972: 515–516). The Kansa attempted to rebuild their villages, but they finally abandoned the Kansas River valley and moved into three villages on the Neosho River near Council Grove (Marshall 2000: 70–71).

THE NEOSHO RIVER VILLAGES

In the vicinity of Council Grove the Kansa occupied three villages from 1847 to 1873. The villages were Hard Chief village, Fool Chief village (not to be confused with earlier villages along the Kansas River), and Big John's village. The social problems that plagued the Kansa society while at Mission Creek continued at Council Grove, where a dramatic decline occurred, "numerically and otherwise" (W. R. Wedel 1946: 15). The list is a depressing result of the effects of disease, social vices, and general disregard. As late as 1836 to 1844, the population was estimated between 1,600 and 1,700 people. The 1869 census records 525 people. The Kansa were removed from Kansas to the Indian Territory in 1873, and by the turn of the century only "97 full bloods and 127 mixed bloods" could be accounted for (W. R. Wedel 1946: 16–17).

The Kansa hunting-and-trading way of life was maintained during the occupation of the Neosho River villages. Small cabins built of stone were erected for individual families, but most preferred to continue to live in their traditional style within the villages (W. R. Wedel 1946: 15). Seasonal hunts continued, during which conflicts ensued with tribes such as the Comanche, the Cheyenne, the Kiowa, and the Arapahoe. Disastrous results of a skirmish with the Cheyenne in 1867 forced the Kansa to finally abandon their western hunting grounds (Staab 1995: 40). Some 60 people were reported to have died on this particular occasion, and an epidemic of smallpox killed more than 400 in 1855 (Staab 1995: 40; W. R. Wedel 1946: 16). The Kansa never fully recovered from these losses.

THE KANSA TODAY

The Kansa have returned to Kansas. The *Topeka Capital-Journal*, on February 18, 2002 (p. 1A), reported that the last band of Kansa was preparing to celebrate their return to the Council Grove vicinity. It reported that 160 acres of land had been purchased two years previous and that plans were being formulated to create an interpretive visitor center, celebrating the return of the Kansa to their homeland after an absence of 130 years. The article reported that hope had been expressed that the Kansa would be able to find their identity again and learn of their past.

SEARCHING FOR A CULTURAL ANTECEDENT

The archaeological evidence that awaits the Kansa is, unfortunately, inconclusive and cloudy. In the early 1900s, F. H. Sterns, who represented the Peabody Museum of Archaeology and Ethnology at Harvard University, conducted excavations at the Blue Earth village and also visited a site on Wolf Creek in Doniphan County that he identified as a Kansa village (Molloy 1993: 187–197; W. R. Wedel 1959: 96). The latter site is listed in the archaeological inventory as the Fanning site, 14DP1.

A goal of the archaeological survey carried out by Waldo Wedel during the summers of 1937, 1939, and 1940 was, as he stated, to "identify the remains of historical tribal groups, such as the Kansa, and to obtain some insight into their antecedents" (1959: 2). The fieldwork he devoted to the Kansa problem was finished in 1937. The results were published 22 years later, but he had realized long before publishing an archaeological report that the archaeological record for the Kansa was very tentative. "Unless," he wrote, "it be at one of their early 18th century sites on the Missouri, the nature of their ceramic tradition, an important point in tracing the tribal cultural origin, may never be conclusively established" (1946: 24).

Three archaeological sites on the Missouri River and within the boundaries of Kansas had been identified as Kansa villages. The earliest occupation was at the Doniphan site, 14DP2, which has been discussed as the village that Bourgmont visited in 1724. Some 30 years later, the Kansa were reported to be in a village adjacent to a French outpost that is known as Fort Cavagnolle. The precise location of the fort is not known, and apparently no physical remains of the fort or the village exist. Wedel (1959: 51) has suggested that the site may have been at the mouth of Salt Creek north of present-day Leavenworth, Kansas.

Wedel first conducted excavations at the Doniphan site, which was only a remnant of what it once was. The excavations revealed that the site was established prior to European contact. The historic occupation was reflected in material recovered from 15 storage pits and several burial pits. The pits were in a location that was thought to be peripheral to the village. Both debris and recognizable items of European manufacture were found in most of the pits. There was, as Wedel (1959: 130) reported, "not much that can be used to set up a Kansa complex: it can only be suggested that there is nothing here to contradict the view that an early post–white contact people resided on the spot, and that this people in light of historic documents were in all likelihood the Kansa."

The Fanning site was visited next, and there the excavations recovered a large amount of native material, as well as a lesser amount of artifacts of European manufacture. The native material was concluded to be representative of the Oneota aspect (Ritterbush, chapter 9, this volume; W. R. Wedel 1959: 600–615). Kansa identification rests upon the late seventeenth- and early eighteenth-century documentation that the Kansa were the residents of the region. Wedel accepted Stern's conclusion that the Fanning site was a Kansa village, and he added that this village predated the Doniphan occupation. He (1959: 170–171) surmised that the Fanning village had been abandoned before 1700.

Wedel moved his survey from northeast Kansas west to investigate sites in Riley and Pottawatomie counties. Limited excavation was done at the Blue Earth village. The hope was that evidence would be found that would allow a Kansa complex to be unequivocally set up, but, as Wedel (1959: 197) stated, "We ran into a dead end." By the time the Kansa had established the Blue Earth village, they were completely dependent on trade and had severed themselves from much of their traditions of manufacture. There was nothing that could relate this village to the Doniphan occupation or to Fanning.

The Historic period component at Doniphan was identified as a Kansa occupation. The Fanning site, based upon a similar style of ceramic manufacture and decoration, was labeled the Wolf Creek focus of the Oneota aspect (W. R. Wedel 1959: 535, 617, 636) and was considered a somewhat earlier Kansa occupation than that at Doniphan. Whether or not there is a local antecedent identifying a Kansa presence prior to European contact remains to be determined.

Roscoe Wilmeth, Kansas' first state archaeologist, reviewed the journals of Isaac McCoy, who in 1828 was searching for a potential reservation for the Potawatomi Indians. McCoy noted several Kansa villages between Junction City and Manhattan, Kansas, that were contemporaneous with the Blue Earth village. Wilmeth (1959: 53–56; 1960: 156–157) hoped to discover a village that was old enough to have items of native manufacture, especially pottery, which then could be related to an archaeological culture. These villages remain unconfirmed.

Wilmeth recommended that excavations be carried out at Hard Chief village, but this did not occur until 1987. Thomas A. Witty, then the Kansas state archaeologist, was afforded the opportunity to excavate by using the site for a Kansas Anthropological Association–sponsored field school. The other historically identified sites—the Methodist Mission, Chouteau's trading post, Fool Chief village, and American Chief village—have yet to be precisely located.

SUMMARY AND CONCLUSIONS

The Kansa appear in history as a culture that had fully adapted to the horse and gun and was reliant upon trade. For decades, the Kansa maintained their way of life as hunters and traders, and their ability to survive is a testament to their character.

Natural disasters, epidemics, intertribal wars, debilitating social vices, and manipulation by a dominant and aggressive European culture eroded Kansa society, but without a defining defeat.

The Kansa remembrances of their own past, which have been included in this chapter as a source that has been neglected by archaeologists, may very well lead to the identification of an archaeological cultural antecedent. The Fanning site, 14DP1, may be a Kansa village that was occupied before the residents were fully impacted by the European trade, but this identification is tentative and inconclusive. The suggestion that the site is a Kansa village has not been disputed, but it has to remain as a late Oneota manifestation waiting to be related to a historically identified tribe (O'Shea and Ludwickson 1992: 16, 72; Ritterbush, chapter 9, this volume).

The different modes of dwellings of the Kansa have been recognized as distinctive features (Bushnell 1922: 97). The limited archaeological excavations have uncovered only the circular lodge pattern with an extended entryway (Marshall 2000: 72–76; W. R. Wedel 1959: 135–136, 190–191). This pattern is that of the earthlodge that is a Pawnee cultural trait and that is a form of dwelling that was first constructed at the beginning of the sixteenth century (O'Shea and Ludwickson 1992: 72).

Bark lodges were also erected. These lodges were rectangular, domed structures covered with bark and hides and were the principal dwelling of the Osage Indians (Din and Nasatir 1983: 18–19). Sibley's description of the Kansa village at the mouth of the Republican River could easily be that of an Osage village. The Omaha and the Otoe Indians had adopted the earthlodge, but they too were once bark lodge–dwellers. The Otoe were using bark lodges as late as 1870 (O'Shea and Ludwickson 1992: 72).

The task confronting archaeologists is to respond to the admonishments of the linguists and the historians that are focused upon the cultural history of the Kansa. The linguist can maintain that, at the present stage of research, "the word is mightier than the sherd" and has stated that an archaeological guideline is lacking (Rankin 2001). Regardless of the problems that archaeologists contend with, a study of James Owen Dorsey's record of the Kansa's own remembrances could contribute significantly to defining a Kansa archaeological guideline. The question of Kansa origins may remain unresolved, but most certainly our appreciation of the extent of the Kansa occupation of the Kansas River valley will be enhanced by a more solid foundation.

14. The Pawnee in Kansas: Ethnohistory and Archaeology

Donna C. Roper

The Pawnee is a Plains horticultural village tribe that occupied a historic homeland in the Loup, Platte, Republican, and upper Blue river valleys of east-central Nebraska and northern Kansas. Speaking a Northern Caddoan language, Pawnee, that is closely related to Arikara, Kitsai, and Wichita (Lesser and Weltfish 1932), the tribe is organized into four bands: *Skiri* or Loup; *Chawi,* or Grand; *Kitkahahki,* or Republican; and *Pitahawirata,* or Tappage. The last three collectively are designated the South Bands, and these people speak the South Band dialect of the language. The Skiri speak the Skiri dialect. In the recent past, each band occupied one or more mudlodge (the Pawnee term for what is elsewhere called the earthlodge) villages during the spring and late summer/early fall and tended fields in which they grew corn, squash, tobacco, and other crops (Dunbar 1880; Weltfish 1965). For part of the summer, as well as during late fall and winter, they conducted extended communal bison hunts through lands to the west and south of the village area, in both Nebraska and western Kansas (Figure 14.1). While on the hunt, they followed the larger rivers along well-established trails and established tipi camps occupied for periods of time ranging from short overnight stops to winter camps occupied for some weeks (Roper 1991b). Raiding or war parties also traveled far beyond the village area, undoubtedly using the same trails. The Pawnee regarded certain landscape features as sacred places (D. R. Parks and Wedel 1985). The Pawnee archaeological record, therefore, is composed of villages, trails, and encampments occupied during the hunt or during extended forays for raiding and warfare, and sacred places.

The four Pawnee bands are known only from the latter third of the eighteenth century. Documentary references, both texts and cartographic representations, for this period are somewhat sporadic and, with really only two exceptions, are secondary through 1806. After that date, references become considerably more abundant, and many are direct. This record shows that Skiri and Chawi village histories are entirely in the Loup and Platte river valleys in Nebraska. Kitkahahki village history is closely tied to the Republican River valley. Pitahawirata village history is sketchy but may be at least in part associated with the Kansas River drainage. All bands, particularly all three South Bands, however, hunted and raided into what is now Kansas, and there is some evidence of interaction with the Wichita of the Great Bend aspect in central Kansas.

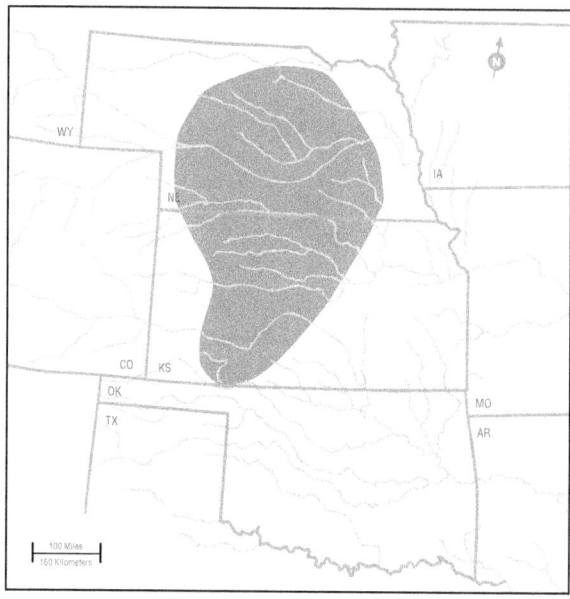

Figure 14.1. Pawnee village areas and maximum hunting territory, late eighteenth and early nineteenth centuries (from Roper 1991b: 209, with slight modification)

KITKAHAHKI VILLAGE ETHNOHISTORY, 1775–1833

The earliest documentary source in which we can specifically identify the Kitkahahki, or Republic (variously also Republica, Republique, or Republican), is the 1775 listing by Piernas of the Republic as one of the nations with whom the Spanish were accustomed to trade (Kinnaird, ed., 1949, 1: 228). Piernas did not say where the Republic were settled, but two years later, in 1777, Cruzat, his successor as lieutenant-governor at St. Louis, said that "La Republica" were about 220 leagues (ca. 527 miles, using the 2.6-mile Spanish *legua legal* [Chardon 1980]) from St. Louis, about 110 leagues (286 miles) from the Missouri River "on the shores of the Cances [Kansas] river," and 40–50 leagues (104–130 miles) from the Cances (Kansa) village (Houck 1909: 143). Similarly, in 1785, Louisiana governor Miró listed "the Indians of the Panis Republic" on the "River Cancés about a hundred and thirty leagues from its mouth" (Nasatir 1952, 1: 126), or about 338 miles. The Republic appear regularly in the records from subsequent years (Nasatir 1942; 1952, 1: 135, 209–211). The incidental location information contained in Truteau's 1794–1795 journal (Nasatir 1952, 1: 261) or MacKay's 1797 table of distances (Nasatir 1952, 2: 488), however, does not add to the earlier accounts.

Neither do the documents, many of which are simply records of trading licenses issued, tell us much about the Kitkahahki people and their culture at that time. From Cruzat, we learn that they numbered 350–400 warriors and that the principal chief was named Escatapé. Miró later said the Republic numbered "two hundred and twenty men capable of bearing arms" (Nasatir 1952, 1: 126). Cruzat also tells us that the Kansa, at that time in the Missouri River valley, "generally cause a great deal of harm to traders who are sent to [the Republic] for they do not allow those traders to ascend the river" (Houck 1909, 1: 143), which may explain the notation "not able to enter" that Piernas made for the Republic two years earlier. This was not new information, though, for Kerlérec had commented on the hostility between the Pawnee and the Kansa as early as 1758 (Nasatir 1952, 1: 52). In no case were these officials writing from firsthand experience, and it is likely that some of the information was at least third- or fourth-hand.

In fact, the first of only two pre-1806 primary records of Pawnee villages is the journal of Pedro Vial's 1793 trip from St. Louis to Santa Fe. Vial had been sent from Santa Fe to St. Louis the previous year, with instructions to return via the Pawnee village. Accordingly, when the time came for the return, Vial and his companion proceeded up the Missouri River to the mouth of the Little Nemaha River, and from there traveled west and southwest to a Pawnee village, spending 12 days there before continuing on to the Comanche and to Santa Fe. From the recorded distances and, sometimes, the direction of a day's travel, in addition to occasional mention of streams and topography, we can approximate Vial's route and place his destination in the Republican River valley. The officials at Santa Fe were seeking to open communications with St. Louis and to make friends with the Indians between the two cities (Loomis and Nasatir 1967: 369). Vial's journal, therefore, also contains useful administrative information. He recorded the chief's name as Sarisere and said the village had 300 warriors. Other Pawnee settlements, he wrote, had another 1,000 men. He recorded distances to Pawnee, Otoe, Kansa, and Osage villages and mentioned who were allies and who were enemies. But information on the village environs, a physical description of the village, or an account of the people and their customs would be superfluous to a government official, so, perhaps not surprisingly, Vial's journal contains no such information (Loomis and Nasatir 1967: 400; A. B. Thomas 1931: 202–203). Vial was again at a Pawnee village—presumably the same one—in June 1795, but, although there is an official two-paragraph administrative record of that mission (Loomis and Nasatir 1967: 413; Nasatir 1952, 1: 329–330), there is no journal or other firsthand account of this trip, and we learn nothing of the village at that time.

The first cartographic representation of the Kitkahahki in the Republican River valley appeared shortly after Vial's 1793 journey. This is Antoine Soulard's 1795 map of the Missouri River drainage and the upper Mississippi River valley (W. R. Wood 1996; 2001: pl. 12). This map, which has been called the first really new map of the Central Plains since 1718 (Ehrenberg 1987: 20), shows three dots portraying the village or villages of the *Republique* on a river that unmistakably is the Republican (Figure 14.2). The map also shows a trail from the mouth of the Little Nemaha River to the village location. This probably is the trail Vial followed, and it seems entirely possible that Vial's journal was one of the sources that Soulard, the surveyor-general at St. Louis, used in preparing the map. Further cartographic representations in the following

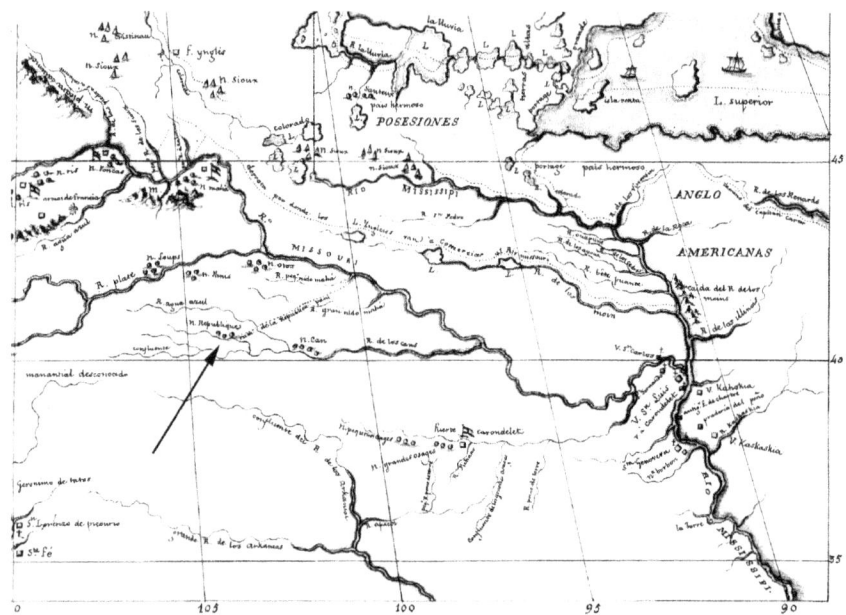

Figure 14.2. A portion of the 1795 Soulard map. Arrow points to the dots portraying the village or villages of the Republique. (Courtesy of the Karpeles Manuscript Library, Santa Barbara, California)

years include the 1802 Perrin du Lac map (W. R. Wood, ed., 1983: pl. 9) that shows the *Village de Republiques* in the same location as on the Soulard map.

Shortly after the time of Perrin du Lac's map, pressure from the Kansa drove the Kitkahahki from the Republican River valley. We have two sources for this. One is the record of Pedro Vial's third trip to the Pawnee, this one in 1804. This time he was at a village on the Platte River, where he mentioned two chiefs, one of whom he named Sartariche, presumably the same man he had met down south in 1793 (Nasatir 1974: 118). More explicitly, Lewis and Clark in 1805 described the streams of the Missouri River drainage and the peoples who lived along them. In the account of the Platte River and its peoples, they indicated that along that river "the Panias Proper [the Grand or Chawi], and Republican Panias reside in one large village" (Moulton 1983–2001, 3: 350). They later explained more fully:

> About ten years since they [the Pania Republicans] withdrew themselves from the mother nation [the Panias Proper], and established a village on a large northwardly branch of the Kanzas, to which they have given name [i.e., the Republican]: they afterwards subdivided and lived in different parts of the country on the waters of Kanzas river; but being harassed by their turbulent neighbors, the Kanzas, they rejoined the Panias proper last spring. (Moulton 1983–2001, 3: 398)

Their maps also showed the Grand and Republic together on the Platte River and an "old village" of the Republican on the Republican River (Moulton 1983–2001, 1: maps 123, 125). The implication in the text that the Republican had become established in the Republican River valley only in the mid-1790s is obviously misleading, for, as we have seen, the French and Spanish documents clearly place them in this position almost two decades earlier. The account, though, strongly implies that the Republican had recently occupied more than one village in the Republican River valley.

The co-residence of the Kitkahahki and the Chawi in the Platte River valley obviously was short, for, in 1806, two expeditions arrived at a Republican village in the Republican River valley. The first expedition, best described in the records of the second (Coues 1895, 2: 410–414), was led by the Spanish lieutenant Facundo Melgares. The second, which arrived a few weeks after Melgares departed, was led by the American lieutenant Zebulon Pike. The story is reasonably well known. The United States had recently acquired the Louisiana Territory, and Pike's was one of a number of expeditions sent to explore it (Lewis and Clark's expedition, of course, was another). Upon arrival at the Kitkahahki village, however, Pike found the Spanish flag flying, left by Melgares, and demanded that it be replaced by the American flag (Coues 1895, 2: 415–416, 543). It was.

For the ethnohistorian, though, there is additional important information in the Pike journal. Pike named the village chief as Caracterish, possibly the same name that Vial rendered as Sarisere/Sartariche, and another chief as Iskatappe, possibly Cruzat's Escatapé. This would make Escatapé a fairly old man at the time of Pike's visit, but thirty years is not impossible. Pike subsequently composed a "Dissertation on Louisiana" in which he described Republican horse-breeding, houses, games, seasonal hunting, and warfare, and thus provided the earliest description of Pawnee culture (Coues 1895, 2: 533–536). He also recorded the route to and from the village and its setting.

Pike's journal in a sense brings the Kitkahahki into written history in a way no previous reference does. Although it would be the 1830s before visits to Pawnee villages became numerous and led to fuller descriptions of villages, peoples, and their customs, the documentary history for the intervening decades nevertheless allows us to outline Kitkahahki history during these apparently turbulent decades. Clamorgan was at a Republican village on the Republican River in 1807 (Nasatir 1942: 112). A few years later, though, a traveler on the Missouri River known only as Dr. Thomas said that in 1809 a Kansa raiding party entered a Republican village and killed the chief and his family (Jackson 1964: 184). This event soon drove the Kitkahahki from the Republican River valley, so that when Sibley arrived at a Pawnee village on the Platte River in 1811 he said that both the Republican and the Grand were living there. He went on to relate that the town "is now inhabited by *three* tribes of the Pawnees, *two* of which formerly dwelt on the north branch of the Konsee [Kansas] River, about 50 miles in a direct course, above the Konsee [Kansa] village. The successive incursions of the Konsees obliged them to abandon their old towns about two years ago" (G. R. Brooks 1965: 180; italics added).

This reference to the simultaneous occupation of two Republican villages in the Republican River valley a few years earlier would be consistent with the implication in Lewis and Clark's account that the Republican had more than one village.

Although the evidence of Kitkahahki whereabouts is poor for the decade of the 1810s, they probably remained in the Loup River valley during that decade. They (the "Pawnee Republic") signed the Treaty of Peace and Friendship with the United States government in 1818 (Kappler 1904, 2: 158), but the text of that treaty does not state where their village was. The Stephen H. Long expedition, however, entered a Kitkahahki village in the Loup River valley in June 1820, saying at that time that the Republican Pawnee had been in "their present situation" for a number of years (Benson 1988: 159). The Kitkahahki returned to the Republican River valley a few years later. In September 1823, Duke Paul of Württemberg was at a Pawnee village on the Platte River and said then that the village "is inhabited by the Great Pawnees, who are divided into two divisions, and another of these people is settled a few miles farther to the west. (One of these bands is called Republican Pawnees by the Americans)" (Wilhelm 1973: 388). Barry (1972: 129) thinks the passing reference to the Republican Pawnee may mean that they had already left the area. Although that is not necessarily what the passage says, at least in the Nitske translation quoted, Barry (1972: 129) also cites a trade license issued that same month for trade with Pawnees on Republic Fork (i.e., the Republican River).

General Henry Atkinson and Agent Benjamin O'Fallon reported the Kitkahahki as still in the Republican River valley in November 1825, and Jedediah Smith wintered with them there for a time in early 1826 on his way west. Smith again went through the villages on his return in 1830 (Barry 1972: 128–129, 175; Clokey 1980: 168–169; Morgan 1953: 346). Supposedly, the Kitkahahki had made peace with their old enemies, the Kansa, in 1822, and perhaps this is what had precipitated their move back to the Republican River valley around that time. In March 1831, however, the Kansa raided the Kitkahahki village, killing several women and children (Barry 1972: 183). This must have been about the last straw for the Kitkahahki in the Republican River valley. In 1833, in council with Indian Treaty Commissioner Henry L. Ellsworth, the four Pawnee bands signed a treaty ceding all lands south of the Platte River (Kappler 1904: 416–418). John Treat Irving was with Ellsworth and described visiting a Republican Pawnee village on the Loup Fork of the Platte River (Irving 1955: 150) during that trip, so clearly the Kitkahahki had moved back north sometime in the previous two years. They would not again live in the Republican River valley.

PITAHAWIRATA ETHNOHISTORY, 1768-1833

The Pitahawirata are much more difficult to follow in the documentary record. The first known use of the specific name of any of the three South Bands is a 1768 record of licensing traders for the "Pani-Topage" (Nasatir 1952, 1: 66), but then the Tappage disappear from the records for over a quarter century. They are not listed in the 1775 or 1777 trade records or in Miró's 1785 letter, nor did Truteau mention them in 1794. They do reappear in that year, however, on a trade list by Jacques Clamorgan (Kinnaird, ed., 1949, 2: 278–279; Nasatir 1952, 1: 209–211), and they were included on several other trade lists for the years 1794–1796 (Nasatir 1952, 2: 530–531). They also were included on a list of Plains tribes the Skiri gave to the Spanish at San Antonio in 1795 (Troike 1964: 384–385). In 1801, however, although they do appear on one trade licensing list for that year (Nasatir 1952, 2: 592), Clamorgan, in a dispatch to the Louisiana governor-general Salcedo, referred to "the three different Panis nations" (Nasatir 1952, 2: 634), apparently, on the basis of other documents from that period, excluding the Tappage. None of the documents in which the Tappage were mentioned gives even the vaguest indication of where the villages were, though, nor do the Soulard or Perrin du Lac maps show Tappage villages.

The suggestion that the Pitahawirata were with the Chawi in the Platte River valley during this time (D. R. Parks 2001: 519) might seem warranted but for a few other bits of contradictory information. John B. Dunbar (1880: 260) said that the Pitahawirata formerly "were known as the Smoky Hill Pawnees from having once resided on that stream in western Kansas" and that during the 1836 summer hunt they pointed out some of their old villages to his father. There is, in fact, a continuing Pitahawirata oral tradition of a village in the Smoky Hill River valley (Blaine 1979, 1990, 1997). Effie Blaine's great-great-great-grandfather lived there, and, since Effie Blaine was born around 1869 (Blaine 1997: 6–7, 227n), this village could date to the late 1700s. No archaeological site has been found that might constitute the remains of this village.

On July 12, 1804, Lewis and Clark passed the mouth of the Little Nehama River. Clark said of it that "the River heads up near the Parnee Village on River Blue a branch of Kansas" (Moulton 1983–2001, 2: 369). This village, and Pawnee occupation in the Blue River valley, is never further mentioned in the Lewis and Clark journals, nor is a Pawnee village shown along the Blue River, although the river is shown on post-expedition maps (Moulton 1983–2001, 1: maps 123, 125). This is credible as a reference to a Tappage village in the Blue River area, though, for it was later reported that the Tappage had been in the Blue Springs, Nebraska, area until about 1825 (Green, cited in Grange 1968: 20).

As had the Kitkahahki, the Pitahawirata signed the Treaty of Peace and Friendship with the United States in 1818 (Kappler 1904, 2: 157–158) and were a party to the Ellsworth treaty of 1833 (Kappler 1904, 2: 416–418). At that time, Irving (1955: 151), although he did not visit it, described the Tappage village as being along the Loup River. The Tappage would remain there with the other three Pawnee bands until 1875 when all the Pawnee gave up their reservation in Nebraska and moved to a new one in Indian Territory.

REPUBLICAN RIVER VALLEY VILLAGE SITES

Four Pawnee village sites—all presumed to be Kitkahahki—are documented from three localities along an approximately 160-mile stretch of the Republican River valley (Figure 14.3). The first recorded is the middle of the three, the Kansas Monument Site (14RP1). Many years ago, Elizabeth Johnson searched for several years for the site of Pike's 1806 visit, an event widely celebrated as the first time the Stars and Stripes were raised west of the Missouri River. When she found the site in 1901, she purchased it and presented it to the State of Kansas as a park (Anonymous 1908: 18). Most of it has never been plowed and now is a state historical site—the Pawnee Indian Village—with a small museum.

The village site lies on the crest of a steep bluff overlooking the confluence of White Rock Creek and the Republican River. It originally contained an estimated 30 to 40 houses and was fortified. The state monument contains 22 of the houses and a portion of the fortifications. The University of Kansas, under the direction of Carlyle S. Smith, excavated two houses in 1949 and tested the fortification and some other features (Roberts 1978; C. S. Smith 1949b, 1950a, 1950b). The Kansas State Historical Society, under the direction of Thomas Witty, excavated another five houses in 1965–1967 (Witty 1968b). The museum is erected over one of these houses with all artifacts and features left in place.

The locality farthest upstream contains two sites, the Hill or Pike-Pawnee site (25WT1) and the Shipman site (25WT7). The Hill site was found in 1923 by A. T. Hill, who earlier concluded that Kansas Monument was not the remains of the Pike village and went in search of a site that more satisfactorily matched the location described in the journals of the Pike expedition (A. T. Hill 1927: 162–164; W. R. Wedel 1936: 34). When Hill found the site, he bought the land containing it and, during 1930 and 1941, directed excavations of 10 houses and 51 burials (Metcalf 1941; W. R. Wedel 1936). The site now is a National Historic Landmark. It is owned by the Nebraska State Historical Society Foundation and is in continuous cultivation.

The Hill site lies on a toe slope and terrace on the south side of the Republican River valley. The Shipman site represents an extension of the Hill site and is separated from it only by a small creek. Hill contains around 100 houses; a few more are found at Shipman. Middens, corral locations, a hoop game field, and trails were visible before the land was cultivated. The burial grounds occupy high points of land behind the village. Early reports of fortifications now are viewed skeptically (Metcalf 1941).

Well downstream from Kansas Monument is the Bogan site (14GE1), by far the smallest and least known of the Republican River valley sites. Floyd Schultz excavated there in 1930, and the University of Nebraska conducted additional work in 1964, working in advance of the construction of Milford Dam and Reservoir (Marshall and Witty 1990: 23). The site is on a low, gentle slope of the Republican River valley on U.S. government land adjoining the Milford Reservoir. It is partially destroyed but probably once contained about a dozen houses, of which about three or

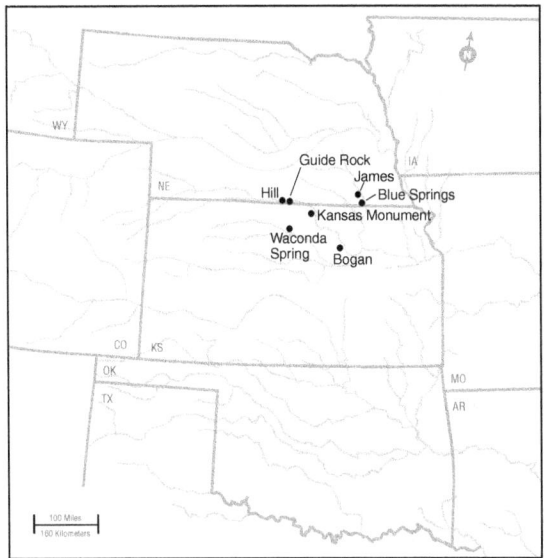

Figure 14.3. Pawnee villages and Nahu'rac in the Kansas River drainage

four now remain. Portions of a fortification can be traced for some distance around the village perimeter. One house has been excavated, and the fortification has been tested (Marshall and Witty 1990: 24–27).

VILLAGE SITE CHRONOLOGY

The Kansas Monument site probably represents the oldest Republican River valley village and the one referred to in the earliest documents that distinctly identify the Kitkahhki. Mean or median dates derived from ceramic formula dating (Grange 1974, 1984) and placement of the site as a whole in seriations of Pawnee sites (Grange 1968; Roberts 1978: 67–75) are misleading. A ceramic formula dating of assemblages from individual houses (Roberts 1978: 76) allows for a more sensitive internal site chronology but is overly precise, probably without being accurate. Comparing Roberts's pottery vessel type identifications for individual excavated houses (Roberts 1978: 84–85) with the externally validated general order of late Protohistoric and early Historic period Pawnee villages developed by Grange (1968), though, suggests that some of the Kansas Monument site lodges were occupied in the latter part of the eighteenth century.

The documentary data support this temporal inference. Cruzat placed the Kitkahahki about 110 leagues, or 286 miles, from the Missouri River, while Miró placed them about 130 leagues, or 338 miles, upriver. A measurement of the modern river course to the Kansas Monument site—which undoubtedly is different in detail from the eighteenth-century course—is about 368 miles, or 142 leagues, using the 2.6-mile league. This is tolerably close to the eighteenth-century estimates, particularly

Miró's, which obviously were made by less precise means, and is closer than the distances to Bogan (243 miles) or Hill (415 miles). A careful evaluation of Vial's 1793 destination using distances traveled both from the mouth of the Little Nemaha River to the village and from the village to the Arkansas River crossing suggest it almost certainly was not the village represented by the Hill site; could have been, but probably was not, the Bogan site village; and most likely was the Kansas Monument site village.

The next chronological signpost is the 1806 Pike expedition. Despite some lingering south-of-the-state-line opposition, Hill's work in the 1920s, which included retracing the route and comparing the site setting with Pike's description, conclusively showed that the Hill site is the ruins of the village that Melgares and Pike visited. The archaeological evidence, particularly from extremely time-sensitive artifacts such as peace medals (Munday 1927: 187), corroborates this identification. When this village was established, and when (or whether) Kansas Monument was abandoned at the same time, is less easy to determine. Lewis and Clark's account, quoted earlier, might indicate that the apparent shift actually represented a division of the village, with some people remaining at Kansas Monument and some establishing the Hill site village, or that Hill represents a second movement of people to the Republican River valley from the Loup River valley. Sibley's intimation of two villages in the Republican River valley prior to abandonment in 1809 is consistent with either scenario. Archaeological evidence at least does not contradict it.

Little is known about the village at the Bogan site. It perhaps was established during the same subdivision in the 1790s that Lewis and Clark reported, and there is a slight chance that this is the village Vial visited in 1793. The collections are small and the pottery is too fragmentary to be identified to type and used in chronological analyses, but Euro-American artifacts are present, and Roberts's (1978: 170) conclusion, based on relative proportions of native and Euro-American artifacts that Bogan dates to the late eighteenth century, probably is correct. The occupation appears to have been short.

It remains to be determined what site or sites the Kitkahahki occupied when they returned to the Republican River valley in the 1820s. Kansas Monument probably was occupied; Bogan probably was not. Again using the ceramic data reported by Roberts (1978: 84–85) in a general sense, a couple of houses are dominated by ceramics that should date those houses to around that time. The Hill site materials are insufficiently analyzed to address this question, although this village probably also was reoccupied.

BLUE RIVER VALLEY VILLAGE SITES

Two Pawnee villages are identified in the upper Big Blue River valley in Gage County, Nebraska, about 10 miles north of the state line. The larger of the two is the Blue

Springs or Wonder site (25GA1). E. E. Blackman (1904: 6–7, 16–17) recorded it in 1903 and more extensively explored it in 1904. The Nebraska State Historical Society, under A. T. Hill, excavated two houses, three middens, and two external pits there in 1935. The site is on a terrace adjacent to the Big Blue River. It contained an estimated 75–100 houses and was fortified. Middens and horse corrals were visible before the land was farmed. The second Blue River site is a short distance north of the Blue Springs site. The site, referred to as the James site (no number), had an estimated couple of dozen houses and was not fortified. No excavations have been conducted. These two sites presumably represent early nineteenth-century Tappage villages. The ceramic types represented and the presence of Euro-American trade goods in fairly small proportion relative to native objects (Grange 1968) are both consistent with this temporal placement.

VILLAGE SITE ARCHAEOLOGY

Pike provided the first descriptions of Pawnee mudlodges (Coues 1895, 2: 533–534) and, of course, did so from observing Kitkahahki lodges at the village represented by the Hill site. Pawnee lodges, like earthlodges throughout the Central and Northern Plains, were circular (Figure 14.4). Excavated lodges range from 26 to 50 feet in diameter. A central hearth is encircled by a ring of interior support posts and, farther out, a ring of wall posts. Ideally, there were four interior support posts, but in actuality the number ranged from six to ten. Entryways of varying lengths ideally extended to the east, but some extended to the southeast or south. An altar holding a buffalo skull was at the back of the lodge, opposite the entryway. Buffalo skulls and occasionally features representing the remnants of altars may be found in excavated houses. Cache pits, typically bell-shaped, are found both inside and outside houses. With one exception, features other than cache pits and middens are not reported outside houses. The exception is a subrectangular unroofed structure at the Hill site that had no interior features or debris and may be a horse corral (W. R. Wedel 1936: 56–57).

Both native-made and Euro-American trade objects are found in the Pawnee sites of the Republican River and Blue River valleys. Native pottery is a grit- or sand-tempered ware fashioned into globular vessels with direct, collared, or braced rims. Exteriors are characteristically simple-stamped, sometimes smoothed, and rarely cord-marked. Incised decoration frequently was applied to rims, shoulders, and/or handles. Vessel lips may be plain, incised, or punctated (Grange 1968; see also Roberts 1978: 47–66; C. S. Smith 1950b; W. R. Wedel 1936: 62–74).

Chipped-stone objects, made from regionally available raw materials, include triangular arrowpoints, scrapers, drills, and a few bifaces. Groundstone objects are more diverse and include hammerstones, metates, manos, mauls, shaft abraders, incised tablets, and pipes. An important bone tool was the scapula hoe. Other bone

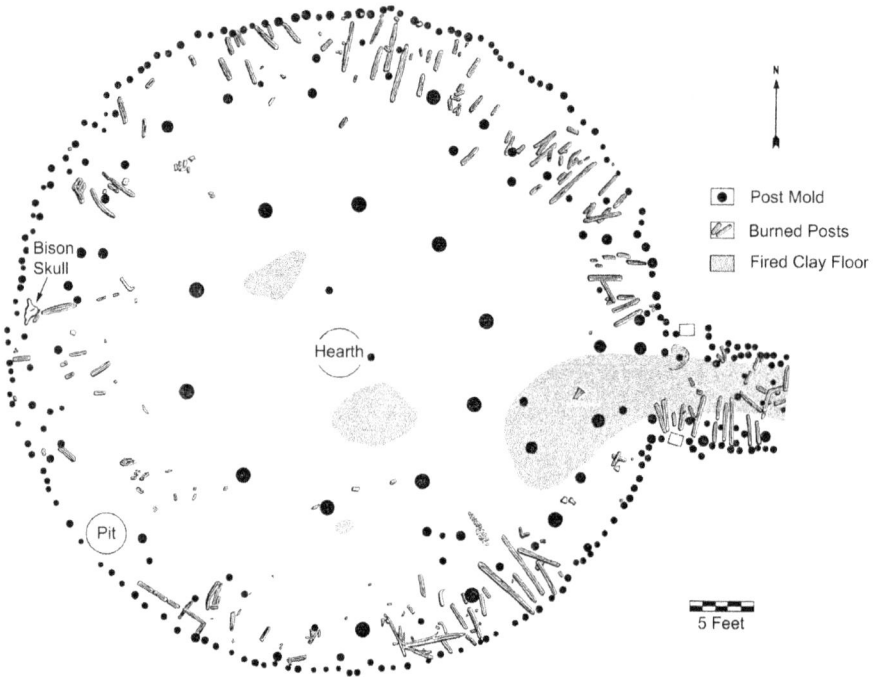

Figure 14.4. Floor plan of a Pawnee mudlodge (Kansas Monument site, House 5). (Courtesy of the Kansas State Historical Society)

tools include awls, shaft wrenches, fleshers, and flakers (Roberts 1978; W. R. Wedel 1936). Wood mortars were found at both the Kansas Monument (Roberts 1978: 115) and Hill (W. R. Wedel 1936: 87–88) sites. Other wood artifacts also were found at Hill (Munday 1927: 192; W. R. Wedel 1936: 88–89).

Trade artifacts did not fully replace native objects until the 1820s/1830s. Trade artifacts appear in even the earliest Pawnee sites in the Loup River valley of Nebraska, however, and are found in every known site, including the Kansas River drainage sites. Documented object types include hoes, knives, axes, kettles, and gun parts (Marshall and Witty 1990: 30; C. S. Smith 1950a). Metal projectile points attest to a continued use of the bow and arrow, even after guns were available. Glass beads are a common artifact type.

A few burials have been excavated at the Kansas Monument site (Witty 1968b: 3–4); more than a few were excavated at the Hill site (Metcalf 1941; W. R. Wedel 1936: 92). Ethnographic information, corroborated by the archaeological record, indicates that burials were individual primary inhumations in cemeteries (O'Shea 1984: 73–75). At the Hill site, and at some of the Platte River drainage villages, the cemeteries were on the hilltops overlooking the village. At hilltop sites such as Kansas Monument, the cemeteries were elsewhere in the village vicinity.

NON-VILLAGE SITES

The Pawnee, like other village tribes on the Plains, conducted several-month-long communal bison hunts during the winter and summer. During the hunt, they moved along well-established trails. The hunting territory of all the South Bands included much of the Kansas River drainage and at times extended at least as far south as the valley of the Arkansas River (Blaine 1990: 72; Holen 1991; Roper 1992); thus, the hunting territory included a substantial portion of modern Kansas. Documented trails known to have been used by the Pawnee for hunting and probably also raiding and trading cross Kansas (Blakeslee 1995; Blakeslee, Blasing, and Garcia 1986). East-west trails followed major rivers; north-south trails cross-cut valleys and interfluves. Trails sometimes are marked by rock cairns and possibly rock art (O'Neill 1981). A few hunting camp sites (e.g., Kinsey 1998; Roper 2001b) have been recorded, and undoubtedly many others are undiscovered or unidentified in museum collections. At the present, these sites are known from surface evidence alone. They may contain either native-made pottery and chipped-stone artifacts or metal projectile points.

At least two major Pawnee *nahu'rac* or animal lodges (G. A. Dorsey 1906; Grinnell 1889, 1893; Murie 1981)—sacred sites—are in the Kansas River drainage (D. R. Parks and Wedel 1985). Waconda Spring was sacred to many tribes. To the Pawnee, it was known as *Kacawi:caku*, the Spring on the Edge of a Bank or Spring Mound. It lies along the Solomon River in Mitchell County and now is submerged by Waconda Lake. Guide Rock, or *Pa:hu:ru'*, the Hill that Points the Way, is a few miles north of the state line. It is on the south side of the Republican River about four and one-half miles east of the Hill village site. Important trails run near both animal lodges.

Occasional Pawnee sherds from Great Bend aspect (i.e., Wichita) villages in central Kansas likely are trade or gift pots and are further evidence of Pawnee activity in this area during the Protohistoric period (Roper 2000d; Udden 1900; S. C. Vehik 2002a: 53). It should be noted, however, that a single pot from the Coal-Oil Canyon site in Logan County, sometimes attributed to the Pawnee (Bowman 1960: 26), probably is really a vessel made locally from poor-quality clay during the Late Prehistoric period.

BEFORE THE MID-EIGHTEENTH CENTURY

The ethnohistoric record of the Pawnee prior to the mid-eighteenth century dates from 1673 but is sporadic and rather murky. One consistency, however, is that prior to the last third of the eighteenth century, the documents, including maps, give names for only two groups now identified as Pawnee: the *Panimaha*, or Skiri, and the *Pani*, or South Bands—other names containing the morpheme Pani are considered to refer to bands now identified with the Wichita. When the documents indicate where the Panimaha and Pani were, they invariably place them in the Platte or Loup

River valley. It seems likely, therefore, that the emergence of the three individual South Bands in the latter third of the eighteenth century marks the time of the movement of some South Bands out of the Platte River drainage. This appearance of a differentiation of the Pani into three individual South Bands and the movement of some bands are consistent with the tradition that the South Bands once were one, the Kawarahki (G. A. Dorsey 1906: 8; Murie 1981: 197).

The converse of the fact that only two band names appear in the early documents is that there are two names in the documents, not one, that refer to the Pawnee as a whole. In fact, until relatively recent times, the Pawnee themselves did not have a name that referred to all four bands collectively (D. R. Parks 2001: 545). Overlooking this, though, scholars have long insisted on constructing a single history for the Pawnee, treating them as a whole and as distinct from the Wichita and Arikara, even as they have recognized both the antiquity of the distinction between the Skiri and the South Bands and the closeness of the relationship among the Wichita, Pawnee, and Arikara. Now, however, it is time to return to a position implicit in Dorsey's (1906: 8–9) introduction to his collection of Pawnee tales, namely, that the South Bands and the Skiri really have separate histories.

A scenario that bears consideration would hold that Skiri and Arikara history, from perhaps sometime in the fifteenth century and through the sixteenth and seventeenth centuries, was played out in south-central South Dakota and parts of Nebraska, with the two bands (Skiri and Arikara) emerging in a process similar to that which a couple centuries later would split the Kawarahki into the three individual South Bands. The contemporary Kawarahki (South Bands) and Wichita history was entirely separate and was played out in central Kansas. Leaving aside the dynamics of the Skiri/Arikara group as beyond the scope of this chapter, the Kawarahki and the several bands now collectively called Wichita formed as peoples previously scattered into small population units, frequently no more than farmsteads, aggregated into villages in the fifteenth and sixteenth centuries. The villages that formed during this aggregation remained autonomous and endogamous, and band identities probably developed in separate, although not necessarily widely spaced, localities at that time. Whether individual bands should be called Pawnee or Wichita is moot; they all spoke Northern Caddoan dialects, they all were called (or at least recorded) by names that included the morpheme Pani, and they probably had no collective identity beyond the band.

It is consistent with this that when Coronado was asked what lay beyond Quivira, the answer was Harahey and that it had "customs, settlement, and size" as at Quivira (Hammond and Rey 1940: 304), the Great Bend aspect villages of Rice County. Harahey (variously also Arae, Arache) is usually considered to be a rendering of the word Awá·hí·h, the Wichita name for the Pawnee. Perhaps, however, it is instead a rendering of the word Kawarahki. The supposition that this is a reference to the early Loup River villages is based on fallacious reasoning and is not supported by archaeological evidence; the documents really do not say where Harahey was, only that it was beyond Quivira. In fact, the documents also say that the houses in Harahey were "some of straw and the rest of hides" (Hammond and Rey 1940: 292), which is not consistent with the obvious use of mudlodges in the early Loup River and Platte River valley villages (Dunlevy 1936). Quite possibly, then, the Kawarahki in the mid-sixteenth century were in central Kansas, and the archaeological designation for their material culture complex is not Lower Loup phase but rather Great Bend aspect. Quite possibly, too, the Kawarahki arrival in the Platte River valley is a result of a seventeenth-century northward movement. It surely is relevant in this regard to note that Holen (1991) found that the predominant lithic raw material in the earliest Nebraska village thought to represent the South Bands, the Gray-Wolfe site (25CX1) in the Platte River valley, is not the Nehawka chert from nearby sources, but Permian chert from the northern Flint Hills—the same lithic raw material that dominates assemblages from some of the northern Great Bend aspect villages (Roper 2000b; Zehnder 1998).

The northern Flint Hills and much of the Kansas River drainage in general would remain within South Bands hunting territory until the signing of the Ellsworth treaty in 1833. In the late eighteenth and early nineteenth centuries, villages were established in this same drainage basin by some of the newly differentiated divisions of the Kawarahki. These villages too would be continually occupied until the 1830s. It is this late Protohistoric and early Historic period occupation that forms the most prominent and readily recognized part of the record of the Pawnee in Kansas. If, however, the scenario laid out above for the earlier centuries has any validity, then Pawnee South Bands history is even more closely tied to Kansas than the ethnohistoric and archaeological record from the late eighteenth and early nineteenth centuries reflects.

15. Paleoethnobotanical Research in Kansas
Mary J. Adair

Paleoethnobotany is the study of the dynamic interrelationship between past populations and their plant world. It requires the methodological recovery and identification of macrobotanical remains, which are plant parts from archaeological deposits that are visible to the naked eye, and the interpretation of the cultural context of these remains. As a critical, and often defining, component of the natural environment, plants were selected for a variety of uses, including food, fuel, building materials, medicine, clothing, and utensils. Plant parts recovered from archaeological deposits are therefore recognized as helping answer questions related to past environments, economic adaptations, crop evolution, plant management, and the human impact on the environment. The reconstruction of diet, however, is perhaps the most common focus in the interpretation of macrobotanical remains. Food is important to everyone, regardless of when, how, or where they lived. At the same time, the ways in which each society meets the need for food often vary and depend on culturally determined standards of production, preparation, consumption, and discard.

These standards also influence the existence and diversity of macrobotanical remains. The mere use of a plant can completely destroy it, while processing or manipulation can reduce a plant to a microscopic element such as pollen, spores, phytoliths, or starch grains. If large plant parts survive the initial intended use, the organic remains are further subjected to deterioration by natural processes. Although some plant parts can survive centuries or even millennia in desiccated or waterlogged environments, few specimens survive in open-air deposits, such as most archaeological sites in the Central Plains, without being partly burned (total burning would reduce the plant to microscopic elements). Carbonized macrobotanical remains retain much of their overall morphological characteristics and can be identified under low-level magnification. The most commonly identified macrobotanical remains are seeds, fruit seeds and pits, nut shells, wood fragments, and grass stems and leaves.

Although visible to the naked eye, macrobotanical, or archaeobotanical, remains vary considerably in size and delicacy and thus require special attention in recovery. Most of the published paleoethnobotanical data, including the data presented in this chapter, would not have been possible to discuss with any certainty without the recovery technique of flotation. First introduced to archaeological excavations in the early-to-mid-1900s, flotation, the gentle separation of plant parts from waterlogged sediments, became increasingly popular in the 1970s and 1980s. This popularity coincided with the significant increase in archaeological work associated with federal legislation and resulted in the recovery of a tremendous volume of archaeobotanical data. Research on these data produced compelling evidence for a North American indigenous seed crop cultivation strategy (Asch and Asch 1985; B. D. Smith 1992a; Yarnell 1978); documented the existence of multiple pathways for the migration of maize (Sánchez González 1994); established the economic and social importance of wild plants to both hunter-gatherers and agriculturalists (Scarry 2003); helped construct regional syntheses of plant use (Adair 1988; Asch 1992; Drass 1995); and, perhaps most important, supported the theoretical argument that the transition from forager to farmer was a complex and diverse process (K. R. Adams 1994; Drass 1995; Ford 1985; Fritz 1990; B. D. Smith 1992b; Woods 1992). Some believe, however, that the greatest contributions in paleoethnobotany to understanding the past will come in future decades as biochemical and genetic analyses are perfected, revealing potential new patterns in plant evolution and highlighting the role of humans in ecosystem reconstruction (Ford 2003).

This chapter focuses on the use of plants, both indigenous species and introduced crops, that at various times contributed to the economies of native populations that once lived within present-day Kansas and surrounding areas, i.e., the Central Plains. The archaeobotanical data are presented in a temporal sequence, from the earliest evidence of occupation to the time of European contact. Specific attention is devoted to the presence of cultivated or domesticated crops and the development of agricultural economies. This emphasis is due in part to the recovery of more archaeobotanical data from ceramic-aged deposits and helps document the aboriginal importance of farming. It also addresses one of the more interesting and remarkable events in the prehistory of the region. Many groups who lived within present-day Kansas practiced farming to some degree at the time of contact. This form of subsistence developed over a period of time and was likely influenced by trade or association with farming populations residing in other areas of North America.

Populations living along the major river drainages of the Midwest may have been particularly responsible for influencing the development of Plains agriculture, especially regarding the domestication of native weedy annuals. Likewise, Archaic foragers living in the higher elevations to the west of the Central Plains and who consumed maize in small quantities may have introduced this crop to Plains populations. There is considerable evidence through time in the form of ceramic designs, lithic resources, and burial practices suggesting that some Central Plains societies interacted with groups to the southwest and the east (Hawley 2000; A. E. Johnson 1992; Reid 1983). These interactions would have provided an established mechanism for the movement of either cultivated plants or the transmission of the corresponding adaptation. As will be discussed below, there is a considerable time difference between the initial cultivation of weedy seeds in the eastern United States and the appearance of maize in the Southwest and the first evidence of any form of cultivation in the Central Plains. We know that agriculture was introduced onto the

Central Plains, but we do not completely understand the timing or the context of the introduction. One tool that has been extremely helpful in establishing a temporal framework for the emergence of Plains agriculture is accelerator mass spectrometry (AMS) dating of the annual crop plants. Radiocarbon dates on plant remains provide one of the best methods of establishing a direct temporal relationship between a crop plant and associated material culture remains.

Crop plants constitute a category that includes both domesticated and cultivated species. Domestication is reserved for plants that undergo some form of genetic modification that requires human intervention for survival during the harvesting or sowing stages. The evidence for initial domestication of native species consists of archaeologically derived seeds that are morphologically different from seeds produced by the same plants today. Statistically larger seed size and/or thinner pericarps (seed coats) are the primary morphological characteristics that differentiate native cultigens from their wild counterparts. Cultivated species do not exhibit morphological changes but are often recovered in large quantities and are usually associated with domesticates.

The cast of crop plants identified in Central Plains archaeological deposits includes the domesticated species of maize (*Zea mays*), common bean (*Phaseolus vulgaris*), bottle gourd (*Lageneria siceraria*), squash (*Cucurbita pepo* var *pepo*), and tobacco (*Nicotiana* sp.) that originally migrated northward from Mesoamerica as domesticated plants; the native domesticated species of gourd (*C. pepo* var *ovifera* var *orzarkana*), marsh elder (*Iva annuus*), and sunflower (*Helianthus annuus*); and the native cultivated species of goosefoot (*Chenopodium berlandieri*), little barley (*Hordeum pusillum*), and maygrass (*Phalaris caroliniana*). Figure 15.1 identifies the archaeological sites where excavations have recovered significant archaeobotanical remains discussed in this chapter.

PALEOINDIAN PERIOD

Applicable evidence for Paleoindian subsistence comes from sites in the western High Plains and mountain foothills and strongly suggests that the primary economic pursuit was hunting large mammals, including mammoth and bison (see chapter 4, this volume). Other smaller animal species offered a more limited contribution, and although the use of plant resources is certainly logical, there is only limited evidence for the use of vegetal foods. The Barton Gulch site in southwest Montana (Aaberg 1993; Davis et al. 1989) provides perhaps the most convincing evidence for the processing of vegetal foods. Excavations of the late Paleoindian living floor exposed 16 discrete feature aggregates, yielding a rich archaeobotanical assemblage, including 36 plant taxa representing food and household (fire-building) products. Weedy annuals, grasses, and seasonal fruits dominate the assemblage and include slimleaf goosefoot (*Chenopodium leptophyllum*), prickly pear cactus (*Opuntia polyacantha*), sun-

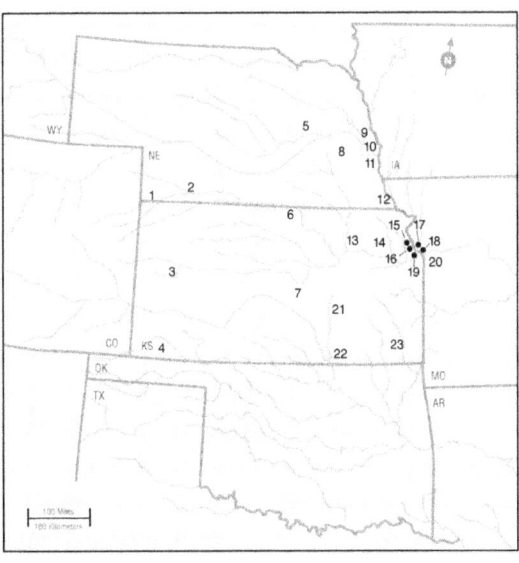

Figure 15.1. Location of archaeological sites discussed in text. 1. Nichols (25DN1); 2. 25FT70 and 25FT22; 3. El Cuartelejo (Scott County Pueblo, 14SC1); 4. Lundeen (14MD306); 5. Beaver Creek (25BO23); 6. Kansas Monument site (14RP1); 7. Little River Great Bend aspect sites (14RC8 and 14RC12); 8. Palmer Johnson (25BU37); 9. Andrews (25DO12); 10. Patterson (25SY31) and 25SY45; 11. Walker-Gilmore (25CC28); 12. 25RH69 and 25RH70; 13. Coffey (14PO1); 14. Avoca (14JN332); 15. DB (14LV1071); 16. Quarry Creek (14LV401); 17. Nebo Hill (23CL11); 18. Crabtree (23CL164) and Katz (23CL163); 19. Trowbridge (14WY1); 20. Traff (23JA159); 21. Two Deer (14BU55); 22. Lower Walnut Great Bend aspect sites (14CO1, 14CO3, 14CO331, 14CO332, 14CO382, 14CO385, 14CO501, 14CO1509); 23. Stigenwalt (14LT351).

flower (*Helianthus* sp.), sedge (*Carex* sp.), plumcherry (*Prunus* sp.), and bulrush (*Scirpus* sp.). Plano period occupations in Colorado and Wyoming have also yielded seeds of sunflower, prickly pear, pine (*Pinus* sp.), juniper (*Juniperus* sp.), pigweed (*Amaranthus* sp.), and chokecherry (Frison 1992). Because Paleoindian sites in the Central Plains usually reflect a short period of occupation, which may be directly related to hunting or butchering practices, the preservation of any plants that may have been used is very limited.

ARCHAIC PERIOD

The widespread occurrence of seasonal or semipermanent structures during the Holocene period (8,000–2,500 years ago) suggests that Archaic groups were developing a new lifestyle different from the preceding Paleoindian period (Blakeslee and Rohn 1986; Larson and Francis 1997). Milling or grinding stones are common in Archaic sites throughout the Central Plains, indirectly suggesting the increased importance of plant foods (Adair and Estep 1991). These artifacts are often recovered in association with fire-cracked rock concentrations. The processing of various abundant roots and tubers in rock-lined earth ovens is well documented in the ethnographic record (Kaye and Moodie 1978; Reid 1977; W. R. Wedel 1978) and has been suggested to explain the fairly wide distribution of archaeological fire-cracked rock features (Francis 1995; Wandsnider 1996, 1997). Within Kansas, grinding stones have been recovered from the Munkers Creek phase occupations at the William Young (14MO304), Williamson (14CF330), Coffey (14PO1), and Cow Killer (14OS347) sites (Schmits 1978, 1980a; Witty 1982) and from the Middle Archaic occupation at the DB site (14LV1071) (Logan 1998a). Direct evidence of the collecting and processing of roots and tubers comes from the Early Archaic occupation at the Stigenwalt site (14LT351) in southeastern Kansas (Figure 15.1), dated to 8810±250 B.P. (TX–6049) (Thies 1990: 109). The site consisted of concentrations of burned limestone, lithic tools, and a variety of faunal remains (Thies 1990). Clustered within the limestone concentrations were complete and fragmented onion (*Allium* sp.) bulbs (Adair 1990). Onion has also been identified from a Middle Archaic occupation in a central Wyoming rockshelter (Morris et al. 1981) and from coprolites associated with a date of ca. 6000 B.P. in the lower Pecos region of southwest Texas (Williams-Dean 1978).

Additional evidence for the use of plants during the Archaic period comes from the Coffey (Schmits 1978) and Nebo Hill (23CL11) (Reid 1983; Root 1979) sites (Figure 15.1), where systematic flotation recovered seeds of goosefoot, smartweed (*Polygonum* sp.), sunflower, bulrush, marsh elder, and grape (*Vitis* sp.), along with black walnut (*Juglans nigra*) and hickory (*Carya* sp.) shells. The presence of weedy annuals, fruits, and nuts suggests that Late Archaic populations were selecting plant resources from several environmental zones, including upland or gallery forests, river margins, and open prairies.

The emergence of ceramics may be associated with the increasing need for storage and processing technology in the intensified use of weedy plants and a corresponding decline in mobility. Baked clay pieces and small fragments of fiber-tempered ceramics have been recovered from Late Archaic sites along the eastern edge of the Central Plains (Artz 1993; Reid 1983; Witty 1982). Thin sections of several ceramics recovered from the Nebo Hill site revealed the use of switchgrass (*Panicum virgatum*), big bluestem (*Andropogon gerardi*), and a monocotyledonous sedge, possibly bulrush (*Scirpus* sp.) for temper (Reid 1983).

A pre-ceramic cultivation and domestication practice is documented on either side of the Central Plains in the greater Southwest and Eastern Woodlands. To the west, maize kernels and cobs were recovered from several high-altitude occupations in eastern and central Colorado, including Recon John shelter (5PE648), LoDaisKa (complex D, 5JF1421), Gooseberry shelter (5PE910), and Medina Rockshelter (5LA22) (Campbell 1976; Irwin and Irwin 1959, 1961; Zier and Kalasz 1991; Zier et al. 1993; Zier et al. 1996). Although none of these remains has been directly dated to the Archaic occupations, the association of maize in a pre-ceramic context is consistent with the cultigen's distribution in the greater Southwest. The northward dispersion of this plant as part of a hunter-gatherer suite of potential resources fits with current research models (K. R. Adams 1994; Zier 1996). The low quantity of maize recovered from the Late Archaic occupations suggests that this plant was not a major dietary item, and its presence in the macrobotanical assemblages does not signify a major shift in subsistence strategies. To date, however, maize has not been identified from a pre-ceramic deposit in the Central Plains, and there is little evidence of contact between Southwest and Plains populations during this time.

To the east of the Central Plains, Archaic societies in several mid-latitude locations were developing a cultivation practice that included several native weedy plants. The floodplain weed theory of plant domestication proposed by B. D. Smith (1992b) focuses on explaining the rise in the cultivation of squash or gourd, marsh elder, and goosefoot (*Chenopodium berlandieri*). The scenario presented suggests that the floodplain locations were ideal habitats for these pioneering plants, which quickly colonized and were opportunistically exploited by middle Holocene populations, creating one of the first stages in the cultivation and domestication of these plant species.

Floodplain-colonizing plants were pre-adapted to domestication in that they rapidly and aggressively colonized along river margins where the soils were frequently disturbed and enriched by spring floods (Cowan and Smith 1993). Human settlements along the river terraces created similar disturbed environments, thus creating a habitat shared by both the plants and humans. Selective pressures associated with the repeated harvesting and deliberate planting of wild plants resulted in a natural progression toward domestication. Seeds with thinner coats germinated faster while larger seeds with a greater stored food reserve grew faster. The archaeobotanical data from several eastern floodplain sites demonstrate the morphological changes in the seeds during the middle Holocene.

For many decades, all squash rind and seed remains were interpreted as representing the tropical cultigen (*Cucurbita pepo*), which migrated northward as a domesticated plant. Recent research, however, argues against a single Mesoamerican origin but documents existence of a long developmental separation between the Mexican and eastern North American branches of the species (B. D. Smith 1992b). Research points to the presence of an indigenous wild *Cucurbita* gourd with a broad geographical range and to an independent domestication of *C. pepo* in eastern North America. Isozymic research provides evidence that the free-living *Cucurbita* gourd, *C. pepo* ssp. *ovifera* var *ozarkana*, represents the ancestral progenitor of the eastern North American domesticated lineage (Decker-Walters et al. 1993). Domesticated varieties of squash developed prehistorically in eastern North America from this indigenous wild gourd. These thin-shelled cucurbit remains are identified as *C. pepo* ssp. *ovifera* var *ozarkana* and are often referred to as gourds. The thick, fleshy-shelled *C. pepo* var *pepo* was first domesticated in Mesoamerica.

The morphological changes associated with the Mesoamerican domesticate, including an increase in rind thickness and changes in seed size and shape, first appear in eastern mid-latitude archaeological deposits dating to ca. 1000–500 B.C. Domestication status for marsh elder (increased seed size) is recognized by ca. 2000 B.C., goosefoot by ca. 1500 B.C. (reduced seed coat), and sunflower by ca. 1500–1000 B.C. (increased seed size). Three other cultivated seed crops are present in the archaeological assemblages by 1000 B.C. This includes knotweed (*Polygonum erectum*), maygrass (*Phalaris caroliniana*), and little barley (*Hordeum pusillum*). A thousand years later, increased quantities of these seven crop plants are recognized over a broad area of the mid-latitude zones, marking the initial intensification of food production in pre-maize farming economies. Maize is introduced and appears in small quantities by ca. A.D. 200 but does not become economically important until after A.D. 800.

In the Central Plains, thin cucurbit rind fragments (0.5–0.8 mm thick) recovered from the Nebo Hill site have been directly dated to 2298–1985 cal B.C. and 2398–2038 cal B.C. (2 sigma ranges) (Table 15.1; Appendix). Similar rind fragments were identified from the DB site in northeastern Kansas (Adair 1998a). All of the middle Holocene *Cucurbita* rind fragments recovered from sites in Illinois, Kentucky, Tennessee, and Missouri (B. D. Smith 1992b: 41) are thin-shelled fragments, averaging less than 2.0 mm in thickness. Based on rind thickness and cultural contexts, it appears that the cucurbit rind fragments from the Central Plains Archaic deposits represent the wild cultivated variety of gourd. To date, this is the only cultivated plant associated with Central Plains Archaic sites.

A broader distribution of cultivated plants, including the native cucurbits, marsh elder, and goosefoot, in Plains Archaic sites would not be surprising, given the prehistoric distribution of early domesticates throughout the mid-continent and northeast (Decker-Walters et al. 1993; Hart and Asch Sidell 1997; Kay, King, and Robinson 1980; Perkl 1998; Peterson and Asch Sidell 1996; B. D. Smith 1992b). This is especially true if one reviews the paleoclimatic evidence for the emergence of "anthropogenic" habitats.

Paleoenvironmental and geomorphological information suggests that the early and middle Holocene periods were times of major bioclimate change on the Plains. The warm, dry Altithermal (Atlantic) climate that prevailed in the Midwest from about 7000–5000 B.P. caused prairies to expand eastward (see chapters 2 and 3, this volume). Spurred by changes in precipitation, these environmental episodes caused significant changes in the dynamics of first- and second-order streams throughout much of the eastern Great Plains. Alluvial/colluvial fans began to develop as erosion of the uplands intensified. By 4,000 years ago, streams began to downcut and migrate laterally, forming new and relatively unstable floodplains (Mandel 1992, 1997). Periods of valley aggradation and stabilization followed. Backwater swamp areas and oxbows developed in stream valleys, creating occupation areas potentially less impacted by the dry winds and erosional forces characteristic of the uplands. Archaic people often used the floodplains and mudflats for resource exploitation, as documented at the Coffey site in northeastern Kansas (Schmits 1978), the Stigenwalt site in southeastern Kansas (Thies 1990), and the Faulconer site in southcentral Kansas

Table 15.1. AMS Dates on Cultigens from Central Plains Sites

Site	Cultigen	Lab #	$^{14}C \pm$ yrs. B.P., ^{13}C corrected	^{13}C	cal B.C./A.D. yrs $\pm$ 2 sigma[a]
Nebo Hill (23CL11)	cucurbit	AA41421	3758±46	-25.4	B.C. 2298 (2196, 2169, 2144) 1985
	cucurbit	AA41422	3782±46	-25.3	B.C. 2398 (2200) 2038
Traff (23JA159)	*Iva annua*	AA36094	2530±40	-27.3	B.C. 800 (764) 455
	Iva annua	AA36093	2535±45	-27.7	B.C. 802 (765) 415
Trowbridge (14WY1)	*Iva annua*	AA36096	1660±45	-25	A.D. 257 (407) 532
	Zea mays	Beta-75015	310±60	-10.5	A.D. 1444 (1531, 1545, 1635) 1945
	Zea mays	Beta-75016	400±60	-11	A.D. 1414 (1468) 1642
	Zea mays	UCR-3357	200±50	-10.7	A.D. 1637 (1668, 1782, 1795) 1950
Quarry Creek (14LV401)	cucurbit	AA36117	1775±45	-25.1	A.D. 130–390
	cucurbit	AA36118	1725±50	-26.1	A.D. 130 (160, 170, 200, 210) 430
	Zea mays	AA36119	930±45	-8.7	A.D. 1020–1220
	Zea mays	AA36120	975±40	-9.8	A.D. 990–1170
	Zea mays	UCR-3356	1880±50	-26.5	A.D. 20–250[b]
Avoca (14JN332)	*Iva annua*	AA36099	985±40	-23.4	A.D. 984 (1024) 1160
	Helianthus annuus	AA36100	1200±40	-28.5	A.D. 691 (782, 790, 815, 842, 859) 960
	Zea mays	AA36101	1165±40	-9.48	A.D. 755 (889) 981
	Zea mays	AA36102	1220±40	-9.4	A.D. 687 (799) 939
Andrews (25DO12)	*Zea mays*	AA36097	1050±40	-9.5	A.D. 895 (997) 1031
	Zea mays	AA36098	1040±40	-8.9	A.D. 898 (1000) 1146
Two Deer (14BU55)	*Helianthus annuus*	AA36111	935±45	-27.1	A.D. 1004 (1041, 1094, 1118, 1141, 1153) 1162
	Iva annua	AA36112	940±35	-25.9	A.D. 1019 (1040, 1100, 1116, 1141, 1151) 1207
	Zea mays	AA36113	925±60	-8.7	A.D. 998 (1044, 1088, 1121, 1139, 1156) 1254
Sterns Creek (25CC28)	C. pepo	AA41425	1194±41	-26.4	A.D. 692 (783, 789, 829, 865) 963
	C. pepo	AA41426	1051±42	-24.9	A.D. 894 (966) 1031
	C. pepo	AA41427	1084±40	-25.5	A.D. 888 (980) 1021
Patterson (25SY31)	*Zea mays*	AA36107	785±40	-9.4	A.D. 1188 (1261) 1290
	Phaseolus vulgaris	AA36108	810±45	-29	A.D. 1159 (1224, 1231, 1239) 1285
	Phaseolus vulgaris	AA36109	780±40	-25.3	A.D. 1190 (1263) 1292
	Phaseolus vulgaris	AA36110	845±45	-26.5	A.D. 1065 (1220) 1282
Beaver Creek (25BO23)	*Phaseolus vulgaris*	AA41430	611±42	-28.9	A.D. 1290 (1322, 1350, 1390) 1415
23PL16	*Phaseolus vulgaris*	AA41431	656±68	-24.7	A.D. 1258 (1300, 1374, 1377) 1418
	Phaseolus vulgaris	AA41432	858±39	-28.5	A.D. 1040 (1193, 1198, 1209) 1264
23CL109	*Phaseolus vulgaris*	AA41434	842±38	-26.9	A.D. 1060 (1215) 1277
23CL115	*Phaseolus vulgaris*	AA41433	804±42	-24.2	A.D. 1161 (1244) 1285
14SC1 (El Cuartelejo)	*Zea mays*	AA36104	350±35		
	Citrullus lanatus	AA36106	200±40		

[a] calibrated using OxCal v.3.8 (Bronk Ramsey 1995, 2001).
[b] sample was not maize.

(Bradley 1973). Rapid alluviation during the late Holocene resulted in the deep burial of these deposits (Mandel 1997; Mandel, chapter 3, this volume).

The assumption that these floodplain locations in the Central Plains provided abundant and disturbed habitat opportunities for pioneering plant species is certainly logical but, as yet, not fully demonstrated. Few mid- to late-Holocene occupations in the Plains have been excavated with sufficiently intensive recovery methods for the retrieval of small, charred seeds, although the limited data from sites such as Coffey and Nebo Hill may suggest that a cultivation strategy was beginning.

WOODLAND PERIOD

Early Woodland occupations dating to ca. 500 B.C. and contemporaneous with habitations on the northeastern Plains have been found on the eastern margin of the Central Plains. Archaeobotanical remains recovered from the Traff site (23JA159) in western Missouri suggest an adaptation that included both the collecting of a variety of wild plants and the tending or gardening of cultivated species. Identified taxa include goosefoot, pigweed, hickory, black walnut, and cultigen marsh elder (Adair 1980). AMS dates on the marsh elder provide solid evidence of the association of this cultigen with the Early Woodland period (Table 15.1).

The archaeobotanical remains associated with the Middle Woodland period (including the Kansas City Hopewell) exhibit an interesting mix of wild plants and cultigens and suggest an increased reliance on local resources by groups that were becoming more sedentary. Although nuts, particularly hickory and hazel (*Corylus* sp.), are well represented in the archaeobotanical record from the Late Archaic to the Middle Woodland, the numbers of small-seeded annuals and fruits increase significantly during this time. Seeds of goosefoot, pigweed, and knotweed, along with plumcherry (*Prunus* sp.), pawpaw (*Diospyros virginiana*), and grape, constitute most of the identified species, with various grasses, including panic grass, bulrush, spurge, and dock (*Rumex* sp.), also present. Remains of cultigen marsh elder and possibly sunflower, along with pepo squash, have been recovered. Maize kernels and cob fragments have been recovered from several Middle Woodland Kansas City Hopewell sites (Adair 1988, 1994) and may represent the earliest presence of this crop on the Central Plains. Described as a Chapalote variety (Adair 1994), the maize from the Trowbridge site (14WY1) was associated with ceramics dated by seriation to A.D. 250–400. Given the temporal distribution of early maize in the eastern mid-latitudes (Chapman and Crites 1987), the Trowbridge sample seemed very consistent with the northward spread of this crop. Recently obtained AMS dates on cultigens from six Middle Woodland sites, including the Trowbridge and Quarry Creek sites (Table 15.1), confirm the association of cultigen marsh elder and pepo squash with the Middle Woodland occupations but document that the maize is associated with later occupations.

For the latter part of the Woodland period, the archaeobotanical remains from Central Plains sites vary extensively between sites. Most of this variation is spatial; less is known about the western Woodland complexes (Figure 15.1), which may be partly due to recovery biases. From several eastern occupations, such as the Radio Lane (14CO385) and Avoca (14JN332) sites, comes evidence for gardening of maize, sunflower, and marsh elder and gathering of a variety of wild seeds, fruits, and nuts. Excellent preservation at the Walker Gilmore site (25CC28) in southeastern Nebraska provides additional evidence of the use of pepo squash, gourd (*Lagenaria siceraria*), and groundnuts (Cutler and Blake 1983). Significant quantities of maize and goosefoot have been recovered from the Loseke Creek occupation at the Andrews site (25DO12) in eastern Nebraska. From the comparably aged Late Woodland Two Deer site (14BU55) in south-central Kansas come remains of cultigen sunflower, marsh elder, and possibly goosefoot, mixed with pepo squash and maize (Adair and Brown 1981). Agricultural implements are lacking at all of these sites. Direct dates on maize from several sites confirm the presence of this domesticate in the Central Plains by the eighth century A.D. (Table 15.1).

Goosefoot seeds are a common element in Woodland archaeobotanical assemblages, often representing one of the most abundant native taxa (Adair 1996, 2003a). Their status as a cultivated plant is largely unknown, although morphological characteristics associated with cultigen chenopod (B. D. Smith 1985, 1992a) have been noted on seeds from the Two Deer and Andrews sites (Adair 1993, 1996). In particular, truncated seed margins and thin pericarps are visible on many randomly sampled specimens.

VILLAGE PERIOD

By the end of the Woodland period, a well-developed farming strategy was established in the eastern part of the Central Plains, and, as discussed below in greater extent, the origins of this strategy appear to have come from contact with eastern societies. The various defined complexes assigned to the Village period all have agriculture as an element of their subsistence. The variability in the quantity of different crops represented in the archaeobotanical assemblages may be due to a combination of recovery biases, seasonal site occupations, and site location, as well as larger issues such as spatial and temporal "patterns" in the economy and links between postulated farmsteads and larger village organizations. Recent research on Nebraska, Itskari, Upper Republican, Steed Kisker, and Plains Border variant sites has produced some of the first systematic flotation samples from Central Plains Village sites (Adair 2003a, 2003b; Asch and Green 1995; Bevitt 1999a; Lopinot 1999a, 1999b; Roper, chapter 7, this volume).

Archaeobotanical assemblages from Nebraska phase sites (including the Patterson site [25SY31], 25RH79, 25RH70, and 25SY45) represent a complex farming practice with the cultivation of native species, including the cool season grasses of little barley and the warm season plants of sunflower, goosefoot, and marsh elder. Maize dominates the assemblages, approaching 100 percent ubiquity, suggesting that this plant formed a strong economic base (Adair 2003b). The common bean, squash, and tobacco are more sporadically represented (Adair 1988, 1998b; Asch 1992; Nickel 1982). The use of various fruits and grasses continues from earlier times. The presence of nuts, particularly black walnut and hickory, suggests that the Nebraska phase people did not abandon their use of this resource but perhaps limited its importance as their use of maize increased (Adair 1996, 2003b). Archaeobotanical data from several Itskari (A.D. 1100–1400) occupations in central and eastern Nebraska, including the Beaver Creek (25BO23) and Palmer Johnson (25BU37) sites, reveal strong similarities with the Nebraska phase (Adair 2003b; Koch 2002: 43–45).

Like goosefoot, the cultivation status of little barley in the Central Plains has not been sufficiently researched. Little barley seeds are often found in concentrations of several hundred grains, suggesting that its presence is not a natural occurrence. Asch (1992) argues that cultivation status can be inferred because little barley has been recovered from sites north and east of its natural range at the time of European contact. Its size is fairly consistent in archaeobotanical contexts (Adair 1998a; Asch and Green 1995), and the grains all lack remnants of adhering bracts.

The Steed Kisker phase displays many similarities to its surrounding Central Plains tradition neighbors. Recently analyzed archaeobotanical assemblages from features at the Crabtree (23CL164) and Katz (23CL163) sites contain domesticated crops of maize, squash, bottle gourd, sunflower, marsh elder, little barley, goosefoot, common bean, and tobacco, as well as maygrass and perhaps knotweed (Lopinot 1999a, 1999b). The latter two crops are more representative of eastern Mississippian occupations, but the common bean is not known from such sites in the American Bottom, southeastern Missouri and northeastern Arkansas. AMS dates (Table 15.1) on the common bean recovered from Steed Kisker, Nebraska, and Itskari phase sites document the presence of this cultigen in the Eastern Plains perhaps 100–200 years earlier than its use in the American Bottom region and the northern Eastern Woodlands (Hart, Asch, and Scarry 2000). It is worth noting that the percentage and density of cultivated seeds from Nebraska and Steed Kisker systematic assemblages are comparable to some of the highest obtained from Late Woodland, Emergent Mississippian, and Early Mississippian sites in the American Bottom (Johannessen 1988).

Archaeobotanical assemblages from Steed Kisker, Nebraska, and Itskari phase sites suggest multicropping residential farmers who occupied one location year-round. The variety of domesticated crops includes both the spring-harvested and the fall-harvested seed-bearing annuals that would have required planting, weeding, tending, and harvesting. These activities would have lasted from mid-spring to mid-to-late fall, and, when supplemented with gathering, hunting, and fishing (all of which are evident in the archaeological remains), a year-round occupation is easily arguable.

Archaeobotanical remains from other sites occupied during the eleventh to thirteenth centuries (including Smoky Hill, Pomona, and Bluff Creek phase occupations) are less well known, due in large part to the recovery techniques, although domesticates have been recovered from sites assigned to these cultural complexes. Upper Republican sites are found in both the mixed prairies and short-grass plains regions of the Central Plains. Corn and domesticated sunflower were recognized from several Upper Republican deposits more than 60 years ago (V. H. Jones 1941), and more recent botanical analyses from sites 25FT70 and 25FT22 in the Medicine Creek vicinity document the addition of beans and squash (Cummings and Rylander 1988; Puseman 1996). A diverse list of wild plant foods from these sites attests to the continued importance of gathering. The western extension of Upper Republican groups (Roper 1990; Scheiber, chapter 8, this volume; W. R. Wood 1990) into eastern Colorado and Wyoming suggests that these people may have been less sedentary than their eastern counterparts and may have relied more on a hunter-gatherer economy utilizing diverse resources instead of food production. At the least, it appears that they may have concentrated their farming energies on fewer crops.

Investigations at the Lundeen site (14MD306) in southwestern Kansas and the Odessa Yates site in northwestern Oklahoma (Bevitt 1999a; Brosowske, Drass, and Maki 2000; Brosowske and Bevitt, chapter 11, this volume) revealed fortified villages whose occupants depended on dry-farming maize agriculture. Hunting was also important, as was the gathering of wild plants, but a reliance on maize in the western plains without the use of irrigation had not been previously documented.

PROTOHISTORIC AND HISTORIC PERIODS

The Protohistoric period spans the time between prehistory and first European contact and is represented in the Central Plains by the White Rock (north-central Kansas), Dismal River (western Kansas), and Great Bend (central and southeastern Kansas) complexes. Although farming remains part of the economic adaptation during this time, changes in settlement patterns, social organization, and trade relations significantly impacted the economies of these societies. The presence of maize in White Rock phase sites is documented (V. H. Jones 1936; Neuman 1963; Rusco 1960), as is the presence of a significant number of bison scapula hoes and antler digging stick tips (Logan 1995), suggesting that maize farming was economically important. Without systematic recovery techniques, however, it is difficult to know if other crops were grown and the importance of farming compared to hunting. The temporal range of the White Rock complex corresponds with the Pacific I climatic episode, which is believed to have caused severe drought conditions and site abandonment throughout the Great Plains (Bryson and Baerreis 1968). Spatially, however, the White Rock core settlement region lies in a pocket area that may have had increased rainfall during the climatic episode (Blakeslee 1993), which would have been sufficient for maize farming.

Maize has also been reported from several Dismal River sites (Adair 1992; V. H. Jones 1941; W. R. Wedel 1986), but the relative importance of farming has been historically downplayed, given the location of sites west of the 100th meridian (where rainfall averages less than 20 inches per year). Again, small pockets or valley regions with sufficient moisture would have been ideal locations for family-oriented households or small hamlets to raise crops. This scenario may explain the relatively abundant quantity of maize cobs recovered from the Nichols site (25DN1), located in extreme southwestern Nebraska.

Excavations of the early eighteenth-century occupation at the El Cuartelejo site (14SC1) in west-central Kansas yielded sizable amounts of maize, watermelon, and melon (Adair 1992, 1994; Cutler and Blake 1973). Watermelons (*Citrullus lanatus*) were introduced into the southwestern and southeastern regions of North America by the Spanish in the 1500s. From these regions, the plant diffused to other areas, adapting quickly to new climates and growing conditions (Blake 1981). The presence of watermelon and melon seeds, in conjunction with Southwestern-style ceramics, at the El Cuartelejo site provides strong evidence of contact with groups to the southwest. AMS dates on the watermelon (Table 15.1) indicate that this contact took place as early as the late 1600s.

Analyses of curated archaeobotanical remains from 14RC8 and 14RC12 and systematic archaeobotanical assemblages from eight Great Bend sites in southeastern Kansas (Figure 15.1) suggest a major economic shift away from the earlier Village period multicropping strategy to a more focused farming of maize (Adair 1998c, 2003a). Beans, squash, tobacco, little barley, and sunflower are also present but in significantly lower quantities than recorded from earlier Village period sites. Various wild plants such as grape, plum, dropseed, and goosefoot (Adair 1989, 1998c; Romine 1996) are often abundant in flotation samples and suggest that wild plant gathering strategies coexisted with a focal maize farming adaptation.

The single Historic-aged occupation included in this chapter is the Kansas Monument site, 14RP1. Located in the Republican River drainage of north-central Kansas (Figure 15.1), it represents one of the southernmost Historic Pawnee villages, with only the Bogan site (14GE1) located farther south (Roper, chapter 14, this volume). Investigations at this site yielded significant amounts of maize, represented by numerous cobs and cob fragments. This archaeobotanical assemblage, along with sizable amounts of maize from earlier Village and Protohistoric sites, provides the opportunity to discuss the type or variety of maize grown by different groups at different times. Unlike other areas of North America, however, extant varieties or races of native maize from Central Plains economies are not available to help us differentiate the presence of different cultivars from the archaeological record. Limited historical records on the maize grown by the Pawnee and Wichita (Will and Hyde 1964) confirm the growing of several varieties, which were used for different purposes, required different growing conditions, had different harvest dates, and were processed or cooked in different ways. Additionally, if we remove the various cultural uses and the distinctive color of many varieties, we are left with the morphological characteristics of row number, cob size and shape, kernel size and shape, and the presence of nubbins as the primary defining components of each type. However, many of these characteristics are common to more than one type, making it difficult to determine a varietal type from one characteristic alone. So, in an attempt to recognize the presence of more than one variety of maize in the archaeological record, our best approach is to record those attributes that have been shown to be most useful for distinguishing corn cultivars (F. B. King 1987) and look for similarities and differences among the archaeological maize samples.

In a recent study (Adair 2004), morphological attributes on maize samples from 22 Central Plains sites were subjected to several statistical measures (descriptive, cluster analysis, and chi-square) in an effort to determine if maize varieties could be identified in archaeological contexts ranging from about A.D. 1000 to A.D. 1800. The morphological attributes of row number, cob size and shape, cupule size, and kernel thickness suggest the presence of at least three maize varieties. Variety 1, found throughout the Central Plains in Village- through Historic-aged deposits, can be characterized as having a mean row number of 9.6, cupule width of 9.5 mm, and kernel thickness of 3.5 mm. The mean cob diameter is almost 16 mm, and pith diameter is 7.3 mm. Variety 2 has a thinner cob (mean diameter of 11.6 mm) with smaller cupules (6.9 mm in width and 3.1 mm in kernel thickness) but with the row number similar to variety 1. Cobs within this cluster have been recovered mainly from sites located in the western portion of the Central Plains and dating from the Village to the Historic period. The third variety is represented by the fewest specimens, but includes the largest cobs. The mean row number is over 10, cob diameter is 20.6 mm, and pith diameter is 8.8 mm. Cupule width is 11.4 mm and kernel thickness is 3.9 mm. All of the cobs in this cluster come from Protohistoric or Historic period sites located in the eastern or central part of the Central Plains. While additional data may alter these findings, this study suggests the presence of three maize varieties that share a relationship with the geography of the Central Plains and less with the chronology of the cultural expressions from which they were recovered.

SUMMARY AND CONCLUSIONS

Most archaeobotanical data from Central Plains sites have been interpreted as remains of food, with even greater attention being paid to those species involved in agricultural developments. Based on evidence provided by currently available archaeobotanical data, cultivation adaptation started in the eastern portion of the Central Plains with indigenous species, developed over time with the adoption of maize, and contributed at some level to almost all native economies before European contact. There are, however, still many gaps in our understanding of the economic role of plant foods; these gaps are spatial, temporal, and theoretical. Our best guess for Paleoindian period foraging is to look at sites in surrounding areas and recognize that the economy was probably more complex than the archaeobotanical data suggest (Aaberg 1993; A. E. Johnson 1987). By late Archaic times, influences from Eastern mid-latitude societies are documented by the appearance of a cultivated native gourd in eastern Central Plains sites. A pre-ceramic use of maize, as seen in the higher elevations to the west in Colorado, is not reflected in Plains economies. Adaptations to stable floodplain habitats may have created ideal situations for the exploitation of several native annuals and may have helped chart the course toward their eventual domestication. Goosefoot seeds often dominate Archaic assemblages and strongly suggest an economic importance, if not cultivation (Asch 1992), of this plant.

Wild marsh elder was identified at the Nebo Hill site, and several hundred years later, the domesticated variety exists within an Early Woodland context. Does the presence of cultivated cucurbits and domesticated marsh elder in archaeological deposits along the eastern fringe of the Central Plains suggest that these societies were on the margin of a broader interior mid-latitude zone of domestication that encompassed a range of river valley and upland settings extending from the Appalachians to central Illinois to central Tennessee (B. D. Smith and Cowan 2003)? While the paucity of archaeobotanical data makes its difficult to fully evaluate this question, a relationship between Plains and Eastern societies can be inferred from the recovery of fiber-tempered ceramics in Late Archaic sites and distinctively styled sand-tempered ceramics from Early Woodland sites in the Central Plains, both of which appear earlier in the East. The interior mid-latitude zone of domestication of native seed crops, as presented by B. D. Smith (1992b: 270), consists of archaeological sites widely scattered over various river valleys, connected by the presence of domesticated native species dated to the third to second millennium B.C. The archaeobotanical data from the Eastern Plains sites reflect a similar pattern in the selection of native weedy annuals, although at a slightly later time. Like the eastern societies, a cultivation strategy developed without the use of maize, making the Plains economies distinctly different from Archaic adaptations of the Southwest.

By the end of the Woodland period, about A.D. 1000, a substantial dependence on agricultural crops had developed. Crops included several native varieties (marsh elder, sunflower, cucurbits, and possibly little barley and goosefoot), along with the introduced cultigens, maize, squash, and gourd. Maize is not the most abundant or ubiquitous species represented, suggesting its dietary importance was not critical. Western Plains Woodland sites are, as of yet, void of these remains. In the higher elevations of the Arkansas and Platte river valleys of northeast New Mexico and southern Colorado, maize has been recovered from several Woodland components located at the intersection of the foothills and the Plains (Zier and Kalasz 1999). As with the earlier Archaic contexts for maize, however, data are not available to indicate a connection between groups occupying the Western Plains and the mountain and foothill region that might have involved the diffusion of maize onto the Central Plains.

The adoption of maize into the economy was once believed to be the prime mover of the Woodland period culture (especially the Hopewellian culture) and the catalyst for population expansion. However, AMS dates fail to demonstrate a clear association between maize and the Middle Woodland Kansas City Hopewell period. Before we conclude that this crop was not used at all by Plains populations until the eighth century, we need to evaluate the reported evidence of maize with other Middle Woodland contexts in the central, northern, and northeastern Plains. If we think that populations living in the Central Plains interacted with groups to the east (as is evident by the Hopewellian-style ceramics), we may suspect that maize entered the Central Plains perhaps as much as a few centuries before A.D. 800 and was absorbed into an economy already well adapted to cultivation. Although research will likely continue to focus on the timing and route/routes of the initial arrival of maize onto the Plains, the data already recovered would suggest that documenting the exact arrival of this crop might be largely peripheral to central questions on the initial development of plant cultivation. It may be more important to expose the environmental conditions that helped create anthropogenic habitats, which allowed the exploitation and eventual cultivation of indigenous species.

We also know that populations identified with the Central Plains Village complexes appeared to have engaged in multicropping and may have structured hunting strategies around the demands of farming. These populations were likely organized around the individual household, and as such, different economic choices may have been made by individual households, resulting in the variability in recovered archaeobotanical remains. During the late Prehistoric period, the large volume of storage space associated with Great Bend sites suggests that farming, especially of maize, may have resulted in a surplus production. The management and allocation of any crop surplus probably had an impact on organizational strategies and social relationships. Maize appears to develop as the major dietary farm plant, with other crops, especially the indigenous species, declining in importance.

16. Kansas Lithic Resources
C. Martin Stein

This chapter identifies sources of stone from bedrock that were or could have been used by prehistoric people with a stone tool technology. Information about the geological occurrence of stone, methods of obtaining it, and studies about identifying stone are also presented. Chert or other siliceous stone that can be knapped to form a variety of useful chipped-stone tools is relatively abundant in Kansas, as are other types of rocks, such as sandstone, which are useful for making groundstone tools. Apart from tool making, other uses of stone in the prehistoric past included using rocks to form hearths or for cooking by stone boiling. Rocks were also heaped up to form burial cairns, and in southeastern Kansas sandstone was used to form mounds for purposes that remain unclear. Hematite and limonite were available for pigments, and harder forms of these minerals, as well as glacially transported pipestone, were available for carving. Crushed stone, minerals, and sand were used as temper in the production of pottery. Depending upon the location in the state, many of these geological resources are readily at hand, and in the case of some chert quarries, there is direct evidence of their use by American Indians.

Because chert and other flakeable stone was so important to prehistoric people and because it is ubiquitous on sites, this chapter emphasizes chert sources in Kansas. The identification of types of chert and an understanding of their sources has a long history in Plains archaeology. A rigorous classification of chert types is beyond the scope of this chapter; readers are referred instead to detailed studies, including L. D. Banks (1990); Blasing (1984); Haury (1984); McLean (1998); and Reid (1984). Still, selected chert types are described to familiarize the reader with the most commonly used chert types in Kansas prehistory.

THE GEOLOGICAL SETTING:
A BRIEF DESCRIPTION OF KANSAS GEOLOGY

The outcropping bedrock of Kansas is almost entirely sedimentary in origin, except for two small localities in the eastern one-third of the state where igneous rocks protrude to the surface. The outcropping rocks represent a span of geological time of approximately 320 million years, with the oldest Mississippian-age limestone outcrops located in the extreme southeastern corner of the state. From that beginning point, alternating layers of limestone and shale predominate in the subsequent exposures of Pennsylvanian and Permian-age rocks forming the surface of the eastern third of the state. West

Table 16.1. Outcropping Rock Units in Kansas

Era	Period	Beginning Point (MYA*)	Stratigraphic units (Series)	Major Constituent Rocks
Cenozoic	Quaternary	1	Pleistocene	Till, aeolian and fluvial deposits, ash, loess
	Tertiary	63	Pliocene	Sand, gravel, silt, chert, caliche, ash, limestone, sandstone, opal
Mesozoic	Cretaceous	135	Upper Cretaceous Lower Cretaceous	Shale, chalk, sandstone, limestone, clay, coal
	Jurassic	181	Upper Jurassic	Undifferentiated sandstone or siltstone
Paleozoic	Permian	280	Upper Permian Lower Permian	Dolomite, sandstone, shale, gypsum, limestone
	Pennsylvanian	320	Upper Pennsylvanian Middle Pennsylvanian	Limestone, shale, sandstone, coal
	Mississippian	345	Upper Mississippian	Limestone

*Millions of years ago

of the Flint Hills and south of the Arkansas River additional Permian deposits of sandstone, shale, gypsum, and dolomite can be found. Stratigraphically above the Permian formations, Jurassic siltstone and sandstone outcrops are found in a limited area in Morton County in extreme southwestern Kansas. More widespread in western Kansas are sandstone, shale, limestone, and chalk formations deposited by Cretaceous seas. Eastward-flowing streams, most originating in the High Plains, have exposed bedrock in many areas. Above these formations are Pliocene deposits of the Ogallala formation, containing sand, gravel, and silt, locally cemented with calcium carbonate, and also containing volcanic ash, opaline sandstone, and limestone, among others, and forming the surface of the High Plains in western Kansas (Table 16.1). In addition to these bedrock sources, potentially useful stone has been carried into the state from distant sources by ancient glaciers. Glacial till, containing igneous and metamorphic rocks, can be found in northeastern Kansas, generally north of the Kansas River and east of the Blue River. Discontinuous deposits of water-lain Pleistocene silt, sand, and gravel are found in stream valleys in all parts of the state (Zeller 1968).

USING GEOLOGY FOR ARCHAEOLOGICAL RESEARCH

The geological literature describes formations and members with stone suitable for prehistoric technologies. The geological identification of stone from archaeological sites serves many purposes in the investigation of prehistoric cultures. Although there are some inconsistencies in the geological terminology used across state boundaries (L. D. Banks 1990: 6), using geological terms for the identification of stone, rather than local names, promotes communication and prevents confusion. Stone was the predominant material used for the manufacture of tools and weapons from the earliest times, ca. 12,000 B.P., to the period following A.D. 1541 when metal tools began to supplant those made of stone. Researchers studying the prehistoric past rely on items of material culture for insights into the lives of the people who produced them, and stone artifacts, being durable and long lasting, provide the basis for many studies: the characterization of trade and exchange; identifying differential access to resources that is often associated with the development of social stratification or the beginning of craft specialization; determining territory location and size; and inferring the nature and degree of prehistoric mobility (Luedtke 1992: Appendix A). These types of studies rely on the correct identification of the sources of stone artifacts, and using geological reports and maps of outcropping rocks to identify specific rock formations is a necessity.

A search of reports and site forms reveals that only sources of knappable stone have been recognized and recorded. There are, for instance, no recorded aboriginal sandstone quarries or workshops associated with other types of rocks or minerals; therefore the sites mentioned in this report are all associated with rocks that could be knapped. The recorded stone sources are described on site forms and in reports as one of three types: quarries where there is evidence of ground disturbance resulting from digging out rock from a bedrock source; collecting stations for gathering rock that has been exposed naturally by weathering at bedrock outcrops or deposited at secondary locations, e.g., gravel bars; and workshops with concentrations of flint-knapping debris near outcrops or collecting stations. Although not technically correct, all types of stone sources are commonly called quarries. The sites reported here were submitted by members of the Kansas Anthropological Association and other members of the public, or were recorded as a result of surveys undertaken for a variety of reasons, such as proposed construction projects, as projects associated with the Kansas Archeology Training Program, or to locate sites eligible for listing on the National Register of Historic Places.

Some reports and many site forms do not identify the geological formation or member of the stone present at the site. In order to compensate for this, quarry or workshop locations were compared with the locations of outcropping rocks shown on geological maps. This was only partly successful, because geological maps were not available for some areas, and in other cases, field observation is needed to determine which outcropping stone is being used when more than one outcrop is present. Therefore, the geological identifications given below are tentative.

The terms "flint" and "chert" are used interchangeably in this chapter. Chert is the term commonly applied by geologists to siliceous rocks regardless of their bedrock matrix, e.g., chalk (Hattin 1982: 19), dolomite (Bailey 2000: 45), and limestone (Zeller 1968) (see also a comprehensive discussion of chert in Luedtke 1992). The outcropping rocks of Kansas are presented in stratigraphic sequence beginning with the Mississippian system in southeastern Kansas and proceeding both upward in the rock column to the Quaternary system and westward geographically from the Missouri border to the Colorado line. Outcrops generally trend northeast/southwest.

OUTCROPPING ROCKS IN THE KANSAS ROCK COLUMN

The Kansas Geological Survey classifies rocks in the following manner: individual rock members are combined into formations, which may then be placed into subgroups or groups. Groups are placed into stages, which are subsumed under a series, and series are combined into systems. As an example, the Winterset Limestone member, the Stark Shale member, and the Canville Limestone member belong to the Dennis formation, which is part of the Bronson subgroup of the Kansas City group. The Kansas City group is part of the Missourian stage of the Upper Pennsylvanian series of the Pennsylvanian system.

It is common practice for archaeologists to identify stone using the member or formation name, e.g., Winterset chert or Foraker chert. Cherie Haury (1981, 1984), in her characterization of the chert found in the southern Flint Hills region, introduced a modified geological terminology by attaching letters in alphabetical sequence to the geological names of formations and members. Blasing (1984), in his description of chert in the northern Flint Hills, also used this system, which is intended to distinguish variations in chert from the same geological context. The terms "Florence A," to distinguish a banded variety, and "Florence B," to denote a nonbanded variety of chert found within the Florence limestone member, are in common use.

Mississippian System

The Spring River enters the state from the east, describes a shallow westward arc within the southeastern part of Cherokee County, and then exits at the Oklahoma border. Encompassed within this arc are the only Mississippian-age rock outcrops in Kansas. Although limited in extent to an area of approximately 60 square miles, there are two chert-bearing limestones of potential importance: the Reeds Spring Limestone formation and the Burlington-Keokuk Limestone formation (Maples 1994: 67–74). Lead and zinc mining in this district has resulted in the accumulation of many acres of tailings, which in turn obscure many outcrops (Seevers 1975). No quarries have been recorded in Mississippian system outcrops in Kansas. Burlington and Reeds Spring cherts, widely used to the east in Missouri, are Mississippian cherts occasionally found in Kansas sites. These cherts, typically white to gray, often contain crinoid fossil segments (McLean 1998: 185–187; Ray 1998).

Table 16.2. Outcropping Chert-Bearing Limestone (Unless Otherwise Noted) in the Pennsylvanian System

Formation	Member
Upper Pennsylvanian	
Foraker limestone	Hughes Creek shale
	Americus limestone
Topeka limestone	Curzon limestone
Deer Creek limestone	Ervine Creek limestone
Oread limestone	Plattsmouth limestone
	Toronto limestone
Stanton limestone	Captain Creek limestone
Plattsburg limestone	Spring Hill limestone
Wyandotte limestone	Argentine limestone
Cherryvale shale	Westerville limestone
Dennis limestone	Winterset limestone
Swope limestone	Bethany Falls limestone
Hertha limestone	Sniabar limestone
Middle Pennsylvanian	
Lenapah limestone	Norfleet limestone
Pawnee limestone	Laberdie limestone

Pennsylvanian System

Middle and Upper Pennsylvanian formations make up the bedrock of eastern Kansas, except for the small area described above, extending from the Missouri state line to approximately 90 miles west to the Flint Hills physiographic province (Figure 16.1). Composed primarily of alternating limestone and shale, the deposits have been described as thin (from 1 to 25 feet thick), but with lateral uniformity; so much so that some rock units can be traced 100 to 400 miles along the outcrop (R. C. Moore 1949: 9). Chert is noted to occur in 13 of the 78 named limestone formations of the Pennsylvanian system (Table 16.2), but the occurrence of chert is not common except in the formations of the Kansas City Group. The outcrops of these rocks occur in a diagonal belt, 25 or more miles wide, from Linn County in the northeast to Montgomery County in the southwest (R. C. Moore 1949: 49–110). Some Pennsylvanian system, Kansas City group, cherts, like Winterset and Westerville, have been long used and are commonly found in prehistoric archaeological sites in the region. Recorded workshops and quarries utilizing the Pennsylvanian system are presented in Table 16.3.

Although chert may be present in other Pennsylvanian limestone outcrops, the quantity may be limited. For instance, the occurrence of chert is described as sparse in the description of the Norfleet Limestone member in Neosho County (Jungmann 1966: 12). Also, the quality of the chert may be poor, making it unsuitable for stone

Table 16.3. Pennsylvanian System, Recorded Quarries and Workshops

County	Site Number	Formation/Member	Comment
Anderson	14AD418	Unknown	Outcropping limestone and chert
Cherokee	14CH315	Unknown	Stone in bottom of gully
Douglas	14DO33	Toronto (?)	
	14DO36	Plattsmouth (?)	
	14DO140	Plattsmouth (?)	
	14DO406	Plattsmouth (?)	Low-grade chert
Elk	14EK320	Foraker	Pits with heat-treated chert
Franklin	14FR435	Spring Hill (?)	
	14FR436	Captain Creek (?)	Gravel deposit
	14FR438	Spring Hill (?)	Rock ledge
	14FR451	Toronto (?)	Rock ledge
	14FR454	Toronto (?)	
Jackson	14JN104	Foraker	
Jefferson	14JF95	Toronto	
Johnson	14JO350	Westerville (?)	
	14JO481	Argentine (?)	Glacial till also present
Leavenworth	14LV1008	Plattsmouth	
Osage	14OS380	Plattsmouth (?)	Gravel deposit
Shawnee	14SH44	Ervine Creek (?)	Gravel deposit
	14SH363	Ervine Creek (?)	Ledge of tan chert

tool production. Furthermore, Pennsylvanian formations are partly masked by glacial deposits in northeastern Kansas and thus have limited exposure. More than one-third of the area of Jackson County is covered by thick glacial drift (Walters 1953: 11), and glacial deposits are present in other northeastern counties.

Descriptions of Kansas City Group Cherts

Pennsylvanian cherts are not widely distributed in Kansas but are common to the east in Missouri. Two Kansas City group varieties, Winterset and Westerville, are well known and were widely used prehistorically. Winterset typically varies from light gray to very dark gray but also can be very pale brown. Abundant veins of white calcite give this chert a zebra-striped appearance (McLean 1998: 179; Reid 1984: 100). Westerville chert is yellowish-brown; its texture is typically medium-grained but ranges from fine to coarse. Fossils, while present, rarely are abundant, and calcite inclusions and veins may be present (McLean 1998: 178; Reid 1984: 100).

Recorded Sites in the Pennsylvanian System

Twenty workshops have been recorded near outcrops or gravel deposits within the Pennsylvanian outcrop region (Table 16.3). Site 14EK320, discovered during

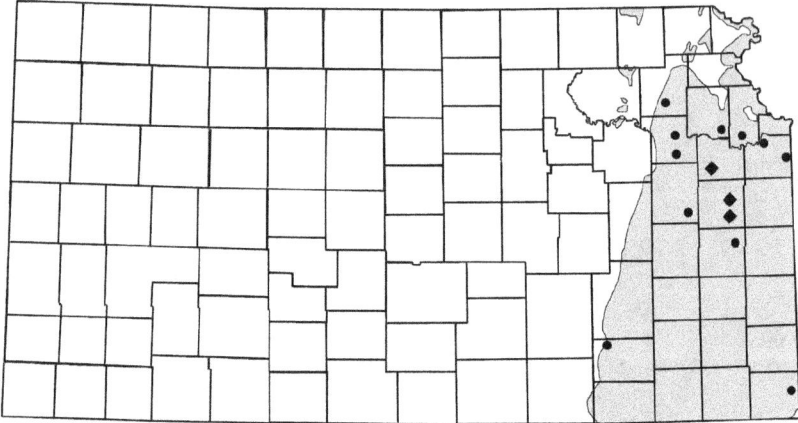

Figure 16.1. Distribution of sites in the Pennsylvanian system. Filled circles indicate single sites; diamonds indicate multiple sites. Pennsylvanian outcrop area is shaded. Mississippian limestone outcrop area is in the extreme southeast corner of the state. (Pennsylvanian outcrop after Zeller 1968: fig. 7).

construction of a watershed dam, apparently had pits with heat-treated chert cobbles, but these features were destroyed before they could be properly documented (Witty 1973).

In addition to chert-bearing limestones, there are 12 sandstone members and 27 other formations and members (primarily shale) that also contain sandstone. The Englevale Sandstone member is also noted as a source of petrified wood (L. W. Howard and Schoewe 1965), but it is not yet known if this material was used prehistorically.

Permian System

Erosion of alternating beds of limestone and shale has formed the Flint Hills Upland, a distinctive and scenic physiographic division that extends from north to south across the state. As its name implies, the Flint Hills is noted for its flint- or chert-bearing limestone formations. Chert-bearing Permian system limestone outcrops are summarized in Table 16.4. In particular, the Florence Limestone member, formerly called the Florence Flint (N. W. Bass 1929), contains abundant nodules of chert. Weathered chert is present on many upland surfaces, and much chert is deposited on stream terraces. Chert is present in 7 of 16 limestone members and formations within the Council Grove and Chase Groups of the Lower Permian. The Pennsylvanian/Permian boundary was moved upward within the rock column in recent years. Formerly placed between the Brownville Limestone member of the Wood Siding formation and the Towle Shale member of the Onaga Shale formation, it was changed to

Table 16.4. Outcropping Chert-Bearing Limestone (and Agatized Dolomite) in the Permian System

Formation	Member
Upper Permian Series	
Day Creek dolomite	
Lower Permian Series	
Nolans limestone	Herington limestone
Winfield limestone	Cresswell limestone
	Stovall limestone
Barneston limestone	Florence limestone
Wreford limestone	Schroyer limestone
	Threemile limestone
Beattie limestone	Cottonwood limestone
Grenola limestone	Neva limestone

the division between the Salem Point Shale member and the Neva Limestone member of the Grenola Limestone, to better correlate the Kansas rock units with those of the Russian type section (Baars et al. 1994: 5–10).

Westward from the southern Flint Hills and south of the Arkansas River, sandstone, shale, gypsum, and dolomite are extensively exposed. The Day Creek Dolomite formation contains agatized dolomite (Figure 16.2).

General Descriptions of Permian Cherts

There are two general classes of Permian cherts that have been described—Wreford and Florence. Three types of Wreford chert have been identified (Blasing 1984; Haury 1984; McLean 1998). Wreford A occurs in the southern Flint Hills. It ranges from tan to buff to gray-buff and has a medium-fine grain. Wreford B is blue-gray to gray and commonly mottled. It is medium- to fine-grained and may contain small white fossil fragments. It is common throughout the Flint Hills (McLean 1998: 184). Descriptions of Wreford C vary (compare McLean 1998: 184 with Haury 1984: 79–80). Its color is typically described as brownish- or bluish-gray (Blasing 1984: 10; McLean 1998: 184) or brown, tan, or yellow (Haury 1984: 79). It is sparsely fossiliferous and medium-grained.

Four varieties of Florence chert have been identified. Florence A, also known as Kay County chert or Maple City chert, is a buff to yellow-gray chert found in the southern Flint Hills. It contains large fusilinid fossils, is fine-grained, and often has bands that resemble fingerprints. Florence B is mottled blue-gray, fine- to medium-grained, and contains fossil fusilinid fragments. It is common throughout the Flint Hills. Florence C is a uniform gray and contains fragments of unidentifiable fossils.

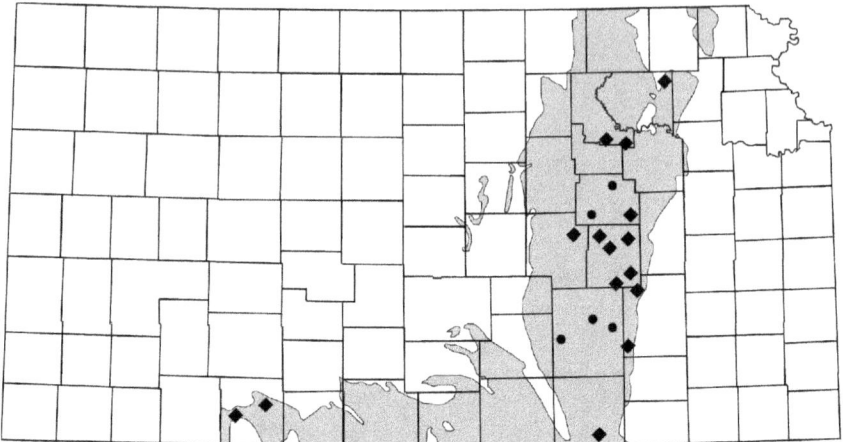

Figure 16.2. Distribution of sites in the Permian system. Filled circles indicate single sites; diamonds indicate multiple sites. Permian outcrop area is shaded. (Permian outcrop after Zeller 1968: fig. 8).

To date it has been found only in secondary contexts (Haury 1984: 76). Florence D is gray to buff and has fine, dark, translucent bands. It is fine-grained and lustrous. Although found throughout the Flint Hills, it is most common in the northern Flint Hills (Haury 1984: 71–77; McLean 1998: 184–185). When heat-treated, some Permian cherts, particularly Florence varieties, turn shades of pink or red (Blasing 1984; Haury 1984).

Recorded Archaeological Sites in the Permian System

Quarries, collecting stations, and workshops are numerous in the Flint Hills, and this region has long been recognized as a source of chipped-stone tools found at archaeological sites in Kansas and surrounding states (W. R. Wedel 1959: 476–482). Sites that have evidence of use of Permian system stone are listed in Table 16.5. Quarrying was by open pit, where topsoil and spoil limestone rock were removed, exposing the chert nodules or chert beds below. Waste rock of limestone and rejected low-grade chert was mixed with flintknapping debitage that was then filled in behind the face of the mining excavation as it progressed. The present-day surfaces of aboriginal quarries in Cowley (L. D. Banks 1990: 99–101) and Pottawatomie (L. D. Banks 1990: 99–101; W. E. Banks 2003) counties have irregular shallow trenches and "fox holes," created by this operation (Figure 16.3). The exploitation of weathered chert gathered from the ground surface or from gravel bar concentrations is less visible, but concentrated areas of flintknapping debris can be found above and along the faces of exposed chert-bearing limestone ledges in Flint Hills pastures and adjacent to gravel bars in the valleys below.

Table 16.5. Permian System, Recorded Quarries and Workshops

County	Site Number	Formation/Member	Comment
Butler	14BU35		
	14BU107		Ledge of chert southeast of site
	14BU343 to 14BU345	All Wreford	
	14BU346	Threemile	
	14BU347 to 14BU355	All Wreford	
	14BU358		
	14BU575	Herrington	
	14BU580	Herrington	
	14BU587	Herrington	Chert outcrop
	14BU589	Florence	Quarry pits
Chase	14CS2	Wreford	Shallow depressions
	14CS3	Wreford	Linear depressions
	14CS108		
	14CS380		
	14CS383 to 14CS385	All Florence	
	14CS391 to 14CS396	All Wreford	
	14CS397	Florence	Archaic (Munkers Creek)
	14CS398		
	14CS406		
	14CS408	Florence	
	14CS409		
	14CS1328 to 14CS1336		
Clark	14CK312 to 14CK318	All Day Creek	
	14CK403	Day Creek	
	14CK405 to 14CK408	All Day Creek	
	14CK411 to 14CK414	All Day Creek	
Cowley	14CO5	Florence	Quarry pits
	14CO352		
	14CO353		
	14CO550 to 14CO554		
Geary	14GE507 to 14GE509		
	14GE511		
	14GE519 to 14GE522		
Greenwood	14GR6		
	14GR310	Wreford	Archaic
	14GR321	Wreford	
	14GR322	Wreford	
Marion	14MN384 to 14MN393	All Florence	
Morris	14MO339		
	14MO347		
	14MO348	Florence	Archaic/Early Ceramic
	14MO351		
	14MO358		
Pottawatomie	14PO56		
	14PO57	Threemile	Quarry pits
	14PO58	Wreford	
	14PO59	Wreford	Eroded quarry pits
	14PO391		
	14PO397		
Riley	14RY503	Florence	Quarry pits
	14RY504	Florence	Quarry pit
Wabaunsee	14WB506	Florence	Quarry pit
	14WB508	Florence	Quarry pits

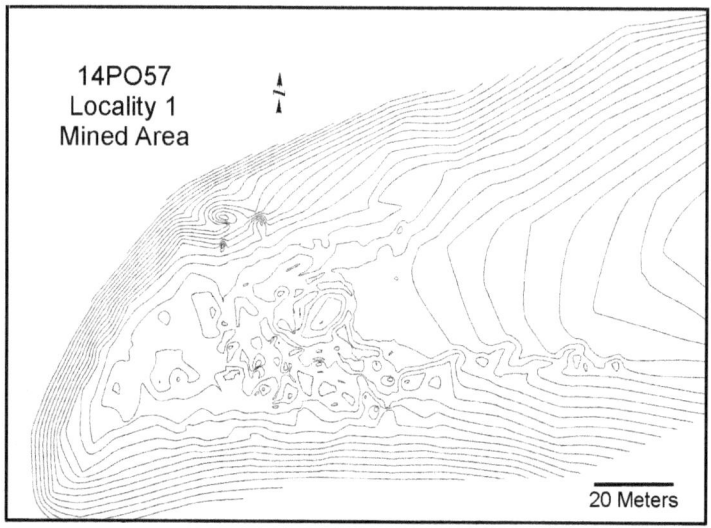

Figure 16.3. Contour map of quarry at 14PO57, showing pits, trenches, and other surface irregularities as a result of mining chert

A survey of the Deep Creek valley in portions of Geary, Riley, and Wabaunsee counties documented 229 sites, including 23 quarries, 102 collection stations, 41 workshops, and 12 stone cairns, some of which may be prehistoric (Blakeslee and Blasing 1985). Collection stations were distinguished from workshops by the amount of lithic debris present. Quarries sometimes had small cairns on the bluff tops above the quarry pits, and most quarry pits were dug into the Florence limestone member.

Archaeological work associated with a series of watershed dams in the upper reaches of Diamond Creek, Middle Creek, and the South Fork of the Cottonwood River in Butler, Chase, Greenwood, Marion, and Morris counties documented 36 workshops. No quarries were recorded. Workshops were located adjacent to Florence or Wreford member limestone outcrops or on stream terraces. Test excavations at two of the workshops showed that the sites were shallow, with no subsurface features, but at another site a hearth was exposed in a cutbank. Diagnostic artifacts from the Middle Archaic through the Early Ceramic periods demonstrate the utilization of these stone resources for thousands of years.

Sites associated with Day Creek dolomite outcrops are located in Clark County, approximately 170 miles west of the southern Flint Hills region. Quarry pits or other mining evidence were not observed on the surface, but one researcher has postulated that stone was removed by digging laterally under the exposed outcrop in order to obtain unweathered cobbles (Bailey 2000: 100–101). A survey in conjunction with the 1989 Kansas Archeology Training Program recorded seven sources in the Day Creek drainage, and Bailey (2000) recorded an additional seven sources of agatized dolomite in Clark County. In addition to chert-bearing limestones, there are six sandstone members and six formations in the Permian system that also contain sandstone.

Jurassic System

Red siltstone and buff, green, and white sandstone occurring in a limited area in southern Morton County mark the extent of outcropping rocks of the Jurassic system in Kansas (Zeller 1968: 54). No lithic procurement sites have been recorded in association with these outcrops.

Cretaceous System

West of the Flint Hills and north of the Arkansas River are most of the state's outcropping Cretaceous rocks, primarily sandstone, limestone, chalk, and shale. In contrast to the numerous limestone deposits present in the older Permian and Pennsylvanian rock series to the east, there are only two limestone members in these Cretaceous rock units. Shale is more commonly exposed, including eight shale members and one shale formation. Three chalk members, two clay members, one sandstone member, and one sandstone formation are also present. The Kiowa formation contains unnamed beds of sandstone, shale, coal, and limestone. Chief among the recorded resources of the Cretaceous system used by prehistoric people are quartzites found within the Cheyenne and Dakota sandstone formations and silicified chalk (Figure 16.4) found in the Smoky Hill chalk member of the Niobrara formation (L. D. Banks 1990: 96). The silicified chalk was widely used prehistorically for chipped-stone tools and has been called a variety of names: Graham, Alma, Republican River, or Smoky Hill jasper (W. R. Wedel 1986: 28); Smoky Hill silicified chalk, Niobrara jasper, or Niobrarite (C. M. Wright 1985); and Quartelejo jasper (L. D. Banks 1990: 96). While the name Smoky Hill silicified chalk is the most accurate description (Holen 1989), the name Smoky Hill jasper is used in this volume for the sake of familiarity and convenience.

General Description of Smoky Hill Jasper

Smoky Hill jasper typically is opaque, but it may be translucent. It is commonly yellow to brown but less commonly is red, green, or white. It may present a solid color or bands of different shades of the same color. Black streaks, patches, wisps, or specks, sometimes in small concentrations, may also be present. It occurs in beds or sheets that erode into relatively thick angular blocks or thin plates or as flattened nodules. Its texture is highly variable, ranging from coarse- to fine-grained. Fossil

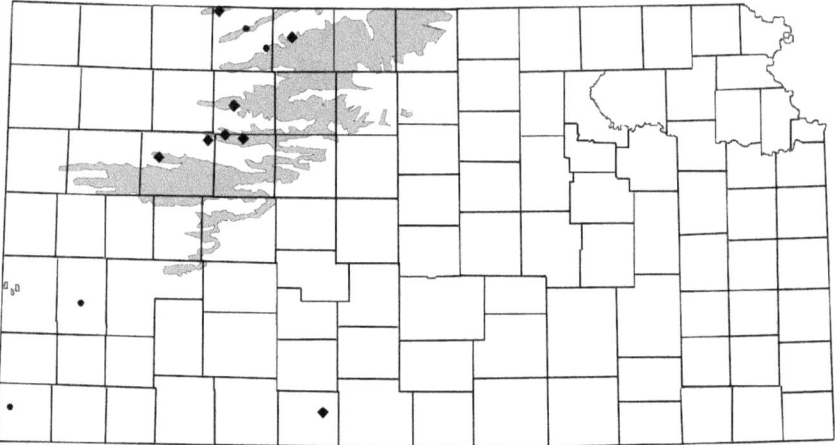

Figure 16.4. Distribution of sites in the Cretaceous system. Filled circles indicate single sites; diamonds indicate multiple sites. The shaded area indicates the extent of outcropping limestone and chalk members of the Niobrara formation. Symbols in unshaded areas mark quartzite outcrops. (Niobrara outcrop after Hattin 1982: fig. 1).

inclusions are rare, but small yellow chalk inclusions are common (Holen 1989: 6; 1991: 401; McLean 1998: 187; Stein 2005; W. R. Wedel 1986: 28–30).

Recorded Quarries and Workshops

A number of stone acquisition sites in association with Cretaceous outcrops have been recorded (Table 16.6), and diagnostic artifacts made from Smoky Hill jasper have been found in all archaeological time periods from Paleoindian to Late Ceramic (Stein 2005). A cache of large bifaces, identified as Paleoindian Hell Gap blanks, was found in northeastern Gove County (Stanford 1997: 40) near outcrops of Smoky Hill jasper. Many exposures of Smoky Hill chalk have been identified, but most show no evidence of silicification. The Walsh Archaeological District in Trego County is an exception. Here are found three Upper Republican sites (14TO304–306) containing large amounts of flintknapping debris in association with outcropping silicified chalk. Hearths and a midden at one of these sites, 14TO304, testify to a relatively lengthy stay at the stone source, though no evidence for quarrying the stone has been found. The lower elevations at site 14TO306 had scalloped areas possibly resulting from digging, but test excavations there found only chalk deposits (Reed 1997). A nearby site, 14TO317, has notches in the outcropping chalk deposits that may represent quarrying activity.

There are also useful minerals present in Cretaceous strata. Hematite and limonite occur in the Dakota sandstone, although not in large deposits. The largest deposit recorded was a bed of hematite 8-feet thick in Russell County (Kinney 1942). Wilson

Table 16.6. Cretaceous System, Recorded Quarries and Workshops

County	Site Number	Formation/Member	Comment
Comanche	14CM306	Cheyenne	
	14CM414	Cheyenne	
	14CM418 to 14CM422	Cheyenne	Small workshops associated with quartzite outcrops
Gove	14GO303	Smoky Hill	
	14GO307	Smoky Hill	
	14GO312	Smoky Hill	
	14GO314	Smoky Hill	
	14GO401	Smoky Hill	
Graham	14GH314	Smoky Hill	
	14GH320	Smoky Hill	
	14GH322	Smoky Hill	
	14GH332	Smoky Hill	
	14GH344	Smoky Hill	
	14GH351	Smoky Hill	
Kearny	14KY303	Dakota	Quartzite cobbles in sandstone matrix
Morton	14MT98	Dakota	Quartzite cobbles
Norton	14NT9	Smoky Hill	Innundated by Keith Sebelius Lake
	14NT315	Smoky Hill	
	14NT322	Smoky Hill	
	14NT606	Smoky Hill	
Phillips	14PH316	Smoky Hill	
	14PH338	Smoky Hill	
	14PH344	Smoky Hill	
Sheridan	14SD404	Smoky Hill	
	14SD406	Smoky Hill	
Trego	14TO306	Smoky Hill	Three Central Plains tradition workshop sites nearby
	14TO317	Smoky Hill	Possible quarry
	14TO325	Smoky Hill	
	14TO339	Smoky Hill	

Lake apparently now covers this bed. Also of importance are veins of calcite, which occur in abundance in Smoky Hill chalk outcrops (for example, see Waite 1947: plate 14). Calcite is a common temper used by Plains Woodland, Keith focus, potters.

Tertiary System

Tertiary rocks are predominantly stream deposits that occur widely in western Kansas and locally in central and eastern Kansas. The principal source of most of these deposits was an area of igneous rocks in the Rocky Mountains and sedimentary rocks located in eastern Colorado and extreme western Kansas (Zeller 1968: 58). One stratigraphic unit, the Ogallala formation, includes all Tertiary rocks. The Ogallala formation of the Tertiary system has three members: Kimball, Ash Hollow, and Valentine. The Ogallala formation covers approximately the western one-third of the state, with its eastern margin presenting a jagged front reflecting the erosional action of downcutting streams. The various members of the Ogallala contain caliche, silt, clay, sand, volcanic ash, diatomaceous marl, gravel, limestone, opaline sandstone, secondary opal, silicified sediment (quartzite), and chert. The quartzite is a green, greenish-brown, or greenish-gray silicified sand that was used for large bifacial cutting, chopping, and scraping tools (Holen 1991: 401; W. R. Wedel 1986: 31).

There are potentially many lithic sources located in the opaline sandstone and gravel deposits of the Ogallala, but only one such source has been recorded: 14GO310, a workshop associated with a gravel deposit in the Smoky Hill River drainage in southeastern Gove County.

Quaternary System

Quaternary deposits, mostly unconsolidated, are found in all parts of the state, though they are discontinuous in their distribution. Pleistocene in age, they include glacial, lacustrine, fluvial, and eolian sediments. Glacial sediments are found only in northeastern Kansas, generally north of the Kansas River and east of the Blue River, as are most of the lacustrine deposits. Sioux quartzite, granite, and greenstone from the glacial till of northeastern Kansas have been found at sites in that region and elsewhere in the state. Sioux quartzite and granite are durable materials that were used for grinding stones and hammerstones. Greenstone was used for ground celts and axes. The dispersed nature of these rocks in the glacial till makes it difficult, if not impossible, to recognize acquisition sites. Understandably none have been recorded.

Holocene Epoch

The phrase "Holocene or Recent" identifies deposits of clay, silt, sand, and gravel in and along the active channels of streams. The composition of these deposits depends upon the source materials available in each drainage basin; therefore, the gravels in these deposits may derive from a number of earlier Pleistocene sources or rocks weathered from Tertiary or earlier systems. No specific procurement sites associated with these Holocene deposits have been identified.

ARCHAEOLOGICAL RESEARCH AND KANSAS LITHIC RESOURCES

Archaeological research into the use of lithic raw material has focused primarily on its use in prehistoric times. After contact with Europeans and later Americans, the

Figure 16.5. Quarry tools found in situ at 14PO57. A large quartzite cobble and two antler wedges lay at the face of a bed of Threemile chert (jagged edge) exposed during the prehistoric mining operation. Arrow is 20 cm long.

use of chipped stone for tools and weapons was phased out as metal replacements became available. Lithic research topics may be organized into three broad categories: obtaining lithic resources, stone-working methods and techniques, and tracing the distribution of stone through time and space in the archaeological record (Andrefsky 1994; Luedtke 1992).

Identifying sources of stone is the first step in most lithic studies. The site rosters noted above in association with the different systems of outcropping rocks represent the current status of this activity in Kansas. Some surveys have been done specifically to locate sources of stone (see Blakeslee and Blasing 1985), but most of the sites were encountered opportunistically. Though incomplete in geographical coverage, the sites recorded thus far indicate that collecting stone from weathered outcrops was more common in Kansas than quarrying stone directly from bedrock (Figure 16.5). Questions that can be answered at the source area include those that pertain to the rock—identifying its geological origin and its mineral, chemical, and physical properties. Other questions pertain to its use. Who were the people using the stone? How was the stone extracted? What was the reduction process? How much of the stone reduction process took place at the source? How did the quarry or stone source fit into the settlement pattern of the people who used it? These are questions that have yet to be answered for most of the recorded stone sources.

STONE SOURCE IDENTIFICATION

Descriptions of the characteristics of some Kansas cherts have been published (Bailey 2000; L. D. Banks 1990; Blasing 1984; Haury 1981, 1984; McLean 1998; Morrow

1994). Although useful to an extent, published descriptions pale in usefulness to well-documented comparative collections. Comparative collections may be found at the Kansas State Historical Society, the University of Kansas, Kansas State University, and Wichita State University. Many Kansas cherts and nonlocal or exotic stone resources can be identified by the naked eye, but it may be difficult or impossible to determine their exact source without determining their chemical or mineralogical composition and comparing it to samples from known source areas. Also, the variability of a particular stone's origin and composition means that no one method can be universally applied to determine its source. A number of destructive and nondestructive methods are available, such as comparative analysis, petrographic analysis (L. D. Banks 1990: 8), scanning electron microscopy, and ultraviolet light fluorescence (Hofman, Todd, and Collins 1991). Techniques used for analysis of chemical composition include instrumental neutron activation analysis (INAA) (Neff 2000), X-ray fluorescence (XRF) (Shackley 1998), X-ray diffraction (XRD) (Gundersen 1993, 2002), or inductively coupled plasma-mass spectrometry (ICP-MS) (Ciurczak 1997). Use of these techniques has helped archaeologists determine the source of exotic stone types, including chert, obsidian, and turquoise found on Kansas sites (Gundersen 1988, 1993, 2002; Gundersen and Tiffany 1986; Hawley 2000; Hawley and Hughes 1999; Hoard et al. 1992; Hoard et al. 1993; Holen 1991, 2001; Logan, Hughes, and Henning 2001; Logan and Banks 1993: Appendix 1; Penman and Gundersen 1999). L. D. Banks (1990: 8) has a brief summary of the different methods used in sourcing stone, and Luedtke (1992: Appendix A) presents an outline of steps that can be taken in chert source analysis.

Source Characterization of Kansas Lithic Resources

Neutron activation analysis was used to identify the raw material source of Smoky Hill jasper artifacts from Great Bend aspect sites located in central Kansas. Samples from a 5-km line of silicified chalk bluffs in the Saline River valley in Trego County were included in the sample, but no uniform trace-element signatures were found that could be used to identify discrete areas within the formation (L. D. Banks 1990: 96). Mineralogical analysis of black rock found in gravel deposits in Trego County and used for flaked tools prehistorically identified the stone as trachite (Blasing 1990). This stone has an origin similar to basalt. Also, artifacts of plagioclase basalt have been found in Woodland and Upper Republican sites in western Kansas (W. R. Wedel 1959: 404–475).

A red argillite commonly known as pipestone was used prehistorically and historically in Kansas and across the mid-continent to make pipes, beads, and other objects. Pipestone occurs in bedrock outcrops in southwestern Minnesota, southeastern South Dakota, and northwestern Wisconsin. Also, glacially redeposited pipestone, referred to as Kansas pipestone, exists in glacial till deposits in southeastern South Dakota, northeastern Nebraska, northwestern Iowa, and northeastern

Kansas (Gundersen and Tiffany 1986: 46). Prehistoric people utilized both the in situ and glacial sources of pipestone. James Gundersen, using X-ray diffraction, has shown these various sources to be distinguishable (Gundersen 1988, 1993, 2002; Gundersen and Tiffany 1986; Ludwickson, Gundersen, and Johnson 1993; Penman and Gundersen 1999).

Catlinite is the name used exclusively to describe the pipestone from southwestern Minnesota, the area now called Pipestone National Monument. The lithological description of catlinite is that it is a muscovite-diospore-pryophyllite argillite. The other two most widely used sources—the Wisconsin bedrock source and Kansas pipestone—are classified as quartz-kaolinite argillite and quartz-pryophyllite argillite, respectively (Gundersen 1993: 561). Establishing the mineralogical composition of these various sources has shown that true catlinite from the pipestone quarry of Minnesota was preferred overwhelmingly by late prehistoric Oneota populations, especially after A.D. 1450, even when closer sources were available (Gundersen 1993: 561; Henning and Shermer 2004: 511), and that it was used almost exclusively by Historic-period people (Gundersen and Tiffany 1986: 63). However, Gundersen's (1993: 561) analysis has demonstrated that Great Bend populations in south-central Kansas used Kansas pipestone almost exclusively, indicating use of near-local materials rather than exotic catlinite.

Source Characterization of Exotic Lithic Resources

As noted elsewhere in this volume, obsidian, a dark-colored volcanic glass, is occasionally found in small quantities in prehistoric Kansas sites. No known sources of obsidian exist in Kansas—most known sources are in the Rocky Mountains or farther west. A handful of studies have been conducted to determine source areas of obsidian found in Kansas sites. Flakes from Kansas Oneota sites 14JW2, 14JW8, and 14JW24 in the Lovewell Reservoir area (known as the Warne locality) have been demonstrated to come from both the Malad, Idaho, and Obsidian Ridge, New Mexico, sources (Logan, Hughes, and Henning 2001; Logan and Banks 1993). Obsidian from Great Bend sites near Arkansas City is most similar chemically to the Obsidian Ridge and Cerro del Medio sources of New Mexico (Hawley 2000: 242–246). Finally, two flakes from the multicomponent Infinity site (14MY305) have been shown to come from the Malad, Idaho, source, though it is not certain if the flakes are from the Cuesta or Pomona component (Hawley and Hughes 1999).

Other exotic tool stone from distant areas is sometimes found on Kansas sites. These include Alibates agatized dolomite and Edwards chert from Texas; Knife River Flint from North Dakota; White River Group silicates, including Flattop chalcedony, from Colorado, Wyoming, and South Dakota; and Hartville chert from Wyoming (L. D. Banks 1990).

Ultimately, understanding the sources of stone found on archaeological sites can help us learn about past patterns of trade or travel. Two studies by Holen, one on the

Lower Loup phase (Holen 1983, 1991) and another on Clovis-age people (Holen 2001), have documented group movements, territory, and acquisition patterns. Blakeslee and Hawley (chapter 10, this volume) and Zehnder (1998) have used the distribution of Kansas stone sources in Great Bend aspect sites to indicate different trade or movement patterns in parts of the Little River focus. By understanding the stone resources available in Kansas, we are able to recognize stone types such as obsidian, turquoise, Alibates agatized dolomite, White River Group silicates, and Knife River flint from outside the state that are evidence of trade or movement and that indicate potential social ties among prehistoric people (Blakeslee and Hawley, chapter 10, this volume; Hawley 2000; Hoard et al. 1992, Hoard et al. 1993; Holen 1991, 2001; Zehnder 1998).

STONE-WORKING TECHNIQUES

The few analyses of flintknapping debris at stone sources have shown that the debitage resulted from both biface and flake production (Ashworth 1982). An experimental archaeology project produced a probable method of making endscrapers from nodular chert cores, by removing flakes in a radial pattern around the perimeter of the nodule (Wilke, Carlson, and Reynolds 2002). This method produced large flakes containing a portion of the higher quality chert that is typically found in Florence A nodules and that can also be seen in archaeological specimens.

Included among stone-working techniques is the process of heat-treating stone to improve its mechanical properties (Sollberger and Hester 1973). Shippee (1963) identified prehistoric heat-treatment pits in the Blue River valley, and, as noted above, another site (14EK320) in the southern Flint Hills also may have had such features. One heat-treating experiment using samples of Florence chert showed that heating the stone to between 500 and 600° F produced useful stone, but that higher temperatures were harmful to the rock (Reynolds, Reed, and Jackson 2001). This same result was obtained in an earlier experiment (Haury 1984).

The opportunities for research into Kansas lithic resources are many and varied, as this brief review has shown. Though the quarry, collecting, and workshop sites noted above were all created for the same purpose—to obtain knappable stone— they are not all identical in content. Extraction methods differ, and the flintknapping techniques used to reduce the stone to usable blanks or tools probably differed as well. Some sites may have evidence of ancillary activities, such as the heat-treating pits seen at site 14EK320, or hearths, such as those exposed in the cutbank in the Cottonwood River drainage, and the hearth and midden at the Walsh sites. Evaluating the information in these sites and integrating it into our understanding of Kansas archaeology has only just begun.

APPENDIX

284 APPENDIX

Site	Lab Number	Sample Material	^{13}C Ratio	Radiocarbon Age BP and Standard Deviation	Median Probability	One Sigma Calibrated Date Range	Two Sigma Calibrated Date Range	References
Paleoarchaic								
Lovewell mammoth 14JW306	UCIAMS-11211	bone collagen	−20.5	19,530±80	CAL B.C. 21,207	CAL B.C. 21,576−20,831	CAL B.C. 21,943−20,526	Kansas archaeological site file
Kanorado vicinity 14SN105	UCIAMS-11214	bone collagen	−18.2	12,375±35	CAL B.C. 12,714	CAL B.C. 13,087−12,638, 12,474−12,185	CAL B.C. 13,475−12,570, 12,515−12,174	Mandel et al. 2005
Kanorado vicinity 14SN105	UCIAMS-11212	bone collagen	−17.3	12,255±40	CAL B.C. 12,425	CAL B.C. 13,064−12,728, 12,420−12,146	CAL B.C. 13,439−12,637, 12,448−12,135, 11,963−11,903	Mandel et al. 2005
Kanorado vicinity 14SN105	UCIAMS-11213	bone collagen	−18.8	12,215±35	CAL B.C. 12,367	CAL B.C. 13,048−12,762, 12,406−12,135, 11,946−11,920	CAL B.C. 13,415−12,657, 12,431−12,124, 11,976−11,895	Mandel et al. 2005
Kanorado vicinity 14SN106	CAMS-112742	bone collagen	—	11,005±50	CAL B.C. 11,064	CAL B.C. 11,187−11,117, 11,104−10,998	CAL B.C. 11,219−10,917, 10,766−10,720	Mandel et al. 2005
Kanorado vicinity 14SN101	CAMS-112741	bone collagen	—	10,950±60	CAL B.C. 11,034	CAL B.C. 11,177−11,126, 11,088−10,946	CAL B.C. 11,202−10,883, 10,771−10,714	Mandel et al. 2005
Kanorado vicinity 14SN105	CAMS-112740	bone collagen	—	10,150±50	CAL B.C. 9862	CAL B.C. 10,826−10,808, 10,684−10,497, 10,492−9231	CAL B.C. 11,172−11,130, 11,080−8516, 8514−8454	Mandel et al. 2005
14LO1	CAMS-16072	bone collagen	—	10,520±70	CAL B.C. 10,552	CAL B.C. 10,867−10,776, 10,709−10,618, 10,590−10,384	CAL B.C. 10,946−10,332, 10,303−10,144, 10,049−10,029	Hofman 1996: 85
14LO1	GX-5812a	bone apatite	—	10,435±260	CAL B.C. 10,316	CAL B.C. 10,875−10,766,	CAL B.C. 10,999−9593,	Rogers and Martin 1984

Site	Lab #	Material	Age BP	Calibrated	Calibrated ranges	Reference
14LO1	GX-5812b	bone gelatin	—		9566-9448, 9444-9390, 9365-9356 10,721-9977, 9859-9816	Rogers and Martin 1984
Simshauser 14KY102	—	soil above bonebed	10,245±335	CAL B.C. 10,024	CAL B.C. 10,665-10,533, 10,424-9597, 9561-9454, 9441-9392	CAL B.C. 11,001-9137, 9126-9125, 8987-8937, 8930-8923	Kansas archaeological site file
14SR319	—	charcoal	10,170±70	CAL B.C. 9870	CAL B.C. 10,138-10,066, 10,019-9680, 9669-9616, 9497-9495	CAL B.C. 10,369-9599, 9557-9528, 9525-9463, 9439-9395	Kansas archaeological site file
		charcoal	9440±90	CAL B.C. 8754	CAL B.C. 9111-9068, 9058-9007, 8997-8995, 8889-8883, 8825-8598, 8586-8584, 8574-8555	CAL B.C. 9158-8518, 8512-8456	
Claussen 14WB322	ISGS-AO479*	charcoal	9225±30	CAL B.C. 8436	CAL B.C. 8535-8514, 8480-8421, 8407-8387, 8384-8348	CAL B.C. 8548-8323	Mandel, Widga, et al. 2004
Claussen 14WB322	ISGS-AO480*	charcoal	9225±35	CAL B.C. 8436	CAL B.C. 8535-8513, 8481-8420, 8408-8347	CAL B.C. 8552-8317	Mandel, Widga, et al. 2004
Winger 14ST401	ISGS-4934	bone	9080±90	CAL B.C. 8290	CAL B.C. 8517-8514, 8453-8202, 8037-8031	CAL B.C. 8551-8157, 8139-7965	Mandel and Hofman 2002, 2003
14SC6	CAMS-16032	bone collagen	9080±60	CAL B.C. 8284	CAL B.C. 8411-8397, 8378-8373, 8358-8353, 8321-8234	CAL B.C. 8522-8508, 8476-8201, 8126-8124, 8039-8027, 7978-7974	Hofman et al. 1995
14LT351	TX-6049	charcoal	8810±250	CAL B.C. 7942	CAL B.C. 8232-7604	CAL B.C. 8686-8672, 8630-7307, 7221-7197	Thies 1990

Site	Lab Number	Sample Material	^{13}C Ratio	Radiocarbon Age BP and Standard Deviation	Median Probability	One Sigma Calibrated Date Range	Two Sigma Calibrated Date Range	References
Claussen 14WB322	ISGS-4684	charcoal	—	8800±150	CAL B.C. 7917	CAL B.C. 8199-8175, 8164-8126, 8123-8101, 8085-8042, 8017-7727, 7722-7711, 7699-7679, 7659-7654	CAL B.C. 8285-8279, 8275-7577, 7555-7554	Mandel, Widga, et al. 2004
Laird 14SN2	CAMS 82397	bone collagen	-8.5	8495±40	CAL B.C. 7555	CAL B.C. 7581-7538	CAL B.C. 7592-7519, 7499-7485	Hofman and Blackmar 2004; Mandel, Hofman, et al. 2004
14LT351	TX-6048	charcoal	—	8130±130	CAL B.C. 7123	CAL B.C. 7448-7437, 7420-7411, 7397-7394, 7348-7028, 7017-7003, 6989-6983, 6968-6949, 6933-6913, 6881-6830	CAL B.C. 7516-7503, 7479-6690	Thies 1990
Sutter 14JN309	SM-1420	charcoal	—	7990±45	CAL B.C. 6913	CAL B.C. 7052-6981, 6970-6946, 6938-6901, 6883-6826	CAL B.C. 7060-6749, 6721-6702	Katz 1973
Lansing 14LV315	GX-586	bone	—	7825±105	CAL B.C. 6702	CAL B.C. 6979-6972, 6898-6884, 6823-6500, 6486-6484	CAL B.C. 7038-6876, 6871-6461	W. M. Bass 1973: 102
Sutter 14JN309	SM-1421	charcoal	—	7818±245	CAL B.C. 6740	CAL B.C. 7039-6875, 6873-6458	CAL B.C. 7449-7434, 7422-7410, 7399-7393, 7350-6215, 6167-6164	Katz 1973
Sutter 14JN3009	SM-1423	charcoal	—	7668±237	CAL B.C. 6562	CAL B.C. 6980-6971, 6946-6939, 6901-6883, 6825-6230	CAL B.C. 7290-7270, 7238-7229, 7181-6006, 6000-5995	Katz 1973

Site	Lab No.	Material	δ13C	BP	CAL B.C.	CAL B.C.	CAL B.C.	Reference
14LT351	TX-6050	charcoal	—	7590±100	CAL B.C. 6428	CAL B.C. 6586-6583, 6566-6556, 6527-6521, 6507-6341, 6312-6258	CAL B.C. 6649-6219	Thies 1990
14LT351	TX-5694	charcoal	—	7410±70	CAL B.C. 6278	CAL B.C. 6387-6215, 6168-6164	CAL B.C. 6420-6158, 6141-6085	Thies 1990
William Young 14MO304	GAK-1735	charcoal	—	7300±2000				Witty 1982: 188
Lansing 14LV315	SI-360	bone	—	6970±200	CAL B.C. 5857	CAL B.C. 6049-6044, 6026-5659, 5651-5640	CAL B.C. 6330-6319, 6248-5477	W. M. Bass 1973: 102
Coffey 14PO1	WIS-715	charcoal	—	6285±145	CAL B.C. 5217	CAL B.C. 5466-5445, 5419-5402, 5380-5050	CAL B.C. 5527-4843, 4819-4809	Schmits 1978: 85
William Young 14MO304	ISGS-5626	charcoal	-26.5	6200±160	CAL B.C. 5126	CAL B.C. 5316-4943, 4866-4864	CAL B.C. 5473-4780	W. E. Banks and Wigand 2005
14DO447	CAMS-87695	bone	—	6160±35	CAL B.C. 5115	CAL B.C. 5209-5165, 5144-5108, 5101-5089, 5083-5039, 5007-5004	CAL B.C. 5258-5239, 5233-5218, 5213-4985, 4975-4960	Hoard et al. 2004: 722
14CT395	—	charcoal	—	6060±90	CAL B.C. 4967	CAL B.C. 5196-5181, 5136-5134, 5064-4834, 4822-4806	CAL B.C. 5258-5239, 5233-5218, 5213-4770, 4753-4723	Kansas archaeological site file
14JF409	Beta-29436	charcoal	—	5710±100	CAL B.C. 4559	CAL B.C. 4687-4630, 4623-4457	CAL B.C. 4774-4748, 4732-4352	Logan 1990b: 95
Lansing 14LV315	M-1890	bone	—	5700±250	CAL B.C. 4565	CAL B.C. 4903-4887, 4880-4874, 4853-4308, 4304-4248	CAL B.C. 5256-5244, 5230-5220, 5212-5158, 5152-3972	W. M. Bass 1973: 102
Coffey 14PO1	N-1550	charcoal	—	5680±130	CAL B.C. 4532	CAL B.C. 4686-4633, 4622-4435, 4423-4363	CAL B.C. 4898-4892, 4848-4817, 4812-4237	Schmits 1978: 85

Site	Lab Number	Sample Material	^{13}C Ratio	Radiocarbon Age BP and Standard Deviation	Median Probability	One Sigma Calibrated Date Range	Two Sigma Calibrated Date Range	References
William Young 14MO304	ISGS-5627	charcoal	-23.7	5630±70	CAL B.C. 4462	CAL B.C. 4523-4508, 4503-4432, 4424-4362	CAL B.C. 4670-4660, 4648-4642, 4617-4339	W. E. Banks and Wigand 2005
Durbin 14EK331	I-8179	charcoal	—	5600±110	CAL B.C. 4445	CAL B.C. 4584-4564, 4554-4330, 4269-4262	CAL B.C. 4769-4753, 4720-4222, 4190-4164, 4117-4113	Barr 1974: 30
Coffey 14PO1	UGa-382	charcoal	—	5505±105	CAL B.C. 4341	CAL B.C. 4487-4480, 4461-4224, 4178-4172	CAL B.C. 4589-4562, 4554-4042	Schmits 1978: 85
14CO1306	—	charcoal	—	5420±60	CAL B.C. 4259	CAL B.C. 4343-4222, 4187-4164, 4116-4114	CAL B.C. 4431-4424, 4362-4216, 4204-4045	Kansas archaeological site file
Coffey 14PO1	WIS-711	charcoal	—	5355±70	CAL B.C. 4174	CAL B.C. 4321-4292, 4252-4218, 4200-4157, 4151-4140, 4128-4048	CAL B.C. 4339-4037, 4022-3996	Schmits 1978: 85
William Young 14MO304	GAK-297	charcoal	—	5340±160				Witty 1982: 188
14MH39	—	charcoal	—	5320±790	CAL B.C. 4068	CAL B.C. 5207-5176, 5140-5126, 5079-3096	CAL B.C. 5967-5953, 5894-1945	K. L. Brown and Simmons 1987
Coffey 14PO1	WIS-629	charcoal	—	5285±70	CAL B.C. 4118	CAL B.C. 4222-4185, 4165-4037, 4021-3996	CAL B.C. 4324-4286, 4255-3963	Schmits 1978: 85
Scott 14LV1082	ISGS-5460	charcoal	—	5270±70	CAL B.C. 4105	CAL B.C. 4221-4195, 4162-4119, 4111-4058, 4054-4035, 4025-3986	CAL B.C. 4317-4298, 4250-3961	Logan 2004: 57
Coffey 14PO1	WIS-636	charcoal	—	5255±70	CAL B.C. 4091	CAL B.C. 4220-4196, 4161-4120,	CAL B.C. 4323-4288,	Schmits 1978: 85

William Young 14MO304	ISGS-A0508	charcoal	-25.1	5255±40	CAL B.C. 4070	4110-4089, 4081-4059, 4053-3979	4254-3942, 3836-3826	W. E. Banks and Wigand 2005
Coffey 14PO1	WIS-624	charcoal	—	5240±70	CAL B.C. 4071	CAL B.C. 4218-4199, 4158-4149, 4142-4125, 4106-4104, 4050-3983	CAL B.C. 4221-4190, 4164-4118, 4112-3977	Schmits 1978: 85
Coffey 14PO1	WIS-623	charcoal	—	5170±70	CAL B.C. 3974	CAL B.C. 4220-4196, 4161-4121, 4109-4093, 4078-4060, 4053-3967	CAL B.C. 4319-4296, 4251-3938, 3859-3812	Schmits 1978: 85
Coffey 14PO1	WIS-628	charcoal	—	5160±70	CAL B.C. 3961	CAL B.C. 4216-4204, 4044-3936, 3877-3804	CAL B.C. 4221-4191, 4164-4118, 4112-3785	Schmits 1978: 85
Coffey 14PO1	WIS-618	charcoal	—	5155±70	CAL B.C. 3954	CAL B.C. 4042-3933, 3921-3914, 3877-3803	CAL B.C. 4221-4194, 4163-4119, 4111-3776	Schmits 1978: 85
Coffey 14PO1	WIS-779	charcoal	—	5140±65	CAL B.C. 3929	CAL B.C. 4041-4016, 4003-3914, 3878-3803	CAL B.C. 4221-4195, 4162-4120, 4110-4087, 4084-3768	Schmits 1978: 85
Coffey 14PO1	WIS-634	charcoal	—	5125±70	CAL B.C. 3906	CAL B.C. 4036-4023, 3993-3914, 3878-3803	CAL B.C. 4219-4198, 4159-4125, 4106-4103, 4068-4064, 4050-3760, 3721-3713	Schmits 1978: 85
Coffey 14PO1	WIS-774	charcoal	—	5080±65	CAL B.C. 3866	CAL B.C. 3984-3893, 3881-3799	CAL B.C. 4217-4201, 4156-4152, 4140-4130, 4047-3710	Schmits 1978: 85
Coffey 14PO1	WIS-778	charcoal	—	5070±70	CAL B.C. 3860	CAL B.C. 3959-3890, 3883-3798	CAL B.C. 4036-4024, 3989-3707	Schmits 1978: 85
						CAL B.C. 3958-3793	CAL B.C. 4036-4023, 3994-3698, 3676-3673	

290 APPENDIX

Site	Lab Number	Sample Material	^{13}C Ratio	Radiocarbon Age BP and Standard Deviation	Median Probability	One Sigma Calibrated Date Range	Two Sigma Calibrated Date Range	References
Coffey 14PO1	WIS-776	charcoal	—	5030±65	CAL B.C. 3831	CAL B.C. 3941-3839, 3822-3759, 3736-3734, 3722-3713	CAL B.C. 3963-3693, 3681-3664	Schmits 1978: 85
Bailey 14OS347	I-12905	charcoal	—	4980±100	CAL B.C. 3779	CAL B.C. 3936-3876, 3867-3864, 3805-3658	CAL B.C. 3979-3631, 3577-3571, 3561-3538	K. L. Brown and Simmons 1987
Coffey 14PO1	N-1549	charcoal	—	4840±95	CAL B.C. 3620	CAL B.C. 3758-3740, 3730-3723, 3712-3517, 3401-3384	CAL B.C. 3931-3923, 3914-3878, 3803-3368	Schmits 1978: 85
Snyder 14BU9	N-1279	charcoal	—	4830±105	CAL B.C. 3604	CAL B.C. 3756-3749, 3712-3504, 3427-3381	CAL B.C. 3938-3861, 3810-3360	Hofman 1996: 85
Lansing 14LV315	SI-360-R	bone	—	4610±200	CAL B.C. 3319	CAL B.C. 3633-3556, 3540-3087, 3060-3037	CAL B.C. 3937-3876, 3868-3864, 3805-2859, 2811-2748, 2723-2699	W. M. Bass 1973: 102
Snyder 14BU9	N-1280	charcoal	—	4600±125	CAL B.C. 3323	CAL B.C. 3616-3613, 3520-3261, 3241-3100	CAL B.C. 3640-3010, 2984-2924	Hofman 1996: 85
Wiseman 14EK343	—	charcoal	—	4600±110	CAL B.C. 3330	CAL B.C. 3518-3306, 3299-3279, 3272-3264, 3238-3168, 3163-3102	CAL B.C. 3638-3016, 2978-2966, 2949-2933	Kansas archaeological site file
Milbourn 14BU25	UGa-2806	charcoal	—	4568±100	CAL B.C. 3271	CAL B.C. 3500-3434, 3378-3255, 3252-3098	CAL B.C. 3628-3582, 3536-3009, 2985-2924	Root 1981: 22
14MH39	—	charcoal	—	4215±180	CAL B.C. 2799	CAL B.C. 3084-3063, 3033-2550, 2542-2490	CAL B.C. 3366-2283, 2249-2232, 2217-2211	Hofman 1996: 85
Snyder 14BU9	N-1551	charcoal	—	4150±110	CAL B.C. 2715	CAL B.C. 2880-2617, 2612-2580	CAL B.C. 3076-3074, 3022-2427,	Hofman 1996: 85

Site	Lab number	Material		RCYBP	CAL B.C.	CAL B.C.	Reference
14MM1	UGa-4085	charcoal	—	4020±90	CAL B.C. 2555	CAL B.C. 2856-2814, 2695-2692, 2680-2455, 2451-2432, 2422-2404, 2362-2353	K. L. Brown and Simmons 1987 2424-2403, 2375-2352
Snyder 14BU9	N-1278	charcoal	—	3980±100	CAL B.C. 2493	CAL B.C. 2829-2823, 2659-2652, 2623-2296	Hofman 1996: 85 CAL B.C. 2876-2292
Snyder 14BU9	N-771	charcoal	—	3910±160	CAL B.C. 2387	CAL B.C. 2827-2824, 2658-2652, 2622-2136, 2078-2067	Grosser 1973 CAL B.C. 2870-2802, 2783-2199, 2158-2152
14MM1	UGa-4084	charcoal	—	3885±135	CAL B.C. 2352	CAL B.C. 2571-2515, 2501-2139	K. L. Brown and Simmons 1987 CAL B.C. 2863-2808, 2777-2773, 2758-2719, 2704-1943
14LY305	GAK-594	charcoal	—	3780±140			K. L. Brown and Simmons 1987
14MY309	GAK-598	charcoal	—	3680±180			K. L. Brown and Simmons 1987
Snyder 14BU9	N-770	charcoal	—	3650±140	CAL B.C. 2033	CAL B.C. 2275-2253, 2228-2222, 2205-1866, 1843-1809, 1801-1775	Grosser 1973 CAL B.C. 2466-1679, 1670-1658, 1652-1636
Williamson 14CF330	GAK-407	charcoal	—	3600±100			Schmits 1987a: 155
Williamson 14CF330	GAK-406	charcoal	—	3500±100			Schmits 1987a: 155
William Young 14MO304	GAK-596	charcoal	—	3400±500			Witty 1982: 188
14GR307	GAK-775	charcoal	—	3250±140			Hofman 1996: 85
Snyder 14BU9	N-1277	charcoal	—	3240±85	CAL B.C. 1520	CAL B.C. 1620-1425, 1423-1414	Hofman 1996: 85 CAL B.C. 1741-1306

292   APPENDIX

Site	Lab Number	Sample Material	^{13}C Ratio	Radiocarbon Age BP and Standard Deviation	Median Probability	One Sigma Calibrated Date Range	Two Sigma Calibrated Date Range	References
William Young 14MO304	GAK-595	charcoal	—	3100±400				Witty 1982: 188
Faulconer 14BU50	N-1552	charcoal	—	3100±165	CAL B.C. 1334	CAL B.C. 1598-1590, 1527-1110, 1100-1076, 1061-1052	CAL B.C. 1745-896, 876-859, 850-844	Bradley 1973: 22
Caenen 14LV1083	ISGS-5654	charcoal	-25.7	2980±70	CAL B.C. 1203	CAL B.C. 1369-1360, 1346-1344, 1316-1113, 1097-1089, 1057-1054	CAL B.C. 1393-1005	Logan 2005c: 48
Lewis 14CS301	GAK-774	charcoal	—	2850±120				Hofman 1996: 85
DB 14LV1071	NSRL-3435	nut shell	-27.9	2610±50	CAL B.C. 794	CAL B.C. 831-762, 678-672	CAL B.C. 897-757, 689-659	Logan 1998: 129
DB 14LV1071	Beta-101875	nut shell	-25.8	2590±50	CAL B.C. 770	CAL B.C. 826-760, 681-667, 612-593, 575-564	CAL B.C. 889-882, 835-742, 723-538, 528-523	Logan 1998: 129
DB 14LV1071	Beta-101874	nut shell	-26.9	2490±70	CAL B.C. 612	CAL B.C. 764-519	CAL B.C. 789-478, 471-411	Logan 1998: 129
Coffey 14PO1	DIC-1358	charcoal	—	2480±55	CAL B.C. 608	CAL B.C. 762-677, 672-518	CAL B.C. 781-478, 471-411	Hofman 1996: 85
DB 14LV1071	NSRL-3436	nut shell	-24.6	2470±50	CAL B.C. 601	CAL B.C. 761-680, 669-610, 595-516, 460-452, 438-431, 417-414	CAL B.C. 764-410	Logan 1998: 129
Stigenwalt 14LT351	TX-5674	soil humates	—	2470±60	CAL B.C. 599	CAL B.C. 761-679, 669-609, 597-515, 462-451, 439-429, 420-414	CAL B.C. 765-408	Thies 1990

Site	Lab No.	Material		Uncorrected BP	CAL	CAL ranges	Reference
14MH1	M-868	charcoal	—	2350±250	CAL B.C. 442	CAL B.C. 796-157, 132-118	CAL B.C. 1111-1099, 1084-1060, 1053 B.C.- CAL A.D. 240	Hofman 1996: 85
Coffey 14PO1	DIC-1357	charcoal	—	2320±60	CAL B.C. 386	CAL B.C. 503-488, 484-463, 450-440, 427-422, 414-351, 316-310, 301-230, 219-209	CAL B.C. 758-683, 660-646, 586-584, 543-199, 186-183	Hofman 1996: 85
Snyder 14BU9	N-1276	charcoal	—	2060±80	CAL B.C. 83	CAL B.C. 197-191, CAL B.C. 175- CAL A.D. 28, CAL A.D. 41-50	CAL B.C. 357-282, 259-241, CAL B.C. 234- CAL A.D. 92, CAL A.D. 97-126	Hofman 1996: 85
Stigenwalt 14LT351	TX-5673	soil humates	—	1970±70	CAL B.C. 29	CAL B.C. 49- CAL A.D. 127	CAL B.C. 166-127, CAL B.C. 123- CAL A.D. 221	Thies 1990
Snyder 14BU9	N-769	charcoal	—	1970±110	CAL B.C. 26	CAL B.C. 151-134-, CAL B.C. 116- CAL A.D. 135, CAL A.D. 155-175, 193-211	CAL B.C. 354-292, 256-252, 232-217, 212 CAL B.C.- CAL A.D. 263, CAL A.D. 276-338	Hofman 1996: 85

Eastern Early Ceramic/ Plains Woodland

Site	Lab No.	Material		Uncorrected BP	CAL	CAL ranges	Reference
14WB504	UGa-4089	—	—	2565±195	CAL B.C. 673	CAL B.C. 896-876, 857-853, 843-406	CAL B.C. 1210-1200, 1192-1176, 1167-1139, 1132-200	Blakeslee and Rohn 1986
14JO46	Beta-38587	—	—	2350±60	CAL B.C. 449	CAL B.C. 741-725, 537-531, 521-362, 271-261	CAL B.C. 760-680, 667-632, 591-577, 559-351, 316-229, 220-208	Logan 1990b
Taylor Mound 14DP3	M-2343	—	—	1940±140	CAL A.D. 62	CAL B.C. 106-98, CAL B.C. 95- CAL A.D. 241	CAL B.C. 353-293, 231-218, CAL B.C. 211- CAL A.D. 403	P. J. O'Brien 1971

294 APPENDIX

Site	Lab Number	Sample Material	^{13}C Ratio	Radiocarbon Age BP and Standard Deviation	Median Probability	One Sigma Calibrated Date Range	Two Sigma Calibrated Date Range	References
Taylor Mound 14DP3	M-2345	—	—	1940±140	CAL A.D. 62	CAL B.C. 106-98, CAL B.C. 95- CAL A.D. 241	CAL B.C. 353-293, 231-218, CAL B.C. 211- CAL A.D. 403	P. J. O'Brien 1971
Macy 14RY38 14LV120	Beta-54313	—	—	1920±80	CAL A.D. 90	CAL B.C. 16-14, CAL A.D. 2-141, 148-177, 191-212	CAL B.C. 106-14, CAL A.D. 258, CAL A.D. 282-289, 299-321	W. E. Banks et al. 2001; Benison et al. 2000
	ISGS-5199	wood charcoal	-24.4	1880±80	CAL A.D. 138	CAL A.D. 33-36, 57-236	CAL B.C. 44- CAL A.D. 264, CAL A.D. 271-340	Latham and Mandel 2002: 50
Quarry Creek 14LV401	UCR-3356	—	—	1880±50	CAL A.D. 134	CAL A.D. 76-178, 190-213	CAL A.D. 5-6, 22-244, 311-315	Logan 1993
14LV120	ISGS-5200	wood charcoal	-24	1850±70	CAL A.D. 171	CAL A.D. 81-241	CAL A.D. 4-10, 19-342, 373-376	Latham and Mandel 2002: 50
Macy 14RY38	Tx-8591	—	—	1830±100	CAL A.D. 194	CAL A.D. 75-261, 278-324	CAL B.C. 39-28, 23-10, CAL B.C. 2- CAL A.D. 419	W. E. Banks et al. 2001; Benison et al. 2000
Trowbridge 14WY1	N-971	—	—	1820±150	CAL A.D. 203	CAL A.D. 31-38, 53-388	CAL B.C. 164-129, CAL B.C. 121- CAL B.C. 541	A. E. Johnson 1976b
Stiles 14WB504	UGa-4088	—	—	1795±145	CAL A.D. 231	CAL A.D. 77-402	CAL B.C. 95- CAL A.D. 563, CAL A.D. 590-596	Blakeslee and Rohn 1986
Quarry Creek 14LV401	Beta-47830	—	—	1780±60	CAL A.D. 250	CAL A.D. 134-159, 171-196, 209-263, 276-338	CAL A.D. 89-100, 125-403	Logan 1993
Macy 14RY38	Tx-8592	—	—	1690±50	CAL A.D. 353	CAL A.D. 261-279, 294-296, 323-415	CAL A.D. 237-441, 449-466, 484-489, 501-509, 517-529	W. E. Banks et al. 2001; Benison et al. 2000

Site	Sample	Material		Date	CAL A.D.	CAL A.D. ranges	CAL A.D. ranges	Reference
Trowbridge 14WY1	N-972	—	—	1690±100	CAL A.D. 714		CAL A.D. 506-935	A. E. Johnson 1976b
Trowbridge 14WY1	Sample 31	—	—	1660±45	CAL A.D. 387	CAL A.D. 263-276, 338-431	CAL A.D. 258-301, 319-471, 479-531	A. E. Johnson 1976b
Taylor Mound 14DP3	M-2344	—	—	1660±140	CAL A.D. 378	CAL A.D. 237-543, 553-556	CAL A.D. 82-646	P. J. O'Brien 1971
Quarry Creek 14LV401	Beta-47828	—	—	1650±80	CAL A.D. 399	CAL A.D. 261-278, 324-331, 336-442, 448-468, 482-530		Logan 1993
Trowbridge 14WY1	N-970	—	—	1630±100	CAL A.D. 420	CAL A.D. 261-278, 324-331, 335-540	CAL A.D. 226-599	A. E. Johnson 1976b
Quarry Creek 14LV401	Beta-47827	—	—	1590±90	CAL A.D. 467	CAL A.D. 385-564, 571-578, 588-597	CAL A.D. 179-190, 213-641	Logan 1993
Trowbridge 14WY1	N-973	—	—	1590±125	CAL A.D. 456	CAL A.D. 342-602	CAL A.D. 257-302, 318-642	A. E. Johnson 1976b
Quarry Creek 14LV401	Beta-47829	—	—	1580±80	CAL A.D. 479	CAL A.D. 405-564, 573-577, 589-597	CAL A.D. 135-158, 171-195, 209-666	Logan 1993
Trowbridge 14WY1	N-974	—	—	1550±105	CAL A.D. 498	CAL A.D. 416-617	CAL A.D. 261-278, 324-641	A. E. Johnson 1976b
14JN349	TX-6483	—	—	1530±170	CAL A.D. 503	CAL A.D. 263-275, 339-665	CAL A.D. 256-303, 317-669	Fosha and Williams 1990; Logan and Fosha 1991
Macy 14RY38	TX-8590	charcoal	—	1490±40	CAL A.D. 576	CAL A.D. 540-619, 634-635	CAL A.D. 130-783, 788-831, 838-872	W. E. Banks et al. 2001; Benison et al. 2000
Richland 14SH101	Beta-18610	—	—	1460±100	CAL A.D. 579	CAL A.D. 440-450, 466-484, 488-501, 509-517, 529-664	CAL A.D. 439-451, 463-518, 529-649	Logan 1987, 1990a
14JO57	TX-8144	wood charcoal	—	1410±60	CAL A.D. 630	CAL A.D. 565-568, 581-587, 597-678	CAL A.D. 389-776	Bevitt 1998
14JO57	TX-8145	wood charcoal	—	1400±70	CAL A.D. 639	CAL A.D. 563-590, 596-688	CAL A.D. 533-724, 740-771	Bevitt 1998

296 APPENDIX

Site	Lab Number	Sample Material	^{13}C Ratio	Radiocarbon Age BP and Standard Deviation	Median Probability	One Sigma Calibrated Date Range	Two Sigma Calibrated Date Range	References
Richland 14SH101	TX-5667	—	—	1400±100	CAL A.D. 639	CAL A.D. 541-717, 748-766	CAL A.D. 429-783, 789-830, 839-866	Logan 1987, 1990a
14AT2	Beta-10120	—	—	1350±60	CAL A.D. 683	CAL A.D. 641-719, 746-767	CAL A.D. 563-591, 596-782, 791-811, 844-851	B. G. Williams 1986
Woodruff 14PH4	C-928	—	—	1343±240	CAL A.D. 698	CAL A.D. 439-452, 463-519, 528-902, 917-962	CAL A.D. 184-186, 217-1193, 1198-1209	Libby 1955
Cow Killer 14OS347	Beta-12906	—	—	1300±100	CAL A.D. 745	CAL A.D. 649-783, 789-828, 840-863	CAL A.D. 563-591, 596-904, 915-976	Reynolds 1982
14WB504	UGa-4091	—	—	1225±75	CAL A.D. 806	CAL A.D. 693-700, 714-750, 762-888	CAL A.D. 664-904, 915-976	Blakeslee and Rohn 1986
Avoca 14JN332	Beta-33220	—	—	1220±50	CAL A.D. 801	CAL A.D. 718-742, 769-881	CAL A.D. 673-897, 922-942	Adair 2000; Baugh 1991: 105
Avoca 14JN332	AA-36102	Zea mays	-9.4	1220±40	CAL A.D. 809	CAL A.D. 728-737, 773-881	CAL A.D. 688-894, 931-935	Adair 2000; Baugh 1991
Kelley 14DP11	N-1058	—	—	1210±100	CAL A.D. 823	CAL A.D. 691-702, 710-752, 759-896, 923-940	CAL A.D. 657-1002, 1012-1016	A. E. Johnson 1976b
Senn's Hill 14JF414	Beta-29434	—	—	1200±60	CAL A.D. 829	CAL A.D. 724-740, 771-894, 925-935	CAL A.D. 689-904, 914-976	Logan 1990c
Avoca 14JN332	AA-36100	Iva annua	-28.5	1200±40	CAL A.D. 830	CAL A.D. 780-883	CAL A.D. 692-701, 714-750, 763-900, 919-959	Adair 2000; Baugh 1991
William Sherwood, Jr. 14MM509	UGa-4090	wood charcoal	—	1195±70	CAL A.D. 834	CAL A.D. 722-742, 770-897, 921-944	CAL A.D. 688-980	Blakeslee and Rohn 1986: 963
Zacharias 14LV380	Beta-36365	—	—	1190±70	CAL A.D. 839	CAL A.D. 727-738, 773-898, 921-955	CAL A.D. 689-981	Logan 1990c
Avoca 14JN332	Beta-33220	—	—	1170±50	CAL A.D. 862	CAL A.D. 780-794, 799-898, 921-944	CAL A.D. 720-745, 768-984	Adair 2000; Baugh 1991

Site	Lab #	Material	δ13C	BP	Cal intercept	Cal 1σ	Cal 2σ	Reference
Avoca 14JN332	AA-36101	Zea mays	-9.48	1165±40	CAL A.D. 870	CAL A.D. 782-791, 809-845, 849-898, 921-944, 953-955	CAL A.D. 777-977	Adair 2000; Baugh 1991
Richland 14SH101	Beta-18609	—	—	1130±60	CAL A.D. 908	CAL A.D. 783-789, 829-839, 864-986	CAL A.D. 775-1019	Logan 1987, 1990a
14MM26	N-1060	—	—	1109±105	CAL A.D. 916	CAL A.D. 782-791, 808-1019	CAL A.D. 687-1070, 1080-1127, 1136-1158	Artz et al. 1975
Kelley 14DP11	N-1059	—	—	1100±100	CAL A.D. 925	CAL A.D. 782-791, 810-844, 854-1022	CAL A.D. 708-753, 758-1071, 1079-1129, 1136-1158	A. E. Johnson 1976b
14AT2	Beta-10122	—	—	1030±60	CAL A.D. 1005	CAL A.D. 899-920, 957-1040, 1100-1116, 1142-1151	CAL A.D. 891-1159	Williams 1986
14JF350	I-11371	—	—	1000±95	CAL A.D. 1044	CAL A.D. 903-915, 964-971, 975-1160	CAL A.D. 783-789, 827-841, 862-1251	Witty 1983
Avoca 14JN332	AA-36099	Iva annua	-23.4	985±40	CAL A.D. 1060	CAL A.D. 1000-1043, 1091-1119, 1140-1155	CAL A.D. 986-1074, 1076-1159	Adair 2000; Baugh 1991
Avoca 14JN332	—	—	—	920±60	CAL A.D. 1113	CAL A.D. 1034-1163, 1174-1178	CAL A.D. 1003-1010, 1016-1224, 1229-1242	Adair 2000; Baugh 1991
14MY2336	Beta-63728	charcoal	—	850±60	CAL A.D. 1180	CAL A.D. 1067-1082, 1124-1137, 1157-1261	CAL A.D. 1039-1142, 1150-1277	Schoen 1993
Zacharias 14LV380	AA-43407	Prunus sp.	-25.3	789±39	CAL A.D. 1244	CAL A.D. 1223-1275	CAL A.D. 1164-1168, 1186-1289	Kansas archaeological site file

Western Early Ceramic/ Plains Woodland

Site	Lab #	Material	δ13C	BP	Cal intercept	Cal 1σ	Cal 2σ	Reference
25HK13	M-181	—	—	2080±250	CAL B.C. 116	CAL B.C. 396-178, 190-213	CAL B.C. 765-423	Unpublished
25RW28	UM-470	—	—	1940±80	CAL A.D. 65	CAL B.C. 43- CAL A.D. 134, CAL A.D. 162-168, 199-207	CAL B.C. 160-131, CAL B.C. 119- CAL A.D. 244, CAL A.D. 312-315	Unpublished

Site	Lab Number	Sample Material	^{13}C Ratio	Radiocarbon Age BP and Standard Deviation	Median Probability	One Sigma Calibrated Date Range	Two Sigma Calibrated Date Range	References
25RW28	UM-549	—	—	1920±70	CAL A.D. 89	CAL A.D. 2-135, 155-174, 193-210	CAL B.C. 88-79, CAL B.C. 55-CAL A.D. 255, CAL A.D. 304-316	Unpublished
25GO2	Beta-28891	—	—	1600±50	CAL A.D. 466	CAL A.D. 415-535	CAL A.D. 265-267, 341-598	Unpublished
25HN174	Beta-10209	—	—	1600±100	CAL A.D. 454	CAL A.D. 343-371, 378-563, 590-596	CAL A.D. 241-645	Unpublished
25FT18	SI-126	—	—	1580±100	CAL A.D. 470	CAL A.D. 360-367, 382-603	CAL A.D. 236-663	Unpublished
25GO2	Beta-28890	—	—	1450±60	CAL A.D. 597	CAL A.D. 544-550, 558-656	CAL A.D. 436-522, 527-685	Unpublished
25RW28	SI-68	—	—	1430±45	CAL A.D. 621	CAL A.D. 598-660	CAL A.D. 541-672	Unpublished
25RW28	UM-466	—	—	1370±100	CAL A.D. 671	CAL A.D. 564-571, 578-588, 597-776	CAL A.D. 438-452, 462-519, 528-889	Unpublished
14SD351	ISGS-5358	charcoal	-25.1	1370±70	CAL A.D. 667	CAL A.D. 604-694, 698-716, 749-765	CAL A.D. 538-782, 791-814, 843-857	Hoard et al. 2005
Woodruff 14PH4	C-928	—	—	1343±240	CAL A.D. 694	CAL A.D. 435-904, 913-976	CAL A.D. 134-163, 167-200, 207-1214	Libby 1955: 104
25FT70	SI-197	—	—	1260±80	CAL A.D. 773	CAL A.D. 679-783, 789-829, 839-864	CAL A.D. 644-903, 916-963	Unpublished
25HN12	UGa-5478	—	—	1250±110	CAL A.D. 791	CAL A.D. 676-887	A.D. 605-1000	Adair and Brown 1987: 96
25HN12	DIC-3325	—	—	1220±55	CAL A.D. 809	CAL A.D. 721-744, 769-887	CAL A.D. 681-899, 919-958	Adair and Brown 1987: 96
25HO23	M-637	—	—	1131±238	CAL A.D. 895	CAL A.D. 663-1072, 1078-1130, 1136-1158	CAL A.D. 412-1322, 1350-1390	Unpublished
25FT18	M-841	—	—	1130±200	CAL A.D. 901	CAL A.D. 683-1040, 1099-1116, 1141-1151	CAL A.D. 544-547, 559-1278	Unpublished

Site	Lab #	Material		BP	CAL A.D.	CAL A.D.	CAL A.D.	Reference
25FT70	SI-50	—		1070±70	CAL A.D. 961	CAL A.D. 893-1022	CAL A.D. 779-1059, 1087-1122, 1138-1156	Unpublished
25HN12	UGa-5482	—		1050±70	CAL A.D. 984	CAL A.D. 894-1034	CAL A.D. 782-790, 812-843, 857-1160	Adair and Brown 1987: 96
25MO86	WIS-1795	—		970±70	CAL A.D. 1083	CAL A.D. 1002-1012, 1016-1159	CAL A.D. 897-922, 943-1223, 1233-1237	Unpublished
25SX405	NWU-61	—		750±90	CAL A.D. 1252	CAL A.D. 1163-1172, 1182-1311, 1354-1387	CAL A.D. 1039-1103, 1115-1142, 1151-1404	Unpublished

Central Plains Tradition

Steed-Kisker Phase

Site	Lab #	Material		BP	CAL A.D.	CAL A.D.	CAL A.D.	Reference
23CL109	UGa-1446	charcoal	—	1260±90	CAL A.D. 776	CAL A.D. 677-783, 788-831, 838-873	CAL A.D. 642-977	P. J. O'Brien 1977
23CL113	GAK-1995	charcoal	—	1190±80				Calabrese 1969; Chapman 1980
Zacharias 14LV380	Beta-36365	—	—	1190±70	CAL A.D. 839	CAL A.D. 727-738, 773-898, 921-955	CAL A.D. 689-981	Logan, ed. 1990c
23CL16	UGa-379	—	—	1180±110	CAL A.D. 848	CAL A.D. 723-741, 771-977	CAL A.D. 646-1037, 1144-1148	Chapman 1980
23CL18	M-2179	charcoal	—	1170±150	CAL A.D. 862	CAL A.D. 692-702, 711-752, 760-996	CAL A.D. 604-1164, 1171-1185	Calabrese 1969; Chapman 1980
23PL13	M-1397	—	—	1090±110	CAL A.D. 933	CAL A.D. 781-793, 802-1029	CAL A.D. 689-1162	Chapman 1980; Shippee 1972
23PL48	M-1182	—	—	1075±150	CAL A.D. 952	CAL A.D. 778-1045, 1052-1055, 1088-1121, 1138-1156	CAL A.D. 667-1223, 1232-1238	Chapman 1980; Shippee 1972
23PL16	UGa-467	—	—	1045±60	CAL A.D. 989	CAL A.D. 897-922, 943-1033	CAL A.D. 784-787, 879-1159	Chapman 1980

APPENDIX

Site	Lab Number	Sample Material	^{13}C Ratio	Radiocarbon Age BP and Standard Deviation	Median Probability	One Sigma Calibrated Date Range	Two Sigma Calibrated Date Range	References
23CL108	UGa-1149	charcoal	—	995±70	CAL A.D. 1053	CAL A.D. 982-1068, 1081-1125, 1137-1158	CAL A.D. 896-923, 939-1210	P. J. O'Brien 1977
23CL113	GAK-1993	charcoal	—	980±90				Calabrese 1969; Chapman 1980
23CL108	UGa-1201	charcoal	—	980±65	CAL A.D. 1074	CAL A.D. 998-1069, 1081-1125, 1136-1158	CAL A.D. 902-917, 961-1213	P. J. O'Brien 1977
23PL13	M-1395b	—	—	950±110	CAL A.D. 1091	CAL A.D. 1000-1193, 1198-1209	CAL A.D. 886-1284	Chapman 1980; Shippee 1972
23CL108	UGa-1200	charcoal	—	920±70	CAL A.D. 1115	CAL A.D. 1032-1164, 1171-1183	CAL A.D. 1001-1254	P. J. O'Brien 1977
Zacharias 14LV380	Beta-36366	—	—	910±50	CAL A.D. 1117	CAL A.D. 1039-1104, 1109-1142, 1150-1164, 1171-1184	CAL A.D. 1021-1221	Logan 1990c
23CL113	GAK-1994	charcoal	—	900±90				Calabrese 1969; Chapman 1980
Zacharias 14LV380	Beta-34371	—	—	900±50	CAL A.D. 1125	CAL A.D. 1041-1097, 1117-1141, 1152-1191, 1201-1207	CAL A.D. 1023-1223, 1232-1239	Logan 1990c
23PL4	M-2347	—	—	880±110	CAL A.D. 1140	CAL A.D. 1037-1144, 1148-1224, 1230-1239	CAL A.D. 902-917, 962-1301, 1372-1378	Chapman 1980; Shippee 1972
23PL13	GAK-590	—	—	870±80				Chapman 1980; Shippee 1972
23CL109	UGa-1445	charcoal	—	865±70	CAL A.D. 1162	CAL A.D. 1044-1089, 1121-1139, 1156-1244	CAL A.D. 1032-1275	P. J. O'Brien 1977

Site	Lab number	Material	δ13C	BP	CAL A.D.	CAL A.D. range	Reference
23CL113	M-9036/7	charcoal	—	850±110	CAL A.D. 1165	CAL A.D. 1042-1092, 1118-1140, 1154-1273	CAL A.D. 982-1308, 1354-1387	Calabrese 1969; Chapman 1980
14WY7	UGa-1454	charcoal	—	845±80	CAL A.D. 1176	CAL A.D. 1060-1086, 1122-1138, 1156-1271	CAL A.D. 1027-1285	Barnes 1977
23PL13	M-1995a	—	—	840±110	CAL A.D. 1172	CAL A.D. 1043-1091, 1120-1139, 1155-1278	CAL A.D. 991-1315, 1353-1387	Chapman 1980; Shippee 1972
23CL109	UGa-1447	charcoal	—	835±75	CAL A.D. 1187	CAL A.D. 1068-1081, 1125-1136, 1158-1277	CAL A.D. 1034-1287	P. J. O'Brien 1977
Scott 14LV1082	OS-44503	burned nutshell	-26.74	770±25	CAL A.D. 1260	CAL A.D. 1246-1281	CAL A.D. 1221-1284	Logan 2004: 50
23PL13	M-1398	—	—	740±100	CAL A.D. 1261	CAL A.D. 1189-1321, 1351-1389	CAL A.D. 1040-1099, 1116-1141, 1151-1409	Chapman 1980; Shippee 1972
23PL13	M-1399	—	—	720±100	CAL A.D. 1279	CAL A.D. 1216-1326, 1347-1392	CAL A.D. 1043-1090, 1120-1139, 1155-1421	Chapman 1980; Shippee 1972
23CL109	UGa-1448	charcoal	—	695±100	CAL A.D. 1300	CAL A.D. 1225-1226, 1243-1331, 1341-1397	CAL A.D. 1066-1083, 1123-1137, 1157-1436	P. J. O'Brien 1977
23PL54	GAK-330	—	—	690±90				Chapman 1980; Shippee 1972
23PL6	GAK-266	—	—	660±80				Chapman 1980; Shippee 1972
23PL4	M-2346	—	—	660±100	CAL A.D. 1327	CAL A.D. 1277-1402	CAL A.D. 1163-1173, 1179-1443	Chapman 1980; Shippee 1972
23PL16	UGa-466	—	—	645±60	CAL A.D. 1345	CAL A.D. 1294-1327, 1347-1392	CAL A.D. 1275-1414	Chapman 1980
23PL16	UGa-392	—	—	635±60	CAL A.D. 1347	CAL A.D. 1297-1328, 1345-1393	CAL A.D. 1279-1414	Chapman 1980
Scott 14LV1082	ISGS-5074	charcoal	-25.9	630±70	CAL A.D. 1347	CAL A.D. 1297-1330, 1342-1396	CAL A.D. 1274-1429	Logan 2004: 50

Site	Lab Number	Sample Material	^{13}C Ratio	Radiocarbon Age BP and Standard Deviation	Median Probability	One Sigma Calibrated Date Range	Two Sigma Calibrated Date Range	References
Scott 14LV1082	ISGS-5540	charcoal	-25.3	610±70	CAL A.D. 1351	CAL A.D. 1301-1334, 1337-1371, 1379-1400	CAL A.D. 1282-1430	Logan 2004: 50
Caenen 14LV1083	OS-49053	nut shell	-28.59	415±25	CAL A.D. 1459	CAL A.D. 1441-1473	CAL A.D. 1434-1501, 1506-1511, 1602-1615	Logan 2005c: 47
Nebraska Phase (note: many other dates have been run from sites in Nebraska and Iowa)								
25RH1	SI-618	charcoal	—	1170±60	CAL A.D. 860	CAL A.D. 780-794, 797-898, 921-955	CAL A.D. 692-700, 714-750, 763-993	Bozell and Ludwickson 1994
14DP10	Wis-326	charcoal	—	860±55	CAL A.D. 1172	CAL A.D. 1064-1084, 1123-1137, 1157-1254	CAL A.D. 1038-1143, 1149-1270	W. R. Wood, ed. 1969
23AN56	Beta-10693	—	—	830±90	CAL A.D. 1185	CAL A.D. 1062-1085, 1123-1138, 1157-1280	CAL A.D. 1020-1300, 1372-1378	Bozell and Ludwickson 1994
23AN56	Beta-10692	—	—	670±70	CAL A.D. 1327	CAL A.D. 1281-1326, 1347-1392	CAL A.D. 1224-1230, 1238-1412	Bozell and Ludwickson 1994
25RH1	SI-619	charcoal	—	620±100	CAL A.D. 1348	CAL A.D. 1292-1407	CAL A.D. 1212-1476	Bozell and Ludwickson 1994
14DP10	GAK-1672	charcoal	—	420±90				W. R. Wood, ed. 1969
14DP13	M-1069	—	—	390±75				Bozell and Ludwickson 1994
14DP10	GAK-1673	charcoal	—	370±90	CAL A.D. 1522	CAL A.D. 1440-1522, 1569-1627	CAL A.D. 1415-1649	W. R. Wood, ed. 1969
Smoky Hill Phase								
14RY3183	ISGS-3135	—	—	14,610±100	CAL B.C. 15,550	CAL B.C. 15,818-15,267	CAL B.C. 16,115-15,010	
14SA403	GAK-2795	charcoal	—	14,40±90				Kansas archaeological site file

Site	Lab number	Material	δ13C	RCYBP	Intercept	2σ range	Reference
14SA403	GAK-2794	charcoal	—	1320±80			Kansas archaeological site file
14RY8	TX-5914	charcoal	—	1090±80	CAL A.D. 937	CAL A.D. 783-788, 831-838, 873-1023	CAL A.D. 722-742, 770-1065, 1084-1124, 1137-1157	Schmits, Mandel, et al. 1987
14JW301	GAK-593	—	—	1040±100			Steinacher 1976
14RY8	TX-5913	charcoal	—	1010±210	CAL A.D. 1010	CAL A.D. 782-790, 816-842, 859-1221	CAL A.D. 646-1322, 1350-1390	Schmits, Mandel, et al. 1987
14LC301	I-509	charcoal	—	963±100	CAL A.D. 1084	CAL A.D. 995-1188	CAL A.D. 891-1268	Witty 1962
14GE21	SI-230	—	—	920±90	CAL A.D. 1115	CAL A.D. 1026-1190, 1203-1206	CAL A.D. 977-1280	Steinacher 1976
Whiteford (Indian Burial Pit) 14SA1	Beta-178533	Zea mays	-8.6	870±40	CAL A.D. 1168	CAL A.D. 1060-1086, 1122-1138, 1156-1221	CAL A.D. 1039-1104, 1109-1142, 1150-1257	Roper 2003
Griffing 14RY21	UGa-465	charcoal	—	860±60	CAL A.D. 1170	CAL A.D. 1061-1086, 1122-1138, 1156-1256	CAL A.D. 1037-1143, 1148-1273	M. E. Brown 1981
14SA403	Beta-177518	charcoal	-23.6	860±60	CAL A.D. 1170	CAL A.D. 1061-1086, 1122-1138, 1156-1256	CAL A.D. 1037-1143, 1148-1273	Roper and Reed 2003
14GE600	UGa-826	charcoal	—	835±65	CAL A.D. 1192	CAL A.D. 1072-1078, 1131-1136, 1158-1276	CAL A.D. 1039-1142, 1150-1283	M. E. Brown 1981
Kohr House 1 14SA414	Beta-178238	Zea mays	-9.7	820±40	CAL A.D. 1224	CAL A.D. 1190-1202, 1207-1265	CAL A.D. 1071-1079, 1125-1136, 1158-1283	Roper and Reed 2003
Griffing 14RY21	UGa-828	charcoal	—	810±60	CAL A.D. 1219	CAL A.D. 1164-1169, 1186-1279	CAL A.D. 1041-1094, 1117-1141, 1153-1295	M. E. Brown 1981
14CY30	M-113	charcoal	—	774±150	CAL A.D. 1219	CAL A.D. 1044-1090, 1120-1139, 1155-1313, 1354-1387	CAL A.D. 978-1440	Witty 1963

304 APPENDIX

Site	Lab Number	Sample Material	^{13}C Ratio	Radiocarbon Age BP and Standard Deviation	Median Probability	One Sigma Calibrated Date Range	Two Sigma Calibrated Date Range	References
14GE21	SI-231	—	—	770±80	CAL A.D. 1240	CAL A.D. 1163-1172, 1182-1299	CAL A.D. 1040-1099, 1116-1141, 1151-1327, 1346-1393	Steinacher 1976
14RY3183	ISGS-3134	—	—	760±70	CAL A.D. 1251	CAL A.D. 1192-1199, 1208-1299	CAL A.D. 1057-1087, 1121-1138, 1156-1328, 1345-1394	Kansas archaeological site file
Budenbender 14PO4	M-869	charcoal	—	760±150	CAL A.D. 1231	CAL A.D. 1061-1086, 1123-1138, 1157-1327, 1346-1393	CAL A.D. 983-1442	A. E. Johnson 1973
14CY30	GAK-295	charcoal	—	750±120				Witty 1963
14RY128	ISGS-3137	—	—	740±240	CAL A.D. 1237	CAL A.D. 1025-1424	CAL A.D. 727-737, 773-1660	Kansas archaeological site file
Minneapolis 14OT5	Beta-16479	charcoal	—	730±70	CAL A.D. 1276	CAL A.D. 1218-1304, 1367-1385	CAL A.D. 1163-1332, 1338-1399	Beck 1998
14OT308	Beta-173317	charcoal	-25.0	730±60	CAL A.D. 1277	CAL A.D. 1223-1233, 1237-1301, 1371-1379	CAL A.D. 1188-1329, 1343-1395	Roper and Reed 2003
14SA415	Beta-177519	charcoal	-25.1	710±60	CAL A.D. 1291	CAL A.D. 1256-1312, 1354-1387	CAL A.D. 1215-1332, 1339-1398	Roper and Reed 2003
14RY3183	ISGS-3138	—	—	700±80	CAL A.D. 1299	CAL A.D. 1255-1327, 1346-1393	CAL A.D. 1164-1169, 1185-1414	Kansas archaeological site file
14GE600	UGa-824	charcoal	—	700±75	CAL A.D. 1300	CAL A.D. 1258-1325, 1349-1391	CAL A.D. 1190-1202, 1206-1411	M. E. Brown 1981
Minneapolis 14OT5	Beta-16480	charcoal	—	680±70	CAL A.D. 1319	CAL A.D. 1277-1326, 1347-1392	CAL A.D. 1222-1407	Beck 1998
Griffing 14RY21	UGa-827	charcoal	—	670±60	CAL A.D. 1329	CAL A.D. 1282-1323, 1350-1390	CAL A.D. 1255-1409	M. E. Brown 1981

Site	Lab number	Material		Date	CAL A.D.	CAL A.D.	CAL A.D.	Reference
14RY383	ISGS-3141	—	—	670±190		CAL A.D. 1068-1081, 1125-1136, 1158-1445	CAL A.D. 981-1649	Kansas archaeological site file
14RY442	UGa-3867	—	—	660±165	CAL A.D. 1314	CAL A.D. 1188-1440	CAL A.D. 1021-1525, 1558-1630	Kansas archaeological site file
14RY383	ISGS-3133	—	—	630±70	CAL A.D. 1347	CAL A.D. 1297-1330, 1342-1396	CAL A.D. 1274-1429	Kansas archaeological site file
14WH319	Beta-45873	charcoal	—	630±50	CAL A.D. 1349	CAL A.D. 1299-1327, 1346-1393	CAL A.D. 1286-1406	Kansas archaeological site file
14GE600	UGa-825	charcoal	—	595±60	CAL A.D. 1353	CAL A.D. 1304-1367, 1384-1403	CAL A.D. 1292-1427	M. E. Brown 1981
14CY17	Beta-46652	charcoal	—	580±50	CAL A.D. 1354	CAL A.D. 1305-1355, 1364-1365, 1386-1410	CAL A.D. 1299-1426	Ritterbush and Logan 1991
14CY102	GAK-803	—	—	420±90				Steinacher 1976
14GE21	SI-232	—	—	410±100	CAL A.D. 1514	CAL A.D. 1426-1525, 1557-1631	CAL A.D. 1306-1365, 1386-1669, 1781-1796	Steinacher 1976
Griffing 14RY21	GAK-1448	charcoal	—	370±70				Steinacher 1976
Griffing 14RY21	GAK-1449	charcoal	—	320±80				Steinacher 1976
Griffing 14RY21	GAK-1446	charcoal	—	320±100				Steinacher 1976
Griffing 14RY21	GAK-1447	charcoal	—	260±70				Steinacher 1976
Griffing 14RY21	GAK-1450	charcoal	—	250±70				Steinacher 1976
14RY442	UGa-3868	—	—	250±440	CAL A.D. 1566	CAL A.D. 1424-1955	CAL A.D. 904-911, 976-1955	Kansas archaeological site file

Waconda Locality

Site	Lab number	Material		Date				Reference
14OB27	GAK-1090	charcoal	—	1380±80				Blakeslee 1999
14OB27	GAK-1536	charcoal	—	1360±70				Blakeslee 1999
14ML15	GAK-804	charcoal	—	1340±90				Blakeslee 1999

306 APPENDIX

Site	Lab Number	Sample Material	^{13}C Ratio	Radiocarbon Age BP and Standard Deviation	Median Probability	One Sigma Calibrated Date Range	Two Sigma Calibrated Date Range	References
14OB27	GAK-1088	charcoal	—	1270±90				Blakeslee 1999
14ML17	GAK-1087	charcoal	—	1140±100				Blakeslee 1999
14ML371	GAK-1091	charcoal	—	1120±80				Blakeslee 1999
14ML15	Beta-54043	charcoal	-26.5	920±70	CAL A.D. 1115	CAL A.D. 1032-1164, 1171-1183	CAL A.D. 1001-1254	Blakeslee 1999
14ML5	Beta-54039	charcoal	-26.6	880±50	CAL A.D. 1149	CAL A.D. 1044-1089, 1120-1139, 1155-1217	CAL A.D. 1035-1254	Blakeslee 1999
14ML15	Beta-54047	charcoal	-27.1	880±50	CAL A.D. 1149	CAL A.D. 1044-1089, 1120-1139, 1155-1217	CAL A.D. 1035-1254	Blakeslee 1999
14ML15	Beta-54046	charcoal	-25.3	870±60	CAL A.D. 1160	CAL A.D. 1043-1091, 1120-1139, 1155-1223, 1232-1238	CAL A.D. 1032-1264	Blakeslee 1999
14ML15	GAK-1089	charcoal	—	860±80				Blakeslee 1999
14ML5	Beta-54040	charcoal	-25.7	860±50	CAL A.D. 1174	CAL A.D. 1065-1084, 1123-1137, 1157-1249	CAL A.D. 1038-1143, 1149-1266	Blakeslee 1999
14ML417	Beta-3334	charcoal	—	850±80	CAL A.D. 1171	CAL A.D. 1045-1047, 1056-1087, 122-1138, 156-264	CAL A.D. 1027-1283	Blakeslee 1999
14ML310	Beta-54050	charcoal	-26.4	820±50	CAL A.D. 1217	CAL A.D. 1164-1167, 1187-1273	CAL A.D. 1044-1089, 1120-1139, 1155-1286	Blakeslee 1999
14ML16	Beta-54048	charcoal	-26.2	800±50	CAL A.D. 1232	CAL A.D. 1194-1196, 1210-1279	CAL A.D. 1067-1082, 1124-1137, 1157-1295	Blakeslee 1999
14ML15	Beta-54045	charcoal	-26.1	780±50	CAL A.D. 1244	CAL A.D. 1220-1281	CAL A.D. 1160-1299, 1374-1376	Blakeslee 1999
14ML16	GAK-638	charcoal	—	760±50				Blakeslee 1999

Site	Lab #	Material	δ13C	BP	CAL A.D.	CAL A.D. (range)	Reference
14ML15	Beta-54044	charcoal	-24.7	740±50	CAL A.D. 1270	CAL A.D. 1224-1228, 1241-1297	CAL A.D. 1191-1201, 1207-1316, 1353-1388	Blakeslee 1999
14ML11	Beta-54042	charcoal	-27.0	720±150	CAL A.D. 1266	CAL A.D. 1163-1404	CAL A.D. 999-1471	Blakeslee 1999
14ML376	Beta-54051	charcoal	-26.5	660±50	CAL A.D. 1343	CAL A.D. 1288-1320, 1351-1389	CAL A.D. 1277-1402	Blakeslee 1999
14ML306	GAK-802	charcoal	—	620±90				Blakeslee 1999
14ML306	Beta-54049	charcoal	-26.7	620±50	CAL A.D. 1349	CAL A.D. 1301-1329, 1343-1372, 1379-1395	CAL A.D. 1289-1410	Blakeslee 1999
14ML5	GAK-639	charcoal	—	610±100				Blakeslee 1999
14ML8	Beta-54041	charcoal	-28.6	560±50	CAL A.D. 1365	CAL A.D. 1317-1353, 1388-1425	CAL A.D. 1301-1372, 1379-1436	Blakeslee 1999
14OB27	GAK-1535	charcoal	—	470±80				Blakeslee 1999
14ML5	GAK-801	charcoal	—	410±80				Blakeslee 1999
14ML5	GAK-640	charcoal	—	230±90				Blakeslee 1999

Medicine Creek Locality

Site	Lab #	Material	δ13C	BP	CAL A.D.	CAL A.D. (range)	Reference
25FT70	SI-50	charcoal	—	1070±70	CAL A.D. 961		CAL A.D. 779-1059, 1087-1122, 1138-1156	Kivett and Metcalf 1997
25FT70	SI-197	charcoal	—	1070±70	CAL A.D. 961		CAL A.D. 779-1059, 1087-1122, 1138-1156	Kivett and Metcalf 1997
25FT13	SI-88	charcoal	—	940±60	CAL A.D. 1102	CAL A.D. 1027-1074, 1076-1133, 1135-1159	CAL A.D. 996-1219	Kivett and Metcalf 1997
25FT16	SI-194	charcoal	—	930±80	CAL A.D. 1109	CAL A.D. 1024-1164, 1170-1185	CAL A.D. 982-1263	Kivett and Metcalf 1997
25FT13	SI-87	charcoal	—	930±60	CAL A.D. 1107	CAL A.D. 1033-1160	CAL A.D. 999-1222	Kivett and Metcalf 1997
25FT35	Wis-324	charcoal	—	930±60	CAL A.D. 1107	CAL A.D. 1033-1160	CAL A.D. 999-1222	W. R. Wood, ed. 1969
25FT17	SI-36	charcoal	—	865±65	CAL A.D. 1163	CAL A.D. 1045-1088, 1121-1139, 1156-1243	CAL A.D. 1034-1272	Kivett and Metcalf 1997

Site	Lab Number	Sample Material	^{13}C Ratio	Radiocarbon Age BP and Standard Deviation	Median Probability	One Sigma Calibrated Date Range	Two Sigma Calibrated Date Range	References
25FT70	SI-53	charcoal	—	845±65	CAL A.D. 1182	CAL A.D. 1066-1083, 1124-1137, 1157-1265	CAL A.D. 1038-1143, 1149-1280	Kivett and Metcalf 1997
25FT17	SI-32	charcoal	—	830±100	CAL A.D. 1182	CAL A.D. 1045-1048, 1056-1087, 1121-1138, 1156-1281	CAL A.D. 1002-1013, 1016-1305, 1355-1358, 1365-1386	Kivett and Metcalf 1997
25FT70	SI-73	charcoal	—	820±50	CAL A.D. 1217	CAL A.D. 1164-1167, 1187-1273	CAL A.D. 1044-1089, 1120-1139, 1155-1286	Kivett and Metcalf 1997
25FT36	SI-193	charcoal	—	800±100	CAL A.D. 1208	CAL A.D. 1064-1085, 1123-1137, 1157-1295	CAL A.D. 1023-1320, 1351-1389	Kivett and Metcalf 1997
25FT70	SI-47	charcoal	—	790±65	CAL A.D. 1231	CAL A.D. 1189-1286	CAL A.D. 1041-1096, 1116-1141, 1152-1302, 1370-1381	Kivett and Metcalf 1997
25FT35	Wis-318	charcoal	—	790±55	CAL A.D. 1236	CAL A.D. 1194-1196, 1210-1283	CAL A.D. 1060-1086, 1122-1138, 1156-1299, 1374-1376	W. R. Wood, ed. 1969
25FT17	I-585	charcoal	—	780±125	CAL A.D. 1219	CAL A.D. 1045-1088, 1121-1138, 1156-1303, 1368-1383	CAL A.D. 1019-1407	Kivett and Metcalf 1997
25FT35	Wis-319	charcoal	—	770±55	CAL A.D. 1249	CAL A.D. 1219-1286,	CAL A.D. 1072-1078, 1128-1136, 1158-1304, 1367-1384	W. R. Wood, ed. 1969
25FT36	SI-192	charcoal	—	750±80	CAL A.D. 1257	CAL A.D. 1190-1203, 1206-1303, 1368-1383	CAL A.D. 1045-1088, 1121-1139, 1156-1333, 1338-1399	Kivett and Metcalf 1997

25FT39	SI-56	charcoal	—	750±80	CAL A.D. 1257	CAL A.D. 1190-1203, 1206-1303, 1368-1383	CAL A.D. 1045-1088, 1121-1139, 1156-1333, 1338-1399	Kivett and Metcalf 1997
25FT16	I-583	charcoal	—	715±125	CAL A.D. 1276	CAL A.D. 1192-1199, 1209-1334, 1337-1400	CAL A.D. 1038-1143, 1149-1433	Kivett and Metcalf 1997
25FT17	SI-40	charcoal	—	710±65	CAL A.D. 1292	CAL A.D. 1253-1316, 1353-1388	CAL A.D. 1194-1197, 1210-1402	Kivett and Metcalf 1997
25FT13	I-584	charcoal	—	510±100	CAL A.D. 1418	CAL A.D. 1303-1368, 1384-1478	CAL A.D. 1288-1528, 1551-1633	Kivett and Metcalf 1997
25FT70	M-844	charcoal	—	500±200	CAL A.D. 1457	CAL A.D. 1291-1533, 1539-1636	CAL A.D. 1074-1076, 1159-1888, 1910-1950	Kivett and Metcalf 1997

Red Willow Locality

25FT80	UM-467	charcoal	—	1457±174	CAL A.D. 578	CAL A.D. 407-727, 738-773	CAL A.D. 232-904, 911-976	Grange 1980
25FT54	SI-70	charcoal	—	640±50	CAL A.D. 1348	CAL A.D. 1297-1325, 1349-1391	CAL A.D. 1284-1403	Grange 1980
25FT32	M-1365	charcoal	—	565±100	CAL A.D. 1374	CAL A.D. 1301-1371, 1380-1432	CAL A.D. 1257-1521, 1586-1625	Grange 1980
25FT80	SI-72	charcoal	—	440±40	CAL A.D. 1454	CAL A.D. 1429-1478	CAL A.D. 1409-1518, 1596-1620	Grange 1980

Other Republican River Valley

25HN36	I-641		—	875±100	CAL A.D. 1146	CAL A.D. 1039-1104, 1112-1142, 1150-1224, 1228-1241	CAL A.D. 986-1295	Newman 1967
25HN36	I-642		—	750±100	CAL A.D. 1252	CAL A.D. 1163-1172, 1182-1312, 1354-1387	CAL A.D. 1039-1103, 1114-1142, 1150-1404	Newman 1967

Site	Lab Number	Sample Material	^{13}C Ratio	Radiocarbon Age BP and Standard Deviation	Median Probability	One Sigma Calibrated Date Range	Two Sigma Calibrated Date Range	References
Other Upper Republican								
Albert Bell 14SD305	Beta-179560	charcoal	-23.5	710±60	CAL A.D. 1291	CAL A.D. 1256-1312, 1354-1387	CAL A.D. 1215-1332, 1339-1398	KSHS archaeological site files
Pomona								
23BE149	GAK-1177	charcoal	—	2070±100				R. Vehik 1978
14CF320	I-11165*	charcoal	—	1770±80	CAL A.D. 258	CAL A.D. 137-199, 206-304	CAL A.D. 71-427	Thies 1981
23BE149	GAK-1176	charcoal	—	1400±100				R. Vehik 1978
14AT2	Beta-10120*	charcoal	—	1350±60	CAL A.D. 677	CAL A.D. 635-715, 744-768	CAL A.D. 569-782, 790-809	B. G. Williams 1986: 43
14BO319	I-12327*	charcoal	—	1230±180	CAL A.D. 810	CAL A.D. 653-984	CAL A.D. 434-493, 507-520, 527-1167	Brogan 1982: 68
14MM506	UGa-2666*	charcoal	—	1175±130	CAL A.D. 852	CAL A.D. 695-696, 708-747, 766-983	CAL A.D. 635-1055, 1077-1154	Blakeslee and Rohn 1986
14JO46	Beta-35858*	—	—	1150±110	CAL A.D. 873	CAL A.D. 728-736, 772-993	CAL A.D. 657-1046, 1090-1121, 1139-1149	Logan, ed. 1990c
14BO319	I-12338*	charcoal	—	1100±90	CAL A.D. 924	CAL A.D. 783-788, 816-843, 859-1022	CAL A.D. 691-750, 762-1052, 1080-1128, 1133-1152	Brogan 1982: 68
Two Deer 14BU55	UGa-2503	charcoal	—	1090±55	CAL A.D. 945	CAL A.D. 894-929, 935-1000	CAL A.D. 782-791, 808-1026	Adair and Brown 1981: 253
14DO32	Beta-1861l*	—	—	1090±50	CAL A.D. 946	CAL A.D. 894-928, 933-994	CAL A.D. 783-788, 812-845, 857-1026	Logan 1987
14DO19	UGa-4705*	charcoal	—	1075±65	CAL A.D. 955	CAL A.D. 894-928, 933-1019	CAL A.D. 778-1046, 1090-1121, 1139-1149	K. L. Brown 1985: 66

Site	Sample	Material		Date B.P.	Calibrated Intercept	1-Sigma Range	2-Sigma Range	Reference
Two Deer 14BU55	UGa-2500	charcoal	—	1065±65	CAL A.D. 967	CAL A.D. 894-925, 935-1023	CAL A.D. 781-792, 804-1057, 1087-1122, 1138-1156	Adair and Brown 1981: 253
14MY316	GAK-599	charcoal	—	1050±100				Marshall 1972: 147
14MM506	UGa-2670*	charcoal	—	1045±130	CAL A.D. 983	CAL A.D. 870-1158	CAL A.D. 689-752, 761-1223	Blakeslee and Rohn 1986
14DO154	GX-6488*	charcoal	—	1040±150	CAL A.D. 986	CAL A.D. 784-787, 825-841, 862-1162	CAL A.D. 688-753, 759-1256	Nathan 1980
14AT2	Beta-10122*	charcoal	—	1030±60	CAL A.D. 1004	CAL A.D. 898-919, 947-1043, 1105-1118, 1144-1146	CAL A.D. 890-1155	B. G. Williams 1986: 43
14CF1320	I-11166*	charcoal	—	990±80	CAL A.D. 1057	CAL A.D. 987-1155	CAL A.D. 891-1216	Thies 1981
14AT427	TX-7774*	—	—	990±60	CAL A.D. 1058	CAL A.D. 990-1052, 1081-1128, 1134-1152	CAL A.D. 898-920, 946-1185, 1202-1205	Logan and Ritterbush 1994: 18
Two Deer 14BU55	UGa-2501	charcoal	—	985±45	CAL A.D. 1063	CAL A.D. 998-1045, 1088-1121, 1138-1156	CAL A.D. 979-1163, 1174-1178	Adair and Brown 1981: 253
Two Deer 14BU55	UGa-1346	charcoal	—	970±80	CAL A.D. 1083	CAL A.D. 1000-1160	CAL A.D. 896-923, 941-1224, 1230-1241	Adair and Brown 1981: 253; Fulmer 1977
14DO19	Beta-19873*	—	—	970±60	CAL A.D. 1084	CAL A.D. 1017-1058, 1073-1155	CAL A.D. 973-1212	Logan 1987
14DO32	UGa-4704*	charcoal	—	950±150	CAL A.D. 1075	CAL A.D. 905-912, 970-1228, 1232-1241, 1247-1251	CAL A.D. 723-739, 770-1299, 1369-1380	K. L. Brown 1985: 66
Two Deer 14BU55	UGa-2504	charcoal	—	950±135	CAL A.D. 1084	CAL A.D. 979-1223, 1233-1237	CAL A.D. 781-792, 805-1292	Adair and Brown 1981: 253
14CF301	GAK-405	charcoal	—	930±150				Schmits 1980b: 161
14CF508	I-9654*	charcoal	—	890±80	CAL A.D. 1135	CAL A.D. 1043-1104, 1118-1215	CAL A.D. 1016-1272	Stein 1978-1979: 12-13
14CF1320	I-11164*	charcoal	—	890±80	CAL A.D. 1135	CAL A.D. 1043-1104, 1118-1215	CAL A.D. 1016-1272	Thies 1981

312 APPENDIX

Site	Lab Number	Sample Material	^{13}C Ratio	Radiocarbon Age BP and Standard Deviation	Median Probability	One Sigma Calibrated Date Range	Two Sigma Calibrated Date Range	References
Two Deer 14BU55	UGa-1345	charcoal	—	890±60	CAL A.D. 1134	CAL A.D. 1041-1095, 1117-1141, 1153-1214	CAL A.D. 1025-1253	Adair and Brown 1981: 253; Fulmer 1977
14OS305	M-1246*	charcoal	—	860±100	CAL A.D. 1157	CAL A.D. 1046-1092, 1121-1140, 1148-1260	CAL A.D. 987-1297, 1374-1376	Wilmeth 1970: 41
14DO154	GX-6487*	charcoal	—	840±150	CAL A.D. 1163	CAL A.D. 1036-1278	CAL A.D. 894-927, 935-1409	Nathan 1980
23JA43	DIC-1522*	charcoal	—	780±90	CAL A.D. 1226	CAL A.D. 1155-1298, 1372-1377	CAL A.D. 1036-1319, 1351-1390	Schmits 1982: 14
14MY335	GAK-600	charcoal	—	760±90				Marshall 1972: 224
23JA43	DIC-1526*	charcoal	—	730±130	CAL A.D. 1260	CAL A.D. 1168-1327, 1342-1395	CAL A.D. 1032-1428	Schmits 1982: 14
23HI172	M-1930*	charcoal	—	720±110	CAL A.D. 1274	CAL A.D. 1208-1328, 1341-1395	CAL A.D. 1044-1098, 1119-1142, 1147-1426	R. Vehik 1978
23JA115	UGa-2353*	charcoal	—	705±55	CAL A.D. 1290	CAL A.D. 1259-1309, 1361-1386	CAL A.D. 1218-1328, 1341-1395	K. L. Brown and Ziegler 1981
14CF508	I-9655*	charcoal	—	705±135	CAL A.D. 1280	CAL A.D. 1190-1196, 1207-1408	CAL A.D. 1031-1444	Stein 1978-1979: 12-13
23JA238	DIC-1603*	charcoal	—	680±65	CAL A.D. 1314	CAL A.D. 1269-1319, 1352-1390	CAL A.D. 1226-1405	Schmits, ed. 1981
14MY305	GAK-876	charcoal	—	640±90				Marshall 1972: 92
23JA115	UGa-2352*	charcoal	—	615±65	CAL A.D. 1348	CAL A.D. 1297-1331, 1338-1374, 1376-1397	CAL A.D. 1278-1423	K. L. Brown and Ziegler 1981
14CF506	I-9656*	charcoal	—	580±150	CAL A.D. 1372	CAL A.D. 1258-1479	CAL A.D. 1053-1079, 1153-1654	Stein 1978-1979: 12-13
14JF303	GAK-1737	charcoal	—	550±110				Witty 1982
14CF511	I-9653*	charcoal	—	490±80	CAL A.D. 1427	CAL A.D. 1315-1355, 1388-1484	CAL A.D. 1295-1524, 1558-1631	Rohn et al. 1977

Site	Lab #	Material	δ13C	RCYBP	Intercept	2σ range	Reference
14JO21A	Beta-3858 5*	—		470±60	CAL A.D. 1438	CAL A.D. 1400-1485	Logan 1990c
14CF506	I-9657*	charcoal		455±145	CAL A.D. 1484	CAL A.D. 1320-1350, 1391-1529, 1542-1634	Stein 1978-1979: 12-13
14JO21A	Beta-3858 4*	—		450±60	CAL A.D. 1456	CAL A.D. 1409-1493, 1602-1614	Logan 1990c
14MO308	GAK-597	charcoal	—	400±110			Witty 1981
14MO308	GAK-598	charcoal	—	390±120			Witty 1981
14JF303	GAK-1736	charcoal	—	350±80			Witty 1982
Two Deer 14BU55	UGa-2502	charcoal	—	325±140	CAL A.D. 1597	CAL A.D. 1434-1676, 1765-1767, 1775-1802, 1939-1946	Adair and Brown 1981: 253

High Plains Upper Republican and Dismal River

Site	Lab #	Material	δ13C	RCYBP	Intercept	2σ range	Reference
Donovan 5LO204	Beta-76915	charcoal	—	1040±80	CAL A.D. 995	CAL A.D. 894-1041, 1097-1117, 1141-1152	Scheiber and Reher 2000
Donovan 5LO204	SR-5464/ CAMS-63095	bone	—	1020±40	CAL A.D. 1010	CAL A.D. 980-1036, 1144-1147	Scheiber 2001
Donovan 5LO204	Beta-76916	charcoal	—	970±90	CAL A.D. 1080	CAL A.D. 992-1163, 1173-1179	Scheiber and Reher 2000
Donovan 5LO204	Beta-76914	charcoal	—	950±60	CAL A.D. 1097	CAL A.D. 1023-1072, 1078-1130, 1136-1158	Scheiber and Reher 2000
Seven Mile 48LA304	B-27038	charcoal	—	930±60	CAL A.D. 1108	CAL A.D. 894-927, 935-1256	Scheiber and Reher 2000
Peavy 5LO1	GX-0318	charcoal	—	810±125	CAL A.D. 1193	CAL A.D. 1042-1092, 1118-1140, 1154-1294	J. J. Wood 1967

Site	Lab Number	Sample Material	^{13}C Ratio	Radiocarbon Age BP and Standard Deviation	Median Probability	One Sigma Calibrated Date Range	Two Sigma Calibrated Date Range	References
Biggs 5WL27	GX-0567	bone	—	735±105	CAL A.D. 1261	CAL A.D. 1164-1168, 1187-1327, 1345-1393	CAL A.D. 1038-1143, 1149-1415	J. J. Wood 1967
Donovan 5LO204	SR-5463/ CAMS-63097	bone	—	720±40	CAL A.D. 1283	CAL A.D. 1258-1301, 1371-1379	CAL A.D. 1220-1317, 1352-1388	Scheiber 2001
Biggs 5WL27	GX-0566	bone	—	695±110	CAL A.D. 1294	CAL A.D. 1221-1334, 1336-1400	CAL A.D. 1039-1103, 1115-1142, 1151-1441	J. J. Wood 1967
Kasper 5LO4	GX-0560	charcoal	—	655±250	CAL A.D. 1317	CAL A.D. 1037-1143, 1148-1490, 1603-1608	CAL A.D. 783-788, 830-838, 868-1694, 1726-1813, 1848-1871, 1918-1949	J. J. Wood 1967
5LO6	GX-0564	charcoal	—	545±150	CAL A.D. 1407	A.D. 1278-1519, 1594-1622	CAL A.D. 1045-1052, 1055-1088, 1121-1138, 1156-1677, 1762-1803, 1938-1946	J. J. Wood 1967
El Cuartelejo 14SC1	AA-36104	Zea mays	-9.7	350±35	CAL A.D. 1557	CAL A.D. 1485-1524, 1563-1629	CAL A.D. 1463-1638	Adair 2003a: 311
El Cuartelejo 14SC1	AA-36106	Citrullus lanatus	-25	200±40	CAL A.D. 1769	CAL A.D. 1656-1679, 1740-1804, 1935-1947	CAL A.D. 1640-1698, 1724-1814, 1833-1878, 1916-1949	Adair 2003a: 311

Oneota

Site	Lab Number	Sample Material	^{13}C Ratio	Radiocarbon Age BP and Standard Deviation	Median Probability	One Sigma Calibrated Date Range	Two Sigma Calibrated Date Range	References
25RH1	SI-618	charcoal	—	1170±60	CAL A.D. 859	CAL A.D. 779-900, 919-958	CAL A.D. 691-702, 711-752, 760-996	Stuckenrath and Mielke 1972: 405
25RH1	UCR-3945	residue	-25	610±110	CAL A.D. 1352	CAL A.D. 1283-1428	CAL A.D. 1162-1522, 1578-1626	Ritterbush 2002a: 261
25RH1	WIS-151	charcoal	—	740±55	CAL A.D. 1269	CAL A.D.	CAL A.D. 1163-	Bender et al. 1967: 534

APPENDIX 315

Site	Lab #	Material	δ13C	14C age BP	Intercept	1σ range	2σ range	Reference
14JW1	Beta-65893	charcoal	-24.7	720±70	CAL A.D. 1283	CAL A.D. 1221-1308, 1354-1387	CAL A.D. 1162-1406	Logan 1995: 101
14JW1	TX-8193	charcoal	-24.5	720±50	CAL A.D. 1284	CAL A.D. 1242-1303, 1368-1383	CAL A.D. 1212-1329, 1344-1395	Logan 1995: 101
14JW24	Beta-53612	charcoal	—	660±80	CAL A.D. 1330	CAL A.D. 1280-1331, 1340-1398	CAL A.D. 1214-1435	Logan 1995: 101
25RH1	BGS-2301	charcoal	-25.83	641±40	CAL A.D. 1349	CAL A.D. 1297-1323, 1350-1390	CAL A.D. 1286-1401	Ritterbush 2002a: 261
25SD147	Beta-133384	charcoal	-25.9	620±50	CAL A.D. 1350	CAL A.D. 1300-1330, 1342-1373, 1378-1396	1221-1299; CAL A.D. 1286-1413 / 1172, 1181-1327, 1346-1393	Pepperl 2000a: 12; 2000b: 63
25RH1	SI-617	charcoal	—	620±100	CAL A.D. 1347	CAL A.D. 1285-1414	CAL A.D. 1163-1492, 1602-1610	Stuckenrath and Mielke 1972: 405
14JW8	ISGS-5631	charcoal	-24.4	580±70	CAL A.D. 1359	CAL A.D. 1304-1367, 1385-1412	CAL A.D. 1289-1439	Logan 2005b
25RH1	BGS-2302	charcoal	-26.36	548±40	CAL A.D. 1391	CAL A.D. 1326-1348, 1392-1429	CAL A.D. 1303-1368, 1384-1438	Ritterbush 2002a: 261
25RH1	WIS-155	charcoal	—	540±55	CAL A.D. 1391	CAL A.D. 1321-1351, 1389-1437	CAL A.D. 1298-1450	Bender et al. 1967: 534
14JW1	TX-7984	charcoal	-24.6	510±40	CAL A.D. 1416	CAL A.D. 1401-1440	CAL A.D. 1315-1354, 1387-1470	Logan 1995: 101
14JW1	Beta-73924	charcoal	-26.3	390±60	CAL A.D. 1519	CAL A.D. 1441-1522, 1578-1626	CAL A.D. 1427-1641	Logan 1995: 101

Great Bend Aspect

Site	Lab #	Material	δ13C	14C age BP	Intercept	1σ range	2σ range	Reference
14CO1509	TX-9266	wood charcoal	-24.2	1540±110	CAL A.D. 505	CAL A.D. 420-621, 631-636	CAL A.D. 252-306, 315-687	Kansas archaeological site file
14CO385	TX-9050	wood charcoal	-26.3	1070±70	CAL A.D. 961	CAL A.D. 893-1022	CAL A.D. 779-1059, 1087-1122, 1138-1156	Kansas archaeological site file
14CO385	TX-9056	wood charcoal	-26.5	920±40	CAL A.D. 1106	CAL A.D. 1039-1104, 1109-1142, 1150-1160	CAL A.D. 1024-1193, 1198-1209	Kansas archaeological site file

Site	Lab Number	Sample Material	^{13}C Ratio	Radiocarbon Age BP and Standard Deviation	Median Probability	One Sigma Calibrated Date Range	Two Sigma Calibrated Date Range	References
14CO385	TX-9059	wood charcoal	-26	880±50	CAL A.D. 1149	CAL A.D. 1044-1089, 1120-1139, 1155-1217	CAL A.D. 1035-1254	Kansas archaeological site file
14CO385	TX-9046	wood charcoal	-26.7	820±90	CAL A.D. 1193	CAL A.D. 1065-1084, 1123-1137, 1157-1284	CAL A.D. 1021-1303, 1369-1382	Kansas archaeological site file
14CO332	TX-9053	wood charcoal	-26	800±70	CAL A.D. 1221	CAL A.D. 1163-1172, 1181-1284	CAL A.D. 1039-1142, 1150-1300, 1374-1377	Kansas archaeological site file
14CO501	Beta-80180	charred material	-25	650±80	CAL A.D. 1339	CAL A.D. 1286-1330, 1342-1396	CAL A.D. 1224-1229, 1239-1430	Kansas archaeological site file
14CO382	Beta-80179	charred material	-25	630±70	CAL A.D. 1347	CAL A.D. 1297-1330, 1342-1396	CAL A.D. 1274-1429	Kansas archaeological site file
14CO1	TX-9058	wood charcoal	-26.1	630±60	CAL A.D. 1348	CAL A.D. 1298-1328, 1344-1394	CAL A.D. 1281-1415	Kansas archaeological site file
14CO385	TX-9047	wood charcoal	-25.3	620±40	CAL A.D. 1349	CAL A.D. 1301-1328, 1344-1371, 1380-1394	CAL A.D. 1295-1404	Kansas archaeological site file
14CO385	TX-9042	wood charcoal	-26.3	600±50	CAL A.D. 1351	CAL A.D. 1304-1334, 1337-1367, 1385-1400	CAL A.D. 1295-1418	Kansas archaeological site file
14MN328	TX-6272*	wood charcoal	—	580±80	CAL A.D. 1358	CAL A.D. 1301-1367, 1382-1417	CAL A.D. 1274-1449	Kansas archaeological site file
Tobias 14RC8	ISGS-A0060*	wood charcoal	-25.4	543±57	CAL A.D. 1385	CAL A.D. 1319-1351, 1390-1433	CAL A.D. 1297-1373, 1377-1445	Kansas archaeological site file
14CO1	TX-9040	wood charcoal	-27.2	520±50	CAL A.D. 1409	CAL A.D. 1330-1342, 1396-1440	CAL A.D. 1303-1369, 1383-1455, 1463-1465	Kansas archaeological site file
Kermit Hayes No 4 14RC306	ISGS-4353*	wood charcoal	-25.7	500±70	CAL A.D. 1418	CAL A.D. 1319-1352, 1390-1457	CAL A.D. 1293-1520, 1592-1619	Kansas archaeological site file

APPENDIX 317

Site	Lab #	Material	δ13C	14C age	CAL A.D.	CAL A.D.	CAL A.D.	Source
C F Thompson 14RC9	ISGS-A0067*	wood charcoal	-25.0	449±52	CAL A.D. 1451	CAL A.D. 1414-1485	CAL A.D. 1334-1336, 1398-1524, 1558-1631	Kansas archaeological site file
14CO1	TX-9057	wood charcoal	-25.7	430±60	CAL A.D. 1477	CAL A.D. 1421-1514, 1600-1615	CAL A.D. 1405-1531, 1545-1635	Kansas archaeological site file
14CO385	TX-9043	wood charcoal	-24.9	430±50	CAL A.D. 1469	CAL A.D. 1423-1494, 1601-1613	CAL A.D. 1409-1525, 1559-1630	Kansas archaeological site file
14CO501	TX-8338	wood and plant charcoal	-23.7	430±50	CAL A.D. 1469	CAL A.D. 1423-1494, 1601-1613	CAL A.D. 1409-1525, 1559-1630	Kansas archaeological site file
14CO332	TX-9054	wood	-27	420±50	CAL A.D. 1477	CAL A.D. 1431-1494, 1499-1511, 1600-1614	CAL A.D. 1414-1527, 1554-1632	Kansas archaeological site file
14CO382	TX-8335	wood and plant charcoal	-24.3	420±50	CAL A.D. 1477	CAL A.D. 1431-1494, 1499-1511, 1600-1614	CAL A.D. 1414-1527, 1554-1632	Kansas archaeological site file
14CO382	TX-8334	wood and plant charcoal	-26.8	420±40	CAL A.D. 1469	CAL A.D. 1433-1491, 1603-1609	CAL A.D. 1419-1522, 1572-1627	Kansas archaeological site file
C F Thompson 14RC9	ISGS-A0066*	wood charcoal	-24.6	404±47	CAL A.D. 1493	CAL A.D. 1439-1515, 1599-1617	CAL A.D. 1426-1529, 1544-1548, 1550-1634	Kansas archaeological site file
14CO382	TX-8333	wood and plant charcoal	-25.9	410±60	CAL A.D. 1498	CAL A.D. 1434-1519, 1593-1622	CAL A.D. 1418-1533, 1540-1636	Kansas archaeological site file
14CO501	TX-8337	wood and plant charcoal	-22.9	410±40	CAL A.D. 1477	CAL A.D. 1437-1494, 1503-1507, 600-1613	CAL A.D. 1426-1524, 1561-1629	Kansas archaeological site file
14CO501	TX-8339	wood and plant charcoal	-25.6	400±50	CAL A.D. 1500	CAL A.D. 1439-1518, 1596-1620	CAL A.D. 1428-1531, 1544-1635	Kansas archaeological site file
Sharps Creek 14MP408	ISGS-4351*	wood charcoal	-26.5	390±70	CAL A.D. 1521	CAL A.D. 1442-1522, 1573-1628	CAL A.D. 1422-1645	Kansas archaeological site file
Max Crandall 14RC420	ISGS-4355*	wood charcoal	-25.1	390±70	CAL A.D. 1521	CAL A.D. 1442-1522, 1573-1628	CAL A.D. 1422-1645	Kansas archaeological site file
Kermit Hayes No 4 14RC306	ISGS-4342*	wood	-25.2	380±70	CAL A.D. 1530	CAL A.D. 1446-1523, 1560-1561, 1572-1630	CAL A.D. 1426-1648	Kansas archaeological site file
14CO501	TX-8340	wood and plant charcoal	-24.6	370±50	CAL A.D. 1534	CAL A.D. 1453-1522, 1576-1626	CAL A.D. 1443-1534, 1537-1637	Kansas archaeological site file

318 APPENDIX

Site	Lab Number	Sample Material	^{13}C Ratio	Radiocarbon Age BP and Standard Deviation	Median Probability	One Sigma Calibrated Date Range	Two Sigma Calibrated Date Range	References
14CO501	TX-8336	wood and plant charcoal	-25.5	360±40	CAL A.D. 1547	CAL A.D. 1476-1523, 1564-1628	CAL A.D. 1450-1533, 1539-1636	Kansas archaeological site file
Tobias 14RC8	ISGS-A0061*	wood charcoal	-24.9	354±52	CAL A.D. 1547	CAL A.D. 1469-1524, 1558-1631	CAL A.D. 1449-1642	Kansas archaeological site file
14CO332	Beta-43532	—	—	350±80	CAL A.D. 1553	CAL A.D. 1475-1533, 1540-1636	CAL A.D. 1417-1672, 1778-1799, 1943-1945	Kansas archaeological site file
14CO3	TX-9045	wood charcoal	-25.6	330±50	CAL A.D. 1559	CAL A.D. 1494-1533, 1540-1601, 1613-1636	CAL A.D. 1456-1650	Kansas archaeological site file
14CO382	TX-8332	wood and plant charcoal	-25.9	310±40	CAL A.D. 1564	CAL A.D. 1518-1596, 1620-1643	CAL A.D. 1482-1654	Kansas archaeological site file
Kermit Hayes No 4 14RC306	ISGS-4354*	wood charcoal	-24.6	320±70	CAL A.D. 1565	CAL A.D. 1490-1603, 1610-1644	CAL A.D. 1438-1676, 1777-1799	Kansas archaeological site file
14CO1	TX-9055	wood charcoal	-27	300±50	CAL A.D. 1569	CAL A.D. 1516-1598, 1617-1652	CAL A.D. 1468-1667, 1782-1795	Kansas archaeological site file
14CO501	TX-8341	wood and plant charcoal	-26	300±60	CAL A.D. 1573	CAL A.D. 1494-1500, 1510-1600, 1614-1653	CAL A.D. 1446-1674, 1777-1800, 1941-1946	Kansas archaeological site file
Sharps Creek 14MP408	ISGS-4352*	wood charcoal	-24.8	290±70	CAL A.D. 1587	CAL A.D. 1490-1603, 1610-1663	CAL A.D. 1447-1683, 1735-1805, 1930-1951	Kansas archaeological site file
14CO1509	TX-9267	wood charcoal	-25.3	270±50	CAL A.D. 1610	CAL A.D. 1520-1589, 1624-1667, 1782-1794	CAL A.D. 1480-1678, 1742-1750, 1758-1804, 1936-1947	Kansas archaeological site file
14CO331	TX-8460	wood charcoal	-24.7	260±50	CAL A.D. 1637	CAL A.D. 1521-1583, 1626-1671, 1779-1798, 1944-1945	CAL A.D. 1486-1681, 1735-1806, 1933-1947	Kansas archaeological site file
14CO332	TX-9052	wood charcoal	-26.5	260±50	CAL A.D. 1637	CAL A.D. 1521-1583, 1626-1671,	CAL A.D. 1486-1681, 1735-1806,	Kansas archaeological site file

Site	Lab number	Material	δ13C	BP	CAL A.D.	1σ ranges	2σ ranges	Reference
Max Crandall	ISGS-A0085* 14RC420	wood charcoal	−26.2	260±52	CAL A.D. 1637		1779-1798, 1944-1945	CAL A.D. 1477-1684, 1734-1806	Kansas archaeological site file
14CO3	TX-8461	wood charcoal	−26.2	250±40	CAL A.D. 1652	CAL A.D. 1521-1578, 1581-1591, 1620-1669, 1780-1789, 1944-1950	CAL A.D. 1516-1598, 1617-1681, 1735-1806, 1932-1947	Kansas archaeological site file
14CO331	TX-8462	wood charcoal	−25.8	230±40	CAL A.D. 1733	CAL A.D. 1528-1552, 1633-1672, 1778-1799, 1943-1945	CAL A.D. 1522-1576, 1626-1689, 1729-1811, 1922-1949	Kansas archaeological site file
14CO1	TX-9041	wood	−25.4	220±50	CAL A.D. 1751	CAL A.D. 1640-1676, 1673-1772, 1775-1802, 1938-1946	CAL A.D. 1522-1576, 1626-1689, 1729-1811, 1922-1949	Kansas archaeological site file
14CO331	TX-8459	wood charcoal	−27.3	200±40	CAL A.D. 1769	CAL A.D. 1641-1680, 1736-1805, 1933-1947	CAL A.D. 1521-1586, 1625-1704, 1721-1817, 1829-1882, 1914-1950	Kansas archaeological site file
14CO385	TX-9051	wood charcoal	−27.1	160±50	CAL A.D. 1789	CAL A.D. 1667-1695, 1725-1783, 1793-1813, 1843-1876, 1917-1949	CAL A.D. 1659-1890, 1909-1950	Kansas archaeological site file

Middle Ceramic, Southern Plains

Odessa phase

Site	Lab number	Material	δ13C	BP	CAL A.D.	1σ ranges	2σ ranges	Reference
41OC43	Beta-20277	wood charcoal	—	840±100	CAL A.D. 1174	CAL A.D. 1045-1052, 1055-1088, 1121-1138, 1156-1277	CAL A.D. 999-1303, 1368-1383	Hughes and Hughes-Jones 1987
41OC27	DIC-3300	wood charcoal	—	800±55	CAL A.D. 1229	CAL A.D. 1192-1200, 1208-1280	CAL A.D. 1045-1049, 1056-1087, 1121-1138, 1156-1297	Hughes and Hughes-Jones 1987

Site	Lab Number	Sample Material	^{13}C Ratio	Radiocarbon Age BP and Standard Deviation	Median Probability	One Sigma Calibrated Date Range	Two Sigma Calibrated Date Range	References
41OC27	Beta-20276	wood charcoal	—	770±80	CAL A.D. 1240	CAL A.D. 1163-1172, 1182-1299	CAL A.D. 1040-1099, 1116-1141, 1151-1327, 1346-1393	Hughes and Hughes-Jones 1987
Lonker 34BV4	Beta-4717	wood charcoal	—	750±40	CAL A.D. 1265	CAL A.D. 1245-1291	CAL A.D. 1212-1300, 1373-1378	R. Brooks 1994a
Handley 41OC1	WIS-90A	wood charcoal	—	740±80	CAL A.D. 1266	CAL A.D. 1194-1197, 1210-1305, 1355-1361, 1365-1386	CAL A.D. 1061-1086, 1122-1138, 1156-1403	Baerreis and Bryson 1965
41OC1	DIC-3338	wood charcoal	—	740±60	CAL A.D. 1269	CAL A.D. 1221-1299	CAL A.D. 1164-1171, 1182-1326, 1347-1392	Hughes and Hughes-Jones 1987
41OC26	DIC-3281	wood charcoal	—	740±50	CAL A.D. 1270	CAL A.D. 1224-1228, 1241-1297	CAL A.D. 1207-1316, 1353-1388	Hughes and Hughes-Jones 1987
41OC29	Beta-185069	wood charcoal	-23.4	740±40	CAL A.D. 1271	CAL A.D. 1245-1246, 1255-1296	CAL A.D. 1215-1302, 1370-1381	Brosowske, unpublished
Odessa Yates 34BV100	Beta-145474	Zea mays	-9.7	720±40	CAL A.D. 1283	CAL A.D. 1261-1300, 1373-1377	CAL A.D. 1221-1309, 1354-1387	Brosowske, unpublished
Lonker 34BV4	Beta-4716	wood charcoal	—	715±50	CAL A.D. 1287	CAL A.D. 1255-1304, 1366-1385	CAL A.D. 1219-1326, 1347-1392	R. Brooks 1994
41OC27	DIC-3301	wood charcoal	—	710±50	CAL A.D. 1290	CAL A.D. 1257-1305, 1365-1386	CAL A.D. 1221-1327, 1346-1393	Hughes and Hughes-Jones 1987
41OC27	DIC-3228	wood charcoal	—	710±50	CAL A.D. 1290	CAL A.D. 1257-1305, 1365-1386	CAL A.D. 1221-1327, 1346-1393	Hughes and Hughes-Jones 1987
41OC29	Beta-185071	Zea mays	-8.4	700±40	CAL A.D. 1294	CAL A.D. 1273-1303, 1368-1384	CAL A.D. 1244-1250, 1256-1327, 1346-1393	Brosowske, unpublished
Lundeen 14MD306	ISGS-4006	wood charcoal	-27.2	670±70	CAL A.D. 1327	CAL A.D. 1281-1326, 1347-1392	CAL A.D. 1224-1230, 1238-1412	Bevitt 1999a

Site	Lab #	Material	δ13C	RCYBP	1-sigma cal	2-sigma cal	Reference
Odessa Yates 34BV100	Beta-133579	wood charcoal	-25.6	670±60	CAL A.D. 1329	CAL A.D. 1282-1323, 1350-1390	CAL A.D. 1255-1409	Brosowske, unpublished
Odessa Yates 34BV100	Beta-153243	wood charcoal	-25.7	670±40	CAL A.D. 1337	CAL A.D. 1284-1310, 1354-1387	CAL A.D. 1277-1330, 1342-1396	Brosowske, unpublished
Odessa Yates 34BV100	Beta-185072	Zea mays	-10.2	660±40	CAL A.D. 1347	CAL A.D. 1290-1316, 1353-1388	CAL A.D. 1280-1331, 1341-1397	Brosowske, unpublished
Handley 41OC1	WIS-90B	wood charcoal	—	640±70	CAL A.D. 1345	CAL A.D. 1294-1329, 1343-1395	CAL A.D. 1264-1424	Baerreis and Bryson 1965
Lundeen 14MD306	ISGS-4007	wood charcoal	-25.9	630±70	CAL A.D. 1347	CAL A.D. 1297-1330, 1342-1396	CAL A.D. 1274-1429	Bevitt 1999a
Lundeen 14MD306	ISGS-4008	wood charcoal	-25.6	630±70	CAL A.D. 1347	CAL A.D. 1297-1330, 1342-1396	CAL A.D. 1274-1429	Bevitt 1999a
Miller 34EL25	Beta-20398	wood charcoal	—	630±60	CAL A.D. 1348	CAL A.D. 1298-1328, 1344-1349	CAL A.D. 1281-1415	Drass and Turner 1989
41OC48	DIC-3302	wood charcoal	—	630±40	CAL A.D. 1350	CAL A.D. 1300-1326, 1348-1373, 1377-1391	CAL A.D. 1292-1401	Hughes and Hughes-Jones 1987
Odessa Yates 34BV100	Beta-153242	Zea mays	-10.1	630±40	CAL A.D. 1350	CAL A.D. 1300-1326, 1348-1373, 1377-1391	CAL A.D. 1292-1401	Brosowske, unpublished
41OC29	Beta-185070	Zea mays	-7.7	620±50	CAL A.D. 1350	CAL A.D. 1300-1326, 1348-1373, 1377-1391	CAL A.D. 1292-1401	Brosowske, unpublished
41OC27	DIC-3227	wood charcoal	—	620±50	CAL A.D. 1349	CAL A.D. 1301-1329, 1343-1372, 1379-1395	CAL A.D. 1289-1410	Hughes and Hughes-Jones 1987
Lundeen 14MD306	ISGS-4009	wood charcoal	-25.3	600±70	CAL A.D. 1353	CAL A.D. 1302-1369, 1381-1403	CAL A.D. 1285-1433	Bevitt 1999a
Seuser 14RH301	—	Zea mays	-25.3	600±40	CAL A.D. 1349	CAL A.D. 1305-1333, 1338-1365, 1386-1399	CAL A.D. 1299-1410	Kansas archaeological site file
41OC1	DIC-3303	wood charcoal	—	590±45	CAL A.D. 1351	CAL A.D. 1305-1355, 1360-1365, 1386-1404	CAL A.D. 1298-1418	Hughes and Hughes-Jones 1987
41OC43	Beta-20871	wood charcoal	—	580±60	CAL A.D. 1357	CAL A.D. 1305-1365, 1386-1410	CAL A.D. 1296-1433	Hughes and Hughes-Jones 1987

Site	Lab Number	Sample Material	^{13}C Ratio	Radiocarbon Age BP and Standard Deviation	Median Probability	One Sigma Calibrated Date Range	Two Sigma Calibrated Date Range	References
Miller 34EL25	Beta-20399	wood charcoal	—	540±50	CAL A.D. 1395	CAL A.D. 1326-1347, 1392-1435	CAL A.D. 1302-1370, 1381-1443	Drass and Turner 1989
Odessa Yates 34BV100	Beta-153241	Zea mays	-11.4	480±50	CAL A.D. 1431	CAL A.D. 1404-1455, 1463-1465	CAL A.D. 1323-1390	Brosowske, unpublished
Odessa Yates 34BV100	Beta-169790	Zea mays	-10.3	390±40	CAL A.D. 1502	CAL A.D. 1444-1516, 1598-1617	CAL A.D. 1437-1528, 1551-1633	Brosowske, unpublished
Odessa Yates 34BV100	Beta-169791	Zea mays	-9.5	390±40	CAL A.D. 1502	CAL A.D. 1444-1516, 1598-1617	CAL A.D. 1437-1528, 1551-1633	Brosowske, unpublished
Handley 41OC1	WIS-97	wood charcoal	—	360±75	CAL A.D. 1547	CAL A.D. 1455-1457, 1465-1528, 1552-1633	CAL A.D. 1423-1664	Baerreis and Bryson 1966
Pratt Complex								
14PT304	TX-7940	wood charcoal	-23.8	650±90	CAL A.D. 1336	CAL A.D. 1284-1332, 1339-1398	CAL A.D. 1217-1438	Kansas archaeological site file
14PT420	TX-8147	wood charcoal	-23.9	470±100	CAL A.D. 1456	CAL A.D. 1326-1347, 1392-1520, 1590-1623	CAL A.D. 1301-1372, 1379-1639	Kansas archaeological site file
Bluff Creek Complex								
14SR303	GAK-2797	wood charcoal	—	1050±110				Kansas archaeological site file
14SR303	GAK-2796	wood charcoal	—	870±90				Kansas archaeological site file
Hallman 14HP524	TX-6448	wood charcoal	—	870±60	CAL A.D. 1238	CAL A.D. 1043-1091, 1120-1139, 1155-1223	CAL A.D. 1032-1264	Berger 2004: 118-119
Armstrong 14HP5	ISGS-5643	wood charcoal	-26.4	820±70	CAL A.D. 1203	CAL A.D. 1159-1281	CAL A.D. 1142-1292	Kansas archaeological site file

Site	Lab #	Material	δ13C	BP	Intercept	Calibrated Range	Reference
Armstrong 14HP5	ISGS-5644	wood charcoal	-25.9	820±70	CAL A.D. 1203	CAL A.D. 1159-1281	Kansas archaeological site file
Hallman 14HP524	ISGS-4301	charcoal	—	780±70	CAL A.D. 1236	CAL A.D. 1224-1228, 1241-1321, 1351-1389	Berger 2004: 118-119
14SR305	GAK-2798	wood charcoal	—	760±110			Kansas archaeological site file
Hallman 14HP524	BETA-13126	wood charcoal	—	710±80	CAL A.D. 1291	CAL A.D. 1189-1292	Berger 2004: 118-119

Unaffiliated Sites

Site	Lab #	Material	δ13C	BP	Intercept	Calibrated Range	Reference
Bell 14CM407	ISGS-4241	wood charcoal	—	860±70	CAL A.D. 1166	CAL A.D. 1045-1047, 1056-1087, 1122-1138, 1156-1257	Kansas archaeological site file
Bell 14CM407	B-12650	wood charcoal	—	780±160	CAL A.D. 1212	CAL A.D. 1041-1097, 1116-1141, 1152-1310, 1354-1387	Kansas archaeological site file
Seuser 14RH301	AA-41420	Zea mays	-10.6	600±40	CAL A.D. 1349	CAL A.D. 1305-1333, 1338-1365, 1386-1399	Adair 2003a: 311
Booth 14CM406	B-35477	wood charcoal	—	440±100	CAL A.D. 1485	CAL A.D. 1405-1523, 1567-1627	Bevitt 1999a
Booth 14CM406	ISGS-4242	wood charcoal	-26.7	430±70	CAL A.D. 1483	CAL A.D. 1417-1518, 1596-1620	Bevitt 1999a

Radiocarbon Assays on Cultigens

Site	Lab #	Material	δ13C	BP	Intercept	Calibrated Range	Reference
Nebo Hill 23CL11	AA-41422	cucurbit	-25.3	3782±46	CAL B.C. 2209	CAL B.C. 2291-2138	Adair 2003a: 284
Nebo Hill 23CL11	AA-41421	cucurbit	-25.4	3758±46	CAL B.C. 2171	CAL B.C. 2280-2251, 2231-2219, 2209-2129, 2082-2043	CAL B.C. 2395-2392, 2336-2319, 2312-2026, 1994-1981 — Adair 2003a: 284

324   APPENDIX

Site	Lab Number	Sample Material	^{13}C Ratio	Radiocarbon Age BP and Standard Deviation	Median Probability	One Sigma Calibrated Date Range	Two Sigma Calibrated Date Range	References
Traff 23JA159	AA-36093	Iva annua	-27.7	2535±45	CAL B.C. 639	CAL B.C. 796-758, 684-660, 646-543	CAL B.C. 803-515, 506-505, 488-484, 464-450, 440-427, 422-413	Adair 2003a: 284
Traff 23JA159	AA-36094	Iva annua	-27.3	2530±40	CAL B.C. 638	CAL B.C. 794-758, 684-661, 644-586, 583-544	CAL B.C. 801-516, 461-451, 439-430, 420-414	Adair 2003a: 284
Quarry Creek 14LV401	UCR-3356	Zea mays	-26.5	1880±50	CAL A.D. 135	CAL A.D. 75-181, 188-215	CAL B.C. 380-86, CAL A.D. 19-255, 304-316	Adair 2003a: 284
Quarry Creek 14LV401	AA-36117	cucurbit	-25.1	1775±45	CAL A.D. 257	CAL A.D. 140-150, 176-192, 212-264, 272-340	CAL A.D. 130-385	Adair 2003a: 284
Quarry Creek 14LV401	AA-36118	cucurbit	-26.1	1725±50	CAL A.D. 316	CAL A.D. 246-305, 315-388	CAL A.D. 135-158, 171-195, 210-427	Adair 2003a: 284
Trowbridge 14WY1	AA-36096	Iva annua	-25	1660±45	CAL A.D. 386	CAL A.D. 262-278, 324-331, 336-433	CAL A.D. 257-302, 318-532	Adair 2003a: 284
Avoca 14JN332	AA-36102	Zea mays	-9.4	1220±40	CAL A.D. 809	CAL A.D. 726-738, 773-882	CAL A.D. 687-896, 923-939	Adair 2003a: 284
Avoca 14JN332	AA-36100	Helianthus annuus	-28.5	1200±40	CAL A.D. 829	CAL A.D. 777-888	CAL A.D. 691-702, 710-752, 760-901, 918-961	Adair 2003a: 284
Walker-Gilmore 25CC28	AA-41425	C. pepo	-26.4	1194±41	CAL A.D. 835	CAL A.D. 777-891	CAL A.D. 692-701, 713-750, 762-903, 916-964, 971-975	Adair 2003a: 284
Avoca 14JN332	AA-36101	Zea mays	-9.48	1165±40	CAL A.D. 869	CAL A.D. 782-791, 808-898, 921-945, 950-955	CAL A.D. 731-736, 774-982	Adair 2003a: 284
Walker-Gilmore 25CC28	AA-41427	C. pepo	-25.5	1084±40	CAL A.D. 956	CAL A.D. 897-922, 943-1000	CAL A.D. 784-787, 833-837, 877-1025	Adair 2003a: 284

Site	Lab #	Taxon	δ13C	BP	1σ cal	2σ cal	Reference
Walker-Gilmore 25CC28	AA-41426	C. pepo	-24.9	1051±42	CAL A.D. 985	CAL A.D. 903-916, 963-1022	CAL A.D. 889-1040, 1100-1116, 1142-1151	Adair 2003a: 284
Andrews 25DO12	AA-36097	Zea mays	-9.5	1050±40	CAL A.D. 987	CAL A.D. 903-916, 964-973, 975-1022	CAL A.D. 890-1039, 1104-1111, 1142-1150	Adair 2003a: 284
Andrews 25DO12	AA-36098	Zea mays	-8.9	1040±40	CAL A.D. 995	CAL A.D. 903-915, 964-970, 975-1026	CAL A.D. 893-1041, 1095-1117, 1141-1153	Adair 2003a: 284
Avoca 14JN332	AA-36099	Iva annua	-23.4	985±40	CAL A.D. 1063	CAL A.D. 998-1045, 1088-1121, 1139-1156	CAL A.D. 980-1162	Adair 2003a: 284
Quarry Creek 14LV401	AA-36120	Zea mays	-9.8	975±40	CAL A.D. 1082	CAL A.D. 1004-1058, 1007, 1017-1058, 1087-1122, 1138-1156	CAL A.D. 985-1163, 1174-1178	Adair 2003a: 284
Two Deer 14BU55	AA-36112	Iva annua	-25.9	940±35	CAL A.D. 1098	CAL A.D. 1031-1067, 1082-1124, 1137-1157	CAL A.D. 1020-1189, 1204-1205	Adair 2003a: 284
Two Deer 14BU55	AA-36111	Helianthus annuus	-27.1	935±45	CAL A.D. 1102	CAL A.D. 1033-1072, 1078-1129, 1136-1158	CAL A.D. 1018-1212	Adair 2003a: 284
Quarry Creek 14LV401	AA-36119	Zea mays	-8.7	930±45	CAL A.D. 1103	CAL A.D. 1036-1133, 1135-1159	CAL A.D. 1020-1213	Adair 2003a: 284
Two Deer 14BU55	AA-36113	Zea mays	-8.7	925±60	CAL A.D. 1111	CAL A.D. 1030-1163, 1174-1177	CAL A.D. 999-1244	Adair 2003a: 284
23PL16	AA-41432	Phaseolus vulgaris	-28.5	858±39	CAL A.D. 1181	CAL A.D. 1070-1080, 1126-1136, 1158-1245	CAL A.D. 1039-1103, 1114-1142, 1150-1268	Adair 2003a: 311
Patterson 25SY31	AA-36110	Phaseolus vulgaris	-26.5	845±45	CAL A.D. 1191	CAL A.D. 1074-1076, 1133-1135, 1159-1262	CAL A.D. 1040-1100, 1116-1142, 1151-1279	Adair 2003a: 311
23CL109	AA-41434	Phaseolus vulgaris	-26.9	842±38	CAL A.D. 1199	CAL A.D. 1163-1174, 1177-1255	CAL A.D. 1043-1090, 1119-1139, 1155-1278	Adair 2003a: 311

Site	Lab Number	Sample Material	^{13}C Ratio	Radiocarbon Age BP and Standard Deviation	Median Probability	One Sigma Calibrated Date Range	Two Sigma Calibrated Date Range	References
Patterson 25SY31	AA-36108	Phaseolus vulgaris	-29	810±45	CAL A.D. 1226	CAL A.D. 1191-1201, 1207-1277	CAL A.D. 1059-1086, 1122-1138, 1156-1291	Adair 2003a: 311
23CL115	AA-41433	Phaseolus vulgaris	-24.2	804±42	CAL A.D. 1232	CAL A.D. 1211-1278	CAL A.D. 1071-1079, 1126-1136, 1158-1291	Adair 2003a: 311
Patterson 25SY31	AA-36107	Zea mays	-9.4	785±40	CAL A.D. 1244	CAL A.D. 1222-1277	CAL A.D. 1163-1171, 1181-1293	Adair 2003a: 311
Patterson 25SY31	AA-36109	Phaseolus vulgaris	-25.3	780±40	CAL A.D. 1247	CAL A.D. 1223-1279	CAL A.D. 1164-1169, 1185-1295	Adair 2003a: 311
23PL16	AA-41431	Phaseolus vulgaris	-24.7	656±68	CAL A.D. 1337	CAL A.D. 1285-1328, 1344-1394	CAL A.D. 1225-1227, 1241-1424	Adair 2003a: 311
Beaver Creek 25BO23	AA-41430	Phaseolus vulgaris	-28.9	611±42	CAL A.D. 1350	CAL A.D. 1302-1331, 1341-1369, 1382-1397	CAL A.D. 1294-1411	Adair 2003a: 311
Trowbridge 14WY1	Beta-75016	Zea mays	-11	400±60	CAL A.D. 1511	CAL A.D. 1437-1521, 1582-1626	CAL A.D. 1422-1639	Adair 2003a: 284
El Cuartelejo 14SC1	AA-36104	Zea mays	-9.7	350±35	CAL A.D. 1557	CAL A.D. 1485-1524, 1563-1629	CAL A.D. 1463-1638	Adair 2003a: 311
Trowbridge 14WY1	Beta-75015	Zea mays	-10.5	310±60	CAL A.D. 1570	CAL A.D. 1493-1601, 1613-1647	CAL A.D. 1441-1675, 1776-1801, 1940-1946	Adair 2003a: 284
Trowbridge 14WY1	UCR-3357	Zea mays	-10.7	200±50	CAL A.D. 1767	CAL A.D. 1646-1687, 1730-1810, 1923-1948	CAL A.D. 1529-1549, 1634-1892, 1907-1951	Adair 2003a
El Cuartelejo 14SC1	AA-36106	Citrullus lanatus	-25	200±40	CAL A.D. 1769	CAL A.D. 1656-1679, 1740-1804, 1935-1947	CAL A.D. 1640-1698, 1724-1814, 1833-1878, 1916-1949	Adair 2003a: 311

– indicates missing data

Gakushuin (GAK) radiocarbon ages are known to be inaccurate and thus are not calibrated in this table.

Many dates are compiled in several references; those listed here are primary sources, to the extent possible. Not all dates are cited in this volume.

All dates (except those marked *) calibrated using CALIB 4.4.2 (Stuiver and Reimer 1993). Samples marked * calibrated with CALIB 5.0 html (Reimer et al. 2004).

REFERENCES CITED

Aaberg, Stephan
  1993   Preliminary Report on Plant Macrofossil Data from the Barton Gulch Site (24MA171). Manuscript on file at the Museum of the Rockies, Montana State University, Bozeman.
Aber, James S.
  1988   West Atchison Drift Section. In *South-Central Section of the Geological Society of America Centennial Field Guide*, vol. 4, edited by O. T. Hayward, pp. 5–10. Geological Society of America, Boulder.
  1991   The Glaciation of Northeastern Kansas. *Boreas* 20: 297–314.
Adair, Mary J.
  1980   Analysis of Carbonized Floral Remains. Appendix B, in *Archaeological Investigations in the Proposed Blue Springs Lake Area, Jackson County, Missouri: The Early Woodland Period*. Submitted to Burns and McDonnell Engineers, Kansas City.
  1988   *Prehistoric Agriculture in the Central Plains*. Publications in Anthropology No. 16. University of Kansas, Lawrence.
  1989   Floral Remains. In *Final Summary Report: 1986 Archeological Investigations at 14MN328, A Great Bend Site along U.S. Highway 56, Marion County, Kansas,* edited by William B. Lees, John D. Reynolds, Terrance J. Martin, Mary J. Adair, and Steven Bozarth, pp. 90–103. Submitted to the Kansas Department of Transportation. Copies available from the Kansas State Historical Society, Topeka.
  1990   Macrobotanical Remains from the Stigenwalt Site. Appendix III, in *The Archeology of the Stigenwalt Site, 14LT351,* by Randall M. Thies, pp. 157–159. Contract Archeology Series No. 7. Kansas State Historical Society, Topeka.
  1991   Macrobotanical Remains from the Avoca Site: The Role of Agriculture during the Early Ceramic Period. In *The Avoca Site (14JN332): Excavation of a Grasshopper Falls Phase Structure, Jackson County, Kansas,* by Timothy G. Baugh, pp. 85–94. Contract Archeology Publications No. 8. Kansas State Historical Society, Topeka.
  1992   Laboratory notes from the analysis of archaeobotanical remains at the University of Michigan, Ethnobotany Laboratory, Ann Arbor. Manuscript in possession of the author.
  1993   Premaize Gardening in the Central Plains. Paper presented at the 58th Annual Meeting of the Society for American Archaeology, St. Louis.
  1994   Corn and Culture History in the Central Plains. In *Corn and Culture in the Prehistoric New World,* edited by Sissel Johannessen and Christine A. Hastorf, pp. 315–334. Westview, Boulder.
  1996   Woodland Complexes in the Central Great Plains. In *Archeology and Paleoecology of the Central Great Plains,* edited by Jack L. Hofman, pp. 101–122. Research Series No. 48. Arkansas Archeological Survey, Fayetteville.
  1998a Macrobotanical Remains. In *Prehistoric Settlement of the Lower Missouri Uplands: The View from the DB Ridge, Fort Leavenworth, Kansas,* edited by Brad Logan, pp. 248–253. Project Report Series No. 98. Museum of Anthropology, University of Kansas, Lawrence.
  1998b Archaeobotanical Analysis. In *Archaeology of the Patterson Site: Three Centuries of Pre-Contact Native American Life in the Lower Platte Valley,* edited by John R. Bozell and John Ludwickson. Nebraska State Historical Society, Highway Archeology Program. Submitted to the Nebraska Department of Roads. Copies available from the State Historic Preservation Officer, Lincoln.

1998c   Great Bend Paleoethnobotany, A.D. 1500–1750. Paper presented at the 56th Annual Plains Conference, Bismarck.

1999   Botanical Remains. In *Archeology of the Patterson Site: Native American Life in the Lower Platte Valley, A.D. 1000–1300*, by John R. Bozell and John Ludwickson, pp. 85–100. Nebraska State Historical Society, Highway Archeology Program. Submitted to the Nebraska Department of Roads. Copies available from the State Historic Preservation Officer, Lincoln.

2000   Ethnobotanical Research in the Central Plains. *Current Archaeology in Kansas* 1: 3–6.

2003a   Great Plains Paleoethnobotany. In *People and Plants in Ancient Eastern North America*, edited by Paul E. Minnis, pp. 258–346. Smithsonian Books, Washington, D.C.

2003b   Becoming Farmers: Crops of the Nebraska Phase. Paper presented at the 61st Plains Anthropological Conference, Fayetteville.

2004   Maize from the Central Great Plains: Introduction and Morphological Variability. Paper presented at the 69th Annual Meeting of the Society for American Archaeology, Montreal, Quebec.

Adair, Mary J., and Marie E. Brown

1981   The Two Deer Site (14BU55): A Plains Woodland–Plains Village Transition. In *Prehistory and History of the El Dorado Lake Area, Kansas (Phase II)*, edited by Mary J. Adair, pp. 237–356. Project Report Series No. 47. Museum of Anthropology, University of Kansas, Lawrence.

Adair, Mary J., and Kenneth L. Brown (editors)

1987   Prehistoric and Historic Cultural Resources of Selected Sites at Harlan County Lake, Harlan County, Nebraska: Test Excavations and Determinations of Significance for 28 Sites. Museum of Anthropology, University of Kansas, Lawrence. Submitted to the U.S. Army Corps of Engineers, Kansas City District.

Adair, Mary J., and Rose Estep

1991   The Archaeobotanical Record from Kansas River Basin Sites. Paper presented at the 49th Plains Anthropological Conference, Lawrence.

Adams, Franklin G.

1904   Reminiscences of Frederick Chouteau. *Kansas Historical Collections, 1903–1904*, vol. 8: 423–434.

Adams, George I.

1903   Physiographic Divisions of Kansas. *Transactions of the Kansas Academy of Science* 18: 109–123.

Adams, Karen R.

1994   A Regional Synthesis of Zea Mays in the Prehistoric American Southwest. In *Corn and Culture in the Prehistoric New World*, edited by Sissel Johannessen and Christine A. Hastorf, pp. 273–302. Westview, Boulder.

Agogino, George A.

1961   A New Point Type from Hell Gap Valley, Eastern Wyoming. *American Antiquity* 26: 558–560.

Ahlbrandt, Thomas S., and S. G. Fryberger

1980   Eolian Deposits in the Nebraska Sand Hills. U.S. Geological Survey Professional Paper 1120 A. Washington, D.C.

Ahlbrandt, Thomas S., James B. Swinehart, and David G. Maroney

1983   The Dynamic Holocene Dune Fields of the Great Plains and Rocky Mountain Basins, U.S.A. In *Eolian Sediments and Processes*, edited by Michael E. Brookfield and Thomas S. Ahlbrandt, pp. 379–406. Elsevier, Amsterdam.

Akersten, William A., Theresea M. Foppe, and George T. Jefferson

1988   New Source of Dietary Data for Extinct Herbivores. *Quaternary Research* 30: 92–97.

Allgood, Ferris P.
　1962　*Soil Survey of Beaver County, Oklahoma.* United States Department of Agriculture, Soil Conservation Service.

Alroy, J.
　2001　A Multispecies Overkill Simulation of the End-Pleistocene Megafaunal Mass Extinction. *Science* 292: 1893–1896.

Anderson, Adrian D.
　1961　The Glenwood Sequence: A Local Sequence for a Series of Archeological Manifestations in Mills County, Iowa. *Journal of the Iowa Archeological Society* 10 (3): 1–101.

Anderson, Adrian D., and Barbara Anderson
　1960　Pottery Types of the Glenwood Foci. *Journal of the Iowa Archeological Society* 9 (4): 12–39.

Andrefsky, William, Jr.
　1994　The Geological Occurrence of Lithic Material and Stone Tool Production Strategies. *Geoarchaeology* 9: 375–391.

Anonymous
　1908　The Centennial Celebration at Pike's Pawnee Village. *Transactions of the Kansas State Historical Society, 1907–1908* 10: 15–19.

Antevs, Ernst
　1955　Geologic-Climatic Dating in the West. *American Antiquity* 20: 317–335.

Arbogast, Alan F.
　1993　Paleoenvironmental Implications of Buried Soils in a South-Central Kansas Lunette. In *Second International Paleopedology Symposium Guidebook,* compiled by William C. Johnson, pp. 9-1–9-7. Open File Report 93-30, Kansas Geological Survey, Lawrence.
　1995　Paleoenvironments and Desertification on the Great Bend Sand Prairie in Kansas. Ph.D. diss., University of Kansas, Lawrence.
　1996　Stratigraphic Evidence for Late-Holocene Aeolian Sand Mobilization and Soil Formation in South-Central Kansas. *Journal of Arid Environments* 34: 403–414.

Artz, Joe A.
　1981　Test Excavations at El Dorado Lake, 1978. In *Prehistory and History of the El Dorado Lake Area, Kansas (Phase II),* edited by Mary J. Adair, pp. 54–168. Project Report Series No. 47. Museum of Anthropology, University of Kansas, Lawrence.
　1983　The Soils and Geomorphology of the East Branch Walnut Valley: Contexts of Human Adaptation in the Kansas Flint Hills. Master's thesis, Department of Anthropology, University of Kansas, Lawrence.
　1985　A Soil-Geomorphic Approach to Locating Buried Late-Archaic Sites in Northeast Oklahoma. *American Archaeology* 5: 142–150.
　1993　Phase II Archaeological Investigations at 13RN59: A Late Archaic Campsite in Ringgold County, Iowa. Project Completion Report No. 53. Highway Archaeology Program, University of Iowa, Iowa City.

Artz, Joe A., J. Manion, James Marshall, and Christopher Wright
　1975　Archaeological Investigations at 14MM26, Hillsdale Reservoir, Eastern Kansas. Report submitted to the Kansas City District, U.S. Army Corps of Engineers. Museum of Anthropology, University of Kansas, Lawrence.

Asch, David
　1992　Prehistoric Agriculture in Iowa. In *Crops of Ancient Iowa: Native Plant Use and Farming Systems,* by David Asch and William Green, pp. 9–108. Report submitted to the Leopold Center for Sustainable Agriculture, Iowa State University. Copies available from the Office of the State Archaeologist, University of Iowa, Iowa City.

Asch, David, and Nancy Asch
　1985　Prehistoric Plant Cultivation in West-Central Illinois. In *Prehistoric Food Production in*

North America, edited by Richard I. Ford, pp. 149–203. Anthropological Papers No. 75. University of Michigan, Museum of Anthropology, Ann Arbor.

Asch, David, and William Green
  1995   Archaeobotanical Analysis. In *Phase III Excavations at 13ML118 and 13ML175, Mills County, Iowa,* by Toby Morrow, pp. 59–73. Contract Completion Report No. 469. Office of the State Archaeologist, University of Iowa, Iowa City.

Ashworth, Kenneth A.
  1982   Phase III Archeological Investigations within the Diamond Creek Watershed. Archeology Department, Kansas State Historical Society, Topeka.

Axelrod, Daniel I.
  1967   Quaternary Extinctions of Large Mammals. *University of California Publications in Geological Sciences* 74: 1–42.

Ayer, Mrs. E. E.
  1965   *The Memorial of Fray Alonso de Benavides 1630.* Horn and Wallace Publishers, Albuquerque.

Baars, D. L., Charles A. Ross, Scott M. Ritter, and C. G. Maples
  1994   Proposed Repositioning of the Pennsylvanian-Permian Boundary in Kansas. In *Revision of Stratigraphic Nomenclature in Kansas,* edited by D. L. Baars, pp. 5–10. Kansas Geological Survey Bulletin 230. University of Kansas, Lawrence.

Baerreis, David A., and Reid A. Bryson
  1965   Climatic Episodes and the Dating of the Mississippian Cultures. *Wisconsin Archaeologist* 46: 203–220.

Bailey, Berkley B.
  2000   The Geoarchaeology of Day Creek Chert: Lithostratigraphy, Petrology, and the Indigenous Landscape of Northwest Oklahoma and Southwest Kansas. Ph.D. diss., University of Oklahoma, Norman. UMI Dissertation Services, Ann Arbor.

Baker, Richard G., Glen G. Fredlund, Rolfe D. Mandel, and E. Arthur Bettis III
  2000   Holocene Environments of the Central Great Plains: Multi-Proxy Evidence from Alluvial Sequences, Southeastern Nebraska. *Quaternary International* 67: 75–88.

Baker, William, and A. V. Kidder
  1937   A Spear Thrower from Oklahoma. *American Antiquity* 3: 51–52.

Bamforth, Douglas
  1988   *Ecology and Human Organization on the Great Plains.* Plenum Press, New York.

Bandy, Phillip
  1976   Lithic Technology: A Reconstruction of a Northern Texas Panhandle Archaeological Assemblage. Master's thesis, Department of Anthropology, Texas Tech University, Lubbock.

Banks, Larry D.
  1990   *From Mountain Peaks to Alligator Stomachs: A Review of Lithic Sources in the Trans-Mississippi South, the Southern Plains, and Adjacent Southwest.* Memoir No. 4. Oklahoma Anthropological Society, Norman.

Banks, William E.
  2003   The Dennis Quarry: 14PO57. National Register of Historic Places nomination submitted to the National Park Service. Copies available from the Kansas State Historical Society, Topeka.

Banks, William E., Rolfe D. Mandel, Donna C. Roper, and Christopher J. Benison
  2001   The Macy Site (14RY38): A Multicomponent Early Ceramic Occupation in Northeastern Kansas. *Plains Anthropologist* 46: 21–37.

Banks, William E., and Peter E. Wigand
  2005   Reassessment of Radiocarbon Age Determinations for the Munkers Creek Phase. *Plains Anthropologist* 50: in press.
Barnes, Ethne J.
  1977   The Calovich Burials (14WY7): Skeletal Analysis of a Plains Mississippian Population. Master's thesis, Department of Anthropology, Wichita State University, Wichita.
Barr, Thomas P.
  1971   KAA Fall Dig, 1971. *Kansas Anthropological Association Newsletter* 17 (3): 1–2.
  1973   Highway Archeological Salvage Site Location and Recommendations. Manuscript on file, Archeology Office, Kansas State Historical Society, Topeka.
  1974   *An Archaeological Assessment of the Durbin Site, 14EK331, in the Lower Elk River Watershed, Southeast Kansas*. Report to the Inter-Agency Archaeological and Paleontological Salvage Program. Kansas State Historical Society, Topeka.
Barry, Louise
  1972   *The Beginning of the West: Annals of the Kansas Gateway to the American West, 1540–1854*. Kansas State Historical Society, Topeka.
Barth, Fredrik
  1969   Introduction. In *Ethnic Groups and Boundaries: The Social Organization of Culture Difference*, edited by Fredrik Barth, pp. 9–38. Little, Brown and Company, Boston.
Bass, N. Wood
  1929   *The Geology of Cowley County, Kansas*. Kansas Geological Survey Bulletin 12. University of Kansas, Lawrence.
Bass, William M.
  1961   1960 Excavations at the Leary Site, 25RH1, Richardson County, Nebraska. *Plains Anthropologist* 6: 201–204.
  1973   Lansing Man: A Half Century Later. *American Journal of Physical Anthropology* 38 (1): 99–104.
Bass, William M., and J. H. Head
  1980   Human Skeletal Material from a Late Archaic Site in Kansas. In *Salvage Archeology of the John Redmond Lake, Kansas*, pp. 174–185. Anthropological Series No. 8. Kansas State Historical Society, Topeka.
Bass, William M., and P. S. Willey
  1966   An Analysis of a Human Skeleton from 14RY302 Riley County, Kansas. *Kansas Anthropological Association Newsletter* 12 (2): 3–5.
Baugh, Timothy G.
  1991   *The Avoca Site (14JN332): Excavation of a Grasshopper Falls Phase Structure, Jackson County, Kansas*. Contract Archeology Publications No. 8. Kansas State Historical Society, Topeka.
Bayne, Charles K.
  1956   *Geology and Ground-Water Resources of Reno County, Kansas*. Kansas Geological Survey Bulletin 120. University of Kansas, Lawrence.
Bayne, Charles K., Howard G. O'Connor, Stanley N. Davis, and Wallace B. Howe
  1971   *Pleistocene Stratigraphy of Missouri River Valley along the Kansas-Missouri Border*. Kansas Geological Survey Special Distribution Publication 53. University of Kansas, Lawrence.
Beaudry, Mary C., Lauren J. Cook, and Stephen A. Mrozowski
  1996   Artifacts and Active Voices: Material Culture as Social Discourse. In *Images of the Recent Past*, edited by Charles E. Orser, pp. 272–310. Alta Mira Press, Walnut Creek, California.
Beaver, Joe
  1998   Geographical Distribution of Hell Gap Projectile Points in Kansas and Oklahoma. *Current Research in the Pleistocene* 15: 4–6.

Beck, Margaret
- 1995 "Mississippian" Ceramics in the Central Plains Tradition: Petrographic Analysis and Interpretive Models. Master's thesis, Department of Anthropology, University of Kansas, Lawrence.
- 1998 Ceramics and Community Structure: A Reanalysis of Material from the Minneapolis Site (14OT5). *Plains Anthropologist* 43: 287–310.
- 2001 Pottery Production at the Mugler Site (14CY1-A): A Central Plains Tradition House in North-Central Kansas. *Plains Anthropologist* 46: 5–20.

Bell, Earl H., and Robert E. Cape
- 1936 The Rock Shelters of Western Nebraska. In *Chapters in Nebraska Archaeology*, vol. 1, edited by Earl H. Bell, pp. 357–399. University of Nebraska, Lincoln.

Bell, Patricia
- 1976 Spatial and Temporal Variability within the Trowbridge Site: A Kansas City Hopewell Village. In *Hopewellian Archaeology in the Lower Missouri Valley*, edited by Alfred E. Johnson, pp. 16–58. Publications in Anthropology No. 8. University of Kansas, Lawrence.

Bell, Robert E., Edward B. Jelks, and William W. Newcomb (editors)
- 1967 A Pilot Study of Wichita Indian Archaeology and Ethnohistory: Final Report. Manuscript on file, National Science Foundation, Washington, D.C.

Bement, Leland B., and Scott D. Brosowske
- 2001 Streams in No Man's Land: A Cultural Resource Survey in Beaver and Texas Counties, Oklahoma. Archeological Resource Survey Report No. 43. Oklahoma Archeological Survey, Norman.

Bement, Leland B., and Kent Buehler (editors)
- 1997 Southern Plains Bison Procurement and Utilization from Paleoindian to Historic. Plains Anthropologist Memoir 29. Vol. 42, No. 159, pp. 1–182.

Bender, Margaret M., Reid A. Bryson, and David A. Baerreis
- 1967 University of Wisconsin Radiocarbon Dates III. *Radiocarbon* 9: 530–544.

Benedict, James B.
- 1978 Getting Away from It All: A Study of Man, Mountains, and the Two-Drought Altithermal. *Southwestern Lore* 45: 1–12.

Benison, Christopher J., William E. Banks, and Rolfe D. Mandel
- 2000 *Phase IV Archeological Investigations at 14RY38: A Multicomponent Early Ceramic Period Campsite near Manhattan, Kansas.* Contract Archeology Publications No. 22. Kansas State Historical Society, Topeka.

Benn, David W.
- 1989 Hawks, Serpents, and Bird-Men: Emergence of the Oneota Mode of Production. *Plains Anthropologist* 34: 233–260.

Benn, David W. (editor)
- 1990 *Woodland Cultures on the Western Prairies: The Rainbow Site Investigations.* Report 18. Office of the State Archaeologist, University of Iowa, Iowa City.

Benson, Maxine (editor)
- 1988 *From Pittsburgh to the Rocky Mountains: Major Stephen Long's Expedition, 1819–1820.* Fulcrum, Golden.

Berger, Shelly
- 2004 Ceramic Artifacts from the Hallman Site (14HP524), A Bluff Creek Complex Site in Harper County, Kansas. *Kansas Anthropologist* 25: 75–124.

Bernabo, J. Christopher
- 1981 Quantitative Estimates of Temperature Changes over the Last 2700 Years in Michigan Based on Pollen Data. *Quaternary Research* 15: 143–159.

Bernstein, J. H.
   2002   First Recipients of Anthropological Doctorates in the United States, 1891–1930. *American Anthropologist* 104: 551–564.

Bettis, E. Arthur, III
   1990   *Holocene Alluvial Stratigraphy and Selected Aspects of the Quaternary History of Western Iowa.* Midwest Friends of the Pleistocene, Iowa Quaternary Studies Group Contribution 36, University of Iowa, Iowa City.

Bettis, E. Arthur, III (editor)
   1995   *Archaeological Geology of the Archaic Period in North America.* Special Paper 297. Geological Society of America, Boulder.

Bettis, E. Arthur, III, and Edwin R. Hajic
   1995   Landscape Development and the Location of Evidence of Archaic Cultures in the Upper Midwest. In *Archaeological Geology of the Archaic Period in North America,* edited by E. Arthur Bettis III, pp. 87–113. Special Paper 297. Geological Society of America, Boulder.

Bettis, E. Arthur, III, and Rolfe D. Mandel
   2002   The Effects of Temporal and Spatial Patterns of Holocene Erosion and Alluviation on the Archaeological Record of the Central and Eastern Great Plains, U.S.A. *Geoarchaeology: An International Journal* 17: 141–154.

Bevitt, C. Tod
   1994   Ceramics of the Wilmore Complex: A Late Prehistoric Manifestation on the Central-Southern Plains Border. Paper presented at the 52nd Annual Plains Anthropological Conference, Lubbock.
   1995   Buresh Site Ceramics: Bluff Creek Complex Connections with Cultures in the Arkansas River Valley and on the Southern Plains. Paper presented at the 17th Annual Flint Hills Conference, Norman.
   1996   Ceramics of the Seuser Site, a Late Prehistoric Occupation in Rush County, Kansas. Paper presented at the 54th Annual Plains Anthropological Conference, Iowa City.
   1997   Late Prehistoric Ceramics: A Perspective from the Central/Southern Plains Border. Paper presented at the 55th Annual Plains Anthropological Conference, Boulder.
   1998   The Lundeen Site (14MD306): Preliminary Results of the 1998 Kansas Archaeology Training Program in Meade County, Kansas. Paper presented at the 56th Annual Plains Anthropological Conference, Bismarck.
   1999a   Life on the High Plains Border: Archaeological Investigation of Three Late Prehistoric Habitation Sites in Southwest Kansas. *Kansas Anthropologist* 20: 1–106.
   1999b   Living on the Edge: The Southern High Plains Border in Late Prehistory and the Proposed Plains Border Variant. Paper presented at the 57th Annual Plains Anthropological Conference, Sioux Falls.
   2005a   *An Analysis of Rim Sherds from Several Buried City Sites.* Unpublished manuscript in the possession of the author.
   2005b   *The Seuser Site: A Late Prehistoric Component in the Walnut Creek Valley, Rush County, Kansas.* Unpublished manuscript in the possession of the author.

Bevitt, C. Tod, Rolfe D. Mandel, and Anne M. Bauer
   2003   *Phase III Archeological Investigations of Site 14BU1305 and 14BU1308 at Whitewater Watershed Structure #29, Butler County, Kansas.* Archeology Office, Kansas State Historical Society, Topeka. Submitted to Whitewater Watershed Joint District No. 22, El Dorado. Copies available from the Kansas State Historic Preservation Office, Topeka.

Billeck, William T.
   1993   Time and Space in the Glenwood Locality: The Nebraska Phase in Western Iowa. Ph.D. diss., Department of Anthropology, University of Missouri–Columbia. University Microfilms, Ann Arbor.

Billings, Melvin O.
- 1882 Ancient Remains in Marion County, Kansas. *Kansas City Review of Science and Industry* 6: 211–212.

Binford, Lewis R.
- 1978a *Nunamuit Ethnoarchaeology.* Academic Press, New York.
- 1978b Dimensional Analysis of Behavior and Site Structure: Learning from an Eskimo Hunting Stand. *American Antiquity* 43: 330–361.
- 1980 Willow Smoke and Dog's Tails: Hunter Gatherer Settlement Systems and Archaeological Site Formation Processes. *American Antiquity* 45: 4–20.
- 1981 *Bones: Ancient Men and Modern Myths.* Academic Press, New York.
- 1983 General Introduction. In *Working at Archaeology,* pp. 31–39. Academic Press, New York. Originally published in *For Theory Building in Archaeology: Essays on Faunal Remains, Aquatic Resources, Spatial Analysis, and Systemic Modeling,* edited by Lewis R. Binford, pp. 1–13, 1977. Academic Press, New York.
- 2001 *Constructing Frames of Reference.* University of California Press, Berkeley.

Birkeland, Peter W.
- 1999 *Soils and Geomorphology.* 3rd ed. Oxford University Press, Oxford.

Blackman, E. E.
- 1904 Report of Department of Archeology, Nebraska State Historical Society, for 1903 and 1904. *Annual Report of the Nebraska State Board of Agriculture for 1904:* 207–229.
- 1930 Nebraska. In Archaeological Field Work in North America during 1929. *American Anthropologist* 32: 357.

Blackmar, Jeannette
- 2001 Regional Variability in Clovis, Folsom, and Cody Land Use. *Plains Anthropologist* 46: 65–94.
- 2002 The Laird Site. Cultures. *Museum of Anthropology Newsletter* 65 (Spring). University of Kansas, Lawrence.

Blaine, Martha R.
- 1979 Mythology and Folklore: Their Possible Use in the Study of Plains Caddoan Origins. *Nebraska History* 60 (2): 240–248.
- 1990 *Pawnee Passage, 1870–1875.* University of Oklahoma Press, Norman.
- 1997 *Some Things Are Not Forgotten: A Pawnee Family Remembers.* University of Nebraska Press, Lincoln.

Blake, Leonard
- 1981 Early Acceptance of Watermelons by Indians of the United States. *Journal of Ethnobiology* 1: 193–199.

Blakeslee, Donald J.
- 1993 Modeling the Abandonment of the Central Plains: Radiocarbon Dates and the Origin of the Initial Coalescent. In *Prehistory and Human Ecology of the Western Prairies and Northern Plains,* edited by Joseph A. Tiffany, pp. 199–214. Plains Anthropologist Memoir 27. Vol. 38, No. 45.
- 1994 Reassessment of Some Radiocarbon Dates from the Central Plains. *Plains Anthropologist* 39: 203–210.
- 1995 *Along Ancient Trails: The Mallet Expedition of 1739.* University Press of Colorado, Niwot.
- 1999 Waconda Lake: Prehistoric Swidden-Foragers in the Central Plains. *Central Plains Archaeology* 7 (1): 1–170.
- 2002 What Do You Mean, Upper Republican? In *Medicine Creek: Seventy Years of Archaeological Investigations,* edited by Donna C. Roper. University of Alabama Press, Tuscaloosa.

Blakeslee, Donald J., and Robert Blasing
- 1985 *Archeological Survey of the Upper Deep Creek Drainage, Kansas.* Department of Anthropology, Wichita State University. Submitted to the Department of the Interior, National

Park Service, NPS Grant No. 20–84–8305. Copies available from the State Historic Preservation Officer, Topeka.

Blakeslee, Donald J., Robert Blasing, and Hector Garcia
- 1986 *Along the Pawnee Trail: Cultural Resources Survey and Testing, Wilson Lake, Kansas.* Report to the U.S. Army Corps of Engineers, Kansas City District.

Blakeslee, Donald J., and Warren W. Caldwell
- 1979 *The Nebraska Phase: An Appraisal.* J & L Reprint Company, Lincoln.

Blakeslee, Donald J., Michelle Peck, and Ronald A. Dorsey
- 2001 Glen Elder: A Western Oneota Bison Hunting Camp. *Midcontinental Journal of Archaeology* 26 (1): 79–104.

Blakeslee, Donald J., and Arthur H. Rohn
- 1986 *Man and Environment in Northeastern Kansas: The Hillsdale Lake Project.* 6 volumes. Wichita State University, Wichita. Submitted to U.S. Corps of Engineers, Kansas City District. Copies available from the Kansas State Historic Preservation Office, Topeka.

Blasing, Robert
- 1984 Prehistoric Sources of Chert in the Flint Hills. Manuscript on file, Department of Anthropology, Wichita State University, Wichita.
- 1990 Mineralogical Identification of Trachyte in Trego County, Kansas. Paper presented at the 48th Annual Plains Anthropological Conference, Oklahoma City.

Bolton, Herbert E.
- 1910 Tawakoni. In *Handbook of American Indians North of Mexico,* edited by F. W. Hodge, pp. 701–704. Bureau of American Ethnology Bulletin 30. Smithsonian Institution, Washington, D.C.
- 1912 The Jumano Indians in Texas, 1650–1771. *Southwestern Historical Quarterly* 15: 66–84.
- 1914a *Athanase de Mézières and the Louisiana-Texas Frontier, 1768–1780,* vol. 1. Arthur C. Clark, Cleveland.
- 1914b *Athanase de Mézières and the Louisiana-Texas Frontier, 1768–1780,* vol. 2. Arthur C. Clark, Cleveland.
- 1917 French Intrusions into New Mexico, 1749–1752. In *The Pacific Ocean in History,* edited by H. M. Stephens and H. E. Bolton, pp. 389–407. Macmillan, New York.
- 1949 *Coronado: Knight of Pueblos and Plains.* Whitley House and the University of New Mexico Press, Albuquerque.

Borchert, James R.
- 1950 The Climate of the Central North American Grassland. *Annals of the Association of American Geographers* 40: 1–30.

Boszhardt, Robert F.
- 1989 Ceramic Analysis and Site Chronology of the Pammel Creek Site. *Wisconsin Archeologist* 70 (1–2): 41–94.
- 1994 Oneota Group Continuity at La Crosse: The Brice Prairie, Pammel Creek, and Valley View Phases. *Wisconsin Archeologist* 75 (3–4): 173–236.
- 1998 Oneota Horizons: A La Crosse Perspective. *Wisconsin Archeologist* 79 (2): 196–226.
- 2000 Turquoise, Rasps, Heartlines: The Oneota Bison Pull. In *Mounds, Modoc, and Mesoamerica: Papers in Honor of Melvin L. Fowler,* edited by S. R. Ahler, pp. 361–373. Illinois State Museum Scientific Papers 28. Illinois State Museum, Springfield.

Bowman, Peter W.
- 1960 *Coal-Oil Canyon (14LO1): Report on Preliminary Investigations.* Bulletin No. 1. Kansas Anthropological Association.
- 1961 The Heil Site, 14GL401. Manuscript on file, Department of Anthropology, University of Kansas, Lawrence.
- 1996 Coal-Oil Canyon (14LO401): Progress Report, Area 7. *Kansas Anthropologist* 17 (2): 33–62.

Boyd, Douglas K.
- 1997 *Caprock Canyonlands Archeology: A Synthesis of the Prehistory of Lake Allen Henry and the Texas Panhandle-Plains.* Report of Investigations No. 110. Prewitt and Associates, Austin.
- 2004 Hank's House 2: A Puzzle Wrapped in Mystery. http://www.texasbeyondhistory.net/villagers/hank2/index.html.

Bozarth, Steven R.
- 1989 Opal Phytoliths. In *Final Summary Report: 1986 Archeological Investigations at 14MN328, A Great Bend Site along U.S. Highway 56, Marion County, Kansas,* edited by W. B. Lees, J. D. Reynolds, T. J. Martin, M. J. Adair, and S. R. Bozarth, pp. 85–90. Kansas State Historical Society. Submitted to the Kansas Department of Transportation. Copies available from the Kansas State Historic Preservation Office, Topeka.
- 1990 Diagnostic Opal Phytoliths from Pods of Selected Varieties of Common Beans (*Phaseolus vulgaris*). *American Antiquity* 55: 98–104.

Bozell, John R.
- 1988 Changes in the Role of the Dog in Protohistoric Pawnee Culture. *Plains Anthropologist* 33: 145–164.
- 1991 Fauna from the Hulme Site and Comments on Central Plains Tradition Subsistence Variability. *Plains Anthropologist* 36: 229–253.
- 1995 Culture, Environment and Bison Populations on the Late Prehistoric and Early Historic Central Plains. *Plains Anthropologist* 40: 145–164.

Bozell, John R., and Gayle F. Carlson
- 1999 Oneota in Nebraska with an Emphasis on the 18th Century Transition to Post-Contact Siouan Tribes. Paper presented at the 57th Annual Plains Anthropological Conference, Sioux Falls.

Bozell, John R., and John Ludwickson
- 1994 *Nebraska Phase Archeology in the South Bend Locality.* Nebraska State Historical Society, Highway Archeology Program. Submitted to the Nebraska Department of Roads. Copies available from the State Historic Preservation Officer, Lincoln.
- 1998a Central Plains Tradition. In *Archaeology of Prehistoric Native America: An Encyclopedia,* edited by Guy Gibbon, pp. 131–132. Garland Publishing, New York.
- 1998b Nebraska Phase. In *Archaeology of Prehistoric Native America: An Encyclopedia,* edited by Guy Gibbon, pp. 556–557. Garland Publishing, New York.
- 1999 *Archeology of the Patterson Site: Native American Life in the Lower Platte Valley,* A.D. 1000–1300. Nebraska State Historical Society, Highway Archeology Program. Submitted to the Nebraska Department of Roads. Copies available from the State Historic Preservation Officer, Lincoln.

Bozell, John R., John Ludwickson, Amy Koch, and Mary J. Adair
- 1999 Perspectives on the Late Prehistory of the South Bend Locality. In *Archeology of the Patterson Site: Native American Life in the Lower Platte Valley,* edited by John R. Bozell and John Ludwickson, pp. 101–141. Nebraska State Historical Society, Highway Archeology Program. Submitted to the Nebraska Department of Roads. Copies available from the State Historic Preservation Officer, Lincoln.

Bozell, John R., and James V. Winfrey
- 1994 A Review of Middle Woodland Archaeology in Nebraska. *Plains Anthropologist* 39: 125–144.

Bozzoli de Wille, María Euginia
- 1958 A Comparative Study of Ceramic Traits within the Central Plains Phase. Master's thesis, Department of Anthropology, University of Kansas, Lawrence.

Bradley, Lawrence E.
- 1973 Subsistence Strategy at a Late Archaic Site in South-Central Kansas. Master's thesis, Department of Anthropology, University of Kansas, Lawrence.

Braun, David P.
- 1977 Middle Woodland–Early Late Woodland Social Change in the Prehistoric Central Midwestern U.S. Ph.D. diss., University of Michigan. University Microfilms, 77–26210, Ann Arbor.
- 1979 Illinois Hopewell Burial Practices and Social Organizations: A Reexamination of the Klunk-Gibson Mound Group. In *Hopewell Archaeology: The Chillicothe Conference*, edited by D. S. Brose and N. Greber, pp. 66–79. Kent State University Press, Kent, Ohio.
- 1983 Pots as Tools. In *Archaeological Hammers and Theories*, edited by J. A. Moore and A. S. Keene, pp. 107–134. Academic Press, New York.
- 1985 Ceramic Decorative Diversity and Illinois Woodland Regional Integration. In *Decoding Prehistoric Ceramics*, edited by B. A. Nelson, pp. 128–153. Southern Illinois University Press, Carbondale.
- 1987 Coevolution of Sedentism, Pottery Technology, and Horticulture in the Central Midwest, 200 B.C.–A.D. 600. In *Emergent Horticultural Economies of the Eastern Woodlands*, edited by W. F. Keegan, pp. 153–181. Occasional Paper No. 7. Center for Archaeological Investigations, Southern Illinois University, Carbondale.
- 1991 Why Decorate a Pot? Midwestern Household Pottery, 200 B.C.–A.D. 600. *Journal of Anthropological Archaeology* 10: 360–397.

Braun, David P., and Stephen Plog
- 1982 Evolution of 'Tribal' Social Networks: Theory and Prehistoric North American Evidence. *American Antiquity* 47: 504–525.

Brogan, William T.
- 1981 *The Cuesta Phase: A Settlement Pattern Study*. Anthropological Series No. 9. Kansas State Historical Society, Topeka.
- 1982 *The Roth Site: An Early Pomona Focus Manifestation in Eastern Kansas*. Contract Archeology Publication No. 1. Kansas State Historical Society, Topeka.

Bronk Ramsey, Christopher
- 1995 Radiocarbon Calibration and Analysis of Stratigraphy: The OxCal Program. *Radiocarbon* 37: 425–430.
- 2001 Development of the Radiocarbon Program OxCal. *Radiocarbon* 43: 355–363.

Brooks, George R.
- 1965 George C. Sibley's Journal of a Trip to the Salines in 1811. *Missouri Historical Society Bulletin* 21 (3): 167–207.

Brooks, Robert
- 1986 Archeological Investigations at the Lonker Site: A Plains Village Settlement in the Oklahoma Panhandle. Paper presented at the 44th Annual Plains Anthropological Conference, Denver.
- 1987 *The Arthur Site: Settlement and Subsistence Structure at a Washita River Phase Village*. Studies in Oklahoma's Past No. 15. Oklahoma Archeological Survey, University of Oklahoma, Norman.
- 1994a Variability in Southern Plains Cultural Complexes: Archaeological Investigations at the Lonker Site in the Oklahoma Panhandle. *Bulletin of the Oklahoma Anthropological Society* 43: 1–27.
- 1994b Warfare on the Southern Plains. In *Skeletal Biology in the Great Plains: Migration, Warfare, Health, and Subsistence*, edited by D. W. Owsley and R. L. Jantz, pp. 317–323. Smithsonian Institution Press, Washington, D.C.

Brooks, Robert L., Michael C. Moore, and Douglas Owsley
- 1992 New Smith, 34RM400: A Plains Village Mortuary Site in Western Oklahoma. *Plains Anthropologist* 37: 59–78.

Brosowske, Scott D.
- 1999 OU Archeological Field School at the Odessa Yates Site. *Oklahoma Archeological Survey Newsletter* 19: 2–3.
- 2000 Results of the 1999 Summer Field School at the Odessa Yates Site in Beaver County. Paper presented at the Oklahoma Anthropological Society Spring Meeting, Norman.
- 2002a Horticulturalists along the Periphery: The Emergence of the Village Economy on the Southern High Plains. Paper presented at the 60th Annual Plains Anthropological Conference, Oklahoma City.
- 2002b What Exactly Is the Zimms Complex? A Review and Synthesis of Architectural and Assemblage Traits. *Oklahoma Archeology: Journal of the Oklahoma Anthropological Society* 50 (4): 20–39.
- 2004 The Emergence of Regional Trade Centers: The Spatial Distribution of Obsidian at Middle Ceramic Settlements of the Southern High Plains. *Council of Texas Archaeologists Newsletter* 28 (2): 16–28.

Brosowske, Scott D., and Leland B. Bement
- 1998a Plains Interaction during the Late Prehistoric: A View from Some New Sites in the Oklahoma Panhandle. Paper presented at the 56th Annual Plains Anthropological Conference, Bismarck.
- 1998b *Pedestrian Survey of Playa Lake Environments in Beaver and Texas Counties, Oklahoma.* Archeological Resource Survey Report No. 39. Oklahoma Archeological Survey, Norman.

Brosowske, Scott D., Richard R. Drass, and David L. Maki
- 2000 The Odessa Yates Project (OYP): Investigation of a Plains Village Period Settlement in the Oklahoma Panhandle. Paper presented at the Joint Midwest Archeological/Plains Anthropological Conference, St. Paul.

Brosowske, Scott D., and David L. Maki
- 2002 *Ground Truthing Geophysical Anomalies at Area 1, Buried City Complex, Ochiltree County, Texas.* Archaeo-Physics Report of Investigations No. 40. Minneapolis.

Brosowske, Scott D., David L. Maki, Susan Vehik, and C. Tod Bevitt
- 2003 What If Stone Houses Had Never Been Found along Wolf Creek? Recent Adventures at Buried City. Paper presented at the 61st Annual Plains Anthropological Conference, Fayetteville.

Brower, Jacob V.
- 1898 *Quivira: Memoirs of Explorations in the Basin of the Mississippi River,* vol. 1. Jacob V. Brower, St. Paul.

Brown, James A., Richard A. Kerber, and Howard D. Winters
- 1990 Trade and the Evolution of Exchange Relations at the Beginning of the Mississippian Period. In *The Mississippian Emergence,* edited by Bruce D. Smith, pp. 251–280. Smithsonian Institution Press, Washington, D.C.

Brown, Kenneth L.
- 1985 Pomona: A Plains Village Variant in Eastern Kansas and Western Missouri. Ph.D. diss., Department of Anthropology, University of Kansas, Lawrence.
- 1987 Other Cultural Complexes and Specific Types of Sites. In *Kansas Prehistoric Archaeological Preservation Plan,* edited by Kenneth L. Brown and Alan H. Simmons, pp. 298–311. Office of Archaeological Research, Museum of Anthropology, and Center for Public Affairs, University of Kansas, Lawrence.

Brown, Kenneth L., and Marie E. Brown
- 1987a The Paleo-Indian Period. In *Kansas Prehistoric Archaeological Preservation Plan,* edited by Kenneth L. Brown and Alan H. Simmons, pp. 2–33. Office of Archaeological Research, Museum of Anthropology, and Center for Public Affairs, University of Kansas, Lawrence.

1987b The Archaic, Ceramic and Historic Periods. In *Kansas Prehistoric Archaeological Preservation Plan*, edited by Kenneth L. Brown and Alan H. Simmons, pp. 34–297. Office of Archaeological Research, Museum of Anthropology, and Center for Public Affairs, University of Kansas, Lawrence.

Brown, Kenneth L., and Brad Logan
1987 The Distribution of Paleoindian Sites in Kansas. In *Quaternary Environments of Kansas*, edited by W. C. Johnson, pp. 189–195. Kansas Geological Survey Guidebook Series 5. University of Kansas, Lawrence.

Brown, Kenneth L., and Alan H. Simmons (editors)
1987 *Kansas Prehistoric Archaeological Preservation Plan*. Office of Archaeological Research, Museum of Anthropology, and Center for Public Affairs, University of Kansas, Lawrence.

Brown, Kenneth L., and Robert J. Ziegler (editors)
1981 *Prehistoric Cultural Resources within the Right-of-Way of the Proposed Little Blue River Channel*. Museum of Anthropology, University of Kansas, Lawrence. U.S. Army Corps of Engineers, Kansas City District.

Brown, Lionel A.
1966 Temporal and Spatial Order in the Central Plains. *Plains Anthropologist* 11: 294–301.
1967 *Pony Creek Archaeology*. Publications in Salvage Archeology No. 5. Smithsonian Institution, River Basin Surveys, Lincoln.

Brown, Marie E.
1982 Cultural Behavior as Reflected in the Vertebrate Faunal Assemblage of Three Smoky Hill Sites. Master's thesis, Department of Anthropology, University of Kansas, Lawrence.

Brunswig, Robert H., Jr.
1995 Apachean Ceramics East of Colorado's Continental Divide: Current Data and New Directions. In *Archaeological Pottery of Colorado: Ceramic Clues to the Prehistoric and Protohistoric Lives of the State's Native Peoples*, edited by Robert H. Brunswig, Jr., Bruce Bradley, and Susan M. Chandler, pp. 172–192. Occasional Papers No. 2. Colorado Council of Professional Archaeologists, Denver.

Brush, G. S.
1967 Pollen Analysis of Late Glacial and Postglacial Sediments in Iowa. In *Quaternary Paleoecology*, edited by Edward J. Cushing and Herbert E. Wright, Jr., pp. 99–115. Yale University Press, New Haven.

Bryson, Reid A.
1966 Air Masses, Streamlines, and the Boreal Forest. *Geographical Bulletin* 8: 228–269.

Bryson, Reid A., and David A. Baerreis
1968 Introduction and Project Summary. In *Climatic Change and the Mill Creek Culture of Iowa*, edited by Dale R. Henning, pp. 1–34. *Journal of the Iowa Archaeological Society* 15.

Bryson, Reid A., and F. Kenneth Hare
1974 *Climates of North America*. Elsevier, New York.

Bryson, Reid A., David A. Baerreis, and Wayne M. Wendland
1970 The Character of Late-Glacial and Post-Glacial Climatic Changes. In *Pleistocene and Recent Environments of the Central Great Plains*, edited by Wakefield Dort, Jr., and J. Knox Jones, Jr., pp. 53–76. University Press of Kansas, Lawrence.

Buckner, Virginia
1970 Kansas Anthropological Association Archeological Site Report for 14ST401. On file at the Kansas State Historical Society, Topeka.
1973 Letter to Thomas Witty (dated November 12, 1973). On file at the Kansas State Historical Society, Topeka.

Buehler, Kent
- 1991 Please Pass the Fetal Stew: Analysis of a Late Prehistoric Trash Pit in Northwest Oklahoma. Paper presented at the 49th Annual Plains Anthropological Conference, Lawrence.
- 1992 Continued Research at Traders Creek: Glimpses of the Protohistoric Period in Northwest Oklahoma. Paper presented at the 50th Annual Plains Anthropological Conference, Lincoln.

Buffalohead, Eric
- 2004 Dhegihan History: A Personal Journey. In *Dhegihan and Chiwere Siouans in the Plains: Historical and Archaeological Perspectives.* Plains Anthropologist Memoir 36. Vol. 49, No. 182, Pt. 1, pp. 327–343.

Buikstra, Jane
- 1976 Hopewell in the Lower Illinois Valley: A Regional Study of Human Biological Variability and Prehistoric Mortuary Behavior. Scientific Papers No. 2, Northwestern University Archeological Program, Evanston, Illinois.

Bushnell, David I., Jr.
- 1922 *Villages of the Algonquian, Siouan, and Caddoan Tribes West of the Mississippi.* Bureau of American Ethnology Bulletin No. 77. Smithsonian Institution, Washington, D.C.

Butler, Todd
- 1997 Lithic Material Availability, Quality, and Selection in the Protohistoric High Plains. Master's thesis, Department of Anthropology, University of Kansas, Lawrence.

Butler, William B.
- 1988 The Woodland Period in Northeastern Colorado. *Plains Anthropologist* 33: 449–465.
- 1997 Cultural and Climatic Patterns in the Faunal Record from Western Plains Archaeological Sites. *Southwestern Lore* 63 (4): 1–36.

Butler, William B., Stephen A. Chomko, and J. Michael Hoffman
- 1986 The Red Creek Burial, El Paso County, Colorado. *Southwestern Lore* 52: 6–27.

Calabrese, Francis A.
- 1967 *The Archeology of the Upper Verdigris Watershed.* Anthropological Series No. 3. Kansas State Historical Society, Topeka.
- 1969 *Doniphan Phase Origins: An Hypothesis Resulting from Archaeological Investigations in the Smithville Reservoir Area, Missouri: 1968.* Report to the National Park Service, Midwest Region. American Archaeology Division, University of Missouri, Columbia.

Campbell, Robert G.
- 1976 *The Panhandle Aspect of the Chaquaqua Plateau.* Graduate Studies No. 11. Texas Tech University, Lubbock.

Carlson, Gayle F.
- 1971 A Local Sequence for Upper Republican Sites in the Glen Elder Reservoir Locality, Kansas. Master's thesis, Department of Anthropology, University of Nebraska, Lincoln.

Cassells, E. Steve
- 1997 *The Archaeology of Colorado.* Johnson Books, Boulder.

Castañeda, C. E.
- 1939 *The Mission Era: The Passing of the Missions, 1762–1782. Our Catholic Heritage in Texas, 1519–1936,* vol. 4. Von Boeckmann-Jones, Austin.

Cattelain, Pierre
- 1989 Un crochet de propulseur de la grotte de Combe-Saunière 1. *Bulletin de la Société Préhistorique Française* 86: 213–216.

Chambers, Mary Elizabeth, and Sally Kress Tompkins, with Robert Lee Humphrey and Cecil R. Brooks
- 1977 *The Cultural Resources of Clinton Lake, Kansas: An Inventory of Archaeology, History and*

Architecture. Report to the U.S. Army Corps of Engineers, Kansas City District. Iroquois Research Institute, Fairfax, Virginia.

Champe, John L.
- 1946 *Ash Hollow Cave:, A Study of Stratigraphic Sequence in the Central Great Plains.* University of Nebraska Studies, n.s., No. 1, Lincoln.
- 1949 White Cat Village. *American Antiquity* 14: 285–292.
- 1950 Archeological Investigations in the Harlan County Reservoir, 1950. River Basin Surveys Reports, Lincoln.

Chapman, Carl H.
- 1948 A Preliminary Survey of Missouri Archaeology, Part IV: Ancient Cultures and Sequence. *Missouri Archaeologist* 10 (4): 133–164.
- 1975 *The Archaeology of Missouri,* vol. 1. University of Missouri Press, Columbia.
- 1980 *The Archeology of Missouri,* vol. 2. University of Missouri Press, Columbia.

Chapman, Jefferson, and Gary Crites
- 1987 Evidence for Early Maize (*Zea mays*) from the Ice-House Bottom Site, Tennessee. *American Antiquity* 52: 352–354.

Chardon, Roland
- 1980 The Linear League in North America. *Annals of the Association of American Geographers* 70 (2): 129–153.

Ciurczak, D. M.
- 1997 Trace Analysis of Archaeological Artifacts Using Nuclear Methods and Inductively Coupled Plasma-Mass Spectrometry. Ph.D. diss., Department of Chemistry, University of Maryland, College Park. University Microfilms, Ann Arbor.

Cleland, Charles E.
- 1976 The Focal-Diffuse Model: An Evolutionary Perspective on the Prehistoric Cultural Adaptations of the Eastern United States. *Midcontinental Journal of Archaeology* 1 (1): 59–76.

Clokey, Richard M.
- 1980 *William H. Ashley: Enterprise and Politics in the Trans-Mississippi West.* University of Oklahoma Press, Norman.

Cobry, Anne M., and Donna C. Roper
- 2002 From Loess Plains to High Plains: The Westward Movement of Upper Republican Pots. In *Geochemical Evidence for Long-Distance Exchange,* edited by Michael D. Glascock, pp. 153–166. Bergin & Garvey, Westport, Connecticut.

COHMAP Members
- 1988 Climatic Change of the Last 18,000 Years: Observations and Model Simulations. *Science* 241: 1043–1052.

Conrad, G. R. (editor and annotator)
- 1971 *Historical Journal of the Settlement of the French in Louisiana.* University of Southwestern Louisiana Series No. 3. Lafayette, Louisiana.

Cook, Eva L.
- 2001 Keeping Up with the Hopewells, or When to Toss the Dishes: A Decorative Analysis of Two Middle Woodland Period Ceramic Assemblages from Delaware County, Oklahoma. Master's thesis, Department of Anthropology, University of Kansas, Lawrence.

Cooper, Paul
- 1937 Field notes on file with the Nebraska State Historical Society, Lincoln.

Coues, Elliott (editor)
- 1895 *The Expeditions of Zebulon Montgomery Pike,* by Francis P. Harper. Facsimile reprint in two volumes, 1987, Dover Publications, New York.

Cowan, C. Wesley, and Bruce D. Smith
    1993   New Perspectives on a Wild Gourd in Eastern North America. *Journal of Ethnobiology* 13: 17–54.

Craine, E. R.
    1956   The Pfaff Site: A Preliminary Report. *Kansas Anthropological Association Newsletter* 1 (6): 2–4.

Creel, Darrell
    1991   Bison Hides in Late Prehistoric Exchange in the Southern Plains. *American Antiquity* 56: 40–49.

Creel, Darrell, Robert F. Scott IV, and Michael B. Collins
    1990   A Faunal Record from West Central Texas and Its Bearing on Late Holocene Bison Population Changes in the Southern Plains. *Plains Anthropologist* 35: 55–69.

Cumming, Robert B., Jr.
    1958   Archeological Investigations at the Tuttle Creek Dam, Kansas. *River Basin Surveys Papers No. 10*. Bulletin 169: 41–78. Bureau of American Ethnology, Smithsonian Institution, Washington, D.C.

Cummings, Linda Scott, and Kate A. Rylander
    1988   Macrobotancial Remains Recovered from 25FT70: A Study of Cultivated Plants. Manuscript prepared for Bureau of Reclamation, Grand Island, Nebraska.

Cutler, Hugh C., and Leonard W. Blake
    1973   *Plants from Archaeological Sites East of the Rockies.* Missouri Botanical Gardens, St. Louis.
    1983   Identified botanical remains. Appendix F, in *Walker-Gilmore: A Stratified Woodland Occupation in Eastern Nebraska.* Notebook No. 6. Division of Archeological Research, Department of Anthropology, University of Nebraska, Lincoln.

Davis, Leslie B., and Michael Wilson
    1980   *Bison Procurement and Utilization: A Symposium.* Plains Anthropologist Memoir 14. Vol. 23, No. 82, Pt. 2, pp. 1–361. Lincoln.

Davis, Leslie, Stephan A. Aaberg, William P. Eckerle, John W. Fisher, Jr., and Sally T. Greiser
    1989   Montane Paleoindian Occupation of the Barton Gulch Site, Ruby Valley, Southwestern Montana. *Current Research in the Pleistocene* 6: 7–9.

Dean, Jeffrey S.
    1997   Dendrochronology. In *Chronometric Dating in Archaeology,* edited by R. E. Taylor and Martin J. Aitken, pp. 31–64. Advances in Archaeological and Museum Science, vol. 2. Plenum Press, New York.

Decker-Walters, Denna S., Terence W. Walters, C. Wesley Cowan, and Bruce D. Smith
    1993   Isozymic Characteristics of Wild Populations of *Cucurbita pepo. Journal of Ethnobiology* 13: 55–72.

Deevey, Edward S., and Richard F. Flint
    1957   Postglacial Hypsithermal Interval. *Science* 125: 182–184.

Delanglez, Jean
    1985   [1700] Tonti Letters. In *Anthology: Selections Useful for Mississippi Valley and Trans-Mississippi American Indian Studies,* edited with an introduction by Mildred Mott Wedel, pp. 209–238. Garland Publishing, New York.
    1985   [1946] The Jolliet Lost Map of the Mississippi. In *Anthology: Selections Useful for Mississippi Valley and Trans-Mississippi American Indian Studies,* edited with an introduction by Mildred Mott Wedel, pp. 67–144. Garland Publishing, New York.

Deuel, Thorne
    1952   The Hopewellian Community. In *Hopewellian Communities in Illinois,* edited by Thorne Deuel, pp. 249–270. Illinois State Museum, Scientific Papers 5, Springfield.

Dillehay, T. D.
　1974　Late Quaternary Bison Population Changes on the Southern Plains. *Plains Anthropologist* 19: 180–196.

Din, Gilbert C., and Abraham P. Nasatir
　1983　*The Imperial Osages: Spanish-Indian Diplomacy in the Mississippi Valley.* University of Oklahoma Press, Norman.

Dorsey, George A.
　1904　*The Mythology of the Wichita.* Carnegie Institution of Washington, Washington, D.C.
　1906　*The Pawnee: Mythology (Part I).* Publication 59. Carnegie Institution of Washington, Washington, D.C.

Dorsey, James Owen
　1882　*James Owen Dorsey Papers.* The National Anthropological Archives, Manuscript No. 4800 (Kansa), Smithsonian Institution, Washington, D.C.

Dort, Wakefield, Jr.
　1966　Nebraskan and Kansan Stades: Complexity and Importance. *Science* 154: 771–772.
　1985　Field Evidence for More Than Two Early Pleistocene Glaciations of the Central Plains. *Ter-Qua Symposium Series* 1: 41–51.
　1987　Salient Aspects of the Terminal Zone of Continental Glaciation in Kansas. In *Quaternary Environments of Kansas,* edited by William C. Johnson, pp. 55–66. Kansas Geological Survey Guidebook Series 5. University of Kansas, Lawrence.

Dragoo, Don W.
　1976　Some Aspects of Eastern North American Prehistory: A Review–1975. *American Antiquity* 41: 3–27.

Drass, Richard R.
　1995　Culture Change on the Eastern Margins of the Southern Plains. Ph.D. diss., Department of Anthropology, University of Oklahoma, Norman.
　1997　*Culture Change on the Eastern Margins of the Southern Plains.* Studies in Oklahoma's Past No. 19 and Oklahoma Anthropological Society Memoir No. 7. Oklahoma Archeological Survey, University of Oklahoma, Norman.
　1998　The Southern Plains Villagers. In *Archaeology on the Great Plains,* edited by W. Raymond Wood, pp. 415–455. University Press of Kansas, Lawrence.
　1999　Two Late Prehistoric Sites in Northwest Oklahoma. *Bulletin of the Oklahoma Anthropological Society* 48: 135–159.

Drass, Richard R., and Peggy Flynn
　1990　Temporal and Geographic Variations in Subsistence Practices for Plains Villagers in the Southern Plains. *Plains Anthropologist* 35: 175–190.

Drass, Richard R., and Christopher L. Turner
　1989　*An Archaeological Reconnaissance of the Wolf Creek Drainage Basin, Ellis County, Oklahoma.* Survey Report No. 35. Oklahoma Archaeological Survey, Norman.

Dreeszen, V. H.
　1970　The Stratigraphic Framework of Pleistocene Glacial and Periglacial Deposits in the Central Plains. In *Pleistocene and Recent Environments of the Central Great Plains,* edited by Wakefield Dort, Jr., and J. Knox Jones, Jr., pp. 9–22. University Press of Kansas, Lawrence.

Dreimanis, Aleksis
　1968　Extinction of Mastodons in Eastern North America: Testing a New Climatic-Environmental Hypothesis. *Ohio Journal of Science* 68: 257–272.

Dunbar, John B.
　1880　The Pawnee Indians: Their History and Ethnology. *Magazine of American History* 4: 241–281.

Dunlevy, Marion Lucille
   1936   A Comparison of the Cultural Manifestations of the Burkett (Nance County) and Gray-Wolfe (Colfax County) Sites. In *Chapters in Nebraska Archaeology,* edited by Earl H. Bell, pp. 147–247. University of Nebraska, Lincoln.

Dunnell, Robert C.
   1971   *Systematics in Prehistory.* Free Press, New York.
   1986   Methodological Issues in Americanist Artifact Classification. In *Advances in Archaeological Method and Theory,* vol. 9, edited by Michael B. Schiffer, pp. 149–207. Academic Press, New York.

Dunnell, Robert C., and William S. Dancey
   1983   The Siteless Survey: A Regional Scale Data Collection Strategy. In *Advances in Archaeological Method and Theory,* vol. 6, edited by Michael B. Schiffer, pp. 267–287. Academic Press, New York.

Durkee, Lenore H.
   1971   A Pollen Profile from Woden Bog in North-Central Iowa. *Ecology* 52: 37–844.

Ebert, James I.
   1992   *Distributional Archaeology.* University of New Mexico Press, Albuquerque.

Echo-Hawk, Roger C.
   2000   Ancient History in the New World: Integrating Oral Traditions and the Archaeological Record. *American Antiquity* 65: 267–290.

Edwards, William E.
   1967   The Late-Pleistocene Extinction and Diminution in Size of Many Mammalian Species. In *Pleistocene Extinctions: The Search for a Cause,* edited by Paul S. Martin and Herbert E. Wright, Jr., pp. 141–154. Yale University Press, New Haven.

Ehrenberg, Ralph E.
   1987   Exploratory Mapping of the Great Plains before 1800. In *Mapping the North American Plains: Essays in the History of Cartography,* edited by Frederick C. Luebke, Frances W. Kaye, and Gary E. Moulton, pp. 3–26. University of Oklahoma Press, Norman.

Eighmy, Jeffrey L.
   1994   The Central High Plains: A Cultural Historical Summary. In *Plains Indians, A.D. 500–1500: The Archaeological Past of Historic Groups,* edited by Karl H. Schlesier, pp. 224–238. University of Oklahoma Press, Norman.

Elcock, D. G., and Patricia J. O'Brien
   1979   *Cultural Resources Survey of Fall River Lake, Kansas.* Report submitted to Tulsa District U.S. Army Corps of Engineers. Copies available from the Kansas State Historic Preservation Office, Topeka.

Ellzey, Tom S.
   1966   *A Panhandle Aspect Site (preliminary report).* Special Bulletin No. 1, pp. 59–65. Midland Archaeological Society, Midland, Texas.
   1985   Field Survey of Archeological Site on Lake Fryer County Park, Ochiltree County, Texas. Paper presented at the 56th Annual Meeting of the Texas Archeological Society, San Antonio.

Emerson, Alice M.
   1977   Evidence for Floodplain Settlement in the Great Bend Aspect of Marion, Kansas. Master's thesis, Department of Anthropology, Wichita State University, Wichita.

Estep, Rose F.
   1993   The R. B. Aker Collection: A Significant Collection for Future Research along the Lower Missouri River Region in Northwestern Missouri. *Missouri Archaeological Society Quarterly* 10 (2): 12–17.

Ewers, John C.
   1955   *The Horse in Blackfoot Culture.* Bureau of American Ethnology Bulletin 159. Washington, D.C.

Eyman, Charles E.
  1966 The Schultz Focus: A Plains Middle Woodland Burial Complex in Eastern Kansas. Master's thesis, Department of Archaeology, University of Alberta, Calgary.
Falk, Carl R.
  1969 The Mowry Bluff Artifacts: Faunal Remains. In *Two House Sites in the Central Plains: An Experiment in Archaeology,* edited by W. Raymond Wood, pp. 44–51. Plains Anthropologist Memoir 6. Vol. 14, No. 44, Pt. 2, pp. 44–51.
Farnham, Thomas Jefferson
  1966 [1843] Travels in the Great Western Prairies, the Anahuac and Rocky Mountains, and in the Oregon Territory. In *Early Western Travels, 1748–1846,* vol. 28, edited by Reuben Gold Thwaites, pp. 26–380. AMS Press, New York.
Feagins, Jim D.
  1988 Nebraska Phase Burials in Northwest Missouri: A Study of Three Localities. *Missouri Archaeologist* 49: 41–56.
  1993 R. B. Aker and the Archaeology of the Kansas City Area: A Personal Perspective. *Missouri Archaeological Society Quarterly* 10 (1): 12–18.
  1996 The Bourbon Complex: A Late Prehistoric Plains Caddoan Subsistence Strategy near the Kansas-Missouri Border. Paper presented at the 54th Annual Plains Anthropological Conference, Iowa City.
Fenenga, Franklin, and Joe B. Wheat
  1940 An Atlatl from the Baylor Rockshelter, Culberson County, Texas. *American Antiquity* 5: 221–223.
Feng, Zhao-dong, William C. Johnson, D. R. Sprowl, and Yan-chou Lu
  1994 Loess Accumulation and Soil Formation in Central Kansas, United States, during the Past 400,000 Years. *Earth Surface Processes and Landforms* 19: 55–67.
Fenneman, Nevin M.
  1931 *Physiography of Western United States.* McGraw-Hill, New York.
Fent, Oscar S.
  1950 Pleistocene Drainage History of Central Kansas. *Transactions of the Kansas Academy of Science* 53: 81–90.
Fiedel, Stuart, and Gary Haynes
  2004 A Premature Burial: Comments on Grayson and Meltzer's "Requiem for Overkill." *Journal of Archaeological Science* 31: 121–131.
Finnegan, Michael
  1977 Osteological Analysis of Skeletal Remains from the Chester Reeves Mound (23CL108), A Steed-Kisker Mississippian Population. In *Cultural Resources Survey of Smithville Lake, Missouri, Volume I: Archeology,* edited by Patricia J. O'Brien, pp. 111–163. Report to the U.S. Army Corps of Engineers, Kansas City District. Department of Sociology, Anthropology, and Social Work, Kansas State University, Manhattan.
  1981 Archaic Skeletal Remains from the Central Plains: Demography and Burial Practices. In *Progress in Skeletal Biology of Plains Population,* edited by R. L. Jantz and D. H. Ubelaker, pp. 85–92. Plains Anthropologist Memoir 17. Vol. 26, No. 94, Pt. 2, pp. 85–92.
Finnegan, Michael, and Dixie L. West
  1990 Faunal Remains from the Stigenwalt Site. Appendix IV, in *The Archeology of the Stigenwalt Site, 14LT351,* edited by Randall M. Thies, pp. 160–184. Contract Archeology Series Publication No. 7. Kansas State Historical Society, Topeka.
Fishel, Richard L. (editor)
  1999a Oneota in Northwest Iowa. In *Bison Hunters of the Western Prairies: Archaeological Investigations at the Dixon Site (13WD8), Woodbury County, Iowa,* edited by Richard L. Fishel, pp. 117–135. Report No. 21. Office of the State Archaeologist, University of Iowa, Iowa City.
  1999b *Bison Hunters of the Western Prairies: Archaeological Investigations at the Dixon Site*

(13WD8), Woodbury County, Iowa. Report 21. Office of the State Archaeologist, University of Iowa, Iowa City.

Flannery, Tim F.
1999   Debating Extinction. *Science* 283: 182–183.

Flores, D. L.
1985   *Journal of an Indian Trader: Anthony Glass and the Texas Trading Frontier, 1790–1810.* Texas A&M University Press, College Station.

Flynn, Peggy
1984   An Analysis of the 1973 Test Excavations at the Zimms Site (34RM72). In *Archaeology of the Mixed Grass Prairie, Phase I: Quartermaster Creek,* edited by Timothy G. Baugh, pp. 215–290. Archaeological Resource Survey Report No. 20. Oklahoma Archaeological Survey, Norman.

Foley, Robert
1981a   *Off-Site Archaeology and Human Adaptation in Eastern Africa: An Analysis of Regional Artifact Density in the Amboseli, Southern Kenya.* Cambridge Monographs in African Archaeology No. 3, BAR International Series No. 97. Oxford.
1981b   Off-Site Archaeology: An Alternative Approach for the Short-Sited. In *Patterns of the Past: Studies in Honour of David Clarke,* edited by Ian Hodder, Glynn Isaac, and Norman Hammond, pp. 157–183. Cambridge University Press, New York.

Ford, Richard I.
1974   Northeastern Archaeology: Past and Future Directions. *Annual Review of Anthropology* 3: 385–413.
2003   Foreword. In *People and Plants in Ancient Eastern North America,* edited by Paul E. Minnis, pp. xii–xvi. Smithsonian Institution Press, Washington, D.C.

Ford, Richard I. (editor)
1985   *Prehistoric Food Production in North America.* Anthropological Papers No. 75. University of Michigan, Museum of Anthropology, Ann Arbor.

Fosha, Michael
1994   A Case Study of Inequality among Smoky Hill Variant Populations. Master's thesis, Department of Anthropology, University of Kansas, Lawrence.

Fosha, Michael, and Barry G. Williams
1990   Dates, Pots, and Pits: A Grasshopper Falls Phase Site in Northeastern Kansas. Paper presented at the 12th Annual Flint Hills Archaeological Conference, Kansas City.

Fowke, Gerard
1922   *Archeological Investigations.* Bulletin 76. Bureau of American Ethnology, Smithsonian Institution, Washington, D.C.

Francis, Julie E.
1995   Root Procurement in the Upper Green River Basin: Archaeological Investigations at 48SU1002. Paper presented at the 53rd Annual Plains Anthropological Conference, Laramie.

Frantz, Wendell
1966   Excavations of the Nebraska State Historical Society at the Leary Site (25RH1), 1965. *Plains Anthropologist* 11 (32): 163.

Fredlund, Glen G.
1992   Analysis of Quaternary Pollen from Cheyenne Bottoms, Kansas: Evidence for Late Quaternary Vegetation and Climates in the Central Great Plains. Ph.D. diss., Department of Geology, University of Kansas, Lawrence.
1995   A Late Quaternary Pollen Record from Cheyenne Bottoms, Kansas. *Quaternary Research* 43: 67–79.

Frison, George C.
- 1965 Spring Creek Cave, Wyoming. *American Antiquity* 32: 81–94.
- 1978 *Prehistoric Hunters of the High Plains.* Academic Press, New York.
- 1991 *Prehistoric Hunters of the High Plains.* 2nd ed. Academic Press, New York.
- 1992 The Foothills-Mountains and the Open Plains: The Dichotomy in Paleoindian Subsistence Strategies between Two Ecosystems. In *Ice Age Hunters of the Rockies*, edited by Dennis J. Stanford and Jane S. Day, pp. 323–342. Denver Museum of Natural History and University Press of Colorado, Niwot.

Frison, George C. (editor)
- 1996 *The Mill Iron Site.* University of New Mexico Press, Albuquerque.

Frison, George C., R. L. Andrews, J. M. Adovasio, R. C. Carlisle, and Robert Edgar.
- 1986 A Late Paleoindian Animal Trapping Net from Northern Wyoming. *American Antiquity* 51: 352–361.

Frison, George C., Michael Wilson, and Diane J. Wilson
- 1976 Fossil Bison and Artifacts from an Early Altithermal Period Arroyo Trap in Wyoming. *American Antiquity* 41: 28–57.

Fritts, Harold C., G. Robert Lofgren, and Geoffrey A. Gordon
- 1979 Variations in Climate since 1602 as Reconstructed from Tree Rings. *Quaternary Research* 12: 18–46.

Fritz, Gayle J.
- 1990 Multiple Pathways to Farming in Precontact Eastern North America. *Journal of World Prehistory* 4 (4): 387–435.

Frye, John C.
- 1946 The High Plains Surface in Kansas. *Transactions of the Kansas Academy of Science* 49: 71–86.
- 1950 *Origin of Kansas Great Plains Depressions.* Kansas Geological Survey Bulletin 85 (1). University of Kansas, Lawrence.

Frye, John C., and A. Byron Leonard
- 1949 Pleistocene Stratigraphic Sequence in Northeastern Kansas. *American Journal of Science* 247: 883–899.
- 1952 *Pleistocene Geology of Kansas.* Kansas Geological Survey Bulletin 99. University of Kansas, Lawrence.

Frye, John C., A. Byron Leonard, and Ada Swineford
- 1956 Stratigraphy of the Ogallala Formation (Neogene) of Northern Kansas. Kansas Geological Survey Bulletin 118. University of Kansas, Lawrence.

Frye, John C., and Kenneth L. Walters
- 1950 *Subsurface Reconnaissance of Glacial Deposits in Northeastern Kansas.* Kansas Geological Survey Bulletin 86, pt. 6, pp. 141–158. University of Kansas, Lawrence.

Fulmer, Darrell W.
- 1976 *Archaeological Excavations within the El Dorado Reservoir Area, Kansas (1974).* Department of the Interior, National Park Service, Interagency Archaeological Services, Denver. Museum of Anthropology, University of Kansas, Lawrence.
- 1977 *Archaeological Investigations in the El Dorado Reservoir Area, Kansas (1975).* Department of the Interior, National Park Service, Interagency Archaeological Services, Denver. Museum of Anthropology, University of Kansas, Lawrence.

Gamble, Clive S.
- 1986 *The Paleolithic Settlement of Europe.* Cambridge University Press, Cambridge.

Garrod, Dorothy
- 1955 Paleolithic Spear-Throwers. *Proceedings of the Prehistoric Society* 21 (3): 21–35.

Garst, Christine D.
    2002   Relative Dating of the Oneota Occupations at the Leary Site (25RH1): A Study of the 1968 Field Season's Ceramic Artifacts. Master's thesis, Department of Anthropology, University of Kansas, Lawrence.

Geisel, Charles A.
    1999   Prehistoric Dwellings on the Great Plains: Investigating Central Plains Tradition Architectural Variation. Master's thesis, Department of Anthropology, University of Nebraska, Lincoln.

Gilbert, B. Miles
    1969   Some Aspects of Diet and Butchering Techniques among Prehistoric Indians in South Dakota. *Plains Anthropologist* 14: 277–294.

Gilder, Robert F.
    1907   Archeology of the Ponca Creek District, Eastern Nebraska. *American Anthropologist* 9, n.s.: 702–719.
    1908   Recent Excavations at Long's Hill, Nebraska. *American Anthropologist* 10, n.s.: 60–73.
    1909   Excavation of Earth-Lodge Ruins in Eastern Nebraska. *American Anthropologist* 11, n.s.: 56–84.
    1911   Discoveries Indicating an Unexploited Culture in Eastern Nebraska. *Records of the Past* 10: 249–259.
    1913   A Prehistoric "Cannibal" House in Nebraska. *Records of the Past* 12 (3): 107–116.
    1926   *The Nebraska Culture Man.* Henry F. Kieser, Omaha.

Gill, George W.
    1991   Human Skeletal Remains on the Northwestern Plains. In *Prehistoric Hunters of the High Plains,* 2nd ed., by George C. Frison, pp. 431–447. Academic Press, New York.

Gill, George W., and Rhoda O. Lewis
    1977   A Plains Woodland Burial from the Badlands of Western Nebraska. *Plains Anthropologist* 22: 67–73.

Gilliland, J. Eric
    2003   Paradigmatic Classification of Medicine Creek Upper Republican Pottery. Master's thesis, Department of Anthropology, University of Missouri, Columbia.

Gilmore, Kevin P.
    1999   Late Prehistoric Stage. In *Colorado Prehistory: A Context for the Platte River Basin.* Submitted by Tate and Associates, Inc. and SWCA Inc., pp. 175–307. Colorado Council of Professional Archaeologists.

Glascock, Michael D., Raymond Kunselman, and Daniel Wolfman
    1999   Intrasource Chemical Differentiation of Obsidian in the Jemez Mountains and Taos Plateau, New Mexico. *Journal of Archaeological Science* 26: 861–868.

Glover, G. F.
    1978   An Analysis of Early Paleo-Indian Projectile Points with New Data from Southwestern Kansas. Master's thesis, Department of Anthropology, Wichita State University, Wichita.

Goodyear, Albert C., III
    1982   The Chronological Position of the Dalton Horizon in the Southeastern United States. *American Antiquity* 47: 382–295.

Gould, Charles N.
    1898a   Prehistoric Mounds in Cowley County. *Transactions of the Kansas Academy of Science* 15: 79–80.
    1898b   The Timbered Mounds of the Kaw Reservation. *Transactions of the Kansas Academy of Science* 15: 78–79.
    1899   Additional Notes on the Timbered Mounds of the Kaw Reservation. *Transactions of the Kansas Academy of Science* 16: 282.

Gould, Ronald
- 1974 The Armstrong site, 14HP5. Manuscript on file, Kansas State Historical Society, Topeka.
- 1975 An Archaeological Survey of the Bluff Creek Drainage System. Master's thesis, Department of Anthropology, Wichita State University, Wichita.

Graham, Martha
- 1994 *Mobile Farmers: An Ethnoarchaeological Approach to Settlement Organization among the Rarámuri of Northwestern Mexico.* Ethnoarchaeological Series 3. International Monographs in Prehistory, Ann Arbor.

Graham, Russell W.
- 1979 Paleoclimates and Late Pleistocene Faunal Provinces in North America. In *Pre-Llano Cultures in the Americas: Paradoxes and Possibilities,* edited by Robert L. Humphrey and Dennis Stanford, pp. 49–69. Anthropological Society of Washington, Washington, D.C.
- 1987 Late Quaternary Mammalian Faunas and Paleoenvironments of the Southwestern Plains of the United States. In *Late Quaternary Mammalian Biogeography and Environments of the Great Plains and Prairies,* edited by R. W. Graham, H. A. Semken, Jr., and M. A. Graham, pp. 24–86. Illinois State Museum, Scientific Papers 22, Springfield.

Graham, Russell W., and Ernest L. Lundelius
- 1984 Coevolutionary Disequilibrium and Pleistocene Extinctions. In *Quaternary Extinctions: A Prehistoric Revolution,* edited by Paul S. Martin and Richard G. Klein, pp. 223–249. University of Arizona Press, Tucson.
- 1994 *FAUNMAP: A Database Documenting Late Quaternary Distribution of Mammalian Species in the United States.* Illinois State Museum, Scientific Papers 25 (2), Springfield.

Graham, Russell W., and Jim I. Mead
- 1987 Environmental Fluctuations and Evolution of Mammalian Faunas during the Last Deglaciation in North America. In *North America and Adjacent Oceans during the Last Deglaciation,* edited by W. F. Ruddiman and E. E. Wright, Jr., pp. 371–402. University of Minnesota Press, Minneapolis.

Grange, Roger T., Jr.
- 1968 *Pawnee and Lower Loup Pottery.* Publications in Anthropology No. 3. Nebraska State Historical Society, Lincoln.
- 1974 Pawnee Potsherds Revisited: Formula Dating of a Non-European Ceramic Tradition. In *The Conference on Historic Site Archaeology Papers,* vol. 7, edited by Stanley South, pp. 318–334. Institute of Archeology and Anthropology, University of South Carolina, Columbia.
- 1980 *Salvage Archeology in the Red Willow Reservoir, Nebraska.* Publications in Anthropology No. 9. Nebraska State Historical Society, Lincoln.
- 1984 Dating Pawnee Sites by the Ceramic Formula Method. *World Archaeology* 15 (3): 274–293.

Grayson, Donald K.
- 1988 Perspectives on the Archaeology of the First Americans. In *Americans before Columbus: Ice-Age Origins,* edited by R. C. Carlisle, pp. 107–123. Ethnology Monograph 12, Department of Anthropology, University of Pittsburgh, Pittsburgh.

Grayson, Donald K., and David J. Meltzer
- 2002 Clovis Hunting and Large Mammal Extinction: A Critical Review of the Evidence. *Journal of World Prehistory* 16: 313–359.
- 2003 A Requiem for North American Overkill. *Journal of Archaeological Science* 30: 585–593.

Greatorex, Linda J.
- 1998 Steed-Kisker and Nebraska Ceramics: A New Interpretation. Master's thesis, Department of Anthropology, University of Kansas, Lawrence.

Green, F. Earl
- 1986 *Report on Archaeological Salvage in the Sanford Reservoir Area.* Publication No. 4. Panhandle Archeological Society, Amarillo.

Greiser, Sally T.
- 1983 A Preliminary Statement about Quarrying Activity at Flattop Mesa. *Southwestern Lore* 49 (4): 6–14.
- 1985 *Predictive Models of Hunter-Gatherer Subsistence and Settlement Strategies on the Central High Plains.* Plains Anthropologist Memoir 20. Vol. 3, No. 110, Pt. 2, pp. v–134.

Griffin, James B.
- 1952 Some Early and Middle Woodland Pottery Types in Illinois. In *Hopewellian Communities in Illinois,* edited by Thorne Deuel, pp. 93–130. Illinois State Museum, Scientific Papers 5, Springfield.

Grinnell, George Bird
- 1889 *Pawnee Hero Stories and Folk-Tales.* Reprinted, 1961, University of Nebraska Press, Lincoln.
- 1893 Pawnee Mythology. *Journal of American Folklore* 6: 113–130.

Grosser, Roger D.
- 1970 The Snyder Site: An Archaic-Woodland Occupation in South-Central Kansas. Master's thesis, Department of Anthropology, University of Kansas, Lawrence.
- 1973 A Tentative Culture Sequence for the Snyder Site, Kansas. *Plains Anthropologist* 18: 228–238.
- 1977 Late Archaic Subsistence Patterns from the Great Plains: A Systemic Model. Ph.D. diss., Department of Anthropology, University of Kansas, Lawrence.

Gruger, Johanna
- 1973 Studies on the Late-Quaternary Vegetation History of Northeastern Kansas. *Geological Society of America Bulletin* 84: 239–250.

Guilday, John E.
- 1967 Differential Extinction during Late Pleistocene and Recent Times. In *Pleistocene Extinctions: The Search for a Cause,* edited by Paul S. Martin and Herbert E. Wright, Jr., pp. 121–140. Yale University Press, New Haven.

Gundersen, James N.
- 1988 Pipestones of the St. Helena Phase. In *The St. Helena Phase: New Data, Fresh Interpretations,* edited by Donald J. Blakeslee, pp. 79–97. J and L Reprint, Lincoln.
- 1993 "Catlinite" and the Spread of the Calumet Ceremony. *American Antiquity* 58: 560–562.
- 2002 The Mineralogical Characterization of *Catlinite* from Its Sole Provenance, Pipestone National Monument, Minnesota. *Central Plains Archeology* 9 (1): 35–60.

Gundersen, James N., and Joseph A. Tiffany
- 1986 Nature and Provenance of Red Pipestone from the Wittrock Site (13OB4), Northwest Iowa. *North American Archaeologist* 7: 45–67.

Gunnerson, Dolores A.
- 1956 The Southern Athabascans: Their Arrival in the Southwest. *El Palacio* 63 (11–12): 346–365.
- 1974 *The Jicarilla Apaches: A Study in Survival.* Northern Illinois University Press, DeKalb.

Gunnerson, James H.
- 1952 Some Nebraska Culture Pottery Types. *Plains Archeological Conference News Letter* 5 (3): 34–44 (pagination from 1961 reprint).
- 1960 *An Introduction to Plains Apache Archaeology: The Dismal River Aspect.* Bureau of American Ethnology Bulletin No. 173. Antrhopological Papers No. 58. Smithsonian Institution, Washington, D.C.
- 1968 Plains Apache Archaeology: A Review. *Plains Anthropologist* 13 (41): 167–189.
- 1987 *Archaeology of the High Plains.* Colorado State Office, Bureau of Land Management, Denver.

Gunnerson, James H., and Dolores A. Gunnerson
- 1971 Apachean Culture: A Study in Unity and Diversity. In *Apachean Culture History and Eth-

nology, edited by Keith Basso and Morris E. Opler, pp. 7–27. Anthropological Papers of the University of Arizona No. 21. University of Arizona Press, Tucson.

Guthrie, R. Dale
- 1986   *Frozen Fauna of the Mammoth Steppe.* University of Chicago Press, Chicago.
- 1990   *Frozen Fauna of the Mammoth Steppe: The Story of Blue Babe.* University of Chicago Press, Chicago.

Habicht-Mauche, Judith A.
- 1987   Southwestern-Style Culinary Ceramics on the Southern Plains: A Case Study of Technological Innovation and Cross-Cultural Interaction. *Plains Anthropologist* 32: 175–189.
- 1992   Coronado's Querechos and Teyas in the Archaeological Record of the Texas Panhandle. *Plains Anthropologist* 37: 247–259.
- 1995   Changing Patterns of Pottery Manufacture and Trade in the Northern Rio Grande Region. In *Ceramic Production in the American Southwest,* edited by Barbara J. Mills and Patricia L. Crown, pp. 167–199. University of Arizona Press, Tucson.

Hackett, C. W.
- 1941   *Pichardo's Treatise on the Limits of Louisiana and Texas,* vol. 3. University of Texas Press, Austin.

Hall, Stephen A.
- 1977   Geology and Palynology of Archaeological Sites and Associated Sediments. In *The Prehistory of the Little Caney River (1976 Field Season),* edited by Donald O. Henry, pp. 13–41. University of Tulsa Contributions in Archaeology No. 1. Tulsa.
- 1982   Late Holocene Paleoecology of the Southern Plains. *Quaternary Research* 17: 391–407.
- 1988   Environment and Archaeology of the Central Osage Plains. *Plains Anthropologist* 33: 203–218.
- 1990   Channel Trenching and Climatic Change in the Southern U.S. Great Plains. *Geology* 18: 342–345.

Hall, Stephen A., and Christopher Lintz
- 1984   Buried Trees, Water Table Fluctuations, and 3000 Years of Changing Climate in West-Central Oklahoma. *Quaternary Research* 22: 129–133.

Hammond, George P., and Agapito Rey
- 1940   *Narratives of the Coronado Expedition, 1540–1542.* University of New Mexico Press, Albuquerque.
- 1953   *Don Juan de Oñate, Colonizer of New Mexico, 1595–1628.* University of New Mexico Press, Albuquerque.

Harrington, Mark R.
- 1971   The Ozark Bluff Dwellers. Indian Notes and Monographs No. 12. Museum of the American Indian, Heye Foundation, New York.

Hart, John P., David L. Asch, and C. Margaret Scarry
- 2000   The Age of Common Beans *(Phaseolus vulgaris)* in the Northern Eastern Woodlands of North America. Paper presented at the Joint Midwest/Plains Anthropological Society Conference, St. Paul.

Hart, John P., and Nancy Asch Sidell
- 1997   Additional Evidence for Early Cucurbit Use in the Northeast Woodlands East of the Allegheny Front. *American Antiquity* 65: 523–537.

Harvey, A. E.
- 1979   *Oneota Culture in Northwestern Iowa.* Report 12. Office of the State Archaeologist, University of Iowa, Iowa City.

Hattin, Donald E.
- 1982   *Stratigraphy and Depositional Environment of Smoky Hill Chalk Member, Niobrara Chalk*

(Upper Cretaceous) of the Type Area, Western Kansas. Kansas Geological Survey Bulletin 225. University of Kansas, Lawrence.

Haury, Cherie E.
- 1981 Chert Types and Terminology of the Upper Walnut River Drainage. In *Prehistory and History of the El Dorado Lake Area, Kansas*. Project Report Series No. 47. Museum of Anthropology, University of Kansas, Lawrence.
- 1984 Availability, Procurement, and Use of Chert Resources by Late Archaic Populations in the Southern Flint Hills of Kansas. Master's thesis, Department of Anthropology, University of Kansas, Lawrence.
- 2005 Analysis of Faunal Material, 14CO331. In Lower Walnut Archeology: Archeological Investigations in the Walnut River Valley (1994–1996), edited by C. Martin Stein. Report in preparation.

Hawley, Marlin F.
- 1993 *A Keen Interest in Indians: Floyd Schultz: The Life and Work of an Amateur Anthropologist*. Bulletin No. 2. Kansas Anthropological Association, Topeka.
- 1994 *Archaeological and Geomorphological Investigations in the Vicinity of Arkansas City, Cowley County, Kansas*. Kansas State Historical Society. Submitted to the Kansas Department of Transportation. Copies available from the Kansas State Historic Preservation Office, Topeka.
- 1995 Revised Archeological Treatment Plan for Sites Affected by the Arkansas City Bypass and Levee Project. Kansas State Historical Society. Document submitted to the Advisory Council on Historic Preservation and U.S. Army Corps of Engineers, Tulsa District. Copies available from the Kansas State Historic Preservation Office, Topeka.
- 2000 European-Contact and Southwestern Artifacts in the Lower Walnut Focus Sites at Arkansas City, Kansas. *Plains Anthropologist* 45: 237–255.

Hawley, Marlin F., and Donald J. Blakeslee
- 2003 An Annotated Bibliography of Great Bend Aspect—Wichita Archaeology and Ethnohistory. *Kansas Anthropologist* 24: 107–145.

Hawley, Marlin F., and Cherie E. Haury
- 1994 Lower Walnut Great Bend: Investigations of Sites near Arkansas City, Kansas: Background and Results. *Kansas Anthropologist* 15 (1): 1–45.

Hawley, Marlin F., and Susan A. Holland
- 1996 Status Report on Archeological Field Work at Arkansas City. *Kansas Anthropological Association Newsletter* 8 (1): 7–10.

Hawley, Marlin F., and Richard E. Hughes
- 1999 A Source Study of Obsidian from the Infinity Site (14MY305), Kansas. *Plains Anthropologist* 44: 297–306

Hawley, Marlin F., Rolfe D. Mandel, Cherie E. Haury, Marsha King, John D. Reynolds, and Timothy Weston
- 1994 Archeological and Geomorphological Investigations of Sites in the Vicinity of Arkansas City, Cowley County, Kansas. Report prepared by the Archeology Office, Kansas State Historical Society. Document submitted to the Kansas Department of Transportation. Copies available from the Kansas State Historic Preservation Office, Topeka.

Haworth, Erasmus
- 1897 *Physiography of Western Kansas*. Kansas Geological Survey, vol. 2, pp. 11–50. University of Kansas, Lawrence.

Haworth, Erasmus, and Joshua W. Beede, Jr.
- 1897 *The McPherson Equus Beds*. Kansas Geological Survey, vol. 2, pp. 287–296. University of Kansas, Lawrence.

Haynes, Gary
    2002   *The Early Settlement of North America: The Clovis Era.* Cambridge University Press, Cambridge.

Hedden, John G.
    1992   Riley Cord Roughened Ceramic Variability as Exhibited by the Assemblages from Ten Smoky Hill Sites in Northcentral Kansas. Master's thesis, Department of Anthropology, University of Kansas, Lawrence.
    1994   Riley Cord Roughened Ceramic Variation from Ten Smoky Hill Variant Sites in North-Central Kansas. *Central Plains Archaeology* 4 (1): 27–42.

Henning, Dale R.
    1961   Oneota Ceramics in Iowa. *Journal of the Iowa Archeological Society* 11 (2).
    1970   Development and Interrelationships of Oneota Culture in the Lower Missouri River Valley. *Missouri Archaeologist* 32.
    1992   A Study of Pottery from the Blood Run Site (13LO2), 1985 Excavations. Report prepared by the Archeological Research Center of Luther College, Decorah, Iowa.
    1998a   The Oneota Tradition. In *Archaeology on the Great Plains,* edited by W. Raymond Wood, pp. 345–414. University Press of Kansas, Lawrence.
    1998b   Oneota: The Western Manifestations. *Wisconsin Archaeologist* 79 (2): 238–247.

Henning, Dale R., and Shirley J. Shermer
    2004   Artifact Analysis. In *Dhegihan and Chiwere Siouans in the Plains: Historical and Archaeological Perspectives,* pt. II: *Central Siouans in the Northeastern Plains: Oneota Archaeology and the Blood Run Site,* edited by Dale R. Henning and Thomas D Thiessen. Plains Anthropologist Memoir 36. Vol. 49, No. 192, Pt. 2, pp. 435–523.

Henning, Dale R., and Thomas D. Thiessen (editors)
    2004   Central Siouans in the Northeastern Plains: Oneota Archaeology and the Blood Run Site. In *Dhegihan and Chiwere Siouans in the Plains: Historical and Archaeological Perspectives.* Plains Anthropologist Memoir 36. Vol. 49, No. 192, Pt. 2, pp. 345–625.

Hester, James J.
    1972   Blackwater Draw Locality No. 1: A Stratified Early Man Site in Eastern New Mexico. Fort Burgwin Research Center Publication 8, Southern Methodist University, Dallas.

Hill, Asa T.
    1927   Mr. A. T. Hill's Own Story. *Nebraska History Magazine* 10 (3): 162–167.

Hill, Asa T., and Paul Cooper
    1937   The Archeological Campaign of 1937. *Nebraska History Magazine* 18 (4): 243–359.

Hill, Asa T., and George Metcalf
    1941   A Site of the Dismal River Aspect in Chase County, Nebraska. *Nebraska History* 22 (2).

Hill, Asa T., and Waldo R. Wedel
    1936   Excavations at the Leary Indian Village and Burial Site, Richardson County, Nebraska. *Nebraska History Magazine* 17 (1): 1–73.

Hill, David, and Donald J. Blakeslee
    1983   Archaeological Assessment of Some Great Bend Aspect Sites in Cowley County, Kansas. Department of Anthropology, Wichita State University. Report to Northwest Central Pipeline, Inc. Copies available from the Kansas State Historic Preservation Office, Topeka.

Hill, Matthew E.
    1994   Paleoindian Archaeology and Taphonomy of the 12 Mile Creek Site in Western Kansas. Master's thesis, Department of Anthropology, University of Kansas, Lawrence.
    1996   Paleoindian Bison Remains from the 12 Mile Creek Site in Western Kansas. *Plains Anthropologist* 41: 359–372.

Hill, Matthew E., Jr., and Jack L. Hofman
- 1992 Faunal remains from the Norton Bonebed (14SC6): A New Paleoindian Site in Western Kansas. Paper presented at the 50th Annual Plains Anthropological Conference, Lincoln.

Hill, Matthew E., Jr., Jack L. Hofman, and Karolyn Kinsey
- 1996 A History of Archeological Research on the Central Plains. In *Archeology and Paleoecology of the Central Great Plains,* edited by Jack L. Hofman, pp. 29–40. Research Series 48. Arkansas Archeological Survey, Fayetteville.

Hill, Matthew E., Jack L. Hofman, and Larry D. Martin
- 1992 A Reinvestigation of the Burntwood Creek Bison Bonebed. *Current Research in the Pleistocene* 9: 9–12.

Hill, Michael G.
- 1997 A Study of Tool Type: Specific Raw Material Quality Differentiations at Three Upper Republican Sites. Paper for Anthropology 625, Independent Readings and Research, Kansas State University, Manhattan.

Hoard, Robert J., William E. Banks, Rolfe D. Mandel, Michael Finnegan, and Jennifer Epperson
- 2004 A Middle Archaic Burial from East Central Kansas. *American Antiquity* 69: 717–739.

Hoard, Robert J., John R. Bozell, Steven R. Holen, Michael D. Glascock, Hector Neff, and J. Michael Elam
- 1993 Source Determination of White Rock Group Silicates from Two Archaeological Sites in the Great Plains. *American Antiquity* 58: 698–710.

Hoard, Robert J., Steven R. Holen, Michael D. Glascock, Hector Neff, and J. Michael Elam
- 1992 Neutron Activation of Stone from the Chadron Formation and a Clovis Site on the Great Plains. *Journal of Archaeological Science* 19: 655–665.

Hoffhaus, Charles E.
- 1984 *Chez les Canses: Three Centuries at Kawsmouth: The French Foundations of Metropolitan Kansas City.* Lowell Press, Kansas City.

Hofman, Jack L.
- 1985 Middle Archaic Ritual and Shell Midden Archaeology: Considering the Significance of Cremations. In *Exploring Tennessee Prehistory,* edited by T. Whyte, C. C. Boyd, Jr., and B. Riggs, pp. 1–21. Report of Investigations 42. Department of Anthropology, University of Tennessee, Knoxville.
- 1986 *Hunter-Gatherer Mortuary Variability: Toward an Explanatory Model.* University Microfilms International, Publication 86-11599, Ann Arbor.
- 1994 Kansas Folsom Evidence. *Kansas Anthropologist* 15 (2): 31–43.
- 1995 The Busse Cache: A Clovis-Age Find in Northwestern Kansas. *Current Research in the Pleistocene* 12: 17–19.
- 1996 Early Hunter-Gatherers of the Central Great Plains: Paleoindian and Mesoindian (Archaic) Cultures. In *Archeology and Paleoecology of the Central Great Plains,* edited by Jack L. Hofman, pp. 41–100. Research Series 48. Arkansas Archeological Survey, Fayetteville.
- 2002 The Allen Technological Complex: New Evidence from the Winger Site. Poster paper presented at the 60th Annual Plains Anthropological Conference, Oklahoma City.
- 2003 Tethered to Stone or Freedom to Move: Folsom Biface Technology in Regional Perspective. In *Multiple Approaches to the Study of Bifacial Technologies,* edited by Marie Soressi and Harold L. Dibble, pp. 229–249. University Museum Monographs 115. Museum of Archaeology and Anthropology, University of Pennsylvania, Philadelphia.

Hofman, Jack L. (editor)
- 1996 *Archeology and Paleoecology of the Central Great Plains.* Research Series No. 48. Arkansas Archeological Survey, Fayetteville.

Hofman, Jack L., and Jeannette M. Blackmar
  1997   The Paleoindian Laird Bison Bone Bed in Northwestern Kansas. *Kansas Anthropologist* 18 (2): 45–58.
  2004   *The Laird Site (14SN2): A Late Paleoindian Bonebed in Northwestern Kansas.* Poster paper presented at the 62nd Annual Plains Anthropological Conference, Billings.
Hofman, Jack L., and Robert L. Brooks
  1989   Summary Discussion: Southern Plains Archaeology in the Late Twentieth Century. In *From Clovis to Comanchero: An Archeological Overview of the Southern Great Plains,* edited by Jack L. Hofman, Robert L. Brooks, Douglas W. Owsley, Richard L. Jantz, Murray K. Marks, and Mary H. Manhein, pp. 175–182. Research Report No. 35. Arkansas Archeological Survey, Fayetteville.
Hofman, Jack L., and Russell W. Graham
  1998   The Paleo-Indian Cultures of the Great Plains. In *Archaeology on the Great Plains,* edited by W. Raymond Wood, pp. 87–139. University Press of Kansas, Lawrence.
Hofman, Jack L., and India S. Hesse
  2002   Clovis in Kansas. *Institute for Tertiary-Quaternary Studies, Ter-Qua Symposium Series* 3: 15–36.
Hofman, Jack L., Matthew E. Hill, William C. Johnson, and Dean Sather
  1995   Norton: An Early-Holocene Bison Bonebed in Western Kansas. *Current Research in the Pleistocene* 12: 19–21.
Hofman, Jack L., Brad Logan, and Mary Adair
  1996   Prehistoric Adaptation Types and Research Problems. In *Archeology and Paleoecology of the Central Great Plains,* edited by Jack L. Hofman, pp. 203–220. Research Series 48. Arkansas Archeological Survey, Fayetteville.
Hofman, Jack L., and Lawrence C. Todd
  2001   Tyranny in the Archaeological Record of Specialized Hunters. In *People and Wildlife in Northern North America: Essays in Honor of R. Dale Guthrie,* edited by S. Craig Gerlach and Maribeth S. Murray, pp. 200–215. BAR International Series 944. Oxford.
Hofman, Jack L., Lawrence C. Todd, and Michael B. Collins
  1991   Identification of Central Texas Edwards Chert at the Folsom and Lindenmeier Sites. *Plains Anthropologist* 36: 297–308.
Holen, Steven R.
  1983   Lower Loup Lithic Procurement Strategy at the Gray Site (25CX1). Master's thesis, Department of Anthropology, University of Nebraska, Lincoln.
  1989   The Smoky Hill Chalk Member of the Niobrara Formation in Kansas: Implications for the Distribution of Smoky Hill Jasper. Copies available from the Kansas State Historic Preservation Office, Topeka.
  1991   Bison Hunting Territories and Lithic Acquisition among the Pawnee: An Ethnohistoric and Archaeological Study. In *Raw Material Economics among Prehistoric Hunter-Gatherers,* edited by Anta Montet-White and Steven R. Holen, pp. 399–411. Publications in Anthropology No. 19. University of Kansas, Lawrence.
  1998   *The Eckles Site, 14JW4: A Clovis Assemblage from the Lovewell Reservoir, Jewell County, Kansas.* Nebraska Archaeology Survey Technical Report 98-03. University of Nebraska State Museum, Lincoln.
  2001   Clovis Mobility and Lithic Procurement on the Central Great Plains of North America. Ph.D. diss., Department of Anthropology, University of Kansas, Lawrence.
Holland, Susan A.
  1998   Evidence of the Spring Planting Ceremony to Evening Star and Her Sacred Garden. *Plains Anthropologist* 43: 411–419.

Holliday, Vance T.
   2000   The Evolution of Paleoindian Geochronology and Typology on the Great Plains. *Geoarchaeology* 15: 227–290.
Hollinger, R. Eric
   2001   Oneota Population Movements: Aggressive Territorial Expansions and Contractions. Paper presented at the 66th Annual Meeting of the Society for American Archaeology, New Orleans.
Houck, Louis
   1909   *The Spanish Regime in Missouri.* 2 volumes. R. R. Donnelley & Sons, Chicago.
Howard, Edgar B.
   1935   Evidence of Early Man in North America. *Museum Journal* 24: 61–171.
Howard, James H.
   1964   *Archeological Investigations in the Toronto Reservoir Area, Kansas.* Bureau of American Ethnology, River Basin Surveys Papers No. 38. Smithsonian Institution, Washington, D.C.
Howard, James N., and Donald N. Brown
   1973   A Puebloid Burial from Western Oklahoma. *Bulletin of Oklahoma Anthropological Society* 22: 207–216.
Howard, Leonard W., and Walter H. Schoewe
   1965   The Englevale Channel Sandstone. *Transactions of the Kansas Academy of Science* 68 (1): 88–106.
Hoyer, Bernard E.
   1980   The Geology of the Cherokee Sewer Site. In *The Cherokee Excavations: Holocene Ecology and Human Adaptations in Northwestern Iowa,* edited by D. C. Anderson and H. A. Semken, Jr., pp. 21–66. Academic Press, New York.
Hrdlička, Aleš
   1903   The Lansing Skeleton. *American Anthropologist* 5: 323–330.
Huebner, Jeffrey A.
   1991   Late Prehistoric Bison Populations in Central and Southern Texas. *Plains Anthropologist* 36: 343–358.
Hughes, David T.
   1991   Investigation of the Buried City, Ochiltree County, Texas: With an Emphasis on the Texas Archeological Society Field Schools of 1987 and 1988. *Bulletin of the Texas Archeological Society* 60: 107–148.
   2002   Decorated Ceramics from Ochiltree County, Texas. Paper presented at the 60th Annual Plains Anthropological Conference, Oklahoma City.
Hughes, David T., and Alicia A. Hughes-Jones
   1987   *The Courson Archeological Project: Final 1985 and Preliminary 1986.* Innovative Publishing, Perryton, Texas.
Hughes, Jack T.
   1968   Prehistory of the Caddoan-Speaking Tribes. Ph.D. diss., Columbia University. University Microfilms, Ann Arbor.
Hughes, Jack T., and Tom S. Ellzey
   1987   Archeological Survey of Wolf Creek Park, Ochiltree County, Texas. Texas Antiquities Committee Permit 527. Draft report on file, Texas Antiquities Committee, Austin.
Hughes, Richard E.
   1995   Source Identification of Obsidian from the Trowbridge Site (14WY1): A Hopewellian Site in Kansas. *Midcontinental Journal of Archaeology* 20: 104–113.
Hughes, Richard E., and William B. Lees
   1991   Provenance Analysis of Obsidian from Two Late Prehistoric Archaeological Sites in Kansas. *Transactions of the Kansas Academy of Science* 94: 38–45.

Hughes, Richard E., and Donna C. Roper
  1999 Source Area Analysis of Obsidian Flakes from a Lower Loup Phase Site in Nebraska. *Plains Anthropologist* 44: 77–82.
Huhnke, Marie H.
  2000 The Hallman Site (14HP524), Harper County, Kansas: New Light on Bluff Creek. *Kansas Anthropologist* 21: 1–33.
Hunt, P. B.
  1881 Report of the Kiowa, Comanche, and Wichita Agency. *Annual Report of the Commissioner of Indian Affairs,* pp. 77–83. U.S. Government Printing Office, Washington, D.C.
Hunt, Robert M., Jr.
  1978 Depositional Setting of a Miocene Mammal Assemblage, Sioux County, Nebraska (U.S.A.). *Paleogeography, Paleoclimatology, Palaeoecology* 24: 1–52.
Hurt, Wesley R., Jr.
  1966 The Altithermal and the Prehistory of the Northern Plains. *Quaternaria* 8: 101–114.
Hutchins, T.
  1797 Appendix I, in *A Topographical Description of the Western Territory of North America,* by G. Imlay, pp. 388–458. J. Debrett, London.
Institute for Public Policy and Business Research
  2000 *Kansas Abstracts.* University of Kansas, Lawrence.
Irving, John T., Jr.
  1955 *Indian Sketches Taken during an Expedition to the Pawnee Tribes.* University of Oklahoma Press, Norman.
Irwin, Cynthia, and Henry Irwin
  1959 *Excavations at LoDaisKa Site in the Denver, Colorado, Area.* Proceedings No. 8. Denver Museum of Natural History, Denver.
  1961 Radiocarbon Dates from the LoDaisKa Site, Colorado. *American Antiquity* 27: 114–115.
Irwin, Henry T.
  1968 The Itama: Early Late Pleistocene Inhabitants of the Plains of the United States and Canada and the American Southwest. Ph.D. diss., Department of Anthropology, Harvard University, Cambridge.
Ives, John C.
  1955 Glenwood Ceramics. *Journal of the Iowa Archeological Society* 4 (3–4).
Jackson, Donald
  1964 Journey to the Mandans, 1809: The Lost Narrative of Dr. Thomas. *Bulletin of the Missouri Historical Society* 20 (3): 179–192.
  1978 *Letters of the Lewis and Clark Expedition with Related Documents, 1783–1854.* 2nd ed. University of Illinois Press, Urbana.
Jackson, Donald, and Mary Lee Spence (editors)
  1970 *The Expeditions of John Clark Fremont, Volume 1: Travels from 1838 to 1844.* University of Illinois Press, Urbana.
Jacobson, G. L., Eric C. Grimm, and T. Webb III
  1987 Patterns and Rates of Vegetation Change in Eastern North America from Full Glacial to Mid-Holocene Time. In *North America and Adjacent Oceans during the Last Deglaciation,* edited by W. F. Ruddiman and H. E. Wright, Jr., pp. 277–288. Geology of North America, vol. K3, Geological Society of America, Boulder.
Jacobson, Jodi A.
  2004 Determining Human Ecology on the Plains through the Identification of Mule Deer (*Odocoileus hemionus*) and White-tailed Deer (*Odocoileus virginianus*) Postcranial Material (Kansas). Ph.D. diss., Department of Anthropology, University of Tennessee, Knoxville.

James, Edwin
    1966   [1823] *Account of an Expedition from Pittsburg to the Rocky Mountains Performed in the Years 1819, 1820*, vols. I and II. March of America Facsimile Series, No. 65. University Microfilms, Ann Arbor.

Jefferson, Thomas
    1852   Expedition of Lewis and Clark. *Annals of the Congress of the United States, Ninth Congress, Second Session, 1806–1807*, pp. 1035–1076. Gales and Seaton, Washington, D.C.

Jelinek, Arthur J.
    1967   Man's Role in the Extinction of Pleistocene Faunas. In *Pleistocene Extinctions: The Search for a Cause*, edited by Paul S. Martin and Herbert E. Wright, Jr., pp. 193–200. Yale University Press, New Haven.

Jennings, Jesse D.
    1974   *Prehistory of North America*. 2nd ed. McGraw Hill, New York.

Jepsen, Glen L.
    1951   Ancient Buffalo Hunters of Northwestern Wyoming. *Southwestern Lore* 9: 19–25.

Johannessen, Sissal
    1988   Plant Remains and Culture Change: Are Paleoethnobotanical Data Better Than We Think? In *Current Paleoethnobotany: Analytical Methods and Cultural Interpretations of Archaeological Plant Remains*, edited by Christine A. Hastorf and Virginia S. Popper, pp. 145–166. University of Chicago Press, Chicago.
    1993   Farmers of the Late Woodland. In *Foraging and Farming in the Eastern Woodlands*, edited by C. Margaret Scarry, pp. 57–77. University Press of Florida, Gainesville.

Johnson, Alfred E.
    1968   *Archaeological Investigations in the Clinton Reservoir Area, Eastern Kansas*. Report submitted to the U.S. Department of the Interior, National Park Service, Midwest Archeological Center. Copies available from the Museum of Anthropology, University of Kansas, Lawrence.
    1973   Archaeological Investigations at the Budenbender Site, Tuttle Creek Reservoir, North-Central Kansas, 1957. *Plains Anthropologist* 18 (62): 271–299.
    1976a   A Model of the Kansas City Hopewell Subsistence-Settlement System. In *Hopewellian Archaeology in the Lower Missouri Valley*, edited by Alfred E. Johnson, pp. 7–15. Publications in Anthropology No. 8. University of Kansas, Lawrence.
    1976b   Introduction. In *Hopewellian Archaeology in the Lower Missouri Valley*, edited by Alfred E. Johnson, pp. 1–6. Publications in Anthropology No. 8. University of Kansas, Lawrence.
    1979   Kansas City Hopewell. In *Hopewell Archaeology: The Chillicothe Conference*, edited by David S. Brose and N'omi Greber, pp. 86–93. Kent State University Press, Kent, Ohio.
    1981   The Kansas City Hopewell Subsistence and Settlement System. *Missouri Archaeologist* 42: 69–76.
    1983   Late Woodland in the Kansas City Locality. *Plains Anthropologist* 28: 99–108.
    1984   Temporal Relationships of Late (Plains) Woodland Components in Eastern Kansas. *Plains Anthropologist* 29: 277–288.
    1987   Late Woodland Adaptive Patterns in Eastern Kansas. *Plains Anthropologist* 32: 390–403.
    1991   Kansa Origins: An Alternative. *Plains Anthropologist* 36: 57–66.
    1992   Early Woodland in the Trans-Missouri West. *Plains Anthropologist* 37: 129–136.
    2001   Plains Woodland Tradition. In *Handbook of North American Indians, Volume 13, Plains*, edited by Raymond J. DeMallie, Part 1 of 2, pp. 159–172. Smithsonian Institution, Washington, D.C.

Johnson, Alfred E., and Ann S. Johnson
    1975   *K*-Means and Temporal Variability in Kansas City Hopewell Ceramics. *American Antiquity* 40: 283–295.

Johnson, Allen W., and Timothy Earle
    2000   *The Evolution of Human Societies: From Foraging Group to Agrarian State.* Stanford University Press, Stanford.

Johnson, Ann M., and Alfred E. Johnson
    1998   The Plains Woodland. In *Archaeology on the Great Plains,* edited by W. Raymond Wood, pp. 201–234. University Press of Kansas, Lawrence.

Johnson, C. P.
    1897   Mound in Cowley County, Kansas. *Antiquarian* 1: 95–96.

Johnson, Paul C.
    1972   Mammalian Remains Associated with Nebraska Phase Earth Lodges in Mills County, Iowa. Master's thesis, Department of Anthropology, University of Iowa, Iowa City.

Johnson, Willard D.
    1901   The High Plains and Their Utilization. U.S. Geological Survey Annual Report 21, pt. 4, pp. 601–741. U.S. Government Printing Office, Washington, D.C.

Johnson, William, and other missionaries
    1925   Letters from the Indian Missions in Kansas. *Kansas Historical Collections, 1923–1925,* vol. 16: 227–271.

Johnson, William C.
    1991   Buried Soil Surfaces beneath the Great Bend Prairie of Central Kansas and Archaeological Implications. *Current Research in the Pleistocene* 8: 108–110.

Johnson, William C., N. Cheney, and C. W. Martin
    1990   The Koehn-Schneider Mammoth Site of Western Kansas. *Current Research in the Pleistocene* 7: 113–115.

Johnson, William C., David W. May, and R. Diekmeyer
    1993   A 600K (?) Record of Loess Deposition and Soil Development. In *Second International Paleopedology Symposium,* INQUA Commission 6, Kansas Geological Survey Open-File Report 93-30, pp. 12-1–12-21.

Johnson, William C., and Kyeong Park
    1996   Late Wisconsin and Holocene Environmental History. In *Archaeology and Paleoecology of the Central Great Plains,* edited by Jack L. Hofman, pp. 3–28. Arkansas Archaeological Survey Research Series No. 48. Fayetteville.

Johnson, William C., and Karen L. Willey
    2000   Isotopic and Rock Magnetic Expression of Environmental Change at the Pleistocene-Holocene Transition in the Central Great Plains. *Quaternary International* 67: 89–106.

Jones, Bruce A., and Thomas A. Witty, Jr.
    1980   The Gilligan Site, 14CF322. In *Salvage Archaeology of the John Redmond Lake, Kansas,* edited by Thomas A. Witty, Jr., pp. 67–132. Anthropological Series No. 8. Kansas State Historical Society, Topeka.

Jones, George T., Charlotte Beck, Eric E. Jones, and Richard E. Hughes
    2003   Lithic Source Use and Paleoarchaic Foraging Territories in the Great Basin. *American Antiquity* 68: 5–38.

Jones, Horace
    1928   Quivira—Rice County, Kansas. *Collections of the Kansas State Historical Society* 17: 535–546.

Jones, Paul A.
    1929   *Quivira.* McCormick-Armstrong, Wichita.
    1937   *Coronado and Quivira.* Lyons Publishing, Lyons, Kansas.

Jones, Volney H.
    1936   *Plant Remains from a Cache Pit, 1 Mile Southwest of Pleasantdale, Seward County, Nebraska.* Ethnobotanical Laboratory Report No. 35. Museum of Anthropology, University of Michigan, Ann Arbor.

1941 *Plant Remains from Dismal River, Upper Republican, Nebraska and Woodland Period Sites, Nebraska.* Ethnobotanical Laboratory Reports Nos. 180–185. Museum of Anthropology, University of Michigan, Ann Arbor.

Jungmann, William L.
  1966 *Geology and Ground-Water Resources of Neosho County, Kansas.* Kansas Geological Survey Bulletin 183. University of Kansas, Lawrence.

Kalasz, Stephan M., Mark Mitchell, and Christian J. Zier
  1999 Late Prehistoric Stage. In *Colorado Prehistory: A Context for the Arkansas River Basin,* by Christian J. Zier and Stephan M. Kalasz, pp. 141–262. Colorado Council of Professional Archaeologists, Denver.

Kappler, Charles J. (editor)
  1904 *Indian Affairs: Laws and Treaties, Volume 2: Treaties.* Reprinted, 1972, Interland, New York.

Katz, Paul R.
  1971 Archaeology of the Sutter Site in Northeastern Kansas. *Plains Anthropologist* 16: 1–19.
  1973 Radiocarbon Dates from the Sutter Site, Northeastern Kansas. *Plains Anthropologist* 18: 167–168.

Kay, Marvin
  1998 The Central and Southern Plains Archaic. In *Archaeology on the Great Plains,* edited by W. Raymond Wood, pp. 173–200. University Press of Kansas, Lawrence.

Kay, Marvin, Francis B. King, and C. Robinson
  1980 Cucurbits from Phillips Spring: New Evidence and Interpretations. *American Antiquity* 45: 806–822.

Kay County Chapter of the Oklahoma Anthropological Society
  1963 The Fred Loomis Site: A Small Group Burial near Freedom, Oklahoma. *Bulletin of Oklahoma Anthropological Society* 11: 123–132.

Kaye, Barry, and D. W. Moodie
  1978 The *Psoralea* Food Resource of the Northern Plains. *Plains Anthropologist* 23: 329–336.

Keeley, Lawrence H.
  1996 *War before Civilization.* Oxford University Press, New York.

Keller, Gordon Nelson
  1961 The Changing Position of the Southern Plains in the Late Prehistory of the Great Plains Area. Ph.D. diss., Department of Anthropology, University of Chicago, Chicago.

Kelly, Robert L.
  1992 Mobility/Sedentism: Concepts, Archaeological Measures, and Effects. *Annual Reviews in Anthropology* 21: 43–66.
  1997 Late Holocene Great Basin Prehistory. *Journal of World Prehistory* 11: 1–49.

Kelly, Robert L., and Lawrence C. Todd
  1988 Coming into the Country: Early Paleoindian Hunting and Mobility. *American Antiquity* 53: 231–244.

Key, P. J.
  1994 Relationships of the Woodland Period on the Northern and Central Plains: The Craniometric Evidence. In *Skeletal Biology in the Great Plains: Migration, Warfare, Health and Subsistence,* edited by Douglas W. Owsley and Richard L. Jantz, pp. 179–188. Smithsonian Institution Press, Washington D.C.

Kilinska, Ewa A.
  1995 Pollen Study of Late Pleistocene and Holocene Sediments from Eastern Nebraska: Paleoecological and Paleoclimatic Implications. Master's thesis, University of Nebraska, Lincoln.

Killion, Thomas W.
  1987 *Agriculture and Residential Site Structure among Campesinos in Southern Veracruz, Mex-*

ico: A Foundation for Archaeological Inference. Ph.D. diss., Department of Anthropology, University of New Mexico, Albuquerque. University Microfilms, Ann Arbor.

King, Francis B.
  1987 Prehistoric Maize in Eastern North America: An Evolutionary Evaluation. Ph.D. diss., Department of Agronomy, University of Illinois, Urbana-Champaign.

King, James E., and W. H. Allen, Jr.
  1977 A Holocene Vegetation Record from the Mississippi River Valley, Southeastern Missouri. *Quaternary Research* 8: 307–323.

King, James E., and Jeffrey J. Saunders
  1984 Environment Insularity and the Extinction of the American Mastodon. In *Quaternary Extinctions: A Prehistoric Revolution*, edited by Paul S. Martin and Richard G. Klein, pp. 315–344. University of Arizona Press, Tucson.

King, Marsha
  1996a *Results of Phase III Archeological Investigations at the Midian Townsite 14BU381, Butler County, Kansas.* Contract Archeology Publications No. 13. Kansas State Historical Society, Topeka.
  1996b *Results of Phase III Archeological Investigations at the Shawnee Mill Site 14JO365, Johnson County, Kansas.* Contract Archeology Publications No. 14. Kansas State Historical Society, Topeka.
  1996c *Results of Phase IIIa Archival Investigations at 14LV389 in Leavenworth Landing Project Area, Leavenworth County, Kansas.* Contract Archeology Publications No. 15. Kansas State Historical Society, Topeka.
  1997 *Fort Harker 14EW310, Ellsworth County, Kansas.* Contract Archeology Publications No. 17. Kansas State Historical Society, Topeka.
  1999a *Results of Phase III Archeological Investigations at Fort Dodge (14FD315), Ford County, Kansas.* Contract Archeology Publications No. 20. Kansas State Historical Society, Topeka.
  1999b *Results of Phase III Archeological Investigations at Fort Wallace (14WC303), Wallace County, Kansas.* Contract Archeology Publications No. 21. Kansas State Historical Society, Topeka.
  2004 *Results of Phase III Historical and Archeological Investigations of Six Historic Sites (14RY380, 14RY381, 14RY382, 14RY383, 14RY384, and 14RY365) in Manhattan, Riley County, Kansas.* Contract Archeology Publications No. 24. Kansas State Historical Society, Topeka.

Kinnaird, Lawrence
  1946 Post War Decade, 1782–1791. In *Spain in the Mississippi Valley, 1765–1794*, vol. 3, pt. 2. Annual Report of the American Historical Association for the Year 1945.

Kinnaird, Lawrence (editor)
  1949 *Spain in the Mississippi Valley, 1765–1794, Pt. I: The Revolutionary Period, 1765–1781.* U.S. Government Printing Office, Washington, D.C.

Kinney, Edward D.
  1942 Iron of Hematite and Limonite. In *Kansas Mineral Resources for Wartime Industries*, edited by John M. Jewett and Walter H. Schoewe, pp. 103–104. Report of Studies, Kansas Geological Survey, University of Kansas, Lawrence.

Kinsey, Karolyn K.
  1998 An Investigation of Metal Projectile Points from the Sheyenne River to the Red River: During the Eighteenth and Nineteenth Centuries. Master's thesis, Department of Anthropology, University of Kansas, Lawrence.

Kivett, Marvin F.
  1947a Preliminary Appraisal of the Archaeological and Paleontological Resources of Harlan County Reservoir, Nebraska. River Basin Surveys Reports, Lincoln.

1947b Preliminary Appraisal of the Archaeological and Paleontological Resources of Medicine Creek Reservoir, Frontier County, Nebraska. River Basin Surveys Reports, Lincoln.
1949   Archeological Investigations in Medicine Creek Reservoir, Nebraska. *American Antiquity* 14: 278–284.
1953   The Woodruff Ossuary: A Prehistoric Burial Site in Phillips County, Kansas. Bureau of American Ethnology Bulletin 154: 103–142. River Basin Surveys Papers No. 3. Smithsonian Institution, Washington, D.C.
1962   Logan Creek Complex. Manuscript on file, Nebraska State Historical Society, Lincoln.
1970   Early Ceramic Environmental Adaptations. In *Pleistocene and Recent Environments of the Central Great Plains,* edited by Wakefield Dort, Jr., and J. Knox Jones, Jr., pp. 93–102. Special Publication No. 3. Department of Geology, University Press of Kansas, Lawrence.

Kivett, Marvin F., and Asa T. Hill
1949   Archeological Investigations along Medicine Creek. In *Proceedings of the Fifth Plains Conference for Archeology,* pp. 25–26. Notebook No. 1, Laboratory of Anthropology, University of Nebraska, Lincoln.

Kivett, Marvin F., and George S. Metcalf
1997   The Prehistoric People of the Medicine Creek Reservoir, Frontier County, Nebraska: An Experiment in Mechanized Archaeology (1946–1948). Plains Anthropologist Memoir 30. Vol. 42, No. 162, pp. 1–218.

Klein, Richard G.
1999   *The Human Career: Human Biological and Cultural Origins.* 2nd ed. Chicago, University of Chicago Press.

Klepinger, Linda
1972   An Early Human Skeleton from the Snyder Site, 14BU9, Butler County, Kansas. *Plains Anthropologist* 17 (55): 71–72.

Klippel, Walter E., and Darcy F. Morey
1986   Contextual and Nutritional Analyses of Freshwater Gastropods from Middle Archaic Deposits at the Hayes Site, Middle Tennessee. *American Antiquity* 51: 799–813.

Klippel, Walter E., and Paul W. Parmalee
1974   Freshwater Mussels as a Prehistoric Food Resource. *American Antiquity* 39: 421–434.

Knox, James C.
1983   Responses of River Systems to Holocene Climates. In *Quaternary Environments of the United States,* edited by Herbert E. Wright, Jr., pp. 26–41. University of Minnesota Press, Minneapolis.

Knudson, Ruthann
2002   Medicine Creek Is a Paleoindian Cultural Ecotone: The Red Smoke Assemblage. In *Medicine Creek: Seventy Years of Archaeological Investigations,* edited by Donna C. Roper, pp. 84–141. University of Alabama Press, Tuscaloosa.

Koch, Amy
2002   Archeology of the Beaver Creek Site, Boone County, Nebraska. Nebraska State Historical Society, Highway Archeology Program. Submitted to the Nebraska Department of Roads. Copies available from the State Historic Preservation Office, Lincoln.
2004   McIntosh: A Late Prehistoric Occupation in the Nebraska Sand Hills. *Central Plains Archeology* 10 (1): 1–167.

Koch, Amy, Trisha Nelson, and John R. Bozell
1999   Modified and Unmodified Fauna. In *Archaeology of the Patterson Site: Native American Life in the Lower Platte Valley, A.D. 1000–1300,* edited by John R. Bozell and John Ludwickson, pp. 71–84. Nebraska State Historical Society, Highway Archeology Program. Submitted to the Nebraska Department of Roads. Copies available from the State Historic Preservation Office, Lincoln.

Kornfeld, Marcel
    1996   The Big Game Focus. *Current Anthropology* 37: 629–657.

Krantz, Grover S.
    1970   Human Activities and Megafaunal Extinction. *American Scientist* 58: 164–170.

Krause, Richard A.
    1969   Correlation of Phases in Central Plains Prehistory. In *Two House Sites in the Central Plains: An Experiment in Archaeology*, edited by W. Raymond Wood, pp. 82–96. Plains Anthropologist Memoir 6. Vol. 14, No. 44, Pt. 2, pp. 82–96.
    1970   Aspects of Adaptation among Upper Republican Subsistence Cultivators. In *Pleistocene and Recent Environments of the Central Great Plains*, edited by Wakefield Dort, Jr., and J. Knox Jones, Jr., pp. 103–115. University Press of Kansas, Lawrence.
    1995a   Attributes, Modes, and Tenth Century Potting in North Central Kansas. *Plains Anthropologist* 40 (154): 307–352.
    1995b   Great Plains Mound Building: A Postprocessual View. In *Beyond Subsistence: Plains Archaeology and the Postprocessual Critique*, edited by Phillip Duke and Michael C. Wilson, pp. 129–142. University of Alabama Press, Tuscaloosa.
    1998   A History of Great Plains Prehistory. In *Archaeology on the Great Plains*, edited by W. Raymond Wood, pp. 48–86. University Press of Kansas, Lawrence.

Kreisa, Paul P.
    1993   Oneota Burial Patterns in Eastern Wisconsin. *Midcontinental Journal of Archaeology* 18: 35–60.

Krieger, Alex D.
    1946   Culture Complexes and Chronology in Northern Texas. Publication No. 4640. University of Texas, Austin.

Kuchler, A. William
    1974   A New Vegetation Map of Kansas. *Ecology* 55: 586–604.

Kutzbach, John E.
    1987   Model Simulations of the Climatic Patterns during the Deglaciation of North America. In *North America and Adjacent Oceans during the Last Deglaciation*, edited by W. F. Ruddimann and Herbert E. Wright, Jr., pp. 425–446. The Geology of North America, vol. K–3. Geological Society of America, Boulder.

Kutzbach, John E., and Peter J. Guetter
    1986   The Influence of Changing Orbital Parameters and Surface Boundary Conditions on Climate Simulations for the Past 18,000 Years. *Journal of Atmospheric Sciences* 43: 1726–1759.

Kutzbach, John E., Peter J. Guetter, Patsy J. Behling, and R. Selin
    1993   Simulated Climatic Changes: Results of the COHMAP Climate-Model Experiments. In *Global Climates since the Last Glacial Maximum*, edited by John E. Kutzbach, Thompson Webb III, William F. Ruddiman, and Patrick J. Bartlein, pp. 24–93. University of Minnesota Press, Minneapolis.

Kutzbach, John E., and Thompson Webb III
    1993   Conceptual Basis for Understanding Late-Quaternary Climates. In *Global Climates Since the Last Glacial Maximum*, edited by John E. Kutzbach, Thompson Webb III, W. F. Ruddiman, F. Alayne Street-Perrott, and Patricia J. Bartlein, pp. 5–11. University of Minnesota Press, Minneapolis.

Laird, Kathleen R., Sherilyn C. Fritz, Brian F. Cumming, and Eric C. Grimm
    1998   Early-Holocene Limnological and Climatic Variability in the Northern Great Plains. *Holocene* 8: 275–285.

Laird, Kathleen R., Sherilyn C. Fritz, Eric C. Grimm, and Pietra G. Mueller
    1996   Century-Scale Paleoclimatic Reconstructions from Moon Lake, a Closed-Basin Lake in the Northern Great Plains. *Limnology and Oceanography* 41: 890–902.

Lamb, G. F.
- 1937 Field notes on file with the Nebraska State Historical Society, Lincoln.

Larson, Mary Lou
- 1990 Early Plains Archaic Technological Organization: The Laddie Creek Example. Ph.D. diss., University of California, Santa Barbara.

Larson, Mary Lou, and Julie Francis (editors)
- 1997 *Changing Perspectives of the Archaic in the Northwestern Plains and Rocky Mountains.* University of South Dakota Press, Vermillion.

Larson, Nadine, Michael Madson, and David Mather
- 2004 *Cultural Resources Investigations at the Hudson (14GR346) and Simair (14GR354) Sites, Greenwood County, Kansas.* Contract Archeology Publications No. 25. Kansas State Historical Society, Topeka.

Latham, Mark A., and Rolfe D. Mandel
- 2002 Archaeological Investigation of Phase I Housing Sites 1, 2, and 3: Including Evaluation and Geomorphological Investigation of a Kansas City Hopewell Site (14LV120) at Fort Leavenworth, Kansas. Burns & McDonnell, Kansas City, Missouri. Copies submitted to the Corps of Engineers, Kansas City District. Copies available from the Kansas State Historic Preservation Office, Topeka.

Latta, Bruce F.
- 1950 Geology and Ground-Water Resources of Barton and Stafford Counties, Kansas. Kansas Geological Survey Bulletin 88. University of Kansas, Lawrence.

Layton, Donald W., and Delmar W. Berry
- 1973 Geology and Ground-Water Resources of Pratt County, Kansas. Kansas Geological Survey Bulletin 205. University of Kansas, Lawrence.

LeBlanc, Stephen A.
- 1999 *Prehistoric Warfare in the American Southwest.* University of Utah Press, Salt Lake City.

Lees, William B.
- 1986 *Jotham Meeker's Farmstead: Historical Archeology at the Ottawa Baptist Mission, Kansas.* Anthropological Series No. 13. Kansas State Historical Society, Topeka.
- 1988 Emergency Salvage Operations at Site 14MN328: A Great Bend Aspect Site at Marion, Kansas. *Journal of the Kansas Anthropological Association* 9: 60–82.
- 1989 Kansas Preservation Plan: Section on Historical Archeology. Archeology Department, Kansas State Historical Society, Topeka.
- 1991 Chronological Placement of the Booth Site: Implications for the Wilmore Complex and Southern Plains Culture History. *Plains Anthropologist* 36: 255–259.

Lees, William B., and Rolfe D. Mandel
- 1993 Origin of the Mounds at Sharps Creek. *Kansas Anthropological Association Newsletter* 5 (4): 6–8.

Lees, William B., John D. Reynolds, T. J. Martin, Mary J. Adair, and Steven R. Bozarth
- 1989 Final Summary Report: 1986 Archeological Investigations at 14MN328: A Great Bend Aspect Site along U.S. Highway 56, Marion County, Kansas. Kansas State Historical Society. Document submitted to Kansas Department of Transportation. Copies available from the Kansas State Historic Preservation Office, Topeka.

Lehmer, Donald J.
- 1954 Archaeological Investigations in the Oahe Dam Area, South Dakota, 1950–1951. Bulletin 158. Bureau of American Ethnology, Smithsonian Institution, Washington, D.C.
- 1954 The Sedentary Horizon of the Northern Plains. *Southwestern Journal of Anthropology* 10 (2): 139–159.
- 1971 Introduction to Middle Missouri Archaeology. National Park Service, Anthropological Papers 1.

Lehmer, Donald J., and Warren W. Caldwell
  1966   Horizon and Tradition in the Northern Plains. *American Antiquity* 31 (4): 511–516.
Le Page du Pratz, Antoine-Simon
  1972   *The History of Louisiana*. Pelican Press, New Orleans.
Lesser, Alexander, and Gene Weltfish
  1932   Composition of the Caddoan Linguistic Stock. Miscellaneous Collections 87 (6). Smithsonian Institution, Washington, D.C.
Libby, Willard F.
  1955   *Radiocarbon Dating*. 2nd ed. University of Chicago Press, Chicago.
Lintz, Christopher R.
  1983   *Stacy Reservoir*. Mariah and Associates, Austin.
  1986   *Architecture and Community Variability within the Antelope Creek Phase*. Studies in Oklahoma's Past No. 14. Oklahoma Archeological Survey, Norman.
  1991   Texas Panhandle–Pueblo Interactions during the 13th through 16th Centuries. In *Farmers, Hunters and Colonists: Interaction between the Southwest and Southern Plains*, edited by K. A. Spielmann, pp. 86–106. University of Arizona Press, Tucson.
Lintz, Christopher R., Abby Treece, and Fred Oglesby
  1995   The Early Archaic Structure at the Turkey Bend Ranch Site (41CC112), Concho County. In *Advances in Texas Archaeology: Contributions from Cultural Resource Management*, edited by James E. Bruseth and Timothy K. Perttula, pp. 155–185. Cultural Resource Management Report 5, Texas Historical Commission, Austin.
Lippincott, Kerry A.
  1976   Settlement Ecology of Solomon River Upper Republican Sites in North Central Kansas. Ph.D. diss., Department of Anthropology, University of Missouri, Columbia.
  1978   Solomon River Upper Republican Settlement Ecology. In *The Central Plains Tradition: Internal Development and External Relationships*, edited by Donald L. Blakeslee, pp. 81–93. Report 11. Office of the State Archaeologist, University of Iowa, Iowa City.
Logan, Brad
  1981   Wiley Site Ceramics: A Description and Spatial Analysis. *Journal of the Kansas Anthropological Association* 2 (3–4): 84–102.
  1985   O-Keet-Sha: Culture History and Its Environmental Context: The Archaeology of Stranger Creek Basin, Northeastern Kansas. Ph.D. diss., Department of Anthropology, University of Kansas, Lawrence.
  1990   The Richland Crematorium: New Evidence of Plains Woodland Mortuary Practices in the Central Plains. *Plains Anthropologist* 35: 103–124.
  1995   Phasing in White Rock: Archaeological Investigation of the White Rock and Warne Sites, Lovewell Reservoir, Jewell County, Kansas, 1994–1995. Project Report Series 90. Museum of Anthropology, University of Kansas, Lawrence.
  1996a The Plains Village Period on the Central Plains. In *Archeology and Paleoecology of the Central Great Plains*, edited by Jack L. Hofman, pp. 123–133. Research Series No. 48. Arkansas Archeological Survey, Fayetteville.
  1996b The Protohistoric Period on the Central Plains. In *Archeology and Paleoecology of the Central Great Plains*, edited by Jack L. Hofman, pp. 134–139. Research Series No. 48. Arkansas Archeological Survey, Fayetteville.
  1998a Oneota Far West: The White Rock Phase. *Wisconsin Archeologist* 79: 248–267.
  1998b The Fat of the Land: White Rock Phase Bison Hunting and Grease Production. *Plains Anthropologist* 43: 349–366.
  2001   Excavation of the Scott Site (14LV1082): A Steed-Kisker Phase House in Stranger Creek Valley. *Current Archaeology in Kansas* 2: 14–19.

2002 Archaeological Investigation of the Scott Site House (14LV1082), Stranger Creek Valley, Northeastern Kansas: A Progress Report. *Current Archaeology in Kansas* 3: 20–25.

2004 Archaeological Investigations at the Evans Locality, Stranger Creek Valley, Northeastern Kansas—2003. Report prepared by the Department of Sociology, Anthropology, and Social Work, Kansas State University, Manhattan. Copies available from the Kansas State Historic Preservation Office, Topeka.

2005a Kansas City Hopewell: Middle Woodland on the Western Frontier. In *Recreating Hopewell*, edited by Douglas K. Charles and Jane E. Buikstra. University Press of Florida (in press).

2005b *Archaeological Investigations at the Johns Creek and Warne Sites, Lovewell Reservoir, Jewell County, Kansas.* Report submitted to the Bureau of Reclamation, Nebraska-Kansas Area Office. Department of Sociology, Anthropology, and Social Work, Kansas State University, Manhattan.

Logan, Brad (editor)

1987 Archaeological Investigations in the Clinton Lake Project Area, Northeastern Kansas: National Register Evaluation of 27 Prehistoric Sites. Kaw Valley Engineering. Submitted to the Kansas City District, U.S. Army Corps of Engineers. Copies available from the State Historic Preservation Office, Topeka.

1990a Archaeological Investigations in the Perry Lake Project Area, Northeastern Kansas: National Register Evaluation of 17 Sites. Kaw Valley Engineering. Submitted to the Kansas City District, U.S. Army Corps of Engineers. Copies available from the State Historic Preservation Office, Topeka.

1990b *Archaeological Investigations in the Plains Village Frontier, Northeastern Kansas.* Project Report Series No. 70. Museum of Anthropology, University of Kansas, Lawrence.

1993 *Quarry Creek: Excavation, Analysis and Prospect of a Kansas City Hopewell Site, Fort Leavenworth, Kansas.* Project Report Series No. 80. Museum of Anthropology, University of Kansas, Lawrence.

1998 *Prehistoric Settlement of the Lower Missouri Uplands: The View from DB Ridge, Northeastern Kansas.* Project Report Series No. 98. Museum of Anthropology, University of Kansas, Lawrence.

Logan, Brad, Alan F. Arbogast, and William C. Johnson

1993 *Geoarchaeology of the Kansas Sand Prairie.* Project Report Series No. 83. Museum of Anthropology, University of Kansas, Lawrence.

Logan, Brad, and William E. Banks

1994 *White Rock Revised: Archaeological Investigation of the White Rock and Warne Sites, Lovewell Reservoir, Jewell County, Kansas, 1993.* Project Report Series No. 85. Museum of Anthropology, University of Kansas, Lawrence.

Logan, Brad, and Margaret E. Beck

1996 Woodland Period Research. In *The Archaeology of Kansas: A Research Guide*, edited by Brad Logan, pp. 55–94. Project Report Series No. 86. Museum of Anthropology, University of Kansas, Lawrence.

Logan, Brad, and Michael Fosha

1991 Quixote and Reichart: Archeological Investigation of Grasshopper Falls Phase Habitation Sites in the Perry Lake Project Area, Northeastern Kansas. *Kansas Anthropologist* 12 (2): 11–31.

Logan, Brad, and John G. Hedden

1990 14JO46. In *Archaeological Investigations in the Plains Village Frontier, Northeastern Kansas,* edited by Brad Logan, pp. 92–110. Project Report Series No. 70. Museum of Anthropology, University of Kansas, Lawrence.

Logan, Brad, and Matthew E. Hill, Jr.

2000 Spatial Analysis of Small Scale Debris from a Late Prehistoric Site in the Lower Missouri Valley, Kansas. *Journal of Field Archaeology* 27 (3): 241–256.

Logan, Brad, Richard E. Hughes, and Dale R. Henning
  2001   Western Oneota Obsidian: Sources and Implications. *Plains Anthropologist* 46: 55–64.
Logan, Brad, and Trever Murawski
  2004   Kansas Archaeological Field School Investigations at the Caenen Site (14LV1083), Stranger Creek Valley, Northeastern Kansas. *Current Archaeology in Kansas* 5: 24–33.
Logan, Brad, and Lauren W. Ritterbush
  1994   Late Prehistoric Cultural Dynamics in the Lower Kansas River Basin. *Central Plains Archaeology* 4: 1–26.
Lohman, Stanley W., and John C. Frye
  1940   Geology and Ground-Water Resources of the "Equus-Beds" Area in South Central Kansas. *Economic Geology* 35: 839–866.
Long, S. H.
  1818   Letter of January 30. National Archives Microcopy 271. *Letters Received by the Office of the Secretary of War Relating to Indian Affairs, 1800–1824.* Roll 2, 1817–1819, Frames 835–841. National Archives and Records Service, General Services Administration, Washington, D.C.
Loomis, Noel M., and Abraham P. Nasatir
  1967   *Pedro Vial and the Roads to Santa Fe.* University of Oklahoma Press, Norman.
Loosle, Byron N.
  1991   Social Interaction among the Late Plains Village Populations in the Central Plains. Ph.D. diss., Department of Anthropology, University of Kansas, Lawrence.
Lopinot, Neal H.
  1999a Archaeobotanical Remains. In *The Crabtree Site: Archaeological Investigations of Site 23CL164, Route 210, Clay County, Missouri,* edited by William Angelbeck and Terrell Martin, pp. 105–119. Report prepared by Missouri Department of Transportation, Jefferson City.
  1999b Archaeobotanical Remains. In *The Katz Site: Archaeological Investigations of Site 23CL163, Route 210, Clay County, Missouri,* edited by Jeffrey J. Berna, pp. 64–69. Report prepared by Missouri Department of Transportation, Jefferson City.
Ludwickson, John
  1978   Central Plains Tradition Settlements in the Lower Loup Basin: The Loup River Phase. In *Central Plains Tradition: Internal Dynamics and External Relationships,* edited by Donald L. Blakeslee, pp. 94–108. Report 11. Office of the State Archaeologist, University of Iowa, Iowa City.
Ludwickson, John, and John R. Bozell
  1998   Upper Republican Phase. In *Archaeology of Prehistoric Native America: An Encyclopedia,* edited by Guy Gibbon, pp. 859–860. Garland Publishing, New York.
Ludwickson, John, James N. Gundersen, and Craig Johnson
  1993   Selected Exotic Artifacts from Cattle Oiler (39ST224): A Middle Missouri Tradition Site in Central South Dakota. Plains Anthropologist Memoir 27, Vol. 38, No. 145, pp. 151–168.
Luedtke, Barbara E.
  1992   *An Archeologist's Guide to Chert and Flint.* Archaeological Research Tools 7, Institute of Archeology, University of California, Los Angeles.
Lundelius, Ernest L., Jr.
  1967   Late-Pleistocene and Holocene Faunal History of Central Texas. In *Pleistocene Extinctions: The Search for a Cause,* edited by Paul S. Martin and Herbert E. Wright, Jr., pp. 287–319. Yale University Press, New Haven.
  1976   Vertebrate Paleontology of the Pleistocene: An Overview. *Geoscience and Man* 13: 45–59.
Lyman, R. Lee, Michael J. O'Brien, and Robert C. Dunnell
  1997   *The Rise and Fall of Culture History.* Plenum Press, New York.

Macy, Jennifer N.
   2002   An Upper Republican Lithic Assemblage from 25FT39: A Study in Variability. Master's thesis, Department of Anthropology, University of Kansas, Lawrence.

Madsen, David B., and Steven R. Simms
   1998   The Fremont Complex: A Behavioral Perspective. *Journal of World Prehistory* 12 (3): 255–336.

Maki, David L.
   2000   Geophysical Investigation of the Buried City Complex. Poster paper presented at the Joint Midwest Archaeological/Plains Anthropological Conference, St. Paul.

Maki, David, Scott D. Brosowske, and Richard Drass
   2003   Archaeological Prospection on the Southern Plains: Results from Some Recent Investigations. Paper presented at the 61st Annual Plains Anthropological Conference, Fayetteville.

Maki, David L., and Geoffry Jones
   1998   A Preliminary Report of a Geophysical Investigation at the Odessa Yates Site (34BV100), Beaver County, Oklahoma. Archaeo-Physics Report of Investigations No. 8. Minneapolis.
   2000   2000 Survey Report of Wolf Creek and Lipps Ranches. Archaeo-Physics Report of Investigations No. 15. Minneapolis.
   2001   An Interim Report Summarizing Buried City Geophysical Research to Date with a Proposed Ground Truthing Research Design and Methodology for Area 1. Archaeo-Physics Report of Investigations No. 22. Minneapolis.

Maki, David L., Geoffry Jones, and Scott D. Brosowske
   1999   A Geophysical Search for House Structures at the Odessa Yates Site: A Southern Plains Village in Western Oklahoma. Poster paper presented at the 57th Annual Plains Anthropological Conference, Sioux Falls.

Mallam, R. Clark
   1982   Site of the Serpent: A Prehistoric Life Metaphor in South Central Kansas. Occasional Publication No. 1. Coronado-Quivira Museum, Lyons, Kansas.

Mallouf, Robert J.
   1994   Sailor-Helton: A Paleoindian Cache from Southwestern Kansas. *Current Research in the Pleistocene* 11: 44–46.

Malouf, Carling
   1958   Indian Tribes of Montana. In *Mountain Almanac,* pp. 106–128. Montana State University Press, Missoula.

Mandel, Rolfe D.
   1987   Late-Quaternary Environments of the Great Plains: Implications for Cultural Resource Management. In *Kansas Prehistoric Archaeological Preservation Plan,* edited by Kenneth L. Brown and Alan H. Simmons, pp. IV-1–IV-28. Office of Archaeological Research, Museum of Anthropology and the Center for Public Affairs, University of Kansas, Lawrence.
   1989   Geomorphological Investigations at Sites 14BU360, 14BU350, and 14BU356. Unpublished manuscript on file at the Kansas State Historical Society, Topeka.
   1990   Geomorphology and Stratigraphy of the Stigenwalt Site. In *The Archeology of the Stigenwalt Site, 14LT351,* edited by R. Thies, pp. 138–145. Contract Archeology Series Publication No. 7. Kansas State Historical Society, Topeka.
   1992   Soils and Holocene Landscape Evolution in Central and Southwestern Kansas. In *Soils in Archaeology,* edited by Vance T. Holliday, pp. 41–117. Smithsonian Institution Press, Washington, D.C.
   1994a   *Holocene Landscape Evolution in Southwestern Kansas.* Kansas Geological Survey and Kansas State Historical Society Bulletin 236. Lawrence.
   1994b   Geomorphology and Stratigraphy of Lower Mill Creek Valley, Johnson County, Kansas.

In *Archeological Test Excavations at Six Prehistoric Sites within the Lower Mill Creek Valley, Johnson County, Kansas,* edited by T. V. Gillen, R. Peter Winham, Edward J. Lueck, and L. Adrian Hannus, pp. 96–125. Archeology Laboratory, Augustana College, Archeology Contract Series No. 99, Sioux Falls, South Dakota.

1995 Geomorphic Controls of the Archaic Record in the Central Plains of the United States. In *Archaeological Geology of the Archaic Period in North America,* edited by E. Arthur Bettis III, pp. 37–66. Special Paper 297, Geological Society of America, Boulder.

1996 Geomorphology of the South Fork Big Nemaha River Valley, Southeastern Nebraska. In *A Geoarchaeological Survey of the South Fork Big Nemaha Drainage, Pawnee and Richardson Counties, Nebraska,* edited by Steven R. Holen, John K. Peterson, and Danial R. Watson, pp. 26–81. Technical Report 96-02. Nebraska Archaeological Survey, University of Nebraska State Museum, Lincoln.

1997 Geoarchaeology of Deeply Stratified Archaic Sites in Southeastern Kansas. Paper presented at the 55th Annual Plains Anthropological Conference, Boulder.

2000 Lithostratigraphy and Geochronology of Playas on the High Plains of Western Kansas. Paper presented at the annual meeting of the Geological Society of America, Reno.

2003 KU-KAA Partnership Studies Ancient Kansans. *Kansas Preservation* 25 (5): 7–8.

2005a Late Quaternary Landscape Evolution in Southeastern and South-Central Kansas: Implications for Archaeological Research. Bulletin. Kansas Geological Survey and Kansas State Historical Society, Lawrence (in press).

2005b Late Quaternary Landscape Evolution in Western Kansas: Implications for Archaeological Research. Bulletin. Kansas Geological Survey and Kansas State Historical Society, Lawrence (in press).

2005c Late Quaternary Landscape Evolution in Northeastern and North-Central Kansas: Implications for Archaeological Research. Bulletin. Kansas Geological Survey and Kansas State Historical Society, Lawrence (in press).

Mandel, Rolfe, and E. Arthur Bettis III

1995a Late Quaternary Landscape Evolution and Stratigraphy in Eastern Nebraska. In *Geologic Field Trips in Nebraska and Adjacent Parts of Kansas and South Dakota,* edited by C. A. Flowerday, pp. 77–90. Guidebook No. 10, Conservation and Survey Division, University of Nebraska, Lincoln.

1995b Alluvial Fans and Archaeological Site Formation Processes in the Eastern Plains of the U.S. In *Abstracts with Programs,* 29th Annual Meeting of the North-Central Section and South-Central Section, Geological Society of America, p. 71.

2001 Late Quaternary Landscape Evolution in the South Fork Big Nemaha River Valley, Southeastern Nebraska and Northeastern Kansas. Guidebook No. 11, Conservation and Survey Division, University of Nebraska, Lincoln.

Mandel, Rolfe D., and Jack L. Hofman

2002 Geoarchaeology of the Winger Site (14ST401): A Late-Paleoindian Bison Bonebed in Southwestern Kansas. *Current Research in the Pleistocene* 19: 61–64.

2003 Geoarchaeological Investigations at the Winger Site: A Late Paleoindian Bison Bonebed in Southwestern Kansas, U.S.A. *Geoarchaeology* 18: 129–144.

Mandel, Rolfe D., Jack L. Hofman, Steven Holen, and Jeannette M. Blackmar

2004 Buried Paleo-Indian Landscapes and Sites on the High Plains of Northwestern Kansas. In *Field Trips in the Southern Rocky Mountains, USA: Geological Society of America Field Guide 5,* edited by Eric P. Nelson and Eric A. Erslev, pp. 69–88. Geological Society of America, Boulder.

Mandel, Rolfe D., Steven Holen, and Jack L. Hofman

2005 Geoarchaeology of Clovis and Possible Pre-Clovis Cultural Deposits at the Kanorado Locality, Northwestern Kansas. *Current Research in the Pleistocene* 22 (in press).

Mandel, Rolfe D., John D. Reynolds, Barry G. Williams, and Virginia A. Wulfkuhle
- 1991 *Upper Delaware River and Tributaries Watershed: Results of Geomorphological and Archeological Studies in Atchison, Brown, Jackson, and Nemaha Counties, Kansas.* Contract Archeology Publications No. 9. Kansas State Historical Society, Topeka.

Mandel, Rolfe D., Chris Widga, Jack L. Hofman, Shannon Ryan, and Kale Brunner
- 2004 The Claussen Site (14WB322). In *The 18th Biennial Meeting of the American Quaternary Association Guidebook*, pp. 4-2–4-9. Kansas Geological Survey, Open-file report. University of Kansas, Lawrence.

Maples, Christopher G.
- 1994 Revision of Mississippian Stratigraphic Nomenclature in Kansas. In *Revision of Stratigraphic Nomenclature in Kansas*, compiled by D. L. Baars, pp. 67–74. Kansas Geological Survey Bulletin 230. University of Kansas, Lawrence.

Marine, I. Wendell, and Stuart L. Schoff
- 1962 *Ground Water Beaver County.* Oklahoma Geological Survey Bulletin 97. University of Oklahoma, Norman.

Marshall, James O.
- 1969 The Glen Elder Focus: The Cultural Affiliations of Archeological Material from the Glen Elder Site, 14ML1. Master's thesis, University of Nebraska, Department of Anthropology. Submitted to the National Park Service, Midwest Region, U.S. Department of the Interior. Copies available from the Midwest Archeological Center, Lincoln.
- 1972 *The Archeology of Elk City Reservoir: A Local Archeological Sequence in Southeast Kansas.* Anthropological Series No. 6. Kansas State Historical Society, Topeka.
- 2000 Archeology at Hard Chief Village: An Introductory Study of the Kansa Indian Experience in the American West, 1806–1846. *Kansas Anthropologist* 21: 57–89.

Marshall, James O., and Thomas A. Witty, Jr.
- 1990 The Bogan Site, 14GE1, An Historic Pawnee Village. *Kansas Anthropologist* 11 (1): 21–32.

Marten, Gerald G.
- 1988 Productivity, Stability, Sustainability, Equitability and Autonomy as Properties for Agroecosystem Assessment. *Agricultural Systems* 26: 291–316.

Martin, Charles W.
- 1993 Radiocarbon Ages on Late Pleistocene Loess Stratigraphy of Nebraska and Kansas, Central Great Plains, U.S.A. *Quaternary Science Reviews* 12: 179–188.

Martin, Handel T.
- 1909 Further Notes on the Pueblo Ruins of Scott County. *Kansas University Science Bulletin* 5 (2): 11–22.

Martin, Henry T.
- 1924 A New Bison from the Pleistocene, with Notice of New Locality for *Bison occidentalis*. *Kansas University Science Bulletin* 15: 273–278.

Martin, Larry D.
- 1996 Paleobiogeography of Post-Sangamonian Vertebrates in the Central Plains. In *Archaeology and Paleoecology of the Central Great Plains*, edited by Jack L. Hofman, pp. 221–227. Research Series No. 48. Arkansas Archeological Survey, Fayetteville.

Martin, Paul S.
- 1967 Prehistoric Overkill. In *Pleistocene Extinctions: The Search for a Cause*, edited by Paul S. Martin and Herbert E. Wright, Jr., pp. 75–120. Yale University Press, New Haven.
- 1973 The Discovery of America. *Science* 179: 969–974.
- 1984 Prehistoric Overkill. In *Quaternary Extinctions*, edited by Paul S. Martin and Richard G. Klein, pp. 354–403. University of Arizona Press, Tucson.

Martin, Paul S., and Richard G. Klein (editors)
- 1984 *Quaternary Extinctions.* University of Arizona Press, Tucson.

Martin, Paul S., and Herbert E. Wright, Jr. (editors)
    1967   *Pleistocene Extinctions: The Search for a Cause.* Yale University Press, New Haven.

Martin, Terrell L.
    1997   The Early Woodland Period in Missouri. *Missouri Archaeologist* 58: entire volume.

Mason, Otis T.
    1881   Mounds in Cowley County. *Annual Report of the Smithsonian Institution for 1880,* p. 446. Smithsonian Institution, Washington, D.C.

Mason, Ronald J.
    1962   The Paleo-Indian Tradition in Eastern North America. *Current Anthropology* 3: 227–278.

Matchen, Paul M.
    2002   Mobility and the Organization of Stone Tool Technology: A Comparison of Tucker Blowout (34TX71) and the Little Deer Site (34CU10) in Western Oklahoma. Master's thesis, Department of Anthropology, University of Oklahoma, Norman.

May, David W., and Steven R. Holen
    1993   Radiocarbon Ages of Soils and Charcoal in Late Wisconsinan Loess, South-Central Nebraska. *Quaternary Research* 39: 55–58.

McClung, Charles E.
    1908   Restoration of the Skeleton of *Bison occidentalis. Kansas University Bulletin* 4: 249–252.

McKern, William C.
    1934   Certain Classification Problems in Middle Western Archaeology. Circular No. 17. National Research Council, Committee on State Archaeological Surveys, Washington, D.C.
    1939   The Midwestern Taxonomic Method as an Aid to Archaeological Study. *American Antiquity* 4: 301–313.

McLean, Janice A.
    1996   Coal-Oil Canyon Revisited: History of Investigations, 1955–1996. *Kansas Anthropologist* 17 (2): 32.
    1998   Lithic Raw Material Use at the DB Site. In *Prehistoric Settlement of the Lower Missouri Uplands: The View from DB Ridge, Fort Leavenworth, Kansas,* edited by Brad Logan, pp. 167–197. Project Report Series No. 98, University of Kansas, Lawrence.

Mead, J. R.
    1890   Camps of Prehistoric People in Sedgwick County, Kansas. *Transactions of the Kansas Academy of Science* 19: 329–330.

Meltzer, David J.
    1993   Is There a Clovis Adaptation? In *From Kostenki to Clovis: Upper Paleolithic-Paleo-Indian Adaptations,* edited by Olga Soffer and N. D. Praslov, pp. 293–310. Plenum Press, New York.

Merriam, Daniel F.
    1963   *The Geologic History of Kansas.* Kansas Geological Survey Bulletin 162. University of Kansas, Lawrence.

Metcalf, George S.
    1941   The Hill Farm or Pike Pawnee Site (Wt1). Manuscript on file at the Nebraska State Historical Society, Lincoln.

Metcalf, Michael, and Kevin Black
    1991   *Archaeological Investigations at the Yarmony Pit House Site, Eagle County, Colorado.* Colorado Cultural Resources Series 31. Bureau of Land Management.

Midgett, Aaron, and Charles A. Reher
    1996   Quantitative Analysis of Stylistic Elements of Upper Republican Rim Sherds: A Comparison of Sites from the Western High Plains and South-Central Nebraska. Paper presented at the 55th Annual Plains Anthropological Conference, Boulder.

Middleton, Jessica L.
   2003   A Nebraska Phase Occupation at the Leary Site. *Kansas Anthropologist* 24: 34–44.
Miller, James C.
   1991   Lithic Resources. In *Prehistoric Hunters of the High Plains,* by George C. Frison, pp. 449–476. 2nd ed. Academic Press, New York.
Moffat, Charles R.
   1998   Oneota in the Central Des Moines Valley. *Wisconsin Archeologist* 79: 165–195.
Moline, Matt
   2002   Kansa Reclaims Tribal Land. *Topeka Capitol Journal,* 18 February: 1A.
Molloy, Paula
   1993   Hunting Practices at an Historic Plains Indian Village: Kansa Ethnoarchaeology and Faunal Analysis. *Plains Anthropologist* 38: 187–197.
Monger, Earl
   1970   A Preliminary Report on the Larned Site. *Kansas Anthropological Association Newsletter* 15 (8): 1–15.
Montet-White, Anta
   1968   *The Lithic Industries of the Illinois Valley in the Early and Middle Woodland Period.* Anthropological Papers No. 35. Museum of Anthropology, University of Michigan, Ann Arbor.
Moore, Petra S., and Walter H. Birkby
   1964   Archeological Investigations in Melvern Reservoir, Osage County, Kansas, 1962. Manuscript on file, University of Kansas, Museum of Anthropology, Lawrence.
Moore, Raymond C.
   1949   *Divisions of the Pennsylvanian System in Kansas.* Kansas Geological Survey Bulletin 83. University of Kansas, Lawrence.
Moorehead, Warren K.
   1931   *Archaeology of the Arkansas River Valley.* Yale University Press, New Haven.
Morehouse, George P.
   1908   History of the Kansa Indians. *Kansas Historical Collections, 1907–1908,* vol. 10: 327–368.
Morgan, Dale L.
   1953   *Jedediah Smith and the Opening of the West.* University of Nebraska Press, Lincoln.
Morris, Elizabeth A., W. M. Witkind, R. L. Dix, and J. Jacobson
   1981   Nutritional Content of Selected Aboriginal Foods in Northeastern Colorado: Buffalo *(Bison bison)* and Wild Onion *(Allium* sp.). *Journal of Ethnobiology* 1: 213–220.
Morrow, Toby
   1994   A Key to the Identification of Chipped-Stone Raw Materials Found on Archeological Sites in Iowa. *Journal of the Iowa Archeological Society* 41: 108–129.
Morse, Dan F.
   1997   *Sloan: A Paleoindian Dalton Cemetery in Arkansas.* Smithsonian Institution Press, Washington, D.C.
Morse, Dan F., and Albert C. Goodyear III
   1973   The Significance of the Dalton Adze in Northeast Arkansas. *Plains Anthropologist* 18: 316–322.
Moulton, Gary E. (editor)
   1983–   *The Journals of the Lewis and Clark Expedition.* 13 vols. University of Nebraska Press,
   2001   Lincoln.
Mudge, Benjamin F.
   1873   Traces of the Mound Builders in Kansas. *Transactions of the Kansas Academy of Science* 2: 5–6.
Mullins, Paul R.
   1997   Race and the Genteel Consumer: Class and African-American Consumption. *Historical Archaeology* 33 (1): 22–38.

Mulloy, William
    1959   The James Allen Site, near Laramie, Wyoming. *American Antiquity* 25: 112–116.
Munday, Frank J.
    1927   Pike-Pawnee Village Site: Review and Summary of the Evidence in the Case. *Nebraska History Magazine* 10 (3): 168–192.
Munsell, Marvin R.
    1961   Anthony: A Kansas-Oklahoma Border Site. *Plains Anthropologist* 6 (pt. 2): 112–114.
Murie, James R.
    1981   *Ceremonies of the Pawnee*. University of Nebraska Press, Lincoln.
Myers, Thomas P., and Ray Lambert
    1983   Meserve Points: Evidence of a Plains-Ward Extension of the Dalton Horizon. *Plains Anthropologist* 28: 109–114.
Nasatir, Abraham P.
    1942   Jacques Clamorgan: Colonial Promoter of the Northern Border of New Spain. *New Mexico Historical Review* 17 (2): 101–112.
    1952   *Before Lewis and Clark: Documents Illustrating the History of the Missouri*. 2 vols. University of Nebraska Press, Lincoln.
    1974   More on Pedro Vial in Upper Louisiana. In *The Spanish in the Mississippi Valley, 1762–1804*, edited by John Francis McDermott, pp. 100–119. University of Illinois Press, Urbana.
Nathan, Michele
    1980   *Survey and Testing of Archaeological Resources at Clinton Lake, Kansas, 1978–1979*. Iroquois Research Institute, Fairfax, Virginia. Report to the U.S. Army Corps of Engineers, Kansas City District.
Neff, Hector
    2000   Neutron Activation Analysis for Provenance Determination in Archaeology. In *Modern Analytical Methods in Art and Archaeology*, edited by E. Ciliberto and G. Spoto, pp. 81–134. John Wiley and Sons, New York.
Nepstad-Thornberry, Curtis, Linda S. Cummings, and Kathryn Puseman
    2002   A Model for Upper Republican Subsistence and Nutrition in the Medicine Creek Locality: A New Look at Extant Data. In *Medicine Creek: Seventy Years of Archaeological Investigations*, edited by Donna C. Roper, pp. 197–211. University of Alabama Press, Tuscaloosa.
Neuman, Robert W.
    1963   Archeological Salvage Investigations in the Lovewell Reservoir Area, Kansas. *Bureau of American Ethnology Bulletin* 185: 257–306.
    1967   Radiocarbon-Dated Archaeological Remains on the Northern and Central Great Plains. *American Antiquity* 32: 71–486.
Newcomb, William W.
    1961   *The Indians of Texas from Prehistoric to Modern Times*. University of Texas Press, Austin.
    1993   Historic Indians of Central Texas. *Bulletin of the Texas Archeological Society* 64: 1–63.
Newcomb, William W., and Thomas N. Campbell
    1982   Southern Plains Ethnohistory: A Re-examination of the Escanjaques, Ahijados, and Cuitoas. In *Pathways to Plains Prehistory: Anthropological Perspectives on Plains Natives and Their Pasts*, edited by Donald G. Wyckoff and Jack L. Hofman, pp. 29–43. Oklahoma Anthropological Society Memoir 3 and Cross Timbers Heritage Association Contributions 1. Norman.
Nickel, Robert K.
    1982   Botanical Remains from Sites in Mills County, Iowa. Manuscript on file, Office of the State Archaeologist, University of Iowa, Iowa City.
Nickels, Martin K.
    1971   An Analysis of the Skeletal Material from Sugar Creek Ossuary (23PL58). Master's thesis, Department of Anthropology, University of Kansas, Lawrence.

Norall, Frank
    1988   *Bourgmont: Explorer of the Missouri, 1698–1725.* University of Nebraska Press, Lincoln.
O'Brien, Michael J., and W. Raymond Wood
    1998   *The Prehistory of Missouri.* University of Missouri Press, Columbia.
O'Brien, Patricia J.
    1971   Valley Focus Mortuary Practices. *Plains Anthropologist* 16: 165–182.
    1972   The Don Wells Site (14RY404): A Hopewellian Site near Manhattan, Kansas, and Its Implications. *Kansas Anthropological Association Newsletter* 17 (5): 1–11.
    1977   *Cultural Resources Survey of Smithville Lake, Missouri.* Report to the U.S. Army Corps of Engineers, Kansas City District. Department of Sociology, Anthropology, and Social Work, Kansas State University, Manhattan.
    1984a   *Archaeology in Kansas.* Public Education Series No. 9. Museum of Natural History, University of Kansas, Lawrence.
    1984b   The Tim Adrian Site (14NT604): A Hell Gap Quarry Site in Norton County, Kansas. *Plains Anthropologist* 29: 41–56.
    1986   Prehistoric Evidence for Pawnee Cosmology. *American Anthropologist* 88: 939–946.
O'Brien, Patricia J., Margaret Caldwell, John Jilka, Lynn Toburen, and Barbara Yeo
    1979   The Ashland Bottoms Site (14RY603): A Kansas City Hopewell Site in North-Central Kansas. *Plains Anthropologist* 24: 1–20.
O'Brien, Patricia J., Pamela Hixon, Beryl Miller, Don Rowlison, Paul Tribble, David Vitt, and J. Pat Young
    1973   A Most Preliminary Report of the Coffey Site, 14PO1: A Plains Archaic Site in Pottawatomie County. *Kansas Anthropological Association Newsletter* 18 (5): 1–38.
O'Brien, Patricia J., Clark Larsen, John O'Grady, Brian O'Neill, and Ann S. Stirland
    1973   The Elliott Site (14GE303): A Preliminary Report. *Plains Anthropologist* 18: 54–72.
O'Bryant, Arch
    1947   Differences in Wichita Indian Camp Sites as Revealed by Stone Artifacts. *Kansas Historical Quarterly* 15 (2): 143–150.
O'Connell, James F.
    1987   Alyawara Site Structure and Its Archaeological Implications. *American Antiquity* 52: 74–108.
Odell, George H.
    2002   *La Harpe's Post: A Tale of French-Wichita Contact on the Eastern Plains.* University of Alabama Press, Tuscaloosa.
O'Gorman, J. A.
    1993   *The Tremaine Site Complex: Oneota Occupation in the La Crosse Locality, Wisconsin, Volume 1: The OT Site (47 Lc–262).* Archaeology Research Series No. 1. Museum Archaeology Program, State Historical Society of Wisconsin, Madison.
    1995   *The Tremaine Site Complex: Oneota Occupation in the La Crosse Locality, Wisconsin, Volume 3: The Tremaine Site (47 Lc–95).* Archaeology Research Series No. 3. Museum Archaeology Program, State Historical Society of Wisconsin, Madison.
Oklahoma Climatological Survey
    2001   Oklahoma Climate. *http://www.climate.ocs.ou.edu* (June 18, 2001).
Olson, Carolyn G., W. Dennis Nettleton, Donna A. Porter, and B. R. Brasher
    1997   Middle Holocene Aeolian Activity on the High Plains of Western Kansas. *Holocene* 7: 255–261.
Olson, Carolyn G., and Donna A. Porter
    2002   Isotopic and Geomorphic Evidence for Holocene Climate, Southwestern Kansas. *Quaternary International* 87: 29–44.
O'Neill, Brian
    1981   *Kansas Rock Art.* Historic Preservation Department, Kansas State Historical Society, Topeka.

Opler, Morris E.
- 1971 Pots, Apache, and the Dismal River Culture Aspect. In *Apachean Culture History and Ethnology*, edited by K. Basso and Morris E. Opler, pp. 29–33. Anthropological Papers of the University of Arizona No. 21. University of Arizona Press, Tucson.
- 1982 The Scott County Pueblo in Historical, Archaeological, and Ethnological Perspective. In *Pathways to Plains Prehistory: Anthropological Perspectives of Plains Natives and Their Pasts*, edited by Don G. Wyckoff and Jack L. Hofman, pp. 135–144. Memoir No. 3 of the Oklahoma Anthropological Society.

O'Shea, John M.
- 1984 *Mortuary Variability: An Archaeological Investigation.* Academic Press, Orlando, Florida.

O'Shea, John M., and John Ludwickson
- 1992 Archaeology and Ethnohistory of the Omaha Indians: The Big Village Site. In *Studies in the Anthropology of North American Indians*. University of Nebraska Press, Lincoln.

Oothoudt, Jerry W.
- 1976 The Gering (25SF10) and Dry Lake (25MP2) Burials: Chronology and Cultural Interpretations. Master's thesis, Department of Anthropology, University of Nebraska, Lincoln.

Owsley, Douglas W.
- 1992 Demography of Prehistoric and Early Historic Northern Plains Populations. In *Disease and Demography in the Americas*, edited by John W. Verano and Douglas H. Ubelaker, pp. 75–86. Smithsonian Institution Press, Washington D.C.
- 1997 Retrospective Analysis and Prospects for the Future. In *Bioarcheology of the North Central United States*, edited by Douglas W. Owsley and Jerome C. Rose, pp. 295–302. A volume in the Central and Northern Plains Archaeological Overview. Arkansas Archeological Survey Research Series 49, Fayetteville.

Owsley, Douglas W., and Karin L. Bruwelheide
- 1996 Bioarcheological Research in Northeastern Colorado, Northern Kansas, Nebraska, and South Dakota. In *Archeology and Paleoecology of the Central Great Plains*, edited by Jack L. Hofman, pp. 150–202. Arkansas Archaeological Survey Research Series 48, Fayetteville.
- 1997 Bioarcheological Research in Northeastern Colorado, Northern Kansas, Nebraska, and South Dakota. In *Bioarcheology of the North Central United States*, edited by Douglas W. Owsley and Jerome C. Rose, pp. 7–56. Arkansas Archaeological Survey Research Series 49, Fayetteville.

Owsley, Douglas W., and Richard L. Jantz
- 1989 A Systematic Approach to the Skeletal Biology of the Southern Plains. In *From Clovis to Comanchero: Archeological Overview of the Southern Great Plains*, edited by Jack L. Hofman, Robert L. Brooks, and Douglas W. Owsley, pp. 137–156. Arkansas Archeological Survey Research Series No. 35, Fayetteville.

Padilla, Matthew J., and Lauren W. Ritterbush
- 2005 White Rock Chipped Stone Technology. *Midcontinental Journal of Archaeology* 29: (in press).

Palmer, Jay W.
- 1992 Migrations of the Apachean Dineh. *North American Archaeologist* 13 (3): 195–218.

Parks, Douglas R.
- 2001 Pawnee. In *Handbook of North American Indians, Volume 13, Plains*, edited by Raymond J. DeMallie, pp. 515–547. Smithsonian Institution, Washington, D.C.

Parks, Douglas R., and Waldo R. Wedel
- 1985 Pawnee Geography: Historical and Sacred. *Great Plains Quarterly* 5 (3): 143–176.

Parks, Sharon G.
- 1978 Test Excavations at 14GE41: A Schultz Focus Habitation Site at Milford Lake, Kansas. Department of Sociology, Anthropology, and Social Work, Kansas State University. Submit-

ted to the Kansas City District, U.S. Army Corps of Engineers. Copies available from the State Historic Preservation Office, Topeka.

Pease, T. C., and E. Jenison
- 1940 *Illinois on the Eve of the Seven Years' War, 1747–1755*. French Series, vol. 3. Collections of the Illinois State Historical Library, vol. 29. Illinois State Historical Library, Springfield.

Peck, Michelle
- 2003 A Study of Great Bend Aspect Hunting Camps within the State of Kansas. Master's thesis, Department of Anthropology, Wichita State University, Wichita.

Penman, John T., and James N. Gundersen
- 1999 Pipestone Artifacts from Upper Mississippi Valley Sites. *Plains Anthropologist* 44: 47–57.

Pepperl, Robert E.
- 2000a Ashland Archeological District, Cass and Saunders Counties, Nebraska. National Register Nomination on file with the Nebraska State Historical Society, Lincoln.
- 2000b *Reassessment of the Ashland Site (25CC1) Complex, Cass and Saunders Counties, Nebraska*, 2 volumes. Copies available from the Archeology Division, Nebraska State Historical Society, Lincoln.

Perkl, Bradley E.
- 1998 *Cucurbita pepo* from King Coulee, Southeastern Minnesota. *American Antiquity* 63: 279–288.

Perttula, Timothy K., Marlin F. Hawley, and Frederick W. Scott
- 2001 Caddo Trade Ceramics from Northeast Texas in Lower Walnut Focus Sites in South Central Kansas. *Southeastern Archaeology* 20 (2): 154–172.

Peterson, James B., and Nancy Asch Sidell
- 1996 Mid-Holocene Evidence of *Cucurbita sp.* from Central Maine. *American Antiquity* 61: 685–698.

Phenice, Terrell W.
- 1969 *An Analysis of the Human Skeletal Material from Burial Mounds in North Central Kansas*. Publications in Anthropology No. 1. University of Kansas, Lawrence.

Phillips, James L., and James A. Brown (editors)
- 1983 *Archaic Hunters and Gatherers in the American Midwest*. Academic Press, New York.

Piazza, Theresa J.
- 1995 The Kaskaskia Manuscripts: French Traders in the Missouri Valley before Lewis and Clark. *Missouri Archeologist* 53: 1–42.

Pike, Zebulon M.
- 1889 *Exploratory Travels through the Western Territories of North America: Comprising a Voyage from St. Louis, on the Mississippi, to the Source of That River and a Journey through the Interior of Louisiana, and the North Eastern Provinces of New Spain*. W. H. Lawrence, Denver.

Ponte, M. R., David B. Loope, and James B. Swinehart
- 1994 Significance of Interbedded Eolian Sand and Peat beneath Interdunes of the Central Nebraska Sand Hills. *Geological Society of America, Abstracts and Program*, p. A–62. Boulder.

Porter, Donna A.
- 1997 Soil Genesis and Landscape Evolution within the Cimarron Bend Area, Southwestern Kansas. Ph.D. diss., Department of Agronomy, Kansas State University, Manhattan.

Pugh, Daniel C.
- 2001 The Aker Site (23PL43): Kansas City Hopewell Settlement Patterns, Aggregation, and Lithic Economy. *Plains Anthropologist* 46: 269–282.

Puseman, Kathryn
- 1996 Macrofloral Remains. In *Toward a New Perspective on Upper Republican Life in the Medicine Creek Valley: The Excavation of 25FT22, House 4, with Testing at Several Nearby Fea-

tures, edited by Donna C. Roper, pp. 251–307. Report to the U.S.D.I. Bureau of Reclamation, Great Plains Region, Grand Island, Nebraska.

Putnam, F. W.
- 1880 Report of the Curator. *Annual Report of the Peabody Museum of American Archaeology and Ethnology* 2 (4): 700–755.

Quigg, J. Michael, Christopher R. Lintz, Fred M. Oglesby, Amy C. Earls, Charles D. Fredrick, W. Nicholas Trierweiler, Douglas W. Owsley, and Karl W. Kibler
- 1993 *Historic and Prehistoric Data Recovery at Palo Duro Reservoir, Hansford County, Texas*. Technical Report 485. Mariah Associates, Austin.

Rankin, Robert L.
- 2000 On Siouan Chronology. Manuscript in the possession of the author, University of Kansas, Lawrence.
- 2001 The Kaw Nation in Prehistory: What the Kaw Language and Place Names Tell Us. Paper presented at the Council Grove Museum of the Kansas State Historical Society, May 5, Council Grove.

Ranney, William H., III
- 1994 Refining the Pratt Complex: Evidence from the Lewis Site. Master's thesis, Department of Anthropology, University of Kansas, Lawrence.

Ray, Jack H.
- 1998 Chert Resource Availability and Utilization. In *The 1997 Excavations at the Big Eddy Site (23CE426) in Southwest Missouri*, edited by Neal H. Lopinot, Jack H. Ray, and Michael D. Conner, pp. 221–265. Center for Archaeological Research, Special Publication No. 2, Southwest Missouri State University, Springfield.

Reed, Harold
- 1997 Field Notes: Site 14TO306. Manuscript on file, Archaeology Office, Kansas State Historical Society, Topeka.

Reeves, Brian O. K.
- 1973 The Concept of an Altithermal Cultural Hiatus in Northern Plains Prehistory. *American Anthropologist* 75: 1221–1253.

Reeves, Corwin C., Jr.
- 1976 Quaternary Stratigraphy and Geologic History of the Southern High Plains. In *Quaternary Stratigraphy of North America*, edited by W. C. Mahaney, pp. 213–234. Dowden, Hutchinson, and Ross; Stroudsburg, Pennsylvania.

Reher, Charles A.
- 1973 A Survey of Ceramic Sites in Southeastern Wyoming. *Wyoming Archaeologist* 16 (1–2).
- 1989 The High Plains Archaeology Project: Interim Report. *Wyoming Archaeologist* 32 (1–2): xviii–xxvi.
- 1991 Large Scale Lithic Quarries and Regional Transport Systems on the High Plains of Eastern Wyoming. In *Raw Material Economies among Prehistoric Hunter-Gatherers*, edited by Anta Montet-White and Steven R. Holen, pp. 251–284. Publications in Anthropology No. 19. University of Kansas, Lawrence.

Reher, Charles A., and Raymond Kunselman
- 1990 Obsidian Source Use in the High Plains of Southeastern Wyoming. Paper presented at the 48th Annual Plains Anthropological Conference, Oklahoma City.

Reher, Charles A., and Laura L. Scheiber
- 1996 Continued Research at the Donovan Site (5LO204): A Stratified Upper Republican Hunting Camp on the Western High Plains. Paper presented at the 54th Annual Plains Anthropological Conference, Iowa City.
- 1999 Test Excavation of a High Plains Upper Republican Fortress: Gurney Peak Revisited. Paper presented at the 57th Annual Plains Anthropological Conference, Sioux Falls.

Reher, Charles A., Laura L. Scheiber, Deborah J. Wyatt, James Miller, and Kathleen O. Maxfield
- 1994 The Donovan Site (5LO204): Interim Report on a Stratified Upper Republican Hunting Camp on the Western High Plains. Paper presented at the 52nd Annual Plains Anthropological Conference, Lubbock.

Reichart, Milton
- 1979 Bourgmont's Route to Central Kansas: A Reexamination. *Kansas History* 2: 96–120.

Reid, Kenneth C.
- 1977 *Psoralea esculenta* as a Prairie Resource. *Plains Anthropologist* 22: 321–327.
- 1980 The Achievement of Sedentism in the Kansas City Region. In *Archaic Prehistory on the Prairie-Plains Border,* edited by Alfred E. Johnson, pp. 29–42. Publications in Anthropology No. 12. University of Kansas, Lawrence.
- 1983 The Nebo Hill Phase: Late Archaic Prehistory in the Lower Missouri River Valley. In *Archaic Hunters and Gatherers in the American Midwest,* edited by James L. Phillips and James A. Brown, pp. 11–39. Academic Press, New York.
- 1984 *Nebo Hill and Late Archaic Prehistory on the Southern Prairie Peninsula.* Publications in Anthropology No. 15. University of Kansas, Lawrence.

Reimer, P. J., M. G. L. Baillie, E. Bard, A. Bayliss, J. W. Beck, C. J. H. Bertrand, P. G. Blackwell, C. E. Buck, G. S. Burr, K. B. Cutler, P. E. Damon, R. L. Edwards, R. G. Fairbanks, M. Friedrich, T. P. Guilderson, A. G. Hogg, K. A. Hughen, B. Kromer, F. G. McCormac, S. W. Manning, C. B. Ramsey, R. W. Reimer, S. Remmele, J. R. Southon, M. Stuiver, S. Talamo, F. W. Taylor, J. van der Plicht, and C. E. Weyhenmeyer
- 2004 IntCal04 Terrestrial Radiocarbon Age Calibration, 26–0 ka BP. *Radiocarbon* 46: 1029–1058.

Reynolds, John D.
- 1977 Preliminary Report of Archeological Investigations at 14ML307, the Range Mound, Glen Elder, Kansas. *Kansas Anthropological Association Newsletter* 23 (2–3): 1–11.
- 1979 *The Grasshopper Falls Phase of the Plains Woodland.* Anthropological Series No. 7. Kansas State Historical Society, Topeka.
- 1981 The Grasshopper Falls Phase: A Newly Defined Plains Woodland Cultural-Historical Integration Phase in the Central Plains. *Missouri Archaeologist* 42: 85–96.
- 1982 *Archaeological Investigations at the Cow-Killer Site, 14OS347.* Kansas State Historical Society. Submitted to the Kansas City District, U.S. Army Corps of Engineers. Copies available from the Kansas State Historic Preservation Office, Topeka.
- 1984 *The Cow-Killer Site: Melvern Lake, Kansas.* Anthropological Series No. 12. Kansas State Historical Society, Topeka.
- 1987 Hard Chief's Village Was Site of 1987 KAA Excavations. *Kansas Preservation* 9 (6): 1–3.
- 1990 Ceremonial Bifaces from the Whiteford Archeological Site, 14SA1. *Kansas Anthropologist* 11 (1): 6–20.
- 1996 The Scott County Pueblo Ruin or El Cuartelejo, the Most Frequently Excavated Site in Kansas. Paper presented at the 54th Annual Plains Anthropological Conference, Iowa City.

Reynolds, John, Harold Reed, and Greg Jackson
- 2001 Experiments in the Heat Treatment of Florence A Chert: A Preliminary Report. *Kansas Anthropologist* 22: 1–13

Richardson, Lynn
- 1997 *1996 Archaeological Investigations at the ForThree Site (14RY3183), Fort Riley, Riley County, Kansas.* USA-CERL. Report to Cultural Resources Division, Directorate of Environment and Safety, Fort Riley, Kansas.

Richey, W. E.
- 1904 Early Spanish Explorations and Indian Implements in Kansas. *Transactions of the Kansas State Historical Society* 8: 152–168.

Ricklis, Robert A.
- 1992 The Spread of a Late Prehistoric Bison Hunting Complex: Evidence from the South-Central Coastal Province of Texas. *Plains Anthropologist* 37: 261–273.

Ritterbush, Lauren W.
- 2001 Temper in White Rock Site Ceramics. *Current Archaeology in Kansas* (2): 7–14.
- 2002a Leary Site Revisited: Oneota and Central Plains Tradition Occupation along the Lower Missouri. *Plains Anthropologist* 47: 251–264.
- 2002b Drawn by the Bison: Late Prehistoric Native Migration into the Central Plains. *Great Plains Quarterly* 22 (4): 259–270.
- 2002c Western Oneota Contact across the Plains. Paper presented at the 60th Annual Plains Conference, Oklahoma City.
- 2003 Analysis of Leary Site Ceramics: Preliminary Results. Paper presented at the 25th Annual Flint Hills Archaeological Conference, Topeka.
- 2005 Oneota Interaction and Impact in the Central Plains. In *Plains Village Archaeology: Bison Hunting Farmers in the Central and Northern Plains,* edited by Stanley A. Ahler and Marvin Kay. University of Utah Press, Salt Lake City (in press).

Ritterbush, Lauren W., and Brad Logan
- 1991 The Schultz Archaeological Project, Phase I: A Survey of Selected Prehistoric Sites in North-Central Kansas. Project Report Series No. 73. Museum of Anthropology, University of Kansas, Lawrence.
- 2000 Late Prehistoric Oneota Population Movement into the Central Plains. *Plains Anthropologist* 45: 257–272.

Roberts, Ricky L.
- 1978 The Archaeology of the Kansas Monument Site: A Study in Historical Archaeology on the Great Plains. Master's thesis, Department of Anthropology, University of Kansas, Lawrence.

Roe, F. G.
- 1951 *The North American Buffalo: A Critical Study of the Species in Its Wild State.* University of Toronto Press, Toronto.

Rogers, Richard A.
- 1984 Kansas Prehistory: An Alluvial Geomorphological Perspective. Ph.D. diss., Department of Anthropology, University of Kansas, Lawrence.

Rogers, Richard A., and Larry D. Martin
- 1983 American Indian Artifacts from the Kansas River. *Transactions of the Nebraska Academy of Sciences* 11: 13–18.
- 1984 The 12 Mile Creek Site: A Reinvestigation. *American Antiquity* 49: 757–764.

Rohn, Arthur H.
- 1994 *Arkansas City Sites 14CO501, 1509, 1510: Survey and Testing.* Report to the U.S. Army Corps of Engineers, Tulsa District. Copies available from the Kansas State Historic Preservation Office, Topeka.

Rohn, Arthur H., and Alice M. Emerson
- 1984 *Great Bend Sites at Marion, Kansas.* Publications in Anthropology No. 1. Wichita State University, Wichita.

Rohn, Arthur H., Beverly M. Larson, and Mark S. Davis
- 1982 *A Survey and Assessment of the Cultural Resources at Kaw Lake, Northern Section (Kansas).* Submitted to the U.S. Army Corps of Engineers, Tulsa District. Copies available from the Kansas State Historic Preservation Office, Topeka.

Rohn, Arthur H., C. Martin Stein, and G. Glover
- 1977 *Wolf Creek Archaeology, Coffey County, Kansas.* Archaeology Laboratory, Wichita State University, Wichita. Report to Kansas Gas and Electric and Kansas City Power and Light Company.

Roll, Thomas E.
  1968 Upper Republican Cultural Relationships. Master's thesis, Department of Anthropology, University of Nebraska, Lincoln.
Romine, John
  1996 Study of the Light Fraction from Pit F454, Sharp's Creek Excavation, 14MP408, 1992–1993. Manuscript on file, Museum of Anthropology, University of Kansas, Lawrence.
Root, Matthew J.
  1979 The Paleoethnobotany of the Nebo Hill Site. *Plains Anthropologist* 24: 239–248.
  1981 The Milbourn Site: Late Archaic Settlement in the Southern Flint Hills. Master's thesis, Department of Anthropology, University of Kansas, Lawrence.
  2000 The Lower Sevenmile Creek Site (14RY115): A Smoky Hill Occupation in the Northern Flint Hills, Kansas. Plateau and Plains Research. Report submitted to Fort Riley, Kansas, and USA-CERL.
Roper, Donna C.
  1984–1985 Notes on Lithic Raw Material from a Dismal River Site in Western Nebraska. *South Dakota Archaeology* 8–9: 40–52.
  1988 Malachite and Turquoise Artifacts from Upper Republican Sites in Nebraska. *Plains Anthropologist* 33: 531–534.
  1990 Artifact Assemblage Composition and the Hunting Camp Interpretation of High Plains Upper Republican Sites. *Southwestern Lore* 56 (4): 1–19.
  1991a *Archaeological Testing of Four Sites, Harry Strunk Lake, Frontier County, Nebraska.* Report to the U.S.D.I. Bureau of Reclamation, Great Plains Region, Grand Island, Nebraska.
  1991b John Dunbar's Journal of the 1834–5 Chawi Winter Hunt and Its Implications for Pawnee Archaeology. *Plains Anthropologist* 36: 193–214.
  1992 Documentary Evidence for Changes in Protohistoric and Early Historic Pawnee Hunting Practices. *Plains Anthropologist* 37: 353–366.
  1993 *Archaeological Investigations at the Marvin Colson Site, 25FT158, Frontier County, Nebraska.* Report to the U.S.D.I. Bureau of Reclamation, Great Plains Region, Grand Island, Nebraska.
  1994 The Material Culture of 25DS21: A Lower Loup Hunting Camp in the Platte River Valley. *Central Plains Archaeology* 4 (1): 55–95.
  1995 Spatial Dynamics and Historical Process in the Central Plains Tradition. *Plains Anthropologist* 40: 203–221.
  1996a *Toward a New Perspective on Upper Republican Life in the Medicine Creek Valley: The Excavation of 25FT22, House 4, with Testing at Several Nearby Features.* Report to the U.S.D.I. Bureau of Reclamation, Great Plains Region, Grand Island, Nebraska.
  1996b An Apachean Pottery Vessel from Coal-Oil Canyon. *Kansas Anthropologist* 17 (2): 63–69.
  1999 The Identification of Clovis Sites from Blade Technology: A Cautionary Note. *Current Research in the Pleistocene* 16: 69–71.
  2000a Non-Mound Schultz Phase Burials from the Elliott Site, Geary County, Kansas. *Kansas Anthropologist* 21: 47–55.
  2000b Investigations of Great Bend Aspect Sites in Marion and McPherson Counties. *Current Archaeology in Kansas* 1: 31–36.
  2000c Radiocarbon Dating Provides Clues to Early Settlement in Marion County. *Kansas Preservation* 22 (5): 8–9, 12.
  2000d Lower Loup Phase Pottery in Great Bend Aspect Sites. *Plains Anthropologist* 45 (172): 169–177.
  2001a Five Smoky Hill Phase Houses in Saline and Ottawa Counties: The Whiteford Excavations, 1934–1945. *Kansas Anthropologist* 22: 83–169.
  2001b A Pawnee Hunting Camp in the Solomon River Valley. *Current Archaeology in Kansas* 2: 19–23.

2002a " . . . Its Turtles All the Way Down": Pre-Federal Upper Republican Site Archaeology at Medicine Creek. In *Medicine Creek: Seventy Years of Archaeological Investigations*, edited by Donna C. Roper, pp. 142–155. University of Alabama Press, Tuscaloosa.
2002b Post–River Basin Surveys Investigations at Upper Republican Sites in the Medicine Creek Valley. In *Medicine Creek: Seventy Years of Archaeological Investigations*, edited by Donna C. Roper, pp. 179–196. University of Alabama Press, Tuscaloosa.
2002c Spatial Variability in Central Plains Tradition Lodges. *Current Archaeology in Kansas* 3: 27–35.
2002d The Marion Great Bend Aspect Sites: Floodplains Settlement on the Plains. *Plains Anthropologist* 47: 17–32.
2003 The Whiteford Family of Salina: Mid-Twentieth Century Avocational Archaeologists. *Kansas History* 25: 244–257.
2005a The Whiteford Site, or Indian Burial Pit: A Smoky Hill Phase Cemetery in Saline County. Manuscript in preparation.
2005b The Origins and Expansion of the Central Plains Tradition. In *Plains Village Archaeology: Bison Hunting Farmers in the Central and Northern Plains*, edited by Stanley A. Ahler and Marvin Kay. In preparation for submittal to University of Utah Press, Salt Lake City.

Roper, Donna C., Robert J. Hoard, Robert J. Speakman, Michael D. Glascock, and Anne M. DiCosola
2004 Instrumental Neutron Activation Analysis of Central Plains Tradition Pottery from Kansas and Nebraska. Paper presented at the 62nd Annual Plains Anthropological Conference, Billings.

Roper, Donna C., and Elizabeth P. Pauls
2005 What, Where, and When Is an Earthlodge? In *Plains Earthlodges: Ethnographic and Archaeological Perspectives*, edited by Donna C. Roper and Elizabeth P. Pauls, pp. 1–31. University of Alabama Press, Tuscaloosa.

Roper, Donna C., and Harold Reed
2003 The 1970 Excavation at 14SA415: A Smoky Hill Phase Lodge. *Kansas Anthropologist* 24: 45–67.

Rosner, Malia L.
1988 The Stratigraphy of the Quaternary Alluvium in the Great Bend Prairie. Master's thesis, University of Kansas, Lawrence.

Ross, E. C.
1928 The Quivira Village. *Collections of the Kansas State Historical Society* 17: 514–534.

Rotman, Deborah L., and Michael S. Nassaney
1994 Class, Gender, and the Built Environment: Deriving Social Relations from Cultural Landscapes in Southwest Michigan. *Historical Archaeology* 31 (2): 42–62.

Rowlison, Don
1977 *A Report of Archeological Investigations at the Big Hill Lake Project, Southeastern Kansas.* Kansas State Historical Society. Submitted to the Tulsa District, U.S. Army Corps of Engineers. Copies available from the Kansas State Historic Preservation Office, Topeka.
1978 *The 1978 Archeological Investigations at the Big Hill Lake, Kansas.* Kansas State Historical Society. Submitted to the Tulsa District, U.S. Army Corps of Engineers. Copies available from the Kansas State Historic Preservation Office, Topeka.
1981 K. A. A. Dig and Kansas Archeology Training Program Uncovers Pithouses Near Lyons. *Journal of the Kansas Anthropological Association* 2 (5–6): 118–120.
1983a Plans for the Kansas Anthropological Association Annual Dig and Kansas Archeology Training Program. *Journal of the Kansas Anthropological Association* 4 (6): 87–92.
1983b Central Kansas Site Is Location of KAA Dig. *Kansas Preservation* 6 (1): 1–3.
1985 A Preliminary Report of the Bell Site and the 1984 Kansas Archaeology Training Program. *Journal of the Kansas Anthropological Association*, 5 (3): 117–128.

Rucker, Marc D.
    1971   Additional Puebloan Sherd Dates from Kansas. *Kansas Anthropological Society Newsletter* 17 (4): 1–6.
Rusco, Mary K.
    1960   *The White Rock Aspect.* Notebook 4. Laboratory of Anthropology, University of Nebraska, Lincoln.
Ryan, Shannon
    2004   Boatstones and Bannerstones on the Central Great Plains: Analysis, Patterns, and Possibilities. Master's thesis, Department of Anthropology, University of Kansas, Lawrence.
Rydjord, Robert L.
    1956   French Frontier and the Indian Trade. In *Kansas, The First Century,* edited by John D. Bright, vol. 1, pp. 22–46. Lewis Historical Publishing Co., New York.
Sánchez González, José Jesús
    1994   Modern Variability and Patterns of Maize Movement in Mesoamerica. In *Corn and Culture in the Prehistoric New World,* edited by Sissel Johannessen and Christine Hastorf, pp. 135–156. Westview, Boulder.
Savage, Sheila B.
    1995   Bison Procurement and Processing Strategies: Contrasts in Two Non-Kill Sites on the Southern Plains. Ph.D. diss., Department of Anthropology, University of Oklahoma, Norman.
Scarry, C. Margaret
    2003   Patterns of Wild Plant Utilization in the Prehistoric Eastern Woodlands. In *People and Plants in Ancient Eastern North America,* edited by Paul E. Minnis, pp. 50–104. Smithsonian Institution, Washington D.C.
Scheiber, Laura L.
    1997   Late Prehistoric Foragers and Farmers on the North American High Plains: A Case Study in Culture Contact. Paper presented at the 55th Annual Plains Anthropological Conference, Boulder.
    2001   Late Prehistoric Daily Practice and Culture Contact on the North American High Plains: A Zooarchaeological Perspective. Ph.D. diss., Department of Anthropology, University of California, Berkeley.
    2005   Late Prehistoric Bison Hide Production and Hunter-Gatherer Identities on the North American Plains. In *Gender and Hide Production,* edited by Lisa Frink and Kathryn Weedman, pp. 57–75. Alta Mira Press, Walnut Creek, California.
Scheiber, Laura L., and Amy C. McCabe
    2003   Upper Republican Bison Processing: A Comparison of Two Faunal Assemblages. Paper presented at the 61st Annual Plains Anthropological Conference, Fayetteville.
Scheiber, Laura L., and Charles A. Reher
    2000   Late Prehistoric Foragers and Farmers on the North American High Plains: A Case Study in Culture Contact. Paper presented at the 65th Annual Meeting for the Society of American Archaeology, Philadelphia.
Schiffer, Michael B.
    1987   *Formation Processes of the Archaeological Record.* University of New Mexico Press, Albuquerque.
Schlesier, Karl H.
    1972   Rethinking the Dismal River Aspect and the Plains Athapaskans, A.D. 1692–1768. *Plains Anthropologist* 17: 101–133.
Schmits, Larry J.
    1976   The Coffey Site: Environment and Cultural Adaptation at a Prairie Plains Archaic Site. Report submitted to the National Park Service, Interagency Archaeological Services, Denver.

1978 The Coffey Site: Environment and Cultural Adaptation at a Prairie-Plains Archaic Site. *Midcontinental Journal of Archaeology* 3: 69–185.

1980a The Williamson Site, 14CF330. In *Salvage Archeology of the John Redmond Lake, Kansas*, edited by Thomas A. Witty, Jr., pp. 13–66. Anthropological Series No. 8. Kansas State Historical Society, Topeka.

1980b The Dead Hickory Site, 14CF301. In *Salvage Archeology of the John Redmond Lake, Kansas*, edited by Thomas A. Witty, Jr., pp. 133–162. Anthropological Series No. 8. Kansas State Historical Society, Topeka.

1981 Archaeological and Geological Investigations at the Coffey Site, Tuttle Creek Lake, Kansas. Report submitted to the interagency Archaeological Services Branch, National Park Service, Denver.

1982 The May Brook Site, Jackson County, Missouri. *Missouri Archaeologist* 43: 1–66.

1987a The Williamson Site and the Late Archaic El Dorado Phase in Eastern Kansas. *Plains Anthropologist* 32: 153–174.

1987b The Diskau Site: A Paleoindian Occupation in Northeast Kansas. *Current Research in the Pleistocene* 4: 69–70.

Schmits, Larry J. (editor)

1981 *Little Blue Prehistory: Archeological Investigations at Blue Springs and Longview Lakes, Jackson County, Missouri.* Soils Systems, Inc.; Overland Park, Kansas. Report to the U.S. Army Corps of Engineers, Kansas City District.

Schmits, Larry J., and Bruce C. Bailey

1989 Prehistoric Chronology and Settlement-Subsistence Patterns in the Little Blue River Valley, Western Missouri. In Prehistory of the Little Blue River Valley, Western Missouri: Archaeological Investigations at Blue Springs Lake, edited by Larry J. Schmits, pp. 221–251. Environmental Systems Analysis, submitted to the Kansas City District, U.S. Army Corps of Engineers. Copies available from the Kansas State Historic Preservation Office, Topeka.

Schmits, Larry J., James A. Donahue, and Rolfe Mandel

1983 Archaeological and Geomorphological Inventory and Evaluation at the Proposed Fort Scott Lake Project, Southeastern Kansas. Environmental Systems Analysis. Report submitted to the Kansas City District, U.S. Army Corps of Engineers.

Schmits, Larry J., Rolfe D. Mandel, Joyce McKay, and John G. Hedden

1987 Archaeological and Historical Investigations at Tuttle Creek Lake, Eastern Kansas. Environmental Systems Analysis, Shawnee Mission, Kansas.

Schmits, Larry J., and John M. Parisi

1987 Summary and Recommendations for Future Cultural Resource Management at Perry Lake. In *Archaeological Survey and Testing at Perry Lake, Jefferson County, Kansas*, edited by Larry J. Schmits, pp. 199–225. Publications in Archaeology No. 2. Environmental Systems Analysis, Shawnee Mission, Kansas.

Schock, Jack M.

1965 14LO8, A Hunting Camp in Logan County, Kansas. *Kansas Anthropological Association Newsletter* 10 (7–9): 6–8.

Schoen, Christopher M.

1993 Phase III Archeological Investigation of 14MY2336 near Independence, Kansas. Archeology Office, Kansas State Historical Society. Report submitted to the Kansas Department of Transportation. Copies available from the Kansas State Historic Preservation Office, Topeka.

1994 *Phase IV Salvage Investigations at the Martin Farmstead (14RP322) in Republic County, Kansas.* Contract Archeology Publications No. 12. Kansas State Historical Society, Topeka.

Schoewe, Walter H.
- 1949 The Geography of Kansas, Part II—Physical Geography. *Transactions of the Kansas Academy of Science* 52 (3): 261–333.

Schoolcraft, H. R.
- 1853 *Information Respecting the History, Condition and Prospects of the Indian Tribes of the United States, Part III.* Lippincott, Grambo and Co., Philadelphia.

Schroeder, Albert H.
- 1962 A Re-analysis of the Routes of Coronado and Oñate into the Plains in 1541 and 1601. *Plains Anthropologist* 7: 2–23.

Schultz, C. Bertrand, and T. Mylan Stout
- 1945 Pleistocene Loess Deposits of Nebraska. *American Journal of Science* 243: 231–244.

Schultz, Floyd, and Albert C. Spaulding
- 1948 A Hopewellian Burial Site in the Lower Republican Valley, Kansas. *American Antiquity* 13: 306–313.

Scott, Frederick W.
- 1995 Tradeware in the Central Plains Tradition: Steed-Kisker Presence, Influence, and Joining of the Central Plains Tradition. *Kansas Anthropologist* 16 (1): 46–68.

Seevers, William J.
- 1975 *Description of the Surficial Rocks in Cherokee County, Southeastern Kansas.* Geology Series No. 1. Kansas Geological Survey, University of Kansas, Lawrence.

Self, Huber
- 1978 *Environment and Man in Kansas.* Regents Press of Kansas, Lawrence.

Sellards, Elias Howard
- 1952 *Early Man in America: A Study of Prehistory.* University of Texas Press, Austin.

Shackley, M. Steven
- 1995 Sources of Archaeological Obsidian in the Greater American Southwest: An Update and Quantitative Analysis. *American Antiquity* 60: 531–551.
- 1998 Archeological Obsidian Studies: Method and Theory. In *Advances in Archaeological and Museum Sciences*, Series 3. Kluwer Academic/Plenum Publishing, New York.
- 1999 Source Provenance of Archaeological Obsidian from the Odessa Yates Site (34BV100), Beaver County, Oklahoma. Report prepared for Scott Brosowske, Department of Anthropology, University of Oklahoma, Norman.
- 2001 Source Provenance of Obsidian Artifacts from Archaic through Late Period Contexts in the Oklahoma Panhandle. Report prepared for the Oklahoma Archeological Survey, University of Oklahoma, Norman.

Shaeffer, Joseph B.
- 1965 Salvage Archaeology in Oklahoma: Papers of the Oklahoma Archaeological Salvage Project No. 8–15. *Bulletin of the Oklahoma Anthropological Society* 13: 131–145.

Shay, Creighton T.
- 1978 Late Prehistoric Bison and Deer Use in the Eastern Prairie-Forest Border. In *Bison Procurement Utilization: A Symposium,* edited by Leslie B. Davis and Michael Wilson, pp. 194–212. Plains Anthropologist Memoir 14. Vol. 23, No. 82, Pt. 2, pp. 194–212.

Shippee, J. Mett
- 1948 Nebo Hill, A Lithic Complex in Western Missouri. *American Antiquity* 14: 29–32.
- 1963 Was Flint Annealed before Flaking? *Plains Anthropologist* 8: 271–272.
- 1972 *Archaeological Remains in the Kansas City Area: The Mississippian Occupation.* Research Series No. 9. Missouri Archaeological Society, Columbia.

Sibley, George C.
- 1927 Extracts from the Diary of Major Sibley. *Chronicles of Oklahoma* 5 (2): 196–218.

Sigstad, John S.
    1969   Pottery. In *Two House Sites in the Central Plains: An Experiment in Archaeology*, edited by W. Raymond Wood, pp. 17–23. Plains Anthropologist Memoir 6. Vol. 14, No. 44, Pt. 2, pp. 17–23.

Simms, Steven R.
    1988   Conceptualizing the Paleoindian and Archaic in the Great Basin. In *Early Human Occupation in Far Western North America: The Clovis-Archaic Interface*, edited by Judith A. Willig, C. Melvin Aikens, and John L. Fagan, pp. 41–52. Anthropological Papers No. 21. Nevada State Museum, Carson City.

Slaughter, Bob H.
    1967   Animal Ranges as a Clue to Late Pleistocene Extinctions. In *Pleistocene Extinctions: The Search for a Cause*, edited by Paul S. Martin and Herbert E. Wright, Jr., pp. 155–168. Yale University Press, New Haven.

Smith, Bruce D.
    1985   *Chenopodium berlandieri* ssp. *jonesianum*: Evidence for a Hopewellian Domesticate from Ash Cave, Ohio. *Southeastern Archaeology* 4: 107–133.
    1987   The Independent Domestication of Indigenous Seed-Bearing Plants in Eastern North America. In *Emergent Horticultural Economies in the Eastern Woodlands*, edited by William F. Keegan, pp. 3–47. Occasional Papers No. 7. Center for Archaeological Investigations, Southern Illinois University, Carbondale.
    1992a   *Rivers of Change: Essays on Early Agriculture in Eastern North America*. Smithsonian Institution Press, Washington, D.C.
    1992b   Prehistoric Plant Husbandry in Eastern North America. In *The Origins of Agriculture: An International Perspective*, edited by C. Wesley Cowan and Patti Jo Watson, pp. 101–120. Smithsonian Institution Press, Washington D.C.
    2001   Low-Level Food Production. *Journal of Archaeological Research* 9: 1–43.

Smith, Bruce D., and C. Wesley Cowan
    2003   Domesticated Crop Plants and the Evolution of Food Production Economies in Eastern North America. In *People and Plants in Ancient Eastern North America*, edited by Paul E. Minnis, pp. 105–125. Smithsonian Institution, Washington D.C.

Smith, Carlyle S.
    1949a   Archaeological Investigations in Ellsworth and Rice Counties, Kansas. *American Antiquity* 14: 292–300.
    1949b   Fieldwork in Kansas, 1949. *Plains Archaeological Conference Newsletter* 2 (4): 38–40.
    1950a   European Trade Material from the Kansas Monument Site. *Plains Archaeological Conference Newsletter* 3 (2): 27–34.
    1950b   The Pottery from the Kansas Monument Site. *Plains Archaeological Conference Newsletter* 3 (4): 49–51.

Smith, Ralph A.
    1959a   Account of the Journey of Bénard de la Harpe: Discovery Made by Him of Several Nations Situated in the West. *Southwestern Historical Quarterly* 62: 525–541.
    1959b   Account of the Journey of Bénard de la Harpe: Discovery Made by Him of Several Nations Situated in the West. *Southwestern Historical Quarterly* 62: 371–385.

Smith, Vernon L.
    1975   The Primitive Hunter Culture, Pleistocene Extinction, and the Rise of Agriculture. *Journal of Politics and Economics* 83: 727–755.

Snyder, Lynn M.
    1991   Barking Mutton: Ethnohistoric and Ethnographic, Archaeological, and Nutritional Evidence Pertaining to the Dog as a Native American Food Resource on the Plains. In *Beamers, Bobwhites, and Blue-Points, Papers in Honor of Paul W. Parmalee*, edited by

James R. Purdue, Walter E. Klippel, and Bonnie W. Styles, pp. 359–378. Illinois State Museum, Scientific Papers 23, Springfield.

Sollberger, J. B., and Thomas R. Hester
- 1973 Some Additional Data on the Thermal Alteration of Siliceous Stone. *Bulletin of the Oklahoma Anthropological Society* 12: 181–186.

Sperry, James E.
- 1965 Cultural Relationships of the Miller and Rush Creek Archaeological Sites on the Lower Republican River of Kansas. Master's thesis, Department of Anthropology, University of Nebraska, Lincoln.

Speth, John D.
- 1983 *Bison Kills and Bone Counts.* University of Chicago Press, Chicago.

Speth, John D., and Katherine A. Spielmann
- 1983 Energy Source, Protein Metabolism, and Hunter-Gatherer Subsistence Strategies. *Journal of Anthropological Archaeology* 2: 1–31.

Spielmann, Katherine A.
- 1983 Late Prehistoric Exchange between the Southwest and the Southern Plains. *Plains Anthropologist* 28: 257–272.
- 1991 *Interdependence in the Prehistoric Southwest: An Ecological Analysis of Plains-Pueblo Interaction.* Garland Publishing, New York.

Staab, Rodney
- 1995 Kansa Presence in the Upper Kansas Valley, 1848–1867. *Kansas Anthropologist* 16 (1): 24–45.

Stafford, C. Russell, and Steven D. Creasman
- 2002 The Hidden Record: Late Holocene Landscapes and Settlement Archaeology in the Lower Ohio River Valley. *Geoarchaeology* 17: 117–140.

Stanford, Dennis
- 1997 The Walsh Cache. In *The Paleoindians of the North American Midcontinent,* edited by Anta Montet-White, pp. 40–43. Musée Départmental de Préhistoire de Solutré, Solutré, France.

Stein, C. Martin
- 1978–1979 Radiocarbon Dates from Coffey County. *Kansas Anthropological Association Newsletter* 24 (4–5): 12–13.
- 1984 Traces of Early Man in Kansas Tantalize Archaeologists. *Kansas Preservation* 6 (2): 5–7. Topeka.
- 1992 Kansas Archeology Training Program Investigates Site in McPherson County. *Kansas Preservation* 14 (5): 1, 2, 3.
- 2005 *Sources of Smoky Hill Silicified Chalk in Northwest Kansas.* Anthropological Papers No. 17. Kansas State Historical Society, Topeka.

Stein, C. Martin (editor)
- 2005 *Lower Walnut Archeology: Archeological Investigations in the Walnut River Valley (1994–1996).* Report in preparation.

Stein, C. Martin, and John Reynolds
- 1994 Querying the Quarry: KATP Lithic Technology Class at 14CO5. *Kansas Anthropological Association Newsletter* 6 (4): 7–10.

Steinacher, Terry L.
- 1976 The Smoky Hill Phase and Its Role in the Central Plains Tradition. Master's thesis, Department of Anthropology, University of Nebraska, Lincoln.

Steinacher, Terry L., and Gayle F. Carlson
- 1998 The Central Plains Tradition. In *Archaeology on the Great Plains,* edited by W. Raymond Wood, pp. 234–268. University Press of Kansas, Lawrence.

Sternberg, Robert S.
- 1997 Archaeomagnetic Dating. In *Chronometric Dating in Archaeology,* edited by R. E. Taylor

and Martin J. Aitken, pp. 323–356. Advances in Archaeological and Museum Science, vol. 2. Plenum Press, New York.

Sterns, Frederick H.
- 1914 Ancient Lodge Sites on the Middle Missouri in Nebraska. *American Anthropologist* 16 (1): 135–137.
- ca. 1915 F. H. Sterns field notes on file at the Peabody Museum, Harvard University, accession file 15–6, pp. 19–21.
- 1915a The Archeology of Eastern Nebraska with Special Reference to the Culture of the Rectangular Earth Lodges. Ph.D. diss., Harvard University, Cambridge.
- 1915b A Stratification of Cultures in Eastern Nebraska. *American Anthropologist* 17: 121–127.

Strahler, Allan N.
- 1964 Quantitative Geomorphology of Drainage Basin and Channel Networks. In *Handbook of Applied Hydrology*, edited by V. T. Chow, pp. 39–76. McGraw-Hill, New York.

Straley, W.
- 1909 *Archaic Gleanings: A Study of the Archaeology of Nuckolls County, Nebraska.* Herald Printery, Nelson, Nebraska.

Strong, William Duncan
- 1932 An Archeological Reconnaissance in the Missouri Valley. *Explorations and Field-work of the Smithsonian Institution in 1931:* 151–158.
- 1933 The Plains Culture Area in the Light of Archaeology. *American Anthropologist* 35: 271–287.
- 1935 *An Introduction to Nebraska Archeology.* Miscellaneous Collections 93 (10): iii–323. Smithsonian Institution, Washington, D.C.

Struever, Stuart
- 1960 The Kamp Mound Group. Master's thesis, Department of Anthropology, University of Chicago, Chicago.
- 1964 The Hopewell Interaction Sphere in Riverine–Western Great Lakes Culture History. In *Hopewellian Studies,* edited by Joseph R. Caldwell and Robert L. Hall, pp. 85–106. Illinois State Museum, Scientific Papers 12, Springfield.

Struever, Stuart, and Gail L. Houart
- 1972 An Analysis of the Hopewell Interaction Sphere. In *Social Exchange and Interaction,* edited by E. N. Wilmsen, pp. 47–49. Anthropological Papers No. 46. Museum of Anthropology, University of Michigan, Ann Arbor.

Stuckenrath, Robert, and James E. Mielke
- 1972 Smithsonian Institution Radiocarbon Measurements VII. *Radiocarbon* 14 (2): 405.

Stuiver, Minze, and Paula J. Reimer
- 1993 Radiocarbon Calibration Program Rev. 3.0.3c. *Radiocarbon* 35: 215–230.

Swain, Albert M.
- 1978 Environmental Change during the Past 2000 Years in North-Central Wisconsin: Analysis of Pollen, Charcoal, and Seeds from Varved Lake Sediments. *Quaternary Research* 10: 55–68.

Swineford, Ada
- 1955 Petrography of Upper Permian Rocks in South-Central Kansas. Kansas Geological Survey Bulletin 111. University of Kansas, Lawrence.

Syms, E. Leigh
- 1969 The McKean Complex as a Horizon Marker in Manitoba and the Northern Great Plains. Master's thesis, University of Manitoba, Winnipeg.

Tainter, Joseph A.
- 1977 Woodland Social Change in West-Central Illinois. *Midcontinental Journal of Archaeology* 2: 67–98.

Taylor, Alan
- 2001 *American Colonies.* Vol. 1 of *The Penguin History of the United States,* edited by Eric Foner. Viking Press, New York.

Taylor, R. E.
- 1987 Radiocarbon Dating: An Archaeological Perspective. Academic Press, New York.
- 1997 Radiocarbon Dating. In *Chronometric Dating in Archaeology,* edited by R. E. Taylor and Martin J. Aitken, pp. 65–96. Advances in Archaeological and Museum Science, vol. 2. Plenum Press, New York.

Teller, H. M.
- 1883 Draft of a Bill to Confirm Title to Certain Land in the Indian Territory to the Cheyenne and Arapahoes, and the Wichitas and Affiliated Bands to Provide for the Issuance of Patents Therefor. Senate Executive Document No. 13, 48th Congress, 1st Session.

Terry, Kenneth, and Ina Terry
- 1961 Chain Mail and Other Exotic Materials from South Central Kansas. *Plains Anthropologist* 6 (12, pt. 2): 126–129.

Thies, Randall M.
- 1981 Archeological Investigations at John Redmond Reservoir, East Central Kansas, 1979. Kansas State Historical Society, Topeka. Report submitted to the U.S. Army Corps of Engineers, Tulsa District.
- 1982 *The Archeology of the Begin Ossuary, 14JW312.* Contract Archeology Publication No. 2. Archeology Department, Kansas State Historical Society, Topeka.
- 1987 From the Pueblos to the Plains: Origins of Certain Southwestern Sherds Found at Saxman and Crandall. *Journal of the Kansas Anthropological Association* 6 (9): 226–232.
- 1988a Hard Chief's Village and the 1987 Kansas Archeology Training Program. *Journal of the Kansas Anthropological Association* 8: 86–108.
- 1988b Excavations at Hard Chief's Village: Results of the 1987 Kansas Archeology Training Program. *Missouri Archaeologist* 49: 67–75.
- 1989 A Preliminary Report on the Hallman Site and the 1988 Kansas Archeology Training Program. *Journal of the Kansas Anthropological Association* 9 (9): 174–199.
- 1990 *The Archaeology of the Stigenwalt Site 14LT351.* Contract Archeology Series No. 7. Kansas State Historical Society, Topeka.
- 1991a Archeological Resources of Selected Portions of the Lower Walnut Valley: Results of the 1990 Investigations. Kansas State Historical Society. Submitted to the U.S. Army Corps of Engineers, Tulsa District. Copies available from the Kansas State Historic Preservation Office, Topeka.
- 1991b New Data on Lower Walnut Sites. Paper presented at the 49th Annual Plains Anthropological Conference, Lawrence.

Thies, Randall M., and Thomas A. Witty, Jr.
- 1992 The Archaic of the Central Plains. *Revista de Arqueología Americana* 5: 137–165.

Thomas, Alfred B.
- 1931 The First Santa Fe Expedition. *Chronicles of Oklahoma* 9 (2): 195–208.
- 1982 *Alonso de Posada Report, 1686.* Perdido Bay Press, Pensacola.

Thomas, Alfred B. (editor)
- 1935 *After Coronado: Spanish Exploration Northeast of New Mexico, 1696–1727.* University of Oklahoma Press, Norman.

Thomas, David H.
- 1975 Nonsite Sampling in Archaeology: Up the Creek without a Site? In *Sampling in Archaeology,* edited by James W. Mueller, pp. 61–81. University of Arizona Press, Tucson.

Thompson, Dean M., and E. Arthur Bettis III
- 1980 Archaeology and Holocene Landscape Evolution in the Missouri Drainage of Iowa. *Journal of the Iowa Archaeological Society* 27: 1–60.

Thoms, Alston V.
- 1989 The Northern Roots of Hunter-Gatherer Intensification: Camas and the Pacific Northwest. Ph.D. diss., Department of Anthropology, Washington State University, Pullman.

Thornthwaite, C. Warren
    1948   An Approach toward a Rational Classification of Climate. *Geographical Review* 38: 55–94.
Thorp, J., W. M. Johnson, and E. C. Reed
    1950   Some Post-Pleistocene Buried Soils of the Central United States. *Journal of Soil Science* 2: 1–19.
Thurmond, Peter J.
    1991   Archeology of Dempsey Divide: A Late Archaic/Woodland Hotspot on the Southern Plains. *Bulletin of the Oklahoma Anthropological Society* 39: 103–157.
Thwaites, Reuben G.
    1905   *Part III of James's Account of S. H. Long's Expedition, 1819–1820. Early Western Travels 1748–1846,* vol. 16. Arthur H. Clark, Cleveland.
    1908   The French Regime in Wisconsin, 1743–1760. *Collections of the State Historical Society of Wisconsin* 18: 1–222.
Tieszen, Larry L., Karl R. Reinhard, Jr., and D. L. Foreshoe
    1997   Application of Stable Isotopes in Analysis of Dietary Patterns. In *Bioarcheology of the North Central United States,* edited by Douglas W. Owsley and Jerome C. Rose, pp. 248–256. Research Series 49. Arkansas Archeological Survey, Fayetteville.
Timberlake, Robert D.
    1983   Phase II Report of Archeological Sites Associated with Structure 23A, South Fork Watershed, Butler County, Kansas. Archeology Office, Kansas State Historical Society. Submitted to the Kansas Department of Transportation. Copies available from the Office of the State Historic Preservation Officer, Topeka.
Troike, Ralph C.
    1964   A Pawnee Visit to San Antonio in 1795. *Ethnohistory* 11 (4): 380–393.
Turnmire, Karen L.
    1996   Unmodified Fauna. In *Toward a New Perspective on Upper Republican Life in the Medicine Creek Valley: The Excavation of 25FT22, House 4, with Testing at Several Nearby Features,* edited by Donna C. Roper, pp. 187–250. Report to the U.S.D.I. Bureau of Reclamation, Great Plains Region, Grand Island, Nebraska.
Udden, Johan August
    1900   *An Old Indian Village.* Lutheran Augustana Book Concern, Printers, Rock Island, Illinois.
Unrau, William E.
    1971   *The Kansa Indians: A History of the Wind People, 1673–1873.* University Press of Oklahoma, Norman.
    1989   *Mixed-Bloods and Tribal Dissolution: Charles Curtis and the Quest for Indian Identity.* University Press of Kansas, Lawrence.
Van Zant, Kent L.
    1979   Late Glacial and Postglacial Pollen and Plant Macrofossils from Lake West Okoboji, Northwestern Iowa. *Quaternary Research* 12: 358–380.
Vehik, Rain
    1967   An Archeological Evaluation of South-Central Kansas. Master's thesis, Department of Anthropology, Wichita State University, Wichita.
    1978   An Analysis of Cultural Variability during the Late Woodland Period in the Ozark Highland of Southwest Missouri. Ph.D. diss., Department of Anthropology, University of Missouri, Columbia.
Vehik, Susan C.
    1976   The Great Bend Aspect: A Multivariate Investigation of Its Origin and Southern Plains Relationships. *Plains Anthropologist* 21: 199–205.
    1986   Oñate's Expedition to the Southern Plains: Routes, Destinations, and Implications for Late Prehistoric Cultural Adaptations. *Plains Anthropologist* 31: 13–33.

1990 Late Prehistoric Plains Trade and Economic Specialization. *Plains Anthropologist* 35: 125–145.

1992 Wichita Culture History. *Plains Anthropologist* 37: 311–332.

2002a Conflict, Trade, and Political Development on the Southern Plains. *American Antiquity* 67: 37–64.

2002b Topics, Themes, and Theories in Little River Archaeology: Research after Udden. *Kansas Anthropologist* 23: 35–44.

2002c "The Barbarian Hammer": Bison Hunters and Farmers on the Plains. Manuscript on file, Department of Anthropology, University of Oklahoma, Norman.

Voorhies, Michael R.
1969 Taphonomy and Population Dynamics of an Early Pliocene Vertebrate Fauna, Knox County, Nebraska. *Contributions to Geology Special Paper No. 1.* University of Wyoming, Laramie.

Waite, Herbert A.
1947 *Geology and Ground Water Resources of Scott County, Kansas.* Kansas Geological Survey Bulletin 66. University of Kansas, Lawrence.

Walker, Danny N.
1982 Early Holocene Vertebrate Fauna. In *The Agate Basin Site: A Record of Paleoindian Occupation of the Northwestern High Plains,* edited by George C. Frison and Dennis J. Stanford, pp. 274–308. Academic Press, New York.

Walters, Kenneth L.
1953 *Geology and Ground-Water Resources of Jackson County, Kansas.* Kansas Geological Survey Bulletin 110. University of Kansas, Lawrence.

Wandsnider, LuAnn
1996 Preliminary Observations on Spatial Structure and Land Use Dynamics associated with Late Prehistoric Pit Hearth Features on the High Plains. Paper presented at the 54th Annual Plains Anthropological Conference, Iowa City.

1997 Good Times? Bad Times: Late Holocene Land Use on the High Plains. Paper presented at the 55th Annual Plains Anthropological Conference, Boulder.

Watson, Danial R.
1996 Summary of Faunal Analysis and Artifacts. In *The Tahaksu Site (25MK15), Merrick County, Nebraska,* edited by John K. Peterson and Steven R. Holen, pp. 128–136. Nebraska Archeological Survey Technical Report 96–03, University of Nebraska State Museum, Lincoln.

Watts, William A., and Herbert E. Wright, Jr.
1966 Late-Wisconsin Pollen and Seed Analysis from the Nebraska Sandhills. *Ecology* 47: 202–210.

Watts, William A., and R. C. Bright
1968 Pollen, Seed, and Mollusk Analysis of a Sediment Core from Pickerel Lake, Northeastern South Dakota. *Geological Society of America Bulletin* 79: 855–876.

Weakly, Harry E.
1946 A Preliminary Report on the Ash Hollow Charcoal. *University of Nebraska Studies* 1: 105–110.

Webb, S. David
1969 Extinction-Organization Equilibria in Late Cenozoic Land Mammals of North America. *Evolution* 23: 688–702.

1977 A History of Savanna Vertebrates in the New World. Part I: North America. *Annual Review of Ecology and Systematics* 8: 355–380.

Webb, Thompson, III, and Reid A. Bryson
1972 Late- and Post-Glacial Climatic Changes in the Northern Midwest, U.S.A.: Quantitative

Estimates Derived from Fossil Pollen Spectra by Multi-Variate Analysis. *Quaternary Research* 2: 358–380.

Weddle, Robert S.
1964 *The San Sabá Mission: Spanish Pivot in Texas*. University of Texas Press, Austin.

Wedel, Mildred M.
1973 Claude-Charles Dutisné: A Review of His 1719 Journeys, Part II. *Great Plains Journal* 12: 147–173.
1979 The Ethnohistoric Approach to Plains Caddoan Origins. *Nebraska History* 60 (2): 183–196.
1981 *The Deer Creek Site, Oklahoma: A Wichita Indian Village Sometimes Called Ferdinandina: An Ethnohistorian's View*. Series in Anthropology No. 5. Oklahoma Historical Society, Norman.
1982 The Wichita Indians in the Arkansas River Basin. In *Plains Indian Studies: A Collection of Essays in Honor of John C. Ewers and Waldo R. Wedel*, edited by D. H. Ubelaker and H. J. Viola, pp. 118–134. Contributions to Anthropology No. 30. Smithsonian Institution, Washington, D.C.

Wedel, Waldo R.
1933 Preliminary Notes on the Archaeology of Medicine Valley in Southwestern Nebraska. *Nebraska History Magazine* 14 (3): 144–166.
1934a Contributions to the Archaeology of the Upper Republican Valley, Nebraska. *Nebraska History Magazine* 15 (4): 132–209.
1934b Minneapolis 1, A Prehistoric Village Site in Ottawa County, Kansas. *Nebraska History Magazine* 15 (2): 210–237.
1935a Preliminary Classification for Nebraska and Kansas Cultures. *Nebraska History Magazine* 15 (3): 251–255.
1935b Contributions to the Archaeology of the Upper Republican Valley, Nebraska. *Nebraska History Magazine* 15 (3): 133–209.
1936 An Introduction to Pawnee Archeology. Bureau of American Ethnology Bulletin 112. Smithsonian Institution, Washington, D.C.
1938a *The Direct-Historical Approach in Pawnee Archaeology*. Smithsonian Miscellaneous Collections, vol. 97, no. 7. Washington, D.C.
1938b Inaugurating an Archeological Survey in Kansas. In *Explorations and Field-Work of the Smithsonian Institution in 1937*, pp. 103–106. Smithsonian Institution, Washington, D.C.
1940 Archeological Explorations in Western Kansas. In *Explorations and Field-Work of the Smithsonian Institution in 1939*, pp. 83–86. Publication 3586. Smithsonian Institution, Washington, D.C.
1942 Archeological Remains in Central Kansas and Their Possible Bearing on the Location of Quivira. *Smithsonian Institution Collections* 101 (7). Smithsonian Institution, Washington, D.C.
1943 *Archeological Investigations in Platte and Clay Counties, Missouri*. Bulletin 183. Smithsonian Institution, United States National Museum, Washington, D.C.
1946 The Kansa Indians. *Transactions of the Kansas Academy of Science* 49 (1): 1–35.
1950 Notes on Plains-Southwestern Contacts in the Light of Archaeology. In *For the Dean: Essays in Honor of Byron Cummings on his 89th Birthday, September 20, 1950*. Edited by E. K. Reed and D. S. King, pp. 99–116. Hohokam Museums Association and the Southwestern Monuments Association, Tucson.
1953 Some Aspects of Human Ecology in the Central Plains. *American Anthropologist* 55: 499–514.
1959 *An Introduction to Kansas Archaeology*. Bureau of American Ethnology, Bulletin 174. Smithsonian Institution, Washington, D.C.

1961 *Prehistoric Man on the Great Plains.* University of Oklahoma Press, Norman.
1963 The High Plains and Their Utilization by the Indians. *American Antiquity* 29: 1–16.
1967 The Council Circles of Central Kansas: Were They Solstice Registers? *American Antiquity* 32: 54–63.
1968 Some Thoughts on Central Plains–Southern Plains Archaeological Relationships. *Great Plains Journal* 7 (2): 53–62.
1970a Coronado's Route to Quivira, 1541. *Plains Anthropologist* 15: 161–168.
1970b Antler Tine Scraper Handles in the Central Plains. *Plains Anthropologist* 15: 36–45.
1970c Some Observations on Two House Sites in the Central Plains: An Experiment in Archaeology. *Nebraska History* 51 (2): 1–28.
1970d A Shield and Spear Petroglyph from Central Kansas: Some Possible Implications. *Plains Anthropologist* 14: 125–129.
1975 Chain Mail in Plains Archaeology. *Plains Anthropologist* 20: 187–196.
1978 Notes on the Prairie Turnip *(Psoralea esculenta)* among the Plains Indians. *Nebraska History* 59: 1–25.
1979 House Floors and Native Settlement Populations in the Central Plains. *Plains Anthropologist* 24: 85–98.
1982 Further Notes on Puebloan–Central Plains Contacts in Light of Archaeology. In *Pathways to Plains Prehistory,* edited by Don G. Wyckoff and Jack L. Hofman, pp. 145–152. Cross Timber Press, Duncan, Oklahoma.
1986 *Central Plains Prehistory: Holocene Environments and Culture Change in the Republican River Basin.* University of Nebraska Press, Lincoln.

Weigand, Phil C., Garman Harbottle, and Edward V. Sayre
1977 Turquoise Sources and Source Analysis: Mesoamerica and the Southwestern U.S.A. In *Exchange Systems in Prehistory,* edited by Timothy K. Earle and Jonathon E. Ericson, pp. 15–34. Academic Press, New York.

Weltfish, Gene
1965 *The Lost Universe.* Ballantine Books, New York.

Wendland, Wayne M.
1978 Holocene Man in North America: The Ecological Setting and Climatic Background. *Plains Anthropologist* 23 (82, pt. 1): 273–287.

West, Judge E. P.
1880 A Buried Race in Kansas. *Kansas City Review of Science and Industry* 4 (2): 86–90.

Weston, Timothy, and William B. Lees
1994 History and Status of an Earthwork Known as "Neodesha Fort," Kansas. *Plains Anthropologist* 39: 415–428.

Wetherill, Bert R.
1995 A Comparative Study of Paleoindian Evidence at the Bonner Springs Locality, Lower Kansas River Basin, Kansas. Master's thesis, Department of Anthropology, University of Kansas, Lawrence.

Wheat, Joe Ben
1972 *The Olsen-Chubbuck Site: A Paleo-Indian Bison Kill.* Memoir 26. Society for American Archaeology.

Wheeler, Richard P.
1954 Selected Projectile Point Types of the United States. *Bulletin of the Oklahoma Anthropological Society* 2: 1–6.

Wheeler, Ryan, James J. Miller, Ray M. McGee, Donna Ruhl, Brenda Swan, and Melissa Memory
2003 Archaic Period Canoes from Newnans Lake, Florida. *American Antiquity* 68: 533–551.

White, Theodore E.
1953 Observations on the Butchering Technique of Some Aboriginal Peoples No. 2. *American Antiquity* 18: 160–164.

1954 Observations on the Butchering Technique of Some Aboriginal Peoples Nos. 3, 4, 5, and 6. *American Antiquity* 19: 254–264.

Whiteford, Guy L.
1937 *Prehistoric Indian Excavations in Saline County, Kansas*. Consolidated Printers, Salina, Kansas.

Whitlock, Cathy, Patrick J. Bartlein, Vera Markgraf, and Allan C. Ashworth
2001 The Midlatitudes of North and South America during the Last Glacial Maximum and Early Holocene: Similar Paleoclimatic Sequences Despite Differing Large-Scale Controls. In *Interhemispheric Climate Linkages,* edited by Vera Markgraf, pp. 391–416. Academic Press, New York.

Widga, Chris, and Jack L. Hofman
2003 Early Holocene Subsistence in the Prairie-Plains Border: Perspectives from the Claussen Site. Poster presented at the 61st Annual Plains Anthropological Conference, Fayetteville.

Wilcox, Ken
1981 *A Descriptive Analysis of the Pratt Ceramics*. Kansas Working Papers in Anthropology 6. Department of Anthropology, University of Kansas, Lawrence.

Wilhelm, Paul, Duke of Württemberg
1973 *Travels in North America, 1822–1824*. Translated by Robert Nitske. Edited by Savoie Lottinville. University of Oklahoma Press, Norman.

Wilke, Phillip J., Gayle F. Carlson, and John D. Reynolds
2002 The Late Prehistoric Percussion-Blade Industry of the Central Plains. *Central Plains Archaeology* 9 (1): 1–24.

Wilkens, L. Doug
2001 The Dykema Canyon Burial (41RB106): A Violent Death in the Texas Panhandle, ca. A.D. 660. *Steward* 6: 81–89.

Will, George F., and George E. Hyde
1964 *Corn among the Indians of the Upper Missouri*. University of Nebraska Press, Lincoln.

Willey, Gordon R.
1966 *An Introduction to American Archaeology: North and Middle America,* vol. 1. Prentice Hall, Englewood Cliffs, New Jersey.

Willey, Gordon R., and Philip Phillips
1958 *Method and Theory in American Archaeology*. University of Chicago Press, Chicago.

Williams, A. C.
1877a Report of the Office of the Wichita Agency, Indian Territory. *Annual Report of the Commissioner of Indian Affairs to the Secretary of the Interior,* pp. 112–113. U.S. Government Printing Office, Washington, D.C.
1877b Letter of August 20. *National Archives Microfilm Publications, Microfilm Publication 856, Records of the Central Superintendency of Indian Affairs, 1813–1878*. Roll 84, Letters Received Relating to the Union and Wichita Agencies, 1877, frames 543–550. National Archives, National Archives and Records Service, General Services Administration, Washington, D.C.

Williams, Barry G.
1986 *Early and Middle Ceramic Remains at 14AT2: A Grasshopper Falls Phase House and Pomona Focus Storage Pits in Northeastern Kansas*. Contract Archeology Publication No. 4. Kansas State Historical Society, Topeka.

Williams, Charles C.
1946 *Ground-Water Conditions in Arkansas River Valley in the Vicinity of Hutchinson, Kansas*. Kansas Geological Survey Bulletin 64, pt. 5. University of Kansas, Lawrence.

Williams-Dean, Glenna J.
1978 Ethnobotany and Cultural Ecology of Prehistoric Man in Southwest Texas. Ph.D. diss., Texas A&M University. University Microfilms, Ann Arbor.

Williston, Samuel W.
- 1899 Some Prehistoric Ruins in Scott County, Kansas. *Kansas University Quarterly, Series B: Philology and History* 7 (4): 109–114.
- 1902 An Arrow-Head Found with Bones of *Bison occidentalis lucas,* in Western Kansas. *American Geologist* 30 (5): 313–315.
- 1905 A Fossil Man in Kansas. *Science* 16: 195–196.

Williston, Samuel W., and Handel T. Martin
- 1900 Some Pueblo Ruins in Scott County, Kansas. *Kansas Historical Collections, 1897–1900,* vol. 6: 124–130.

Wilmeth, Roscoe
- 1959 Present Status of the Archeology of the Kansa Indians. *Kansas Anthropological Association Newsletter* 4 (7): 53–56.
- 1960 Kansa Village Locations in the Light of McCoy's 1828 Journal. *Kansas Historical Quarterly* 26 (2): 152–157.
- 1970 *Excavations in the Pomona Reservoir.* Anthropological Series No. 5. Kansas State Historical Society, Topeka.

Wilson, Frank W.
- 1984 Landscapes: A Geologic Diary. In *Kansas Geology,* edited by Rex Buchanan, pp. 9–39. University Press of Kansas, Lawrence.

Wilson, Gilbert L.
- 1924 *The Horse and the Dog in Hidatsa Culture.* Anthropological Papers of the American Museum of Natural History 15 (2), New York.
- 1934 *The Hidatsa Earthlodge.* Anthropological Papers of the American Museum of Natural History, New York, 33 (5): 341–420.

Winfrey, James V.
- 1991 Spatial Distribution of Cultural Material and Post-Depositional Disturbances at the Wallace Site (25GO2): A Plains Woodland Occupation in South Central Nebraska. Master's thesis, Department of Anthropology, University of Nebraska, Lincoln.

Winship, George P.
- 1896 *The Coronado Expedition, 1540–1542.* 14th Annual Report of the Bureau of American Ethnology, pt. 1. Smithsonian Institution, Washington, D.C.
- 1990 [1904] *The Journey of Coronado, 1540–1542.* Reprint. Fulcrum Publishing, Golden, Colorado.

Winterhalder, Bruce, and Eric A. Smith
- 1981 *Hunter-Gatherer Foraging Strategies: Ethnographic and Archeological Analyses.* University of Chicago Press, Chicago.

Witty, Thomas A., Jr.
- 1962 *Archeological Investigations of the Hell Creek Valley in the Wilson Reservoir, Russell and Lincoln Counties, Kansas.* Anthropological Series No. 1. Kansas State Historical Society, Topeka.
- 1963 *The Woods, Avery and Streeter Archeological Sites, Milford Reservoir, Kansas.* Anthropological Series No. 2. Kansas State Historical Society, Topeka.
- 1966 The West Island Site, 14PH10: A Keith Focus Plains Woodland Site in Kirwin Reservoir, Phillips County, Kansas. *Plains Anthropologist* 11: 127–135.
- 1967 The Pomona Focus. *Kansas Anthropological Association Newsletter* 12 (9): 1–5. Topeka.
- 1968a Notes from the Editor. *Kansas Anthropological Association Newsletter* 14 (1): 7–8.
- 1968b The Pawnee Indian Village Museum Project. *Kansas Anthropological Association Newsletter* 13 (5): 1–6.
- 1969a The K.A.A. Fall Dig, 1969. *Kansas Anthropological Association Newsletter* 15 (3): 1–5.
- 1969b The Caldwell Dig. *Kansas Anthropological Association Newsletter* 15 (2): 1–3.

1970 K.A.A. Spring Dig, 1970. *Kansas Anthropological Association Newsletter* 16 (1): 1–2.
1971 Reconstruction of the Scott County Pueblo Ruins. *Kansas Anthropological Association Newsletter* 16 (8): 1–3.
1973 Progress report, 14EK320. Manuscript on file, Kansas State Historical Society, Topeka.
1974 K.A.A. Dig, 1973: The Minneapolis Site, One More Time. *Kansas Anthropological Association Newsletter* 19 (5): 1–5.
1977 The 1977 Kansas Anthropological Association Dig and Kansas Archeology Training Program: The Tobias Dig. *Kansas Anthropological Association Newsletter* 23 (1): 1–7.
1978 Along the Southern Edge: The Central Plains Tradition in Kansas. In *The Central Plains Tradition: Internal Development and External Relationships,* edited by Donald J. Blakeslee, pp. 56–66. Report 11. Office of the State Archaeologist, Iowa City.
1981 The Pomona Focus, Known and Unknown. *Missouri Archaeologist* 42: 77–83.
1982 *The Slough Creek, Two Dog, and William Young Sites, Council Grove Lake, Kansas.* Anthropological Series No. 10. Kansas State Historical Society, Topeka.
1983a *Four Archeological Sites of the Perry Lake, Kansas.* Anthropological Series No. 11. Kansas State Historical Society, Topeka.
1983b An Archaeological Review of the Scott County Pueblo. *Bulletin of the Oklahoma Anthropological Society* 32: 99–106.
1986 1986 Society Dig Held at C. F. Thompson Site in Rice County. *Kansas Preservation* 8 (6): 5–6.
1992 *Archeological Investigations in the Upper Little Arkansas Watershed, Rice and McPherson Counties, Kansas.* Report to the U.S. Army Corps of Engineers, Tulsa District. Copies available from the Kansas State Historic Preservation Office, Topeka.
1999 *Cuesta Phase Sites of the Big Hill Lake Area, Southeast Kansas.* Contract Archeology Publications No. 19. Kansas State Historical Society, Topeka.

Witty, Thomas A., and Wendell P. Frantz
1964 The Historic Uses of Dogs among Plains Indians. *Kansas Anthropological Association Newsletter* 9 (4–5): 1–8.

Wood, John J.
1967 Archeological Investigations in Northeastern Colorado. Ph.D. diss., University of Colorado, Boulder.

Wood, W. Raymond
1967 An Interpretation of Mandan Culture History. River Basin Survey Papers No. 39. *Bureau of American Ethnology Bulletin* 198. Smithsonian Institution, Washington, D.C.
1969 Ethnographic Reconstructions. In *Two House Sites in the Central Plains: An Experiment in Archaeology,* edited by W. Raymond Wood, pp. 102–108. Plains Anthropologist Memoir 6. Vol. 14, No. 44, Pt. 2, pp. 102–108.
1971 Pottery Sites near Limon, Colorado. *Southwestern Lore* 37 (3): 53–85.
1990 A Query on Upper Republican Archaeology in Colorado. *Southwestern Lore* 56 (3): 3–7.
1996 The Missouri River Basin on the 1795 Soulard Map: A Cartographic Landmark. *Great Plains Quarterly* 16 (3): 183–198.

Wood, W. Raymond (editor)
1969 Two House Sites in the Central Plains: An Experiment in Archaeology. Plains Anthropologist Memoir 6. Vol. 14, No. 44, Pt. 2, pp. iv–132.
1983 *An Atlas of Early Maps of the American Midwest.* Illinois State Museum, Springfield.
1998 *Archaeology on the Great Plains.* University Press of Kansas, Lawrence.
2001 *An Atlas of Early Maps of the American Midwest: Part II.* Illinois State Museum, Springfield.

Woods, William I. (editor)
1992 *Late Prehistoric Agriculture: Observations from the Midwest.* Studies in Illinois Archaeology No. 8. Illinois Historic Preservation Agency, Springfield.

Word, James H.
  1994 Coronado's Route in the Texas Panhandle. Paper presented at the 52nd Annual Plains Anthropological Conference, Lubbock.
Wormington, H. Marie, and Richard G. Forbis
  1965 An Introduction to the Archaeology of Alberta, Canada. Proceedings No. 11. Museum of Natural History, Denver.
Wright, Carl M.
  1985 The Complex Aspects of the "Smoky Hill Jasper," Now Known as Niobrarite. *Journal of the Kansas Anthropological Association* 5 (3): 87–90.
Wright, Christopher A.
  1980 Archaeological Investigations in the Proposed Blue Springs Lake Area, Jackson County, Missouri: The Early Woodland Period. Museum of Anthropology, University of Kansas. Submitted to the Kansas City District, U.S. Army Corps of Engineers. Copies available from the Kansas State Historic Preservation Office, Topeka.
Wright, Herbert E., Jr.,
  1968 History of the Prairie Peninsula. In *The Quaternary of Illinois,* edited by R. Bergstrom, pp. 78–88. Special Report No. 14. College of Agriculture, University of Illinois, Champaign-Urbana.
  1970 History of the Prairie Peninsula. In *Pleistocene and Recent Environments of the Central Great Plains,* edited by Wakefield Dort, Jr., and J. Knox Jones, Jr., pp. 78–88. University Press of Kansas, Lawrence.
  1971 Late Quaternary Vegetation History of North America. In *Late Cenozoic Glacial Ages,* edited by Karl K. Turekian, pp. 425–462. Yale University Press, New Haven.
  1976 The Dynamic Nature of Holocene Vegetation: A Problem in Paleoclimatology, Biogeography, and Stratigraphic Nomenclature. *Quaternary Research* 6: 581–596.
Wulfkuhle, Virginia
  1993 KATP Returns to Sharps Creek. *Kansas Preservation* 15 (6): 1–3.
Wyckoff, Don G.
  1993 Gravel Sources of Knappable Alibates Silicified Dolomite. *Geoarchaeology* 8: 35–58.
Wyckoff, Don G., and James Jackman
  1988 Shadid: A New Arrow Point for the Plains. *Bulletin of the Oklahoma Anthropological Society* 37: 111–135.
Yaple, Dennis D.
  1968 Preliminary Research on the Paleo-Indian Occupation of Kansas. *Kansas Anthropological Association Newsletter* 13 (7): 1–9.
Yarnell, Richard A.
  1978 Domestication of Sunflower and Sumpweed in Eastern North America. In *The Nature and Status of Ethnobotany,* edited by Richard I. Ford, pp. 285–299. Anthropological Papers No. 67. University of Michigan, Museum of Anthropology, Ann Arbor.
Yellen, John E.
  1977 *Archaeological Approaches to the Present: Models for Reconstructing the Past.* Academic Press, New York.
Zehnder, Jon P.
  1998 Relationships between Two Little River Focus Sites in McPherson and Rice Counties of Central Kansas Based on Excavated Lithic Debitage. Master's thesis, Department of Anthropology, Wichita State University, Wichita.
Zeller, Doris (editor)
  1968 *The Stratigraphic Succession in Kansas.* Kansas Geological Survey Bulletin 189. University of Kansas, Lawrence.

Zier, Christian J.
  1996   Archaic Stage. In *Colorado Prehistory: A Context for the Arkansas River Basin,* by Christian J. Zier and Stephen M. Kalasz, pp. 100–140. Colorado Council of Professional Archaeologists, Denver.
Zier, Christian J., Robert F. Carrillo, Stephen A. Brown, William R. Arbogast, Kathryn Puseman, and Jan Saysette
  1996   *Excavation of Four Prehistoric Sites and Historic Archaeological Investigations on the Bucci Ranch, Huerfano County, Colorado.* Prepared for Farm Service Agency and National Park Service by Centennial Archaeology, Fort Collins.
Zier, Christian J., Daniel A. Jepson, Michael McFaul, and William Doering
  1993   Archaeology and Geomorphology of the Clovis-Age Klein Site near Kerset, Colorado. *Plains Anthropologist* 38: 203–210.
Zier, Christian J., and Stephen M. Kalasz
  1991   Recon John Shelter and the Archaic-Woodland Transition in Southeastern Colorado. *Plains Anthropologist* 36: 111–138.
  1999   *Colorado Prehistory: A Context for the Arkansas River Basin.* Colorado Council of Professional Archaeologists, Denver.
Zimmerman, Mark
  1918   The Ground-House Indians and Stone-Cist Grave Builders of Kansas and Nebraska. *Collections of the Kansas State Historical Society, 1915–1918,* vol. 14: 471–487.
Zvelebil, Marek
  1986   Mesolithic Prelude and Neolithic Revolution. In *Hunters in Transition: Mesolithic Societies of Temperate Eurasia and Their Transition to Farming,* edited by Marek Zvelebil, pp. 5–15. Cambridge University Press, Cambridge.
  1996   The Agricultural Frontier and the Transition to Farming in the Circum-Baltic Region. In *The Origins and Spread of Agriculture and Pastoralism in Eurasia,* edited by David R. Harris, pp. 323–345. Smithsonian Institution Press, Washington, D.C.
Zvelebil, Marek, and Malcolm Lillie
  2000   Transition to Agriculture in Eastern Europe. In *Europe's First Farmers,* edited by T. Douglas Price, pp. 57–92. Cambridge University Press, Cambridge.

THE CONTRIBUTORS

Mary J. Adair is the interim director of the Museum of Anthropology at the University of Kansas. She has interpreted plant remains from archaeological sites in the Great Plains for over twenty-five years. Although her primary focus has been the recognition of early cultivated and domesticated plants within the prehistoric Central Plains region, her research has included the analysis of early Archaic to Euro-American botanical deposits.

William E. Banks earned his B.A. in anthropology from the University of Wyoming and his M.A. and Ph.D. degrees in anthropology from the University of Kansas. He has worked in the Northwestern High Plains and the Central Plains for over a decade and has also conducted field and lab research on Middle and Upper Paleolithic sites in France. He is a specialist in high-power lithic use-wear methodologies and conducts research on old- and new-world lithic technologies, lithic economies, and hunter-gatherer adaptations. He is currently an archaeologist with the Centre National de la Recherche Scientifique (CNRS) in Talence, France.

C. Tod Bevitt has had an interest in the archaeology of Kansas, his lifelong home, since childhood. He is a member of the Kansas Anthropological Association and in 1987, at the age of fifteen, participated in his first excavation through that organization. Childhood and avocational interests fostered future academic pursuits and a professional career. Majoring in anthropology, he received a B.A. from the University of Kansas (1994) and an M.A. from Wichita State University (1999), where his thesis focused on Plains Village period sites in southern Kansas. His research interests include the study of prehistoric ceramics, lithic caches and caching behavior, trade/exchange, and environmental reconstruction.

Jeannette M. Blackmar served as the collections manager at the University of Kansas Museum of Anthropology and faculty coordinator for the anthropology track of the Museum Studies Program. She received a master's degree in anthropology and a master's degree in Museum Studies from the University of Kansas. Prior to working at the Museum of Anthropology, Jeannette served as curator in anthropology at the Nebraska State Historical Society. Her research interests include Paleoindian archaeology, zooarchaeology, and curation of archaeological collections.

John R. Bozell is a lifelong Nebraska resident and received bachelor's and master's degrees in anthropology from the University of Nebraska–Lincoln. He is an archaeologist and is associate director of the Nebraska State Historical Society where he has been employed for over twenty years. Bozell's professional interests include Native American and early Euro-American culture change, climate change, subsistence, cultural resource management, and public archaeology.

Scott D. Brosowske is currently a research archaeologist for Courson Oil and Gas of Perryton, Texas, and an adjunct curator for the Panhandle-Plains Historical Museum. His research interests include foraging and horticultural societies, subsistence economies, exchange, settlement patterns, and archaeological method and theory. He is currently involved in fieldwork that examines Middle Ceramic period horticultural societies and Historic period buffalo hunters and equestrian nomads of the Southern Plains.

Marlin F. Hawley, a native Kansan, earned his B.A. in anthropology at Kansas State University and his M.A. in anthropology at the University of Kansas; he has worked in both state and private sector cultural resources management. He currently is an assistant curator of archaeology at the Wisconsin Historical Society, Museum Archaeology Program. He has a keen interest in the history of archaeology.

Robert J. Hoard holds degrees in anthropology from the University of Nebraska–Lincoln (1982), the University of Oregon (1985), and the University of Missouri–Columbia (1992). He has worked in Florida, the Southwest, the Great Basin, the Midwest, the Great Plains, and Micronesia. His interests include analysis of the performance characteristics of archaeological tools and the use of trace element analysis to determine the geological sources of archaeological materials. He currently is the Kansas State Archeologist.

Jack L. Hofman has been involved in the archaeology of the Plains region since 1971 and attended the universities of Oklahoma, Wyoming, and Tennessee. After completing his Ph.D. at the University of Tennessee he worked with the Oklahoma Archaeological Survey and the University of Oklahoma for several years. He has taught archaeology at the University of Kansas since 1991. His primary research pertains to Paleoindian archaeology on the Plains.

Alfred E. Johnson earned his B.A. from the University of Kansas and his M.A. and Ph.D. degrees from the University of Arizona. He currently is Professor Emeritus in the Department of Anthropology, University of Kansas, with which he has been affiliated since 1965. He also served as curator, then director, of the Museum of Anthropology at the University of Kansas for over thirty years. He has conducted archaeological fieldwork in Kansas, Arizona, South Dakota, Missouri, Saskatchewan, Yugoslavia, and Sonora, Mexico. His publications include the chapter "Plains Woodland Tradition" in the *Handbook of North American Indians*, volume 13.

Brad Logan received his M.A. in anthropology from the University of Nevada, Reno (1977), and his Ph.D. from the University of Kansas (1985). From 1985 to 2003 he was director of the Office of Archaeological Research at the University of Kansas Museum of Anthropology. From 1998 to 2003 he was senior curator at the museum, and since 1998 he has been research associate professor at Kansas State University. He has more than thirty years of archaeological experience, including fieldwork in the Great Plains and Great Basin, as well as in France and Austria.

Rolfe D. Mandel is executive director of the Odyssey Archaeological Research Program at the Kansas Geological Survey and an associate professor in the Department of Anthropology, University of Kansas. He has spent over twenty-five years working with archaeologists on projects throughout the United States and eastern Mediterranean, but his research has focused on the Great Plains. He is especially interested in the effects of geologic processes on the archaeological record and has published work in a number of books and professional journals.

James O. Marshall received a B.A. degree (1960) from St. Lawrence University, Canton, New York, and an M.A. degree (1967) from the University of Nebraska–Lincoln. Archaeology of the Central Plains has been a primary field of research for him at the Kansas State Historical Society, the Nebraska State Historical Society, and the University of Nebraska. Most of the research has been funded by archaeological salvage projects such as the Missouri River Basin Archaeological and Paleontological Salvage Program. Other professional experience has been with the Museum of New Mexico, Santa Fe, as an archaeologist on the Navajo reservoir project. His first experience in archaeology was his participation in the excavations at the baronial home of Sir William Johnson at Johnstown, New York.

Lauren W. Ritterbush is associate professor of anthropology/archaeology at Kansas State University and has a long-standing interest in the archaeology and ethnohistory of the Great Plains, topics with which she has worked for the past twenty-seven years. She was introduced to Kansas archaeology during her graduate education at the University of Kansas, from which she earned her master's degree (1984) and Ph.D. (1990) in anthropology. Prior to accepting her present position at Kansas State University, she served as research assistant professor with the University of Kansas Museum of Anthropology.

Donna C. Roper received her Ph.D. in anthropology in 1975 from the University of Missouri–Columbia. She is a research associate professor at Kansas State University and an independent researcher and consultant. Much of her current work is concerned with the Central Plains tradition in central and western Kansas and southwestern Nebraska. Recently, she has been the editor of *Medicine Creek: Seventy Years* of *Archaeological Investigations* and co-editor of *Plains Earthlodges: Ethnographic and Archaeological Perspectives*.

Laura L. Scheiber is an assistant professor in the Anthropology Department at Indiana University. In her research she addresses long-term social dynamics on the Plains by considering culture contact studies, household production, and micro-scale daily activities. She recently has been studying the intersection between food processing and cultural identity during the Late Prehistoric and Protohistoric, trying to unravel relationships among High Plains hunter-gatherers and Central Plains villagers. With the help of many students, she is analyzing faunal material from several sites, including the Donovan site in northeastern Colorado and the Albert Bell site in western Kansas.

C. Martin Stein has been an archaeologist at the Kansas State Historical Society for over twenty years. One of his long-term research goals has been to discover and describe lithic resource sites in Kansas and to place them in the context of the cultural/historical units defined for the state. To this end he has directed surveys, during selected Kansas Archeology Training Program events, to locate quarries and workshops, and he has also conducted excavations to gather information about the content and research potential of a selected number of sites.

Susan C. Vehik is an associate professor of anthropology at the University of Oklahoma where she has taught since 1977. She received her B.A. (1969) from Wichita State University and her M.A. (1972) and Ph.D. (1975) degrees from the University of Missouri–Columbia. Her major research interest is the political, economic, and ritual lifeways of people who lived on the Great Plains during the Late Prehistoric period.

INDEX

Accelerator mass spectrometry (AMS), 3, 250
Adams Ranch alluvial fan, 30 (fig.), 32
Afton site, 52 (fig.)
Agate Basin complex, 49, 52, 53, 55 (fig.), 71
Agriculture
    Archaic, 252–54
    Central Plains tradition and, 121, 122, 126–27, 128–29, 257–59
    development of, in Plains, 249–50
    Great Bend aspect, 173, 259, 263
    Protohistoric, 259–61
    Village period, 257–59, 263
    Woodland, 256–57, 262–63
    See also Horticulture
Ahouaho, 210, 215, 216, 216 (fig.)
Aijaos, 210, 212, 213, 214
Aker, R. B., ix
Aker site, xi
Alberta complex, 49
Albert Bell site, 114 (fig.), 118, 120, 122, 129
Alibates agatized dolomite, 116, 131, 147, 153, 161, 169, 174, 180, 188, 189–90, 194, 198, 202, 281, 282
Alibates Quarry, 144 (fig.)
Allen site, 50 (fig.), 52 (fig.)
Allen-Frederick complex, 4 (fig.), 48, 49, 52, 55 (fig.), 56, 60, 63, 65, 68, 70 (fig.)
Alluvium
    Holocene, 29, 35–36, 38, 39
    Pleistocene-Holocene transition, 29, 31, 32, 33 (fig.), 34
Altithermal interval, 37, 43, 44, 57, 254
American Chief village, 225, 226, 227
Anahouo, 216, 216 (fig.)
Anderson site, 86
Andrews, 251 (fig.), 255, 257
Animals. *See* Fauna
Antelope Creek phase, 180, 181, 181 (fig.), 189, 201, 202, 207 (fig.)
Anthony site, 196
Apaches, 4 (fig.), 144, 148, 221
Arapahoe, 4 (fig.)
Archaeological dating, 2–5

Archaeology in Kansas (O'Brien), ix
Archaic period, 43, 47, 273
    ceramics, 252, 262
    distribution of sites in, 51–53, 56 (fig.), 57 (fig.)
    flora, 251–56, 262
    geologic processes during, 24, 28, 43
    Late, 8 (fig.)
    See also Paleoarchaic period
Architecture
    Central Plains tradition, 111, 118–20, 134
    Dismal River complex, 143, 144–45
    Great Bend aspect, 168, 171–73
    High Plains Upper Republican complex, 134
    Kansa, 223, 224, 228, 229, 232
    Middle Ceramic (Plains Border region), 181, 184–86, 192, 193 (fig.), 196, 199 (fig.)
    Middle Woodland, 82
    Oneota, 156–57, 158, 159
    Paleoarchaic, 69–71
    Pawnee, 243, 244 (fig.)
    Plains Woodland, 95–96
    Pomona, 125, 126
Arikara, 131, 233, 246
Arkansas City sites, 166, 170
Arkansas phase, 94, 96
Arkansas River Lowlands, 4 (fig.), 14
Armstrong site, 196
Arnold Research cave, 58
Arrowpoints. *See* Projectile points
Art, 168–69, 170 (fig.)
Artifacts, definition of, 5. *See also* Ceramic artifacts and technology; Chipped-stone artifacts; Groundstone artifacts; *individual cultures*
Ash Hollow Cave site, 110, 134 (fig.), 136, 144 (fig.)
Ash Hollow Cord-Roughened ware, 98
Ashland site, 151, 151 (fig.), 158, 163
Aspect, definition of, 6, 105
Atkinson, Henry, 238
Atlatl, 58, 62
Aucanis, 210, 215, 216 (fig.)

405

Augusta site (14BU306), 30 (fig.)
Augusta sites (Great Bend aspect), 166, 167
Avoca site, 86, 87 (fig.), 251 (fig.), 255, 257

Baca, Alonzo, 212
Bahntge Ranch alluvial fan, 30 (fig.), 33
Base, definition of, 7
Beads, 100 (fig.), 118
Beaver Creek site, 251 (fig.), 255, 258
Bell site, 199, 199 (fig.)
Bemis Creek phase, 84
Big Eddy site, 52 (fig.)
Biggs site, 134 (fig.)
Big John's village, 229
Bignell loess, 34
Bison, 67–69, 96, 98, 122, 137–38, 161–62, 187, 192, 197, 207–8, 209, 245
Blackman, E. E., 243
Black Sand cultures, 78, 91
Black Vermillion phase, 48, 49
Blackwater Draw site, 52 (fig.)
Blaine, Effie, 239
Blue Earth village, 222, 223, 225, 230, 231
Blue Springs site, 241 (fig.), 242–43
Blue Stone site, 151 (fig.), 159, 161
Bluff Creek complex (phase), 4 (fig.), 126, 179, 180, 193 (fig.), 195–201, 202, 203, 207 (fig.), 259
Boatstones, 58, 62
Bogan site, 240, 241 (fig.), 242
Bone artifacts and technology, 58, 100, 117 (fig.), 118, 154, 178, 179 (fig.), 193, 200 (fig.), 243–44
Bonner Springs locality, 53, 56
Booth site, 199
Bourgmont, Etienne de Véniard, 221–22, 230
Bow and arrow technology (Woodland), 85, 99
Bowlin phase, 78
Bowman, Peter, 136
Brady soil, 34
Brown, Lionel, 105
Bryson-Paddock site, 218
Buckner Creek site, 30 (fig.)
Bureau of American Ethnology (Smithsonian Institution), 142
Buresh site, 195
Burial mounds, 80–81, 83 (fig.), 87, 108
Burials. *See* Mortuary practices
Buried City complex, 181, 181 (fig.), 183, 184, 186, 207 (fig.), 208–9

Burntwood Creek site, 60, 67, 68
Busse Cache site, 60
Busse site, 52 (fig.), 53
Butler phase, 84, 87

Calovich Mound, 108
Caracterish, 237
Catlinite, 281
Cattle Guard site, 52 (fig.)
Cavagnolle, Fort, 230
Caves, 58
Central Lowland, 11
Central Plains tradition
  agriculture, 121, 122, 126–27, 128–29
  architecture, 111, 118–20
  ceramics, 111–14
  chipped-stone artifacts, 114–16
  chronology, 110–11
  groundstone artifacts, 116–18
  High Plains cultures and, 135
  mortuary practices, 111, 122–24
  and Oneota tradition, 130, 131, 156–58, 163–64
  Plains Border region and, 202
  settlement patterns, 118–21, 129–30
  sites, 106–10
  subsistence, 121–22, 129–30
  taxonomy of, 105–6, 130–31
Ceramic artifacts and technology
  Archaic, 252, 262
  Central Plains tradition, 111–14
  Dismal River complex, 142, 143 (fig.), 145
  High Plains Upper Republican complex, 136–37
  Kansas City Hopewell, 79 (fig.), 80, 81, 84
  Middle Ceramic (Plains Border region), 187 (fig.), 188–89, 194–95, 198, 200 (fig.), 202
  Oneota, 154–55, 157, 160–61, 162
  Pawnee, 243
  Plains Woodland, 98, 99 (fig.), 103, 277
  Pomona, 124
  Woodland, 77, 79 (fig.), 80, 81, 82, 84, 84 (fig.), 85, 85 (fig.), 87, 88–91, 262
Ceramic period
  Early, 4 (fig.), 7, 8, 8 (fig.), 273
  Late, 4 (fig.), 7, 8 (fig.), 133, 141
  Middle, 4 (fig.), 7, 8, 105, 133, 180–205
Champe, John, 7, 8, 110, 142
Chautauqua Hills, 13, 21

Chawi (Grand) band, 233, 236, 237, 239
Chelsea complex (phase), 4 (fig.), 48, 49, 60
Cherokee, 4 (fig.)
Cherokee Lowlands, 13
Chert, 264, 279–80
    definition of, 266–67
    Edwards, 281
    Flint Hills, 14, 116, 131, 161, 193, 202, 270, 271–72, 282
    Hartville, 134 (fig.), 144 (fig.), 147–48, 281
    Mississippian-age, 267
    Pennsylvanian-age, 153, 268–70
    Permian-age, 116, 153, 270, 271–72
Cheyenne, 4 (fig.), 220, 229
Cheyenne Bottoms, 15, 22, 24, 25
Chipped-stone artifacts, 279
    Central-Plains tradition, 114–16
    Dismal River complex, 142 (fig.)
    Great Bend aspect, 174, 177 (fig.)
    Middle Ceramic (Plains Border region), 189–90, 193, 194 (fig.), 197 (fig.), 200 (fig.)
    Oneota, 153
    Paleoarchaic, 47, 50 (fig.), 59, 60–61, 62, 64
    Pawnee, 243
    Plains Woodland, 99–100
    Pomona, 124, 126
Chippewa, 4 (fig.)
Chiwere Souian group, xi
Chouteau, Frederick, 225, 226, 227
Cimarron Bend, 34, 37, 38, 42
Clamorgan, Jacques, 237, 239
Clary Ranch site, 52 (fig.)
Classic Horizon, 155, 158
Classification systems, 6–9
Claussen site, 30 (fig.), 31, 37, 43, 48, 65, 66
Claypool site, 52 (fig.)
Clements Section, 30 (fig.), 36
Climate
    Holocene, 22, 23, 24, 25, 26, 30, 35, 37, 40, 57, 254
    modern Kansas, 18–20
    Pleistocene-Holocene transition, 22, 30
    Protohistoric, 259
    Woodland tradition, 93–94
Clovis complex, 48, 49, 50 (fig.), 51–52, 53 (fig.), 55 (fig.), 56, 60, 64, 68
Coal-Oil Canyon site, 93, 134 (fig.), 136, 137, 245
Cody complex, 4 (fig.), 48, 49, 50 (fig.), 52, 53, 55 (fig.), 56, 60, 65, 68

Coffey site, 48, 52 (fig.), 58, 59, 60, 63, 64, 65, 66, 67, 68, 70, 251 (fig.), 252, 254, 256
Collecting station sites, 266, 272, 274, 282
Colvin phase, 49
Comanche, 4 (fig.)
Component, definition of, 6
Cooper, Paul, 159
Cooper site, 52 (fig.)
Cooper variant, 79, 82
Copan Paleosol, 40, 41
Coronado, 166, 211, 246
Cow Killer site, 48, 52 (fig.), 60, 63, 64, 65, 67, 68, 70 (fig.), 89, 252
Crabtree site, 251 (fig.), 258
Cretaceous system, 16, 17, 265 (fig.), 275–77
Cuartelejo Apache, 4 (fig.), 144, 148
Cuesta phase, 4 (fig.), 79, 82
Curry site, 87
Custer/Turkey Creek complex, 201, 207 (fig.)

Dakota Formation, 16, 116, 117, 175, 276
Dalton complex, 4 (fig.), 47, 48, 49, 50 (fig.), 52, 53, 55 (fig.), 60, 68
DB site, 59, 67, 108, 251 (fig.), 252, 254
Deer Creek phase, 84, 86
Deer Creek site, 218
Delaney site, 30 (fig.), 36, 37
Delaware, 4 (fig.)
Dent site, 52 (fig.)
Developmental Horizon, 155, 158
Dhegiha Siouan group, xi, 219
Diamond Creek site, 30 (fig.), 36
Dipper Gap site, 52 (fig.)
Direct Historical Approach, x
Diskau site, 52 (fig.), 53, 60, 64
Dismal River complex, xi, 4 (fig.), 133, 141–48, 259, 260
Dissected Till Plains, 4 (fig.), 55, 110, 124, 128, 265
Domebo site, 52 (fig.)
Doniphan site, 221, 222, 230, 231
Donovan site, 134 (fig.), 136, 137, 139, 140
Dooley site, 107
Dorsey, James Owen, 219, 225, 226
Doyle site, 96 (fig.)
Droughts, 20
Dry Creek rockshelter, 57
Dunbar, John B., 239
Durbin site, 70 (fig.)
Dustiné, Claude-Charles, 215, 216

Eagle's Roost site, 30 (fig.), 38
Early Archaic sites, 24, 43
Early Ceramic period, 4 (fig.), 7, 8, 8 (fig.), 273
Early Holocene, 23–24, 35–37, 43–44, 47, 54, 56, 69
Early Woodland tradition, 8, 8 (fig.), 77–78, 256, 262
Eastern Woodland tradition, 76
Eckles site, 48, 52 (fig.), 53, 59, 60, 70
Edwards chert, 281
Edwardsville phase, 80
El Cuartelejo (Scott County Pueblo), 142, 142 (fig.), 144–45, 146, 147, 251 (fig.), 255, 260
El Dorado complex, 4 (fig.), 48, 49, 60, 63, 65, 68, 70 (fig.), 73
Ellsworth, Henry L., 238
Ellsworth treaty, 238, 239, 247
Equus beds, 16
Ernie's rockshelter, 57
Escanjaque, 210, 211 (fig.), 212, 213
Escatapé, 234, 237
Etzanoa, 210, 211, 211 (fig.)
Eureka site, 65, 66
European/Euro-American contacts
    American expeditions, 222–23, 236, 237, 238, 239, 240, 242, 243
    French, 214, 215–16, 220, 221–22, 224
    Kansa and, 222–24, 228, 230
    Lewis and Clark expedition, 222–23, 236, 239, 242
    Pawnee and, 234–38
    Pike expedition, 237, 240, 242, 243
    Spanish, 166, 178, 209, 212–13, 214, 220, 234–36, 237
    Wichita and, 209, 212–13, 214, 215–16
Extended Coalescent variant, 131

Fanning site, 230–31, 232
Farnham, Thomas Jefferson, 228
Faulconer site, 60, 65, 66, 70 (fig.), 254
Fauna
    Central Plains tradition and, 122
    Great Bend aspect, 173–74, 207–8, 209
    Late Prehistoric, 137, 138, 161–62
    Middle Ceramic, 186–87, 192–93, 197
    Paleoarchaic, 64–69
    Plains Woodland, 94, 96, 98
    Pleistocene, 23
    Pomona, 125
Feature, definition of, 5
Flattop Butte, 134 (fig.), 144 (fig.)

Flattop chalcedony, 116, 281
Flint Hills, 4 (fig.)
    Central Plains culture in, 116
    chert, 14, 116, 131, 161, 193, 202, 270, 271–72, 282
    environment, 13–14, 20, 34, 55
    Paleoarchaic complexes in, 49
    Woodland culture in, 77, 87
Flint Hills Conference, ix
Flora
    Central Plains tradition, 121–22, 126–27
    Dismal River complex, 259–60
    Great Bend aspect, 173, 259–60, 263
    Great Plains, 20–22
    Middle Ceramic (Odessa phase), 186
    Paleoarchaic, 62, 65, 67, 250–56, 262
    Pomona, 125, 126
    Village period, 257–59
    Woodland tradition, 256–57, 262, 263
    See also Vegetation
Flotation technique, 248
Focus, definition of, 6
Folsom complex, 49, 50 (fig.), 51–52, 53, 55 (fig.), 56, 60, 68
Folsom site, 65, 66
Food
    Central Plains tradition, 121–22, 126–27, 129
    Dismal River complex, 145, 146–47, 260
    Great Bend aspect, 173, 260, 263
    Paleoarchaic, 62, 64–67, 70, 250, 251–54
    Upper Republican complex, 138, 259
    Village period, 257–59, 260
    Woodland tradition, 98, 256–57
    See also Agriculture; Horticulture; Maize
Fool Chief village, 225, 227, 229
Forest communities in Kansas, 21–22. *See also* Prairie-forest region
Frederick complex, 4 (fig.), 53
Fred Loomis site, 199
French contacts, 214, 215–16, 220, 221–22, 224
Ft. Dodge alluvial fan, 30 (fig.), 36
Ft. Riley alluvial fans, 30 (fig.)

Gakushuin laboratory, 4
Gardiner site, 67, 68
Garza complex, 208, 208 (fig.), 210, 211
Geology
    archaeology research and, 28–29, 265–67, 278–82
    Kansas, 10–18, 264–65, 267–68

rock classifications in, 265 (fig.), 267
    See also Lithic resources
Gilder, Robert F., 105
Glaciated Region, 11–12, 265, 278
Glen Elder site, 151 (fig.), 159, 161
Glenwood locality, 110, 113, 127, 163
Gooseberry shelter, 252
Graham Research cave, 58
Grand (Chawi) band, 233, 236, 237, 239
Grand Osage, 216
Grasshopper Falls phase, 4 (fig.), 84, 85 (fig.), 86, 87, 87 (fig.), 90, 90 (figs.)
Gray-Wolfe site, 247
Great Bend aspect, viii, 4 (fig.), 211, 281
    architecture, 168, 171–73
    ceramics, 130–31, 175–76
    chronology of, 130–31, 166–67
    economy, 173–75, 245, 259, 260, 263
    flora and, 173, 259–60, 263
    hunting camps, 165 (fig.), 167–68, 172 (fig.), 209
    mortuary practices, 170–71
    settlement pattern, 167–71, 208 (fig.)
    sites, 165, 167–71, 246, 251 (fig.)
    stone sources, 174, 280, 281, 282
    tools, 176–78, 179 (fig.)
    Wichita and, xi, 132, 165, 167, 171, 214, 233
Great Bend Sand Prairie, 34, 37, 38, 41–42
Great Oasis population, 102
Great Plains
    climate of, 18–20
    physiographic provinces of, 11
    vegetation of, 20–22
Great Plains Archaeological Field School, 81
Greenhorn Formation, 16
Green Plum site, 151 (fig.), 159, 161
Greenwood phase, 4 (fig.), 84, 84 (fig.), 87, 88, 89
Greenwood pottery, 84 (fig.), 88, 89
Griffing site, 107
Groundstone artifacts
    Central Plains tradition, 116–18
    Great Bend aspect, 175, 177, 178, 178 (fig.)
    Paleoarchaic, 62, 63
    Pawnee, 243
    Pomona, 125
Guide Rock site, 241 (fig.), 245
Gunnerson, James, 142, 145
Gurney Peak sites, 134 (fig.), 136, 139

Hallman site, 196
Harahey, 246, 247

Hard Chief village, 225, 226, 227, 229, 231
Harlan Cord-Roughened ware, 88, 98
Hart site, 125
Hartville Uplift, 134 (fig.), 144 (fig.)
Havana Hopewell, 79, 81, 91
Hays site, 170
Hearths
    Great Bend aspect, 172–73
    Paleoarchaic, 69–70
Hedding site, 199, 199 (fig.)
Hell Gap complex, 49, 52, 53, 55 (fig.), 56, 60, 71, 276
Herl site, 73
Hertha phase, 84
High Plains
    cultures in, 4 (fig.)
    environment, 17–18, 20, 32, 40, 42, 54, 57, 265
    Late prehistoric complexes in, 133–150
    Middle Ceramic period in, 180–205
    Southern Plains complexes in, 207 (fig.), 208 (fig.)
    See also Plains Woodland tradition
High Plains Upper Republican complex, 133–41, 259, 276, 280
Hill, A. T., 240, 243
Hill site, 240, 241 (fig.), 242, 243, 244
Historic period, 4 (fig.), 8 (fig.)
Holocene
    bison in, 69
    environment, 22–27, 55–57, 254, 278
    Paleoarchaic sites from, 52–57, 251
    See also Early Holocene; Late Holocene environment; Middle Holocene; Pleistocene-Holocene transition
Hopewellian cultures, 76, 79, 81. *See also* Kansas City Hopewell culture
Horizon, definition of, 7
Horticulture
    Archaic, 251–56
    Dismal River complex, 147, 260
    Kansa, 223, 224, 228
    Middle Ceramic (Plains Border region), 183, 186, 193, 196–97, 203, 259
    Plains Village tradition, 206–7, 257–59
    Upper Republican complex, 138
    See also Agriculture
Hudson-Meng site, 52 (fig.)
Hulme site, 134 (fig.), 140
Humphreys/Matthews site, 144 (fig.)
Hunter-gatherer technology, 58–64

Individual Frontier Mobility, 128
Infinity site, 281
Initial Coalescent variant, 105, 130, 131, 132, 163
Intermill site, 151 (fig.), 159
Introduction to Kansas Archaeology (Wedel), vii
Iowa, 4 (fig.)
Irving, John Treat, 238
Iscani, 206, 208, 210, 211, 212, 215
Iskatappe, 237
Itskari phase, 105, 257, 258

Jake's Bluff site, 52 (fig.)
James site, 241 (fig.), 243
Johnson, Elizabeth, 240
Jones Miller site, 52 (fig.)
Jumano, 210, 212, 213, 214, 218
Jurassic system, 265 (fig.), 275
Jurgens site, 52 (fig.)

Kamschroeder site, 86
Kanorado locality sites, 30 (fig.), 32, 48, 52 (fig.), 60, 64, 72
Kansa, 4 (fig.)
 architecture, 223, 224, 228, 229, 232
 clothing, 224–25
 description of villages, 223, 224
 Doniphan village, 221, 222, 230, 231
 horticulture, 223, 224, 228
 hunting, 228
 modern-day, 229–30
 movement of, 219–23, 225
 Neosho River villages, 229
 origins of, 220–21, 230–31
 Pawnee and, 235, 236, 237, 238
 reservation life, 228–29
 settlements, xi, 221, 223–27
 trade, 224, 231
Kansas Anthropological Association (KAA), viii, xiii, 107, 136, 231, 266
Kansas Archaeological Preservation Plan (1987), 51
Kansas Archeology Training Program (KATP), 107, 166, 196, 266, 274–75
Kansas City Group cherts, 269
Kansas City Hopewell culture, 4 (fig.)
 burials, 80–81
 ceramics, 79 (fig.), 80, 81, 82, 84
 establishment of, 76–77, 78, 79–81, 83
 flora and, 256, 263
 projectile points from, 80, 82
 settlement pattern, xi, 80, 88
 similarities to other Woodland cultures, 79, 81–83, 93, 102
Kansas City phase, 80
Kansas Monument site, 240, 241–42, 241 (fig.), 244, 251 (fig.), 260
Kansas State Historical Society, vii, viii–ix, 145, 166, 192, 196, 219, 240, 280
Kansas State University, vii, 280
Kansas Unmarked Burial Sites Preservation Act, viii, 123
Kaskaskia, 4 (fig.)
Katz site, 251 (fig.), 258
Kawarahki, 132, 246, 247
Keen site, 90
Keith phase (variant/focus), 4 (fig.), 87, 88, 94, 95, 97, 98, 99 (figs.), 100 (fig.), 101 (fig.), 102, 103, 277
Kickapoo, 4 (fig.)
Kiowa, 4 (fig.)
Kiowa-Apache, 4 (fig.)
Kitkahahki (Republican) band, 233, 234–38, 240, 241, 242
Kitsai, 233
Knife River flint, 281, 282
Knives, 61 (fig.), 99 (fig.), 115, 117 (fig.), 124, 142 (fig.), 176–77
Knudsen playa, 34
Kohr House site, 112 (fig.), 114 (fig.)
Kulbom sites, 163

La Harpe, Jean Baptiste Bénard de, 215, 216
Laird site, 48, 52 (fig.), 60, 67, 68
Lake Theo site, 52 (fig.)
Lamb, George, 159
Lamb Spring site, 52 (fig.)
Lansing Man, 73
Late Archaic period, 8 (fig.)
Late Ceramic period, 4 (fig.), 7, 8 (fig.), 133, 141
Late (Classic) Horizon I, 155
Late Holocene environment 24–27, 39–42, 44, 55, 62
Late Prehistoric period, High Plains, 133
Late Quaternary environments, 10, 22–27, 28–45
Late Woodland tradition, 8 (fig.)
 ceramics, 77, 84, 85, 87, 88–91
 flora, 257, 258, 262
 mortuary practices, 85, 86, 87

phases, 84
population changes, 88, 91
projectile points, 85, 86, 87 (fig.)
See also Plains Woodland tradition
Leary site, 151, 151 (fig.), 152–58, 163
Lehmer, Donald J., 7, 105
Lemon Ranch site, 192
Lewis and Clark expedition, 222–23, 236, 238, 239, 242
Lewis site, 131, 168, 191, 192, 193, 194
Libby, Willard F., 3
Lime Creek site, 52 (fig.)
Lindenmeier site, 52 (fig.)
Lipscomb site, 52 (fig.)
Lithic resources
 exotic, 281–82
 identification methods, 279–81
 outcropping rock units in Kansas, 264, 265 (fig.), 267–78
 quarries, collecting station, and workshops, 266, 269, 269 (fig.), 272–74, 276–77, 279 (fig.), 282
 stone-working techniques, 282
 See also Alibates agatized dolomite; Chert; Chipped-stone artifacts; Dakota Formation; Edwards chert; Flattop chalcedony; Groundstone artifacts; Hartville chert; Obsidian; Quartzite; Smoky Hill jasper
Little River focus, 130, 165, 166, 167, 168, 172 (fig.), 174, 176, 176 (fig.), 184, 203, 204, 208, 208 (fig.), 209, 210, 211, 212, 213, 215, 216, 251 (fig.), 282
LoDaisKa site, 252
Loess, 34
Logan Creek complex (phase), 4 (fig.), 48, 49, 50 (fig.)
Logan Creek site, 52 (fig.)
Long expedition, 238
Lonker site, 182, 186
Lost Creek site, 107
Loup (Skiri) band, 131, 233, 239, 245, 246
Lovitt site, 142, 144 (fig.)
Lower Mill Creek site, 30 (fig.)
Lower Walnut focus, 165, 166, 167, 169, 172 (fig.), 174, 176, 176 (fig.), 208, 208 (fig.), 210, 211, 214
Lower Walnut Great Bend sites, 251 (fig.)
Lubbock Lake site, 52 (fig.)
Lundeen site, 182, 186, 251 (fig.), 259

Macy site, 84
Maize (corn), 203, 249, 252–53, 254, 256, 258, 259–61, 262–63
 Central Plains tradition and, 121, 126, 127
Maple City quarry, 174
Marion Great Bend aspect sites, 165, 166, 167, 172 (fig.), 176, 176 (fig.), 208, 208 (fig.), 210, 212, 214
Markley site, 130
Martin, Handel T., 145
Matter Mound site, 73
Mattox Draw, 32 (fig.), 33
McCoy, Isaac, 231
McKean complex, 4 (fig.), 48
McKern, W. C., 6–7
Medicine Creek localities, 112, 122, 123, 129, 134 (fig.), 139, 140, 259
Medina Rockshelter, 252
Meek site, 151 (fig.), 159
Melgares, Facundo, 237
Mento, 215, 217
Meserve complex, 52, 52 (fig.), 53, 55 (fig.)
Method and Theory in American Archaeology (Willey and Phillips), 7
Miami, 4 (fig.)
Miami site, 52 (fig.)
Middle Archaic sites, 24, 43
Middle Ceramic period, 4 (fig.), 7, 8, 105, 133, 180. *See also* Plains Border region
Middle Holocene
 ceramics, 64
 environment, 23–24, 37–39, 44, 57, 254
 flora in, 253–54
Middle (Developmental) Horizon I, 155
Middle Missouri tradition, 102, 105, 131
Middle-range theory, 5
Middle Woodland tradition, 8 (fig.)
 ceramics, 77, 79 (fig.), 80, 81, 82, 84, 88
 flora in, 256, 263
 Plains Woodland tradition and, 95
 sites, 76, 79–84
Midwestern Taxonomic Method (MTM), 6–7, 105
Miguel, 211, 212
Milbourn site, 56 (fig.), 60, 63, 65, 67, 68, 70
Mile Creek site, 52 (fig.)
Miller site, 182, 186
Milnesand complex, 53
Minneapolis site, 112 (figs.), 114 (fig.)
Mississippian period, 8, 8 (fig.), 127

Mississippian system, 265 (fig.), 267–68
Mixed-grass prairies, 20, 25
    Paleoarchaic sites and, 51 (fig.), 53, 54 (fig.), 55, 55 (fig.), 56 (fig.), 57 (fig.)
Mortality rates, Plains Woodland, 97
Mortuary practices
    Central Plains tradition, 111, 122–24
    Great Bend aspect, 170–71
    Hopewellian mounds for, 80–81, 83 (figs.), 87
    Late Woodland, 85, 86, 87
    Middle Ceramic (Plains Border region), 190–91, 195, 198
    Oneota, 153
    Paleoarchaic, 71–72, 73 (fig.)
    Pawnee, 244
    Plains Woodland, 101–2
    Pomona, 125–26
    Wichita, 171
Mounds
    Calovich, 108
    Great Bend aspect, 167, 168
    Hopewellian burial, 80–81, 83 (figs.), 87
    Taylor, 81
    Younkin, 83 (figs.)
Mowry Bluff site, 134 (fig.), 140
Muddy Creek site, 96
Munkers Creek complex (phase), 4 (fig.), 48, 49, 50 (fig.), 60, 63, 65, 68, 70 (fig.), 252, 273
Muscotah Marsh, 22, 24, 25

Nall site, 52 (fig.)
National Historic Preservation Act, 1
Native American Graves Protection and Repatriation Act, 123
Nebo Hill complex (phase), 4 (fig.), 49, 50 (fig.), 52 (fig.), 74, 78, 251 (fig.), 252, 254, 255, 256, 262
Nebraska aspect (phase/variant), 4 (fig.), 105, 106, 108, 110, 112, 113, 114, 115, 116, 120, 121, 122–23, 139, 257–58
Nebraska Sand Hills, 25
Nebraska State Historical Society, 142, 152, 153, 156, 159, 166, 243
Nelson site, 199
Neosho focus, 4 (fig.)
Neosho River Group of Wichita, 217
Neosho River villages, 228
Niastor, 217

Nichols Ranch site, 199
Nichols site, 144 (fig.), 260
Niobrara Formation, 17, 276 (fig.)
Nolan site, 52 (fig.)
Northern Caddoan, 132, 233, 246
Northern Rio Grande Pueblos site, 134 (fig.), 144 (fig.)
Norton site, 48, 52 (fig.), 60, 65, 67, 68
Nulik site, 195
Nuzum site, 108

O'Brien, Patricia J., ix, 7, 81
O'Fallon, Benjamin, 238
Obsidian, 116, 142 (fig.), 148, 161, 281
Odessa phase, 4 (fig.), 181–91, 202, 203, 207 (fig.)
Odessa Yates site, 182, 184, 186, 259
Ogallala Formation, 17, 117, 265, 278
Olsen-Chubbuck site, 52 (fig.)
Omaha, 219, 220, 221, 232
Oñate, Juan de, 211
Oneota tradition, xi, 4 (fig.), 219
    architecture, 156–57, 158, 159
    artifacts, 153–55, 157, 161, 231, 281
    Ashland site, 151, 158, 163
    burials, 153
    Central Plains tradition and, 130, 131, 156–58, 163–64
    ceramics, 154–55, 157, 160–61, 162
    Leary site, 151, 152–58, 163
    site distribution, 151 (fig. 1)
    subsistence, 161–62, 163
    westward movement of, 163
    White Rock phase, 4 (fig.), 130, 131, 151, 151 (fig.), 154, 159–62, 163, 259
Osage, 4 (fig.), 168, 216, 219, 220, 221, 232
Osage Cuestas, 4 (fig.), 12–13, 49, 87, 124
Otoes, 222, 232
Ottawa, 4 (fig.)
Ouitsitas, 210, 215, 216 (fig.)
Ozark Plateau, 11, 21

Packard site, 52 (fig.)
Padouca, 221, 222
Paint Creek site, 166, 176
Paleoarchaic period, 4 (fig.)
    architecture, 69–71
    artifacts, 47, 50 (fig.), 58, 59, 60–61, 62, 63, 64, 73
    burials, 71–72, 73 (fig.)

chipped-stone technology, 47, 50 (fig.), 59, 60–61, 62, 64
cultivation practices, 251–56
economies of, 46–47, 64–69
groundstone technology, 62, 63
projectile points, 47, 50 (fig.), 53 (fig.), 58, 59, 62
site distribution in, 48–49, 51–52, 54, 55–56, 57 (fig.)
transportation, 59
See also Archaic period; Paleoindian period
Paleoethnobotany, definition of, 248
Paleoindian period, 47
architecture, 69–71
distribution of sites in, 51–52, 54, 54 (fig.), 55 (fig.), 56, 57 (fig.)
economy of, 64–69, 262
flora in, 67, 250–51
See also Paleoarchaic period
Palmer Johnson, 251 (fig.), 258
Pana villages, 214–16
Pani, 245, 246
Panimaha, 245
Pani Noir, 210, 218
Paniouassa, 210, 215, 216
Panis Blanc, 210, 216–17
Panis Picques, 210, 216, 217, 218
Paoli/Washita River complex, 201, 207 (fig.)
Parks, Ed, 81
Pat Allen site, 68
Pattern, definition of, 6, 7
Patterson site, 251 (fig.), 255, 257
Paul, Duke of Württemberg, 238
Pawnee, 4 (fig.), 217
architecture, 243, 244 (fig.)
bands, 233
in Blue River valley, 239, 242–43
burials, 244
ceramics, 243
chronology, 131–32, 241–42
hunting, 234 (fig.), 245
Kansa and, 235, 236, 237, 238
in Kansas River drainage, 241 (fig.), 244, 245
in Loup River valley, 238, 239, 242, 244, 245–46, 247
Nahu'rac, 241 (fig.), 245
in Platte River valley, 239, 244, 245–46, 247
in Republican River valley, 235–38, 240, 241, 242, 243, 260
in Smoky Hill River valley, 239

South Bands, 132, 233, 245, 246, 247
territory of, 234 (fig.)
tools, 243–44
trade, 234–35, 239, 243, 244
treaties, 238, 239, 247
Wichita and, 132, 233, 246
Pawnee Lower Loup phase, 131
Pawnee Village (Republic County), viii
PDT site, 53
Peavy site, 134 (fig.)
Pennsylvanian system, 12–13, 265 (fig.), 268–70
Peoria, 4 (fig.)
Peoria loess, 34
Permian system, 12, 15–16, 265 (fig.), 270–75
Perrin du Lac map, 236, 239
Petroglyphs, 169
Petsch Springs site, 144 (fig.)
Peverly site, 169
Pfaff site, 93, 100 (fig.), 101 (fig.)
Phase, definition of, 6, 7, 105
Phillips, Philip, 7
Physiographic provinces of Kansas, 4, 10–18
Pike expedition, 237, 240, 242, 243
Pike-Pawnee site, 240
Pike Ranch site, 30 (fig.), 31
Pipes, 118, 177–78, 188 (fig.)
Pipestone, 280–81. *See also* Catlinite
Pipestone National Monument, 281
Pitahawirata (Tappage) band, 233, 238–39, 243
Plains Anthropological Conference, ix
Plains Apache (Padouca), xi, 221, 222
Plains Border region
agriculture, 129, 257
architecture, 181, 184–86, 192, 193 (fig.), 196, 199 (fig.)
ceramics, 162, 187 (fig.), 188–89, 194–95, 198, 200 (fig.), 202
definition of, 180
mortuary practices, 190–91, 195, 198
sites and settlement patterns, 182–84, 191–92, 196, 198–201, 203, 204, 205, 207 (fig.)
subsistence, 186–88, 192–93, 196–97
tools, 188 (fig.), 189, 190, 193 (fig.), 197 (fig.), 200 (figs.), 203
Plains Village tradition, xi, 8, 97, 105, 204
Southern, 180, 206–7
Plains Woodland tradition
ceramics, 98, 99 (fig.), 103, 277
economy of, 97–98

Plains Woodland tradition, *continued*
  environment, 93–94
  fauna, 94
  material culture, 98–100
  mortuary practices 101–2
  origin of, 8, 102
  physical anthropology, 97
  projectile points, 99–100
  settlement and architecture, 95–96, 100
  social and political structure, 100–102
  taxonomy, 8 (fig.), 94–95, 103
Plainview complex, 49, 52, 53, 55 (fig.), 56
Plants. *See* Flora
Playas, 18, 34–35, 36, 38–39, 42, 43–44
Pleistocene-Holocene transition
  environment, 22–23, 30–35, 36, 42, 52, 54
  Paleoarchaic period and, 47
Pleistocene period, 2, 47, 52, 54, 56, 64, 278
Pomona complex (phase/variant), xi, 4 (fig.), 77, 89, 90, 91, 124–26, 128, 130, 207 (fig.), 259
Ponca, 219, 220
Potawatomi, 4 (fig.)
Pottery. *See* Ceramics
Pottorff site, 93, 134 (fig.), 136
Prairies. *See* Mixed-grass prairie; Prairie-forest region; Short-grass prairie; Tall-grass prairie
Prairie-forest region, 21–22
  Paleoarchaic sites in, 51 (fig.), 53, 54 (fig.), 55–56, 55 (fig.), 56 (fig.), 57 (fig.), 68
Pratt complex, 4 (fig.), 130, 131, 179, 180, 181 (fig.), 191–95, 202, 203, 205, 207 (fig.), 208–9
Prehistoric period, 4 (fig.)
Professional Archaeologists of Kansas (PAK), x, xiii
Projectile points
  Central Plains tradition, 114, 116
  Dismal River complex, 142
  Great Bend aspect, 176, 177 (fig.)
  Kansas City Hopewell, 80, 82
  Late Woodland, 85, 86, 87, 87 (Fig.)
  Odessa phase (Middle Ceramic), 189
  Paleoarchaic, 47, 50 (fig.), 53 (fig.), 58, 59, 62
  Pawnee, 244
  Plains Woodland, 99–100
  Pomona, 124
Protohistoric period, 4 (fig.), 141, 146, 259, 260

Quapaw, 219, 220, 221
Quarries, 266, 269 (fig.), 272–74, 276–77, 279 (fig.), 282
Quarry Creek site, 79, 80, 251 (fig.), 255, 256
Quartzite, 276 (fig.), 278, 279 (fig.)
Quaternary period
  in Arkansas River Lowlands, 14–15
  environments in Kansas, 10, 22–27, 28–45
  rock units in, 265 (fig.), 278
Quivira, 210, 211 (fig.), 211, 212, 213, 214, 215, 246

Radiocarbon dating, 3–5, 32 (fig.), 35 (fig.), 250
Radio Lane site, 174, 257
Range Mound site, 73
Reany site, 151 (fig.), 159
Recon John shelter, 252
Redbud variant, 188
Red Hills, 16
Red Smoke site, 52 (fig.)
Religion, Plains Woodland, 101
Republican (Kitkahahki) band, 233, 234–38, 240, 241, 242
Republican River valley, Pawnee in, 235–38, 240, 241, 242, 243, 260
Richland site, 86
Riley cord-roughened pottery, 113, 131
River Basin Surveys (RBS), 107, 142
Rock art, 169
Rocks
  outcropping, 265 (fig.), 267–78
  See also Geology; Lithic resources
Rockshelters, 57, 58, 169
Rodgers Shelter site, 52 (fig.)
Rogers site, 199
Root site, 120
Rosebud site, 22
Roth site, 125
Roy Smith site, 189
Ruby site, 96

Sac and Fox, 4 (fig.)
Sailor-Helton site, 52 (fig.), 60
Salina Burial Pit (Whiteford site), 107, 115, 123, 131
Sand dunes/sheets, 18, 37, 38, 44
Sarisere (Sartariche), 235, 236, 237
Schultz, Floyd, 123, 240
Schultz phase, 4 (fig.), 79, 80, 82, 83 (fig.)
Schwab site, 182

Scott County Pueblo (El Cuartelejo), 142, 142 (fig.), 144–45, 146, 147, 251 (fig.), 255, 260
Scott phase, 143
Scottsbluff complex, 53
Scottsbluff site, 52 (fig.)
Scott site, 108
Selby/Dutton site, 52 (fig.)
Settlement patterns
  Central Plains tradition, 118–21, 129–30
  Great Bend aspect, 167–71, 208
  High Plains Upper Republican complex, 140–41
  Kansa, xi, 221, 223–27
  Kansas City Hopewell, xi, 80, 88
  Middle Ceramic (Plains Border region), 182–84, 191–92, 196, 198–201, 203, 204, 205, 207 (fig.)
  Plains Woodland, 95–96, 100
Seuser site, 192, 199
Seven Mile Point site, 134 (fig.)
Shadid site, 199
Shawnee, 4 (fig.)
Shell artifacts
  Central Plains tradition, 117 (fig.), 118
  Plains Woodland, 100, 101 (fig.)
Shellfish, 66–67
Shields site, 78
Shipman site, 240
Shone-ge-ne-gare, 223
Short-grass prairie, 20, 25
  Paleoarchaic sites and, 51 (fig.), 53, 54, 54 (fig.), 55 (fig.), 56 (fig.), 57 (fig.), 68
Shrope site, 218
Sibley, George, 223, 228, 237, 242
Signal Butte site, 52 (fig.), 134 (fig.), 136
Simshauser alluvial fan, 30 (fig.), 33
Simshauser site, 68
Siouan groups, xi, 4 (fig.), 219
Skiri (Loup) band, 131, 233, 239, 245, 246
Smith, Carlyle S., 240
Smith, Jedediah, 238
Smithsonian institution, 142, 166
Smoky Hills, 16–17
Smoky Hill aspect (phase/variant), 4 (fig.), 105, 106, 107, 108–9, 113, 114, 115, 116, 121, 130, 131, 207 (fig.), 208–9, 259
Smoky Hill chalk, 277
Smoky Hill jasper, 116, 134 (fig.), 139, 144 (fig.), 147, 153, 161, 174, 193, 202, 275, 276, 280

Snyder site, 48, 52 (fig.), 58, 59, 60, 63, 65, 66, 67, 68, 70 (fig.), 73
Soil
  Holocene, 35–45
  Odessa phase and, 183
  Pleistocene-Holocene transition, 30–35
  stratigraphy, 29, 31 (fig.), 33 (fig.), 35 (fig.), 39 (fig.)
Solomon River locality, 134 (fig.), 140
Soulard map, 235, 236 (fig.), 239
Southern Plains cultures, 181–82, 201, 202, 206–8
South Fork Big Nemaha River valley, 23, 24, 25, 26
South Platte phase, 94, 95, 96, 98, 103
Spanish contacts, 166, 167, 178
  with Kansa, 220, 221–22
  with Pawnee, 234
  with Wichita, 209, 212–13, 214, 215–16
Spillway site, 151 (fig.), 159
Spiro site, 131
Sprague site, 182
Spring Creek site, 52 (fig.)
Stamper site, 189
Steed-Kisker phase (variant), 4 (fig.), 89, 90, 90 (figs.), 105, 106, 108, 110, 112, 113, 116, 121, 123, 127, 157, 257, 258
Steed-Kisker site, 107, 108
Sterns, F. H., 121, 230
Sterns Creek site, 255
St. Helena phase, 105, 130
Stingenwalt complex, 4 (fig.), 60, 63, 65, 70 (fig.), 73
Stingenwalt site, 30 (fig.), 36, 48, 49, 52 (fig.), 58, 59, 60, 63, 65, 66, 67, 70, 70 (fig.), 73 (fig.), 251 (fig.), 252, 254
Stinking Water phase, 142
Stone sources. *See* Lithic resources
Stream classification system, 29
Strong, William Duncan, 105, 106, 121
Structures. *See* Architecture
Sullivan playa, 34
Sutter site, 48, 52 (fig.), 60, 62, 63, 65, 68, 70 (fig.)

Tall-grass prairie, 20, 25
  Paleoarchaic sites and, 51 (fig.), 53, 54 (fig.), 55, 55 (fig.), 56 (fig.), 57 (fig.), 68
Tanoca, 210, 211 (fig.), 212
Taovaya, 206, 210, 212, 214, 215, 216, 217, 218

Tappage (Pitahawirata) band, 233, 238–39, 243
Tawakoni, 206, 210, 211, 212, 215, 216, 217, 218
Taxonomic systems, 6–8, 105
Taylor Mound, 81
Tertiary system, 265 (fig.), 277–78
Teya, 210, 211 (fig.)
Tierra Blanca complex, 208 (fig.), 209
Till Plains region, 4 (fig.), 55, 110, 124, 128, 265
Tim Adrian site, 60
Tobias site, viii, 167, 168, 168 (fig.), 169, 170, 173
Tonti, Henry de, 221
Tools
    Central Plains tradition, 114–17
    Great Bend aspect, 176–78, 179 (fig.)
    High Plains Late Prehistoric, 137, 142, 142 (fig.)
    Middle Ceramic (Plains Border region), 188 (fig.), 189, 190, 193, 194 (fig.), 197 (fig.)
    Paleoarchaic, 47, 50 (fig.), 58, 59, 60–61, 62, 63, 64
    Pawnee, 243–44
    Plains Woodland, 98–100
    Pomona, 125
    quarry, 279 (fig.)
    quartzite, 278
    See also Chipped-stone artifacts; Groundstone artifacts
Touacara, 210, 215, 216, 216 (fig.)
Touajas, 210, 215, 216 (fig.)
Trade
    Great Bend aspect, 175
    High Plains Late Prehistoric, 139–40, 147–48
    Kansa, 224, 231
    Middle Ceramic (Plains Border region), 188 (fig.), 189–90
    Oneota, 161
    Pawnee, 234–35, 239, 243, 244
    stone sources and, 281–82
Trader's Creek site, 199
Tradition, definition of, 7
Traff site, 78, 251 (fig.), 255, 256
Transportation technology, Paleoarchaic, 59
Trowbridge phase, 80
Trowbridge site, 79, 79 (fig.), 251 (fig.), 255, 256
12 Mile Creek site, 48, 53, 60, 67, 68
Two Deer site, 126, 128, 251 (fig.), 255, 257
Two Sisters site, 189

Uayam, 210, 212
Udden, Johan, 166

Uncas complex, 179
University of Kansas, vii, 142, 145, 152, 196, 198, 240, 280
    Museum of Anthropology, ix–x
University of Nebraska, 142, 240
Upper Canark site, 188
Upper Mississippian complex, 151
Upper Republican aspect (phase/variant)
    in Central Plains, 102, 105, 106, 107, 109, 113, 114, 115, 116, 118, 120, 122, 130, 137, 138, 139, 257, 259
    in High Plains, 133–40, 259, 276, 280

Valley variant (phase), 4 (fig.), 79, 81, 94, 102
Variant, definition of, 7, 105
Vegetation
    Holocene, 22–27, 30, 52–57
    modern Kansas, 20–22, 52
    Paleoarchaic sites and, 52–57, 68
    Plains Woodland tradition, 94
    Pleistocene-Holocene transition, 22, 30
    See also Flora
Verdigris ware, 84 (fig.), 88, 89
Vermillion phase, 4 (fig.)
Vial, Pedro, 235, 236, 242
Village period, 257–59, 260, 263. *See also* Plains Village tradition
Vohs site, 93

Waco, 206, 211, 212, 215, 216, 217
Waconda Lake locality, 112, 113, 120
Waconda Spring site, 241 (fig.), 245
Wakarusa phase, 84, 86, 87
Walker-Gilmore, 251 (fig.), 257
Walnut complex (phase), 4 (fig.), 48, 49, 60, 77
Walsh Archaeological District, 276, 282
Walter Hutchinson site, 169, 170 (fig.)
Wardell site, 96
Warne site, 151 (fig.), 159, 163, 281
Waugh site, 52 (fig.), 69, 71
Wea and Piankeshaw, 4 (fig.)
Wedel, Waldo, vii, 105, 107, 109, 145, 165, 166, 168, 203, 223, 230, 231
Wellington-McPherson Lowlands, 15–16
Westfall site, 52 (fig.)
West Island site, 93
Wheeler phase, 208, 208 (fig.), 209, 210, 212
White Cat Village site, 142, 144 (fig.), 147
Whiteford site (Salina Burial Pit), 107, 115, 123, 131

White Plume, 227
White River Group silicates. *See* Flattop chalcedony
White Rock phase (aspect), 4 (fig.), 130, 131, 151, 151 (fig.), 154, 159–62, 163, 259
White Rock site, 159, 163
Wichita bands, 4 (fig.)
    definition of, 206
    early historic, 209–18
    Great Bend aspect and, xi, 132, 165, 171, 233
    mortuary practices of, 171
    Pawnee and, 132, 233, 246
    prehistoric, 206–9
    subdivisions of, 206, 210
Wichita State University, vii, 280
Wichita subdivision, 206, 210, 212, 215, 217, 218
Wiley site, 89
Willey, Gordon R., 7
Williamson site, 48, 52 (fig.), 58, 59, 60, 63, 65, 66, 68, 70 (fig.), 73, 252
William Young site, 48, 52 (fig.), 60, 63, 64, 65, 66, 68, 70 (fig.), 252
Williston, S. W., 145
Wilmeth, Roscoe, vii, 231
Wilson site, 199
Winfield site (Archaic), 65, 66
Winfield sites (Great Bend aspect), 167
Winger site, 30 (fig.), 34–35, 44, 48, 52 (fig.), 60, 67, 68, 70 (fig.), 71
Wiseman site, 65, 66
Wislizenus, Frederick Adolph, 227

Witty, Thomas, Jr., 7, 145, 231, 240
Wolf Creek focus, 231
Wonder site, 243
Woodland tradition, 8, 28
    agriculture, 256–57, 262–63
    artifacts, 280
    definition of, 76, 93
    Eastern, 76
    environment, 93–94
    flora and, 256–57, 262–63
    Plains, 93–104
    See also Early Woodland tradition; Late Woodland tradition; Middle Woodland tradition
Woodruff Ossuary site, 93, 97, 101, 101 (fig.), 102
Woodson County rockshelters, 169
Wood technology, Paleoarchaic, 58
Workshop sites, 266, 269, 269 (fig.), 272–74, 276–77, 282
Works Project Administration (WPA), 142
Wyandotte, 4 (fig.)

Young site, 93
Younkin Mound, 83 (figs.)

Zacharias site, 90, 90 (figs.), 91
Zimmerman, Mark, 81
Zimms complex, 201, 202, 207 (fig.)
Zyba site, 167, 170

www.ingramcontent.com/pod-product-compliance
Lightning Source LLC
Chambersburg PA
CBHW050133240426
43673CB00043B/1656